New Perspectives on

MICROSOFT®
ACCESS 2000
WITH VISUAL BASIC
FOR APPLICATIONS

Advanced

KRISTIE L. OXFORD
Santa Rosa Junior College

COURSE
TECHNOLOGY

Thomson Learning™

ONE MAIN STREET, CAMBRIDGE, MA 02142

Australia • Canada • Denmark • Japan • Mexico • New Zealand • Philippines
Puerto Rico • Singapore • South Africa • Spain • United Kingdom • United States

New Perspectives on Microsoft Access 2000 with Visual Basic for Applications—Advanced is published by Course Technology.

Managing Editor	Greg Donald
Senior Editor	Donna Gridley
Senior Product Manager	Rachel A. Crapser
Product Managers	Catherine V. Donaldson
	Karen Shortill
Associate Product Manager	Melissa Dezotell
Editorial Assistant	Jill Kirn
Developmental Editor	Betsy Newberry
Academic Advisor	Joseph J. Adamski
Production Editor	Megan Cap-Renzi
Text Designer	Meral Dabcovich
Cover Designer	Douglas Goodman

© 2001 by Course Technology, a division of Thomson Learning

For more information contact:

Course Technology
One Main Street
Cambridge, MA 02142
Or find us on the World Wide Web at: http://www.course.com.

For permission to use material from this text or product, contact us by

■ **Web: www.thomsonrights.com**

■ **Phone: 1-800-730-2214**

■ **Fax: 1-800-730-2215**

Trademarks

Course Technology and the Open Book logo are registered trademarks and CourseKits is a trademark of Course Technology. Custom Edition is a registered trademark of Thomson Learning.

The Thomson Learning logo is a registered trademark used herein under license.

Some of the product names and company names used in this book have been used for identification purposes only and may be trademarks or registered trademarks of their respective manufacturers and sellers.

Disclaimer

Course Technology reserves the right to revise this publication and make changes from time to time in its content without notice.

ISBN 0-619-01915-8

Printed in the United States of America

1 2 3 4 5 6 7 8 9 10 BM 05 04 03 02 01

PREFACE

The New Perspectives Series

About New Perspectives

Course Technology's **New Perspectives Series** is an integrated system of instruction that combines text and technology products to teach computer concepts, the Internet, and microcomputer applications. Users consistently praise this series for its innovative pedagogy, use of interactive technology, creativity, accuracy, and supportive and engaging style.

How is the New Perspectives Series different from other series?

The **New Perspectives Series** distinguishes itself through **innovative technology**, from the renowned Course Labs to the state-of-the-art multimedia that is integrated with our Concepts texts. Other distinguishing features include **sound instructional design, proven pedagogy, and consistent quality**. Each tutorial teaches students in the context of solving a realistic case problem rather than simply a laundry list of features. With the **New Perspectives Series**, instructors report that students have a complete, integrative learning experience that stays with them. They credit this high retention and competency to the fact that this series incorporates critical thinking and problem-solving with computer skills mastery. In addition, we work hard to ensure accuracy by using a multi-step quality assurance process during all stages of development. Instructors focus on teaching and students spend more time learning.

Choose the coverage that's right for you .

New Perspectives applications books are available in the following categories:

Brief
2-4 tutorials

Brief: approximately 150 pages long, two to four "Level I" tutorials, teaches basic application skills.

Introductory
6 or 7 tutorials, or Brief + 2 or 3 more tutorials

Introductory: approximately 300 pages long, four to seven tutorials, goes beyond the basic skills. These books often build out of the Brief books, adding two or three additional "Level II" tutorials.

Comprehensive
Introductory + 4 or 5 more tutorials. Includes Brief Windows tutorials and Additional Cases

Comprehensive: approximately 600 pages long, eight to twelve tutorials—all tutorials included in the Introductory text plus higher-level "Level III" topics. Also includes two Windows tutorials and three or four fully developed Additional Cases.

Advanced
Quick Review of basics + in-depth, high-level coverage

Advanced: approximately 400 to 600 pages long, covers topics similar to those in the Comprehensive books, but offers the highest-level coverage in the series. Advanced books assume students already know the basics, and therefore go into more depth at a more accelerated rate than the Comprehensive titles. Advanced books are ideal for a second, more technical course. The book you are holding is an Advanced book.

Office
Quick Review of basics + in-depth, high-level coverage

Office: approximately 800 pages long, covers all components of the Office suite as well as integrating the individual software packages with one another and the Internet.

Custom Editions

Choose from any of the
above to build your own
Custom Editions or
CourseKits

Custom Books: The New Perspectives Series offers you two ways to customize a New Perspectives text to fit your course exactly. *CourseKits™* are two or more texts shrink-wrapped together, and offer significant price discounts. *Custom Editions®* offer you flexibility in designing your concepts, Internet, and applications courses. You can build your own book by ordering a combination of topics bound together to cover only the subjects you want. There is no minimum order, and books are spiral bound. Contact your Course Technology sales representative for more information.

What course is this book appropriate for?

New Perspectives on Microsoft Access 2000 with Visual Basic for Applications—Advanced can be used in any course in which you want students to learn some of the most important topics of Access 2000 and Visual Basic for Applications, including Reviewing Database Objects, Designing and Documenting a Database, Using Import Wizards, Action Queries and SQL, Designing Complex Forms, Creating Complex Reports and Queries, Customizing the User Interface, Using Visual Basic for Applications, Error Handling, Combo Box Programming and ActiveX Controls, Data Access Object Model, ActiveX Data Object Model and Security, and Connecting to the Web. It is particularly recommended for a full semester course on Access 2000 with VBA. This book assumes that students have learned basic Access skills and Windows navigation and file management skills from Course Technology's *New Perspectives on Microsoft Windows 95—Brief*, or the equivalent book for Windows 98 or NT.

Proven Pedagogy

CASE

Tutorial Case Each tutorial begins with a problem presented in a case that is meaningful to students. The case turns the task of learning how to use an application into a problem-solving process.

45-Minute Sessions Each tutorial is divided into sessions that can be completed in about 45 minutes to an hour. Sessions allow instructors to more accurately allocate time in their syllabus, and students to better manage their own study time.

1.

2.

3.

Step-by-Step Methodology We make sure students can differentiate between what they are to *do* and what they are to *read*. Through numbered steps—clearly identified by a gray shaded background—students are constantly guided in solving the case problem. In addition, the numerous screen shots with callouts direct students' attention to what they should look at on the screen.

TROUBLE?

TROUBLE? Paragraphs These paragraphs anticipate the mistakes or problems that students may have and help them continue with the tutorial.

Tutorial Tips Page This page, following the Table of Contents, offers students suggestions on how to effectively plan their study and lab time, what to do when they make a mistake, and how to use the Reference Windows, MOUS grids, Quick Checks, and other features of the New Perspectives series.

Read This Before You Begin Page Located opposite the first tutorial's opening page for each level of the text, the Read This Before You Begin Page helps introduce technology into the classroom. Technical considerations and assumptions about software are listed to save time and eliminate unnecessary aggravation. Notes about the Data Disks help instructors and students get the right files in the right places, so students get started on the right foot.

QUICK CHECK

Quick Check Questions Each session concludes with meaningful, conceptual Quick Check questions that test students' understanding of what they learned in the session. Answers to the Quick Check questions are provided at the end of each tutorial.

RW

TASK REFERENCE

REVIEW

CASE

Explore ▶

Reference Windows Reference Windows are succinct summaries of the most important tasks covered in a tutorial and they preview actions students will perform in the steps to follow.

Task Reference Located as a table at the end of the book, the Task Reference contains a summary of how to perform common tasks using the most efficient method, as well as references to pages where the task is discussed in more detail.

End-of-Tutorial Review Assignments and Case Problems Review Assignments provide students with additional hands-on practice of the skills they learned in the tutorial using the same case presented in the tutorial. These Assignments are followed by three to four Case Problems that have approximately the same scope as the tutorial case but use a different scenario. In addition, some of the Review Assignments or Case Problems may include Exploration Exercises that challenge students and encourage them to explore the capabilities of the program they are using, and/or further extend their knowledge.

File Finder Chart This chart, located in the back of the book, visually explains how a student should set up the data disk, what files should go in what folders, and what they'll be saving the files as in the course of their work.

New Perspectives on Microsoft Access 2000 with VBA—Advanced Instructor's Resource Kit contains:

- Electronic Instructor's Manual
- Data Files
- Solution Files
- Course Test Manager Testbank
- Course Test Manager Engine
- Figure Files
- Sample Syllabus

These supplements come on CD-ROM. If you don't have access to a CD-ROM drive, contact your Course Technology customer service representative for more information.

The New Perspectives Supplements Package

Electronic Instructor's Manual Our Instructor's Manuals include tutorial overviews and outlines, technical notes, lecture notes, solutions, and Extra Case Problems. Many instructors use the Extra Case Problems for performance-based exams or extra credit projects. The Instructor's Manual is available as an electronic file, which you can get from the Instructor Resource Kit (IRK) CD-ROM, or you can download it from www.course.com.

Data Files Data Files contain all of the data that students will use to complete the tutorials, Review Assignments, and Case Problems. A Readme file includes instructions for using the files. See the Read This Before You Begin Page for more information on Data Files.

Solution Files Solution Files contain every file students are asked to create or modify in the Tutorials, Review Assignments, Case Problems, and Extra Case Problems. A Help file on the Instructor's Resource Kit includes information for using the Solution files.

Figure Files Many figures in the text are provided on the IRK CD-ROM to help illustrate key topics or concepts. Instructors can create traditional overhead transparencies by printing the figure files. Or they can create electronic slide shows by using the figures in a presentation program such as PowerPoint.

Course Test Manager: Testing and Practice at the Computer or on Paper Course Test Manager is cutting-edge, Windows-based testing software that helps instructors design and administer practice tests and actual examinations. Course Test Manager can automatically grade the tests students take at the computer and can generate statistical information on individual as well as group performance.

Online Companions: Dedicated to Keeping You and Your Students Up-to-Date Visit our faculty sites and student sites on the World Wide Web at www.course.com. Here instructors can browse this text's password-protected Faculty Online Companion to obtain an online Instructor's Manual, Solution Files, Data Files, and more.

Acknowledgments

I would like to thank the following reviewers for their helpful feedback: Roy Ageloff, University of Rhode Island; Sue Krimm, Los Angeles Pierce College; and Carrie Budd. My thanks to all of the Course Technology staff: Jill Kirn, Editorial Assistant; Melissa Dezotell, Associate Product Manager; all the Quality Assurance testers: John Freitas, Jeff Schwartz, Nicole Ashton, and Justin Rand; and especially Catherine Donaldson for all her help, guidance, and patience in managing the production process. I'd also like to thank Christine Guivernau for her support and faith in me from the beginning. Special thanks to Betsy Newberry for her outstanding editorial contributions and hard work and to Joe Adamski for his incredible attention to detail, editorial expertise, guidance, support, and friendship. I could not have done it without him. Finally, I want to thank Tim, Jon, and Justin for their love and support, hard work, and tolerance of all the lost weekends, evenings, and holidays. You guys are the best.

Kristie L. Oxford
14 April 2000

Preface   iii

Microsoft Access 2000 with Visual Basic for Applications—Advanced Tutorials   AC 1

Tutorial 1   AC 3

Reviewing Database Objects   SESSION 1.1   AC 4
                                   SESSION 1.2   AC 18

Tutorial 2   AC 33

Designing and Documenting a Database   SESSION 2.1   AC 34
                                              SESSION 2.2   AC 49

Tutorial 3   AC 73

Using Import Wizards, Action Queries, and SQL   SESSION 3.1   AC 74
                                                       SESSION 3.2   AC 88
                                                       SESSION 3.3   AC 103

Tutorial 4   AC 117

Designing Complex Forms   SESSION 4.1   AC 118
                                 SESSION 4.2   AC 136

Tutorial 5   AC 165

Creating Complex Reports and Queries   SESSION 5.1   AC 166
                                              SESSION 5.2   AC 182

Tutorial 6   AC 217

Customizing the User Interface   SESSION 6.1   AC 218
                                        SESSION 6.2   AC 231

Tutorial 7   AC 263

Using Visual Basic for Applications   SESSION 7.1   AC 264
                                             SESSION 7.2   AC 280

Tutorial 8   **AC 319**

Trapping Errors and Automating   SESSION 8.1   AC 320
ActiveX Controls with VBA   SESSION 8.2   AC 334

Tutorial 9   **AC 361**

Working with Object Models and   SESSION 9.1   AC 362
Securing the Database   SESSION 9.2   AC 378

Tutorial 10   **AC 407**

Connecting to the World Wide Web   SESSION 10.1   AC 408
    SESSION 10.2   AC 419

Task References

Index

TABLE OF CONTENTS

| Preface | iii |
| Reference Windows | xv |

Microsoft Access 2000 with Visual Basic for Applications—Advanced Tutorials ... AC 1.1

Read this Before you Begin ... AC 1.2

Tutorial 1   AC 3

Reviewing Database Objects

Exploring the Database for MovieCam Technologies

SESSION 1.1	**AC 4**
Introduction to Database Management Systems	AC 4
Opening the MovieCam Technologies Database	AC 5
Naming Conventions	AC 5
The Database Window	AC 7
Tables	AC 8
Table and Field Properties	AC 9
Field Properties	AC 13
Queries	**AC 15**
Select Queries and Expressions	AC 15
Parameter Queries	AC 17
Crosstab Queries	AC 17
Action Queries	AC 17
SQL-Specific Queries	AC 17
Quick Check	**AC 17**

SESSION 1.2	**AC 18**
Forms	**AC 18**
Reports	**AC 25**
Pages	**AC 29**
Macros	**AC 29**
Modules	**AC 29**
Quick Check	**AC 29**
Review Assignments	**AC 29**
Case Problems	**AC 30**
Quick Check Answers	**AC 32**

Tutorial 2   AC 33

Designing and Documenting a Database

Completing the tables and establishing relationships in the MovieCam Technologies database

SESSION 2.1	**AC 34**
Database Design	AC 34
Creating Tables	AC 36
Primary Keys, Foreign Keys, and Indexing	AC 38
Setting Relationships	**AC 41**
One-to-One Relationships	AC 42
One-to-Many Relationships	AC 42
Many-to-Many Relationships	AC 43
Referential Integrity	AC 43
Cascade Update and Cascade Delete	AC 45
Quick Check	**AC 48**

SESSION 2.2	**AC 49**
Entering Records in Tables	**AC 49**
Combo Box Properties	AC 51
Subdatasheets	AC 57
Dates in Access	AC 58
Documenting Your Database	**AC 61**
Quick Check	**AC 67**
Review Assignments	**AC 67**
Case Problems	**AC 68**
Quick Check Answers	**AC 72**

Tutorial 3   AC 73

Using Import Wizards, Action Queries, and SQL

Importing and Archiving Data for the MovieCam Technologies Database

SESSION 3.1	**AC 74**
Introduction	AC 74
Importing and Linking Data	AC 76
Using the Import Text Wizard	AC 76
Creating an Append Query	AC 79
Using Text-Manipulation Functions	AC 79
Quick Check	AC 88
SESSION 3.2	**AC 88**
Importing an Access Object	AC 88
Creating an Update Query	AC 90
Using the Import Spreadsheet Wizard	AC 91
Query Properties	AC 94
Archiving Data	AC 97
Quick Check	AC 102
SESSION 3.3	**AC 103**
SQL-Specific Queries	AC 103
Pass-Through Queries	AC 103
Data-Definition Queries	AC 103
Union Queries	AC 103
Access SQL Statements and Clauses	AC 104
The Select Statement	AC 104
DistinctRow and Distinct Keywords	AC 104
The From Clause	AC 105
The Where Clause	AC 105
The Order By Clause	AC 106
The Join Clause	AC 107
The Union Statement	AC 109
Quick Check	AC 111
Review Assignments	AC 112
Case Problems	AC 113
Quick Check Answers	AC 116

Tutorial 4   AC 117

Designing Complex Forms

Building the User Interface for MovieCam Technologies

SESSION 4.1	**AC 118**
Introduction to Forms	AC 118
Form Design	AC 119
Creating a Form Template	AC 121
Changing Default Properties of Toolbox Controls	AC 123
Creating Form Masters	AC 124
Creating Data Entry Forms	AC 127
Identifier Operators	AC 130
Working with Subforms	AC 133
Quick Check	AC 136
SESSION 4.2	**AC 136**
Creating Switchboards	AC 136
Working with Macros	AC 142
Naming Macros and Macro Groups	AC 143
Events	AC 143
Creating Macros	AC 143
Using the Command Button Wizard	AC 153
Comparing Macros to VBA	AC 157
Quick Check	AC 159
Review Assignments	AC 159
Case Problems	AC 161
Quick Check Answers	AC 164

Tutorial 5   AC 165

Creating Complex Reports and Queries

Reporting on Data in the MovieCam Technologies Database

SESSION 5.1	**AC 166**
Introduction	AC 166
Creating a Report Master	AC 166
Domain Aggregate Functions	AC 167

Report Sections AC 169
   Grouping Records in a Report AC 170
   Creating a Query with a Self-Join AC 170
   Can Grow and Can Shrink Properties AC 175
Quick Check AC 182

SESSION 5.2 AC 182
Event Properties AC 182
   The Print Events AC 183
   Using the NoData Event AC 183
   Converting Macros to VBA Code AC 186
Creating Numbered Lists AC 191
   The Running Sum Property AC 191
Subreports AC 194
   Charting AC 200
   Page Numbering AC 204
   Adding Blank Rows to a Report AC 206
   Using an If...Then...Else Statement AC 207
Quick Check AC 209
Review Assignments AC 209
Case Problems AC 211
Quick Check Answers AC 215

Tutorial 6   AC 217

Customizing the User Interface

Redesigning the User Interface in the MovieCam Technologies Database

SESSION 6.1
Objects, Methods, and Properties AC 218
   Collections and Classes AC 218
   Data Event Properties AC 219
Validating Data Using an Event Procedure AC 220
   Canceling the Default Behavior Following
      an Event AC 221
   The DoCmd Object AC 224
Control Structures for Decision Processing AC 225
   If...Then...Else AC 225
   ElseIf AC 225
   Select Case AC 225
Adding an Event Procedure to the
   frmDataSwitchboard Form AC 226
   The With Statement AC 227
Quick Check AC 230

SESSION 6.2 AC 231
Introduction to Menus and Toolbars AC 231
Creating and Customizing Menus and Toolbars AC 233
   Customizing Toolbars AC 234
   Creating a Custom Menu Bar AC 237
   Creating a Custom Shortcut Menu AC 241
Startup Properties AC 245
Disabling the Bypass Key AC 247
   Using Code Samples in Visual Basic Help AC 248
AutoKeys Macro Group AC 251
Splitting the Database AC 254
Quick Check AC 258
Review Assignments AC 258
Case Problems AC 259
Quick Check Answers AC 262

Tutorial 7   AC 263

Using Visual Basic for Applications

Creating the Reports Switchboard for the MovieCam Database

SESSION 7.1 AC 264
Introduction AC 264
Modules AC 264
   Sub Procedures and Functions AC 265
   Indenting and Spacing Procedures AC 266
   Procedure Scope AC 266
Creating the Reports Switchboard AC 267
   OpenReport Method AC 269
   Compiling Code AC 272
   Adding Comments AC 272
Variables AC 273
   Variable Scope AC 275
   Declaring Variables AC 275
   Variable Data Types AC 276
   Variant Data Type AC 277
   Variable Naming Conventions AC 277
Declaring Constants AC 278
Quick Check AC 280

SESSION 7.2 AC 280
Creating the Wherecondition for
   Employee Reports AC 280
   Creating Combo Boxes AC 280
   Building the WhereCondition AC 283
   Writing the Code AC 285

Using the Immediate Window	AC 289
Setting Breakpoints in Code	AC 291
Reviewing Code Line by Line	AC 293
The Locals Window	AC 293
Modifying the Code for Employee Reports	AC 298
Adding to the Wherecondition for Job Reports	AC 305
Using the Line Continuation Character	AC 307
Quick Check	AC 312
Review Assignments	AC 312
Case Problems	AC 313
Quick Check Answers	AC 317

Tutorial 8　　　　　　　　AC 319

Trapping Errors and Automating ActiveX Controls with VBA

Trapping Errors and Refining Forms in the MovieCam Database

SESSION 8.1	AC 320
Control Structures for Decision Processing and Looping	AC 320
Do...Loop	AC 320
For...Next Loop	AC 321
For Each...Next Loop	AC 321
Testing and Refining the Reports Switchboard	AC 321
Collections	AC 328
Dot vs. Bang Notation	AC 329
Me Keyword	AC 329
CodeContextObject Property	AC 329
The Screen Object	AC 330
Controls Collection	AC 330
Object Variables	AC 330
Quick Check	AC 333
SESSION 8.2	AC 334
Syntax Errors	AC 334
Run-Time Errors	AC 334
Logic Errors	AC 335
Trapping Run-Time Errors	AC 335
VBA Errors	AC 335
The On Error Statement	AC 335
The Resume Statement	AC 336
The Err Object	AC 336

Access Errors	AC 340
Error and Timing Events	AC 340
Determining the Error Number	AC 340
Combo Box Programming	AC 344
DoCmd.GoToControl	AC 347
DoCmd.FindRecord	AC 347
NotInList Event Procedure	AC 348
ActiveX Controls	AC 350
Registering an ActiveX Control	AC 351
Using the Calendar ActiveX Control	AC 351
Quick Check	AC 356
Review Assignments	AC 357
Case Problems	AC 357
Quick Check Answers	AC 360

Tutorial 9　　　　　　　　AC 361

Working with Object Models and Securing the Database

Working with DAO and Implementing User-Level Security in the MovieCam Technologies Database

SESSION 9.1	AC 362
Introduction to Object Models	AC 362
DAO vs. ADO	AC 362
ADO	AC 364
DAO	AC 364
The DBEngine Object	AC 364
The Workspace Object	AC 364
The Database Object	AC 365
The Recordset Collection	AC 367
Changing the Object Library Reference	AC 372
Writing Code Using the Recordset Object	AC 374
RecordsetClone Property	AC 374
FindFirst, FindLast, FindNext, and FindPrevious Methods	AC 374
Bookmark Property	AC 375
Quick Check	AC 378
SESSION 9.2	AC 378
Overview of Security	AC 378
Workgroup Information File	AC 379
Creating a Workgroup Information File	AC 379
Rebuilding a Workgroup Information File	AC 381

Security Accounts   **AC 381**

Creating a New User   AC 382

Setting a Password   AC 384

User-Level Security Wizard   **AC 385**

Running the User-Level Security Wizard   AC 385

Testing User-Level Security   AC 389

Joining the Default Workgroup   AC 392

Creating a Shortcut to an Access Database and its Workgroup Information File   **AC 394**

Assigning Permissions   **AC 396**

Owners   AC 396

Changing Permissions   AC 396

Setting Passwords   AC 399

Removing User-Level Security   **AC 400**

Quick Check   **AC 400**

Review Assignments   **AC 401**

Case Problems   **AC 402**

Quick Check Answers   **AC 405**

Tutorial 10   AC 407

Connecting to the World Wide Web

Working with Hyperlinks and Data Access Pages in the MovieCam Technologies Database

SESSION 10.1   **AC 408**

Introduction   **AC 408**

Using Hyperlinks on a Form   **AC 408**

Creating a Lightweight Switchboard   AC 409

Using Hyperlinks on a Menu Bar   **AC 416**

Quick Check   **AC 419**

SESSION 10.2   **AC 419**

Data Access Pages   **AC 419**

Creating a Read-Only Data Access Page   AC 419

Formatting the Data Access Page   AC 423

Applying Themes to Data Access Pages   AC 424

Grouping in Data Access Pages   AC 426

Changing Sorting and Grouping Properties   AC 428

Changing Navigation Toolbar Properties   AC 430

Creating an Updateable Data Access Page   AC 433

Testing the Data Access Pages   AC 437

Adding a Hyperlink to Another Page   AC 439

Exporting to the Web   **AC 440**

Importing from the Web   **AC 441**

Quick Check   **AC 442**

Review Assignments   **AC 442**

Case Problems   **AC 443**

Quick Check Answers   **AC 446**

Reference Window List

Creating a Table Validation Rule	AC 10
Creating a Field Validation Rule	AC 12
Changing Form Properties	AC 20
Adding a Rectangle to a Form	AC 22
Applying the Force New Page Property	AC 26
Specifying a Composite Primary Key	AC 40
Creating a Relationship Between Tables	AC 46
Adding a Combo Box to a Table Using the Lookup Wizard	AC 51
Forcing a Four-Digit Year	AC 59
Using the Database Documenter	AC 62
Using the Import Text Wizard	AC 76
Using the Expression Builder	AC 81
Creating an Append Query	AC 87
Importing Access Objects	AC 89
Creating an Update Query	AC 90
Using the Import Spreadsheet Wizard	AC 92
Querying for Unique Values	AC 95
Copying and Pasting a Table Structure	AC 97
Creating a Delete Query	AC 100
Creating a Query Using SQL	AC 105
Creating a Form Template	AC 121
Adding a Picture to a Form	AC 125
Creating a Form from a Master	AC 127
Creating an Expression in a Form	AC 131
Using the Option Group Wizard	AC 139
Changing Default Macro Settings	AC 147
Using the Control Wizard to Add a Command Button to a Form	AC 154
Creating a Self-Join Query	AC 171
Applying the Can Grow Property	AC 175
Modifying the Query from the Report Window	AC 178
Sending a Report in Snapshot Format	AC 180
Changing the NoData Event Property	AC 184
Converting a Macro to VBA	AC 186
Using the Code Builder	AC 189
Using the Running Sum Property to Number Items in a Report	AC 192
Inserting a Record-Bound Chart in a Report	AC 200
Adding Page Numbering to a Report	AC 204
Bypassing the Choose Builder Dialog Box	AC 220
Displaying the Full Set of Menu Commands	AC 231
Customizing a Toolbar	AC 234
Creating a New Menu Bar and Menu Items	AC 237
Adding Commands to a Menu Item	AC 239
Creating a Custom Shortcut Menu	AC 241
Setting the Database Startup Properties	AC 246
Using the Database Splitter Wizard	AC 255
Using the Linked Table Manager	AC 256
Adding an Event Procedure	AC 270
Testing a Function in the Immediate Window	AC 290
Using Breakpoints to Step Through a Procedure	AC 291
Determining the Number of an Access Error	AC 341
Adding an ActiveX Control to a Form	AC 351
Changing the Object Library Reference	AC 373
Creating a Workgroup Information File	AC 380
Changing Permissions	AC 396
Clearing a Password	AC 399
Creating a Hyperlink to Open a Form	AC 409
Assigning a Hyperlink to a Menu Command	AC 417
Creating a Data Access Page Using the Wizard	AC 421
Applying a Theme to a Data Access Page	AC 424
Adding a Group to a Data Access Page	AC 426
Exporting an Access Query to an HTML Document	AC 440

Tutorial Tips

These tutorials will help you learn about Access 2000 with Visual Basic for Applications. The tutorials are designed to be worked through at a computer. Each tutorial is divided into sessions. Watch for the session headings, such as Session 1.1 and Session 1.2. Each session is designed to be completed in about 45 minutes, but take as much time as you need. It's also a good idea to take a break between sessions.

To use the tutorials effectively, read the following questions and answers before you begin.

Where do I start?

Each tutorial begins with a case, which sets the scene for the tutorial and gives you background information to help you understand what you will be doing. Read the case before you go to the lab. In the lab, begin with the first session of a tutorial.

How do I know what to do on the computer?

Each session contains steps that you will perform on the computer to learn how to use Access 2000 and Visual Basic for Applications. Read the text that introduces each series of steps. The steps you need to do on the computer are numbered and are set against a shaded background. Read each step carefully and completely before you try it.

How do I know if I did the step correctly?

As you work, compare your computer screen with the corresponding figure in the tutorial. Don't worry if your screen display is somewhat different from the figure. The important parts of the screen display are labeled in each figure. Check to make sure these parts are on your screen.

What if I make a mistake?

Don't worry about making mistakes—they are part of the learning process. Paragraphs labeled "TROUBLE?" identify common problems and explain how to get back on track. Follow the steps in a TROUBLE? paragraph only if you are having the problem described. If you run into other problems:

- Carefully consider the current state of your system, the position of the pointer, and any messages on the screen.

- Complete the sentence, "Now I want to…" Be specific, because identifying your goal will help you rethink the steps you need to take to reach that goal.

- If you are working on a particular piece of software, consult the Help system.

- If the suggestions above don't solve your problem, consult your technical support person for assistance.

How do I use the Reference Windows?

Reference Windows summarize the procedures you will learn in the tutorial steps. Do not complete the actions in the Reference Windows when you are working through the tutorial. Instead, refer to the Reference Windows while you are working on the assignments at the end of the tutorial.

How can I test my understanding of the material I learned in the tutorial?

At the end of each session, you can answer the Quick Check questions. The answers for the Quick Checks are at the end of that tutorial. After you have completed the entire tutorial, you should complete the Review Assignments and Case Problems. They are carefully structured so that you will review what you have learned and then apply your knowledge to new situations.

What if I can't remember how to do something?

You should refer to the Task Reference at the end of the book; it summarizes how to accomplish tasks using the most efficient method.

Before you begin the tutorials, you should know the basics about your computer's operating system. You should also know how to use the menus, dialog boxes, Help system, and My Computer.

Now that you've read the Tutorial Tips, you are ready to begin.

New Perspectives on

MICROSOFT ACCESS 2000 WITH VISUAL BASIC FOR APPLICATIONS

TUTORIAL 1   AC 3
Reviewing Database Objects
Exploring the Database for MovieCam Technologies

TUTORIAL 2   AC 33
Designing and Documenting a Database
Completing the tables and establishing relationships in the MovieCam Technologies database

TUTORIAL 3   AC 73
Using Import Wizards, Action Queries, and SQL
Importing and Archiving Data for the MovieCam Technologies Database

TUTORIAL 4   AC 117
Designing Complex Forms
Building the User Interface for MovieCam Technologies

TUTORIAL 5   AC 165
Creating Complex Reports and Queries
Reporting on Data in the MovieCam Technologies Database

TUTORIAL 6   AC 217
Customizing the User Interface
Redesigning the User Interface in the MovieCam Technologies Database

TUTORIAL 7   AC 263
Using Visual Basic for Applications
Creating the Reports Switchboard for the MovieCam Database

TUTORIAL 8   AC 319
Trapping Errors and Automating ActiveX Controls with VBA
Trapping Errors and Refining Forms in the MovieCam Database

TUTORIAL 9   AC 361
Working with Object Models and Securing the Database
Working with DAO and Implementing User-Level Security in the MovieCam Technologies Database

TUTORIAL 10   AC 407
Connecting to the World Wide Web
Working with Hyperlinks and Data Access Pages in the MovieCam Technologies Database

Read This Before You Begin

To the Student

Data Disks

To complete the tutorials, Review Assignments, and Case Problems in this book, you will need access to a folder on your computer's local hard drive or a personal network drive. If you must complete work using a floppy disk, you may not be able to complete some of the steps due to space limitations. Your instructor will either provide you with these Data Disk files or ask you to make your own.

You will need to copy a set of folders from a file server, standalone computer, or the Web, to your folder. Your instructor will tell you which computer, drive letter, and folders contain the files you need. You could also download the files by going to www.course.com, clicking Data Disk Files, and following the instructions on the screen.

The following list shows you how to set up your Data Files in the folder that you will use to store them. (If you are storing your Data Files on floppy disks, put each database on a separate disk.)

Contents for the Data Files folder

Put this folder in the Data Files folder:
Tutorial.01

It will contain the following files:
Movie1, Hours1, Edward1, ISD1, Homes1, Sonoma1

Put this folder in the Data Files folder:
Tutorial.02

It will contain the following files:
Movie2, Hours2, Edward2, ISD2, Homes2, Sonoma2

Put this folder in the Data Files folder:
Tutorial.03

It will contain the following files
Movie3 (Access file), Movie3 (text file), Movie3 (Excel file), Hours3 (Access file), Hours3 (Excel file), Edward3 (Access file), Edward3 (text file), ISD3 (Access file), ISD3 (Excel file), Homes3 (Access file), Homes3 (text file), Sonoma3 (Access file), Sonoma3 (Excel file), Samples (Access file)

Put this folder in the Data Files folder:
Tutorial.04

It will contain the following files:
Movie4, Logo, Hours4, Edward4, ISD4, Homes4, H4Logo, Sonoma4

Put this folder in the Data Files folder:
Tutorial.05

It will contain the following files:
Movie5, Logo, Hours5, Edward5, ISD5, Homes5, H5Logo, Sonoma5

Put this folder in the Data Files folder:
Tutorial.06

It will contain the following files:
Movie6, MovieCam, Hours6, Edward6, ISD6, Homes6, Sonoma6

Put this folder in the Data Files folder:
Tutorial.07

It will contain the following files:
Movie7, Hours7, Edward7, ISD7, Homes7, Sonoma7

Put this folder in the Data Files folder:
Tutorial.08

It will contain the following files:
Movie8, Hours8, Edward8, ISD8, Homes8, Sonoma8

Put this folder in the Data Files folder:
Tutorial.09

It will contain the following files:
Movie9, Hours9, HOURSECURE, Edward9, Edward9.bak, EDWARDSECURE, ISD9, Homes9, Sonoma9

Put this folder in the Data Files folder:
Tutorial.10

It will contain the following files:
Movie10, Hours10, Edward10, ISD10, Homes10, Sonoma10

When you begin each tutorial, be sure you are using the correct files. Refer to the File Finder Chart at the back of this text for more detailed information on which files are used in which tutorials. See the inside front or inside back cover of this book for more information on Data Files, or ask your instructor or technical support person for assistance.

Using Your Own Computer

If you are going to work through this book using your own computer, you need:

- **Computer System** Access 2000 must be installed on your computer. This book assumes a complete installation of Access 2000.

- **Data Files** You will not be able to complete the tutorials or exercises in this book using your own computer until you have your Data Files. It is highly recommended that you work off your computer's hard drive or your personal network drive.

Visit Our World Wide Web Site

Additional materials designed especially for you are available on the World Wide Web. Go to www.course.com.

To the Instructor

The Data Files are available on the Instructor's Resource Kit for this title. Follow the instructions in the Help file on the CD-ROM to install the programs to your network or standalone computer. For information on creating Data Disks, see the To the Student section above.

You are granted a license to copy the Data Files to any computer or computer network used by students who have purchased this book.

In this tutorial you will:

- Review standard database-naming conventions

- Add a group to the database window

- Add table and field validation rules to an existing table

- Explore an existing query

- Create a query expression to use for sorting

- Explore existing forms and their design

- Change the cycle property of a form

- Add a text expression to a form

- Explore an existing report and its design

- Add a page break to a group footer

- Add an expression to a report

REVIEWING DATABASE OBJECTS

Exploring the Database for MovieCam Technologies

CASE

MovieCam Technologies

MovieCam Technologies specializes in the development and manufacture of state-of-the-art imaging systems for the entertainment industry. MovieCam, which is based in northern California, has grown rapidly over the past five years, from a small consulting firm to a sophisticated engineering and manufacturing firm which produces cameras that mount to virtually any type of moving platform, including helicopters, boats, and camera cars. Computer systems have been used in all aspects of business operations since the company's inception, but many of their methods and procedures are now outdated and ineffective.

One of the problems that MovieCam is experiencing is how to track and manage a growing number of orders for standard and custom-engineered camera systems. Currently, a product manager is responsible for coordinating the engineering and production of these camera systems from the time that a bid is requested through the final date of completion. Product managers traditionally have used spreadsheets to track the jobs for which they are responsible; however, this has led to long hours at the computer entering and compiling time card information. And, some managers who are not proficient with spreadsheets have opted to track products the old-fashioned way—making mental notes and acting on their gut feelings!

MovieCam management decided that an employee, labor, and product tracking system should be designed and written in the database program Microsoft Access 2000. Jason Thompson, an Access developer, began a prototype system, but left the company before completing it.

Amanda Tyson, director of Information Systems, has asked you to help complete the system. Earlier this week you met with her and the product managers to discuss the objectives for the database. The list of objectives that the group compiled follows:

- The database should store employee, time card, hours worked, and product data.
- Product managers, company officers, and other personnel should be able to access reports on employees, products, and total hours spent on particular projects.
- Employees should be able to update some portions of the system via the company intranet.

SESSION 1.1

In this session you will review key database terms and concepts, learn to use a naming convention for Access objects, and review table design. You will create table-level and field-level validation rules, create an expression in a query, and sort a query based on that expression.

Introduction to Database Management Systems

Microsoft Access 2000 is a **database management system (DBMS)** that is used to manage, store, retrieve, and order large amounts of information. Unlike many desktop database management systems, in Access all the objects required to make the database operational are stored in one file. Access also is a **relational database management system (RDBMS)**. In an RDBMS, you can link tables through a common field, and thereby combine data in new objects and minimize data duplication. An RDBMS also can store a large amount of information; an Access database can be up to two gigabytes in size.

MovieCam Technologies needs an RDBMS to manage labor and product information. This would allow managers to design tables to contain data that's specific to a certain subject, such as employees, time cards, products, and projects or jobs.

The spreadsheet that MovieCam managers use to track data on employees and time cards is shown in Figure 1-1. It is repetitive and difficult to understand.

| Figure 1-1 | SPREADSHEET |

Figure 1-2 shows how the data can be organized in a database. One table contains data on employees and another table stores data on time cards. As shown in Figure 1-2, the tables have a common field—EmpNo—on which they can be joined so that other database objects can be generated using data from both tables.

Figure 1-2   EMPLOYEE AND TIME CARD DATA IN TWO TABLES

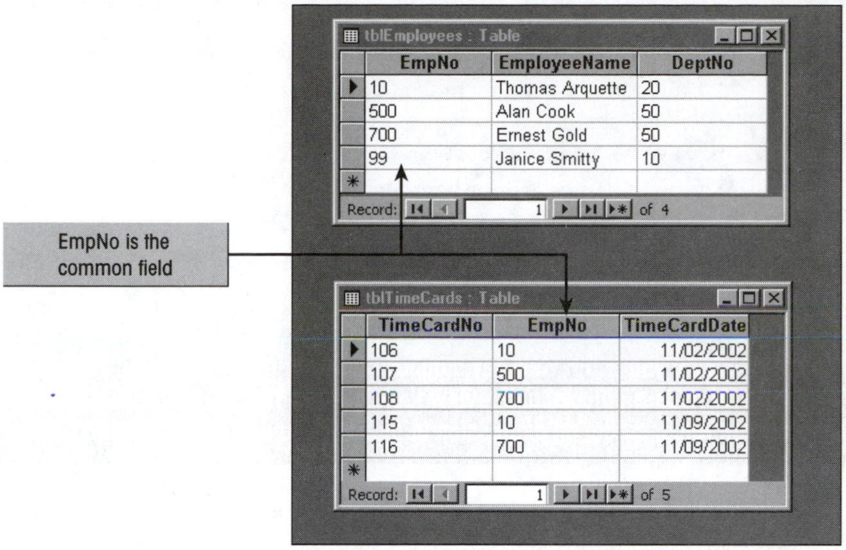

tblEmployees : Table

EmpNo	EmployeeName	DeptNo
10	Thomas Arquette	20
500	Alan Cook	50
700	Ernest Gold	50
99	Janice Smitty	10
*		

Record: ◄◄ ◄   1   ► ►I ►* of 4

EmpNo is the common field

tblTimeCards : Table

TimeCardNo	EmpNo	TimeCardDate
106	10	11/02/2002
107	500	11/02/2002
108	700	11/02/2002
115	10	11/09/2002
116	700	11/09/2002
*		

Record: ◄◄ ◄   1   ► ►I ►* of 5

Opening the MovieCam Technologies Database

Amanda has asked you to take a look at the database Jason started before leaving the company.

To open the MovieCam Technologies database:

1. Make sure that the data files have been copied to the local or network drive on which you will be working.

   TROUBLE? If the data files have not been copied to your local or network drive, you must do so before you can proceed. Read the "Read This Before You Begin" section on page 2, or ask your instructor for help.

2. Start Access and open the **Movie1** database located in the **Tutorial.01** folder on your local hard drive or network drive.

The Movie1 database is displayed in the Access window. The Tables option on the Objects bar of the Database window is selected, so you see the four tables that Jason created. You notice that he named the tables with "tbl" preceding each descriptive name. This naming convention will be discussed next.

Naming Conventions

Even the simplest Access database can have hundreds of objects. For that reason, you should develop a naming convention or standard that clearly defines the type and purpose of each object. A name also can help make the relationship between objects clear, as in the case of a linking table in a many-to-many relationship. A consistent naming convention will bring order to your database, aid in documentation, and make it easier for you and others to understand the database.

Before you can develop a naming convention, you need to understand the Access requirements for naming objects:

- Object names can be up to 64 characters long.
- Object names can include any combination of letters, numbers, spaces, and special characters, except a period (.), an exclamation point (!), an accent grave (`), and brackets ([ ]).
- Object names cannot begin with a space.
- Object names cannot include control characters (ASCII values 0 through 31).
- Table, view, or stored procedure names cannot include a double quotation mark (").
- Table and query names must be unique in the database. However, other objects can have the same name. For example, it is possible to name a table and a form "Customer", but it is not possible to name a table and a query "Customer". Although possible, naming different objects with the same name is confusing and is *not* recommended.

Following are the suggested naming standards that many developers use. Examples of objects named using this convention are shown in Figure 1-3.

- Include a tag in lowercase letters at the beginning of the object name to identify the type of object; for example, "tbl" preceding each table name. This tag is typically three characters long except in instances where a prefix is added. Some developers include a tag in field names to specify in which table the field is located.
- Add a prefix to the tag to further identify an object. For example, a form tag is "frm", but if it is a subform, the prefix "s" could be added to "frm" to further identify the type of form. Another prefix that might be added to the form name and tag is "zt". It is used to specify temporary objects in the database.
- Include a descriptive name that contains no spaces or special characters. Capitalize each word to make the name easier to read.
- Keep object names short to avoid misspellings and excessive typing in expressions and Visual Basic for Applications (VBA) code.
- Table names should be plural—tblEmployees as opposed to tblEmployee.

Figure 1-3	SAMPLE OBJECT NAMES			
OBJECT TYPE	**TAG**	**DESCRIPTIVE NAME**	**NAME**	
Table	tbl	Employees	tblEmployees	
*Field	emp	FirstName	empFirstName	
Query	qry	EmployeesCurrent	qryEmployeesCurrent	
Form	frm	Employees	frmEmployees	
Report	rpt	EmployeesByDept	rptEmployeesByDept	
Macros	mcr	Global	mcrGlobal	
**Macro group (prefix added)	mfrm	MainSwitchboard	mfrmMainSwitchboard	
Modules	bas or mdl	DateFunctions	basDateFunctions	

* In all instances, the tag represents the object type except in naming a field. The object name represents the table name in which the field is found.

** The tag "mfrm" and the use of the form name helps identify which form the macros are used in. The "m" designates macro and "frmMainSwitchboard" is the name of the form.

There are certainly exceptions and variations to the preceding guidelines. Some developers include tags in the names of all objects in the database except tables. Others forego using tags in field names or use singular names for their tables. There is, however, one consistent rule that developers follow: no spaces in any names. Spaces in field and object names create more work when you write expressions and can produce naming conflicts in VBA and in expressions.

It also is a good idea to make sure that object names don't duplicate the name of properties or keywords reserved for special purposes in Access. For example, the Name property is used in Access to name properties so that you can refer to them in macros, expressions, and in VBA, as well as for documentation purposes. You should not name a field in one of your tables Name because this can produce unexpected behavior in some circumstances. Keywords reserved by Access for use in Structured Query Language (SQL) and VBA will be introduced as they apply to topics presented in these tutorials.

The naming convention used in these tutorials follows the guidelines listed above, with the exception of using tags in field names. Tags and prefixes precede all other object names.

The Database Window

An Access database consists of the following objects: tables, queries, forms, reports, pages, macros, and modules. The **Database window** shown in Figure 1-4 is what you see when you open an Access file. It is the command center for working with objects.

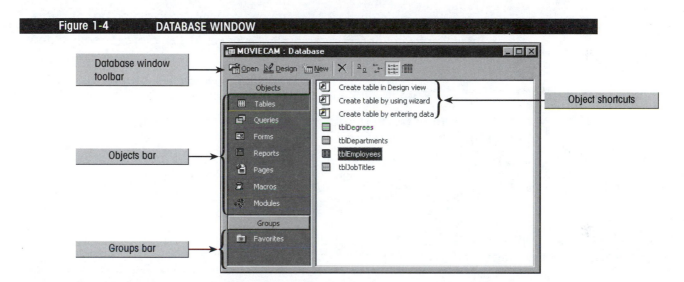

Figure 1-4   DATABASE WINDOW

The **Database window toolbar** contains buttons for opening, creating, and deleting objects, and for changing views.

The **Objects bar** along the left side of the window contains buttons for viewing each database object. **Object shortcuts** provide a quick method for creating an object. To remove these shortcuts from the Database window, select Options on the Tools menu, select the View tab, and deselect the New object shortcuts option.

The **Groups bar** is handy for organizing database objects according to subject. For example, you might create a group to contain all the queries and reports relating to employees. It becomes difficult to keep track of these objects when you have 10 or more in the database. The Favorites group that you see on the Groups bar cannot be removed.

In your initial review of the MovieCam database, you think it would be a good idea to create a new group to contain reports and queries related to employee data. These objects will then be easier to access.

To create the EmployeeReports group:

1. Right-click in the Groups bar to display the shortcut menu. See Figure 1-5.

Figure 1-5   **SHORTCUT MENU**

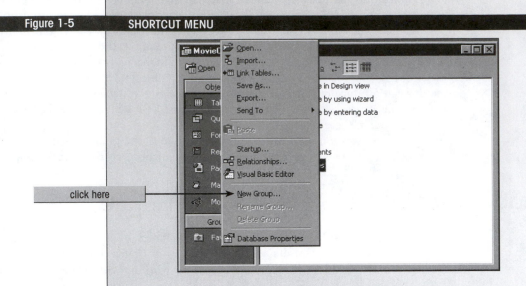

2. Click **New Group** on the shortcut menu. The New Group dialog box appears.

3. Type **EmployeeReports** and press the **Enter** key. The *EmployeeReports* folder appears below Favorites in the Groups bar.

4. Click **Queries** in the Objects bar. Drag the **qryEmployeesCurrent** query into the EmployeeReports group.

5. Click **Reports** in the Objects bar. Drag the **rptEmployeesByDept** report into the group.

6. Click the **EmployeeReports** group on the Groups bar. The two objects— qryEmployeesCurrent and rptEmployeesByDept—are now listed in the Database window.

Tables

Now that you are familiar with the Database window, you want to review the various objects in the database. You start with tables, which are the foundation of the database. Tables store data, in the form of **records**, that is used to generate all the other objects in the database. The properties associated with tables and with their fields allow you to streamline the data entry process and validate data as it is entered.

The MovieCam database contains four tables. Human resource, accounting, and labor-related information is stored in the tblEmployees table. The tblDepartments, tblDegrees, and tblJobTitles tables contain data on the company's departments, employees' academic degrees, and job titles. The tables and their current relationships are shown in Figure 1-6.

Figure 1-6   **MOVIECAM TABLES AND RELATIONSHIPS**

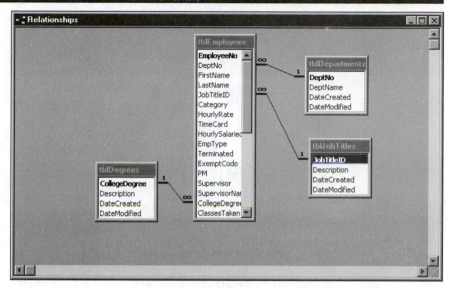

Table and Field Properties

You already know that tables, forms, and reports are considered objects in Access. Likewise, fields, controls, relationships, and indexes are considered objects as well. All objects in Access have properties that describe them and allow you to manipulate them. You can think of objects as nouns and properties as their adjectives.

To view the properties of a table, you must open it in Design view. The properties for the tblEmployees table are shown in Figure 1-7. As you can see, there are properties for validating data, filtering, and working with subdatasheets. (Subdatasheets will be discussed in Tutorial 2.)

Figure 1-7   **TBLEMPLOYEES PROPERTIES**

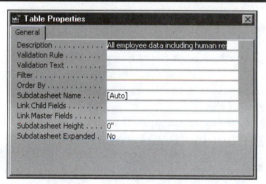

A **validation rule** is an optional expression (formula) that can be created at the table or field level. **Table validation rules** allow you to test the validity of one field compared to another. **Field validation rules** allow you to validate a field compared to a constant. **Validation text** appears in the warning message box that opens if the validation rule is violated. Figure 1-8 shows some sample validation rules and validation text for both tables and fields.

Figure 1-8	SAMPLE VALIDATION RULES FOR TABLES AND FIELDS

TABLE/FIELD	FIELD(S) USED	VALIDATION RULE	VALIDATION TEXT
Field	EmpType	"R" Or "P" Or "T" Or "C"	You must enter an R, P, T, or C code into this field.
Field	HourlyRate	Between 7 And 150	You must enter a value between $7.00 and $150.00.
Field	DateModified	>=#1/1/1900# Or Is Null	This date must be January 1, 1900, or higher, or left blank.
Table	DateCreated and HireDate	[DateCreated]>=[HireDate]	The DateCreated must be the same or higher than the HireDate.

Next you'll open tblEmployees table in Design view and browse through some of the fields to see which properties Jason set.

To examine field properties of the tblEmployees table:

1. Make sure that **Tables** is selected on the Objects bar of the Database window, click **tblEmployees**, and then click the **Design** button in the Database window toolbar.

2. Scroll down. When you see the **HireDate** field, click it.

   You see that Jason set the Required property for the HireDate field to *Yes*. You also note the other properties that Jason set for this field. The Caption property contains *Hire Date* to make the field name easier to read in Datasheet view. The Format property is set to *mm/dd/yyyy*, a custom format designed to display a four-digit year.

3. Click the **BirthDate** field. This field also has the Required property set to *Yes*, its Caption property changed to *Birth Date*, and its Format property set to *mm/dd/yyyy*.

Because both fields must have entries as specified by the Required property, it is logical to expect that the date of hire will always be later than the date of birth. It is not possible to test these dates against each other in a field validation rule, so you must create the validation rule at the table level.

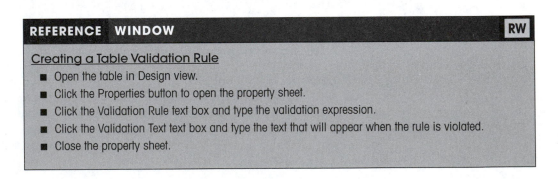

REFERENCE WINDOW   **RW**

Creating a Table Validation Rule
- Open the table in Design view.
- Click the Properties button to open the property sheet.
- Click the Validation Rule text box and type the validation expression.
- Click the Validation Text text box and type the text that will appear when the rule is violated.
- Close the property sheet.

Now you will create a table validation rule to test these dates against each other.

To create a table validation rule:

1. Click the **Properties** button 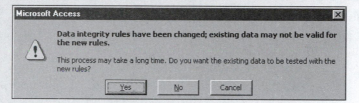 on the toolbar to display the Table Properties dialog box.

2. Type **[HireDate]>[BirthDate]** in the Validation Rule text box and press the **Enter** key.

3. Type **The hire date must be later than the birth date of the employee** in the Validation Text text box.

4. Close the Table Properties dialog box and switch to Datasheet view. You are asked to save the table.

5. Click the **Yes** button.

   A warning message displays as shown in Figure 1-9. The message states that data integrity rules have changed, and asks if you would like to test the existing data against the new rules.

Figure 1-9	DATA INTEGRITY WARNING MESSAGE

Microsoft Access ✕

⚠ **Data integrity rules have been changed; existing data may not be valid for the new rules.**

This process may take a long time. Do you want the existing data to be tested with the new rules?

[Yes]   [No]   [Cancel]

6. Click the **Yes** button to continue.

   Access tests the existing records against the new validation rule. If any of the records violate the rule, an error message will be displayed and you will be prompted to continue testing or abandon the new rule.

Next you will open the table in Datasheet view to test the validation rule.

To test the table validation rule:

1. Scroll to the Birth Date field, select the entry for the first record, and enter today's date.

2. Press the ↓ key to move out of the record. The error message you entered in the Validation Text text box should appear.

   TROUBLE? If a warning message did not appear, you might not have typed the square brackets around each field name. If you did not type the brackets, Access places quotation marks around the field names, and your validation rule will not work. Return to Design view. Be sure that square brackets rather than quotation marks enclose the field names.

3. Click the **OK** button, and then click the **Undo** button ↶ on the toolbar to cancel your change.

4. To return to Design view, click the **View** button.

Because MovieCam has been in business since Feb. 1, 1994, it is impossible for any employee to have been hired prior to that date. You now will create a field validation rule to that effect for the HireDate field.

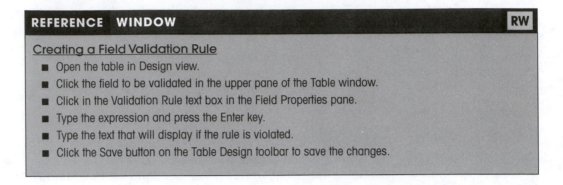

REFERENCE WINDOW **RW**

Creating a Field Validation Rule
- Open the table in Design view.
- Click the field to be validated in the upper pane of the Table window.
- Click in the Validation Rule text box in the Field Properties pane.
- Type the expression and press the Enter key.
- Type the text that will display if the rule is violated.
- Click the Save button on the Table Design toolbar to save the changes.

You will use the Date function to write this Validation Rule. A **function** is a built-in procedure that returns a value and usually requires you to specify one or more pieces of information, called **arguments**. The Date() function returns the current date from the system clock in your computer and does not require any arguments.

To create a field validation rule:

1. Click the **HireDate** field name in the upper pane.

2. Press the **F6** key to move the insertion point to the Field Properties pane of the window. Press the **Enter** key until the insertion point is in the Validation Rule text box.

3. Type **Between 2/1/94 and Date()** and then press the **Enter** key. The insertion point is now in the Validation Text text box, and the Validation Rule value has changed to Between #02/01/1994# And Date().

   TROUBLE? Depending on your system settings, the year in the Validation Rule text box might contain only two digits.

4. Type **The hire date must be between February 1, 1994 and today's date** and then press the **Enter** key. Figure 1-10 shows the Validation Rule and Validation Text properties.

Figure 1-10   HIREDATE FIELD PROPERTIES

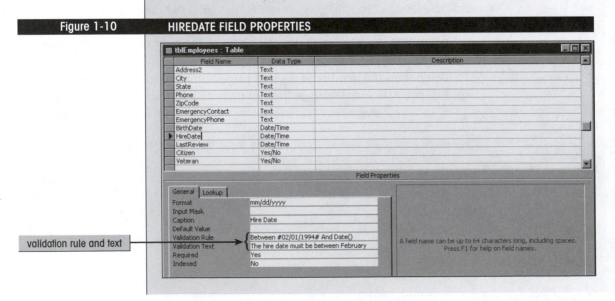

validation rule and text

5. Click the **View** button ▦ on the toolbar to switch to Datasheet view.

6. Click the **Yes** button when prompted to save the table.

7. Click the **Yes** button to continue after the warning message advises you that data integrity rules have changed and that the existing data will be tested with the new rules.

8. Scroll to the right and highlight the first entry in the Hire Date field. Type **2/1/93** and press the **Enter** key. The validation error message should be displayed.

9. Click the **OK** button, and then press the **Esc** key to remove 2/1/93 and replace it with the original entry.

10. Click the **Close** button ☒ on the Table window title bar to close the table and return to the Database window.

Field Properties

Validation rules and text are only two of many types of field properties. Each data type has a set of field properties that apply to it. For example, Date/Time properties are different from Text properties. Additional field properties are defined below:

- **Field Size.** The number of characters a field can contain.

- **Format.** Standard predefined formats for Number, Date/Time, and other types of fields. Custom formats may also be entered. A commonly used format in Text fields is the > symbol, which forces all characters to uppercase. The Format property does not affect the way data must be entered, only how it will be displayed after it is entered.

- **New Value.** This property can be applied only to fields of AutoNumber data type. You can choose Increment or Random. The Increment choice automatically generates new numbers in the AutoNumber field by adding one to the highest existing value. If you choose Random, Access generates a random integer for this value.

- **Precision.** This property can be applied only to fields of Number data type where the Field Size property has been changed to Decimal. It defines the total number of digits used to represent a numeric value.

- **Scale.** This property can be applied only to fields of Number data type where the Field Size property has been changed to Decimal. It is used to determine the number of decimal places to the right of the decimal point.

- **Decimal Places.** This property applies to Number and Currency fields and determines the number of decimal places displayed to the right of the decimal point. If you choose Auto, the number of decimal places to the right of the decimal point depends on the choice made in the Format property. You also may choose a number from the drop-down list or type in a value.

- **Input Mask.** The input mask controls how data is actually entered into a field, opposed to how it is displayed after it is entered (Format property). An input mask is composed of a string of characters that act as placeholders for the characters that will be entered into the field. The Input Mask Wizard has a number of predefined input masks from which you can choose, including masks for zip codes and Social Security numbers, as shown in Figure 1-11.

Figure 1-11   INPUT MASK WIZARD

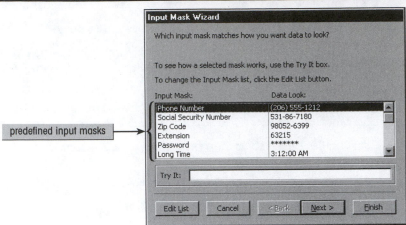

predefined input masks

- **Caption.** This property displays text other than the field name as the column heading in Datasheet view when you open a table or query. When you create a form or report from the table, the caption is used as the label for the control. There are no restrictions on using punctuation symbols in captions.

- **Default Value.** When you enter a value in the Default Value text box, Access automatically enters that value in each new record. For fields of Number or Currency data types, Access inserts a default value of zero. No entry is interpreted as null, so number data types should never be left empty. Null propagates through expressions (formulas), so if a value in an expression is null, the result of the expression is null. If you add two fields and one is null, the result will be null. This is called propagation of null values.

- **Required.** If you set this property to Yes, text or a value must be entered into the field.

- **Allow Zero Length.** This property applies to Text, Memo, and Hyperlink fields. If you set it to Yes, a zero length string may be entered. To enter a zero length string, type a set of two quotation marks next to one another. A zero length string and null both appear as an empty or blank field; however, each has a different meaning. A zero length string indicates that the data doesn't exist, while null indicates that the data exists but is unknown. For example, if you know that a customer has no e-mail address, you might choose to enter a zero length string in the field because the e-mail address doesn't exist. Another customer might have an e-mail address, but because you don't know what it is, the field is left blank or null.

- **Indexed.** Indexes speed up the process of searching and sorting on a particular field, but they can slow updates (data entry). You'll probably want to index the fields on which you plan to sort or search frequently. (Indexes, in conjunction with primary keys, foreign keys, and setting up relationships will be discussed in more detail in Tutorial 2.)

- **Unicode Compression.** Microsoft Access 2000 uses the Unicode character-encoding scheme to represent data in a Text, Memo, or Hyperlink field. In Unicode, each character is represented by two bytes instead of by a single byte. When you set the Unicode Compression property of a field to Yes, any character whose first byte is 0 is compressed from two bytes to one byte when it is stored, and uncompressed back to two bytes when it is retrieved.

Queries

Queries are a powerful tool in database management systems. Queries are used to find records that meet a condition or criterion. They also are commonly used to filter data from a single table, group data with totals, combine fields from more than one table, update or delete data, append data from one table to another, or create an entirely new table. The results (or the records found) of a query—referred to as the **recordset**— can be used to generate other objects in the database.

Select Queries and Expressions

Select queries are commonly used to combine fields from more than one table into a single object. Up to 16 different tables can be used in the construction of one select query.

The MovieCam database contains a select query (qryEmployeesCurrent) that is used as the basis for the report that lists employees by department (rptEmployeesByDept). It is based on the tblEmployees table and finds records for current employees. The query now contains one field expression.

An **expression** is a combination of symbols and values that produces a result. A few examples of how expressions are used in Access follow:

- Set a property that establishes a validation rule or sets a default field property.
- Enter a criteria expression in a query.
- Create a calculated field in a query.
- Set a condition for carrying out an action(s) in a macro.
- Construct functions or procedures in VBA.
- Edit a SQL query.

You should use the following guidelines to write expressions in queries:

- Separate the name of the expression from the actual expression (formula) by a colon.
- Do not include spaces or special characters in the name of the expression. Although spaces and some special characters are allowed, this practice is discouraged. Capitalize each word in the name so that it is easy to read.
- You do not need to type brackets around field names referenced in expressions if you do not use spaces and special characters in the name of the field.

The qryEmployeesCurrent query contains an expression that **concatenates**, or joins, the FirstName and LastName text fields using the ampersand (&) operator and the Space(x) function, where x is the number of spaces desired between the first and last name. The expression looks like the following:

Name:[FirstName]&Space(1)&[LastName]

Now that you've reviewed the tblEmployees table and made some changes, you take a look at the query that Jason created.

To review qryEmployeesCurrent:

1. Click **Queries** in the Objects bar.

2. Click **qryEmployeesCurrent** in the Database window and click the **Open** button.

    Notice that the records are displayed in ascending order by the EmployeeNo field. Although the query does not specify a sort on this field, EmployeeNo is the primary key for this table and Access automatically sorts data in ascending order by the primary key. However, as shown in Figure 1-12, because EmployeeNo is a text field, 99 appears at the bottom of the list instead of in numerical order.

Figure 1-12	QRYEMPLOYEESCURRENT

qryEmployeesCurrent : Select Query

Employee No	Dept No	Name	Job Title	Hourly/Salary
10	Engineering	Thomas Arquette	Engineering Manager	S
150	Accounting	Carolyn Valdez	Accountant	S
210	Product Management	Martin Woodward	Product Manager	S
500	Production	Alan Cook	Electronic Assembler	H
600	Engineering	Gloria Cauldwell	Mechanical Engineer	H
700	Production	Ernest Gold	Production/Assembly	H
800	Accounting	Ann Garcia	Accounting Clerk	H
99	Accounting	Janice Smitty	Accountant	S
*			0	H

text field does not sort in numerical order

You think the report based on this query would be clearer if the employee numbers were sorted in numerical order. You decide to create an expression in the query that will convert the EmployeeNo field from text to a number type.

The **CInt function** is used to convert a text or date field to an integer. The syntax of the CInt function is: CInt([fieldname])

To create a field expression in a query:

1. Click **DeptNo** in the lower pane of the window.

2. Click **Insert** on the menu bar, and then click **Columns**. A blank column is now positioned to the left of the DeptNo column.

3. In the **Field** text box of the column you added, type **EmpNoInt:CInt(EmployeeNo)** and then press the ▼ key twice.

    EmpNoInt is the name of the field expression. *CInt(EmployeeNo)* is the function that converts the EmployeeNo field to an integer.

4. Type **a** to select **Ascending** from the drop-down list as shown in Figure 1-13.

Figure 1-13	QRYEMPLOYEESCURRENT

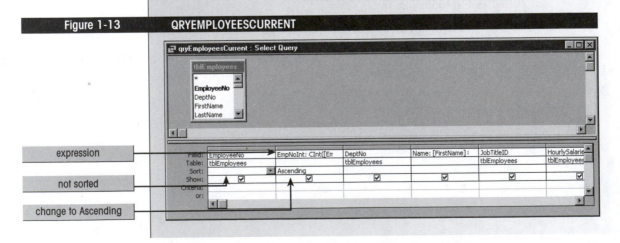

expression

not sorted

change to Ascending

5. Click the **Run** button ☐ on the toolbar. The employee numbers are now sorted from smallest to largest, instead of on the first character of the entry.

6. Close the query and save your changes.

Parameter Queries

Parameter queries allow you to substitute a prompt for criteria. When a parameter query is run, the prompt for information displays on the screen and the criteria is entered at that time. This allows you to repeatedly run one query for different conditions.

Crosstab Queries

Crosstab queries display summarized values from one or more tables in a spreadsheet format. You can group data by column and by row so that summary data, such as monthly or yearly totals or averages, can be generated for a specific group of records.

Action Queries

Action queries include update, delete, append, and make-table queries. They are different from select queries in that they modify the data in the underlying table when they are run. Action queries are frequently used to archive data. A Yes/No field can identify inactive records, and an Append query can be run to append them to another table. A delete query might then be run to delete inactive records from the active table. An archive table can be created initially using a make-table query. (These queries and the process of archiving will be explored in greater detail in Tutorial 3.)

SQL-Specific Queries

SQL-specific queries are written in SQL. They cannot be created in the QBE (Query By Example) grid like other types of queries. They must be written in SQL view. SQL view is accessed in the query's Design View. You would click View on the menu bar and then click SQL View. You then create the query by entering SQL statements and clauses. There are three types of SQL queries: union, pass-through, and data definition. Pass-through and data-definition queries will not be covered in these tutorials.

Union queries let you query for similar data from two or more unrelated tables. For example, you might want to compile a list of names and addresses of your vendors and customers for a mailing. The data for each is found in two separate, unrelated tables. A union query could be written to bring data together from these two tables. (Union queries will be discussed in greater detail in Tutorial 3.)

Session 1.1 QUICK | CHECK

1. A(n) ——————— is used to manage, store, retrieve, and order large amounts of information.

2. The ——————— character forces all characters to uppercase when it is used to format a text field.

3. The ——————— operator is used to concatenate text fields in an expression.

4. The ——————— function can be used to convert data in a text field to an integer.

5. What is the purpose of a crosstab query?

6. List the four types of action queries.

7. List the three types of SQL queries.

SESSION 1.2

In this session you will review forms and their design. You will change the cycle property of a form, add rectangles for grouping controls, and add a text expression to a form. You will review reports, add an expression to a report to count the number of records in each group, and add a page break to a grouping footer.

Forms

Forms are used to display, edit, and enter data on screen. A form is basically a different way to display records; however, it can incorporate pictures, graphs, music, narration, and other controls that you do not see in a table or query. Forms are also used to create the user interface for a database. (You'll learn more about the user interface in Tutorial 4.)

The MovieCam database includes two forms. The frmEmployees(page_break) form, as shown in Figure 1-14, is designed with a page break that splits the data from the tblEmployees table between two screens. You click the *Human Resource Info* button at the bottom of the form to display the second screen.

| Figure 1-14 | FRMEMPLOYEES (PAGE_BREAK) |

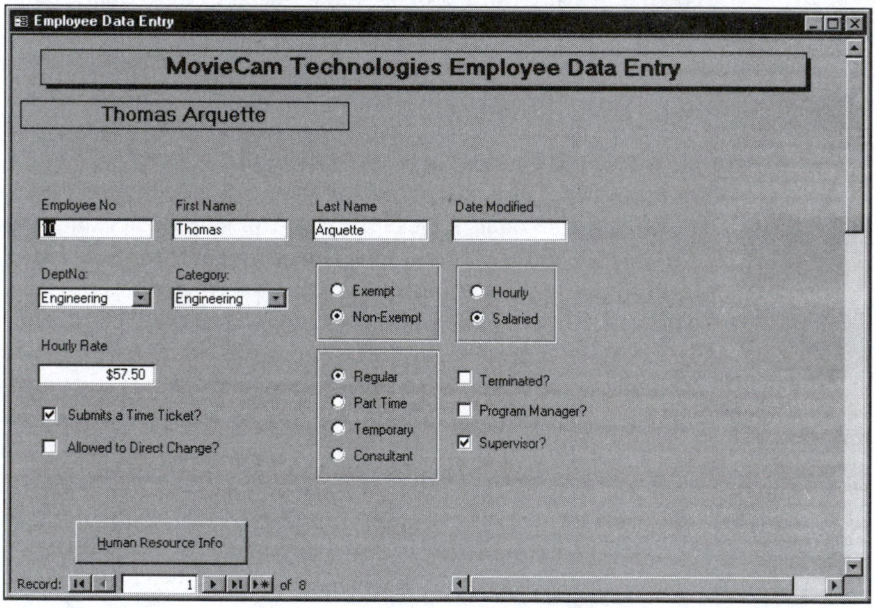

The frmEmployees form, as shown in Figure 1-15, uses a tab control to present the two categories of data from the tblEmployees table.

Figure 1-15   **FRMEMPLOYEES**

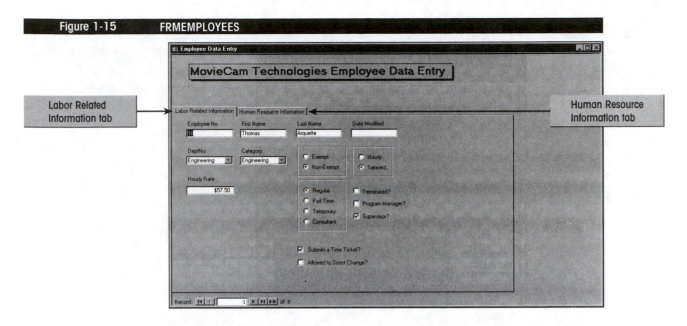

A form that uses the tab control is helpful when you want to segregate data or organize data when the underlying table has many fields. But the tab control can cause the form to load more slowly than a form that uses a page break. When you use a tab control, the tabs are created on the form, and then the text box, combo box, and check box controls are placed on top of the form. Overlapping controls in this manner causes the decrease in the form's performance.

You understand that Jason created the forms to show users of the database two options for entering and viewing records. Ultimately, you will retain the option that performs the best.

To explore the frmEmployees(page_break) form:

1. Make sure that Access is running, that the **Movie1** database located in the Tutorial.01 folder on your local or network drive is open, and that **Forms** is selected in the Objects bar of the Database window.

2. Click **frmEmployees(page_break)**, and then click the **Open** button.

3. Click the **Human Resource Info** button at the bottom of the form. The second page of the form displays, and the button at the bottom changes to a Labor Related Info button.

4. Click the **Labor Related Info** button to return to the first page of the form.

5. Press the **Tab** key to tab through the controls on the form until the insertion point is in the Address Line 1 text box. The first page and a portion of the second page of the form should be displayed as shown in Figure 1-16.

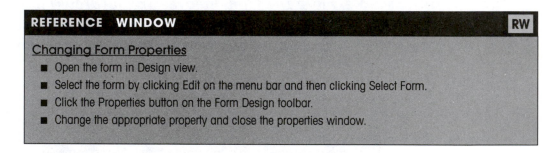

Figure 1-16 VIEWING TWO PAGES OF A FORM

You can apply the **Cycle property** to a form to control the order in which you tab through fields and records in a form. The default is All Records, which in a form with a page break causes a portion of two pages to display on the screen simultaneously. In this form, you prefer to cycle through the Current Page only, and use the command buttons to move between pages.

REFERENCE WINDOW **RW**

<u>Changing Form Properties</u>
- Open the form in Design view.
- Select the form by clicking Edit on the menu bar and then clicking Select Form.
- Click the Properties button on the Form Design toolbar.
- Change the appropriate property and close the properties window.

Next you'll change the Cycle property of the frmEmployees(page_break) form to Current Page.

To change the Cycle property of a form:

1. Switch to Design view.

2. Open the **Edit** menu and then click **Select Form**.

3. Click the **Properties** button on the Form Design toolbar.

4. If necessary, click the **Other** tab in the Form properties dialog box.

5. Change the **Cycle** property to **Current Page** as shown in Figure 1-17.

| Figure 1-17 | FORM PROPERTIES DIALOG BOX |

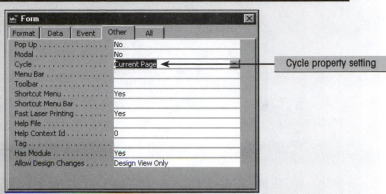

To test the change you made, you will open the frmEmployees(page_break) form in Form view and tab through its controls.

6. Close the Form properties dialog box.

7. Switch to Form view and press the **Tab** key to move through the controls on the first page.

The focus returns to the first control on the form after the command button at the bottom. When the command button has the focus, the user can click it or press the Enter key to move to the second page of the form and display the entire page. The command button has the focus when a dotted line outlines the text on the button.

8. Close the form and save your changes.

Now you want to take a look at the frmEmployees form to determine its ease of use.

To explore the frmEmployees form:

1. Open the **frmEmployees** form in Form view. It contains tab controls with the data divided into two categories.

2. Click the **Human Resource Information** tab at the top of the form to view the controls. Notice that the *Home Address* and *Identification* sections on the form are accented with a rectangle that is formatted with a sunken special effect.

3. Switch to Design view, and click the **Human Resource Information** tab.

You determine that the form's design could be improved if the Job Related Information and Education & Training controls were boxed in the same manner as the Home Address and Identification sections.

REFERENCE   WINDOW   RW

Adding a Rectangle to a Form
■ Open the form in Design view.
■ Display the toolbox by clicking View on the menu bar and then clicking Toolbox, or by clicking the
  Toolbox button on the toolbar.
■ Click the Rectangle button on the toolbox and draw the box on the form by clicking and dragging.

Next, you will add rectangles to the form.

To add rectangles to the form:

1. If necessary, display the toolbox by clicking the **Toolbox** button 🛠 on the
   Form Design toolbar.

2. Click the **Rectangle** button 🔲 on the toolbox. When you position the mouse
   pointer on the form, the pointer changes to a ⁺🔲 shape.

3. Click and drag to create a rectangle around the Job Related Information controls as shown in Figure 1-18.

Figure 1-18   ADDING A RECTANGLE TO FRMEMPLOYEES

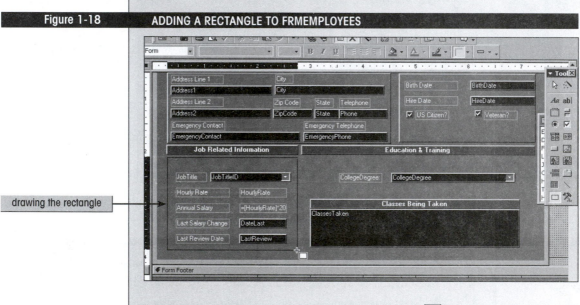

drawing the rectangle

4. Click the **arrow** on the **Special Effect** button 🔲 on the toolbar and
   click **Sunken**.

   TROUBLE? Your Special Effect button might have a different special effect
   symbol depending on which of its options was previously chosen.

5. Create a rectangle to enclose the Education & Training controls as shown in
   Figure 1-19, and then apply the **Sunken** effect.

| Figure 1-19 | COMPLETED FRMEMPLOYEES |

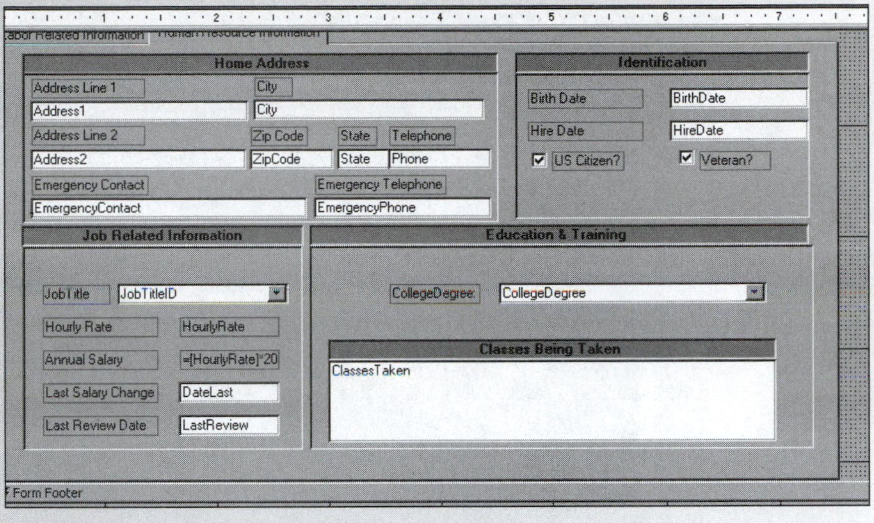

6. Click the **Save** button to save your changes to the form.

The frmEmployees(page_break) form has a text box at the top of the form that displays the employee first and last name. The text box value is a text expression that concatenates the values of the FirstName and LastName fields with a space between them. You decide to add this same expression to the frmEmployees form so that the employee's name shows regardless of which tab of the form is displayed.

To add a text expression to a form:

1. If necessary, display the toolbox by clicking the **Toolbox** button on the Form Design toolbar, and then click the **Text Box** button on the toolbox.

2. To create a text box, click below the *MovieCam Technologies Employee Data Entry* label in the Form Header section. A label control and an unbound text box appear.

3. To delete the label, click it and press the **Del** key, and then position the insertion point inside the text box.

4. Type **=FirstName&Space(1)&LastName** and press the **Enter** key.

5. Size the label so that it is approximately **2"** wide and ¼" tall as shown in Figure 1-20.

Figure 1-20   FRMEMPLOYEES

text box

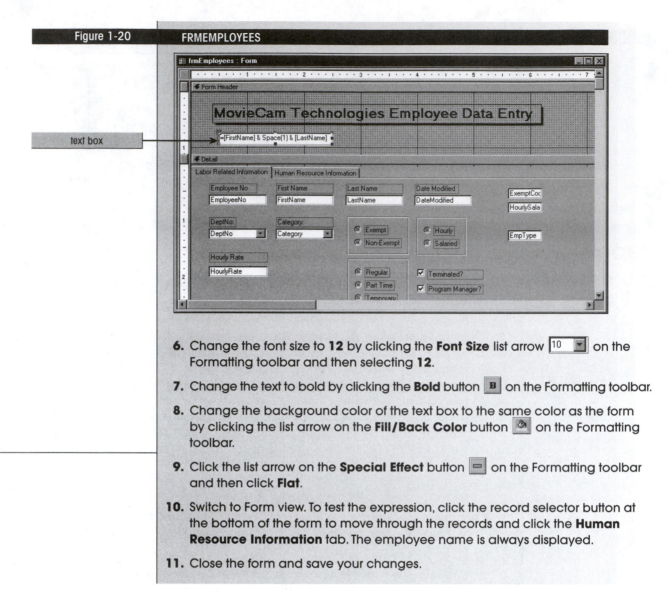

6. Change the font size to **12** by clicking the **Font Size** list arrow 10 ▼ on the Formatting toolbar and then selecting **12**.

7. Change the text to bold by clicking the **Bold** button **B** on the Formatting toolbar.

8. Change the background color of the text box to the same color as the form by clicking the list arrow on the **Fill/Back Color** button 🎨 on the Formatting toolbar.

9. Click the list arrow on the **Special Effect** button ▭ on the Formatting toolbar and then click **Flat**.

10. Switch to Form view. To test the expression, click the record selector button at the bottom of the form to move through the records and click the **Human Resource Information** tab. The employee name is always displayed.

11. Close the form and save your changes.

You prefer the layout of the form with tabs to the page break form and are satisfied with its performance, but you are not sure which layout the users will prefer. Do not delete any objects from the database that might come in handy later on. You decide to rename the frmEmployees(page_break) form with a name that indicates it is a temporary object. If the users prefer it, or if you need to refer to it again, it will be available.

The prefix *zt* is used in front of object names and tags to specify a temporary object, such as a test object or an object saved for reference purposes. The letter *z* is used because all the objects that begin with *z* sort to the bottom of the list in the Database window. When you finish developing the MovieCam application, you will delete all temporary objects that have the prefix *zt*.

Next, you will add this prefix to the name of the form.

To change the name of a form:

1. Make sure that **Forms** is selected in the Objects bar of the Database window.

2. Right-click **frmEmployees(page_break)** in the Database window, and then click **Rename** on the shortcut menu.

3. Press the **Home** key to position the insertion point at the beginning of the name, and then type *zt*. The form name should now read *ztfrmEmployees(page_break)*.

TROUBLE? If a message box opens warning that the section width is greater than the page width, click the OK button to continue.

4. Press the **Enter** key to accept your changes.

You have completed your review of the forms in the database. You now decide to examine the report that Jason created.

Reports

Reports are used primarily for printing records in an organized, attractive format. A report may be based on the contents of a table, the results of a saved query, or a SQL statement.

Jason created one report in the MovieCam database. It is a list of all employees grouped by the department in which they work, and contains information such as their job title, salary, and labor category. The Product Managers use the report to project job costs based on employees' current earnings.

To preview a report:

1. Click **Reports** in the Objects bar.

2. Click **rptEmployeesByDept** and click the **Preview** button 🔍 on the Database window toolbar.

TROUBLE? If a message box opens warning that the section width is greater than the page width, click the OK button to continue.

You recall that you already modified the query on which this report is based by changing the sort order of the EmployeeNo field. The sort order in this report needs to reflect the changes you made in the query. This report is grouped on DeptNo so that all of the employees from a particular department print in one group. It is then sorted by EmployeeNo so that each group or department of employees is sorted in ascending order by this number. Because EmployeeNo is a text field which doesn't sort in true numerical order, you will change the Sorting and Grouping options so that the data is sorted by EmpNoInt instead.

To change the sort order in the rptEmployeesByDept report:

1. Switch to Design view.

2. To display the Sorting and Grouping options of the report, click **View** on the menu bar and then click **Sorting and Grouping**.

3. Click **EmployeeNo** in the Field/Expression text box, click its list arrow, and then click **EmpNoInt**, as shown in Figure 1-21. You now have changed the sort order of the report from *EmployeeNo* (a text field) to *EmpNoInt* (an integer).

Figure 1-21   **SORTING AND GROUPING DIALOG BOX**

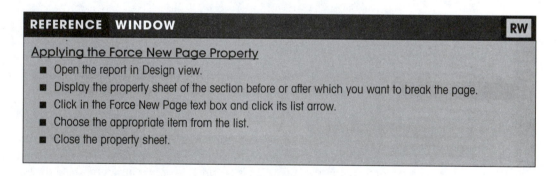

change to EmpNoInt

4. Close the Sorting and Grouping dialog box.

5. Preview the report and note that the data within each group now sorts in numerical order.

   TROUBLE? If a message box opens warning that the section width is greater than the page width, click the OK button to continue.

When you preview the rptEmployeesByDept report, you notice that all the departments print on one page. The report will be easier to read if each new department begins on a separate page.

REFERENCE   WINDOW   **RW**

<u>Applying the Force New Page Property</u>
- Open the report in Design view.
- Display the property sheet of the section before or after which you want to break the page.
- Click in the Force New Page text box and click its list arrow.
- Choose the appropriate item from the list.
- Close the property sheet.

You will change the Force New Page property of the DeptNo Footer to add page breaks between each department.

To use the Force New Page property:

1. Switch to Design view.

2. Right-click the **DeptNo Footer** section band to display the shortcut menu, and then click **Properties** to open the Section Properties dialog box.

3. Click the **All** tab and scroll to the top of the dialog box, if necessary.

4. Click in the **Force New Page** text box and click its list arrow.

5. Click **After Section**, as shown in Figure 1-22, and then close the property sheet.

| Figure 1-22 | **SECTION PROPERTIES** |

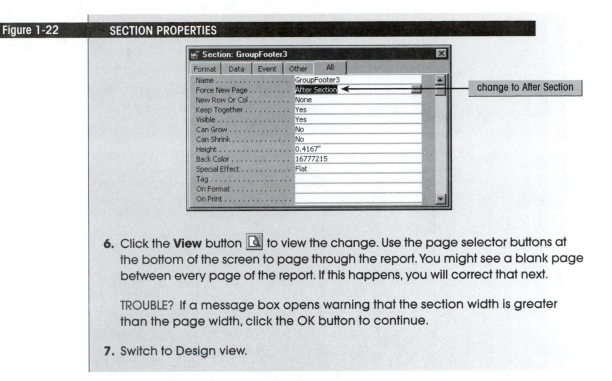

6. Click the **View** button 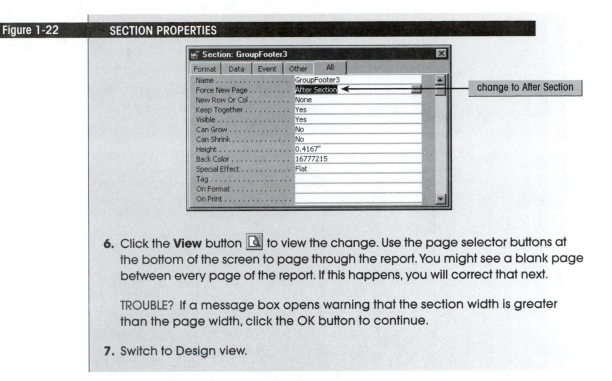 to view the change. Use the page selector buttons at the bottom of the screen to page through the report. You might see a blank page between every page of the report. If this happens, you will correct that next.

   TROUBLE? If a message box opens warning that the section width is greater than the page width, click the OK button to continue.

7. Switch to Design view.

Jason didn't size the report properly to fit on one page, so the extra width of the report is printing on an additional page. The horizontal ruler bar along the top of the report shows the width of the report. This report is designed to print on 8½ x 11-inch paper. The default top, bottom, left, and right margins in Access reports are one inch each. If this report is going to print on 8½-inch wide paper with a one-inch margin on the left and the right, it can be only 6½-inches wide.

Next you'll drag the right border of the report to make it narrower, and adjust the left and right margins to eliminate blank pages between each page of the report.

To size a report and change its margins:

1. Position your mouse pointer on the right border of the report as shown in Figure 1-23.

| Figure 1-23 | **RPTEMPLOYEESBYDEPT** |

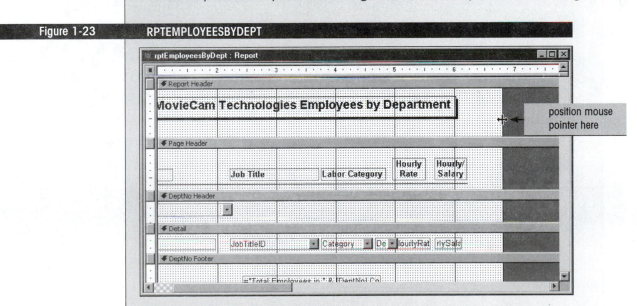

2. Click and drag the mouse to the left to size the report so that it is 6½-inches wide.

   For most printers, this change will eliminate the blank page. You also will change the margin settings just to be sure.

3. Click **File** on the menu bar and then click **Page Setup**.

4. Type **.75** in the **Left** and **Right** text boxes and then click the **OK** button.

5. Preview the report to be sure that the blank pages are gone.

   TROUBLE? If the report still displays blank pages, it might be due to the printer you are using. Repeat steps 3 and 4 and change the Left and Right margins to .5.

6. Switch to Design view.

Jason included a label control in the DeptNo Footer section for the total number of employees, but he did not include the control to calculate and display that total. Next you will add the control that totals the number of employees in each department.

To create an expression in a report:

1. Click the **Text Box** button ![abl] on the toolbox.

2. Click in the blank area at the right of the DeptNo footer. A label control and its Unbound text box control appear.

3. Click the **label** and press the **Delete** key. Next, you'll type the expression to total the number of employees in the Unbound text box control as shown in Figure 1-24.

| Figure 1-24 | CREATING AN EXPRESSION IN THE RPTEMPLOYEESBYDEPT REPORT |

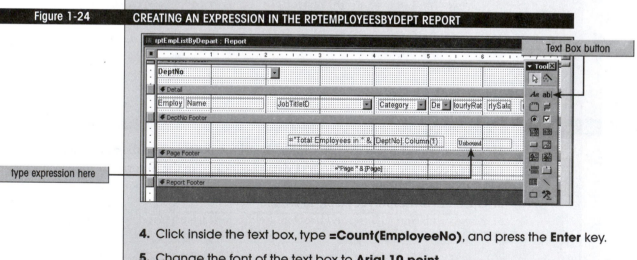

type expression here

4. Click inside the text box, type **=Count(EmployeeNo)**, and press the **Enter** key.

5. Change the font of the text box to **Arial 10 point**.

6. Resize both text boxes in the DeptNo footer section so they are the same height.

7. Align the tops of the text boxes using their top borders.

8. Preview your results. Save your changes.

9. Close the database and exit Access.

Pages

You can display a database object as a data access page that can be published to the Internet or an intranet. The page serves as a live link to that data. Data access pages are a new feature in Access 2000. They are written in HTML and are stored outside the database file. (You will work with data access pages in Tutorial 10.)

Macros

Macros are used with forms and reports to automate database operations. Although not the only method of automation, macros are the easiest to learn. To program with macros at the simplest level, you choose from a list of macro actions that parallel manual actions a user might take to perform a task. After those actions are listed and saved, you can run the macro from a command button or a combo box on a form, to name a few options. Macros will be explored in depth later in these tutorials as an introduction to working with VBA.

Modules

A module is a small compact program written in VBA and is a more flexible and powerful tool than a macro. VBA is a better choice to automate your applications. VBA code runs faster and keeps getting easier to use with each new release. It also allows developers to **trap errors**, which means that when a developer anticipates an error that could occur, the default response of Access can be trapped and replaced with custom messages and actions. It is not possible to trap errors using macro actions, although steps can be taken to avoid them. VBA will be covered in depth in the last several Tutorials.

Session 1.2 QUICK CHECK

1. What is the purpose of a form?
2. On which objects can a report be based?
3. The section property in a report used to create a page break is called
   _____.
4. In what language are data access pages written?
5. In what ways is VBA programming superior to macro programming?
6. What is a module?

REVIEW ASSIGNMENTS

In the Review Assignments, you'll work with the **Hours** database, which is similar to the MovieCam database you worked with in the Tutorial. Complete the following:

1. Start Access and open the **Hours1** database located in the Tutorial.01 folder on your local or network drive.
2. Open the **tblEmployees** table in Design view.
3. Add a validation rule to the HireDate field to test whether it is later than April 1, 1993. Add validation text to explain what the user is doing wrong if they violate the rule.
4. Switch to Datasheet view and save the table when prompted to do so. Click the Yes button to continue after the warning message advises you that data integrity rules have changed.
5. Test the rule to be sure that it works by typing a date in HireDate that is prior to April 1, 1993.
6. Close the table and save your changes.
7. Open the **frmEmployees** form in Design view.
8. Add a text box to the Form Header below the label containing *Employee Data Entry*.
9. Delete the label control that is created with the text box.
10. Position the insertion point inside the text box, type **FirstName&Space(1)&LastName**, and press the Enter key.

11. Format the text box containing the expression so it has the same background color and font as the label control in the Form Header section. Change the font size to 12 point and the special effect to Flat. Switch to Form view to test the expression.
12. Return to Design view and size the text box as necessary to accommodate the contents.
13. Click the Human Resource Information tab.
14. Add rectangles to enclose the Home Address, Identification, and Job Related Information sections.
15. Change the effect of the rectangles to Sunken.
16. Return to Form view to test your changes.
17. Print one page of the form that has the Human Resource Information tab displayed.
18. Close the form and save your changes.
19. Close the database and exit Access.

CASE PROBLEMS

Case 1. Edwards and Company   Edwards and Company is a CPA firm that provides: tax planning and preparation services to individuals and businesses; real estate, finance, and investment consulting; estate and financial planning; and small business consulting. Managing partner Jack Edwards contacted you regarding the firm's database needs. His company needs a database to track employees, contractors, clients, and client services.
Complete the following:
1. Start Access and open the **Edward1** database located in the **Tutorial.01** folder on your local or network drive.
2. Open the **tblConsultants** table in Design view.
3. Add a table validation rule to test whether BirthDate is prior to HireDate.
4. Add validation text to let the user know how to correct the error if the validation rule is violated.
5. Change the Field Size property of the State field to 2.
6. Change the Format property of the State field so that all characters are forced to upper-case after being entered.

Explore   7. Apply a validation rule to the ConsultantType field so that only R or C may be entered. (R stands for regular employee and C stands for consultant.)
8. Add validation text to tell the user what the error is if the validation rule is violated.
9. Test the rule to be sure that it works by typing a letter other than R or C in the ConsultantType field.
10. Close the table and save your changes.

Explore   11. Now you'll use the documenter to print the table properties. Open the Tools menu, select Analyze, and then click Documenter. Click tblConsultants to mark it for printing, and then click the Options button to change the print options. Uncheck the Relationships and Permissions by User and Group options and then click OK to close the Options dialog box. Click OK to close the Documenter. After a moment, a report opens in Preview mode. Click the Print button on the toolbar.
12. Close the report and the database, and then exit Access.

Case 2. San Diego County Information Systems   You are the training coordinator and lead trainer for the San Diego County Information Systems Department. Your job includes planning, coordinating, and training all county employees on computer systems and applications. You develop classes, write course material, train other instructors, and publish a class schedule in the county newsletter each month. You also work closely with the PC team to schedule training for entire departments during major conversions or upgrades of software. To keep track of students and the classes they take, you have developed an Access database.
Complete the following:
1. Start Access and open the **ISD1** database located in the **Tutorial.01** folder on your network or local drive.

2. Click Queries in the Objects bar.

3. Open the **qryEmployeesByDept** query in Design view.

4. Add a column to the query following the DeptNo field and enter the following expression: **DeptNoInt:CInt([tblDepartments]![DeptNo])**. The name of the table is required because there is a field in each table with the name DeptNo.

5. Run the query to test the expression. The results display the DeptNo as an integer rather than as text.

6. Switch back to Design view and delete the column DeptNo.

7. Change the column DeptNoInt sort text box to Ascending.

8. Run the query to test your changes. Notice that department number 50 now displays at the top of the results, instead of after department 400.

9. Switch back to Design view.

10. Add another column to the query after the DeptNoInt column and enter an expression named "StudentName" that concatenates FirstName to LastName with a space between the two fields.

11. Run the query to test your expression.

12. Delete the first and last name columns from the query.

13. Print the query results.

14. Close the query and save your changes.

15. Close the database and exit Access.

Case 3. Christenson Homes   Christenson Homes is a builder and developer of custom homes. At any given time, two or three different subdivisions might be under construction. As office manager, it is your responsibility to keep track of the homes under construction based on lot number and subdivision location. In addition, each home comes with standard options such as doors, carpeting, and showers. Customers may choose from a variety of purchase options, which upgrade the standard options and carry an added cost. To track all of the purchase options for each lot in each subdivision, you have begun an Access database. Complete the following:

1. Start Access and open **Homes1** located in the **Tutorial.01** folder on your local or network drive.

2. Click Reports in the Objects bar.

3. Open the **rptLotsBySub** report in Design view.

4. Change the grouping properties of the SubdivisonID Footer section so that the report breaks after this section.

5. Using the toolbox, add a text box that is approximately .25 inches deep to the SubdivisionID Footer section beneath the Elevation control in the Detail section.

6. Display the property sheet for the text box.

7. Change the Name property to txtCount.

8. Click the Control Source property of the text box, type **=Count([LotNo])**, and press the Enter key.

9. Delete the label that is created when you created the text box.

10. Draw another text box to the left of txtCount. It should be below LotNo and approximately one inch wide.

11. Delete the label that is created when you created the text box.

12. Be sure that the text box properties are displayed.

13. Change the Name property to txtLabel.

14. Click in the Control Source property of the text box and type **="Total Lots in " & [SubdivisionID].[column](1)**. This will display the subdivision name concatenated to the words Total Lots in. Include a space between the word *in* and the quotation mark.

15. Format the new text boxes to be Arial 8 point bold, and size the text boxes to display all of the text.

16. Save and preview the report.

17. Print the report.

18. Close the report and the database, and exit Access.

Case 4. Sonoma Farms   Sonoma Farms is a family-owned and -operated cheese factory located in Sonoma County. Known for their award-winning cheeses, Sonoma Farms attracts thousands of visitors each year. Visitors may observe the cheese being processed, sample from over 20 different kinds of cheese, or simply enjoy the picturesque setting. As marketing manager for Sonoma Farms, you work directly with the regional distributors and end consumers of the Sonoma Farms products. You need to track the customers each distributor is responsible for servicing the customer information for use in product announcements and mailings, and the promotional visits by customers to the factory.

Complete the following:

1. Start Access and open **Sonoma1** located in the **Tutorial.01** folder on your local or network drive.

2. Click Reports in the Objects bar.

3. Open the **rptDistributors** report in Design view.

4. The Detail section has a text box that contains a formula that concatenates Address and City. It is missing the State and Zip Code. Add these two fields of information by typing **&", "&State&", "&ZipCode** after [City].

5. Preview the report to test your results.

6. Return to Design view and add a text box to the Report Footer section to count the total number of distributors.

7. Change the label of the text box to Total.

8. Change the format of the text box and label to Arial 12-point, bold.

9. Save your changes.

10. Preview the report and print it. Then close the report.

Explore ▶   11. Open the **frmCustomers** form and, using the command button wizard, add buttons to the footer of the form. The buttons should move to the first, previous, next, and last record. If you need assistance, open the Access Help system and look up information on how to create a command button in the text box label. Click the link for creating a button using a wizard.

12. Close the database and exit Access.

QUICK | CHECK ANSWERS

Session 1.1

   1. database

   2. >

   3. &

   4. CInt

   5. Crosstab queries display summarized values from one or more tables in a spreadsheet format.

   6. The four types of action queries are make-table, delete, append, and update.

   7. Three three types of SQL are union, data definition, and pass-through.

Session 1.2

   1. Forms are used to display, edit, and enter data onscreen.

   2. A report can be based on the contents of a table, the results of a saved query, or a SQL statement.

   3. Force New Page

   4. Data access pages are written in HTML.

   5. VBA is more flexible and powerful than macros.

   6. A module is a small compact program written in VBA.

OBJECTIVES

In this tutorial you will:

- Create tables in Datasheet and Design view

- Learn about data redundancy

- Study primary keys, foreign keys, and indexes

- Create primary keys and indexes

- Identify one-to-one, one-to-many, and many-to-many relationships

- Learn about referential integrity and apply it when you establish relationships

- Create combo boxes and learn about their properties

- Add data using a subdatasheet

- Explore how Access handles dates and set properties to manage date issues

- Document your database using the Database Documenter and printing relationships

DESIGNING
AND DOCUMENTING A DATABASE

Completing the tables and establishing relationships in the MovieCam Technologies database

CASE

MovieCam Technologies

Amanda has assigned another member of the department, Carolyn White, to work with you on the MovieCam project. She wants you and Carolyn to finalize the database's design by completing the tables and establishing relationships between them. She has requested that you use the Database Documenter tool to provide detailed information on the database's design and structure.

In your preliminary review of the MovieCam database, you found the following: the tblEmployees table is the central table in the database. The tblDepartments, tblDegrees, and tblJobTitles tables contain data on departments, academic degrees, and job titles, respectively, and are each related to the tblEmployees table.

Using what you've learned from reviewing the MovieCam database, and understanding the objectives that Amanda and the other product managers have for it, you and Carolyn begin formulating the complete design of the database.

SESSION 2.1

In this session, you will add tables to the MovieCam database. You also will set primary keys and indexes, and you will establish relationships between tables.

Database Design

As you learned in Tutorial 1, a database management system is designed to manage, store, retrieve, and order large amounts of information. Some databases accomplish this with a single table, sometimes referred to as a flat file. Most real-world databases, however, contain numerous tables that store many records. This is where relational database management systems become essential.

One advantage of using a relational database is its capability to link tables, thus reducing the amount of data duplication. Duplication of data is referred to as **redundancy**. Some duplication of data is always necessary, but the goal of good database design is to eliminate as much redundancy as possible.

The sample spreadsheet shown in Figure 2-1 is an example of a flat file. This file, you may recall from Tutorial 1, represents what MovieCam's product managers use to track time spent on jobs. It is considered a flat file because it is not possible to create and link more than one table in a spreadsheet program like it is in a relational database.

Figure 2-1   SPREADSHEET TO TRACK TIME SPENT ON JOBS

	A	B	C	D	E	F	G	H	I
1	Emp No	EmployeeName	TimeCard No	TimeCard Date	Dept No	DeptName	Line Item	Hours Worked	JobNo
2	10	Thomas Arquette	106	11/02/2002	20	Engineering	1	10	99562
3	10	Thomas Arquette	106	11/02/2002	20	Engineering	2	12	98378
4	10	Thomas Arquette	106	11/02/2002	20	Engineering	3	8	99899
5	10	Thomas Arquette	115	11/09/2002	20	Engineering	1	3	99562
6	99	Janice Smitty			10	Accounting			
7	500	Alan Cook	107	11/02/2002	50	Production	1	7	99562
8	500	Alan Cook	107	11/02/2002	50	Production	2	12	98378
9	700	Ernest Gold	108	11/02/2002	50	Production	1	4	99562
10	700	Ernest Gold	116	11/09/2002	50	Production	1	8	99562
11	700	Ernest Gold	116	11/09/2002	50	Production	2	4	98378
12									

Notice the redundancy of information in practically every column of the spreadsheet file. This file contains only 10 records. Imagine the data redundancy problem you'd have if you were dealing with thousands of records. In Figure 2-1, the term Engineering occurs four times. Assume that you're dealing with 100,000 records, and the term *Engineering* occurs 50,000 times. The department name *Engineering* uses approximately 10 characters, so if Engineering is entered 49,999 times more than necessary, you would enter 499,990 characters. If each character requires two bytes of storage, the duplication of just one department name takes up 999,980 bytes!

In addition to wasting storage space, data redundancy can result in inefficiency and inaccurate data. For example, if Thomas Arquette and his address are stored in a single table or spreadsheet 2,000 times, that information had to be typed each one of those times. What would happen if his address changed? All of the records containing his address would have to be changed. If one or two records were missed, it would be difficult to tell which was the correct address.

With a relational database, you can reorganize data into separate tables to eliminate the redundant storage of data. You and Carolyn have come up with a plan for completing the table design for the MovieCam database. Ultimately, you want the database to include the following tables:

- **tblEmployees**: This table contains one record for each employee, and has data such as the employee's name, address, title, salary, and start date. This table has already been created by Jason and includes sample records.

- **tblDepartments**: This table contains one record for each department. It is related to the tblEmployees table via the DeptNo field. This means you can create another database object using fields from both tables. This table has already been created by Jason and includes sample records.

- **tblDegrees**: This table contains one record for the four types of academic degrees an employee might have. It also is related to the tblEmployees table via the CollegeDegree field. The table has been created by Jason and includes sample records.

- **tblJobTitles**: This table contains one record for each job title at MovieCam. It is related to the tblEmployees table via the JobTitleID field. This table has been created by Jason and includes sample records.

- **tblTimeCards**: This table has not yet been created. It will contain one record for each time card filled out for each pay period by each employee who uses a time card. It will contain fields for the time card number, the time card date, and the employee's identification number. Information will be entered in the table using the employee's actual time card, which is shown in Figure 2-2.

Figure 2-2	EMPLOYEE TIME CARD

MovieCam Technologies Time Card # 106	Weekly Time Ticket For:		Thomas Arquette							Emp # 10
	Week Ending (Saturday):		02-Nov-2002							Dept# 20
Line Item	**Job#**	**Task Description**	**S**	**M**	**T**	**W**	**Th**	**F**	**S**	**Total**
1										
2										
3										
4										
5										
6										
7										
8										
9										
10										
11										
12										
13										
14										
15										
16										
17										
18										
19	99998	Personal Time								
20	99999	Holidays								
		Total Time								

Signature:	Supervisor:

This time ticket must be filled out daily in blue or black ink and signed by your supervisor at the end of the week. Report time in 15-minute increments. All time tickets are to be turned in to your supervisor by the end of work on Friday or Saturday. Supervisors must review and sign time tickets. Submit to Accounting no later than 9:30 a.m. Monday.

■ ***tblHours*:** This table has not yet been created. It will contain a record for each line item on the time card (see Figure 2-2), including the time card number, the line item number, the hours worked, and the job number.

■ ***tblJobs*:** This table has not yet been created. It will contain a record for each job or product made by MovieCam, and the product's model number.

When the database design phase is completed, the table structure for the database should look like that shown in Figure 2-3.

Figure 2-3   DESIGN FOR THE MOVIECAM DATABASE

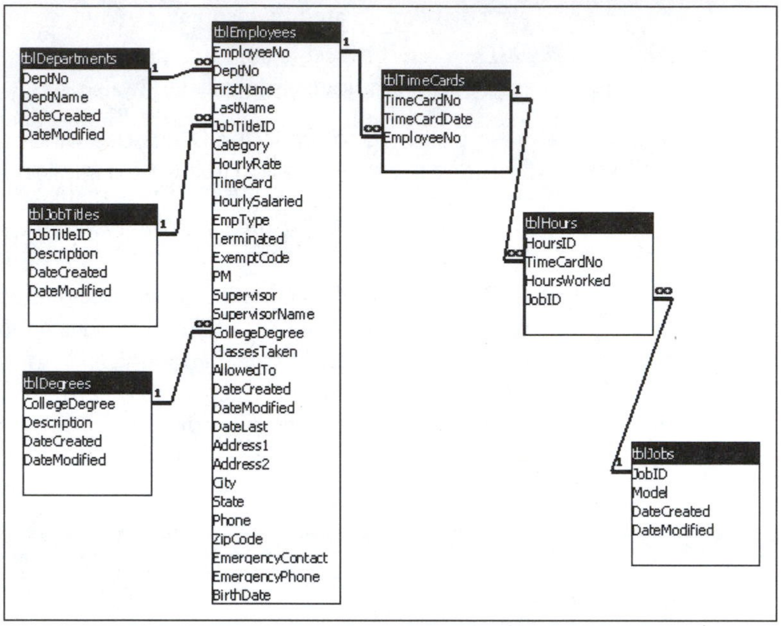

Creating Tables

You and Carolyn are ready to complete the design of the tables in the database. You start by creating the tblTimeCards table.

To create a table in Datasheet view:

1. Make sure that the data files have been copied to the local or network drive on which you will be working.

   TROUBLE? If the data files have not been copied to your local or network drive, you must do so before you can proceed. Read the *Read This Before You Begin* section on page 2, or ask your instructor for help.

2. Start Access and open the **Movie2** database located in the Tutorial.02 folder on your local or network drive.

3. If necessary, click **Tables** in the Objects bar of the Database window.

4. Double-click **Create table by entering data**. A new table opens in Datasheet view.

5. Right-click the **Field1** field name, and then click **Rename Column** on the shortcut menu.

6. Type **TimeCardNo** and press the **Enter** key.

7. Change the name of Field2 to **TimeCardDate**.

8. Change the name of Field3 to **EmployeeNo**.

9. Close the table. When you are prompted to save the table, click the **Yes** button. Enter the name **tblTimeCards** in the Save As dialog box, and click the **OK** button. A message box like that shown in Figure 2-4 warns you that there is no primary key for this table and asks if you'd like to create one now.

10. Click the **No** button to return to the Database window. You will set the primary key and modify the table design in the next section.

| Figure 2-4 | PRIMARY KEY MESSAGE BOX |

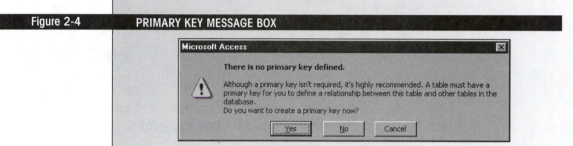

You must open a table in Design view to set a primary key and modify its design. When you create a table using the shortcut, as you did in the previous set of steps, the fields are defined by default as Text type, and the field size is automatically set to 50. You want to assign a primary key, change the data type for the TimeCardDate field from Text to Date/Time, and set the Caption property for each of the three fields in the table.

To modify the table design:

1. Open the **tblTimeCards** table in Design view.

2. Click **TimeCardNo** and click the **Primary Key** button on the toolbar.

3. Click **TimeCardDate** and change the data type to **Date/Time**.

4. Click **TimeCardNo**. In the Field Properties pane, type **Time Card No** in the Caption text box.

5. Repeat Step 4 to set the Caption property for the TimeCardDate field to **Time Card Date**, and EmployeeNo to **Employee No**.

6. Close the table and save your changes.

Next, you need to create the tblJobs table to keep track of MovieCam's jobs.

To create the tblJobs table:

1. Create a new table in Design view.

2. Define the fields as shown in Figure 2-5.

Figure 2-5   **TBLJOBS TABLE**

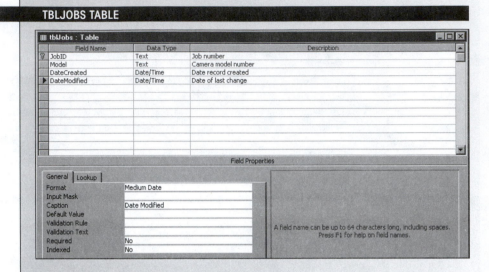

3. Change the Caption property of *JobID*, *DateCreated*, and *DateModified* to **Job ID**, **Date Created**, and **Date Modified**, respectively.

4. Change the Format property for both date fields to **Medium Date**.

5. Set **JobID** as the primary key.

6. Set the caption, close the table, and save it as **tblJobs**.

Before you can set relationships between the tables, you need to review primary keys and indexing.

Primary Keys, Foreign Keys, and Indexing

A field that is used for identification purposes is called a key. In Access, the field (or fields) that uniquely identifies a record in a table is called a **primary key**. Each table can have only one primary key, even if more than one field is unique. For example, if both a Social Security number and an employee number were stored in an employee table, each of these fields could contain unique data, but only one can be set as the primary key. A primary key that consists of two or more fields is a **composite key**. Sometimes one field by itself is not unique, but combined with another field it is. The tblHours table in the MovieCam database has a composite key. As illustrated in Figure 2-6, the TimeCardNo field is not unique because the same number can be entered many times. However, when the data in this field is combined with the data in the LineItem field, it is unique. For example, there is only one record for TimeCardNo 106 and LineItem 1.

Figure 2-6	COMPOSITE KEY IN THE TBLHOURS TABLE

these two fields
combined are unique

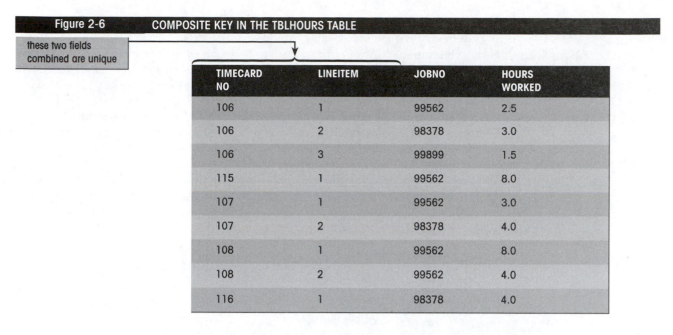

TIMECARD NO	LINEITEM	JOBNO	HOURS WORKED
106	1	99562	2.5
106	2	98378	3.0
106	3	99899	1.5
115	1	99562	8.0
107	1	99562	3.0
107	2	98378	4.0
108	1	99562	8.0
108	2	99562	4.0
116	1	98378	4.0

Another type of key field is a **foreign key**. It exists only in terms of the relationship between two tables because there is no method for *setting* a foreign key. This is the join field in the secondary table in a relationship. It refers to the primary key field in the primary table. Figure 2-7 identifies a primary key and foreign key in a relationship. The DeptNo field is used to create the relationship between the tblDepartments table and the tblEmployees table. It is the primary key in the tblDepartments table and the foreign key in the tblEmployees table.

Figure 2-7	DEPTNO AS PRIMARY KEY AND FOREIGN KEY

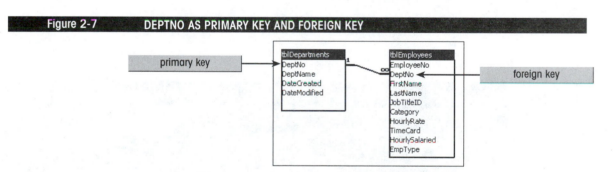

primary key

foreign key

When you set a primary key, Access automatically creates an **index** that is based on the primary key field. An index is a separate hidden table that consists of pointers to records or groups of records, and is designed to make sorting and searching more efficient. Each table can have a maximum of 32 indexes. When relationships are created between tables, Access creates a hidden index on the foreign key field. The Indexed property for this field does not change.

Indexes speed up the performance of queries you run on records, but they slow down updates. For each record that you add, the indexes must be updated as well. For each record that is edited, Access must also update the indexed fields affected by the edit. For this reason, it is recommended that you limit the number of indexes in tables, especially for those tables that are considered transactional.

A **transactional** table is one in which the data entry process is ongoing. Orders entered in an order entry system, for example, would be transactional data. The tblTimeCards and tblHours tables in the MovieCam database are examples of transactional tables because new records will be entered into these tables on a regular basis. However, tables that are not changed or updated frequently can support many indexes. An example of such a table is the tblEmployees table in the MovieCam database because data in this table is changed only when new employees are hired, or when an employee's address or salary changes.

Generally, you should index fields that you plan to sort, set criteria for, group, or on which you will establish relationships. Indexes can be set at any time in the development of the database. You might find that you need indexes when you generate a query and/or report.

You and Carolyn anticipate that you will query the tblTimeCards table frequently. The product managers told you that they will need reports based on cumulative hours for each pay period or time card date. For this reason, you decide to index the TimeCardDate field.

To create an index:

1. Open the **tblTimeCards** table in Design view.

2. Click the **TimeCardDate** field. The Field Properties for TimeCardDate are visible in the lower pane of the window.

3. Change the Indexed property to **Yes (Duplicates OK)**.

   You need to set the indexed property to Yes (Duplicates OK) because the same date will be entered into this field for many records. The Yes (No Duplicates) property option is typically used for primary keys only, although it can be used to restrict duplicate entries in a field that is not the primary key field.

4. Close the table and save your changes.

Next, you will create the tblHours table and set the primary key, which will be a composite key.

REFERENCE WINDOW   RW

Specifying a Composite Primary Key
- In the table's Design view, click the row selector of the first field you've chosen for the primary key, and drag over the row selector of the second field. You may click the first field and hold down the Ctrl key while you click the second field.
- Click the Primary Key button on the toolbar.

Now you will create the tblHours table and set the primary key, which will be a composite key. You also will assign captions for each of the field names.

To create the tblHours table and set a composite primary key:

1. Create a new table in Design view.

2. Define the fields as shown in Figure 2-8.

Figure 2-8   SETTING A COMPOSITE PRIMARY KEY

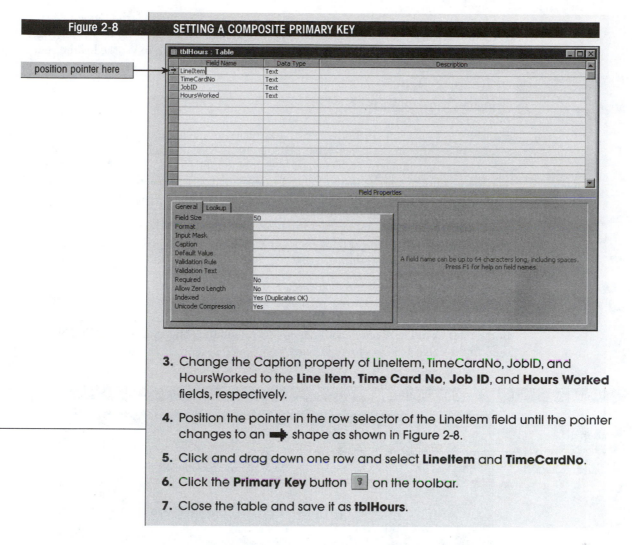

position pointer here

3. Change the Caption property of LineItem, TimeCardNo, JobID, and HoursWorked to the **Line Item**, **Time Card No**, **Job ID**, and **Hours Worked** fields, respectively.

4. Position the pointer in the row selector of the LineItem field until the pointer changes to an ➡ shape as shown in Figure 2-8.

5. Click and drag down one row and select **LineItem** and **TimeCardNo**.

6. Click the **Primary Key** button 🗝 on the toolbar.

7. Close the table and save it as **tblHours**.

Next, you and Carolyn will establish the relationships between the tables in the database.

Setting Relationships

Relationships are a necessary byproduct of working with a relational database and storing data in multiple tables.

After relationships between tables have been established, you can build queries, forms, and reports that pull together information from the various tables. Relationships between tables are established in the Relationships window.

The following syntax is commonly used to identify tables and their fields in a database. In this syntax, primary keys are underlined, the foreign key(s) is italicized and normally follows the primary key, and the remaining fields follow the foreign key(s). This method of notation is used to further define relationships.

TableName (<u>Field1</u>, Field2, Field3, Field4, Field5…)

If you applied the above notation to tblHours in the MovieCam database, it would look like this:

tblHours (<u>LineItem</u>, TimeCardNo, JobID, HoursWorked)

LineItem and TimeCardNo is the composite primary key, JobID is the foreign key that will be used to relate the tblHours table to the tblJobs table, TimeCardNo is the foreign key that will relate the tblHours table to the tblTimeCards table, and HoursWorked is the remaining field in the table.

One-to-One Relationships

A **one-to-one relationship** between two tables exists when one entry in each table corresponds to only one entry in the other table. This is not a common relationship because in many instances the data in the two tables could be combined and stored more efficiently in one table. The few exceptions where separate tables are appropriate are the following:

■ To avoid exceeding the 255 field number maximum per table

■ To control access to fields in a table that are particularly sensitive or confidential

■ To store data in a separate table when only a small group or subset of the records will use those fields

An example of the appropriate use of a one-to-one relationship would be the tblEmployees table in the MovieCam database. You might split the table into two tables, one of which would contain confidential salary information that you want only certain users to be able to access. Both tables would have one record per employee and the primary key for each table would be the EmployeeNo field as shown in Figure 2-9.

| Figure 2-9 | ONE-TO-ONE RELATIONSHIP |

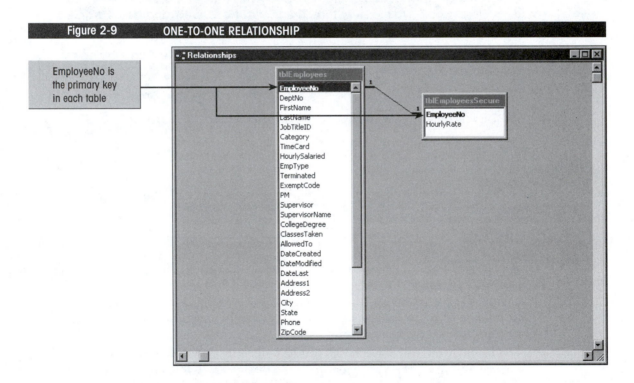

EmployeeNo is the primary key in each table

One-to-Many Relationships

A **one-to-many relationship** is the most common type of relationship between tables. It exists between two tables when a **related table** has many records that relate to a single record in the **primary table**. The term primary table describes the table that contains data about a person or object when there is only one record that can be associated with that person or object. The tblEmployees table is one example of a primary table.

For example, one customer places many orders with a business, one employee submits many time cards, and one publisher publishes many books. When you implement a one-to-many relationship in Access, the join field in the table on the one side of the relationship must be unique. In almost all cases, it is the primary key.

In the MovieCam database, there are numerous examples of one-to-many relationships: tblDepartments has a one-to-many relationship with tblEmployees; tblDegrees has a one-to-many relationship with tblEmployees; tblEmployees has a one-to-many relationship with tblTimeCards; and tblTimeCards has a one-to-many relationship with tblHours.

Many-to-Many Relationships

A many-to-many relationship is defined between two tables and a third table, referred to as a **junction table**. A junction table contains common fields from two tables. It is on the many side of a one-to-many relationship with the other two tables. An example of a many-to-many relationship is that between students and classes. The relationship would consist of three tables: a students table containing fields such as names and addresses that describe the students; a classes table containing fields such as descriptions, dates, and times that describe the classes offered; and a students and classes table that contains links to the other two tables. Figure 2-10 illustrates a many-to-many relationship.

Figure 2-10	MANY-TO-MANY RELATIONSHIP

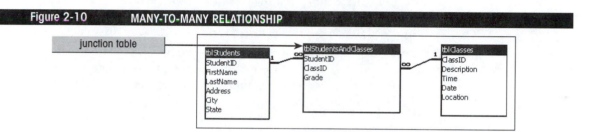

Junction tables are often named so that the two tables for which they provide the link is obvious. In the example in Figure 2-10, tblStudents has a one-to-many relationship with tblStudentsAndClasses and tblClasses also has a one-to-many relationship with tblStudentsAndClasses.

Referential Integrity

Referential integrity requires that a foreign key value in a related table matches the value of the primary key for some row in the primary table. This requirement prevents the occurrence of orphaned records. (Remember, a primary key is a field that is indexed and does not allow duplicates.) An **orphan record** is a record in the related table that does not contain a record in the primary table. An example of an orphan record is a time card record in the tblTimeCards table that refers to an employee number that doesn't exist in the tblEmployees table.

Referential integrity also controls the order of operations in your database. For example, if a user tries to enter a time card for a new employee before the employee is entered into the system, referential integrity between the two tables does not allow the time card to be entered.

Access enforces a series of rules to make sure that relationships between records in related tables are valid and that you don't accidentally change or delete related data. When a relationship is created between two tables, the option to set referential integrity is displayed. The following conditions must be met in order to enforce referential integrity:

- The field on the one side of the relationship (in the primary table) must be a primary key.
- The fields on which the tables are joined must be the same data type with the following exceptions: An AutoNumber field can be related to a Number field that has its field size property set to Long Integer; an AutoNumber field that has a field size property set to Replication ID can be related to a Number field to which the same Replication ID field size property has been applied.
- Both of the tables that are related must be part of the same database. Referential integrity cannot be enforced for linked tables from databases in other formats, although you can set referential integrity on Access linked tables in the database file in which they exist.

The following rules apply to tables on which referential integrity has been set:

- You cannot enter a value in the foreign key field of a related table if the primary table doesn't contain that particular value. For example, you cannot enter an employee number in the tblTimeCards table for an employee who doesn't exist in the tblEmployees table. You can, however, enter *null* in the foreign key to indicate that the record is not related to any record in the primary table. A null value in the EmployeeNo field specifies that the time card is assigned to no one, rather than to an employee who doesn't exist.
- You cannot delete a record from a primary table if there are matching records in the related table. For example, you cannot delete an employee from the tblEmployees table if time cards for that employee exist in the tblTimeCards table. See Figure 2-11.

| Figure 2-11 | ENFORCING REFERENTIAL INTEGRITY WHEN DELETING A RECORD |

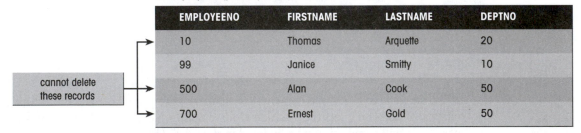

tblEmployees (primary table)

EMPLOYEENO	FIRSTNAME	LASTNAME	DEPTNO
10	Thomas	Arquette	20
99	Janice	Smitty	10
500	Alan	Cook	50
700	Ernest	Gold	50

cannot delete these records

related foreign key values

tblTimeCards (related table)

TIMECARD NO	TIMECARD DATE	EMPLOYEE NO
106	11/2/2002	10
115	11/2/2002	10
107	11/2/2002	500
108	11/2/2002	700
116	11/9/2002	700

■ You cannot change the value in the primary key field if there is a related record(s) in the related table. EmployeeNo in the tblEmployees table cannot be changed if time cards exist for that employee number in the tblTimeCards table. See Figure 2-12.

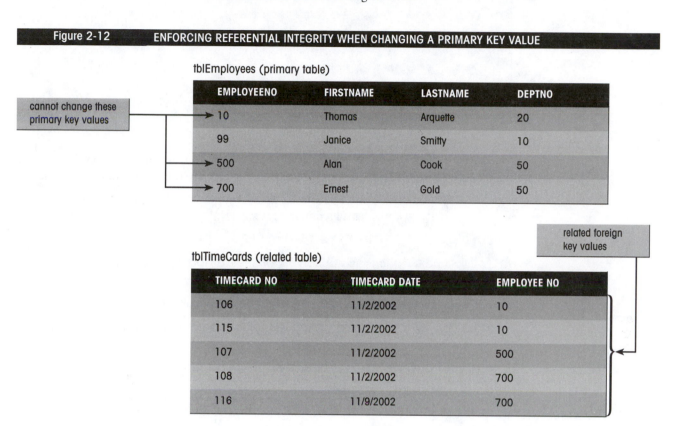

Figure 2-12	ENFORCING REFERENTIAL INTEGRITY WHEN CHANGING A PRIMARY KEY VALUE

tblEmployees (primary table)

cannot change these primary key values

EMPLOYEENO	FIRSTNAME	LASTNAME	DEPTNO
10	Thomas	Arquette	20
99	Janice	Smitty	10
500	Alan	Cook	50
700	Ernest	Gold	50

related foreign key values

tblTimeCards (related table)

TIMECARD NO	TIMECARD DATE	EMPLOYEE NO
106	11/2/2002	10
115	11/2/2002	10
107	11/2/2002	500
108	11/2/2002	700
116	11/9/2002	700

Some restrictions, such as deleting from a primary table those records that have matching records in a related table, and changing the value of the key in the primary table, can be overridden with the Cascade Update and Cascade Delete options.

Cascade Update and Cascade Delete

When enforcing referential integrity, you can apply the Cascade Update and Cascade Delete options. When you select the Cascade Update option, a change in the primary key of the primary table will automatically be updated in the related table. For example, when you change an employee number in the tblEmployees table, that employee number will be updated for each record in the tblTimeCards table.

If the primary key in the primary table is an AutoNumber field, setting this option will have no effect because you cannot change entries in AutoNumber fields.

When you select the Cascade Delete option, deleting a record in the primary table automatically deletes any related records in the related table. For example, if you delete an employee record from the tblEmployees table, any related time card records are deleted from the tblTimeCards table.

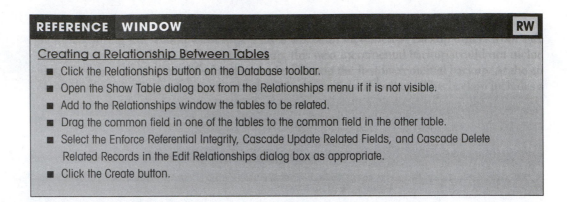

Creating a Relationship Between Tables
- Click the Relationships button on the Database toolbar.
- Open the Show Table dialog box from the Relationships menu if it is not visible.
- Add to the Relationships window the tables to be related.
- Drag the common field in one of the tables to the common field in the other table.
- Select the Enforce Referential Integrity, Cascade Update Related Fields, and Cascade Delete Related Records in the Edit Relationships dialog box as appropriate.
- Click the Create button.

You and Carolyn are now prepared to establish relationships in the MovieCam database. You'll start by creating a relationship between the tblEmployees and tblTimeCards tables.

To create a relationship between the tblEmployees and tblTimeCards tables:

1. Click the **Relationships** button on the Database toolbar. The Relationships window opens.

2. Click the **Show Table** button on the Relationship toolbar.

3. Double-click **tblHours** and **tblTimeCards** to add them to the Relationships window.

4. Click the **Close** button to close the Show Table dialog box.

5. If necessary, reposition the tblHours and tblTimeCards field lists as shown in Figure 2-13.

Figure 2-13   RELATIONSHIPS WINDOW

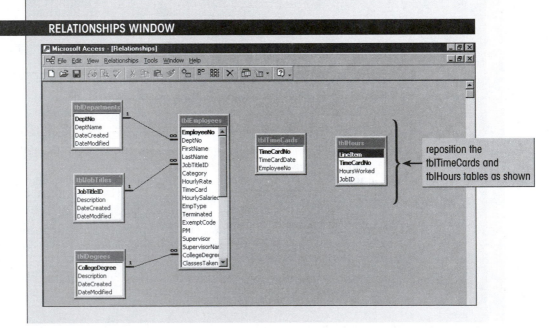

6. Select the **EmployeeNo** field in tblEmployees and drag it to the EmployeeNo field in tblTimeCards. The Edit Relationships dialog box appears. See Figure 2-14.

Figure 2-14	EDIT RELATIONSHIPS DIALOG BOX

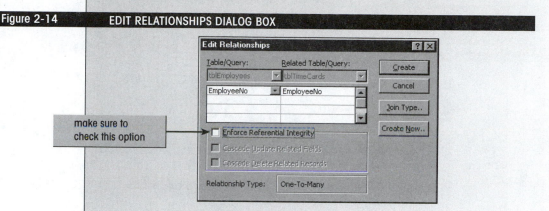

make sure to check this option

7. Click the **Enforce Referential Integrity** check box. Selecting this option prevents modifications to the EmployeeNo of an employee in the tblEmployees table that has a related time card(s) in the tblTimeCards table. Enforce Referential Integrity also ensures that the record for that employee cannot be deleted.

8. Click the **Cascade Update Related Fields** check box. Selecting this option allows you to change an employee number in the EmployeeNo field of the tblEmployees table and have that change automatically occur in a related record in the tblTimeCards table. Do not click the Cascade Delete option for this relationship because you do not want employees with existing time cards to be deleted from the database.

9. Click the **Create** button.

Next, you will establish the relationship between the tblTimeCards and tblHours tables.

To create a relationship between the tblTimeCards and tblHours tables:

1. Click the **TimeCardNo** field in the tblTimeCards field list and drag it to the TimeCardNo field in the tblHours field list.

2. Click the **Enforce Referential Integrity** check box in the Edit Relationships dialog box.

3. Click both the **Cascade Update Related Fields** and **Cascade Delete Related Records** check boxes as shown in Figure 2-15. You set the Cascade Update Related Fields option to allow a change to incorrectly entered data in the TimeCardNo field in the tblTimeCards table even if there are related records in the tblHours table. You set the Cascade Delete Related Records option to allow an erroneous entry in the tblTimeCards table to be deleted even if hours have been entered in the tblHours table for that time card number.

Figure 2-15	CASCADE UPDATE AND CASCADE DELETE OPTIONS

select these options

4. Click the **Create** button to create the relationship.

Finally, you will create the relationship between the tblHours and tblJobs tables. The tblJobs table will have a one-to-many relationship with the tblHours table, because one job may have hours applied to it from many days and/or from many employees. If a record is deleted from the tblJobs table, you don't want all of the records for the hours worked on that job deleted, so you will *not* select the Cascade Delete option. This prevents a user from deleting a job that has related records. However, you decide that changing a job number (*JobID*) may be necessary in a situation where records have been entered against it in the tblHours table, so you select the Cascade Update option.

To create the relationship between the tblJobs and tblHours tables:

1. Add **tblJobs** to the Relationships window.

2. Click the **JobID** field in tblJobs and drag it to **JobID** in tblHours.

3. Click the **Enforce Referential Integrity** check box.

4. Click the **Cascade Update Related Fields** check box, and then click the **Create** button.

5. Close the Relationships window, saving your changes.

Other than making some minor changes to field properties, you and Carolyn have finished the tables for the MovieCam database. Now that the structure is complete and the relationships are established, you can test the database, add any necessary finishing touches, and document the database to complete Amanda's request.

Session 2.1 QUICK CHECK

1. Define the term redundancy.

2. Access automatically creates a hidden index on _____ key fields.

3. The maximum number of indexes in a table is _____.

4. What is the benefit of adding indexes to a table?

5. A(n) _____ relationship exists between two tables when only one entry in each table corresponds to only one entry in the other table.

6. What is the most common type of relationship between tables?

7. Which relationship requires a junction table?

8. What is an orphaned record?

SESSION 2.2

In this session you will add data to the tables you created and refine the tables' design by changing field properties. You will learn about subdatasheets and how to use them. You also will document your work by printing relationships and using the Database Documenter.

Entering Records in Tables

You and Carolyn decide to add sample data to the tables that you created, so you can test the tables' relationship settings. Adding sample data will also help you determine field properties that might need to be set. Figure 2-16 shows the sample records you will enter into the tblTimeCards table.

| Figure 2-16 | RECORDS TO ADD TO THE TBLTIMECARDS TABLE |

Time Card No	Time Card Date	Employee No
106	02/02/2002	10
107	02/02/2002	500
108	02/02/2002	700

To enter data in the tblTimeCards table:

1. Make sure that Access is running, that the **Movie2** database located in the Tutorial.02 folder on your local or network drive is open, and that **Tables** is selected in the Objects bar of the Database window.

2. Open the **tblTimeCards** table in Datasheet view.

3. Type the first record shown in Figure 2-16, and press the **Enter** key to move to the second record.

4. Type **107** in the Time Card No field for the second record, and press the **Enter** key.

5. Press **Ctrl+'** [Ctrl+apostrophe] in the Time Card Date field to copy the previous entry in this field. Press the **Enter** key to move to the next column.

6. Type **501** in the Employee No field and press **Enter**. You will see an error message like the one in Figure 2-17. Because there is no EmployeeNo 501 in the tblEmployees table, the rules of referential integrity prohibit you from entering the value in this field.

Figure 2-17 | REFERENTIAL INTEGRITY ERROR MESSAGE

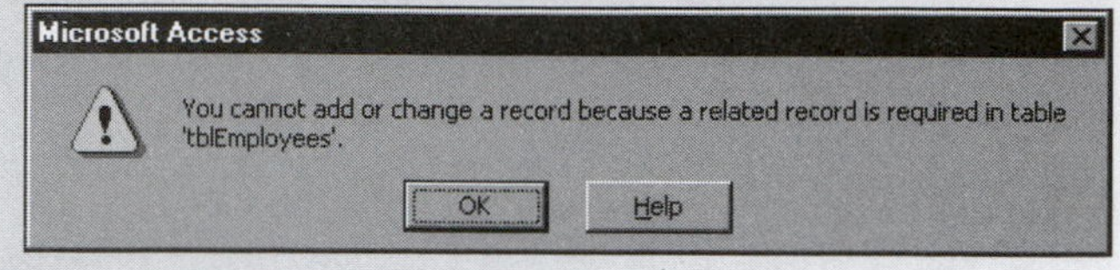

7. Click the **OK** button and change the entry to **500**.

8. Enter the third record as shown in Figure 2-16.

9. Close the table.

   Next, you will enter the sample records from Figure 2-18 into the tblJobs table.

Because the relationships that were set earlier control the order of data entry, you must enter records into the tblJobs table before you can enter them into the tblHours table. Otherwise you'll get an error similar to the one you got when you tried to enter a nonexistent employee into the tblTimeCards table.

To add data to the tblJobs table:

1. Open the **tblJobs** table in Datasheet view.

2. Refer to Figure 2-18, and type the data for the Job ID and Model fields for the first record. Press the **Enter** key to position the insertion point in the Date Created field.

Figure 2-18 | RECORDS TO ADD TO THE TBLJOBS TABLE

Job ID	Model	Date Created	Date Modified
98378	XCAM1080SB	11/02/2002	
99562	ZTSM 1022	11/02/2002	

3. Press **Ctrl+;** [Ctrl+semicolon] to automatically insert the current date into the **Date Created** field. This is a good place to include a field property to default to the current date. You'll switch to Design view and make that change before you complete the data entry.

4. Switch to Design view.

5. Click the **DateCreated** field and click the **Default Value** property text box.

6. Type **=Date()** and then press the **Enter** key.

7. Switch to Datasheet view and save your changes.

8. Refer to Figure 2-18 and complete the data entry for the second record.

9. Close the table.

Finally, you will add the sample records from Figure 2-19 to the *tblHours* table.

| Figure 2-19 | RECORDS TO ADD TO THE TBLHOURS TABLE |

Line Item	Time Card No	Job ID	Hours Worked
1	106	99562	2.5
1	107	99562	3.0

To add data to tblHours:

1. Open the **tblHours** table in Datasheet view.

2. Add the two records listed in Figure 2-19.

3. Switch to Design view.

You and Carolyn decide it would be simpler to enter the JobID number in the tblHours table if the field is defined as a combo box that displays the possible job numbers from which to choose.

Combo Box Properties

Combo boxes can be created on forms or in tables. A **combo box** is a drop-down list of items from which you can select. You select an item by clicking it or by typing the first character or two of the item (referred to as the type-ahead feature). A combo box is handy for limiting the entries in a field, for ensuring that data is entered correctly, and for looking up information.

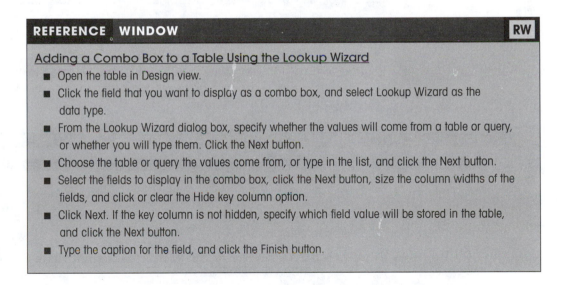

REFERENCE WINDOW   **RW**

Adding a Combo Box to a Table Using the Lookup Wizard
- Open the table in Design view.
- Click the field that you want to display as a combo box, and select Lookup Wizard as the data type.
- From the Lookup Wizard dialog box, specify whether the values will come from a table or query, or whether you will type them. Click the Next button.
- Choose the table or query the values come from, or type in the list, and click the Next button.
- Select the fields to display in the combo box, click the Next button, size the column widths of the fields, and click or clear the Hide key column option.
- Click Next. If the key column is not hidden, specify which field value will be stored in the table, and click the Next button.
- Type the caption for the field, and click the Finish button.

You and Carolyn will now change the data type of the JobID field in the tblHours table to a lookup field that uses a combo box.

To create a combo box using the Lookup Wizard:

1. Click in the Data Type text box for the JobID field, click the list arrow, and then click **Lookup Wizard**. The first Lookup Wizard dialog box opens as shown in Figure 2-20.

Figure 2-20   LOOKUP WIZARD DIALOG BOX

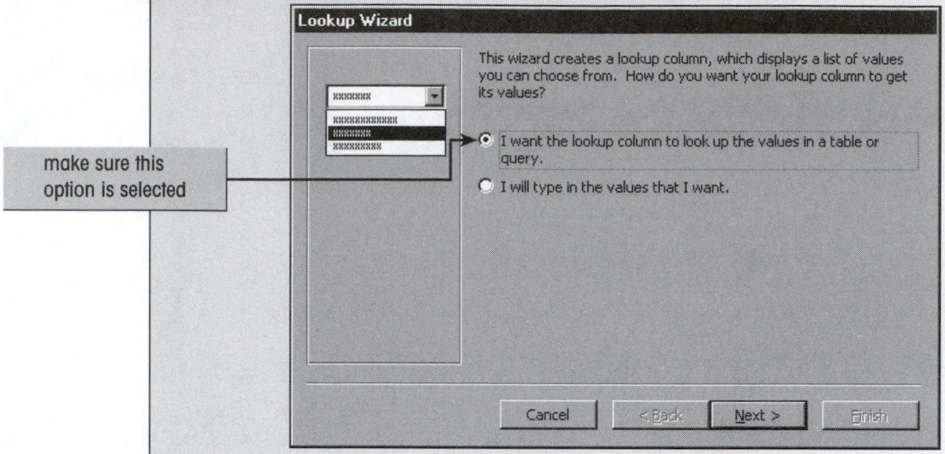

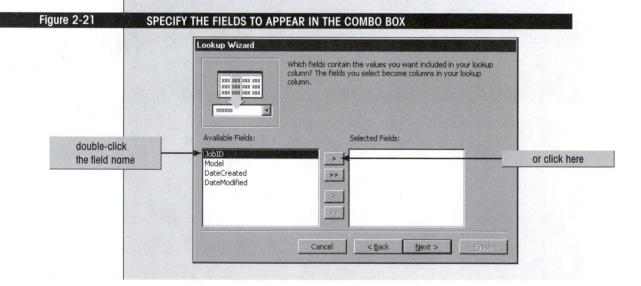

make sure this option is selected

This dialog box lets you specify a list of values that are allowed for the JobID value in a record in the tblHours table. You can specify a table or query from which the value is selected, or you can enter a new list of values. You want the JobID number to come from the tblJobs table.

2. Make sure the option for looking up the values in a table or query is selected, and then click the **Next** button to display the next dialog box.

3. Select **tblJobs** from the list of tables shown in the next dialog box, and then click the **Next** button.

The next Look Wizard dialog box, shown in Figure 2-21, lets you specify which fields you want to appear in the combo box. You will include JobID and Model. The value in JobID from the tblJobs table will be stored in this field. Model will be next to it in the combo box so that users can verify that they have chosen the correct JobID field values.

Figure 2-21   SPECIFY THE FIELDS TO APPEAR IN THE COMBO BOX

double-click the field name

or click here

4. Double-click **JobID** and **Model** to move them into the Selected Fields list box. Click the **Next** button.

In the next dialog box you can specify whether the key column (the primary key from the tblJobs table) will be displayed in the combo box. Most often you will create a combo box that includes two or more columns: the primary key of the table from which the combo box gets its data, and a descriptive field from that table. You include the descriptive field so the user can verify that the correct data is being selected. However, the primary key column will contain the data that is actually stored in the combo box field. If you select the **Hide key column** option, the first column of the combo box will be stored but not displayed. You also can adjust the size of the fields in this dialog box.

5. If necessary, deselect the **Hide key column** option so that the JobID will display in the combo box. Drag the column borders so that they are approximately the same size as shown in Figure 2-22. Click the **Next** button.

Figure 2-22	DETERMINING THE WIDTH OF COLUMNS

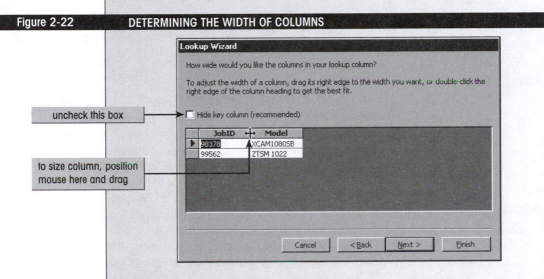

The next dialog box lets you specify the value of the field that will be stored in the tblHours table. You would like to store the JobID rather than the Model in the tblHours table.

6. Be sure that **JobID** is selected, and then click the **Next** button.

The last dialog box asks you to specify a label for the lookup column. You will use this label to set the Caption property for this field.

7. Type **Job ID** (with a space between Job and ID), and then click the **Finish** button.

8. Click the **Yes** button when prompted to save the table.

9. Close the table.

You and Carolyn want users of the tblTimeCards table to be able to look up an employee name sorted alphabetically by last name from the tblEmployees table. The combo box will then store the EmployeeNo field value in the tblTimeCards table after the name is selected from the combo box.

To add a combo box to a table:

1. Open the **tblTimeCards** table in Design view.

2. Click **EmployeeNo** in the Field Name column and click the **Lookup** tab in the Field Properties pane.

Initially, the only property on the Lookup tab is the Display Control property. It contains a drop-down list of the available controls for the selected field. For Text or Number data type fields, this property can be set to Text Box, List Box, or Combo Box. For Yes/No data type fields, this property can be set to Check Box, Text Box, or Combo Box. When you select a control for this property, the other properties that apply to the control type are displayed on the Lookup tab.

3. Click in the Display Control text box and select **Combo Box** from the drop-down list.

When you select Combo Box from the Display Control text box, the properties shown are specific to combo boxes. The Row Source Type property determines whether the combo box is based on a table or a query, a value list, or a field list.

If you choose value list, you can specify a list of values to be displayed by the combo box in the Row Source property. If you choose field list, you can specify a table or query in the Row Source property from which you want the field names displayed. If you accept the default, which is Table/Query, you can then specify in the Row Source property the table or query name from which the fields and records will come.

You also can choose to use a SQL statement by creating it in the Row Source property text box. All queries are really SQL statements. You normally create queries using the Query By Example (QBE) grid (query Design view) to simplify the process. Using the Build button in the Row Source property box of a combo box opens the Query Builder window, which is similar to the QBE grid. The Query Builder window allows you to construct a query, which is then converted to a SQL statement and used as the basis for the combo box.

To create a SQL statement for the Row Source property:

1. Click in the **Row Source** text box and click the **Build** button [...]. The Query Builder window and Show Table dialog box open, as shown in Figure 2-23.

| Figure 2-23 | QUERY BUILDER WINDOW AND SHOW TABLE DIALOG BOX |

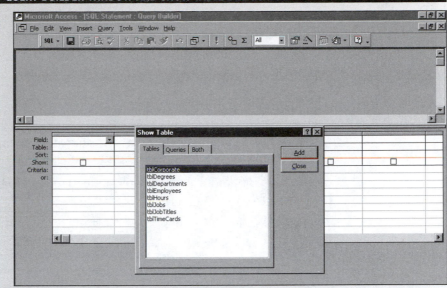

2. Click **tblEmployees** in the Show Table dialog box, click the **Add** button, and then close the Show Table dialog box.

3. Double-click **EmployeeNo** in the tblEmployees field list to move it into the first column of the design grid and then press the **Tab** key to move one column to the right.

4. Right-click the **Field** text box for the second column, and then click **Zoom** on the shortcut menu to open the Zoom window.

5. Type **EmpName:[FirstName]&Space(1)&[LastName]** and then press the **Enter** key to close the Zoom window. Be sure to enclose the FirstName and LastName fields in square brackets.

6. Press the **Tab** key to move one column to the right, click the field drop-down list arrow, and then click **LastName**.

7. Press the down arrow key ↓ twice and type **A** to choose Ascending from the Sort drop-down list.

8. Close the Query Builder window, and click the **Yes** button when prompted to save your changes. The SQL statement which represents the query you constructed in the Query Builder window is now visible in the Row Source text box.

Now you'll set the remaining properties to complete the combo box.

To complete the combo box in the tblTimeCards table:

1. If necessary, click in the **Bound Column** property text box and type the number **1**.

   The Bound Column property determines which column's values to use as the value of the control. If the combo box is bound to a field in a table, the Bound Column's data is stored in the field. Setting this property to 1 stores the EmployeeNo in the tblTimeCards table, rather than storing the employee name, which is displayed in the second column.

2. Change the Column Count property value to the number **3**, and then press the **Enter** key.

   You use the Column Count property to specify the number of columns to be included in the combo box—whether or not they are displayed. This query or SQL statement includes three columns: EmployeeNo, EmpName (the expression which concatenates first and last name), and LastName.

3. Be sure that the Column Heads property is set to **No** and press the **Enter** key. The Column Heads property lets you display the field names or captions from the underlying table or query.

4. Type **0";1.25";0"** in the Column Widths property text box, and then press the **Enter** key.

   The Column Widths property specifies the width of each column in a multiple-column combo box. You also can use this property to hide one or more columns by setting the width of that column to 0". With your setting for the Column Widths property, the EmployeeNo field will be hidden, the EmpName expression will be visible, and the LastName field (used to determine the sort order) will be hidden.

5. Press the **Enter** key again. The List Row property defaults to 8, which is fine for this combo box. The List Row property sets the maximum number of rows listed when the combo box list is displayed.

6. Type **1.25"** in the List Width text box, and press the **Enter** key. The List Width property determines the total width of the combo box.

7. If necessary, set the Limit To List property to **Yes**, and press the **Enter** key.

   You use this property to limit the combo box's values to the listed items. You do not want any employee numbers entered in the tblTimeCards table that do not exist in the tblEmployees table. The relationship between these tables enforces this rule, but you will set it to *Yes* because it is a good practice to follow. The final properties set for the EmployeeNo field are shown in Figure 2-24.

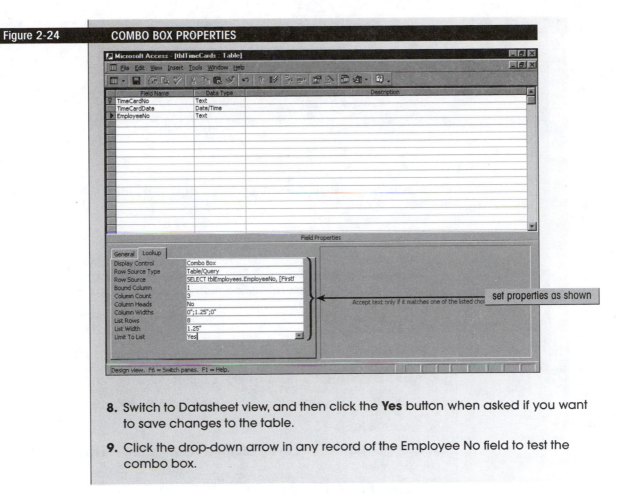

Figure 2-24 **COMBO BOX PROPERTIES**

8. Switch to Datasheet view, and then click the **Yes** button when asked if you want to save changes to the table.

9. Click the drop-down arrow in any record of the Employee No field to test the combo box.

The plus sign to the left of the first field in the tblTimeCards table in Datasheet view is called an expand indicator, and indicates a subdatasheet.

Subdatasheets

A **subdatasheet** is a datasheet that is nested within another datasheet and contains data related or joined to the first datasheet. A subdatasheet allows you to view or edit related or joined data in a table, query, form datasheet, or subform. Access automatically creates a subdatasheet in a table that is in a one-to-one or a one-to many relationship, as long as the Subdatasheet property of the table is set to Auto, which is the default. The tblTimeCards table is the primary table in a one-to-many relationship with the tblHours table. Because the Subdatasheet table property has not been changed, a subdatasheet for the *tblHours* table was created. You now can click the expand indicator (plus sign) to the left of TimeCardNo as shown in Figure 2-25, to see any records from the tblHours table that relate to the selected record in the tblTimeCards table.

Figure 2-25   SUBDATASHEET

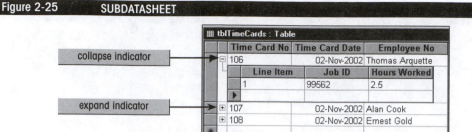

You will now change the sample data in the tblHours table while working in the tblTimeCards table.

To add data using a subdatasheet:

1. Click the expand indicator ⊞ for the Time Card No 106 record. The sub-datasheet for TimeCardNo 106 opens.

2. Click in the Line Item field for the second row, type the number **2** and then press the **Enter** key.

3. Type **98378** in the Job ID field and press the **Enter** key.

4. Type **3.0** in the Hours Worked field and press the **Enter** key.

5. Click the collapse indicator ⊟ for Time Card No 106.

6. Close the table.

7. Open the **tblHours** table in Datasheet view. You see the new record you entered.

8. Close the **tblHours** table.

Dates in Access

The way Access handles dates can influence the way you set the properties for Date/Time fields. Most users type dates in the short format—MM/DD/YY. When a user types 1/1/29, Access interprets this as January 1, 2029. When a user types 1/1/30, Access interprets this as January 1, 1930. A two-digit year can include only a 100-year time span, and that time span is defined as January 1, 1930, through December 31, 2029.

However, a Windows file (named OLEAUT32.DLL) controls this time span. If that file is damaged, Access could erroneously interpret two-digit years as falling into the range of January 1, 1900, through December 31, 1999.

There are three levels of precautions that you can take to prevent users from entering an incorrect date. First, you can set Access to always display a four-digit year. Second, you can force users to enter a four-digit year. Third, you can add validation rules to test dates that are entered, and to display an error message if a date is entered incorrectly.

The least restrictive approach to handling dates is to format all date fields so that a four-digit year is displayed. However, this method relies on the user to spot entries where Access makes an incorrect assumption about the century.

A more restrictive approach is to apply an input mask for all date fields. The input mask would require users to enter all four digits of the year. This isn't the most desirable option because input masks are effective only on new data, not on data that's already entered. Also, a validation rule limits the entries to a particular range of years based on the system date.

Access 2000 has a feature that allows you to force all date formats to display a four-digit year.

Amanda prefers that you take a conservative approach on matters like these. She believes that taking the most precautions is the best course of action, considering the end users of this system. You decide to force all date formats to display four digits. You also include input masks that require four-digit year data entry, and you write validation rules for dates wherever possible.

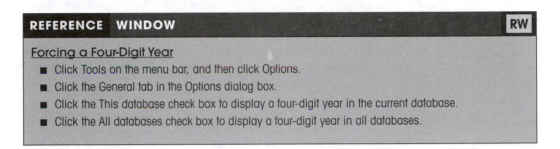

REFERENCE WINDOW   RW

Forcing a Four-Digit Year
- Click Tools on the menu bar, and then click Options.
- Click the General tab in the Options dialog box.
- Click the This database check box to display a four-digit year in the current database.
- Click the All databases check box to display a four-digit year in all databases.

You start by changing this database's default date display option to a four-digit year.

To display four-digit dates in the MovieCam database:

1. Click **Tools** on the menu bar and then click **Options**.

2. Click the **General** tab in the Options dialog box to display date formatting options as shown in Figure 2-26.

Figure 2-26   DATE FORMATTING OPTIONS

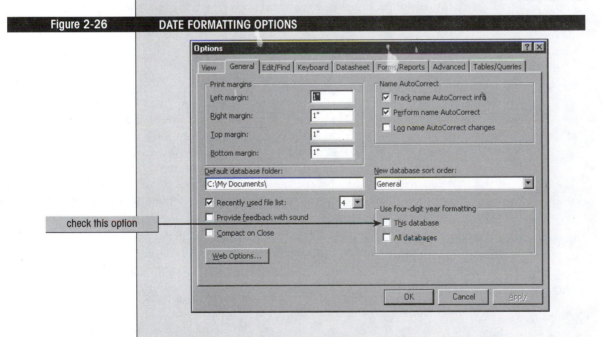

check this option

Note that in the *Use four-digit year formatting* options, you can apply the formatting to the database in which you are currently working. If you want to apply the formatting to all databases, Access will add a Registry entry to your computer to force four-digit year formatting on any Access 2000 database.

3. Click the **This database** check box.

4. Click the **OK** button to return to the Database window.

Next, you'll change the format for the TimeCardDate field to Medium Date, which displays and prints dates in a format similar to 19-Apr-2002.

To change date field properties in the tblTimeCards table:

1. Open the **tblTimeCards** table in Design view.

2. Change the Format property of the TimeCardDate field to **Medium Date**.

3. Switch to Datasheet view and save the table.

4. To test the way that Access handles dates, type **1/1/29** in the TimeCardDate field in the first record. Notice that it interprets this as the year 2029.

5. Now type **1/1/30** into the TimeCardDate field in the second record. This time Access interprets the year as 1930.

6. Change both dates to **11/2/02**.

7. Switch back to Design view.

You now will create an input mask for the TimeCardDate field in the tblTimeCards table that requires the user to enter a four-digit year.

To create an input mask in the TimeCardDate field:

1. Click the **TimeCardDate** field.

2. Click in the **Input Mask** property text box and type the following input mask: **99/99/0000;0;_**. Make sure you do not type the period at the end of the input mask.

An input mask is composed of three parts separated by semicolons. The first part represents the placeholders for the data to be entered. In the above step, the placeholders are 99/99/0000.

The 9s stand for optional numbers from 0 to 9, and the 0s stand for required numbers from 0 to 9. The slashes are character separators that are used for date input masks.

The second part of the input mask can be 0 or 1. In this case, it is 0. This means that Access will store any literals that are included in the input mask. A **literal** is a character in the mask that you don't have to type, such as dashes in a Social Security number—555-55-5555.

The date input mask does not have any literals, only separators for the month, day, and year. The 0 is a default value. It is a good idea to store literals when you create an input mask, because when you query the data, you will probably type the literal character. If you haven't stored it, the query won't find the value you are looking for. A 1 in this position would indicate that only the typed data would be stored. In the case of the Social Security number example, Access would store 555555555.

The last part of the input mask is the placeholder character that you want to use. The placeholder character is the character that appears in the field and represents the number of characters the user should type. In this case, the placeholder is the underscore.

To test the TimeCardDate field's input mask:

1. Switch to Datasheet view and save your changes.

2. Test the input mask by typing **1/1/29** in the TimeCardDate field for the first record and then pressing the **Tab** key. You should see the error message shown in Figure 2-27.

Figure 2-27	INPUT MASK ERROR MESSAGE

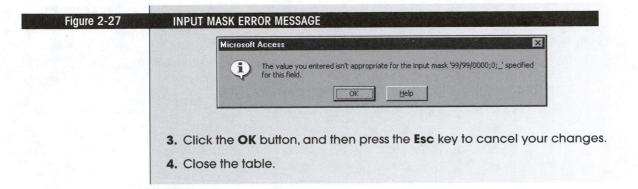

3. Click the **OK** button, and then press the **Esc** key to cancel your changes.

4. Close the table.

Documenting Your Database

Amanda asks you and Carolyn to begin documenting the database that you are developing for MovieCam Technologies. She wants you to gather documents which include: the objectives for the database; the information that you have compiled from your interviews with the product managers; notes you have taken at meetings; and the original system printouts, including the sample spreadsheet and the time card used by employees. She also wants you to print a report of the relationships between the tables you have developed and a data dictionary of the fields and their properties.

A **data dictionary** is a list and definition of the individual fields included in each of the tables in your database. It may also include table and field properties, such as primary keys, foreign keys, indexes, field data types, and validation rules.

The **Database Documenter** allows you to create a data dictionary quickly and easily. It generates a document that clearly identifies the objects in the database and their related properties.

Figure 2-28 shows one page of the data dictionary for the tblEmployees table in the MovieCam Technologies database. The actual document is 13 pages long and doesn't even include all the information on the table! In fact, if you were to print documentation for all the properties applied to all the objects in a database like MovieCam's, you could end up with a document that's hundreds of pages long! In most cases, it's necessary to print only the documentation for the tables in the database.

Figure 2-28	PARTIAL DATA DICTIONARY

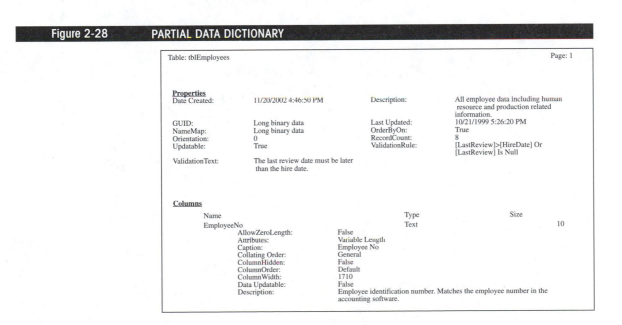

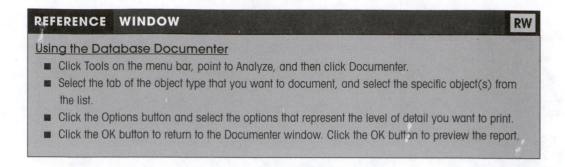

REFERENCE   WINDOW   **RW**

Using the Database Documenter
- Click Tools on the menu bar, point to Analyze, and then click Documenter.
- Select the tab of the object type that you want to document, and select the specific object(s) from the list.
- Click the Options button and select the options that represent the level of detail you want to print.
- Click the OK button to return to the Documenter window. Click the OK button to preview the report.

Earlier in the week, Carolyn added field descriptions to the tblEmployees table as shown in Figure 2-29. Field descriptions print as a part of the documentation, as do table descriptions and properties. For this reason, it is a good idea to add them whenever possible. Carolyn also printed the data dictionary for all of the tables except tblEmployees, tblTimeCards, tblHours, and tblJobs. You will complete the data dictionary for these tables next.

Figure 2-29	TBLEMPLOYEES TABLE WITH FIELD DESCRIPTIONS

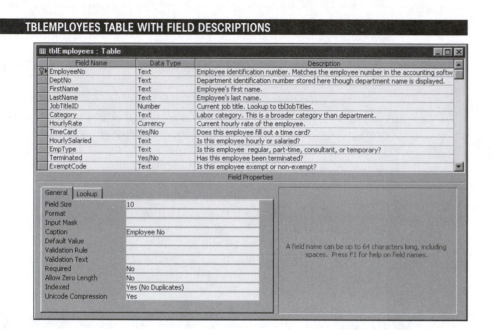

To use the Database Documenter:

1. In the Database window, click **Tools** on the menu bar, point to Analyze, and then click **Documenter**. The Documenter dialog box opens with the Tables tab selected, as shown in Figure 2-30.

Figure 2-30   **DATABASE DOCUMENTER**

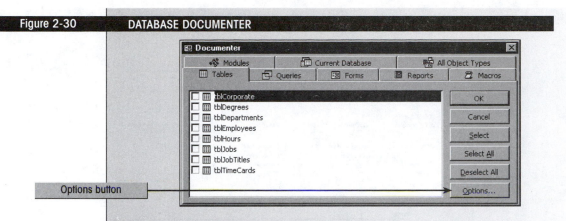

Options button

2. Click the **tblEmployees** check box and then click the **Options** button to open the Print Table Definition dialog box, as shown in Figure 2-31.

Figure 2-31   **PRINT TABLE DEFINITION DIALOG BOX**

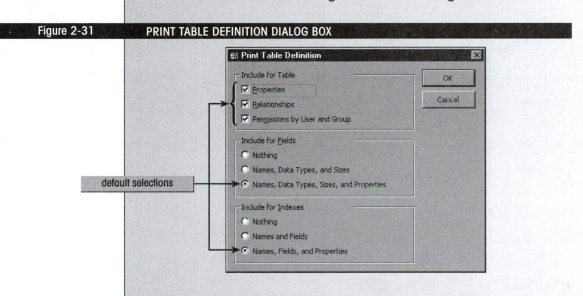

default selections

Access defaults to print all of the possible options for tables. If you have used the Database Documenter before, the options that you selected then will still be displayed. Otherwise, all of the options will be checked by default.

3. If necessary, clear the check boxes for **Relationships** and **Permissions by User and Group**.

4. If necessary, click the **Names, Data Types, Sizes, and Properties** option button in the Include for Fields section.

5. If necessary, click the **Names and Fields** option button in the Include for Indexes section, and then click the **OK** button.

6. Click the **OK** button in the Documenter dialog box. After a few moments, an Object Definition report opens in Print Preview as shown in Figure 2-32.

Figure 2-32   OBJECT DEFINITION REPORT

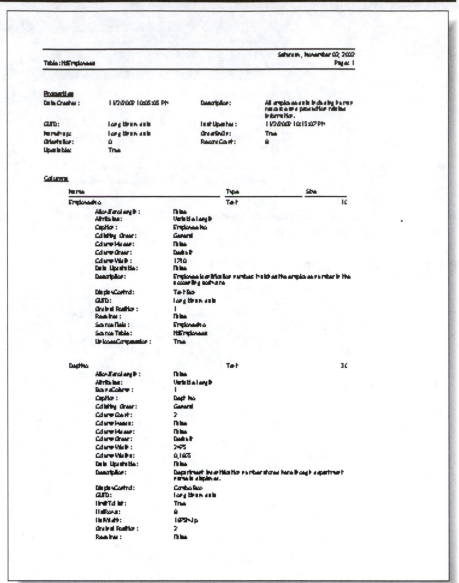

Rather than print the report, you and Carolyn export it to Word and save it with your other files. Because it is 13 pages long, you'll print it later.

To export the Object Definition report to Word:

1. Click the **OfficeLinks** list arrow, and then click **Publish It with MS Word**.

2. Word opens and displays a document named doc_rptObjects. Select **Save As** from the **File** menu. From the Save as type drop-down list, select **Word Document**. Save the document to the same folder containing the Movie2 database.

3. Close Word and return to Access.

4. Close the Object Definition window.

Next, you'll add descriptions to the tblTimeCards, tblHours, and tblJobs tables and then print the data dictionary for these three tables.

To add field descriptions:

1. Open the **tblTimeCards** table in Design view.

2. Add the following field descriptions by typing the values in each field's description column:

TimeCardNo	**Time card number**
TimeCardDate	**Week ending date**
EmployeeNo	**Employee number, lookup to tblEmployees**

3. Close the table and save your changes.

4. Open the **tblHours** table in Design view.

5. Add the following field descriptions:

LineItem	**Line item number from time card**
TimeCardNo	**Time card number**
JobID	**Job number from time card, lookup to tblJobs**
HoursWorked	**Total hours worked column from time card**

6. Close the table and save your changes.

7. Open the **tblJobs** table in Design view.

8. Add the following field descriptions:

JobID	**Job number**
Model	**Camera model number**
DateCreated	**Date record created**
DateModifed	**Date of last change**

9. Close the table and save your changes.

Now you will print the Database Documenter report for these three tables.

To print the Database Documenter report:

1. In the Database window, click **Tools** on the menu bar, point to **Analyze**, and then click **Documenter**. The Documenter dialog box opens with the Tables tab selected.

2. Click the check box for **tblTimeCards**, **tblHours**, and **tblJobs** and click the **Options** button to display the Print Table Definition dialog box.

3. Be sure that the check boxes for **Relationships** and **Permissions by User and Group** are cleared.

4. Be sure that the **Names, Data Types, Sizes, and Properties** option in the Include for Fields section is selected.

5. Be sure that the **Names and Fields** option in the Include for Indexes section is selected, and click the **OK** button.

6. Click the **OK** button in the Documenter opening dialog box. After a few moments, an Object Definition report opens in Print Preview.

7. Click the **Print** button on the Print Preview toolbar.

8. Close the Object Definition window.

The last thing you need to do for documentation is print the Relationships window, which graphically illustrates the relationships among all the tables. One relationship was automatically created by the Lookup Wizard. It is the relationship between the tblHours and tblJobs tables.

To print the relationships report:

1. Click **Tools** on the menu bar, and then click **Relationships** to display the Relationships window.

Note that there are two representations of tblJobs as shown in Figure 2-33. The table tblJobs_1 is an alias that the Lookup Wizard created when the tblJobs table was identified as the Row Source for looking up the JobID in the tblHours table.

Figure 2-33   RELATIONSHIPS WINDOW

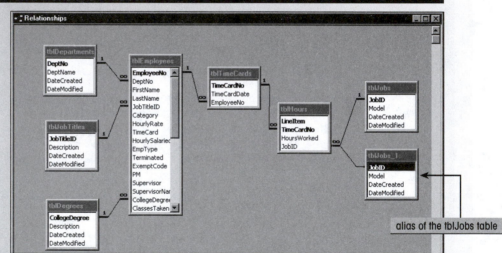

2. Click **File** on the menu bar, and then click **Print Relationships**.

3. Click the **Print** button on the Print Preview toolbar to print the report.

4. Close the report to return to the Database window.

5. Close the Movie2 database and exit Access.

You and Carolyn have now compiled a data dictionary for all the tables in the Movie2 database. You have printed a report of the relationships between each set of tables in the database. You have a copy of the original time card, a copy of the original sample spreadsheet, handwritten notes of your interviews with product managers, and notes taken at meetings. You complete Amanda's request by compiling this documentation into a binder. You will add more to it as you continue to develop the database in later tutorials.

Session 2.2 QUICK CHECK

1. What are the benefits of using a combo box?

2. The _____ Column property of a combo box determines which column's data is stored in the field.

3. What is a subdatasheet?

4. What is the range of years that Access uses when a user types a two-digit year?

5. A(n) _____ is a character you don't have to type that is included in an input mask.

6. What is a data dictionary?

7. The _____ lets you create a data dictionary quickly and easily.

REVIEW ASSIGNMENTS

You have been asked to complete the tables for the Hours database and to set the relationships between the tables. The design is similar to the Movie2 database you worked on in this tutorial. Complete the following:

1. Open the **Hours2** database located in the Tutorial.02 folder on your local or network drive.

2. Create the following tables in the Hours2 database, setting the indicated primary keys:

    tblTimeCards (<u>TimeCardNo</u>, TimeCardDate, *EmployeeNo*)
    tblHours (<u>LineItem</u>, *TimeCardNo*, HoursWorked, ProductNo)

3. Open the **tblTimeCards** table in Design view.

4. The data type of TimeCardNo should be text; TimeCardDate should be date/time; and EmployeeNo should be text.

5. Type a caption (with a space between each word) for each field. For example, Time Card No is the caption for the TimeCardNo field.

6. Add the following field descriptions to the fields in the **tblTimeCards** table:

TimeCardNo	Time card number from the original time card document
TimeCardDate	Period ending date
EmployeeNo	Employee number

7. Format the TimeCardDate field as a medium date.

8. Create an input mask so that a four-digit year must be entered in the TimeCardDate field.

Explore ▷ 9. Create a validation rule so that only dates between March 1, 1995, and the current day's date can be entered.

Explore ▷ 10. Enter validation text to notify users of what is wrong if they enter incorrect dates.

11. Close the **tblTimeCards** table and save your changes.

12. Click **Tools** on the menu bar, click **Options**, and then click the **General** tab. Select the option for this database to display four-digit years in the date/time fields.

13. Open the **tblHours** table in Design view.

14. Define HoursWorked as a number field with the Field Size property set to **Double**.

Explore 15. Format HoursWorked to display positive numbers in #,###.00 format in black, negative numbers in red with the same format but enclosed by parentheses, and zero values as the word "Zero". (*Hint*: Click the Format property text box, press the F1 key, and then click the link to "Number and Currency Data Types" to get help.)

Explore 16. Use the Lookup Wizard to convert ProductNo to a combo box that looks up a value list supplied by you. (Store the first column in the table, and use the default label.) The values are:

98877	Camera Optics Upgrade
93455	Sensor Integration
87990	Stinger Motors

17. The remaining fields in the tblHours table should be text fields. Create captions for each of the fields. Use a space between each word of the field name, such as Line Item No for the LineItemNo field.

18. Add the following field descriptions to the fields in the tblHours table:

LineItemNo	Line item from time card
TimeCardNo	Time card number from the original time card
HoursWorked	Total hours worked per project
ProductNo	Product number

19. Close the **tblHours** table and save your changes.

20. Open the Relationships window and create the relationships between the tblTimeCards and tblHours tables on the TimeCardNo field, and between the tblEmployees and tblTimeCards tables on the EmployeeNo field. Set referential integrity for each relationship and apply the Cascade Update Related Fields option to each.

21. Print the Relationships window report and save it as **rptRelationships**.

22. Close the **Hours2** database and exit Access.

CASE PROBLEMS

Case 1. Edwards and Company You completed the tblConsultants table for the Edwards and Company database, and now you need to complete the tblClients table. One consultant in the database can have many clients, so these tables have a one-to-many relationship between them. Jack Edwards wants the users of the system to be able to enter a consultant into the client table by picking the correct consultant name from a displayed list rather than having to use the consultant number.

You decide to create a combo box that displays the consultant's first and last name sorted alphabetically by last name and that stores the consultant number in the ConsultantID field of the tblClients table.

1. Start Access and open **Edward2** located in the **Tutorial.02** folder on your local or network drive.

2. Open the **tblClients** table in Design view.

Explore 3. Format the **Address2** field to display text that is entered and to display the word "None" when the filed is empty (null). (*Hint:* Press the F1 key in the Format property text box and then click the link to "Text and Memo Data Types" for help.)

Explore

4. Create a custom input mask for the ZipCode field that requires the entry of five digits with a placeholder of @. (*Hint:* Press the F1 key in the Input Mask property text box for help.)

5. Click **ConsultantID** in the field list, click the Lookup tab in the Field Properties pane, and then create a combo box for the field as follows:
   a. Set the Display Control property to **Combo Box**.
   b. Click in the Row Source text box, click its **Build** button, add the **tblConsultants** table to the Query Builder window, and then close the Show Table dialog box.
   c. Add the **ConsultantID** field to the first column's Field text box and, in the second column's Field text box, type ConsultantName:[FirstName]&" "&[LastName].
   d. Add the **LastName** field to the third column's Field text box, and then set its Sort property to **Ascending**.
   e. Close the Query Builder window and save the changes.
   f. Set the Column Count property to **3**, and then type **0";.75";0"** in the Column Widths text box.
   g. Close the table and save your changes.

6. Open the **tblClients** table in Datasheet view, test the combo box, and then widen the column to display the name more clearly.

7. Open the Database Documenter, select the tblClients table, click the Options button, and then select the Names, Data Types, Sizes, and Properties option in the Include for Fields section. Click the OK button, click the OK button, and then print your results.

8. Close the **Edward2** database and exit Access.

Case 2. San Diego County Information Systems You have developed the tables and the test data for your database, which tracks students and classes. The tables need a few more changes, the documentation needs to be completed, and relationships between tables need to be established. When you consider the options for setting relationships, note that the following conditions must be met:

■ If a student stops taking classes or is entered by mistake, you would like to allow them to be deleted, but not if enrollment records for that student exist.

■ If a student ID is entered incorrectly, you would like to correct that error in the tblStudents table and have the correction made in all of the related records for classes that student has taken.

■ If a class is deleted from the schedule (the tblClasses table), you would like all related student enrollment records for that class to be deleted as well.

■ If a class number is changed in the tblClasses table, you would like all related records in the tblStudentsAndClasses table to be updated also.

1. Open the **ISD2** database located in the Tutorial.02 folder on your local or network drive.

2. Open the **tblClasses** table in Design view.

3. Format the Date field as a Medium Date.

Explore

4. Create a custom format for the StartTime and EndTime fields. The times should be displayed with hours and minutes and am or pm should be in lowercase. (*Hint:* Press the F1 key in the Format property text box, and then click the link for Date/Time Data Type to get help.)

5. Use the Input Mask Wizard for the Date field to create an input mask that requires a four-digit year to be entered.

6. Click in the Indexed property text box of the Date field and click Yes (Duplicates OK) from the drop-down list.

7. Set an identical index for the ClassName field.

8. Close the table and save your changes.

9. Open the Database Documenter, select the tblClasses table, click the Options button, and then select the Names, Data Types, Sizes, and Properties option in the Include for Fields section. Click the OK button, click the OK button, and then print your results.

10. Open the Relationships window, and set the relationships for all tables in the database. Select the options for Cascade Update Related Fields and Cascade Delete Related Records based on the criteria listed at the beginning of this case.

11. Click File, Print Relationships to print the report, and then save it as **rptRelationships**.

12. Close the **ISD2** database, and then exit Access.

Case 3. Christenson Homes You decide that it would be easier to enter the subdivision ID information in the tblLots table if the SubdivisionID field were a lookup to the tblSubdivisions table. You will create the combo box and set the relationships between the tables.

1. Open **Homes2** database located in the **Tutorial.02** folder on your local or network drive.

2. Open the **tblLots** table in Design view.

Explore

3. Use the Lookup Wizard to convert the Plan field to a combo box that looks up a value list you supply. Set the Limit to List property so that only these values can be entered. The values are: 1, 2, 3, and 4.

4. Click SubdivisionID in the field list, click the Lookup tab in the Field Properties pane, and then create a combo box for the field as follows:

   a. Set the Display Control property to Combo Box.

   b. Click in the Row Source text box, click its Build button, add the **tblSubdivisions** table to the Query Builder window, and then close the Show Table dialog box.

   c. Add the SubdivisionID field to the first column's Field text box and the SubdivisionName field to the second column's Field text box.

   d. Close the Query Builder window and save your changes.

   e. Set the Column Count property number to 2, set the Column Widths property to 0";1", and then set the Limit To List property to Yes.

   f. Close the table and save your changes.

5. Open the **tblLots** table in Datasheet view and test the combo box.

6. Open the Relationships window and set the relationship between the tblLots and tblSubdivisions tables on the common field. In the Edit Relationships dialog box, set Referential Integrity and select the option to allow changes to the primary key in the primary table to be updated in the related table.

7. Click File, click Print Relationships, print the report, and then save it as **rptRelationships**.

8. Close the **Homes2** database, and then exit Access.

Case 4. Sonoma Farms The Sonoma Farms database is only partially completed. You have completed the tblCustomers and tblDistributors tables, but you need to finish the design of the database and the remaining tables. You also want to store information about customer visits to the winery. You've listed the following attributes to include in the remaining tables: VisitDate, CustomerID, VisitorFirstName, VisitorLastName, Accommodations, Meals, and Gifts.

1. Open the **Sonoma2** database located in the Tutorial.02 folder on your local or network drive.

2. Create the **tblVisits** table and structure it as follows:

    tblVisits (VisitID, VisitDate, *CustomerNo*, Accomodations, Meals, Gifts)

3. Define VisitID as an AutoNumber data type and the primary key. Define VisitDate as a date/time field. Define CustomerNo as a number field with the Long Integer format. The remaining fields are text data types.

Explore

4. Create a custom format for the Date field in the Format property text box. The date should be formatted to the full name of the month, the day, and a four-digit year. (*Hint:* Press the F1 key in the Format property text box, and then click the link to "Date/Time Data Types" to get help.)

5. Create an input mask for the Date field requiring a four-digit year.

6. Create a combo box for the CustomerNo field which looks up the CustomerID and CompanyName fields from the tblCustomers table. Only the CompanyName field should be displayed by the combo box. The CustomerID field should be stored in the field.

7. Close the **tblVisits** table and save your changes.

8. Create the **tblVisitors** table and structure it as follows:

    tblVisitors (VisitorID, *VisitID*, VisitorFirst, VisitorLast)

9. Define VisitorID as an AutoNumber data type and the primary key. Define VisitID as a number data type (Long Integer), and the remaining fields as text data types.

10. Close the **tblVisitors** table and save your changes.

11. Set a relationship between the **tblCustomers** and **tblVisits** tables and the **tblVisits** and **tblVisitors** tables. Use the common field between each pair of tables.

12. Set referential integrity, but do not select the Cascade Update or Cascade Delete options for either relationship.

13. Click File, and then click Print Relationships to create the relationships report.

14. Print the report and save it as **rptRelationships**.

15. Open the Database Documenter, select the tblVisits and tblVisitors tables, click the Options button, select the Names, Data Types, Sizes, and Properties option in the Include for Fields section. Do not select anything for the Indexes section, and do not print the Relationships or Permissions information. Click the OK button, click the OK button, and then print your results.

16. Close the **Sonoma2** database and exit Access.

QUICK | CHECK ANSWERS

Session 2.1

1. Redundancy is the term for duplication of data.
2. "foreign"
3. "32"
4. The benefit of adding indexes to a table is that they speed sorting and searching.
5. "one-to-one"
6. The most common type of relationship between tables is a one-to-many relationship.
7. Many-to-many relationships require a junction table.
8. An orphaned record is a record in a related table that does not contain a record in the primary table.

Session 2.2

1. The benefits of using a combo box are that they are useful for: limiting the entries in a field of a table; ensuring that data is entered correctly; and looking up information.
2. "bound"
3. A subdatasheet is a datasheet that is nested within another datasheet and contains data related or joined to the first datasheet.
4. The range of years that Access uses when a user types a two-digit year is 1/1/1930 through 12/31/2029.
5. "literal"
6. A data dictionary is a list and definition of the individual fields that comprise each of the tables in your database.
7. "Database Documenter"

OBJECTIVES

In this tutorial you will:

- Use the Import Text Wizard to import a tab-delimited text file

- Create expressions using text manipulation functions in a query

- Create append, update, and delete queries

- Import a standard module from another Access database

- Import data from an Excel worksheet

- Learn about query properties

- Create a query for unique values

- Learn about SQL-specific queries and write a union query in SQL

- Export query results to an Excel worksheet

USING
IMPORT WIZARDS, ACTION QUERIES, AND SQL

Importing and Archiving Data for the MovieCam Technologies Database

CASE

MovieCam Technologies

MovieCam Technologies has accumulated a significant amount of employee data, production data, and other historical data that needs to be incorporated in its new database. Amanda asks you and Carolyn to determine the best method to import this existing data into the MovieCam database. As you have learned, much of the data, including time cards and employee information, exists in Excel spreadsheets. Other data, such as personnel and payroll information, has been entered in MovieCam's accounting software program.

The company's accounting software is an older version of ACC90, and does not export to a format recognized by Access. Randy Harper, an ACC90 consultant, has already exported some of the data to a tab-delimited text file. Amanda asks you to work out the importing process with the sample accounting file Randy has provided, and with the sample Excel data provided to you by the product managers.

She also wants you to develop queries for archiving data that is more than a year old. The time card and hours data go back three years. Amanda wants you to optimize performance by storing the outdated transactional data in separate tables.

Finally, Amanda wants you to develop the query to integrate the archived records with the active records for those situations when the product managers need to compile statistics from all the data. She then wants you to demonstrate to a product manager how to export this data back to Excel for statistical analysis.

SESSION 3.1

In this session, you will use the Import Text Wizard to import a tab-delimited text file. You then will write text manipulation expressions to extract first and last names to separate fields, and append the imported data to an existing table.

Introduction

You and Carolyn decide to import *sample* records to use to develop the rest of the database. While you develop the remaining objects and write code, you will need sample data to work with. After the database is completed, tested, and documented, you will delete the sample records and import all the records to date. The queries for populating tables and archiving inactive records can then be run and the database distributed for use. The Excel worksheet data and the ACC90 accounting software data will continue to be updated while you complete the database design, so it is neither necessary nor efficient to import all the data at this point. Figure 3-1 illustrates your plan for importing and appending employee text data from ACC90.

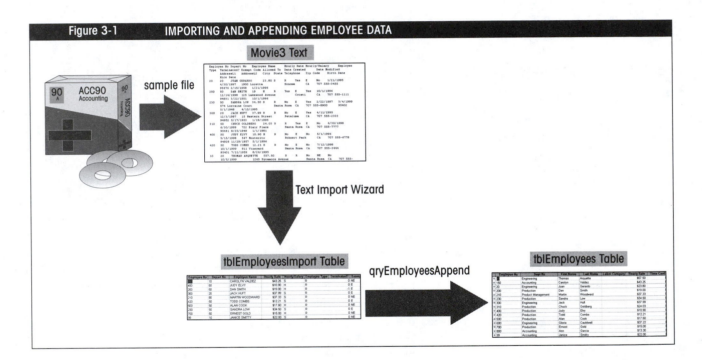

Figure 3-1   IMPORTING AND APPENDING EMPLOYEE DATA

Figure 3-2 shows how you plan to import, append, and archive time card and hours data from Excel.

Figure 3-2   IMPORTING, APPENDING, AND ARCHIVING HOURS AND TIME CARD DATA

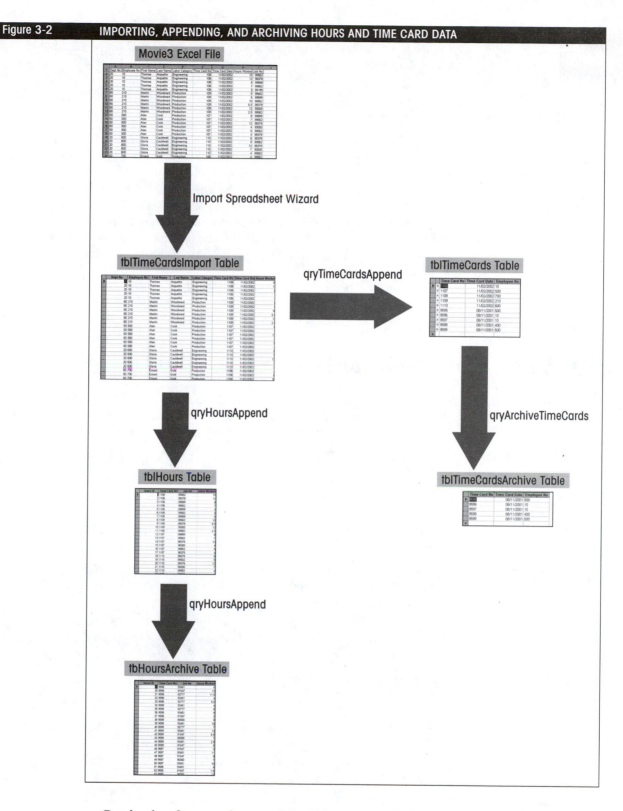

Carolyn has fine-tuned some of the objects in the database over the last few days. The tblHours table no longer contains a composite key field. She changed the name of its LineItem field to HoursID, and she changed the HoursID field type to AutoNumber so that each record added to the table is automatically assigned a unique number. Changing the HoursID field to an AutoNumber field will save data entry time. It can also be set as the primary key. Carolyn changed a few other field names and properties, but the structure of the database is consistent with the one developed in Tutorial 2.

Importing and Linking Data

You can pull data into an Access database from an external source by using one of two methods: importing or linking. Importing brings the data into Access, usually into a new table. Linking leaves data in its current format and location.

Linking is a good alternate method if the data is going to be used both in its original format and in Access. When you use Access to link to another RDBMS, Access acts as a database front end. The **front end** is one file that contains the queries, forms, reports, macros, and modules. Tables are stored in another file and location referred to as the **back end**. Access can link to dBASE, Paradox, and FoxPro RDBMS database files. Access also can link to Excel, Outlook, and text files.

Importing is a better method than linking if you know that you will be using the data only in Access and not in its original format. You can import data into an Access database from the same programs and file types to which you can link Access.

Using the Import Text Wizard

You and Carolyn begin by importing the sample tab-delimited text file that Randy created.

The term **delimiter** refers to the characters that identify the end of one field and the beginning of another field in a text file. The term **tab-delimited** refers to text files in which the fields are separated by tabs, and each record begins on a new line. Access also supports comma-delimited, space-delimited, and fixed-width files. In comma-delimited and space-delimited text files, fields are separated by commas and spaces, respectively. In a fixed-width text file, the fields are fixed in size so that a delimiter is not necessary.

To import the tab-delimited text file to the Movie3 database, you will use the Import Text Wizard.

REFERENCE WINDOW   **RW**

Using the Import Text Wizard
- Start Access and open the database to which you want to import the text file.
- Click File on the menu bar, point to Get External Data, and then click Import.
- In the File Name text box, type the filename. Click the Files of Type list arrow, click Text Files, and then click Import.
- The Import Text Wizard dialog box opens. Navigate to the drive and folder that contains the file you want to import.
- Complete the Wizard dialog boxes to select delimited or fixed-width fields, choose a delimiter if necessary, mark the first row as field names or not, and choose the table to which you want to import the data. You will need to change the field options as necessary, choose whether you want to add a primary key or not, and name the table if you're importing to a new table.

Next, you will open the Movie3 database and start the Import Text Wizard.

To import a tab-delimited text file:

1. Start Access and open the **Movie3** database located in the Tutorial.03 folder on your local or network drive.

2. Click **File** on the menu bar, point to **Get External Data**, and then click **Import**.

3. Click the **Files of type** list arrow, and then click **Text Files**.

4. Be sure that the files from the Tutorial folder on your local or network drive are visible, click the **Movie3** text file, and then click the **Import** button. The Import Text Wizard dialog box opens. See Figure 3-3.

Figure 3-3   **FIRST IMPORT TEXT WIZARD DIALOG BOX**

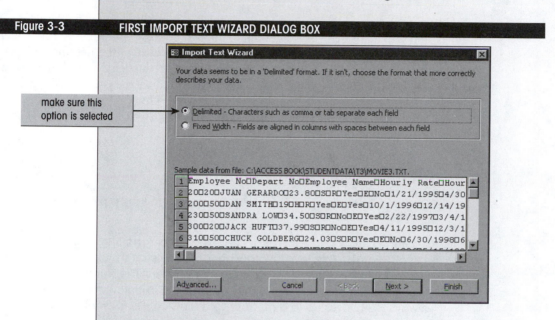

5. Be sure that the **Delimited** option button is selected, and then click the **Next** button.

6. Be sure that the **Tab** option button is selected, and then click the **First Row Contains Field Names** check box to select it, as shown in Figure 3-4.

Figure 3-4   **CHOOSING A DELIMITER**

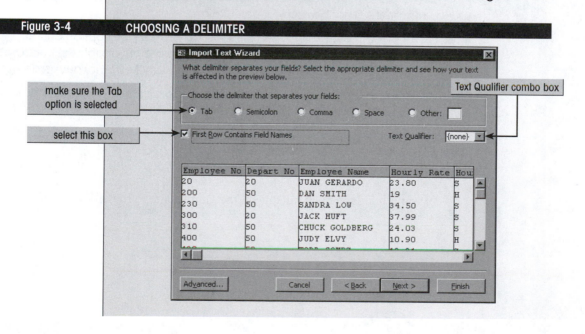

You choose the character that distinguishes text data from numeric data in the Text Qualifier combo box. Some programs use quotation marks to enclose all data in a comma-delimited format; others that export to a comma-delimited format enclose only text data in quotation marks.

7. Qualifiers are not used in tab-delimited files, so make sure that **None** is selected in the Text Qualifier Combo box, and then click the **Next** button.

8. Be sure the **In a New Table** option button is selected, and then click the **Next** button.

In the next dialog box, you can change field names, add indexes to fields, change field data types, and skip fields that you don't want to import. Because you will import the data to a new table and then append it to existing tables, you won't change the field names. The table to which you are importing this data will be temporary, so the name of each field is not critical. Changing the data types is a good idea, however, to reduce the risk of losing data during the import process. For example, the currency data in the Hourly Rate field or the dates in date fields might not import properly if these fields are not changed from text fields. You will change the data types next.

To change field data types:

1. Click the **Data Type** list arrow, and then change the Employee No data type to **Text**.

2. Click the **Depart No** field name, click the **Data Type** list arrow, and then select **Text**. The Employee No and Depart No fields should be Text data types because these fields contain reference numbers. The Number data type should be used only for fields that will be used in calculations. A text field can always be converted to a number field temporarily for sorting purposes.

3. Repeat Step 2 to change the data types for the following: Hourly Rate to **Currency**, Terminated? to **Yes/No**, Allowed To to **Yes/No**, and Zip Code to **Text**. The Hourly Rate field is changed to Currency because it is a dollar value. The Terminated? and Allowed To fields are set as Yes/No fields because the data stored in them is always either Yes or No. The Zip Code field is changed to Text because it will not be used for calculations.

4. Click the **Next** button and then click the **No primary key** option button. Because you'll use this table's records to populate other tables in the database and you will eventually delete the table, a primary key is not necessary.

5. Click the **Next** button, type **tblEmployeesImport** as the name of the new table, and then click the **Finish** button.

6. Click the **OK** button in the message box that tells you that Access has finished importing the file.

Next you'll build the query to append the sample data to the tblEmployees table.

Creating an Append Query

You have successfully imported the sample employee data into Access. The data imported smoothly but the employee name information is not yet in the format you want. The first name and last name are in one field, as shown in Figure 3-5; you want the names to appear in two separate fields.

Figure 3-5	EMPLOYEE FIRST AND LAST NAMES ARE IN ONE FIELD

first and last name needs to be extracted from Employee Name

tblEmployeesImport : Table

Employee No	Depart No	Employee Name	Hourly Rate	Hourly/Salary	Employe
150	10	CAROLYN VALDEZ	$43.25	S	R
400	50	JUDY ELVY	$10.90	H	R
200	50	DAN SMITH	$19.00	H	R
300	20	JACK HUFT	$37.99	S	R
210	80	MARTIN WOODWARD	$37.33	S	R
420	50	TODD COMBS	$12.21	S	R
500	50	ALAN COOK	$17.60	H	R
230	50	SANDRA LOW	$34.50	S	R
700	50	ERNEST GOLD	$15.00	H	R
99	10	JANICE SMITTY	$22.00	S	R
10	20	THOMAS ARQUETTE	$57.50	S	R
310	50	CHUCK GOLDBERG	$24.03	S	R
600	20	GLORIA CAULDWELL	$37.22	H	R
20	20	JUAN GERARDO	$23.80	S	R
800	10	ANN GARCIA	$13.30	H	H

You will write field expressions to extract first name and last name from the Employee Name field in the same query you create to append this data to the tblEmployees table. Before you do this, however, you want to be certain that the sample records Jason created in the tblEmployees table have all been deleted.

To check for records in the tblEmployees table:

1. Click **Tables** in the Objects bar of the Database window.

2. Double-click the **tblEmployees** table. It does not contain any records.

3. Close the table.

Using Text-Manipulation Functions

Before you can write the field expressions to extract first and last name from the Employee Name field in the imported data, you need to know more about working with functions in Access, and about string functions in particular.

Functions return a value and are used to build validation rule expressions in tables, field expressions in queries, and text box expressions in forms and reports. Functions also are used to construct macros and in VBA programming. They will be discussed throughout these tutorials. Approximately 150 functions in Access and VBA are grouped into categories based on their purpose. The following is a list of functions commonly used in queries:

- *Date and time*: Used for manipulating dates and times, for example, adding values to dates, subtracting one date from another, extracting the month or year from a date, and extracting hours or minutes from the time.

■ *Text manipulation*: Functions for manipulating strings of text, for example, trimming leading and trailing spaces from a string of text, extracting part of a string of text from another string of text, and counting the number of characters in a string of text. Commonly used text manipulation functions are listed in Figure 3-6.

Figure 3-6	COMMONLY USED TEXT MANIPULATION FUNCTIONS		
FUNCTION	**DESCRIPTION**	**EXAMPLE**	**RETURNS**
InStr	Returns the position of one string within another	InStr("Jones","o")	2
LCase	Returns the lowercase version of a string	LCase("JONES")	jones
UCase	Returns the uppercase version of a string	UCase("jones")	JONES
Len	Returns the number of characters in a string	Len("Jones")	5
Left	Returns the leftmost character(s) of a string	Left("jones",2)	jo
Right	Returns the rightmost character(s) of a string	Right("jones",2)	es
Mid	Returns a portion of a string	Mid("jones",2,2)	on
LTrim	Removes leading spaces from the string	LTrim(" jones")	jones
RTrim	Removes trailing spaces from a string	RTrim("jones ")	jones
Space	Returns a string that consists of the specified number of spaces	Space(3)	returns 3 spaces

■ *Data type conversion*: Functions that let you force a particular data type, for example, CInt (which you used in Tutorial 1 to force a text data type to an integer) is a data type conversion function.

To extract first name and last name from the Employee Name field, you need to find a common character in each entry that indicates where the first name ends and the last name begins. The obvious choice in this instance is the space. In other instances where you extract one string of text from another, it might be a comma, a dash character, or a slash character. You will use the InStr function to find the position of the space in each entry.

You will use the Expression Builder (see Figure 3-7) to create the expression to extract first and last name from the *Employee Name* field. The Expression Builder is a useful tool for creating field expressions because it provides a list of built-in Access functions, and thus helps you avoid syntax errors. It does not always provide you with the exact syntax that you must use in these functions, however. For example, quotation marks are required around arguments for some functions, and the Expression Builder does not include them when it displays the syntax of these functions. You should double-check the Access Help system for the correct syntax of functions, even if you use the Expression Builder.

Figure 3-7   **EXPRESSION BUILDER**

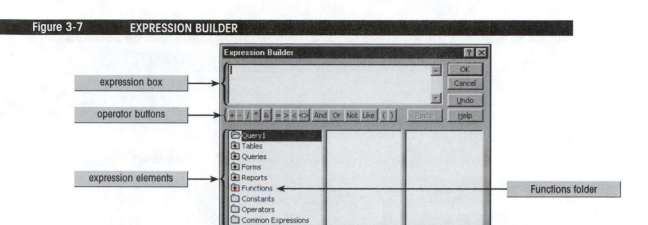

REFERENCE WINDOW   **RW**

Using the Expression Builder

- Display the query in Design view.
- Position the insertion point in the Field text box of the field in which you want to create the expression.
- Click the Build button on the Query Design toolbar.
- Use the expression elements and operators to build the expression, or type the expression in the expression box.
- Click the OK button.

You will create a new query and use the Expression Builder to build an InStr function which will determine the position of the space in the Employee Name field. Later you will use the results of this formula to extract first name and last name from the Employee Name field.

To use the Expression Builder:

1. Create a new query in Design view, add the **tblEmployeesImport** table to the Query window, and then close the Show Table dialog box.

2. Be sure that the insertion point is in the first Field text box, and then click the **Build** button ⚟ on the Query Design toolbar. The Expression Builder dialog box opens.

3. Double-click the **Functions** folder in the list of expression elements. The Built-In Functions and Movie3 folders appear below the Functions folder.

4. Click the **Built-In Functions** folder. A list of function categories is visible in the center list box, and you will see all functions in the right list box.

5. Scroll down in the center list box, click the **Text** function category, click the **InStr** function in the right list box, and then click the **Paste** button to paste the function into the expression box. See Figure 3-8.

Figure 3-8   **BUILDING THE INSTR EXPRESSION**

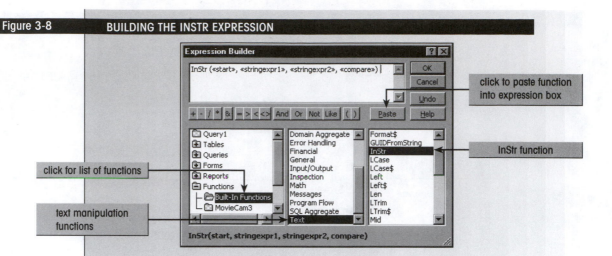

Notice that the first argument—<<start>>—is the starting position of the search and is optional. Because you want to start at the beginning of the string and that is the default for this argument, you will omit this first argument. To delete or replace any argument in the expression box, click the argument to highlight it.

6. Select **<<start>>** in the expression box, and then press the **Delete** key three times to delete the argument, comma, and space.

   The second argument in the function—*<<stringexp1>>*—is required. It represents the string that you are searching.

7. Click **<<stringexpr1>>** in the expression box to select it, and double-click the **Tables** folder in the first list box.

8. Click **tblEmployeesImport** in the left list box, click **Employee Name** in the middle list box, and then click the **Paste** button.

   The third argument in the function—*<<stringexp2>>*—is also required. It represents the string for which you are searching.

9. Click **<<stringexpr2>>** to select it, and then type **" "** (quotation mark, space, quotation mark) to indicate that you are searching for a space.

10. Delete the remaining comma. Also, delete **<<compare>>**, which is the last argument. (This argument is for conducting a binary or textual non-case-sensitive comparison, neither of which apply here.) Do *not* delete the closing parenthesis.

11. Click the **OK** button in the Expression Builder dialog box and then click the **Run** button 🔘 on the Query Design toolbar to run the query.

The result of the InStr function is a number that represents the position of the space character between the first and last names in the Employee Name string. Next you will create another string function that uses this position as one of its arguments. Before you do that, however, you need to give a more meaningful name to the expression you just created.

To name the expression:

1. Switch to Design view.

2. In the Field text box, delete the word **Expr1** from the beginning of the expression and then type **NameSpace** in its place. Do not delete the colon or the formula won't work. (Do not use the word "space" by itself as an object name because space is also the name of an Access function.)

3. Run the query again to be sure that it still works. *NameSpace* now appears as the name of the field expression.

4. Switch to Design view to prepare to build the next expression.

Now that you've located the space in each employee name, you'll use the Left function to extract the first name from the Employee Name string. For its first argument, the Left function requires the string from which you want to extract the leftmost characters; the second argument represents the number of characters to return.

To use the Left function to extract the first name:

1. Click the **Field** text box in the column to the right of the *NameSpace* expression.

2. Right-click and then click **Zoom** on the shortcut menu to open the Zoom window.

3. Type **FirstName:Left([Employee Name],NameSpace-1)** as shown in Figure 3-9, and then click the **OK** button.

| Figure 3-9 | FIRSTNAME EXPRESSION |

You must include square brackets around *Employee Name* because it contains a space. NameSpace does not, so Access automatically adds the brackets. You must subtract one from the second argument because NameSpace counts the position up to and including the space and you don't want the space included at the end of the first name.

4. Run the query to test the expression. The first name should appear in the second column.

5. Return to Design view to write the expression to extract the last name.

The last name requires using two additional functions. To extract the rightmost characters from the Employee Name value, you need to know the number of characters in the value, starting with the space and counting to the end of the string. To determine this value, calculate the total number of characters in Employee Name using the Len function, and then subtract the value of NameSpace from the total. See Figure 3-10. You then use the Right function to extract the rightmost characters from the Employee Name field.

Figure 3-10	CALCULATING TOTAL STRING LENGTH LESS NAMESPACE

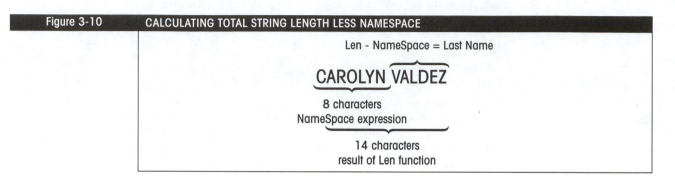

To use the Len function and the Right function to extract the last name:

1. Click the **Field** text box one column to the right of the FirstName expression.

2. Open the Zoom window and type **NameLen:Len([Employee Name])** and then click the **OK** button. Be sure to include the brackets around Employee Name.

3. Run the query to test the expression. The total number of characters in each employee name is displayed in the NameLen column.

4. Return to Design view and then click the **Field** text box one column to the right of the NameLen expression.

5. Open the Zoom window, type **LastName:Right([Employee Name],NameLen-NameSpace)**, and then click the **OK** button to close the Zoom window.

6. Run the query to test the expression. Your results should look like those shown in Figure 3-11.

Figure 3-11	RESULTS OF LASTNAME EXPRESSION

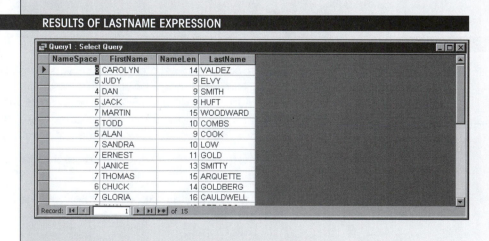

You and Carolyn want to combine the four expressions you just created into two expressions you will then use to update the tblEmployees table. You will now copy and paste the expressions for the NameSpace and NameLen fields in place of their names in the FirstName and LastName field expressions.

To complete the FirstName and LastName expressions:

1. Switch to Design view, click the **NameSpace** expression, and open the Zoom window. Click and drag from the **I** in InStr to the end of the expression to select it, as shown in Figure 3-12.

Figure 3-12	SELECTING THE INSTR FUNCTION

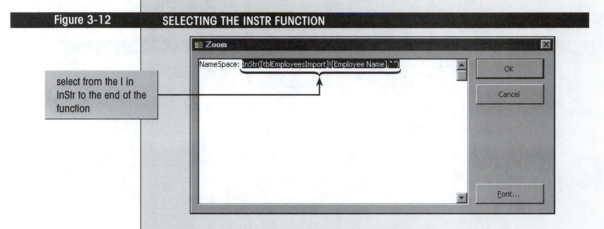

select from the I in InStr to the end of the function

TROUBLE? If you have trouble selecting the characters with the mouse, click at the beginning of the I, then hold down the Shift key while you press the right arrow to select one character at a time to the end of the expression.

2. Right-click the selected expression, click **Copy** on the shortcut menu to copy the formula into the Clipboard, and then click the **Cancel** button to close the Zoom window.

3. Click the **FirstName** expression, open the Zoom window, and then select **[NameSpace]**.

4. Right-click the selected expression and then click **Paste** on the shortcut menu. Make sure the operation to subtract 1 remains at the end of the expression. See Figure 3-13. Click the **OK** button to close the Zoom window.

Figure 3-13	PASTING NAMESPACE IN THE FIRSTNAME EXPRESSION

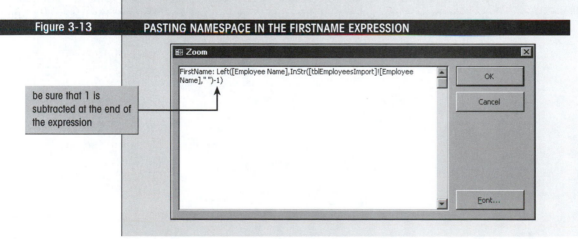

be sure that 1 is subtracted at the end of the expression

5. Save the query as **qryEmployeesAppend** before you continue.

6. Click the **LastName** expression, open the Zoom window, select [**NameSpace**], right-click the selected expression, and then click **Paste**. Click the **OK** button to close the Zoom window.

7. Click **NameLen** and open the Zoom window. Copy the function (excluding the name and the colon) into the Clipboard just like you did for NameSpace in Steps 1 and 2.

8. Click the **LastName** expression, open the Zoom window, select [**NameLen**], right-click the selected expression, and then click **Paste** on the shortcut menu. The expression should look like that shown in Figure 3-14.

Figure 3-14	PASTING NAMESPACE IN THE LASTNAME EXPRESSION

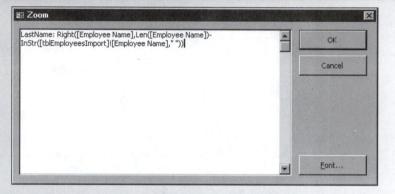

9. Click the **OK** button to close the Zoom window, and run the query to be sure that both expressions still work, and then return to Design view.

10. Position the mouse pointer in the gray bar above the NameSpace expression so that it looks like ↓, click, and then press the **Delete** key.

11. Repeat Step 10 to delete the NameLen expression.

12. Click the **Save** button 🖫 on the toolbar to save your changes.

Review what you've completed so far. You imported the sample text file into Access as the tblEmployeesImport table. You created a query that extracts the first name and last name from the Employee Name column of this table. Now you need to complete the query by adding the other fields you'll append to the tblEmployees table. You'll then convert the query to an append query.

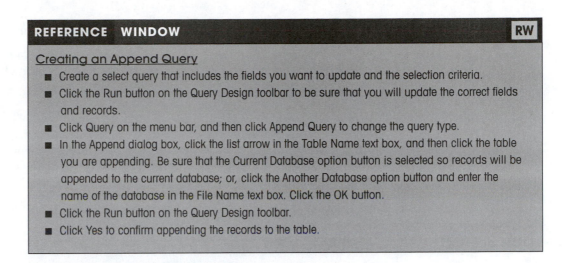

REFERENCE   WINDOW   **RW**

Creating an Append Query
- Create a select query that includes the fields you want to update and the selection criteria.
- Click the Run button on the Query Design toolbar to be sure that you will update the correct fields and records.
- Click Query on the menu bar, and then click Append Query to change the query type.
- In the Append dialog box, click the list arrow in the Table Name text box, and then click the table you are appending. Be sure that the Current Database option button is selected so records will be appended to the current database; or, click the Another Database option button and enter the name of the database in the File Name text box. Click the OK button.
- Click the Run button on the Query Design toolbar.
- Click Yes to confirm appending the records to the table.

The query is almost complete. Next you will append the data to the tblEmployees table.

To create the Append query:

1. Add all the fields in the tblEmployeesImport table, except for the Employee Name field, to the **qryEmployeesAppend** query design grid.

2. Click **Query** on the menu bar and then click **Append Query**.

3. In the Append dialog box, click the list arrow of the **Table Name** text box to display the list of table names, click **tblEmployees**, and then click the **OK** button to close the Append dialog box.

4. Click the list arrow in each column of the Append To row (fourth row in the grid) and choose the field that corresponds to each of the field names in the top row. See Figure 3-15.

| Figure 3-15 | COMPLETING THE QRYEMPLOYEESAPPEND QUERY |

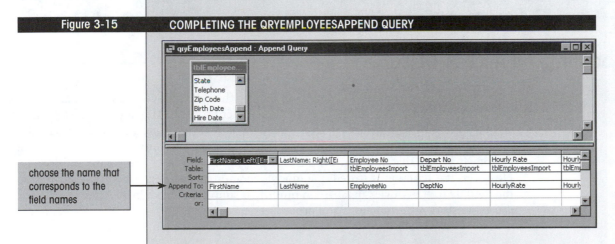

choose the name that corresponds to the field names

5. Run the query to append the rows to the tblEmployees table. When the message box appears and warns you that you cannot undo the append, click the **Yes** button.

6. Close the query and save your changes.

7. Click **Tables** in the Objects bar of the Database window, and then open the **tblEmployees** table.

8. You should see 15 records appended to the table. Close the table to return to the Database window.

You and Carolyn have completed the first part of Amanda's request—you successfully imported the data from the accounting software program and appended it to the tblEmployees table. Now you'll focus on reformatting the data you've imported, and on importing the Excel data.

Session 3.1 QUICK CHECK

1. If data is going to be used in its original format, which is a better method: linking or importing?

2. The term _____ is used to refer to characters that identify the end of one field and the beginning of another field in a text file.

3. _____ functions allow you to force a particular data type, and are commonly used in queries.

4. Which function returns the position of a particular character in a string?

5. The _____ function returns the number of characters in a string of text.

SESSION 3.2

In this session, you will import a standard module from another database and write an expression in an update query using a custom function in the module. You also will use the Import Spreadsheet Wizard to import data from Excel, and write action queries to append and archive the data.

Importing an Access Object

Now that you've appended the employee data to the tblEmployees table, you and Carolyn decide to write an update query to correct one other problem. When you imported the data from the accounting software to Access, the data in the FirstName and LastName fields was in all capital letters. You want to convert it to uppercase and lowercase. Carolyn created a custom function that will convert all caps to a combination of uppercase and lowercase. However, the function is stored in a module in another database, so you'll want to import the module to the Movie3 database. A **module** is simply an object in an Access database that is used to store VBA functions and procedures.

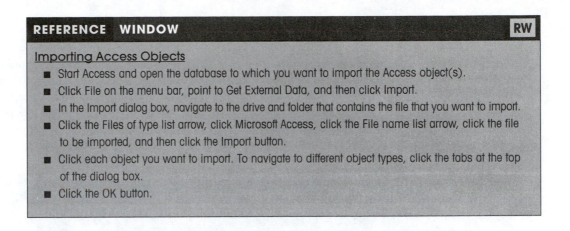

REFERENCE   WINDOW   **RW**

Importing Access Objects

- Start Access and open the database to which you want to import the Access object(s).
- Click File on the menu bar, point to Get External Data, and then click Import.
- In the Import dialog box, navigate to the drive and folder that contains the file that you want to import.
- Click the Files of type list arrow, click Microsoft Access, click the File name list arrow, click the file to be imported, and then click the Import button.
- Click each object you want to import. To navigate to different object types, click the tabs at the top of the dialog box.
- Click the OK button.

Now, you will import the basUtilityFunctions module from the Samples database.

To import a standard module from another Access database:

1. Make sure that Access is running and that the **Movie3** database from the Tutorial.03 folder on your local or network drive is open.

2. Click **File** on the menu bar, point to **Get External Data**, and then click **Import**.

3. In the Import dialog box, if necessary, click the **Files of type** list arrow, and then click **Microsoft Access**.

4. Be sure that the files in the Tutorial.03 folder on your local or network drive are visible, click **Samples**, and then click the **Import** button.

5. Click the **Modules** tab in the Import Objects dialog box. See Figure 3-16.

| Figure 3-16 | IMPORTING THE BASUTILITYFUNCTIONS MODULE |

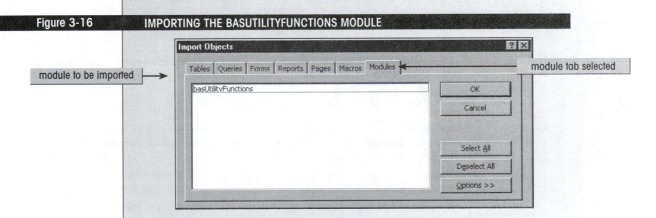

module to be imported

module tab selected

6. Click **basUtilityFunctions** and then click the **OK** button. The bas tag preceding the module name stands for basic. Some developers name modules using mdl. Either is fine as long as you are consistent.

The basUtilityFunctions module contains Carolyn's custom function, which you can use in the same way that you use the built-in functions of Access. Next you'll write an update query using this function.

Creating an Update Query

In most cases, it is a good idea to make a copy of the table you plan to update, delete, or append to before you run the action query to do so. If you make an error, you cannot undo the results. Restoring a backup from the previous day or two is time-consuming and can result in lost data. In this instance, it is not necessary to make a copy of the tblEmployees table because you have the imported data, you've saved the append query, and you can always run the query again if something goes wrong during the update.

REFERENCE WINDOW   **RW**

Creating an Update Query

- Make a copy of the table you plan to update, or be sure that you have a current backup of the database file.
- Create a select query that includes the fields you want to update and the selection criteria.
- Click the Run button on the Query Design toolbar to be sure that you update the correct fields and records.
- Click Query on the menu bar, and then click Update Query to change the query type.
- Enter the expression for the new value(s) in the Update To rows for the field(s) you want to update.
- Click the Run button on the Query Design toolbar and click Yes to confirm updating the records.

You do not need to make a copy of the table, so you are ready to write the update query to convert the FirstName and LastName fields to uppercase and lowercase.

To create an update query using a custom function:

1. Create a new query in Design view, add the **tblEmployees** table to the query window, and close the Show Table dialog box.

2. Drag the **FirstName** and **LastName** fields into the first two columns of the query grid.

3. Click **Query** on the menu bar, and then click **Update Query**.

4. Click in the **Update To** text box in the **FirstName** column, type **ProperCase([FirstName])**, and then press the **Tab** key to move to the next column. Remember to type the square brackets around FirstName. It is sometimes not necessary to type the square brackets around a field name that has no spaces in it. However, in this instance, you are working with a custom function that accepts either a field or a string of text as its argument. If you do not include the square brackets, Access will assume that the data you are modifying is a string, and it would convert the FirstName string to Firstname. The brackets indicate that you are referring to a field and not a string of text.

5. Type **ProperCase([LastName])**. Again, be sure to type the square brackets around LastName. See Figure 3-17.

Figure 3-17	USING A CUSTOM FUNCTION IN AN UPDATE QUERY

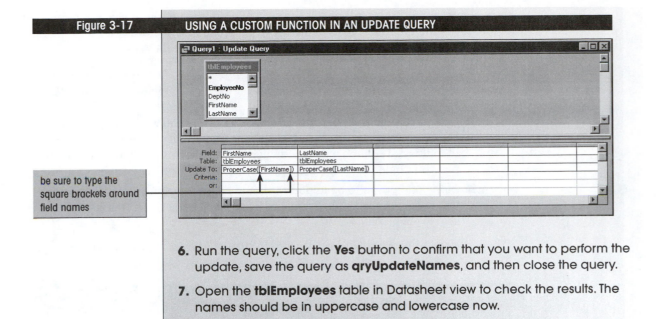

be sure to type the
square brackets around
field names

6. Run the query, click the **Yes** button to confirm that you want to perform the update, save the query as **qryUpdateNames**, and then close the query.

7. Open the **tblEmployees** table in Datasheet view to check the results. The names should be in uppercase and lowercase now.

8. Close the table to return to the Database window.

You've imported an Access object and a text file to the Movie3 database. Now you'll import the Excel spreadsheet data.

Using the Import Spreadsheet Wizard

Martin Woodward, one of MovieCam's product managers, has provided you with an Excel spreadsheet file that contains sample data used to track time cards and hours. See Figure 3-18.

Figure 3-18	SAMPLE SPREADSHEET DATA

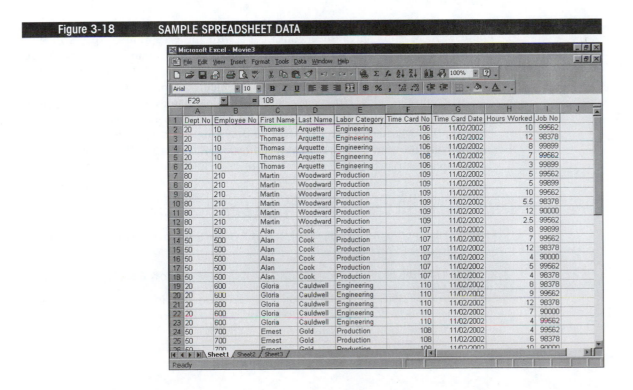

You plan to import this table and then use it to write the queries needed to populate the tblTimeCards and tblHours tables in the MovieCam database. Before you begin the import process, you examine the data in the Excel worksheet for the following:

- The data should be arranged in rows, and the same type of data should be entered in each column. For example, dates and text data should not be entered in the same column.

- Column headings should appear in the top row of the worksheet, with no blank rows above them. You might also want to remove spaces between words in multiword column names, although this can be done in Access. For example, you would use EmployeeName rather than Employee Name.

- None of the cells to be imported should contain formulas. If they do, you will need to replace the formula with its calculated value. This is referred to as freezing.

You'll use the Import Spreadsheet Wizard to import Martin's Spreadsheet file.

REFERENCE WINDOW | **RW**

Using the Import Spreadsheet Wizard
- Start Access and open the database to which you want to import the text file.
- Click File on the menu bar, point to Get External Data, and then click Import.
- In the Import dialog box, navigate to the drive and folder that contain the file you want to import.
- Click the Files of type list arrow, click Microsoft Excel, click the file to be imported, and then click the Import button.
- Complete the Wizard dialog boxes to select the worksheet and named range, mark the first row as field names or not, and choose a new table or the table name of an existing table. You will need to change the field options as necessary, choose if you want to add a primary key, and name the table if you're importing to a new table.

The data in Martin's spreadsheet looks good with the exception of spaces in the field names. You decide to leave those the way they are for now. If the names in the worksheet are the same as the field names in the table you plan to append to, creating the append query is simpler. Access automatically determines to which fields to append the data and you don't have to match up the fields. However, changing the field names in the spreadsheet is just as time-consuming as assigning the correct field names in the append query when you create it.

The data that Martin gave you is a sampling of time cards from this year and last. You wanted both so that you can work out the archive queries that you'll need after all the data has been imported.

To import an Excel spreadsheet into Access:

1. Click **File** on the menu bar, point to **Get External Data**, and then click **Import**. The Import dialog box opens.

2. Click the **Files of type** list arrow, and then click **Microsoft Excel**.

3. Be sure that the files from the Tutorial.03 folder on your local or network drive are displayed, click **Movie3** in the Import dialog box, and then click the **Import** button. The Import Spreadsheet Wizard starts, as shown in Figure 3-19.

Figure 3-19   **IMPORT SPREADSHEET WIZARD**

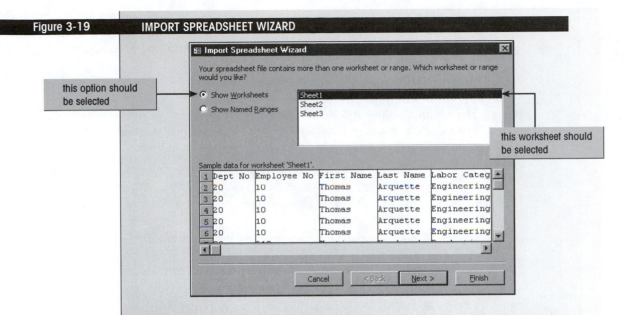

this option should be selected

this worksheet should be selected

If you have a large spreadsheet that includes cells you do not want to import to Access, you should name the range in the Excel file that you plan to import. Any ranges you name in the Excel file will appear in the first Import Spreadsheet Wizard dialog box after you select the Show Named Ranges option. In this instance, you want to import all the data on the worksheet (Sheet1).

4. Be sure that the **Show Worksheets** option button is selected and that **Sheet1** is selected, as shown in Figure 3-19, and then click the **Next** button.

   In the next dialog box, you discover the reason for a single row of column headings in the Excel worksheet. If more than one row contains column headings, Access assumes the second row of data represents the first record.

5. Be sure that the **First Row Contains Column Headings** option is checked, and then click the **Next** button.

6. Be sure that the **In a New Table** option button is selected, and then click the **Next** button.

   In this next dialog box, you can change field names and add indexes. It is not necessary to make changes here because the table you are creating is temporary.

7. Click the **Next** button.

   Again, because this is a temporary table you will delete when you are finished with it, a primary key is unnecessary.

8. Click the **No primary key** option button, and then click the **Next** button.

9. Type **tblTimeCardsImport** as the new table's name, and then click the **Finish** button.

10. Click the **OK** button in the message box that informs you Access has finished importing the data.

   Now that the transactional data is successfully imported to the database, you want to transfer it to the tables that you and Carolyn created. You will start by appending data to the tblTimeCards table.

As you already determined, storing data in the Excel file led to a lot of data duplication. Now that same redundant data appears in the table to which you imported it. To minimize duplicate data in a table, you apply the Unique Values property in a query.

Query Properties

The Unique Values and Record Locks query properties are particularly useful when you write action queries. Other query properties are helpful to understand when you work with external data files. An explanation of these properties follows:

- *Output All Fields*: Use this property to show all the fields in the query's underlying data source. When this property is set to Yes, the only fields you need to include in the design grid are the fields that you want to sort by or specify criteria on.

- *Unique Values*: Use this property when you want to include only unique results when the query is run. If the query results contain more than one field, only the records that are unique given the combination of all the included fields will be displayed.

- *Unique Records*: Use this property to return from the underlying data source only the unique records that are based on all the fields in the data source, not just the ones displayed in the query results. This property is ignored when the query uses only one table.

- *Source Database and Source Connect Str*: Use these properties when you want to access external data that cannot be linked to your database. The Source Database property specifies the external source database where the data resides. The Source Connect Str specifies the name of the program used to create the external file. For an Access database, the source database property is the path and database name, such as C:\Clients\MovieCam. Access adds the .mdb file extension automatically. The Source Connect Str is not necessary for an Access database. For a database created by another program, such as dBASE, the source database property is also the path and the Source Connect Str is the specifier for the database type, such as dBASE III; or dBASE IV;. (The semicolon should be included.)

- *Destination Table, Destination DB, Dest Connect Str*: These are properties of append and make-table queries. The Destination Table property represents the name of the table that you are appending to. The Destination DB property is the name and path of the database that you are appending to, if it is outside the current database. The Dest Connect Str property is the specifier for the destination database, such as dBASE IV. If you are appending to the current database, Destination DB would be the current database, and Dest Connect Str would not be used.

- *Record Locks*: This property specifies whether the records in a multiuser environment are locked so that other users cannot access them while the query is being run. This property is typically set for action queries, so it is of particular importance when you create queries to import and archive records. There are three choices for locking records. The No Locks option, the default for select queries, means that the records aren't locked while the query is being run. The All Records option allows users to read records but prevents editing, adding to, or deleting from the underlying record source until the query has finished running. The Edited Record option, the default for action queries, locks a page of records as soon as the query is run. A page is a portion of the database that is 4 KB in size in Access 2000 and 2 KB in Access 97. Depending on its size, a page may contain more than one record. You can change this property, but be aware that it affects record locking in forms and reports as well.

You'll create a query to append to the tblTimeCards table only those records with unique Values.

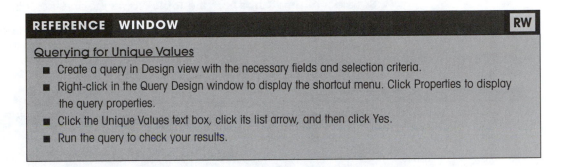

Querying for Unique Values
- Create a query in Design view with the necessary fields and selection criteria.
- Right-click in the Query Design window to display the shortcut menu. Click Properties to display the query properties.
- Click the Unique Values text box, click its list arrow, and then click Yes.
- Run the query to check your results.

Next you'll create the append query to append the imported records to the tblTimeCards table.

To append unique data to the tblTimeCards table:

1. Create a new query in Design view, add the **tblTimeCardsImport** table to the query window, and close the Show Table dialog box.

2. Add the **Time Card No**, **Time Card Date**, and **Employee No** fields to the grid in the lower pane of the query window.

3. Run the query to test the results. There should be 56 records in the results.

4. Switch to Design view, and then right-click a blank area of the upper pane of the Query Design window. See Figure 3-20.

| Figure 3-20 | DESIGNING THE APPEND QUERY |

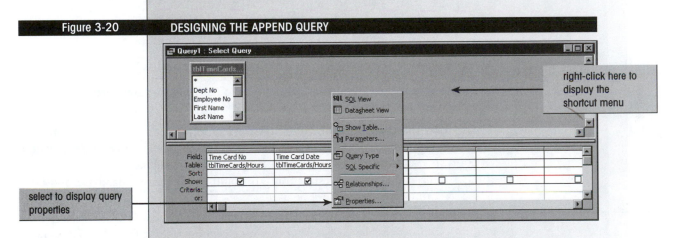

5. Click **Properties** on the shortcut menu, and then change the Unique Values property to **Yes**.

   The Unique Values property applies to select queries and make-table and append action queries. After this property is changed, the query results, or recordset, can no longer be updated. This means that you cannot change the data in the recordset in Datasheet view. Most, but not all, queries can be used to change the data in the underlying table or tables (recordset) in Datasheet view. The Help system contains detailed information regarding which type of query can and cannot be changed.

6. Run the query again. Now the recordset should display 10 unique records.

7. Return to Design view, close the Properties window, click **Query** on the menu bar, and then click **Append Query**.

8. Select **tblTimeCards** from the **Table Name** list, and then click the **OK** button.

9. In the design grid, click the list arrow in the **Append To** text box in each of the three columns, and choose the corresponding fields from the **tblTimeCards** table. See Figure 3-21.

Figure 3-21   **CHANGING QUERY PROPERTIES**

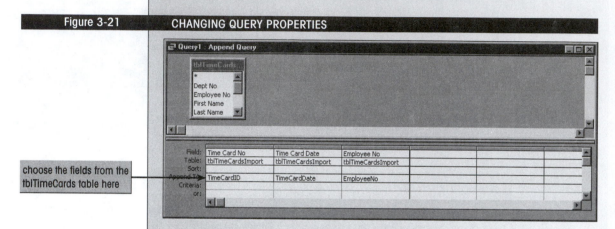

choose the fields from the tblTimeCards table here

10. Run the query, click the **Yes** button in the message box that appears, save the query as **qryTimeCardsAppend**, and then close the query.

11. Open the **tblTimeCards** table to check your results. You should have 10 records.

12. Close the table to return to the Database window.

Now you will append the hours data to the tblHours table.

To append sample data to the tblHours table:

1. Create a new query in Design view, add the **tblTimeCardsImport** table to the query window, and close the Show Table dialog box.

2. Add the **Time Card No**, **Job No**, and **Hours Worked** fields to the query grid. You do not need to include the HoursID field. It is an AutoNumber field that has been set as the primary key and will populate automatically.

3. Click **Query** on the menu bar and then click **Append Query**.

4. Select **tblHours** from the Table Name list, and then click the **OK** button.

5. In the design grid, click the list arrow in the Append To text box in each of the three columns, and choose the corresponding field. The Time Card No field will be appended to TimeCardID and the Job No field to JobID.

6. Run the query, click the **Yes** button in the message box, save the query as **qryHoursAppend**, and then close the query.

7. Open the **tblHours** table to check the results. There should be 56 records in the table.

8. Close the table to return to the Database window.

Next you will work out the archiving queries that Amanda requested.

Archiving Data

The tblTimeCards and tblHours tables in the MovieCam Technologies database will contain the most records. Because time cards and hours are entered for many employees each week of the year, these tables grow quite rapidly. To optimize the performance of queries, forms, and reports, Amanda wants to store only the current year's data in the active tables.

You and Carolyn question whether to store the archive tables in this database or another. If you store them in another database, you have to run only the append queries so that the records are appended to the other database file. However, you decide it will be simpler if all the tables are stored in the same database file. Then you can include the data in the archive tables when you create comprehensive reports and queries.

The Movie3 database already contains an archive table, named tblTimeCardsArchive. This table was created simply by copying and pasting the structure of the tblTimeCards table to a new table, and saving it with a new name. You need to create the archive table for the tblHours table. You will use the same method of copying and pasting. Then you will change the HoursID field in the archive table from an AutoNumber type to a Number field. That way, the data from the tblHours table can be appended to the archive table without error. You cannot add data to an AutoNumber field; it increments automatically. Because you want the HoursID field in the archive table to contain the same number it had in the tblHours table, the HoursID field must be changed to a Number data type.

The first time you archive data, you can create make-table queries to create the tables and write the records all in one step. In this instance, however, you will run the queries over and over to archive data as time goes by. If you use a make-table query rather than an append query, the existing data will be overwritten each time you run the query. The purpose of creating the queries is for future use, so you will create the tables first, and then write and save the append and delete queries.

REFERENCE WINDOW **RW**

Copying and Pasting a Table Structure
- In the Database window, select the table to be copied.
- Click Edit on the menu bar, and then select Copy.
- Click Edit on the menu bar, and then select Paste.
- Select the Structure Only paste option.
- Type the table name and click the OK button.

You will create the tblHoursArchive table and its structure by copying and pasting the tblHours table structure.

To copy and paste the tblHours table structure:

1. Click the **tblHours** table in the Database window to select it.

2. Click the **Copy** button 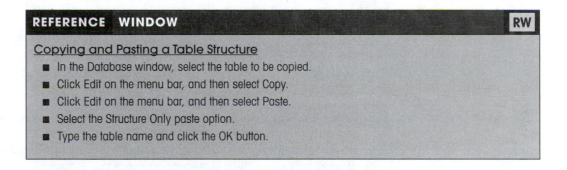 on the Database toolbar.

3. Click the **Paste** button on the Database toolbar.

4. Type **tblHoursArchive** in the Table Name text box, click the **Structure Only** option button, and then click the **OK** button.

5. Open the **tblHoursArchive** table in Design view and change the data type of the HoursID field to **Number**.

6. Close and save the table.

Now that you have created the archive tables, you'll write the append queries. The append queries will contain a prompt that requests the user to enter the date. All records prior to that date will then be archived. This allows the query to be used over and over.

To create the append query from the tblTimeCards table:

1. Create a new query in Design view, add the **tblTimeCards** table to the query window, and close the Show Table dialog box.

2. Double-click the title bar of the tblTimeCards field list to select all the fields, as shown in Figure 3-22.

| Figure 3-22 | SELECTING ALL FIELDS |

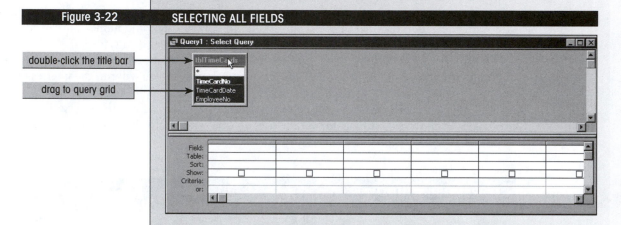

double-click the title bar

drag to query grid

3. Drag the selected fields to the first column of the design grid. All the fields appear in the design grid.

4. Click the **Criteria** text box for the TimeCardDate column, type **<[Enter the first date of the current year]** and then run the query to be sure you are archiving the correct records. Creating this query as a parameter query enables the users to archive records over and over using one query. The less than (<) symbol indicates that all records entered before the date the user types in will be found.

5. When you are prompted to enter the first date of the current year, type **1/1/2002**, and then press the **Enter** key. Check to see that the records from the year 2001 are displayed.

6. Switch to Design view, click **Query** on the menu bar, and then click **Append Query**.

7. Type **tblTimeCardsArchive** in the Table Name text box and then click the **OK** button. The Append To row fills in automatically because all the fields in both tables have the same name.

8. Run the query, type **1/1/2002** when prompted for the date, press the **Enter** key, and then click the **Yes** button to append the five rows.

9. Close the query and save it as **qryArchiveTimeCards**.

Now that the records from the previous year are archived to the tblTimeCardsArchive table, you need to write a query to delete the records that were archived from the active table. However, you must consider the relationship between the tblTimeCards and tblHours tables. Remember that in Tutorial 2, you applied the *Cascade Update* and *Cascade Delete* options to this relationship. If you delete the records from the tblTimeCards table before you archive the records from the tblHours table, the related records in the tblHours table will be deleted also.

With this in mind, you write the append query for the tblHours table *before* you delete records from the tblTimeCards table.

To create the append query from the tblHours table:

1. Create a new query in Design view, add the **tblTimeCards** and **tblHours** tables to the query window, and close the Show Table dialog box.

2. Add the **TimeCardDate** field from the tblTimeCards table, and then add all the fields from the **tblHours** table to the design grid.

3. Type **<[Enter the first date of the current year]** in the Criteria text box for the TimeCardDate field. Your query should look like that shown in Figure 3-23.

Figure 3-23	APPENDING TO THE TBLHOURSARCHIVE TABLE

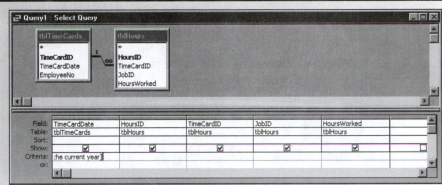

4. Run the query, type **1/1/2002** when prompted to enter the first date of the current year, and press the **Enter** key. The recordset should display 28 records.

5. Switch to Design view, change the query to an **Append** query, type **tblHoursArchive** in the Table Name text box, and then click the **OK** button.

6. Right-click a blank area of the query window, and then click **Properties** on the shortcut menu.

7. Change the Record Locks property to **All Records** so the records cannot be accessed until the query has finished running, and then close the Properties dialog box. This is a good idea for all append queries, but especially for those run on transactional tables that might contain many records.

8. Run the query, type **12/1/2002** when prompted for the date, press the **Enter** key, click **Yes** to confirm that you want to append the records, and then close the query and save it as **qryArchiveHours**.

REFERENCE WINDOW   **RW**

Creating a Delete Query
- Make a copy of the table you plan to update, or be sure that you have a current backup of the database file.
- Create a select query that includes the fields you want to update and the selection criteria.
- Click the Run button on the Query Design toolbar to be sure you are deleting the correct fields and records.
- Click Query on the menu bar, and then select Delete Query to change the query type.
- Click the Run button on the Query Design toolbar. Click Yes to confirm updating the records.

The last step in the archiving process is to create a query to delete the records from the tblTimeCards table that were archived to the tblTimeCardsArchive table. The related records in the tblHours table will be deleted as a result of the Cascade Delete option set in the Relationships window. See Figure 3-24.

Figure 3-24	RELATIONSHIP BETWEEN THE TBLTIMECARDS AND TBLHOURS TABLES

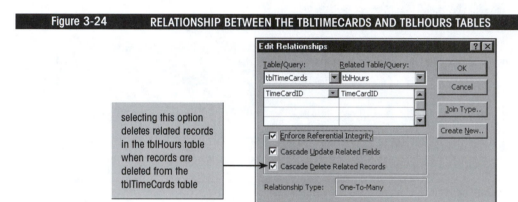

selecting this option deletes related records in the tblHours table when records are deleted from the tblTimeCards table

To delete the archived records from the active tables:

1. Create a new query in Design view and add the **tblTimeCards** table to the query window.

2. Add all the fields to the design grid, and type **<[Enter the first date of the current year]** in the Criteria text box for the TimeCardDate field.

3. Run the query as a select query to be sure you delete the correct records. Type **1/1/2002** when you are prompted to enter the first date of the current year. Check the dates of the five records. They should all be prior to Jan. 1, 2002.

4. Switch to Design view, click **Query** on the menu bar, and then click **Delete Query**. The delete query is displayed in Figure 3-25.

Figure 3-25   **QUERY TO DELETE ARCHIVED RECORDS**

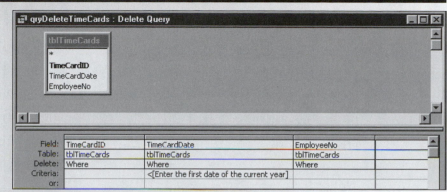

5. Right-click in the upper pane of the Query Design window, and then click **Properties** on the shortcut menu.

6. Change the Record Locks property to **All Records** so that the records cannot be accessed until the query has finished running, and then close the properties dialog box.

7. Run the query, type **1/1/2002** when you are prompted to enter the first date of the current year, press the **Enter** key, click the **Yes** button to confirm the deletion of five rows from the specified table, save the query as **qryDeleteTimeCards**, and then close it.

8. Open the **tblTimeCards** table, press the F11 key, and then open the **tblHours** table to check the records. The tblTimeCards table should contain five records, all dated in the year 2002. The tblHours table should contain 28 records.

9. Close the tables.

When you work with action queries, take the following safeguards. Copy a table you plan to delete from or update to before you run the query. Run action queries that contain criteria as select queries first, as you did in the queries to archive and delete time cards and hours. A final precaution is to hide action queries in the Database window. You will document and hide the queries next.

To hide an object in the Database window:

1. Right-click the **qryHoursAppend** query, and then click **Properties** on the short-cut menu.

2. In the Description text box, type **Appends records to tblHours from imported data stored in tblTimeCardsImport**. (Do not type the period.)

3. Click the **Hidden** Attributes check box, as shown in Figure 3-26, and then click the **OK** button. The query disappears from the Database window.

TROUBLE? If the query is still visible but dimmed in the Database window, the option to display hidden objects in the Options dialog box (opened from the Tools menu) may have already been selected.

Figure 3-26   HIDING AN OBJECT IN THE DATABASE WINDOW

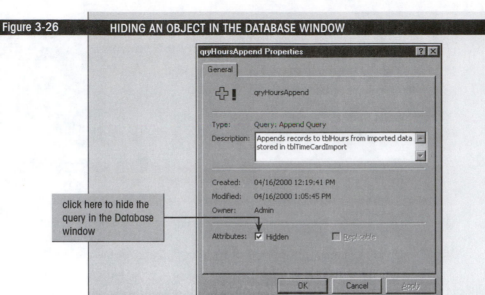

click here to hide the query in the Database window

After you've hidden an object, you still need to be able to display it to run or to modify it. Next you'll redisplay the hidden query.

4. Click **Tools** on the menu bar and then click **Options**.

5. On the View tab, click the **Hidden objects** check box to select it, and then click the **OK** button. In the Database window, you see that the qryHoursAppend query is visible but dimmed.

You and Carolyn have completed the procedure for importing data, cleaning up imported data, and archiving, but you have a few more queries to write. Amanda asked you to recombine the data from the active tables with the archive tables, and demonstrate to Martin and the other product managers how to export that data to Excel for statistical analysis. The product managers are concerned that they won't know the new system well enough to generate the statistics they are using now in Excel.

You can combine the data from the tblTimeCards table with the tblTimeCardsArchive table, and the tblHours table with the tblHoursArchive table by using a union query. You will create those queries in the next session.

Session 3.2 QUICK CHECK

1. The _____ query property is used when you want to include only unique results when the query is run.

2. How do you keep users from accessing records while an action query is being run?

3. It is a good idea to _____ a table before you run an update query that will change its data.

4. How do you hide an object in the Database window?

SESSION 3.3

In this session, you will learn about SQL-specific queries and study basic statements and clauses of Access SQL. You also will write a union query and export its results to Excel.

SQL-Specific Queries

Access uses a form of query language known as **Structured Query Language**, or SQL (frequently pronounced *sequel*). SQL is the most common database query language used today, but it is more than just a query language. It is a complete database management system language because it gives you the capability to create components of a database, as well as to manipulate them. SQL has three components:

- A data definition language to allow the creation of database components, such as tables
- A data manipulation language to allow manipulation of database components, such as queries
- A data control language to provide internal security for a database

SQL 92 is the current version of SQL. Access SQL is a dialect of SQL. It does not implement the complete SQL 92 standard, and adds some features of its own to the language. Access SQL is the language that underlies all your queries.

Whether you use a query wizard or QBE to create your queries, they all come down to SQL. However, SQL-specific queries cannot be created by using either wizards or the QBE grid. They must be written in SQL. The following sections define the three types of SQL-specific queries.

Pass-Through Queries

A pass-through query passes an uninterpreted SQL statement through to an external database server. As mentioned earlier in this tutorial, Access can act as a front end to various back-end databases. The back end is the data and could be a product that uses a completely different dialect of SQL than does Access. A pass-through query is not interpreted by Access, but is passed through to the back-end server for interpretation. These queries are useful if the action you want to take is supported by your back-end database server but not by Access SQL.

Data-Definition Queries

Data-definition queries use the data-definition language component of SQL to create objects such as tables and indexes. The data-definition commands in Access SQL include Create Table, Alter Table, Drop Table, and Create Index. You will not create tables and indexes in SQL in the Movie3 database, so you won't create any data-definition queries. However, it is worthwhile for you to know what they are and how they are used.

Union Queries

A union query is a query that creates the union of two or more tables. In other words, this query allows you to combine data (records) from two tables with similar or the same structure. Consider the tblHours and tblHoursArchive tables. You could create a union query to merge the records in these two tables into one table for reporting purposes. Another example of a union query might be a mailing list composed of all the vendors stored in one table in your database and all the customers stored in another table. A union query allows you to produce a recordset that contains all the names and addresses from both tables in one listing.

Access SQL Statements and Clauses

SQL has very few verbs. Knowledge of the basic constructs of SQL will allow you to create queries that cannot be created using wizards or the QBE grid, and will help you understand how all your queries work.

The Select Statement

The SELECT statement is used to specify the fields you want to retrieve from a table whose data is being returned to the recordset. The simplest SELECT statement, to retrieve all fields from a table, is:

SELECT *

If you use the statement in a query that contains more than one table, include the table name and a period before the asterisk:

SELECT tblHours.*

This SELECT statement returns all fields, but if you want to retrieve particular fields, such as TimeCardID and JobID, the statement would be:

SELECT TimeCardID, JobID

If the query contains more than one table, it might be:

SELECT tblHours.TimeCardID, tblHours.JobID

You also can include expressions in your SELECT statement, just as you have done in the QBE grid. The following statement, for example, retrieves the EmployeeNo field, concatenates FirstName and LastName and names it EmployeeName, and retrieves the DeptNo field:

SELECT EmployeeNo, FirstName & " " & LastName AS EmployeeName, DeptNo

DistinctRow and Distinct Keywords

When you use the DISTINCT keyword, Access eliminates duplicate rows, based on the fields that you include in the query results. This also happens when you set the Unique Values property to *Yes* in the query Properties dialog box.

When you use the DISTINCTROW keyword, Access eliminates any duplicate rows based on all fields of all tables you include in the query (whether they appear in the query results or not). This also happens when you set the Unique Records property to *Yes* in the Properties dialog box.

For example, earlier in this tutorial you built a query to append unique values from the tblTimeCardsImport table to the tblTimeCards table. You changed the Unique Values property to *Yes* in that query. To write the same query in SQL, you use the DISTINCT keyword because you want all the fields displayed to be unique. Note the use of brackets around both the table name and the field name of those fields containing spaces.

SELECT DISTINCT [tblTimeCardsImport].[Time Card No], [tblTimeCardsImport].[Time Card Date], [tblTimeCardsImport].[Employee No] FROM tblTimeCardsImport;

The From Clause

You use the FROM clause to specify the table or query *from which* the SELECT statement takes its records. For example, the following SELECT statement retrieves all fields from the tblHours table:

SELECT * FROM tblHours

Again, in the case of more than one table in the query, you include the table name as follows:

SELECT tblHours.* FROM tblHours

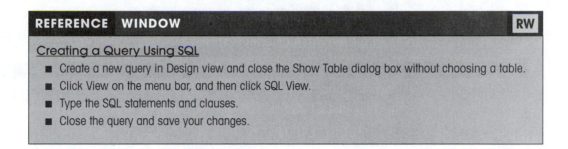

REFERENCE   WINDOW   **RW**

Creating a Query Using SQL
- Create a new query in Design view and close the Show Table dialog box without choosing a table.
- Click View on the menu bar, and then click SQL View.
- Type the SQL statements and clauses.
- Close the query and save your changes.

Next you'll begin writing the union query to combine records from the tblTimeCards and tblTimeCardsArchive tables.

To write a query in SQL:

1. Make sure that Access is running, that the **Movie3** database from the Tutorial.03 folder on your local or network drive is open, and that **Queries** is selected in the Objects bar of the Database window.

2. Create a new query in Design view, and then close the Show Table dialog box without choosing a table.

3. Click the **View** button on the toolbar. The Query window opens in SQL view.

4. Type **SELECT tblHours.* FROM tblHours** and then run the query to check the results. The recordset contains 28 records and four fields from the tblHours table.

5. Switch to SQL view.

Now you will add a WHERE clause to the query.

The Where Clause

You use the WHERE clause to limit the records that are retrieved by the SELECT statement. A WHERE clause can include up to 40 fields combined by the keywords AND and OR. A simple WHERE clause that limits the TimeCardID field in the results to 106 is:

WHERE TimeCardID = "106"

To specify which table the TimeCardID field comes from, the same clause would be written:

WHERE tblHours.TimeCardID = "106"

To put together a SELECT statement, FROM clause, and WHERE clause you would write:

SELECT tblHours.* FROM tblHours WHERE tblHours.TimeCardID = "106"

If only one table were included in the query, the following statement would have the same result:

SELECT * FROM tblHours WHERE TimeCardID = "106"

To add a WHERE clause in SQL:

1. Position the insertion point at the end of the statement **SELECT tblHours.* FROM tblHours** and then press the **Enter** key.

2. Type **WHERE tblHours.TimeCardID = "106"**, as shown in Figure 3-27.

Figure 3-27   SELECT STATEMENT, FROM CLAUSE, AND WHERE CLAUSE

Quotation marks are required around the number because the TimeCardID field is a text field.

3. Run the query to check your results. You see all of the fields from the tblHours table where the TimeCardID is 106.

4. Switch to SQL view.

Next you want to sort the results by the JobID field and then by the TimeCardID field. In SQL, you use the ORDER BY clause to sort the data.

The Order By Clause

The ORDER BY clause determines the order in which the returned records will be sorted. It is an optional clause, and an example of the ORDER BY clause is:

ORDER BY TimeCardID

The ORDER BY clause can include more than one field. When more than one field is used, just as in QBE, the leftmost field is the first sorted. For example, the following would first sort by the JobID field, and then by the TimeCardID field:

ORDER BY tblHours.JobID, tblHours.TimeCardID

If you combine the ORDER BY clause with earlier statements and clauses, you get:

SELECT tblHours.*
FROM tblHours
WHERE tblHours.TimeCardID = "106"
ORDER BY tblHours.JobID, tblHours.TimeCardID

Next you will change the query to add the ORDER BY clause.

To use the ORDER BY clause in SQL:

1. Click at the end of the WHERE clause and press **Enter**.

2. Type **ORDER BY tblHours.JobID, tblHours.TimeCardID**, as shown in Figure 3-28.

Figure 3-28 ORDER BY CLAUSE

```
Query1 : Select Query                                    _ □ ×
SELECT tblHours.* FROM tblHours
WHERE tblHours.TimeCardID = "106"
ORDER BY tblHours.JobID, tblHours.TimeCardID
```

3. Run the query and check the results.

4. Switch to SQL view.

Next you need to join the records from the tblTimeCards table to the tblHours table. Then you need to join the records from the tblTimeCardsArchive table to the tblHoursArchive table. First you will look at the JOIN clause, and review the different types of joins possible.

The Join Clause

You often need to build SELECT statements that retrieve data from more than one table. When you build a SELECT statement on more than one table, you must join the tables using a JOIN clause. The JOIN clause varies depending on whether you're using an inner join, left outer join, or right outer join.

The inner join property, the default when creating a query in the design grid, includes all the records or rows where the joined fields from both tables are equal. See Figure 3-29.

Figure 3-29 JOIN PROPERTIES DIALOG BOX

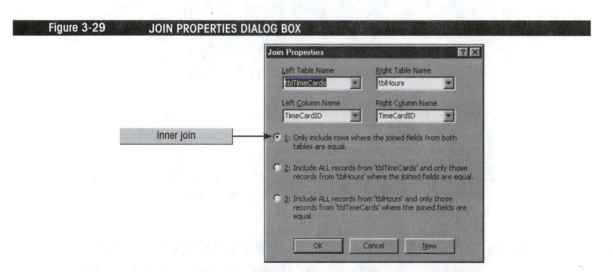

To create an inner join in SQL, you use the INNER JOIN clause. For example, to join the tblTimeCards table to the tblHours table using an inner join, you would type the following:

tblTimeCards INNER JOIN tblHours ON tblTimeCards.TimeCardID = tblHours.TimeCardID

The outer joins, left and right, are created in Design view by viewing the join properties and choosing the appropriate join. A left outer join includes all records from the primary table and only the records from the related table where the joined fields from both tables are equal, as shown in Figure 3-30.

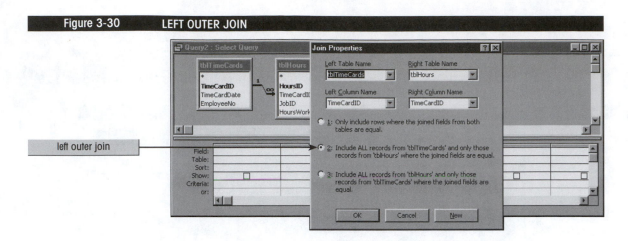

Figure 3-30 　　LEFT OUTER JOIN

A right outer join includes all records from the related table and only the records from the primary table where the joined fields from both tables are equal, as shown in Figure 3-31. The SQL clause for these are LEFT JOIN and RIGHT JOIN, respectively.

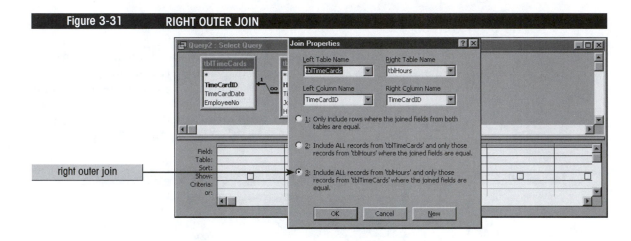

Figure 3-31 　　RIGHT OUTER JOIN

You will create the inner join between the tblTimeCards and tblHours tables next.

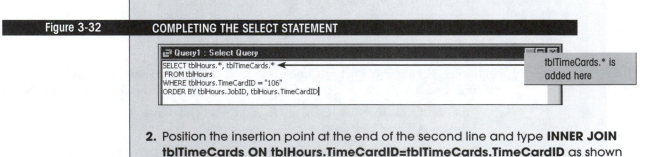

To use the JOIN clause in SQL:

1. Position the insertion point at the end of SELECT tblHours.*, type **,** (a comma), type **tblTimeCards.***, and then press the **Enter** key (see Figure 3-32). Do not run the query yet.

Figure 3-32 　　COMPLETING THE SELECT STATEMENT

```
Query1 : Select Query
SELECT tblHours.*, tblTimeCards.*   ◄
 FROM tblHours
 WHERE tblHours.TimeCardID = "106"
 ORDER BY tblHours.JobID, tblHours.TimeCardID
```

tblTimeCards.* is added here

2. Position the insertion point at the end of the second line and type **INNER JOIN tblTimeCards ON tblHours.TimeCardID=tblTimeCards.TimeCardID** as shown in Figure 3-33.

Figure 3-33   **COMPLETING THE INNER JOIN CLAUSE**

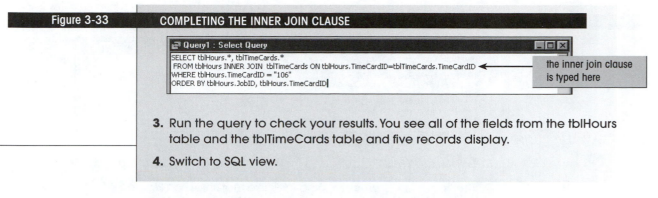

3. Run the query to check your results. You see all of the fields from the tblHours table and the tblTimeCards table and five records display.

4. Switch to SQL view.

Finally you will "union" these two tables to the archive tables. You've decided that you won't need the WHERE clause or the ORDER BY clause in the query you need to write. The product managers want to see all the records now, although they might want them filtered and sorted at a later time.

The Union Statement

You use the UNION statement to create the union of two or more tables. The ALL option forces Access to include all records. Without this option, Access does not include duplicate rows. The use of the ALL option also improves performance because the query runs faster. For example, to union the tblHours table to the tblHoursArchive table, you would use:

    SELECT *
    FROM tblHours
    UNION ALL
    SELECT *
    FROM tblHoursArchive

This statement is in its simplest form and does not include references to tables, except in the FROM clauses. In the query you are creating, you need to add the UNION ALL statement. You then will construct the last half of the query that will select all the fields from both of the archive tables and join them together on the common field—TimeCardID.

You'll complete the query next.

To complete the union query:

1. Position the insertion point at the end of the line that contains the ORDER BY clause, and press the **Enter** key.

2. Type **UNION ALL** and press the **Enter** key.

3. Type **SELECT tblHoursArchive.*,tblTimeCardsArchive.*** as shown in Figure 3-34, and press the **Enter** key.

Figure 3-34   **COMPLETING THE UNION ALL AND SECOND SELECT STATEMENT**

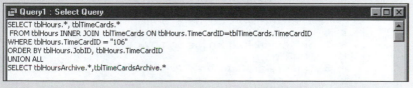

4. Type **FROM tblHoursArchive INNER JOIN tblTimeCardsArchive ON tblHoursArchive.TimeCardID=tblTimeCardsArchive.TimeCardID** as shown in Figure 3-35.

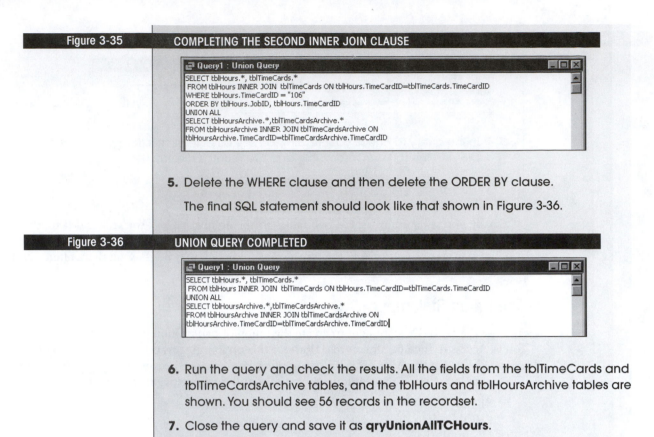

| Figure 3-35 | COMPLETING THE SECOND INNER JOIN CLAUSE |

```
Query1 : Union Query
SELECT tblHours.*, tblTimeCards.*
 FROM tblHours INNER JOIN  tblTimeCards ON tblHours.TimeCardID=tblTimeCards.TimeCardID
WHERE tblHours.TimeCardID = "106"
ORDER BY tblHours.JobID, tblHours.TimeCardID
UNION ALL
SELECT tblHoursArchive.*,tblTimeCardsArchive.*
FROM tblHoursArchive INNER JOIN tblTimeCardsArchive ON
tblHoursArchive.TimeCardID=tblTimeCardsArchive.TimeCardID
```

5. Delete the WHERE clause and then delete the ORDER BY clause.

The final SQL statement should look like that shown in Figure 3-36.

| Figure 3-36 | UNION QUERY COMPLETED |

```
Query1 : Union Query
SELECT tblHours.*, tblTimeCards.*
 FROM tblHours INNER JOIN  tblTimeCards ON tblHours.TimeCardID=tblTimeCards.TimeCardID
UNION ALL
SELECT tblHoursArchive.*,tblTimeCardsArchive.*
FROM tblHoursArchive INNER JOIN tblTimeCardsArchive ON
tblHoursArchive.TimeCardID=tblTimeCardsArchive.TimeCardID
```

6. Run the query and check the results. All the fields from the tblTimeCards and tblTimeCardsArchive tables, and the tblHours and tblHoursArchive tables are shown. You should see 56 records in the recordset.

7. Close the query and save it as **qryUnionAllTCHours**.

You and Carolyn will now export the results of the union query to Excel so that Martin can use the data with this program. You ask Martin to join you so that he can observe the process.

To analyze query results with Excel:

1. Run the query **qryUnionAllTCHours** so that the resulting recordset is displayed.

2. Click **Tools** on the menu bar, point to **Office Links**, and then click **Analyze It with MS Excel**.

Martin is delighted. He walks you through the way he works with the data in Excel. He wants to be able to sort it in various ways and to calculate subtotals. For example, he frequently sorts by the JobID field and then by the TimeCardDate field to get a subtotal of all the hours to date worked on the jobs.

To sort and subtotal the data in Excel:

1. Click **Data** on the menu bar and then click **Sort**.

2. Select **JobID** from the Sort by combo box.

3. Select **TimeCardDate** from the Then by combo box, and then click the **OK** button.

4. Click **Data** on the menu bar, and then click **Subtotals**.

5. Click **JobID** in the At each change in combo box.

6. Click **Sum** in the Use function combo box.

7. Check **HoursWorked** in the Add subtotal to list box. Make sure the other boxes are not checked and then click the **OK** button. The subtotals display as shown in Figure 3-37.

Figure 3-37   CREATING SUBTOTALS IN AN EXCEL WORKSHEET

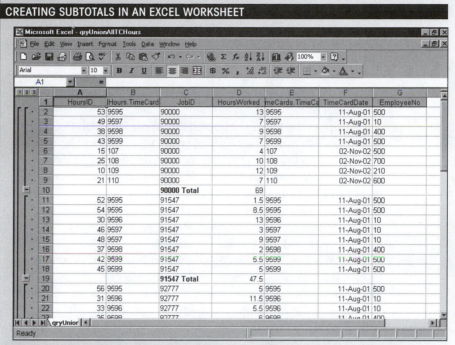

8. Click **Data** on the menu bar, and then **Subtotals**. Click the **Remove All** button.

9. Close Excel to return to Access. Do not save your changes.

10. Close the **Movie3** database, and then exit Access.

Now that you've completed the queries to append, archive, and compile the data, the actual importing and conversion of the historical data should run smoothly.

Session 3.3 Q**UICK** C**HECK**

1. The current version of SQL is _____.

2. Which queries are SQL-specific?

3. The SELECT statement in SQL is used to specify the _____.

4. Using the DISTINCT keyword is the same as setting the _____ property in a query.

5. The WHERE clause is used to limit the records retrieved by the _____ statement.

6. What is an inner join?

7. What is a right outer join?

8. The _____ statement in SQL is used to create the union of two or more tables.

REVIEW ASSIGNMENTS

The Hours3 database has been modified slightly from Tutorial 2. It was determined that the tblTimeCards table was not necessary because the week-ending date isn't used for reporting purposes and the time card numbers are not tracked. The hours that an employee works will be entered directly into the tblHours table. This table is related on the many side of a one-to-many relationship with the tblEmployees table. In this assignment, you will import data from an Excel worksheet and write the append queries to append the data to the tblEmployees and tblHours tables.

Complete the following:

1. Start Access and open the **Hours3** database located in the Tutorial.03 folder on your local or network drive.
2. Import the **Hours3** Excel file from the Tutorial.03 folder on your local or network drive. Be sure to set Files of type to Excel files. The first row contains field names. Do not set a primary key. Import the data to a new table named **tblEmloyeesImport**.
3. Create a select query and add the **tblEmloyeesImport** table to the query window.
4. Create the following expressions in the query:
   NameSpace:InStr([EmployeeName]," ")
   FirstName:Left([EmployeeName],NameSpace-1)
   NameLen:Len([EmployeeName])
   LastName:Right([EmployeeName],NameLen-NameSpace)
5. Copy and paste the expressions for NameSpace and NameLen into the expressions FirstName and LastName. When completed the expressions should look like the following:
   FirstName: Left([EmployeeName],InStr([EmployeeName]," ")-1)
   LastName: Right([EmployeeName],Len([EmployeeName])-InStr([EmployeeName]," "))
6. Delete the NameSpace and NameLen columns from the grid.
7. Add the remaining fields to the query, *except* the DateWorked, HoursWorked, and ProductNo fields.
8. Run the query to test the results, click File on the menu bar, and then click Print.
9. Return to Design view and change the Unique Values property to Yes. Run the query to test the results, click File on the menu bar, and then click Print.
10. Change the query to an Append query and type **tblEmployees** in the Table Name text box. All fields match up automatically because the names in the Excel file match the names in the table.
11. Run the query to append the records, save the query as **qryEmployeesAppend**, and then close the query.
12. Create another select query, add the **tblEmployeesImport** table to the Query window, and add the EmployeeNo, DateWorked, HoursWorked, and ProductNo fields to the design grid.
13. Change the query to an append query. Type **tblHours** in the Table Name text box.
14. Run the query, save it as **qryHoursAppend**, and then close the query.
15. Copy and paste the structure of the **tblHours** table to the **tblHoursArchive** table.
16. Open the **tblHoursArchive** table in Design view and change the HoursID field from AutoNumber type to a Number data type. Close the table and save your changes.
17. Create a new query to append the old data to the archive table. Add the **tblHours** table to the Query window and drag all the fields to the design grid. Type **< 1/1/02** in the DateWorked column, change the query to an Append query, type **tblHoursArchive** in the Table Name text box, make sure that the fields match, and run the query. Save the query as **qryHoursArchive**, and then close the query.
18. Create a new query to delete the data that you archived. It will be just like the one in Step 17 except it will be a delete query, not an append query. The criteria will be the same. Run the query, save it as **qryDeleteArchive**, and then close the query.

19. Create a union query to union the records in the **tblHours** table with the records in the **tblHoursArchive** table. The query should be written as follows:
    SELECT * FROM tblHours
    UNION ALL
    SELECT * FROM tblHoursArchive

20. Run the query to test the results, click File on the menu bar, and then click Print. Save the query as **qryUnionHours**, and then close the query.

Explore 21. Create another union query that is identical to qryUnionHours except that it is sorted in Descending order by the EmployeeNo field. Save the query as **qryUnionHoursSort**.

22. Close the **Hours3** database and exit Access.

CASE PROBLEMS

Case 1. Edwards and Company Jack Edwards has a list of clients that he exported from another software program into a text file. He wants you to import this data before he creates a complete listing for you. The file is a tab-delimited text file.

He then wants you to create a mailing list and run labels for all the clients and consultants in the database. He plans to do several different mailings to these people and wants the list sorted in ascending order by ZipCode. He wants the CompanyName field in the **tblClients** table, the FirstName field concatenated to the LastName field from the **tbConsultants** table in one field, and the Address, City, State, and ZipCode data in the remaining fields. You need to build a union query to accomplish this task.

Complete the following:

1. Start Access and open the Edward3 database located in the Tutorial.03 folder on your local or network drive.

2. Click File, point to Get External Data, and then click Import.

3. Click the Files of type list box, and then click Text Files.

4. Select the text file **Edward3** from the Tutorial.03 folder on your local or network drive, and then click Import. Make sure that Delimited is selected, click Next, click the option First Row Contains Field Names, and then click Next.

5. Make sure that In a New Table is selected, click Next, change the ConsultantID and ZipCode fields to a Text data type, click Next, click No primary key, and then save the data in a new table named **tblClientsImport**.

6. Open the **tblClientsImport** table in Datasheet view, click File on the menu bar, and then click Print to print the imported records. Close the table.

7. Create a new query in Design view and add the **tblClientsImport** table to the Query window. Add all the fields to the design grid except ClientID. Change the query to an append query, type **tblClients** in the Table Name text box. Run the query. Save the query as **qryClientsAppend**, and then close the query.

8. Create a new query, do not add any tables to the design window, and then switch to SQL view.

9. Type the following: "SELECT CompanyName, Address1, City, State, ZipCode FROM tblClients" and then press the Enter key.

10. Type "UNION All" and then press the Enter key.

11. Press Enter again, type "SELECT FirstName&" "&LastName, Address, City, State, ZipCode FROM tblConsultants", and then press the Enter key.

12. Type "ORDER BY ZipCode" and then run the query to check the results. Click File on the menu bar, and then click Print.

13. Save the query as **qryUnionClientsConsultants**, and then close the query.

Explore

14. Create another union query that selects CompanyName, Address1, City & " " & State & " " & ZipCode AS Address2 from the tblClients table and unions it to FirstName & " " & LastName, Address, City & " " & State & " " & ZipCode AS Address2 from the tblConsultants table. Do not sort the results. The resulting query will display three columns: CompanyName, Address1, Address2. Save the query as **qryUnionClientsConsultants2**.

15. Close the **Edward3** database and exit Access.

Case 2. San Diego County Information Systems   Richard Johnson from Personnel recently e-mailed you an Excel spreadsheet that contains employee data. The file has some of the same data that you track for students who are employees of the county. He wants to share information after you complete your database and will send you a complete list of employees if this one is helpful to you.

You will import the data and write the queries necessary to update and append the appropriate tables. Complete the following:

1. Start Access and open the **ISD3** database located in the Tutorial.03 folder on your local or network drive.

2. Click File on the menu bar, point to Get External Data, click Import, and click Microsoft Excel from the Files of type list box.

3. Click ISD3 in the Tutorial.03 folder on your local or network drive, click the Import button, click the First Row Contains Column Headings option, and then click the Next button.

4. Make sure that In a New Table is selected, click the Next button twice, click No primary key, click the Next button, type **tblStudentsImport**, and then click the Finish button.

5. Open the **tblStudentsImport** table in Datasheet view, click File on the menu bar, then click Print to print the imported records. Close the table.

6. Create a select query and add the **tblStudentsImport** table to the Query window.

7. Create the following expressions in the query:
   NameSpace:InStr([EmployeeName]," ")
   FirstName:Left([EmployeeName],NameSpace-1)
   NameLen:Len([EmployeeName])
   LastName:Right([EmployeeName],NameLen-NameSpace)

8. Copy and paste the expressions for NameSpace and NameLen into the expressions FirstName and LastName. They will look like the following when completed:
   FirstName: Left([EmployeeName],InStr([EmployeeName]," ")-1)
   LastName: Right([EmployeeName],Len([EmployeeName])-InStr([EmployeeName]," ")

9. Delete the NameSpace and NameLen columns from the grid.

10. Add the EMPLOYEEID, DEPARMENT, and TELEPHONE fields to the design grid.

11. Change the query to an append query, type **tblStudents** in the Table Name text box, click the OK button, and make sure that the fields match up to the fields in the table (EMPLOYEEID should be appended to StudentNo).

12. Run the query, close the query, and save it as **qryStudentsAppend**.

13. Click File on the menu bar, point to Get External Data, click Import, click the Files of type list box, and then click Microsoft Access. Select the **Samples** database from the Tutorial.03 folder on your local or network drive, and import the basUtilityFunctions module.

14. Right-click the **tblStudents** table, click Copy, right-click in the Database window, and then click Paste. Type **tblStudentsCopy** in the Table Name text box, make sure that Structure and Data is selected, and click the OK button. This copy is a backup in case you make a mistake in the update query you will write next.

15. Create a new query and add the **tblStudents** table to the Query window. Add FirstName and LastName to the design grid, change the query to an update query and type the following expressions in the Update To row of the query grid:
   =ProperCase([FirstName])
   =ProperCase([LastName])

16. Run the query, save it as **qryUpdateNames**, and then close the query.

17. Open the **tblStudents** table in Datasheet view, click File on the menu bar, and then click Print to print the updated records. Close the table.

Explore

18. You will research the Strconv function and then use it rather than the ProperCase function to convert text to proper case:
   a. Open the basUtilityFunctions module in Design view. Click Help in the menu bar and then click Microsoft Visual Basic Help. Click the Answer Wizards tab and then type in Strconv in the What would you like to do? text box. Determine from the Help window the syntax that would be required to convert EmployeeName to proper case. Close Help, close the Visual Basic window, and then close the basUtilityFunctions module.
   b. Create a new query and add the tblStudentsImport table to the query window. Create an expression named NameProper that uses the Strconv function to convert the EMPLOYEENAME field to proper case. Run the query to check the results and save it as **qryEmployeeNames**.
19. Close the **ISD3** database and exit Access.

Case 3. Christenson Homes   After you met with Roberta Christenson to discuss the design you created for her database, you made a few changes to the earlier structure. You added a table for customer data because there is often more than one buyer of a home. The relationship between the **tblLots** and **tblCustomers** tables is a one-to-many relationship to allow for additional buyers. The primary key in the **tblLots** table is now an AutoNumber field because the lot number is not critical data to store, and you can assign a unique value with the AutoNumber data type to each record in this table.

Roberta exported some of the data from her accounting system to a tab-delimited text file and asks you to import it into Access. You will then write queries to format the data the way she asked to see it in the database. Complete the following:

1. Start Access and open the **Homes3** database located in the Tutorial.03 folder on your local or network drive.
2. Import the **Homes3** tab-delimited text file from the Tutorial.03 folder on your local or network drive. Set Files of type to Text Files. The first row contains field names. Change the ZipCode field to a Text data type. Do not set a primary key. Import the data to a new table named **tblCustomersImport**.
3. Open the **tblCustomersImport** table in Datasheet view, click File on the menu bar, and then click Print to print the imported records. Close the table.
4. Create a new query in Design view and add the **tblCustomersImport** table to the Query window.
5. Use the string functions from this tutorial as a guide, and create expressions in the query to extract first and last name from the CUSTOMERNAME field. Then add the remaining fields to the query.
6. Change the query to an append query and type **tblCustomers** as the table to append to.
7. Close the query and save it as **qryCustomersAppend**.
8. Import the module **basUtilityFunctions** from the **Samples** database located in the Tutorial.03 folder on your local or network drive.
9. Make a copy of the **tblCustomers** table in the current database; include structure and data, and name it **tblCustomersCopy**.
10. Write an update query. Use the ProperCase function in expressions to update all the text fields that are in uppercase. Use the functions in this tutorial as a guide.
11. Run the query, save it as **qryUpdateNames**, and then close the query.
12. Close the **Homes3** database and exit Access.

Case 4. Sonoma Farms   The Sonoma Farms database has been redesigned to eliminate the **tblVisits** table. After you work with sample data, you decide that the **tblVisits** table information is not necessary, but a new record in the **tblVisitors** table that includes the CustomerID will meet your needs.

Now you want to import some historical data from one of your spreadsheets. Then you will construct a query to combine data from the **tblDistributors** and **tblCustomers** tables. You will use the data for a promotional mailing. Complete the following:

1. Start Access and open the **Sonoma3** database located in the Tutorial.03 folder on your local or network drive.

2. Use the Spreadsheet Import Wizard to import the **Sonoma3** Excel file in the Tutorial.03 folder on your local or network drive. Do not set a primary key. Save the file as **tblVisitorsImport**.

3. Open the **tblVisitorsImport** table in Datasheet view, click File on the menu bar, and then click Print to print the imported records. Close the table.

4. Write a query to extract FirstName and LastName from the VISITORNAME field, and then append these two fields plus the remaining fields to the **tblVisitors** table.

5. Save the query as **qryVisitorsAppend**, and then close the query.

6. Import the module **basUtilityFunctions** from the **Samples** database located in the Tutorial.03 folder on your local or network drive.

7. Write an update query using the ProperCase function to convert the FirstName and LastName in the **tblVisitors** table to the proper case.

Explore

8. Save the query as **qryUpdateNames**, and then close the query.

9. Convert the data in the Gifts field to lowercase. (*Hint*: Use the Format property of the field in the table.)

10. Write a union query in SQL to create a list from the **tblCustomers** and **tblDistributors** tables. The list should include the Name, Address1, City, State, and ZipCode fields from each table.

11. Sort the query by ZipCode, run it to check the results, click File on the menu bar, and then click Print.

12. Save the query as **qryUnionCustomersDistributors**, and then close the query.

13. Close the **Sonoma3** database and exit Access.

QUICK | CHECK ANSWERS

Session 3.1

1. Linking is a better method if the data is going to be used in its original format and in Access.
2. delimiter
3. data conversion
4. The InStr function returns the position of a particular character from a string of text.
5. Len

Session 3.2

1. Unique Values
2. The Record Locks query property specifies whether the records in a multiuser environment are locked so that users cannot access them while a query is being run.
3. copy
4. After action queries are created and saved, you can change their hidden attribute property so they don't display in the Database window.

Session 3.3

1. SQL 92.
2. SQL-specific queries include data-definition queries, union queries, and pass-through queries.
3. columns you want to retrieve.
4. Unique Values
5. SELECT
6. An inner join includes all the records from the two tables where the joined fields are equal.
7. A right outer join includes all the records from the related table and only the records from the related table and the records from the primary table where the joined fields are equal.
8. UNION

OBJECTIVES

In this tutorial you will:

- Review form design guidelines
- Create a form template
- Create form masters
- Use templates and masters to create data entry forms
- Apply expressions to refer to a subform
- Use the column property of a combo box
- Create a switchboard containing an option group
- Understand macros and macro group-naming conventions
- Write a macro containing a conditional expression
- Create buttons using the Command Button Wizard
- Compare macros to VBA code

DESIGNING COMPLEX FORMS

Building the User Interface for MovieCam Technologies

CASE

MovieCam Technologies

Amanda is pleased with the progress that you and Carolyn have made on the MovieCam Technologies database. She approved the design and is satisfied that the importing and archiving processes will run smoothly.

Amanda asks that you now begin work on the forms for the user interface of the database. She wants you to identify and create the forms necessary for data entry, keeping in mind that the users of the system are not familiar with Access and do not have a lot of time to learn more about it. She also wants you to design switchboards that will prevent users from seeing the Database window, thereby eliminating the possibility of them unintentionally modifying or deleting an object.

Your goal therefore, is to develop standardized forms that do not require a significant amount of training to use, and to design switchboards that contain all the controls end users need to work within the database.

SESSION 4.1

In this session, you will study form design guidelines. You will create a form template that you will set as the database default and create a form master to use as the basis for data entry forms. You then will create data entry forms based on the template and master, add a subform to a main form, and make form changes based on the design guidelines. You also will work with expressions designed to further enhance the user-friendliness of forms.

Introduction to Forms

Access forms are classified as either bound or unbound. **Bound forms** are tied to a table or a query. They are used for editing, entering, and reviewing data in those underlying tables and queries. **Unbound forms** are not tied to a table or query and are used to create an interface that provides the users controlled access to the application. An unbound form that is used to navigate to other forms and reports in the database is referred to as a **switchboard**. In most cases, you design a switchboard to open instead of the Database window. Then on that switchboard you place controls for only those objects to which you want the user to have access. Figure 4-1 shows the design and format of a typical switchboard. It includes a command button to open the data entry forms switchboard, a command button to open the Reports switchboard, and a command button to exit Access.

Figure 4-1   SAMPLE SWITCHBOARD

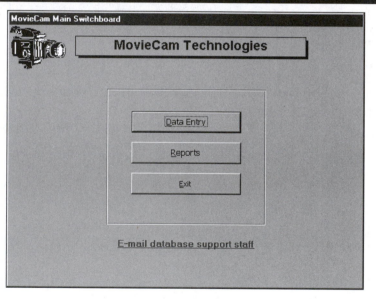

A splash screen is another type of unbound form. A **splash screen** form opens automatically when a database is opened, and is designed to give the user something to do while the application is loading. A sample splash screen is shown in Figure 4-2.

Figure 4-2   SAMPLE SPLASH SCREEN

Carolyn and Jason have already created some of the data entry forms for the MovieCam Technologies database. However, changing the same properties over and over and adding the same controls to the forms have been tedious. You suggest that it would be prudent to develop a form template you and Carolyn can use to design the rest of the forms. You can apply all the common properties that are characteristic of the forms to the form template, and then build individual forms using the template's basic structure and design. You also decide to create a form master, which can contain items like a company logo, company name, and other standard controls that you want to be part of newly created forms and switchboards.

Form Design

The user interface is one of the most important features you need to consider as you design forms. The **user interface** is the mechanism by which the user communicates and interacts with the application. From the user's perspective, the user interface *is* the application. In most instances, you design the user interface assuming the end user does not want to spend a lot of time learning how to use the application. Some design guidelines for meeting this goal are:

- If the application runs on the Windows platform, design your interface to look and feel like Windows. Because Access runs on Windows, Access database forms should look similar to the dialog boxes you see in the Access application, as well as other Office applications. For example, use option groups when you want the user to select only one option, and check boxes when the user can select several options. Text boxes in which the user enters or edits data should have a white background and the sunken special effect. For controls the users cannot change use flat text boxes with the same background color as the form. Figure 4-3 illustrates these examples.

Figure 4-3   **THE MICROSOFT WORD PRINT DIALOG BOX**

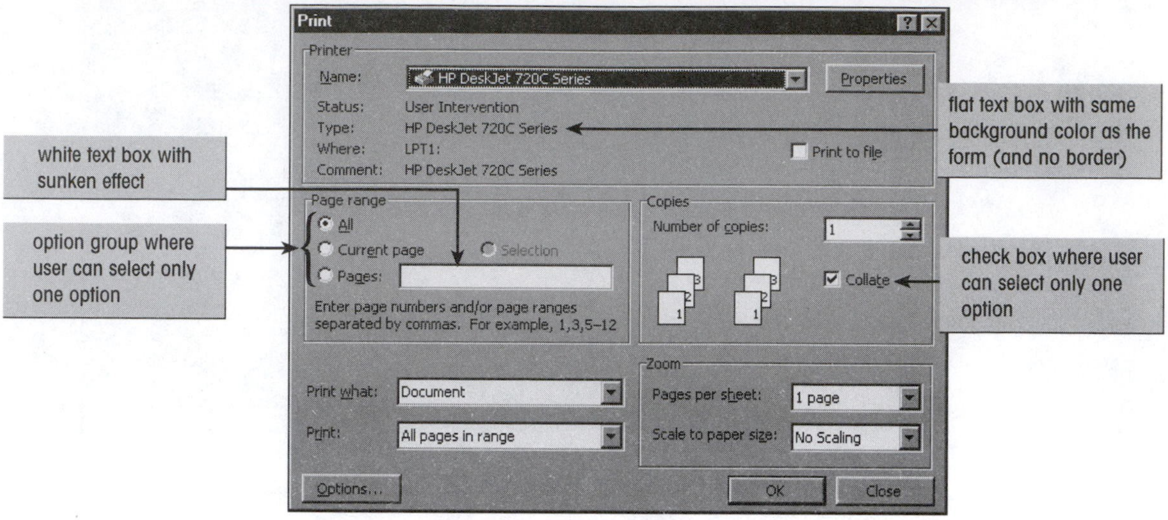

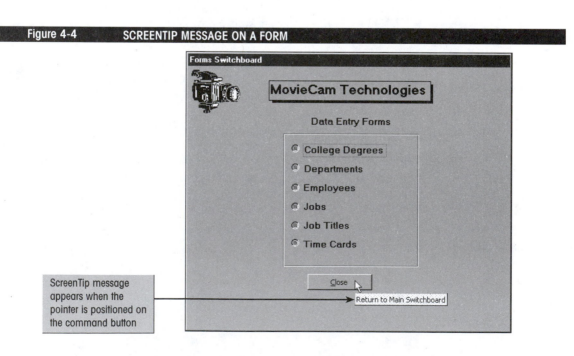

white text box with
sunken effect

option group where
user can select only
one option

flat text box with same
background color as the
form (and no border)

check box where user
can select only one
option

■ Simple is better. Avoid the use of too many colors or fonts. It is visually confusing. Align controls and use rectangles to group information. The standard Windows look includes gray forms, as illustrated in the Print dialog box shown in Figure 4-3.

■ Be direct. Provide linear, intuitive ways to accomplish tasks. Apply tab order (the order in which the insertion point moves from one control to the next) on forms to reinforce the visual order of the controls. Organize controls logically, based on how the user enters the data. Add keystroke shortcuts to command buttons, menu commands, and labels.

■ Provide users with feedback. Create ScreenTip messages, like that shown in Figure 4-4. A **ScreenTip** is a message that appears when the pointer is positioned on a control on a form or on a button on a toolbar. Messages should be short and informative.

Figure 4-4   **SCREENTIP MESSAGE ON A FORM**

ScreenTip message
appears when the
pointer is positioned on
the command button

Visual consistency is another important consideration in form design. All forms in a database application should have the same color scheme and font properties, and the same consistent visual cues for controls. Form templates and masters help you achieve this consistency.

Creating a Form Template

A **form template** is a form on which you base other forms you create in the database. The template determines which sections a form will have and defines the dimensions of each section. It also contains the default property settings for the form, its sections, and controls.

When you create a form without using a wizard, Access uses the default template named *Normal* to determine the characteristics mentioned above. Creating a custom form template with new property settings and identifying it as your database's default template allows you to standardize properties for all forms in your database. You can reset the default template on the Forms/Reports tab in the Options dialog box.

REFERENCE WINDOW **RW**

Creating a Form Template
- In the Database window, click Forms on the Objects bar.
- Double-click the Create form in Design view option.
- If necessary, display the toolbox and then click the Properties button on the toolbar.
- Change default control, section, and form properties as desired.
- Save your changes and close the form.
- Click Tools on the menu bar and then click Options.
- Click the Forms/Reports tab in the Options dialog box and type the template form name in the Form template text box.

You now will create the form template for MovieCam Technologies. The template will contain a Form Header/Footer section. You will set a size for it, and you will set properties to eliminate record selectors and dividing lines.

To create a form template:

1. Start Access and then open the **Movie4** database located in the Tutorial.04 folder on your local or network drive.

2. Click **Forms** on the Objects bar in the Database window, and then double-click **Create form in Design view**.

3. Click **View** on the menu bar and then click **Form Header/Footer**.

4. Maximize the form window to make it easier to size the form.

5. Position the pointer at the bottom edge of the Form Header section until it changes to the ✛ shape, and then click and drag down to the ¾" mark on the vertical ruler.

6. Position the pointer on the right edge of the form until it changes to the ↔ shape, and then drag to the 6½" mark on the horizontal ruler.

7. Position the pointer at the bottom edge of the Detail section until it changes to the ✛ shape, and then drag down to the 3" mark on the vertical ruler.

8. Position the pointer on the bottom edge of the Form Footer section until it changes to the ✛ shape, and then drag down to the ½" mark on the vertical ruler.

9. Select the form by clicking the form selector, which is the box in the upper-left corner of the form where the two ruler bars meet (see Figure 4-5), and then, if necessary, click the **Properties** button 🗐 on the Form Design toolbar.

Figure 4-5	THE FORM'S PROPERTY SHEET

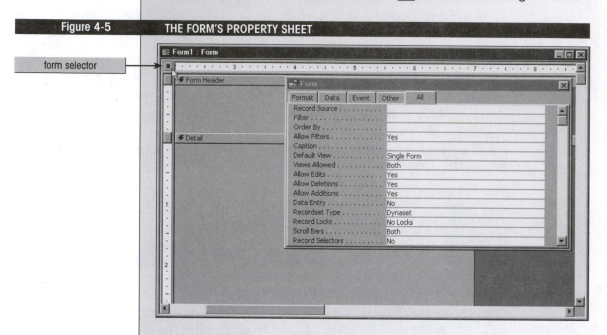

10. Click the **All** tab on the property sheet if necessary, change the Record Selectors property to **No**, and the Dividing Lines property to **No**. This action removes the objects identified in Figure 4-6. Record selectors are useful when there is more than one record on one page of a form. All the MovieCam database forms will have only one record per page. Dividing lines show the end of one form section and the beginning of another.

Figure 4-6	ELIMINATING RECORD SELECTORS AND DIVIDING LINES

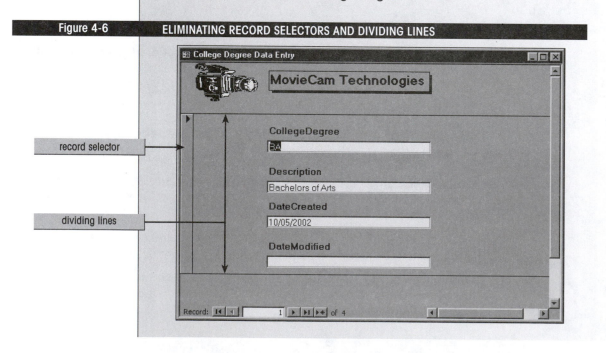

11. Save the form as **zsfrmTemplate**. The tag prefix zs is commonly used to identify objects that are part of the development and maintenance of your database application. End users normally do not work with these objects. The z is used so that the object sorts to the bottom of the Database window. The s denotes a system object.

Now you will focus on customizing the template's properties.

Changing Default Properties of Toolbox Controls

The properties of a toolbox control can be changed by selecting the toolbox control and then opening its property sheet. Modifying the properties of a control in the form template affects the use of that control in new forms based on the template.

Next you'll change some of the default controls on the template you created. The default Font Size of labels and text boxes is 8 point, which you think is too small. The default Font Weight is normal, but you and Carolyn want the labels to be semi-bold. When you insert a text box, the default position of its label is to the left of the text box. You and Carolyn want the label positioned above the text box.

To change the default properties of controls:

1. Be sure that the toolbox is visible, and then click the **Label** button [Aa] on the toolbox. The Default Label properties are listed in the property sheet, as shown in Figure 4-7.

| Figure 4-7 | PROPERTIES OF THE TOOLBOX'S DEFAULT LABEL BUTTON |

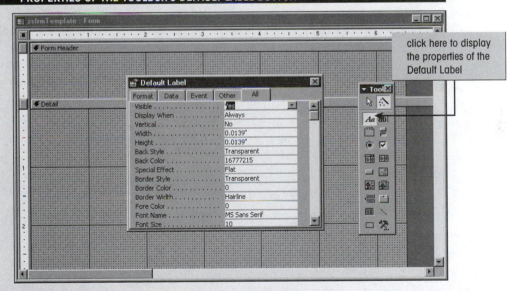

2. Change the Font Size property to **10**, scroll to the Font Weight property, and change it to **Semi-bold**.

3. Click the **Text Box** button [abl] on the toolbox. The default Text Box properties are visible in the property sheet.

4. Change the Font Size property to **10**.

5. Change the Label X property to **0** and the Label Y property to **-0.25**. Now when you add a Text Box control to a form, its accompanying label control will be positioned above the text box, instead of to its left.

6. Change the Text Align and Label Align properties to **Left**.

7. Change the Add Colon property to **No** to eliminate the colon in the label.

8. Restore the form window, close the property sheet, and then close the toolbox.

9. Save your changes and close the form.

After you complete the design of the form template, you will set it as the default for any new forms you and Carolyn create.

To set the zsfrmTemplate as the default:

1. Click **Tools** on the menu bar and then click **Options**.

2. Click the **Forms/Report** tab in the Options dialog box.

3. Click the **Form template** text box and then delete **Normal**.

4. Type **zsfrmTemplate** and then press the **Enter** key.

Creating Form Masters

A custom form template represents the basic structure for all forms in the database and determines the dimensions, properties, and form sections of new forms. It cannot contain any controls, however. To add the same controls, such as a label control for the company name or an image control for a company logo, to forms in a database, you can create a form master. A **form master** is a form that contains the controls that are common to all forms in the database. Unlike a template, new forms created in the database do not inherit the characteristics of the form master. However, the form master can be copied and pasted to create new forms. You and Carolyn decide that all data entry forms should contain the company logo and the company name.

To create a master data entry form:

1. Create a new form in Design view. It will automatically be based on zsfrmTemplate.

2. If necessary, click the **Toolbox** button [⚒] on the Form Design toolbar so the toolbox is visible.

3. Click the **Label** button [Aa] on the toolbox, and then click and drag near the top center of the Form Header section to create a label approximately 2½" wide and ¼" tall.

4. Type **MovieCam Technologies** inside the label and then press the **Enter** key.

5. Click the **Font Size** list arrow on the Formatting toolbar, click **14**, and then click the **Bold** button [B] on the Formatting toolbar.

6. Click the list arrow on the **Special Effect** button [▭▾] on the Formatting toolbar, and then click **Shadowed**.

7. Size and position the label as shown in Figure 4-8.

Figure 4-8 SIZING THE LABEL ON THE FORM MASTER

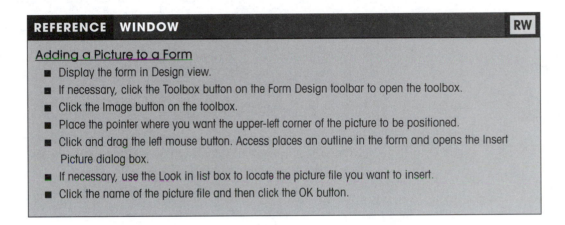

8. Save the form as **zsfrmMaster**.

Next you will use the Image button on the toolbox to embed the company logo in the form master.

REFERENCE WINDOW | RW

Adding a Picture to a Form

■ Display the form in Design view.
■ If necessary, click the Toolbox button on the Form Design toolbar to open the toolbox.
■ Click the Image button on the toolbox.
■ Place the pointer where you want the upper-left corner of the picture to be positioned.
■ Click and drag the left mouse button. Access places an outline in the form and opens the Insert Picture dialog box.
■ If necessary, use the Look in list box to locate the picture file you want to insert.
■ Click the name of the picture file and then click the OK button.

In addition to the company name, you and Carolyn decide to insert the company logo in the Form Header of the master.

To add a picture to a form:

1. Click the **Image** button  on the toolbox, and then click and drag inside the Form Header section to create an image box that's ¾" wide by ¾" tall in the upper-left corner of the section. The Insert Picture dialog box opens, as shown in Figure 4-9.

Figure 4-9 | **INSERT PICTURE DIALOG BOX**

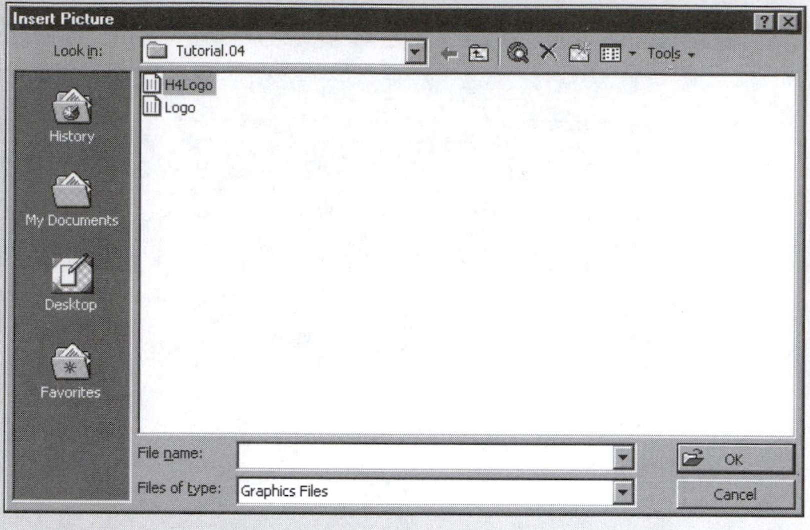

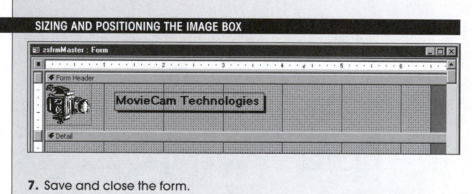

2. If necessary, click the **Look in** list arrow and navigate to the Tutorial.04 folder on your local or network drive.

3. Click the **Logo** file and then click the **OK** button. The image is now visible on the form.

4. Right-click the **Image** box and then click **Properties** on the shortcut menu.

5. Set the Size Mode property to **Stretch**. The default Size Mode setting is Clip, which means that the picture will be cropped to fit inside the image box that is created. You want to stretch the logo to fit in the image box.

6. Close the property sheet, and then size and position the image box and label as shown in Figure 4-10.

Figure 4-10 | **SIZING AND POSITIONING THE IMAGE BOX**

7. Save and close the form.

You and Carolyn have put together a list of data entry forms that you want the MovieCam database to contain. The form template and form master are completed, so you'll now create the remaining data entry forms.

Creating Data Entry Forms

The data entry forms that you and Carolyn plan for the database include the following:

- The frmDegrees form for data on college degrees. Carolyn has already created this form.
- The frmDepartments form for data on company departments. It has not yet been created.
- The frmEmployees form for data on employees. Jason created this form before he left. Carolyn has modified it so that its style matches the template and master.
- The frmJobs form for data on MovieCam's jobs. It will be used by management to review hours spent to date on existing jobs. Carolyn has already created the form. It contains a read-only subform that lists the hours spent on each job. The hours spent information comes from the tblHours table. Because this data is entered with the time card data on the frmTimeCards form, the data is read-only so the managers cannot change it.
- The frmJobTitles form for data on job titles. Carolyn has already created this form.
- The frmTimeCards form for data on labor and projects. The frmTimeCards form is the central form in the database. It will be used to enter data into both the tblTimeCards and tblHours tables. The tblTimeCards table is the record source for the main form Carolyn has begun. She has completed the sfrmHours subform, which is based on the tblHours table.

The frmDepartments form needs to be created, and the frmTimeCards form needs to be completed. You will work on these forms next.

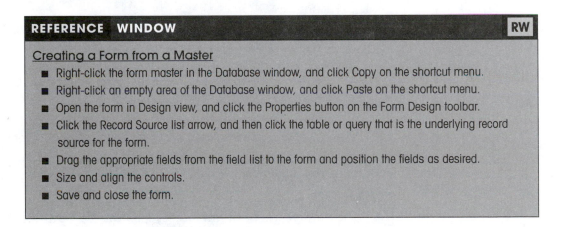

REFERENCE   WINDOW   RW

Creating a Form from a Master

- Right-click the form master in the Database window, and click Copy on the shortcut menu.
- Right-click an empty area of the Database window, and click Paste on the shortcut menu.
- Open the form in Design view, and click the Properties button on the Form Design toolbar.
- Click the Record Source list arrow, and then click the table or query that is the underlying record source for the form.
- Drag the appropriate fields from the field list to the form and position the fields as desired.
- Size and align the controls.
- Save and close the form.

You will create the frmDepartments form first.

To create a form using the master:

1. Click the **zsfrmMaster** form in the Database window, and then click the **Copy** button on the Database toolbar.

2. Click in a blank area of the Database window, and then click the **Paste** button on the Database toolbar.

3. Type **frmDepartments** in the Paste As dialog box, and press the **Enter** key.

4. Open the **frmDepartments** form in Design view, and then open the form's property sheet by clicking the **Properties** button on the Form Design toolbar.

5. Change the Record Source property to **tblDepartments** and the Caption property to **Department Data Entry**, and then close the property sheet. The tblDepartments table field list should be visible.

6. Drag each field from the field list onto the form in the order shown in Figure 4-11, and then close the field list.

Figure 4-11	ADDING FIELDS TO THE FORM

7. After you've positioned the fields on the form, select them by dragging a rectangle around all the controls.

8. Point to the selected controls so that your pointer changes to a 🖐 shape, right-click, point to **Align**, and then click **Left** on the shortcut menu.

9. Deselect the controls, and then size and position the labels and text boxes as shown in Figure 4-12.

10. Click the **DeptNo** label and change it to **Dept No**, click the **DeptName** label and change it to **Dept Name**, click the **DateCreated** label and change it to **Date Created**, and then click the **DateModified** label and change it to **Date Modified**, as shown in Figure 4-12.

Figure 4-12	SIZING AND POSITIONING CONTROLS

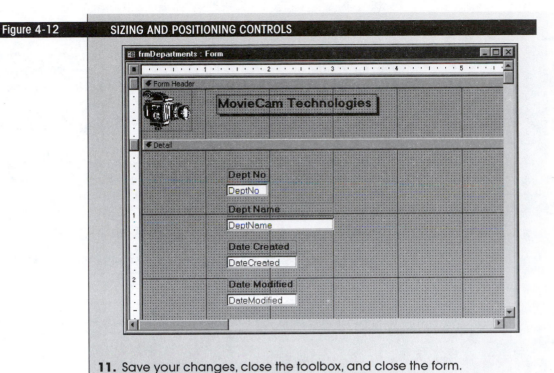

11. Save your changes, close the toolbox, and close the form.

You and Carolyn will now complete the frmTimeCards form. Carolyn's design of the form is shown in Figure 4-13. It consists of a main form that will be used to enter data into the tblTimeCards table, and a subform that will be used to enter data in the tblHours table. The main form contains a formula that adds all the hours worked as noted on the subform for each time card.

Figure 4-13	PRELIMINARY DESIGN OF THE FRMTIMECARDS FORM

(MovieCam Technologies Image)   (Title)

Time Card No	Time Card Date	Employee No	Employee Name
XXX	XX/XX/XXXX	XXX	XXXXX XXXXXXX

Time Card No	Job No	Hours Worked
XXX	XXXXX	XXX
XXX	XXXXX	XXX
XXX	XXXXX	XXX
XXX	XXXXX	XXX
XXX	XXXXX	XXX
XXX	XXXXX	XXX
XXX	XXXXX	XXX

	Total Hours	XXXX

Carolyn has completed the subform and named it sfrmHours. She has begun work on the main form and has named it frmTimeCards. You will complete this form next.

To complete the frmTimeCards form:

1. Open the **frmTimeCards** form in Design view. Carolyn created the form by copying the master, as you did for the frmDepartments form. She then added a text box control for the TimeCardNo and TimeCardDate fields, and a combo box control for the EmployeeNo field.

2. Click the **EmployeeNo** combo box, and then click the **Properties** button on the Form Design toolbar.

3. Click the **Row Source** property, and then click its **Build** button. EmployeeNo is the first column of the combo box. The expression Name, which contains FirstName and LastName, is the second column. LastName is the third column and is included for sorting purposes.

4. Close the Query Builder window to return to the form.

5. Change the **Name** property for the combo box to **cboEmployeeNo**. You will use this name in expressions or when you set the tab order of the form.

6. Save the form and then close the property sheet.

7. Switch to Form view, click the **Employee No** list arrow to see the options, and then press the **Esc** key to cancel.

8. Switch to Design view.

Identifier Operators

Identifier operators are used in expressions, macros, and VBA code to identify objects and their properties.

The **!** (exclamation point, referred to as the **bang operator**) is used to separate one object from another or from the object collection. A **collection** is an object that contains a set of related objects (collections will be discussed in greater detail in Tutorial 6). For example, the Forms collection is the group of all open forms in the database, and the Reports collection is all the open reports.

The **.** (period, referred to as the **dot operator**) is used to separate an object from its property or method (methods will be discussed in greater detail in Tutorial 7). Some examples of how identifier operators are used include the following:

- Combine the names of object collections and object names to select a specific object. For example, *Forms!frmTimeCards* identifies the frmTimeCards form in the MovieCam database. This identification is necessary because developers who do not use a naming convention might give a report the same name as a form.

- Combine object names with properties to select a specific property. For example, *txtTotalHours.Visible = False* specifies that the Visible property of the text box, txtTotalHours, is false.

- Identify specific fields in tables or controls on forms and reports. For example, *Forms!frmTimeCards!cboEmployeeName* identifies the combo box on the frmTimeCards form and *tblEmployees!FirstName* identifies the FirstName field in the tblEmployees table.

You will use a dot operator in an expression to display a particular column from the cboEmployeeNo combo box in the frmTimeCards form. The Column property of a combo box returns the value contained in a particular column of the combo box. It is **zero-based**, meaning it begins counting with the number 0. The first column is 0, the second column is 1, and so forth.

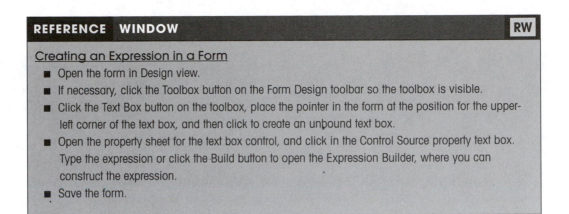

REFERENCE WINDOW   **RW**

Creating an Expression in a Form

- Open the form in Design view.
- If necessary, click the Toolbox button on the Form Design toolbar so the toolbox is visible.
- Click the Text Box button on the toolbox, place the pointer in the form at the position for the upper-left corner of the text box, and then click to create an unbound text box.
- Open the property sheet for the text box control, and click in the Control Source property text box. Type the expression or click the Build button to open the Expression Builder, where you can construct the expression.
- Save the form.

You might have noticed when you tested the cboEmployeeNo combo box in Form view, that only the employee number was visible, even though the number and the name of the employee were on the drop-down list. Amanda wants you to add a control to show the employee name as well. This control will be based on an expression that refers to the combo box.

To add an expression to the form:

1. Open the toolbox, click the **Text Box** button on the toolbox, and then click in the form to the right of the cboEmployeeNo combo box. An unbound text box control is inserted on the form. It is referred to as unbound because it is not bound to a field in the underlying record source (table or query).

2. Position the insertion point inside the unbound text box, type **=[cboEmployeeNo].Column(1)** and then press the **Enter** key. The expression will appear as shown Figure 4-14. The expression specifies that the value appearing in the text box will be column 1 of the cboEmployeeNo combo box. Remember that column 1 is actually the second column because the property is zero-based, and this column contains the employee's name.

3. Click the **Label** button on the toolbox, click and drag to create a label above the text box, type **Employee Name** in the label, and then press the **Enter** key.

Figure 4-14   CREATING AN EXPRESSION IN THE FRMTIMECARDS FORM

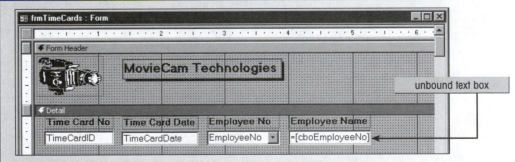

4. Switch to Form view to test the results of the expression. The text box contains an employee name.

5. Switch to Design view, click the text box containing the expression, open its property sheet, and then set the Name property to **txtEmployee**.

6. Close the property sheet. Select the new **txtEmployee** text box and the **EmployeeNo** combo box to the left of the text box.

7. Right-click the selected controls, point to **Size**, and then click **To Widest**. Repeat this procedure to size the controls **To Tallest**.

8. Right-click the selected controls, point to **Align**, and then click **Top** on the short-cut menu.

9. Select the **Employee Name** label and the **Employee No** label to the left of it, and repeat Steps 7 and 8 to size and align the labels.

10. Save your form changes.

Because the txtEmployee text box contains an expression and is not a control in which data can be entered, you will change a few of the text box's properties to differentiate it from the other text box controls. You want the control to be flat and have the same background color as the form. You also will remove it from the tab order so that the user is restricted from entering data in it.

To change properties of the txtEmployee control:

1. If necessary, open the property sheet of the txtEmployee text box.

2. Click the **Format** tab on the property sheet, click the **Back Color** text box, and then click its **Build** button ⌷.

3. Click the **gray color** in the Color dialog box that matches the background color of the form, and then click the **OK** button. The text box's color will not change until you set the next property.

4. Click the **Special Effect: Flat** ⌷ button on the toolbar.

5. Click the **Other** tab on the property sheet, change the Tab Stop property to **No**, and then close the property sheet.

6. Save the changes and then switch to Form view. The form should look like that shown in Figure 4-15.

| Figure 4-15 | DISPLAYING THE EMPLOYEE NAME ON THE FORM |

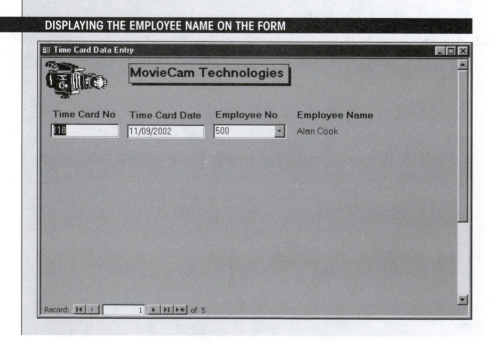

7. Test the form by pressing the **Tab** key to move through the controls. Notice that you skip the Employee name field when you tab.

8. Switch to Design view.

Working with Subforms

Next you will insert the sfrmHours subform in the frmTimeCards form. You will do this simply by dragging the subform from the Database window to the frmTimeCards form in Design view.

To insert the sfrmHours subform in the frmTimeCards form:

1. Resize and position the frmTimeCards window as shown in Figure 4-16.

Figure 4-16	POSITIONING THE FORM TO UNBLOCK THE DATABASE WINDOW

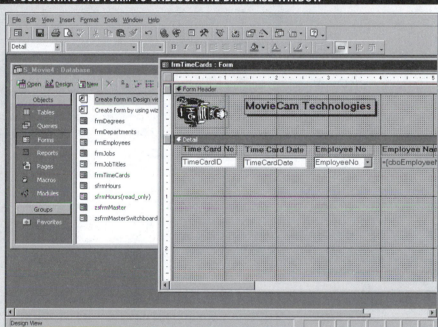

2. In the Database window, click the **sfrmHours** form and drag it to a blank area below the other controls in the Detail section of the frmTimeCards form.

3. Select the label control above the subform that contains the text tblHours, and press the **Delete** key.

4. Size the main form so the entire subform is visible, select the subform control, position the pointer on the lower-right corner handle so that it has a ↖ shape, and resize it to approximately 3¾" wide and 2½" tall, as shown in Figure 4-17.

Figure 4-17	RESIZING THE SUBFORM

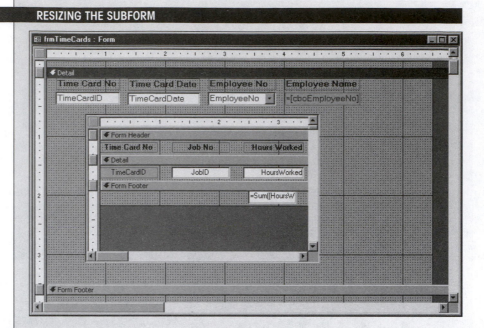

5. Center the subform control below the other four controls.

6. Click the **Properties** button [icon] on the Form Design toolbar. Change the Name property to **sfrmHours**. (It currently is named tblHours.) Close the property sheet.

7. Click the **Save** button [icon] on the Form Design toolbar.

Next you'll add to the frmTimeCards form an expression that will calculate total hours worked. This data is displayed on the subform. Carolyn included an expression—named txtTotalHours—in the footer of the subform that sums the HoursWorked field in the subform. The expression you'll add will be set equal to the txtTotalHours control. The txtTotalHours expression will look like this:

```
-sfrmHours.Form!txtTotalHours
```

In the expression above, the control in the frmTimeCards form that contains the subform is named sfrmHours. The subform also has the name sfrmHours, but in this syntax you are referring to the control rather than the subform itself. Form refers to the Form property of the control and specifies that you are now referring to the subform and not the control. The last part of the expression, txtTotalHours, represents the name of the subform control that totals the HoursWorked field.

To refer to a subform in an expression:

1. Click the **Text Box** button [abl] on the toolbox, and click below the subform in the Detail section to create another unbound text box. Carolyn changed the default properties of the Text Box control on this form so that no label is drawn with the text box. You will add the label later.

2. Click the **unbound text box**, type **=sfrmHours.Form!txtTotalHours**, and then press the **Enter** key. See Figure 4-18.

Figure 4-18   EXPRESSION TO TOTAL RECORDS IN A SUBFORM

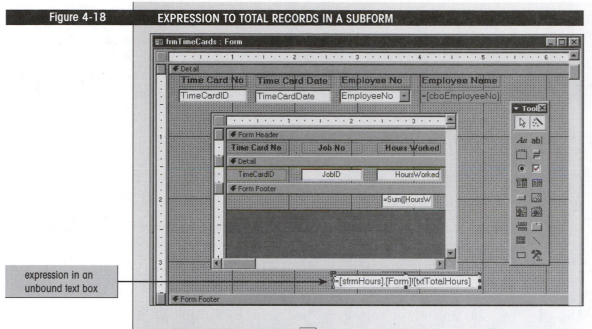

expression in an
unbound text box

3. Click the **Label** button on the toolbox, click to the left of the text box, type
   Total Hours, and then press **Enter**.

4. Size the Total Hours label and the text box so that each is approximately 1" wide.

5. Click the **EmployeeName** combo box, click the **Format Painter** button on
   the Form Design toolbar, and then click the text box you just created. It now is
   formatted the same as the Employee Name text box.

6. Click the **Properties** button on the Form Design toolbar, and change the
   name of the new text box to **txtTotalHours**. Rename the label **Total Hours**, and
   then close the property sheet. The form should look like that shown in Figure 4-19.

7. Save your changes and close the form.

Figure 4-19   MODIFIED DESIGN OF THE FORM WITH A SUBFORM

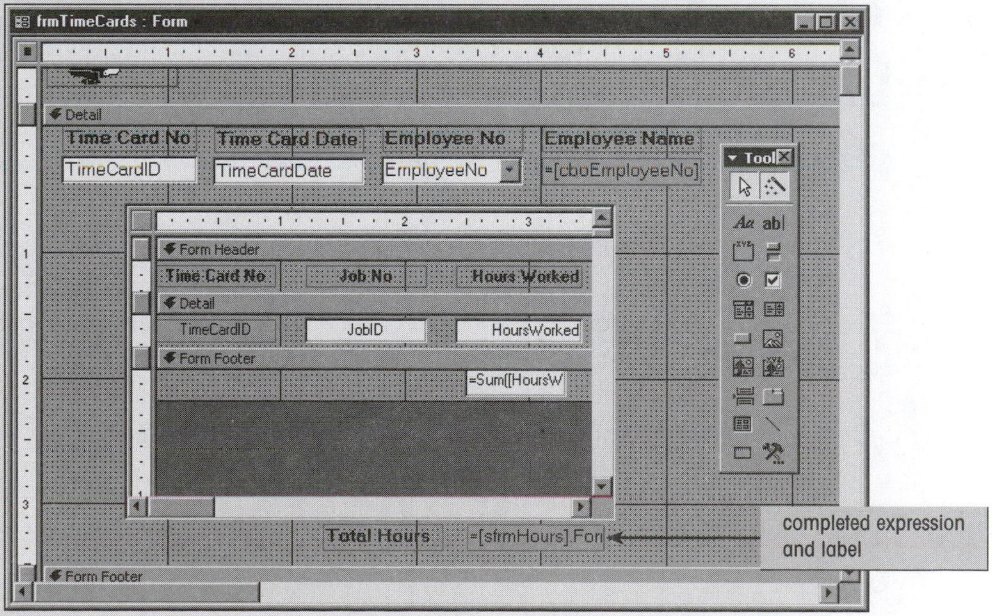

completed expression
and label

You and Carolyn have completed the template, the master, and the data entry forms for the database. Next you will plan the database's switchboard forms and macros.

Session 4.1 QUICK CHECK

1. What is the purpose of a splash screen?

2. The _____ is the mechanism by which the user communicates and interacts with the computer program.

3. What is the drawback to using too many colors on a form?

4. How does a form template differ from a form master?

5. _____ forms are not tied to a table or query and are used to create an interface that provides the users controlled access to the program.

6. What are the identifier operators?

7. What does the term zero-based mean?

8. All the open forms in the database belong to the Forms _____.

SESSION 4.2

In this session, you will create a switchboard master and a switchboard. You will learn more about macros and macro groups, and about macro naming conventions. You also will examine the Macro window. You will write a conditional macro and test it, and then you will be introduced to event properties and use them to run macros. Lastly you will compare Visual Basic code for an event to a macro performing the same function.

Creating Switchboards

As you and Carolyn decided, you will create a number of switchboard forms in the database. The design of the switchboards will be different from the design of the other forms in the database, so you determine that you'll need a different form master as well. The switchboard will contain the logo and company name just like the zsfrmMaster form, but these items will be included in the body of the form instead of in the header. The switchboards will also have a different set of properties. Next you'll design a master for the switchboards that will be created in the database. To do this, you will copy and rename the zsfrmMaster form and then modify it for use with switchboards.

To create the switchboard master:

1. Make sure that Access is running, that the **Movie4** database from the Tutorial.04 folder on your local or network drive is open, and that **Forms** is selected on the Objects bar of the Database window. Right-click the **zsfrmMaster** form in the Database window, and then click **Copy** on the shortcut menu.

2. Right-click below the last form listed in the Database window, and then click **Paste** on the shortcut menu.

3. In the Paste As dialog box, type **zsfrmMasterSwitchboard**, and then press the **Enter** key. The new form master is displayed in the Database window.

4. Open the **zsfrmMasterSwitchboard** form in Design view.

5. Click the image box containing the logo to select it, hold down the **Shift** key, and then click the **MovieCam Technologies** label to select both controls.

6. Click the **Cut** button ✂ on the Form Design toolbar, and then click anywhere in the **Detail** section of the form.

7. Click the **Paste** button 📋 on the Form Design toolbar to paste the two controls into the Detail section.

8. Click **View** on the menu bar, and then click **Form Header/Footer** to remove the header and footer sections from the form. You will not need header and footer sections in the switchboard forms.

9. Save your changes.

The form properties for switchboard forms differ somewhat from those for other forms in a database. You and Carolyn will now adjust the property settings in the switchboard master.

To change form properties of the zsfrmMasterSwitchboard:

1. If necessary, click the form selector (the box in the corner of the form where the two rulers meet).

2. Click the **Properties** button 🗐 on the Form Design toolbar to open the property sheet. If necessary, click the **All** tab.

3. Change the Scroll Bars property to **Neither** because the switchboards will be designed so that all controls fit on the screen and scrolling will not be necessary.

4. Change the Navigation Buttons property to **No**. Switchboards have no underlying records to navigate through.

5. Change the Auto Center property to **Yes** so that open switchboards will be centered on the screen.

6. Change the Border Style property to **Dialog** so that users cannot change the size of the form.

7. Change the Control Box property to **No** to remove the control box from the upper-left corner of the window.

8. Change the Min Max Buttons property to **None** so that the user cannot minimize or maximize the form.

9. Finally, change the Close Button property to **No**. You and Carolyn will design the switchboards so that users can navigate only where you want them to go. Eliminating the buttons for closing or minimizing the switchboards gives you more control of the database areas to which users have access.

10. Close the property sheet, and then switch to Form view. Your form should look like that shown in Figure 4-20. If it does not, switch to Design view and size the form so it looks similar to the form shown in Figure 4-20.

Figure 4-20	COMPLETED ZSFRMMASTERSWITCHBOARD

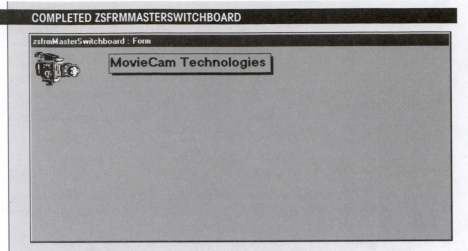

11. Click **File** on the menu bar, click **Close** to close the form, and click **Yes** to save your changes.

You and Carolyn are planning three switchboards for the MovieCam Technologies database. You will create a main switchboard that opens when a user opens the database, a switchboard for data entry forms, and another for reports.

You'll create the data entry forms switchboard first. This switchboard will contain the company logo and company name, and an option group with buttons to open each data entry form.

To create the data entry forms switchboard:

1. Right-click the **zsfrmMasterSwitchboard** form in the Database window, and then click **Copy** on the shortcut menu.

2. Right-click an empty area of the Database window, and then click **Paste** on the shortcut menu.

3. In the Paste As dialog box, type **frmDataSwitchboard** in the Form Name text box, and then press the **Enter** key.

4. Open the **frmDataSwitchboard** form in Design view and, if necessary, open the toolbox.

You can manually create an option group and the option buttons in it, but it is much simpler to use the Option Group Wizard. The wizard automatically assigns numbers to each button in the group and then prompts you for the names of each item in the group. The Wizard also prompts you for a default button, the style of the option group, and the option group's caption.

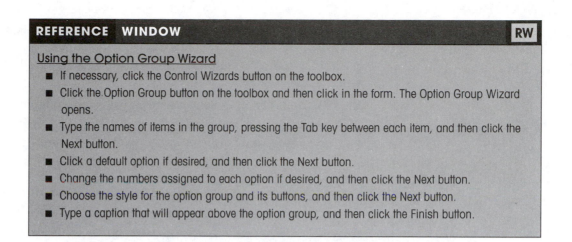

You will add an option group to the switchboard. The buttons, or options, in the option group will represent the data entry forms in the database.

1. If necessary, click the **Control Wizards** button on the toolbox to select it, and then click the **Option Group** button on the toolbox.

2. Click and drag to draw a form box that is approximately 2" tall and 2" wide. The Option Group Wizard dialog box opens, and you are instructed to enter the labels, or names, for each option in the option group.

3. Type the label names as shown in Figure 4-21. Each label represents the name of a data entry form in the database. After you type a label name, be sure to press the **Tab** key and *not* the Enter key. After you have entered all the label names, click the **Next** button. The next dialog box asks if you want the option group to show one choice as the default.

Figure 4-21   ADDING LABELS (FORM NAMES) FOR EACH OPTION

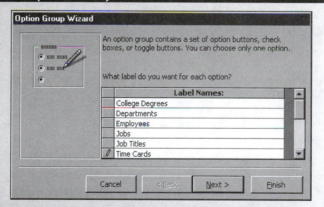

4. Click the **No, I don't want a default** option button, and then click the **Next** button. The next dialog box shows the numbers the wizard will assign to each choice in the option group. When the user clicks a button in the group, the value of the option group itself becomes the number that corresponds to the option button selected by the user. This allows you to test the value of the option group in a macro and then open the appropriate form.

5. Click the **Next** button to accept the numbers the wizard assigned to each option and continue. The next dialog box lists several style options. You accept the default etched option buttons selection, which is the standard Windows style for option groups.

6. Click the **Next** button to continue. In this last dialog box, you enter the caption, or heading, that you want to appear above the option group on the form.

7. Type **Data Entry Forms** and then click the **Finish** button.

Next you will enhance the appearance of the option group.

To move controls on a form:

1. Drag the bottom border of the form down so that it is approximately 4" in height.

2. Position the pointer on the lower-center handle of the option group frame, and click and drag down approximately ½", as shown in Figure 4-22.

| Figure 4-22 | SIZING THE OPTION GROUP FRAME |

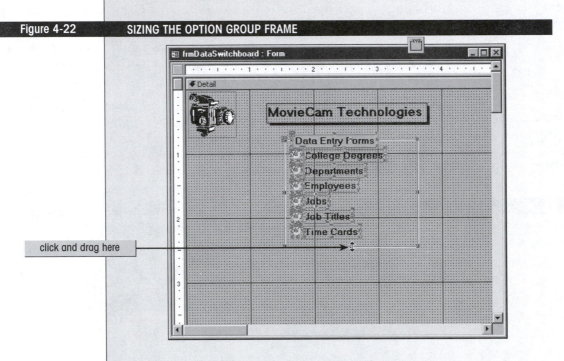

3. Drag around the option group, its label and contents to select them all and then drag down so that the top border of the label Data Entry Forms is approximately even with the 1" mark on the vertical ruler bar. See Figure 4-23. Click a blank area of the form to deselect the option group.

4. Drag around all the options in the option group, except College Degrees, to select them. (See Figure 4-23.)

Figure 4-23   SELECTING AND MOVING OPTION BUTTONS

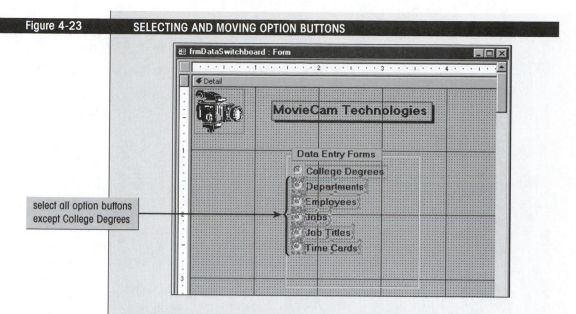

select all option buttons
except College Degrees

5. Hold down the **Ctrl** key and press ↓ five times. This moves down the selected options in slight increments.

6. Drag around all the options in the option group, except College Degrees and Departments, to select them, hold down the **Ctrl** key, and press ↓ five times.

7. Drag around the **Jobs**, **Job Titles**, and **Time Cards** options, hold down the **Ctrl** key, and press ↓ five times.

8. Repeat this process to insert the same amount of space between the remaining options in the option group.

9. Click the **Data Entry Forms** label, position the pointer on the upper-left corner handle until it has a  shape, and then click and drag to move the label above the option group. Size the label to the width of the option group frame, and click the **Center** button on the Formatting toolbar. Your screen should look similar to Figure 4-24.

Figure 4-24   MODIFYING THE OPTION GROUP LABEL

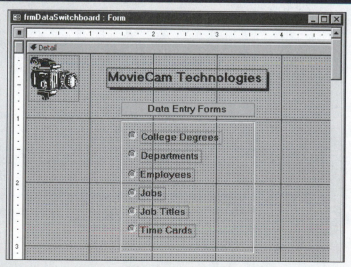

10. Select the option group frame, click the **Properties** button 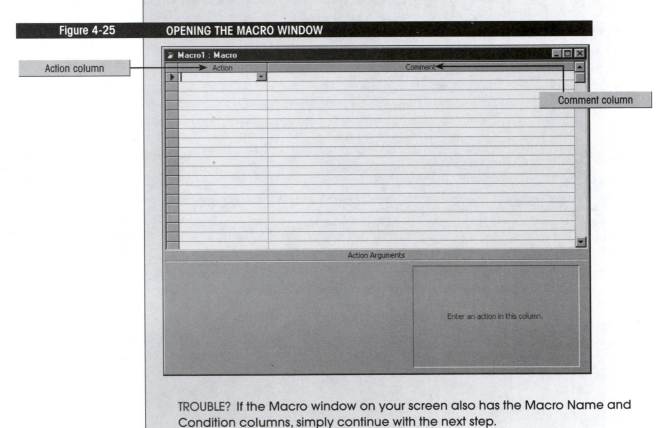 on the Form Design toolbar, and then change the Name property to **grpForms**.

11. Save your changes, close the property sheet, and then close the form.

You and Carolyn now turn your attention to creating the macro that will open each form listed in the option group.

Working with Macros

A **macro** is a command or series of commands that you want Access to perform automatically for you. In Access, these commands are called **actions**. Some common actions you might want a macro to perform are opening a form, closing a form, exiting the database, finding a record, and so forth. The goal of macro programming is to duplicate those steps you take when you work interactively with the database, so that you don't have to repeatedly execute the steps.

You and Carolyn decide to explore the macro window and brush up on macro concepts.

To explore the Macro window:

1. Click **Macros** on the Objects bar of the Database window and then click the **New** button. The Macro window opens, as shown in Figure 4-25.

Figure 4-25   OPENING THE MACRO WINDOW

Action column →

Comment column

Macro1 : Macro

Action	Comment

Action Arguments

Enter an action in this column.

TROUBLE? If the Macro window on your screen also has the Macro Name and Condition columns, simply continue with the next step.

In its default setting, the Macro window consists of the Action and Comment columns. You also want to display the Macro Name and Condition columns.

2. Click the **Macro Name** button ⊞ on the Macro Design toolbar to add the Macro Name column to the Macro window.

3. Click the **Conditions** button ⊡ on the Macro Design toolbar to add the Condition column to the Macro window.

In the **Condition** column, you enter conditional expressions, which determine if an action will be carried out when the macro is run. If you want to create more than one macro in the Macro window, you enter the names of the individual macros in the **Macro Name** column. You can then organize the individual macros into a group. That group name is displayed in the Database window when Macros is selected on the Objects bar.

Naming Macros and Macro Groups

You and Carolyn will organize the macros you create for the frmDataSwitchboard form in a macro group. You have applied a naming convention to the objects with which you've worked so far in the database, and you also need to develop a standard naming convention for macros and macro groups.

You decide to name an individual macro according to the name of the object that initiates the macro, followed by the object's event property. Event properties are discussed in more detail below. For example, if the click event of a command button named cmdNext executes a macro, the name of the macro should be cmdNext_Click.

You decide to name a macro group with the same name as the form with which it is associated, preceded by the letter m. The macro group that contains the macros for the frmDataSwitchboard form would be named mfrmDataSwitchboard. It is common to use the name mcrGlobal for a group of generic macros to be used on many different forms or reports.

Before you start designing macros, however, it's important that you understand event properties.

Events

Events are actions that are recognized by an object and for which you can define a response. Some events are the result of an action that the user takes; others are related to the retrieval or updating of data. Events include button clicks, opening a form, closing a form, keystrokes in text boxes, record updates, and more. Each event has an associated **event property** that specifies how an object responds when the event occurs. These event properties are listed in the property sheet for forms, reports, form and report sections, and form and report controls. Tables and queries do not have event properties. You can specify a macro name (or the name of a VBA procedure, which is discussed later in this tutorial) in the event property of an object, and that macro or procedure runs when the event occurs. The use of event properties to run macros or to execute VBA code is called **event-driven programming**. (Event properties will be discussed in greater detail in Tutorial 6.)

Creating Macros

You and Carolyn are ready to begin writing the macro for the option group you created on the frmDataSwitchboard form. The macro will test the value of the option group grpForms to determine which option button was selected, and then, based on that value, open the form that corresponds to the button. You will use the OpenForm action in this macro and you will provide this action's required argument, which is Form Name. The arguments for the OpenForm action are summarized following:

- The **Form Name** argument is a required argument for the OpenForm action, and is the name of the form to open.

- The **View** argument lets you specify Form, Design, Print Preview, or Datasheet view when you open the form.

- The **Filter Name** argument lets you specify the name of a filter you save as a query to filter the records that open in the form.

- The **Where Condition** argument lets you type a SQL statement that filters the records that open in the form. Remember that a query is expressed as a statement in SQL.

- The **Data Mode** argument lets you specify that the form will accept only new records (Add), that the form is Read Only, or the default is Edit, and allows you to enter, edit, and delete records. These settings correspond to the form properties Allow Edits, Allow Deletions, Allow Additions, and Data Entry. Add is the same as changing the Data Entry property to Yes. Read Only is the same as changing Allow Edits, Allow Deletions, and Allow Additions to No.

- The **Window Mode** lets you set the form so that it is Minimized, Hidden (it isn't visible even though it is open), or Dialog—which sets the Modal and Pop Up properties to Yes. Modal means that other windows in Access are disabled until the form is closed. Pop Up means that the form stays on top of other open windows, and the toolbars and menus are disabled until the form is closed. The default is Normal, which means the form opens as it normally would from the Database window if the properties haven't been changed.

To create a macro:

1. Click the **Macro Name** text box in the first row, type **grpForms_AfterUpdate**, and then press **Tab** to move to the Condition column. The macro name indicates that you are using the AfterUpdate event property of the grpForms option group to execute the macro. The AfterUpdate event property sets the macro to execute *after* the user chooses an option from the group. As you recall, the grpForms option group contains a value based on the option selected by the user. Therefore, you are allowed to test what that value is and then open the appropriate form.

2. Type **grpForms=1** in the **Condition** text box, and then press the **Tab** key to move to the Action column. Access will add the square brackets around grpForms automatically so it is not necessary to type them. This expression tests to see if the value of the grpForms option group is equal to 1. If it is, you want to open the frmDegrees form. When you want to repeat the condition for the next action so that it is also executed conditionally, you don't have to retype the condition. Simply type **...** to represent the same condition.

3. Click the **Action** list arrow, scroll through the list, click **OpenForm**, and press the **Tab** key. Type **Open frmDegrees form** to document the macro action as shown in Figure 4-26, and then press the **F6** key to move to the Action Arguments section of the Macro window. The arguments are additional information that might or might not be needed to complete the macro action. The description of the selected argument is shown in the right portion of the Action Arguments section.

Figure 4-26	CREATING A MACRO

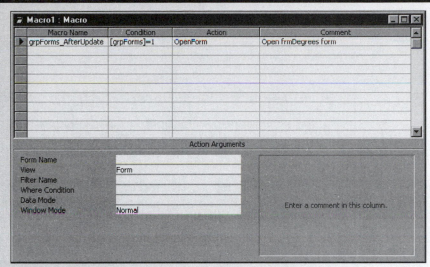

4. Click the **Form Name** list arrow, and then click **frmDegrees**.

5. Click the **Condition** text box in the second row, type **grpForms=2**, press the **Tab** key, and click the **Action** list arrow. Click **OpenForm**, press the **Tab** key, and then type **Open frmDepartments form**.

6. In the Action Arguments section, click the **Form Name** text box, click the **list arrow**, and then click **frmDepartments**.

7. Click the **Condition** text box in the third row, type **grpForms=3**, press the **Tab** key, click the **Action** list arrow, and click **OpenForm**. Press the **Tab** key, type **Open frmEmployees form**, press **F6**, click the **Form Name** list arrow, and then click **frmEmployees**.

8. Save the macro as **mfrmDataSwitchboard**.

9. Create macro actions just like those you created in Steps 1–4 for opening the frmJobs, frmJobTitles, and frmTimeCards forms. Use Figure 4-27 as a guide for entering the conditions, actions, and comments for the three macro actions.

Figure 4-27	CREATING MACROS FOR THE OPTION GROUP

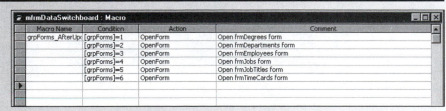

10. Click the next **Action** text box, click its list arrow, and then click **SetValue**.

11. In the Action Arguments section, click the **Item** text box, type **grpForms**, press the **Tab** key, and then type **Null** in the Expression text box. This macro action and its arguments set the value of the option group back to null after the form is opened. Then when you return to the switchboard to select another form, the option group will be ready.

12. Save your changes and close the Macro window.

Next you will open the frmDataSwitchboard form and set the AfterEvent property of the grpForms option group to execute the macro you created.

To set the AfterUpdate property of the grpForms option group:

1. Open the **frmDataSwitchboard** form in Design view.

2. Click the **grpForms** option group frame, and click the **Properties** button 🔲 on the Form Design toolbar.

3. Click the **Event** tab on the property sheet, click the **After Update** text box, click its list arrow, and then click **mfrmDataSwitchboard.grpForms_AfterUpdate**. This is the name of the macro group separated from the name of the macro by a . (period).

4. Select the form by clicking the form selector, click the **All** tab on the property sheet, and then type **Forms Switchboard** in the Caption text box.

5. Resize the form so it is 5" wide, and then resize the form window so it is the same size as the form (see Figure 4-28).

Figure 4-28	FINE-TUNING THE DESIGN OF THE FRMDATASWITCHBOARD FORM

6. Close the form and save the changes.

7. Open the form in Form view. It should look like the form shown in Figure 4-29. Click the **College Degrees** option button to test the macro. The College Degrees data entry form should open in Form view. Close the form to return to the switchboard.

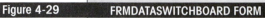

| Figure 4-29 | FRMDATASWITCHBOARD FORM |

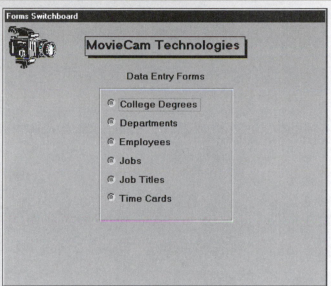

8. Open each form from the switchboard, and then close each form.

9. Close the frmDataSwitchboard form to return to the Database window.

You can change the default settings of the Macro window so that the Condition and Macro Name columns are included by default in each new macro you create. This is helpful if you plan to store your macros in groups, or when you want to test a condition before you execute it.

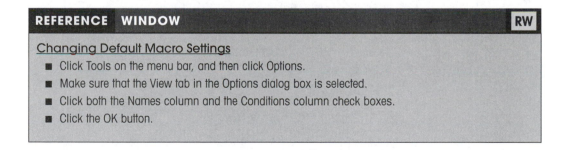

REFERENCE WINDOW   RW

Changing Default Macro Settings
- Click Tools on the menu bar, and then click Options.
- Make sure that the View tab in the Options dialog box is selected.
- Click both the Names column and the Conditions column check boxes.
- Click the OK button.

Next you will change the default options for the Macro window.

To change macro design default options:

1. In the Database window, click **Tools** on the menu bar, and then click **Options**.

2. Make sure that the **View** tab in the Options dialog box is selected.

3. Click the **Names column** check box and the **Conditions column** check box, as shown in Figure 4-30.

| Figure 4-30 | CHANGING MACRO DESIGN DEFAULT OPTIONS |

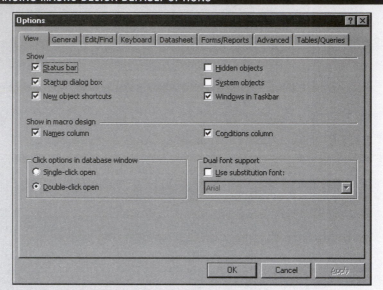

4. Click the **OK** button to return to the Database window.

Because switchboards do not have a Close button in the upper-right corner, you and Carolyn want to add a command button that users can click to close the frmDataSwitchboard form. You now will create that macro as part of a new macro group, and then assign that macro to the On Click Event property of the new button.

This macro can be used on all the forms, so you will save it in a macro group named mcrGlobal. You will use the Macro Builder to create this macro.

To create a macro to close objects:

1. Open the **frmDataSwitchboard** form in Design view and, if necessary, display the toolbox.

2. Click the **Control Wizards** button on the toolbox to *deselect* it.

3. If necessary, enlarge the Detail section to make room for the button, click the **Command Button** button on the toolbox, and then click once below the option group to insert a command button control as shown in Figure 4-31.

Figure 4-31   **CREATING THE COMMAND BUTTON**

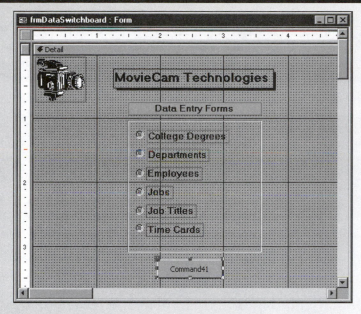

4. If necessary, click the **Properties** button 🖹 on the Form Design toolbar, and then click the **Event** tab on the property sheet.

5. Click the **On Click** text box, and then click its **Build** button ⋯ as shown in Figure 4-32.

TROUBLE? If the Visual Basic window opens automatically when you click the Build button, it is because the Always use event procedures option is checked in the Options dialog box. To disable this, click Tools on the menu bar, click the Forms/Reports tab, and then deselect the Always use event procedures option.

Figure 4-32   **OPENING THE MACRO BUILDER**

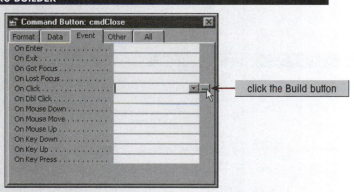

6. Click **Macro Builder** in the Choose Builder dialog box, and then click the **OK** button

7. In the Save As dialog box, type **mcrGlobal** and then click the **OK** button.

8. Type **cmdClose_Click** in the Macro Name text box, press the **Tab** key twice, click the **Action** list arrow, click **Close**, press the **Tab** key, and then type **Close the active window**. The button used to execute this macro will be named cmdClose in any form in which it is used and the event property will always be On Click. The caption of the button, what the user sees, will display Close.

9. Save your changes and close the macro to return to the frmDataSwitchboard form.

Lastly, you'll add some finishing touches to the frmDataSwitchboard form. To make the form easier to work with, you will add a caption and a ScreenTip to the command button. The caption is what the user will see on the button in Form view and the ScreenTip will display when the user points to the button with the mouse.

To complete the frmDataSwitchboard form:

1. If necessary, click the **command button** control to select it, and then click the **Properties** button 🖹 on the Form Design toolbar.

2. Click the **All** tab, change the Name property to **cmdClose**, and change the Caption property to **&Close**. The ampersand (&) indicates that the letter C will be underscored on the button, so the user can press Alt+C on the keyboard to execute the action, and not have to click the button. This is referred to as a **keyboard shortcut**. If you want the ampersand character to be visible in a label or a text box, you must type && (two ampersands). Otherwise, the only thing visible is the underscored character.

3. Click the **Other** tab on the property sheet, click the **ControlTip Text** text box, and then type **Return to Main Switchboard**. You will create the Main Switchboard in Tutorial 10, and it will be designed so you can open the frmDataSwitchboard form from it.

4. Click the **option group** frame to display its properties in the dialog box, click in the **ControlTip Text** text box, type **Select a data entry form**, as shown in Figure 4-33, and then close the property sheet. Now you'll test the form.

| Figure 4-33 | SETTING THE CONTROLTIP TEXT PROPERTY FOR THE OPTION GROUP |

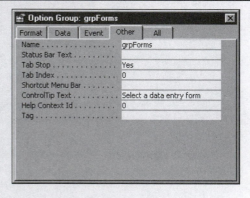

5. Save your changes, and then switch to Form view.

6. Position the pointer on the center of the option group so that the ScreenTip text is visible.

7. Position the pointer on the **Close** command button to test it.

8. Press **Alt+C** to close the form.

9. Open the form again and then click the **Close** command button to return to the Database window.

Next you and Carolyn will add command buttons to the data entry forms. The standard record navigation buttons in Access forms do not allow for keyboard shortcuts. However, you can design custom buttons that are associated with keyboard shortcuts for navigating records in a form.

To add command buttons for record navigation:

1. Open the **frmTimeCards** form in Design view, open the toolbox if necessary, make sure the Control Wizards button is deselected, and then make sure the form's Form Footer section is visible.

2. Click the **Command Button** button on the toolbox, and click in the far-left side of the Form Footer section.

3. Click **Edit** on the menu bar and then click **Duplicate**. Another command button is now visible below the first button.

4. Click and drag the second command button to the right of the first, as shown in Figure 4-34.

Figure 4-34   CREATING COMMAND BUTTONS

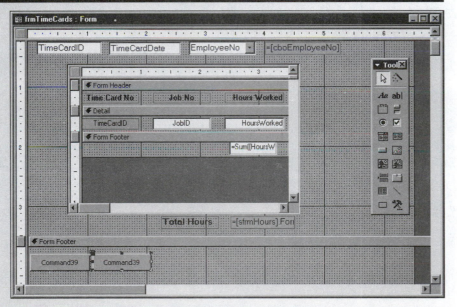

5. With the second command button selected, click **Edit** on the menu bar, and then click **Duplicate**. A third command button appears to the right of the second button.

6. Open the property sheet for the command button at the far left, change the Name property to **cmdFirst**, the Caption property to **&First**, and then click the **second command button**. If necessary, reposition the properties dialog box so that you can see all three command buttons.

7. Change the Name property to **cmdPrevious**, and the Caption property to **&Previous**.

8. Click the **third command button** and change the Name property to **cmdNext**, and the Caption property to **&Next**. You'll create and test the macros for these three buttons before completing them.

9. Save your changes, close the property sheet, and close the form.

Next you'll write the macros for the first two record navigation buttons in the mcrGlobal macro. Then you will return to the form and assign the macros to their event properties.

To create the macros for form record navigation buttons:

1. Open the **mcrGlobal** macro in Design view, and then click the third row of the **Macro Name** column. (It's easier to read the macro group if you leave a blank row between macros.)

2. Type **cmdFirst_Click**, press the **Tab** key twice, click the **Action** list arrow, scroll down, click **GoToRecord**, press the **Tab** key, and then type **Go to first record**. For a thorough explanation of each Action Argument, click in the Action Argument text box and press the **F1** key. A brief description is displayed in the Action Arguments pane.

3. In the Action Arguments section, click the **Record** text box, click its list arrow, and then click **First**.

4. Click the fifth row of the **Macro Name** column, type **cmdPrevious_Click**, press the **Tab** key twice, click the **Action** list arrow, click **GoToRecord**, press the **Tab** key, and then type **Go to previous record**.

5. In the Action Arguments section, click the **Record** text box, click its list arrow, and then click **Previous**.

6. Click the seventh row of the **Macro Name** column, type **cmdNext_Click**, press the **Tab** key twice, click the **Action list arrow**, click **GoToRecord**, press the **Tab** key, and then type **Go to next record**. In the Action Arguments section, the Record text box contains Next by default, so you will not change it.

7. Save your changes, and then close the macro.

Next you will assign the macros to the command buttons on the frmTimeCards form. You also will test the macros.

To assign macros to command buttons:

1. Open the **frmTimeCards** form in Design view.

2. Open the property sheet for the button labeled First, click the **Event** tab, click the **On Click** text box, click its list arrow, and then click **mcrGlobal.cmdFirst_Click**. Leave the property sheet open, and make sure it is positioned so you can see all three command buttons.

3. Click the button labeled **Previous**, and then set the **On Click** property to **mcrGlobal.cmdPrevious_Click**.

4. Click the button labeled **Next**, and then set the **On Click** property to **mcrGlobal.cmdNext_Click**.

5. Close the property sheet, and then switch to Form view to test the buttons. Click the **Next** button twice to move forward two records.

6. Click the **First** button. The first record is now visible. Click the **Previous** button. You will receive an error message because there is no record previous to the first record.

7. Click the **OK** button. You will see an Action Failed dialog box like that shown in Figure 4-35.

Figure 4-35	**ACTION FAILED DIALOG BOX**

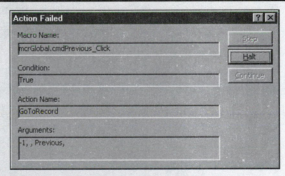

8. Click the **Halt** button to return to the form.

Using the Command Button Wizard

You and Carolyn are concerned that database users will panic if they see an Action Failed dialog box like the one shown in Figure 4-35. Carolyn suggests replacing the command buttons with those you can create using the Command Button Wizard. The Command Button Wizard uses VBA error-trapping code to ward off failure and error messages such as that in the Action Failed dialog box.

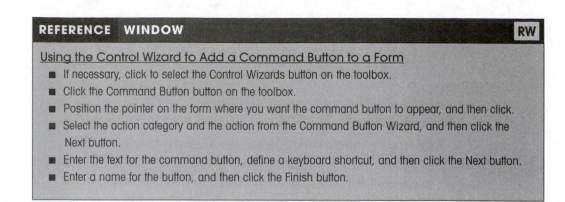

REFERENCE WINDOW **RW**

Using the Control Wizard to Add a Command Button to a Form
- If necessary, click to select the Control Wizards button on the toolbox.
- Click the Command Button button on the toolbox.
- Position the pointer on the form where you want the command button to appear, and then click.
- Select the action category and the action from the Command Button Wizard, and then click the Next button.
- Enter the text for the command button, define a keyboard shortcut, and then click the Next button.
- Enter a name for the button, and then click the Finish button.

Next you'll create buttons using the Command Button Wizard.

To use the Command Button Wizard:

1. Switch to Design view, click the **First** button in the Form Footer, and press the **Delete** key.

2. If necessary, click the **Control Wizards** button on the toolbox to select it, and then click the **Command Button** button on the toolbox.

3. Click the far-left area of the **Form Footer** section to start the Command Button Wizard. The first dialog box of the Wizard offers a choice of categories of actions you want the button to perform. The dialog box also lists the actions in each category.

4. Make sure that **Record Navigation** is selected in the Categories list box, click **Goto First Record** in the Actions list box as shown in Figure 4-36, and then click the **Next** button.

Figure 4-36 • **COMMAND BUTTON WIZARD**

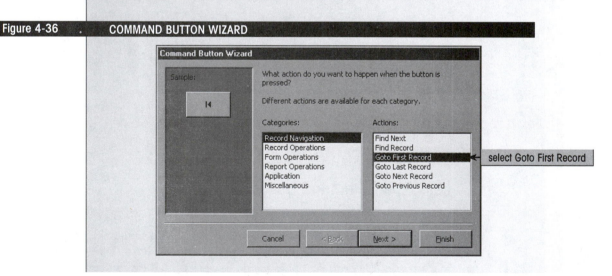

The next dialog box gives you the choice of using a text caption or a picture on the button. You'll use text so that you can incorporate keyboard shortcuts.

5. Click the **Text** option button, type **&First** in the Text text box as shown in Figure 4-37, and then click the **Next** button.

Figure 4-37   **ASSIGNING TEXT TO THE BUTTON**

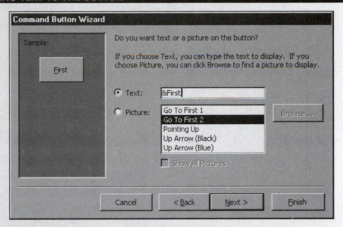

The next dialog box prompts you for a name for the button. You will use the same naming convention you used when you created the buttons manually.

6. Type **cmdFirst** to name the button, and then click the **Finish** button.

7. Click the **Previous** button and press the **Delete** key, click the **Command Button** button on the toolbox, and then click in the form to the right of the **First** button.

8. Click **Goto Previous Record** in the Actions list box, click the **Next** button, type **&Previous** in the Text text box, click the **Next** button, type **cmdPrevious** to name the button, and then click the **Finish** button.

9. Click the **Next** button in the Form Footer section, hold down the **Shift** key, click the **First** button, and then click the **Previous** button to select all three buttons.

10. Right-click one of the buttons, point to **Size**, click **To Widest**, right-click one of the buttons, point to **Size**, click **To Tallest**, right-click one of the buttons, point to **Align**, and then click **Top**. If necessary, move the buttons so they don't overlap.

Next you'll test the buttons to see how errors are handled.

To test record navigation command buttons:

1. Switch to Form view, click the **Next** button twice to move forward two records, and then click the **Previous** button once so that record 2 is visible.

2. Click the **First** button to move to the first record in the form, and then click the **Previous** button. You will see an error message that advises that you can't go to the desired record.

3. Click the **OK** button. (This error message is less alarming than the Action Failed dialog box that the macro displayed in a previous set of steps.) You and Carolyn decide to complete the buttons using the Command Button Wizard.

4. Switch to Design view and delete the **Next** button on the form.

5. Click the **Command Button** button on the toolbox, click to the right of the **Previous** button, click **Goto Next Record** in the Actions list box, and click the **Next** button. Click the **Text** option, type **&Next** in the Text text box, click the **Next** button, type **cmdNext** to name the button, and then click the **Finish** button.

6. Click the **Command Button** button on the toolbox, click to the right of the **Next** button, click **Goto Last Record** in the Actions list box, click the **Next** button, and click the **Text** option. Type **&Last** in the Text text box, click the **Next** button, type **cmdLast** to name the button, and then click the **Finish** button.

7. Click the **Command Button** button on the toolbox, click to the right of the **Last** button, click **Record Operations** in the Categories list box, and make sure that **Add New Record** in the **Actions** list box is selected. Click the **Next** button, click the **Text** option, type **Ne&w** in the Text text box, click the **Next** button, type **cmdNew** to name the button, and then click the **Finish** button.

The ampersand is placed in front of the w on the New button because you have already used the keyboard shortcut Alt+N on this form. Only one particular combination on a given form will work. If two buttons both used the same keystroke combinations for a shortcut, the first one in the tab order would execute and no error message would display.

8. Size and align the buttons so they look like those shown in Figure 4-38.

Figure 4-38	COMPLETED COMMAND BUTTONS

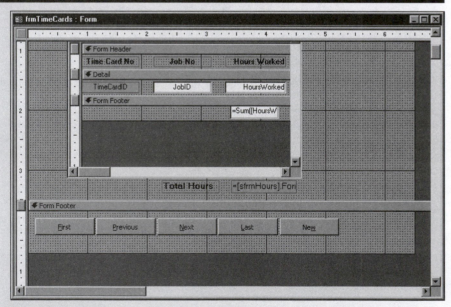

9. Save your changes and switch to Form view to test the buttons. Click each button to be sure that it works properly.

Comparing Macros to VBA

You and Carolyn want to learn more about the VBA code used by the Command Button Wizard to create the buttons.

To examine VBA code:

1. Switch to Design view, and then click the **Properties** button 🔲 on the Form Design toolbar.

2. Click the **First** button in the Form Footer section, click the **Event** tab in the properties dialog box, click in the **On Click** property text box, and then click the **Build** button ⌐. The Visual Basic window opens, as shown in Figure 4-39.

   TROUBLE? If other windows such as the Immediate window appear in your Visual Basic window, click the Close button ☒ to close them.

| Figure 4-39 | EXAMINING CODE FOR THE FIRST COMMAND BUTTON |

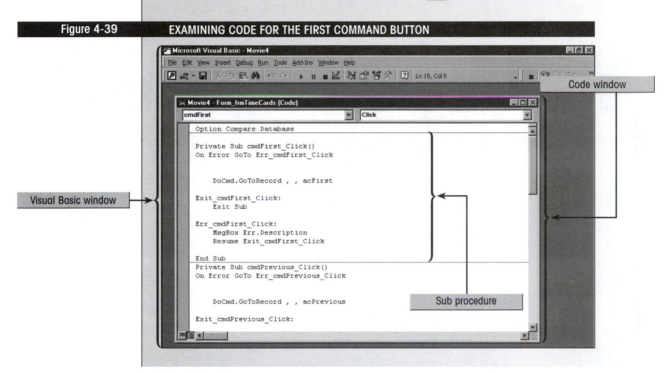

The event procedure that automates the First button is shown in the Visual Basic window. An **event procedure** is a group of statements that execute when an event occurs, and is part of a larger category of procedures called **sub procedures**. You create, modify, and display VBA code in the Code window, which is contained in the Visual Basic window. (The Code window and related terms will be discussed in greater detail in Tutorial 6.)

Compare the procedure in the Code window to the macro that you created earlier to automate the First button. The group of statements that make up a procedure are somewhat similar to the actions that make up a macro. This particular procedure includes a statement that reads:

```
DoCmd.GoToRecord , , acFirst
```

The DoCmd.GoToRecord statement corresponds to the GoToRecord macro action. The commas in this statement represent the position of optional arguments. The first argument is blank, the second argument is blank, and the third argument is acFirst. The acFirst argument is a constant, and represents the first record in the form. Figure 4-40 displays the macro you created earlier and its arguments. Note in the Action Arguments section that the first two arguments are blank and the third is First.

Figure 4-40   MCRGLOBAL MACRO

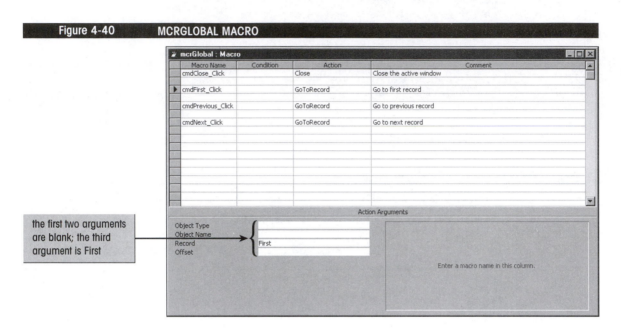

the first two arguments are blank; the third argument is First

The procedure contains other statements. However, the DoCmd statement is the one that automates the button. Some standard error-trapping code is included. It specifies that if an error occurs, you will see a message box containing the description of the error, and the procedure will be exited.

The procedure contains an opening statement called a Sub statement and a closing statement called an End Sub statement. The procedure is separated from other procedures in the Code window by a horizontal line. The End Sub statement simply ends the procedure. The opening statement of Private Sub cmdFirst_Click() indicates with the word Private that the procedure is available only to this form. The cmdFirst_Click code follows the same naming convention that you used to name macros, where cmdFirst is the name of the button, and Click is the event property that executes the procedure. The opening and closing parentheses enclose argument(s) that could be supplied to the procedure.

To close the Visual Basic window and the form:

1. Click **File** on the menu bar, and then click **Close and Return to Microsoft Access** to close the Visual Basic window.

2. Close the property sheet.

3. Close the form. If prompted to save your changes, click the **No** button.

4. Close the **Movie4** database and exit Access.

You, Carolyn, and Amanda are pleased with the frmDataEntrySwitchboard form and the command buttons on the frmTimeCards form. Your next challenge is to design reports and complete the remaining switchboards.

Session 4.2 QUICK CHECK

1. A(n) _____ is an instruction or sequence of instructions that is carried out as a unit.

2. _____ are actions that are recognized by an object and for which you can define a response.

3. What is the purpose of the Condition column in the Macro window?

4. What is a macro group?

5. Which character precedes a letter on a command button to create a keyboard shortcut?

6. A(n) _____ is a group of statements that execute when an event occurs.

7. You create, modify, and display VBA code in the _____ window.

REVIEW ASSIGNMENTS

Create a form template, a switchboard, and macros in the Hours4 database, which is similar to the MovieCam Technologies database you worked on in this tutorial.

1. Start Access and open the **Hours4** database located in the Tutorial.04 folder on your local or network drive.

2. Make sure Forms is selected on the Objects bar of the Database window, and double-click Create form in Design view.

3. Click View on the menu bar, and then click Form Header/Footer.

4. Size the form so it is 6½" wide, the Form Header section so that it is ½" tall, the Detail section so that it is 3" tall, and the Form Footer section so that it is ½" tall.

5. Open the form's property sheet, change the Record Selectors property to No, the Dividing Lines property to No, and the Auto Center property to Yes.

6. If necessary, make the toolbox visible, click the Label button on the toolbox, and in the label properties dialog box, change the Font Size property to 9, and the Font Weight property to Medium.

7. Click the Text Box button on the toolbox, and in its properties dialog box change the Font Size property to 9, the Label X property to -0.25, the Text Align and Label Align properties to Right, and the Add Colon property to No.

8. Save the form as "zsfrmTemplate" and close it. Click Tools on the menu bar, click Options, click the Forms/Reports tab, replace Normal with "zsfrmTemplate", and then click the OK button.

9. Create an unbound form in Design view. Save it as **frmMainSwitchboard**.

10. Open the form's property sheet, change the Caption property to "Main Switchboard", the Navigation Buttons property to No, the Min Max Buttons property to None, the Close Button property to No, and the Border Style property to Dialog.

11. Make sure that the Control Wizards button on the toolbox is selected, click the Option Group button on the toolbox, and then click to create an option group on the form.

12. Type "Department Data Entry", "Employee Data Entry", "Job Title Data Entry", and "Close" as the Label Names. Be sure to press the Tab key between each label name entry, and then click the Next button. Click No, I don't want a default, and then click the Next button three times to accept the default choices in the next two dialog boxes.

13. Type "Select from the following options:" as the caption for the option group, and then click the Finish button.

14. Size the option group, and position the buttons and labels so that none overlap and they are easy to read.

15. Display the properties of the option group, change the Name property to "grpOptions", click the Event tab in the properties dialog box, click the Build button in the After Update property text box, click Macro Builder, click OK and save the macro as **mfrmMainSwitchboard**.

16. Click the first row of the Macro Name column, type "grpOptions_AfterUpdate", press the Tab key to move to the Condition column, type "grpOptions=1", press the Tab key, click in the Action text box and click its list arrow. Click OpenForm, press Tab, type "Open frmDepartments form", click the list arrow in the Form Name text box in the Action Arguments section, and then click frmDepartments.

17. Repeat this process to create the macro action to open the frmEmployees form and the frmJobTitles form.

18. In the fourth row of the Condition column, type "grpOptions=4", select Close as the Macro Action, and type "Close frmMainSwitchboard" in the Comment column.

19. In the fifth row of the Action column, select SetValue as the macro action, type "Set the option group to null" in the Comment column, set the Item Action Argument to grpOptions, and set the Expression Action Argument to Null.

20. Save the changes, close the macro, and test the option group.

Explore 21. Create a button below the option group using the Command Button Wizard, that closes the database and exits Access.

22. Click Tools on the menu bar, click Analyze, and then click Documenter. Click the Macros tab, click the mfmMainSwitchboard macro, click the Options button, make sure that only the Actions and Arguments option is checked, and then click the OK button. Click the OK button and then print the report.

23. Save and close the form.

24. Close the **Hours4** database and exit Access.

CASE PROBLEMS

Case 1. Edwards and Company   Jack Edwards has asked you to replace the navigation buttons in the frmClients form with command buttons that include keyboard shortcuts. He also wants a command button to close the form and a command button to delete a record. Complete the following:

1. Start Access and open the **Edward4** database located in the Tutorial.04 folder on your local or network drive.

2. Select Forms on the Objects bar, and open the **frmClients** form in Design view.

3. Make sure that the toolbox is open and that the Control Wizards button on the toolbox is selected, click the Command Button button on the toolbox, and then click in the far-left area of the Form Footer section to create a command button.

4. Make sure that Record Navigation is selected in the Categories list box of the Command Button Wizard, click Goto First Record in the Actions list box, and then click the Next button.

5. Click the Text option, type "&First" in the Text text box, and then click the Next button. Type "cmdFirst" to name the button, and then click the Finish button.

6. Repeat Steps 4 and 5 to create a button labeled "&Previous" and named "cmdPrevious", one labeled "&Next" and named "cmdNext", one labeled "&Last" and named "cmdLast", and one from the Record Operations category labeled "Ne&w" and named "cmdNew".

7. Size the buttons to approximately 1" wide and ¼" tall. Align them and be sure that they don't overlap.

Explore 8. Add a command button that uses the wizard to close the form. Add another command button to delete a record. The Close Form action is in the Form Operations category, and the Delete Record action is in the Record Operations category.

9. Open the form's property sheet, change the Navigation Buttons property to No, the Auto Center property to Yes, the Modal and Pop Up properties to Yes, and the Border Style to Dialog.

Explore 10. Click the Code button on the toolbar to open the Visual Basic window, click File on the menu bar in the Visual Basic window, and then click Print to print your code.

11. Switch to Form view and test your changes.

12. Save your changes and close the form.

13. Close the **Edward4** database and exit Access.

Case 2. San Diego County Information Systems   You have started the forms for the training database. So far you have completed a main form that contains data from the tblClasses table and a subform which is based on a query. The query contains all the fields from the tblStudents table. It also contains the ClassID field from the tblStudentsAndClasses table so that you can link the main form on the ClassID field. You have created the subform and named it sfrmStudents. The subform contains a footer text box named txtTotal. You want the text box to be visible on the main form. The txtTotal text box is the expression Count([StudentID]), and is designed to count the total number of students in each class. Complete the following:

1. Start Access and open the **ISD4** database located in the Tutorial.04 folder on your local or network drive.

2. Open the **frmClasses** form in Design view. Size the window that contains the form so that you can see the Database window. Point to the sfrmStudents form, click and drag it to the frmClasses form, and position it below the other controls in the Detail section.

3. Select the label control above the subform containing the text tblStudentsAndClasses, press the Delete key, select the subform control, size the control so that it is approximately 5" wide and 3" tall, and then position the subform control so that is centered below the other controls.

4. Change the Name property of the subform control to "sfrmStudents", change the Record Selectors property of the frmClasses form to No, the Caption property to "ISD Classes", and then save the form.

5. Size the Detail section to be 5½" tall so that there is room to add the text box below the subform.

6. Open the toolbox (if necessary), click the Text Box button in the toolbox, and click in the Detail section below the subform to create an unbound text box.

7. Click the unbound text box and type "=sfrmStudents.Form!txtTotal", and then press the Enter key.

8. Size the label and text box to be roughly the same size as the other controls in the main form.

9. Type "Total Students" in the label, click the unbound text box, open its property sheet (if necessary), and change the Name property of the new text box to "txtTotalStudents".

10. Click the Format tab in the property sheet, click the Back Color property text box, click the Build button, and then change the background color so it matches the form.

11. Change the Special Effect property to Flat, click the Other tab in the property sheet, change the Tab Stop property to No, and then close the property sheet.

12. Switch to Form view to test your changes.

Explore ▷ 13. Click Tools on the menu bar, point to Analyze, and then click Documenter. Click the Forms tab, click the frmClasses form option, click the Options button, make sure that only the Properties option is checked, and then click the OK button and then print the report.

14. Save your changes and close the form.

15. Close the **ISD4** database and exit Access.

Case 3. Christenson Homes   The forms for Christenson Homes are not yet completed. You have created one of the data entry forms, but now Roberta is considering adding tables to track the options for each new home that is sold. Being able to track those options will expand the use of the database program, but will require creating a number of new data entry forms. While Roberta works out the specifications for these new tables, you decide to create a form template and a master for the data entry forms. The template and master will contain the default property settings, the company name, and the company logo. Complete the following:

1. Start Access and open the **Homes4** database located in the Tutorial.04 folder on your local or network drive.

2. Create a template for data entry forms. Add a form header and footer, and size the Form Header section so it is ¾" tall. Make the form 6½" wide, the Detail section 2" tall, and the Form Footer section ½" tall.

3. Change the form properties as follows: Scroll Bars to Neither, Record Selectors to No, Dividing Lines to No, Auto Center to Yes, Border Style to Dialog, and Min Max Buttons to None.

4. Change the Label button properties as follows: Font Size to 10 and Font Weight to Semi-bold.

5. Change the Text Box button properties as follows: Font Size to 10, Label X to 0, Label Y to -0.25, Text Align and Label Align to Left, and Add Colon to No.

6. Save the form as "zsfrmTemplate" and close it.

7. Set the form as the default template in the database.

8. Create a new form in Design view. Create a label in the form header that contains the company name, Christenson Homes, size the name to 16 points, and add an image to the left of the label in the form header. Use the **H4Logo** file located in the Tutorial.04 folder on your local or network drive.

9. Change the Size Mode property of the image to Stretch.

10. Save the form as **zsfrmMaster**.

Explore   11. Open the frmLots form in Design view and then open the zsfrmMaster form in Design view. Copy and paste the label containing the company name and the picture from zsfrmMaster to the Form Header section in frmLots. Align the controls so they do not overlap, and then save and close the frmLots form.

12. Close the **Homes4** database and exit Access.

Case 4. Sonoma Farms   The Sonoma Farms database has three data entry forms. To make the application easier to work with, you will develop a switchboard that enables users to access each of the three forms or exit the database. Complete the following:

1. Start Access and open the **Sonoma4** database located in the Tutorial.04 folder on your local or network drive.

2. Create a new form in Design view. Change the form properties as follows: Scroll Bars to Neither, Record Selectors to No, Dividing Lines to No, Auto Center to Yes, Border Style to Dialog, Min Max Buttons to None, and Close Button to No.

3. Create an option group on the form with options for Customer Data Entry, Distributor Data Entry, and Visitor Data Entry. These will be the frmCustomers, frmDistributors, and frmVisitors forms in the macro.

4. Name the option group "grpForms".

5. Name the form **frmMainSwitchboard**.

6. Write a macro named **grpForms_AfterUpdate** to open each of the forms or close the form. Save the macro group as "mfrmMainSwitchboard".

7. Type the macro name in the After Update property of the option group.

8. Use the Command Button Wizard to create a Close button on the form.

9. Add a label with the text "Sonoma Farms" to the top of the switchboard form.

10. Test the switchboard to be sure that all the forms open.

Explore   11. Create a button next to the Close button using the Command Button Wizard, that closes the database and exits Access.

12. Save the form.

13. Click Tools on the menu bar, point to Analyze, and then click Documenter. Click the Macros tab, click the mfmMainSwitchboard macro, click the Options button, make sure that only the Actions and Arguments option is checked, and then click the OK button. Click the OK button and then print the report.

14. Close the **Sonoma4** database and exit Access.

QUICK | CHECK ANSWERS

Session 4.1

1. A splash screen is designed to give the user something to do while the application loads.

2. user interface

3. The drawback to using too many colors on a form is that it is visually confusing.

4. A form template allows you to change form, section, and toolbox button properties. A template automatically affects all new forms if it is set as the default template. A form master contains controls common to many of the forms on your database.

5. Unbound

6. The identifier operators are the bang (!) and the dot (.).

7. Zero-based means that the first item in a group is numbered 0.

8. collection

Session 4.2

1. macro

2. Events

3. The Condition column in the Macro window is used to create a conditional expression to determine if an action will be carried out when a macro is run.

4. A macro group is a group of macros saved as a unit.

5. The ampersand character precedes a letter on a command button to create a keyboard shortcut.

6. event procedure

7. You create, modify, and display VBA code in the Visual Basic window.

In this tutorial you will:

- Create a report master using the DLookup function

- Study report sections

- Create a self-join in a query

- Send a report as a snapshot file via e-mail

- Study event properties

- Use print events to run macros and code from reports

- Convert a macro to a VBA function

- Use the Chart Wizard to embed a chart in a report

- Write VBA code to calculate an expression in a page footer

- Use the Running Sum property to add a line item to a report

- Add blank rows to a report using report properties and VBA code

CREATING
COMPLEX REPORTS AND QUERIES

Reporting on Data in the MovieCam Technologies Database

CASE

MovieCam Technologies

You and Carolyn have completed most of the forms for the MovieCam Technologies database, and now turn your attention to reports. Just as you can create a form template, you also can design a template for the reports in a database. Carolyn has already created a report template for the MovieCam database. You'll use that template to develop the various reports that Amanda and other managers have requested.

Martin Woodward, for example, has requested a report on employees, categorized by supervisor. The report should contain data such as name, department, hourly rate, and whether the employee has to complete a time card. Each supervisor can then compare the report data to the time cards that employees turn in at the end of each week.

The product managers need a report that contains detailed information on the number of hours and the total dollars spent to date on each job. This report should include a summary of hours and dollars for each job. The summary needs to be broken down by each quarter of the year and illustrated in a chart.

Daniel Jenkins, MovieCam's human resources manager, has requested two reports. One report will list active employees and the other will list terminated employees. Those reports will then be compared to the quarterly reports generated by the ACC90 payroll module. Both of the reports for Daniel Jenkins should contain employee number, employee name, job title, labor category, whether employees are hourly or salaried, and hourly rate of pay.

You and Carolyn must consider one more requirement before you design the database's reports. In a staff meeting earlier in the week, it was announced that MovieCam Technologies is being purchased by TechCam Incorporated, a large corporation located in Southern California. It is uncertain whether the MovieCam Technologies name and logo will be retained once the buyout is completed. Amanda suggests that you design future forms and reports so that they can be updated easily in the event the company name changes.

SESSION 5.1

In this session, you will create a new table that contains the company information (name and logo) that will be displayed on reports. You will create a report master that uses a domain aggregate function to look up the company name and logo in the new table. You also will work with report sections, learn to group records in a report based on a query containing a self-join, and e-mail a report as a *snapshot* file.

Introduction

Reports are often the only component of a database that upper management or customers ever see. Most database administrators will tell you that reports generally require a great deal of maintenance and ongoing development. That's because management typically requests new reports or modifications to existing reports on a regular basis.

For this reason, you should strive for efficient report design. Report templates and report masters can help you achieve that efficiency.

Creating a Report Master

You create a report template and a report master following the same basic steps you followed to create templates and masters for forms. Carolyn created a report template, named zsrptTemplate, and set it as the default report template. She formatted the default controls to be in Arial 10 point.

She has also started work on a report master. She has formatted the default controls, and has added the company logo to the report master. Now you need to complete the design of the report master. Your first step is to create a new table that contains the company name and address information. If the MovieCam company name changes when TechCam takes over, you can easily modify this in the table, and those modifications will be reflected in the reports.

To create the table to contain the company name and logo:

1. Start Access and open the **Movie5** database located in the Tutorial.05 folder on your local or network drive.

2. Make sure that **Tables** is selected on the Objects bar of the Database window, and then double-click **Create table in Design view**.

3. Create the following fields: **CompanyName**, **Address**, **City**, **State**, **ZipCode**, **Telephone**, and **FAX**. Set all the fields to be Text data types.

4. Insert a caption of **Company Name** for the CompanyName field, and a caption of **Zip Code** for the ZipCode field.

5. Switch to Datasheet view and save the table as **tblCorporate**. (As you have learned, widely accepted naming conventions specify plural table names, but because this table will contain only one record, singular is more appropriate.)

6. When you see a message box that asks if you want to define a primary key, click the **Yes** button. Access automatically adds a new field named ID to the table, assigns it the AutoNumber data type, and sets it as the primary key.

7. Add the record shown in Figure 5-1 to the table.

Figure 5-1	DATA FOR THE TBLCORPORATE TABLE							
ID	Company Name	Address	City	State	Zip Code	Telephone	FAX	Logo
1	MovieCam Technologies	1521 5th Street	Windsor	CA	95492	(707) 555-1111	(707) 555-2222	

8. Close the table.

You will use the domain aggregate function, DLookup, to look up the report master objects in the new table.

Domain Aggregate Functions

Domain aggregate functions provide statistical information about a set of records, or **domain**. The set of records can be a table or query. The arguments required are the same for all of these functions: DFunction("Expression","Domain","Criteria").

The Expression argument is required and is the field you want returned. The Domain argument is required and is the name of the table or query being searched. The Criteria argument is optional and is a condition that you specify. If the Criteria argument is not included, all the records will be returned. Each argument must be enclosed in quotation marks.

The domain aggregate functions include:

- **DLookup( )**, which returns the value in the specified field.
- **DMin( )**, **DMax( )**, which returns the minimum or maximum value in the specified field.
- **DFirst( )**, **DLast( )**, which returns the value in the specified field from the first or last physical record.
- **DAvg( )**, which returns the arithmetical average of the values in the specified field.
- **DSum( )**, which returns the sum of the values in the specified field.
- **DCount( )**, which returns the number of records with nonnull values in the specified field.

The DLookup function also is used to look up data in a table that is unrelated to the form or report in which the function has been entered. An example of the DLookup function is: DLookUp("CompanyName","tblCorporate","ID=1").

The Dlookup function looks up and returns the CompanyName field value from the tblCorporate table when the ID field value is equal to 1. This is the expression that you and Carolyn will use on MovieCam reports. To change the company name or address on reports, all you have to do is change the data in the underlying table, and the changes are automatically reflected in the reports.

To complete the report master with the DLookup function:

1. Click **Tools** on the menu bar, click **Options**, click the **Forms/Reports** tab, type **zsrptTemplate** in the Report template text box (to replace the default value of Normal), and then press the **Enter** key. All new reports you create in this database will be based on this template Carolyn created earlier.

2. In the Database window, click **Reports** on the Objects bar, click **zsrptMaster**, and then click the **Design** button. The report looks like that shown in Figure 5-2.

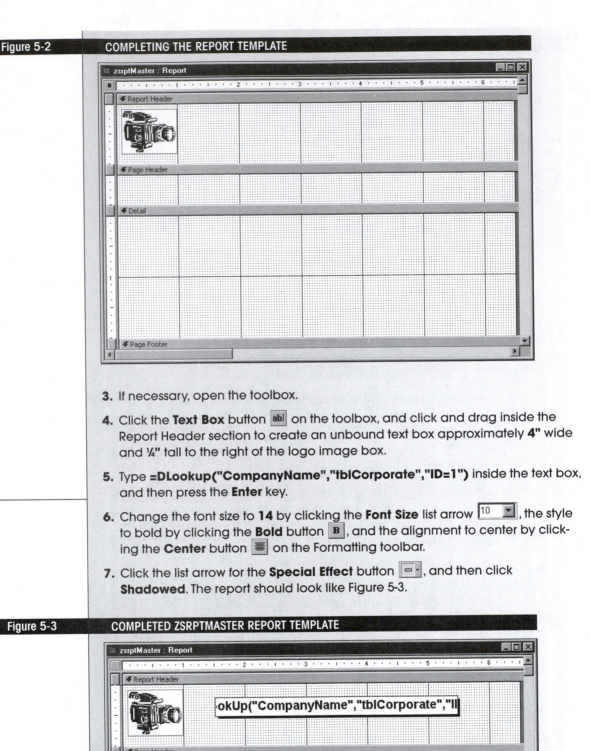

Figure 5-2   COMPLETING THE REPORT TEMPLATE

3. If necessary, open the toolbox.

4. Click the **Text Box** button [abl] on the toolbox, and click and drag inside the Report Header section to create an unbound text box approximately **4"** wide and ¼" tall to the right of the logo image box.

5. Type **=DLookup("CompanyName","tblCorporate","ID=1")** inside the text box, and then press the **Enter** key.

6. Change the font size to **14** by clicking the **Font Size** list arrow [10 ▼], the style to bold by clicking the **Bold** button [B], and the alignment to center by clicking the **Center** button [≡] on the Formatting toolbar.

7. Click the list arrow for the **Special Effect** button [□ ▾], and then click **Shadowed**. The report should look like Figure 5-3.

Figure 5-3   COMPLETED ZSRPTMASTER REPORT TEMPLATE

8. Click the **Save** [💾] button and then close the report.

Now that the report master is complete, you and Carolyn can use it as the basis for new reports. To test the DLookup function you used to show the CompanyName field in the master, you will change the name in the table and then view the report to see the result.

To test the DLookup function in the report master:

1. Open the **tblCorporate** table in Datasheet view.

2. Change the value in the Company Name field to **TechCam Incorporated**, and close the table.

3. Open the **zsrptMaster** report in Print Preview. It should look similar to that shown in Figure 5-4.

| Figure 5-4 | VIEWING CHANGES TO THE MASTER REPORT |

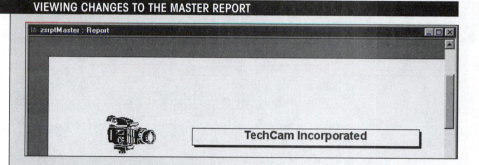

4. Close the report, open the **tblCorporate** table in Datasheet view, and then change the Company Name field entry back to **MovieCam Technologies**.

5. Close the table.

Because the report master is now complete, you are ready to create reports. You will review report sections next, and then you'll work on Martin Woodward's employee-by-supervisor report.

Report Sections

In Design view, a report's sections are represented as bands. An explanation of the various sections follows:

- The **Report Header** section appears once at the beginning of a report. This section might contain information such as a company logo, report title, and company name and address. The report header can be either a single page or multiple pages.

- The **Page Header** section prints at the top of every page of the report. You might use the Page Header to print column headers or the report title on each page.

- The **Detail** section is the main body of the report. It prints one time for each record in the report's underlying record source (table or query).

- The **Page Footer** section appears at the bottom of every page of the report. Use the Page Footer section for items such as the date, time, and page numbers. Do not include numeric expressions, such as totals or averages, in the Page Footer section or an error will result. If you want to total a field in the report, that expression should be entered in the Group Footer section (discussed more in the next section) or the Report Footer section. If you absolutely must total a field at the bottom of each page, you have to write VBA code to do so.

■ The **Report Footer** section appears once at the end of the report. You can use it to show the results of expressions such as totals or averages. The Report Footer section is the bottom section in the report's Design view, but it prints *before* the Page Footer on the last page of the report.

Grouping Records in a Report

By grouping records that share a common value, you can calculate subtotals and make reports easier to read. You can group on up to 10 expressions or values in a single report. When you choose to group on a field or expression, two other sections might appear on the report:

■ A **Group Header** section appears at the beginning of a new group of records. You can use it to show information that applies to the group, such as a group name or a picture.

■ A **Group Footer** section appears at the end of a group of records. You can use it to show calculations, such as a total or average of the records in the group.

The first report that Martin Woodward requested for the product managers is a list of employees grouped by supervisor. He asked that the supervisor's name and department appear at the beginning of each group of employees that report to that supervisor. He also wants each group to print on a separate page. Carolyn has roughed out the report, as shown in Figure 5-5.

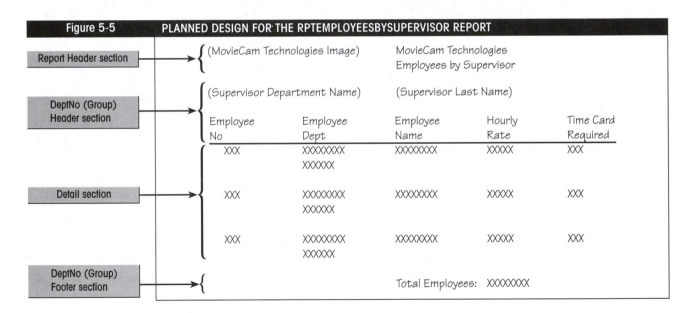

Figure 5-5   PLANNED DESIGN FOR THE RPTEMPLOYEESBYSUPERVISOR REPORT

Creating a Query with a Self-Join

The rptEmployeesBySupervisor report will contain data from the tblEmployees table and the tblDepartments table. It will contain a Group Header section based on the employee number of the supervisor, and a Group Footer section. You and Carolyn are struggling with the Group Header section. If you set the header to group on the DeptNo field, the report will group employees by their respective departments. In some cases, the supervisor's department name is different from the employee's. For example, Carolyn Valdez, supervisor in the Administrative and Accounting department, supervises Ann Garcia, who is in the Accounting department. See Figure 5-6.

Figure 5-6   **REVIEWING THE DIFFERENT MOVIECAM DEPARTMENTS**

Carolyn's department

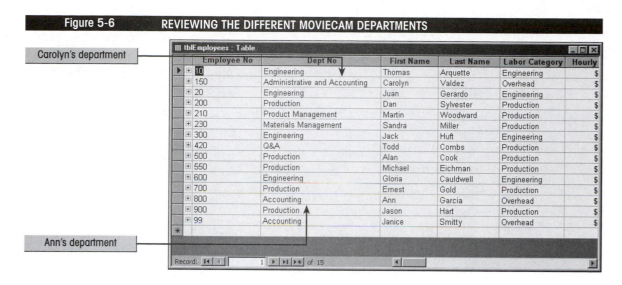

Employee No	Dept No	First Name	Last Name	Labor Category	Hourly
10	Engineering	Thomas	Arquette	Engineering	$
150	Administrative and Accounting	Carolyn	Valdez	Overhead	$
20	Engineering	Juan	Gerardo	Engineering	$
200	Production	Dan	Sylvester	Production	$
210	Product Management	Martin	Woodward	Production	$
230	Materials Management	Sandra	Miller	Production	$
300	Engineering	Jack	Huft	Engineering	$
420	Q&A	Todd	Combs	Production	$
500	Production	Alan	Cook	Production	$
550	Production	Michael	Eichman	Production	$
600	Engineering	Gloria	Cauldwell	Engineering	$
700	Production	Ernest	Gold	Production	$
800	Accounting	Ann	Garcia	Overhead	$
900	Production	Jason	Hart	Production	$
99	Accounting	Janice	Smitty	Overhead	$

Ann's department

Record: 1 of 15

The other problem you're struggling with is how to show the supervisor's name in the report's Group Header section. Again, if you add the FirstName and/or LastName fields from the tblEmployees table to the Group Header Report Header section, then each employee's name will appear in the header instead of only the supervisor.

If the records for supervisors were stored in a separate table, this would be a simple task. Because they are not, your solution is to create a query with a self-join. Joining a table to itself in a query is referred to as a **self-join**.

A self-join can be either an inner or outer join. Remember from Tutorial 3 that an inner join is the default join type and is the one in which all the records with equal field values are displayed. Because each employee has a supervisor, this is the type of join you will use for this query.

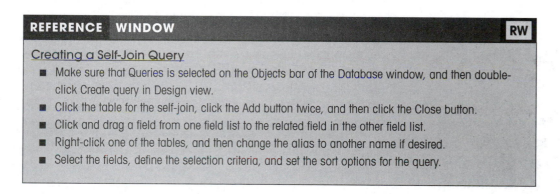

REFERENCE   WINDOW   **RW**

Creating a Self-Join Query
- Make sure that Queries is selected on the Objects bar of the Database window, and then double-click Create query in Design view.
- Click the table for the self-join, click the Add button twice, and then click the Close button.
- Click and drag a field from one field list to the related field in the other field list.
- Right-click one of the tables, and then change the alias to another name if desired.
- Select the fields, define the selection criteria, and set the sort options for the query.

You will include the tblEmployees table twice in the query, and join the EmployeeNo field to the SupervisorNo field. You also will include the tblDepartments table twice, once for each of the tblEmployees tables. One table will be used to display the DeptName field for the employee, and the other will be used to display the DeptName field for the supervisor.

To create a query with a self-join:

1. Make sure that **Queries** is selected on the Objects bar of the Database window, double-click **Create query in Design view**, click the **tblDepartments** table in the Show Table dialog box, and then click the **Add** button.

2. Click the **tblEmployees** table in the Show Table dialog box, and then click the **Add** button *twice*.

3. Click the **tblDepartments** table again, click the **Add** button, and then close the Show Table dialog box.

   Now you have four tables in the Query window, as shown in Figure 5-7.

Figure 5-7   ADDING THE TWO TABLES TWICE FOR A SELF-JOIN

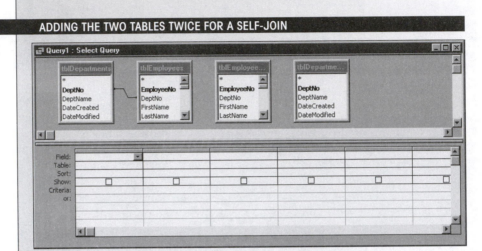

The two tables on the left will be used to display data about the employees, and the two tables on the right will be used to display data about the supervisors.

4. In the left-most tblEmployees table, click the **SupervisorNo** field, and then drag it to the **EmployeeNo** field in the other tblEmployees table (tblEmployees_1) to create the join, as shown in Figure 5-8.

Figure 5-8   CREATING THE SELF-JOIN

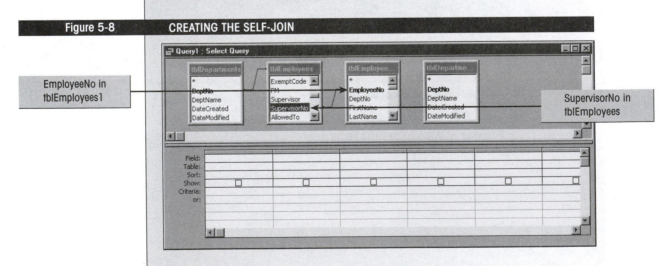

EmployeeNo in tblEmployees1

SupervisorNo in tblEmployees

5. Click and drag the **DeptNo** field in the tblEmployees_1 table to the **DeptNo** field in the right-most tblDepartments table (tblDepartments_1) to create a join.

6. Right-click the **title bar** of the **tblEmployees_1** table, click **Properties** on the shortcut menu, type **tblSupervisors** in the Alias text box, and then press the **Enter** key. This will make it clear which fields contain the supervisor data and which fields contain employee data when you build the report.

7. Click the **title bar** of the tblDepartments_1 table, and then type **tblSupervisorsDept** in the Alias property text box.

8. Close the property sheet, add the **EmployeeNo**, **LastName**, **HourlyRate**, and **TimeCard** fields from the tblEmployees table to the design grid, and then add the **DeptName** field from the tblDepartments table to the design grid.

9. Add the **DeptNo** and **LastName** fields from the tblSupervisors table to the design grid, and then add the **DeptName** field from the tblSupervisorsDept table to the design grid. The query should look like that shown in Figure 5-9.

| Figure 5-9 | COMPLETING THE SELF-JOIN QUERY |

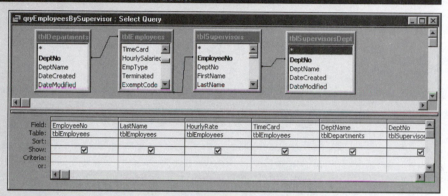

10. Run the query. There should be 15 records in the query results. Save it as **qryEmployeesBySupervisor**, and then close it.

Now you're ready to create the report. You will copy the report master and rename it, and you will specify the qryEmployeesBySupervisor query as the record source.

To create the rptEmployeesBySupervisor report:

1. Make sure that **Reports** is selected on the Objects bar of the Database window, right-click the **zsrptMaster** report, click **Copy** on the shortcut menu, right-click an empty area of the Database window, and then click **Paste** on the shortcut menu.

2. Type **rptEmployeesBySupervisor** in the Report Name text box, and then press the **Enter** key.

3. Open the new report in Design view and, if necessary, click the **Properties** button on the toolbar.

4. Click the **Record Source** list arrow, and then click **qryEmployeeBySupervisor**. The field list for the query is visible, as shown in Figure 5-10. In the field list, any fields with the same name are preceded by the table name.

Figure 5-10	DESIGNING THE RPTEMPLOYEESBYSUPERVISOR REPORT

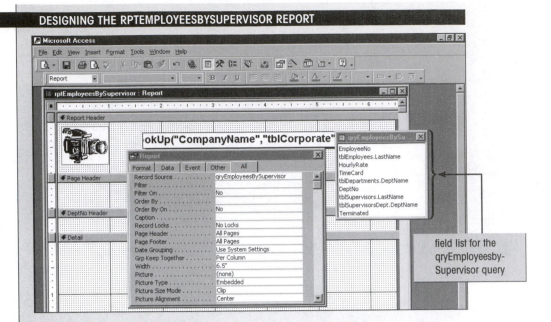

field list for the qryEmployeesby-Supervisor query

5. Close the property sheet, click the **Sorting and Grouping** button [≡] on the Report Design toolbar, click the first row's **Field/Expression** list arrow, and then click **DeptNo**. This is the supervisor's department number.

6. In the Group Properties section of the Sorting and Grouping dialog box, change Group Header to **Yes**, and change Group Footer to **Yes**. Do not change any other properties. A Group Header section and a Group Footer section for the DeptNo field are added to the report.

The **Group On** property lets you group on Prefix Characters, such as the first letter in a company name, rather than on the entire field. The **Group Interval** property is used to indicate the number of characters you want to group on if you select the Prefix Characters setting for the Group On property. The **Keep Together** property is used to keep a group together so it prints on one page. Don't change the Keep Together property because each group in this report begins on a new page.

7. Close the Sorting and Grouping dialog box.

8. Drag the **tblSupervisorDepts.DeptName** field and the **tblSupervisors.LastName** field to the DeptNo Header section.

9. Drag the **EmployeeNo**, **tblDepartments.DeptName**, **tblEmployees.LastName**, **HourlyRate**, and **TimeCard** fields to the Detail section, and align and arrange the fields as shown in Figure 5-11.

Figure 5-11   ADDING CONTROLS TO THE REPORT

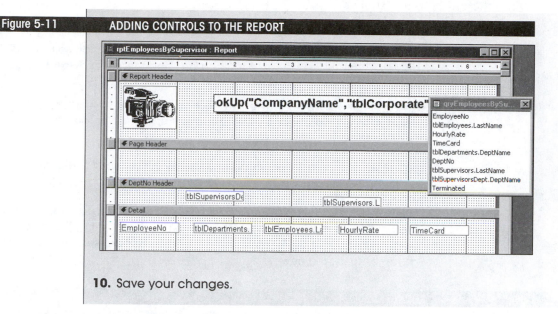

10. Save your changes.

Next you will add labels to the report and align the labels with the fields in the Detail section. You also will change a property setting so that the full name of each employee's department is visible.

Can Grow and Can Shrink Properties

You can use the Can Grow and Can Shrink properties of sections or controls on printed or previewed forms and reports. Setting the Can Grow property to Yes enables the section or control to grow vertically so all of the data is visible. This is useful when the data in a few records is much longer than the data in the majority of records. Setting the Can Shrink property to Yes shrinks the section or control vertically to avoid printing blank lines.

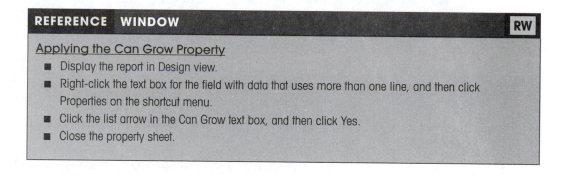

REFERENCE WINDOW   RW

Applying the Can Grow Property
- Display the report in Design view.
- Right-click the text box for the field with data that uses more than one line, and then click Properties on the shortcut menu.
- Click the list arrow in the Can Grow text box, and then click Yes.
- Close the property sheet.

Now you will make some formatting changes to the report's design, and change the Can Grow property for the tblDepartments.DeptName field to Yes so that it wraps to two lines.

To format the rptEmployeesBySupervisor report:

1. Close the Field List window, size the **DeptNo Header** section so that it is approximately 1" tall, click **View** on the menu bar, and then click **Page Header/Footer** to delete these sections from the report.

2. Add a label below the MovieCam Technologies text box control in the Report Header, type **Employees By Supervisor,** change the font size to **14,** and change the alignment to **Center.**

   TROUBLE? If all the characters do not display in the label, position the mouse pointer on one of the label's handles and double-click.

3. Insert field labels in the DeptNo Header section as shown in Figure 5-12. To create a new line in a label, press **Ctrl+Enter.** You are inserting the labels in the DeptNo Header section instead of in the Page Header section because each group begins on a new page.

Figure 5-12	ADDING LABELS TO THE REPORT

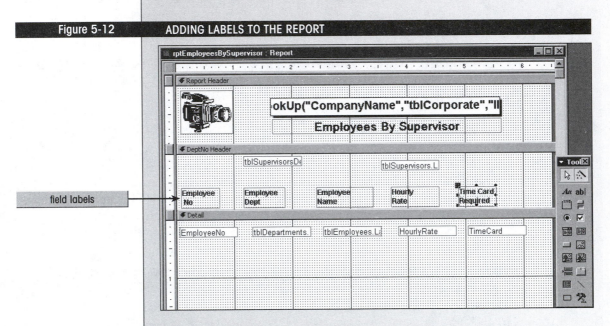

field labels

4. Click the **Line** button on the toolbox, hold down the **Shift** key, and drag below the labels to create a straight horizontal line.

5. Drag the Detail section of the report up so that it is approximately ¼" high, as shown in Figure 5-13.

6. Left-align the text boxes in the Detail section with their labels in the DeptNo Header section, as shown in Figure 5-13, and adjust their width to be the same as the labels'. Change the font size of the field labels in the DeptNo Header section to **9.** The labels should be bold because default labels in the template are bold.

7. Size and align the **tblSupervisorDept.DeptName** and **tblSupervisors.LastName** fields in the DeptNo Header section as shown in Figure 5-13, and then apply the bold style to both fields. Leave the font size at 10.

| Figure 5-13 | ALIGNING CONTROLS ON THE RPTEMPLOYEESBYSUPERVISOR REPORT |

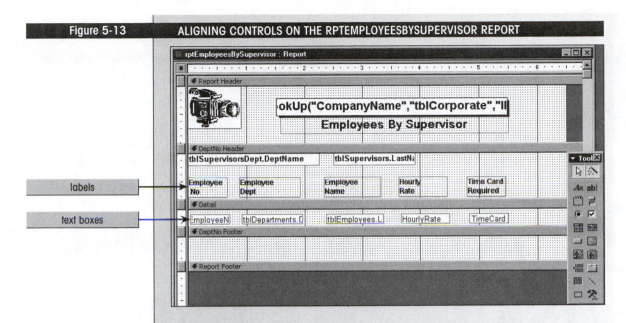

8. Center the alignment of the **Employee No** and **Time Card Required** labels and their corresponding text box controls. The rest of the labels and text boxes should be left-aligned.

9. Click the **tblDepartments.DeptName** text box in the Detail section of the report, click the **Properties** button on the toolbar, and change the Can Grow property to **Yes**.

10. Click the **DeptNo Footer** section and change the Force New Page property to **After Section**, and then close the property sheet.

11. Create a text box in the DeptNo Footer section that contains the expression =Count(EmployeeNo), and then create a label to the left of the text box and type **Total Employees**, as shown in Figure 5-14.

| Figure 5-14 | ADDING AN EXPRESSION TO THE DEPTNO FOOTER SECTION |

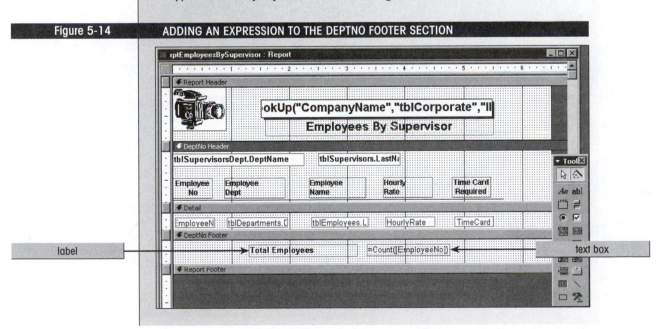

12. Preview the report. Use the navigation buttons at the bottom to move between pages. Note that the logo, company name, and title appear only on the first page. This is because these items are in the Report Header section of the report.

13. Save your changes, and then return to Design view.

You and Carolyn realized two things when you previewed the report. One is that because these pages will be distributed to various supervisors, the data in the Report Header section should be moved to the DeptNo Header section. Then it will appear on each page of the report. You also realized that you did not include criteria in the query so that only active employees are included in the report.

REFERENCE WINDOW   RW

Modifying the Query from the Report Window
- Open the report in Design view.
- Click the Properties button on the toolbar so the report properties are visible.
- Click the Record Source text box, and then click its Build button to open the query the report uses as its record source.
- Make the necessary changes to the query fields, criteria, or sort order.
- Save the changes and then close the query.
- Save the changes and then close the report.

All the test records in the tblEmployees table include active employees. However, the final data will include terminated employees. You need to add the field and criteria to the query to designate only active employees in this report.

To change the query of the report from Design view:

1. Click the report selector (the box in the left corner of the report where the rulers meet) to select the report, and then click the **Properties** button 🖼 on the toolbar.

2. Click the **Record Source** property text box, and click its **Build** button ⋯ . The qryEmployeesBySupervisor query opens.

3. Scroll down the tblEmployees table field list, and then add the **Terminated** field to the query grid.

4. Click the **Criteria** row in the Terminated column, and type **No**.

5. Close the query and then click the **Yes** button when prompted to save the changes. See Figure 5-15.

Figure 5-15	SAVING CHANGES TO THE QUERY DESIGN

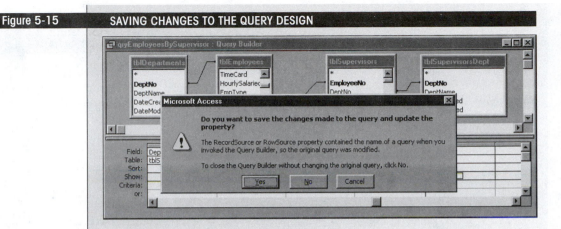

6. Close the property sheet, size the DeptNo Header section so that it is approximately **2"** tall, and select all the controls in the section, as shown in Figure 5-16. Be sure to select the horizontal line below the labels, as well.

Figure 5-16	SELECTING THE CONTROLS IN THE DEPTNO HEADER SECTION

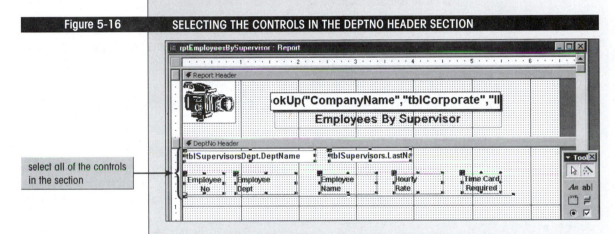

select all of the controls in the section

7. Drag all the controls to the bottom of the section, select all the controls in the Report Header section, right-click, and click **Cut**.

8. Right-click in the **DeptNo Header** section, click **Paste**, click **View** on the menu bar, and then click **Report Header/Footer** to deselect it. Your report should look like that shown in Figure 5-17.

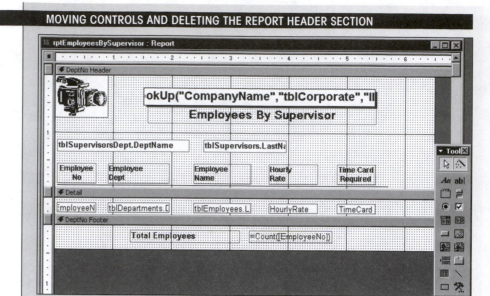

Figure 5-17   MOVING CONTROLS AND DELETING THE REPORT HEADER SECTION

9. If necessary, click the **Logo control** in the DeptNo Header section, click the **Properties** button on the toolbar, and change the Size Mode property to **Stretch**. (It may have changed back to Clip when you cut and pasted the control.)

10. Close the property sheet, save your changes, and then preview the report.

Now that you have completed the report for the product managers, you want Martin Woodward to take a look at it. Carolyn suggests e-mailing it to him in a snapshot format because she's not sure if he has Access installed on his computer. This way he can look at the report and then e-mail a response at his convenience.

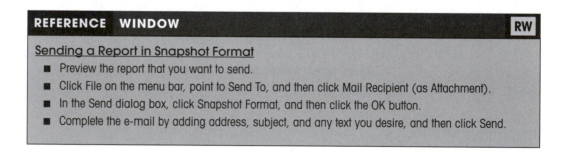

REFERENCE WINDOW   RW

Sending a Report in Snapshot Format
- Preview the report that you want to send.
- Click File on the menu bar, point to Send To, and then click Mail Recipient (as Attachment).
- In the Send dialog box, click Snapshot Format, and then click the OK button.
- Complete the e-mail by adding address, subject, and any text you desire, and then click Send.

The Report Snapshot feature is built into Access 2000. The advantage to sending a report snapshot is that the recipient doesn't need Access to view the report. If the recipient does not have the Snapshot Viewer installed, he or she can download it from the Microsoft Web site: *www.microsoft.com/accessdev/prodinfo/snapshot.htm*. This Web site also provides additional information about working with snapshots.

To send the report in snapshot format:

1. Make sure that your e-mail program is operational. You must have a functioning e-mail system to export a report snapshot.

2. In the Print Preview window, click **File** on the menu bar, point to **Send To**, and then click **Mail Recipient (as Attachment)**.

3. In the Send dialog box, click **Snapshot Format**, and then click the **OK** button.

4. Microsoft Outlook should open with the report attached, as shown in Figure 5-18.

Figure 5-18   E-MAILING A SNAPSHOT ATTACHMENT

report attachment

5. Address the e-mail to your instructor, and type **MovieCam Technologies Report** in the subject line.

6. Complete the e-mail as shown in Figure 5-19 and send it.

Figure 5-19   SENDING AN E-MAIL

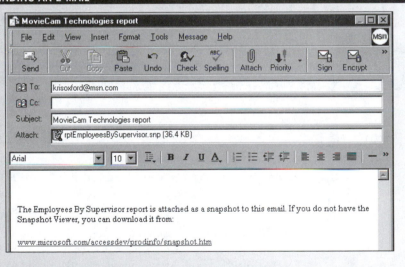

7. Close the report.

You and Carolyn have completed the report master and the first report for Martin. You will now direct your attention to a report for Daniel Jenkins. This report requires that you work with event properties. You will review event properties and design the remaining report in the next session.

Session 5.1 QUICK CHECK

1. What is the purpose of domain aggregate functions?

2. The _____ argument in DLookup is optional. If it is not included, all records will be returned.

3. What does the DAvg function return?

4. Which type of image control should be used for an object that will be updated automatically when the source file is changed?

5. The Report Header is printed before the _____ on the first page of the report.

6. What is the Detail section of a report?

7. In which sections of a report can expressions be included without you having to write a macro or Visual Basic code?

8. What is a self-join?

9. What is the effect of setting the Can Grow property of a control to Yes?

10. Explain the advantage of sending a report as a snapshot.

SESSION 5.2

In this session, you will learn more about event properties and use the print event properties of reports to execute macros and VBA code. You will create a report that contains a summary subreport, add a chart to a report, and create an expression in a Page Footer section using VBA code. You also will create a macro to cancel printing a blank report and then convert the macro to a VBA function. Then you will add line items to a report using the Running Sum property, and learn a technique for adding blank rows to the Detail section of a report.

Event Properties

Events and event properties were discussed briefly in Tutorial 4. Remember that forms, reports, and controls and sections on forms and reports, have event properties. Tables and queries do not. An explanation of the categories of events follows:

■ **Data events:** These events occur when data is entered, deleted, or changed in a form or control. They also occur when the focus moves from one record to another. The AfterUpdate event you used to run a macro in Tutorial 4 falls into this category. Some other data events include Current, BeforeUpdate, Dirty, and Delete.

■ **Error and timing events:** These events are used for error-handling and synchronizing data on forms or reports. They include the Error event found on forms and reports and the Timer event found on forms.

- **Filter events:** These events occur when you apply or create a filter on a form. The ApplyFilter and Filter events are included in this category.
- **Focus events:** These events occur when a form or control loses or gains the focus. They also occur when a form or report becomes the active or inactive window. **Focus** is the ability to receive mouse or user input through mouse or keyboard actions. In the Windows environment, only one item at a time can have the focus. If you try to type a string into a text box, but some other item on the form has the focus, the input is not accepted. You must click the text box so that it has the focus, and then type the string. Examples include the Activate, Deactive, GotFocus, and LostFocus events.
- **Keyboard events:** These events occur when you type on a keyboard. They also occur when keystrokes that use the Sendkeys macro action or the Sendkeys statement in VBA are sent to a form or a control on a form. Some examples of keyboard events are KeyDown, KeyUp, and KeyPress.
- **Mouse events:** These events occur in a form or in a control on a form as a result of a mouse action, such as pressing down or clicking the mouse button. The Click event that you used in Tutorial 4 falls into this category. Other mouse events include DblClick, MouseDown, and MouseMove.
- **Print events:** These events are found on reports and report sections, and occur when a report is being printed or is being formatted for printing. Examples are the NoData and Print events, which you will apply in this tutorial.
- **Window events:** These events occur when you open, resize, or close a form or report. Some examples of these events are Open, Close, and Load.

The Print Events

The Print events, which are triggered by reports and report sections, include the following:

- **Format:** This event occurs when Access determines what data goes in a report section, but happens before the section is formatted for previewing or for printing.
- **NoData:** This event occurs after Access formats a report for printing when the report has no data (the underlying recordset contains no records), but before the report is printed. This event is used to cancel printing a blank report.
- **Page:** This event occurs after Access formats a page for printing, but before the page is printed.
- **Print:** This event occurs after Access has formatted the data in a report section, but before the section is printed.
- **Retreat:** This event occurs when Access must back up past one or more report sections on a page in order to perform multiple formatting passes. Retreat occurs after the section's Format event, but before the Print event. The retreat event for each section occurs *as* Access backs up past the section. This allows you to undo any changes you have made during the Format event for the section.

Using the NoData Event

Carolyn has created the report of terminated employees that Daniel Jenkins requested. It is named rptTermEmployees and uses the qryTermEmployees query for its record source. Although records for terminated employees will be stored in the final database, the sample records that you and Carolyn are working with do not include data on terminated employees; so this report contains no records. In the future, terminated employees might be archived out at year end, so at times there will be no records in this report.

REFERENCE   WINDOW   **RW**

Changing the NoData Event Property
- Open the report in Design view and open the property sheet.
- Click the Event tab in the property sheet, click the On No Data text box, and then click the Build button.
- Click Macro Builder, click the OK button, type a macro group name, and then click the OK button.
- If necessary, type a macro name in the first column, click the Action list arrow, click Msgbox, and then type a comment in the last column.
- In the Action Argument section, click the Message text box and type a message that tells the user the report has no data. If desired, change the Type argument to Information.
- Click the next row of the Action column, click the Action list arrow, and then click CancelEvent.
- Type a comment in the third column, and then save and close the macro.

You will create a macro that uses the NoData print event which, as you learned, stops the printing or previewing of a report that contains no data. This macro will be saved in the mcrGlobal macro and can be used by any of the reports in the database.

To change the NoData event:

1. Make sure that Access is running, that the **Movie5** database located in the Tutorial.05 folder on your local or network drive is open, and that **Reports** is selected on the Objects bar of the Database window. Click the **rptTermEmployees** report, and then click **Preview**.

   The report opens with no records and shows an error in the expression in the Report Footer section that counts the total number of employees.

2. Switch to Design view and click the **Properties** button 🖼 on the toolbar.

3. Click the **Event** tab in the property sheet, click the **On No Data** text box, and then click its **Build** button ⸬ .

4. Click **Macro Builder**, click the **OK** button, type **mcrGlobal** for the macro name, and then press the **Enter** key.

5. Type **Report_NoData** in the Macro Name column, click the **Action** list arrow, click **Msgbox**, press the **Tab** key, and then type **Displays a message box stating that there are no records in the report**.

   TROUBLE? If the Macro Name column is not displayed, click View on the menu bar and click Macro Name. You can change the default settings so that the Macro Name column is always displayed by clicking Tools on the menu bar, clicking the Options command, clicking the View tab, and then clicking the Names column option.

   The first argument of the Msgbox action is Message. You can enter up to 255 characters or an expression that you want shown in the message box.

The second argument, Beep, can be Yes or No and specifies whether your computer beeps when the message is shown.

The third argument, Type, specifies a type of icon that will be in the message box. The choices are None, Critical, Warning?, Warning!, or Information. The default is None.

The fourth argument, Title, specifies the text you want in the title bar of the message dialog box. If it is left blank, "Microsoft Access" is used in the title bar.

6. In the Action Arguments section, click the **Message** text box, type **This report has no data**, click the **Type** list arrow, and then click **Information**, as shown in Figure 5-20.

Figure 5-20   SETTING THE ARGUMENTS FOR THE MSGBOX ACTION

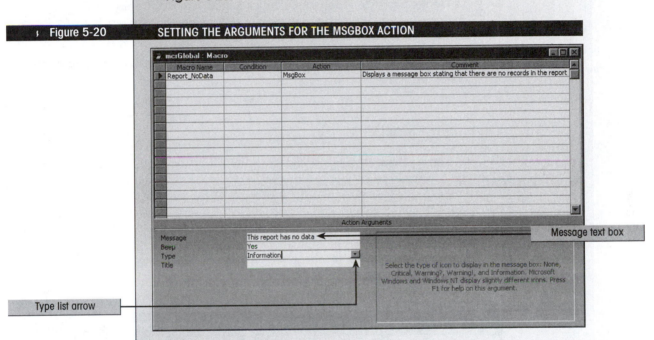

7. Click the **second row** of the Action column, click the **Action** list arrow, click **CancelEvent**, press the **Tab** key, type **Cancels printing or previewing of the report**, and then save your changes and close the macro. The CancelEvent action has no arguments and cancels the event—which is previewing the report—that caused this macro to run.

8. In the property sheet, click the **On No Data** list arrow and then click **mcrGlobal.Report_NoData** to select from the mcrGlobal macro the specific macro that you want to run, as shown in Figure 5-21.

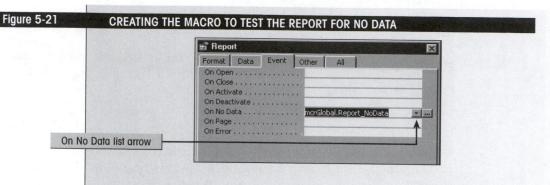

Figure 5-21   CREATING THE MACRO TO TEST THE REPORT FOR NO DATA

On No Data list arrow

9. Close the property sheet, save your changes, close the report, select the **rptTermEmployees** report, and then click **Preview** to test the macro. A message box opens and advises that there are no records.

10. Click the **OK** button to acknowledge the error message, and cancel the previewing event.

Converting Macros to VBA Code

You and Carolyn decide that you would rather use VBA code in place of macros whenever possible. Macros might be simpler to write, but you understand that macros exist in Access 2000 only for the sake of backward compatibility with earlier versions of the program. You know that Microsoft will not be adding new functionality to the macro language.

Access can automatically convert macros to VBA event procedures or to modules that perform equivalent actions. You can convert macros on a form or report, or you can convert global macros that aren't attached to a specific form or report. You will convert the mcrGlobal macro you just wrote.

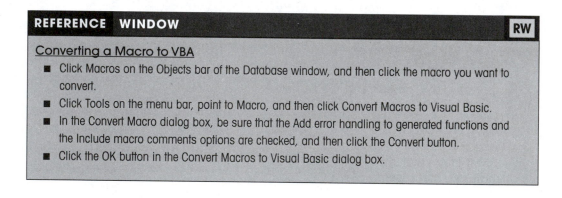

REFERENCE WINDOW   **RW**

Converting a Macro to VBA

■ Click Macros on the Objects bar of the Database window, and then click the macro you want to convert.

■ Click Tools on the menu bar, point to Macro, and then click Convert Macros to Visual Basic.

■ In the Convert Macro dialog box, be sure that the Add error handling to generated functions and the Include macro comments options are checked, and then click the Convert button.

■ Click the OK button in the Convert Macros to Visual Basic dialog box.

Because the macro you are converting is a global macro, Access automatically converts it to a function in a standard module. A **function** procedure, often just called a function, returns a value, such as the result of a calculation. In addition to the Access built-in functions, you can create your own custom functions. A **sub procedure**, on the other hand, is a series of VBA statements that performs actions but does not return a value. Sub procedures and event procedures were introduced at the end of Tutorial 4.

Because functions return values, you can use them in expressions, property settings, or as criteria in queries and filters. Although the macro you will convert to a function does not need to return a value, it still needs to be a function rather than a sub procedure so that it can be run from a property setting in a report.

To convert a macro to VBA:

1. Click **Macros** on the Objects bar of the Database window, and then click the **mcrGlobal** macro to select it.

2. Click **Tools** on the menu bar, point to **Macro**, and then click **Convert Macros to Visual Basic**.

3. In the Convert macro dialog box, be sure that the **Add error handling to generated functions** and **Include macro comments** options are checked (see Figure 5-22), and then click the **Convert** button.

Figure 5-22	CONVERT MACRO DIALOG BOX

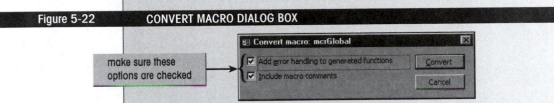

make sure these options are checked

These options will add some generic error handling to the function and add descriptions that are the same as those included in the macro.

4. Click the **OK** button in the Convert macros to Visual Basic dialog box, and then click the **Visual Basic** button on the taskbar to maximize the Visual Basic window.

   TROUBLE? If other windows such as the Immediate window are displayed in the Visual Basic window, click their Close buttons ⊠.

5. Click **Edit** on the menu bar, click **Replace**, type **mcrGlobal_Report_NoData** in the **Find What** text box, type **Report_NoData** in the **Replace With** text box, click the **Replace All** button, and then click the **OK** button in the message box that tells you six replacements were made. This search-and-replace procedure eliminates the mcrGlobal string, which can look confusing in the code.

6. Close the Replace dialog box. The procedure should now look like that shown in Figure 5-23.

Figure 5-23   REPORT_NODATA FUNCTION

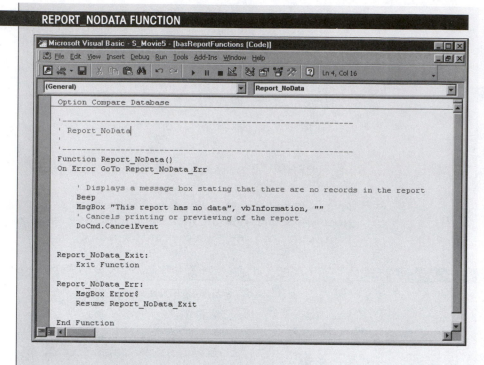

7. Close the Visual Basic window, click **Modules** on the Objects bar of the Database window, right-click the **Converted Macro-mcrGlobal** module, click **Rename**, type **basReportFunctions**, and then press the **Enter** key. This name better describes the type of function contained in this module. The bas tag is an abbreviation for Basic. The mdl tag is also used for modules by some developers.

Next you want to test the function. Before you delete the mcrGlobal macro, you and Carolyn will change the NoData event property of the rptTermEmployees report to the function name instead of the macro name, and then preview the report to test the function.

To assign a VBA function to an event property:

1. Click **Reports** on the Objects bar of the Database window and open the **rptTermEmployees** report in Design view.

2. If necessary, open the property sheet and then click the **Event** tab.

3. Delete **mcrGlobal.Report_NoData** from the On NoData event property text box, and then type **=Report_NoData()** in its place.

4. Save the changes and close the report.

5. Preview the report. A message box like that shown in Figure 5-24 opens.

Figure 5-24   ERROR MESSAGE DIALOG BOX

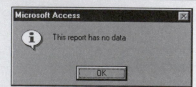

6. Click the **OK** button.

Daniel Jenkins also requested a report on all active employees. It is similar to the rptTermEmployees report. Carolyn has designed the report, but she still needs to add an expression to count the number of employees. This report has no grouping levels, so only the Report Footer section can contain the expression. However, the Report Footer prints on the last page of the report, and Daniel wants to have the number of employees shown on each page of the report.

When you include a calculated expression in a Report Footer or a Group Footer, Access knows to which records the expression applies, and does the calculation for the expression before laying out the pages of the report in memory. If you try to calculate an expression in a Page Footer, an error results because Access does not know which records to include in the calculation of the expression until after the page has been laid out. To overcome this limitation you can create a macro or write VBA code to perform the calculation.

You can use the Print event to run the code that will perform calculations for a text box contained in a Page Footer. A report section recognizes the Print event after the section has been laid out, but before the section is printed or displayed in Print Preview.

To calculate a count of employees on each page, you can place an unbound text box in the Page Footer section. Use the unbound text box to tabulate the total number of employees on the page as Access lays out the records. A new page starts after Access recognizes the Print event as it lays out the Page Header. So you will use the Print event of the Page Header to initialize the unbound text box. You will set the value of the unbound text box to 0 before any records are added, and then add a 1 to the value of the text box for each record that is laid out.

The Print event of the Detail section is recognized each time a record is laid out in the Detail section, but before the record is printed. You will use this event to run a line of code that increments the value of the text box by 1 for each record in the Detail section. Then by the time all the records are laid out in a page of the report, the value in the text box will be equal to the total number of records on that page.

REFERENCE WINDOW   **RW**

Using the Code Builder
- Use Design view to open the form or report for which you are writing the VBA code.
- Click the control or section that will run the code.
- Open the property sheet, click the Event tab, and click the Build button in the text box of the property that will run the code.
- Click Code Builder, and then click the OK button.
- Type the code, and then close the Visual Basic window.

You will use the Code Builder to create two event procedures. Remember from Tutorial 4 that an event procedure is a group of statements that executes when an event occurs. You also will create these event procedures in a **form class module**. A form class module is saved as part of a form and contains one or many procedures that apply specifically to that form. (Form class modules will be discussed in greater detail in Tutorial 7.)

To create the report module for a page record count:

1. Open the **rptActiveEmployees** report in Design view, open the toolbox if necessary, click the **Text Box** button ab| on the toolbox, and then click in the **Page Footer** section.

2. If necessary, click the **Properties** button 🔲 on the toolbar, and change the Name property to **txtCount**. Leave the property sheet open.

3. Insert a label control to the left of the text box and type **Total Employees**, as shown in Figure 5-25.

Figure 5-25   INSERTING A LABEL IN THE REPORT

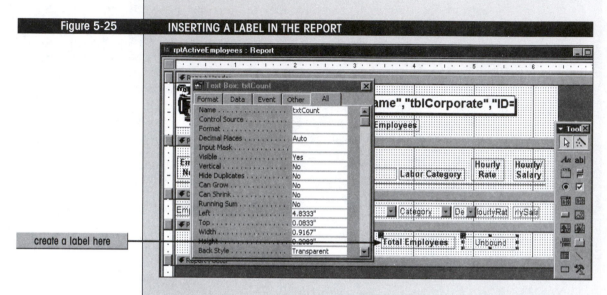

create a label here

4. Click the **PageHeader** section band, and then click the **Event** tab on the property sheet.

5. Click on the **On Print** text box, click its **Build** button 🔲 , click **Code Builder** in the Choose Builder dialog box, and then click the **OK** button. The Code window opens and the first and last line of the event procedure are created automatically, as shown in Figure 5-26.

Figure 5-26   CODE WINDOW

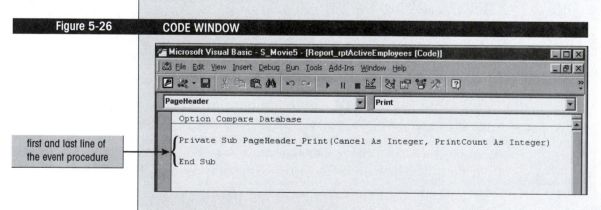

first and last line of the event procedure

6. Press the **Tab** key to indent the line, and type **txtCount = 0** as shown in Figure 5-27. This statement sets the txtCount text box in the Page Footer equal to zero at the beginning of each new page.

7. Close the Visual Basic window, and then save your changes.

8. Click the **Detail** section band, click the **On Print** text box, click its **Build** button ..., click **Code Builder**, and then click the **OK** button.

9. Press the **Tab** key to indent the line, and type **txtCount = txtCount + 1**, as shown in Figure 5-27. This statement increments the value of the txtCount text box by 1 each time a record on the page is laid out.

Figure 5-27   **ENTERING CODE FOR THE EVENT PROCEDURE**

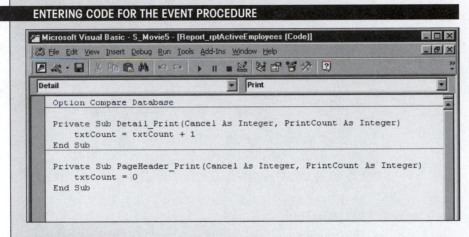

10. Close the Visual Basic window, and then save your changes.

11. Preview the report, scroll down to see the contents of the expression, and then close the report.

You and Carolyn need to create one last report for the product managers. It will show a detailed listing of hours by job, and a summary of hours by quarter of the year.

Creating **Numbered Lists**

Carolyn has begun the design of the report, which she named rptHoursByJob. The report's record source is the qryHoursByJob query. This query contains a list of hours for each job by each employee. The report groups records on the JobID field. A page break has been inserted after the Group Footer section so each job number begins on a new page. The product managers want a line item number for each entry on the report to serve as a point of reference.

As you know, records are not numbered in the report—they simply appear in the order determined by the underlying query or table, or by the settings applied in the Sorting and Grouping dialog box. To create a reference number for each record, you need to insert a text box and use the Running Sum property to increment the text box's value.

The Running Sum Property

You use the Running Sum property to calculate record-by-record totals or group-by-group totals in a report. You can specify that the text box display a running total, and you can set the range over which values are accumulated.

For example, in the rptEmployeesByDept report, an expression in the DeptNo Footer section counts the number of employees in each department. If you set the Running Sum property on this control to Over All, it counts the number in the first group and continues counting all the records in each successive group, instead of starting over with each group. The value accumulates to the end of the report.

When you set the Running Sum property to Over Group, the running sum value accumulates until another group is encountered.

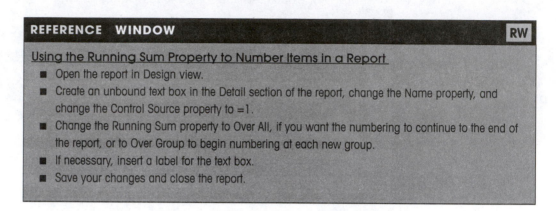

REFERENCE   WINDOW   RW

Using the Running Sum Property to Number Items in a Report

- Open the report in Design view.
- Create an unbound text box in the Detail section of the report, change the Name property, and change the Control Source property to =1.
- Change the Running Sum property to Over All, if you want the numbering to continue to the end of the report, or to Over Group to begin numbering at each new group.
- If necessary, insert a label for the text box.
- Save your changes and close the report.

Setting the Record Source property of a text box in the Detail section of a report to =1 will increment the value in the text box by 1 for each detail record.

To number each Detail section line in a report:

1. Open the **rptHoursByJob** report in Design view.

2. Make sure that the toolbox is open, and then click the **Text Box** button [abl] on the toolbox.

3. Click to the left of the TimeCardDate control in the Detail section of the report to create a new unbound text box.

4. Make sure the property sheet is open, click the **All** tab, change the Name property to **txtLineItem**, type **=1** in the Control Source text box, and then change the Running Sum property to **Over Group**.

5. Close the property sheet and then preview the report. Each page should have numbered line items and the numbers should start over for each page.

6. Return to Design view, size the txtLineItem text box so that it is the same height as the other controls in the Detail section of the report, and then reposition the text box so it is aligned with the other controls, as shown in Figure 5-28.

Figure 5-28	ADDING A COUNTER TO THE REPORT

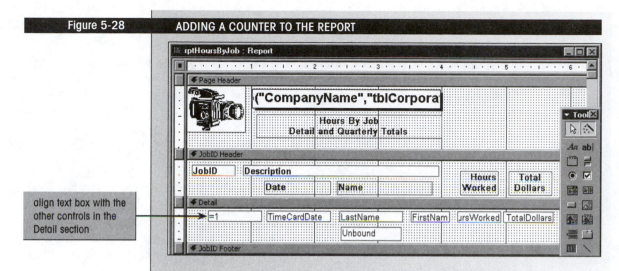

align text box with the other controls in the Detail section

7. Add a label to the JobID Header section. Position the label beneath the Job ID label, and align it with the txtLineItem control you just added in the Detail section.

8. Type **Line Item** in the label box, save your changes, and then preview the report. Page five of the final report should look like that shown in Figure 5-29.

Figure 5-29	ADDING LINE ITEM NUMBERS TO THE REPORT

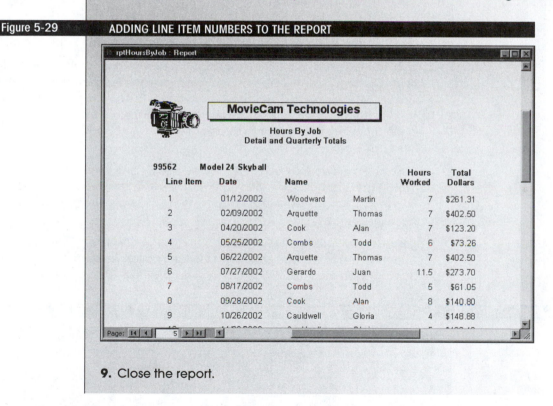

9. Close the report.

You and Carolyn now modify the report so that it sums the hours worked on a job during a specified quarter of the year. The quarterly totals can be calculated in a query, and then the query can be used to create a subreport on the main report.

Subreports

A subreport is a report that is inserted in another report. When you combine reports, one must be the main report. The main report can be bound to an underlying table, query, or SQL statement, or it can be unbound. An unbound main report can serve as a container for unrelated subreports that you want to combine. A bound report must contain a field in its record source that is also a field in its subreport(s).

A main report can contain several levels of subreports; there is no limit to the number of subreports a main report can contain.

Subreports are often used to show summary data that is related to the detail data in the main report. In this way, subreports are similar to subforms and main forms. For example, when you view the page in the rptHoursByJob report for a specific job, you can include a subreport that has a summary of hours and dollars spent on that job during a calendar quarter.

The subreport will be based on a query you create that calculates total hours and dollars by quarter for each job. You will use the DatePart function in an aggregate query to perform these calculations.

To create a totals query for the subreport:

1. Make sure that **Queries** is selected on the Objects bar of the Database window, and create a new query in Design view.

2. Add the following tables to the Query window: **tblEmployees**, **tblHours**, **tblJobs**, and **tblTimeCards**, and then close the Show Table dialog box.

3. Add the **JobID** in the tblJobs field list to the design grid, click the **Field** text box of the second column in the design grid, and then type **Quarter: "Qtr" & Space(1) & DatePart("q",[TimeCardDate])**. This formula joins the abbreviation Qtr (for quarter) to the DatePart function that returns the quarter of the year in the TimeCardDate field. The quarter of the year value will be an integer value from 1 to 4.

4. Add the **HoursWorked** field in the tblHours field list to the third column of the design grid, right-click the third column, click **Properties** on the shortcut menu, and then change the Format property to **Fixed**. Leave the property sheet open.

5. Click the **Field** text box of the fourth column in the design grid, type **TotalDollars: Sum([HoursWorked]*[HourlyRate])**, and then change the Format property to Currency. This expression calculates the total dollars by quarter for each job. The query design should look like that shown in Figure 5-30.

| Figure 5-30 | DESIGNING A QUERY ON WHICH TO BASE THE SUBREPORT |

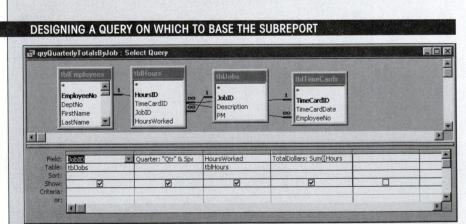

6. Click the **Totals** button Σ on the Report Design toolbar. In the Total row in the design grid, change the HoursWorked column to **Sum**, and change the TotalDollars column to **Expression**. The design grid should look like that shown in Figure 5-31.

Figure 5-31   **GROUPING IN THE QUERY DESIGN**

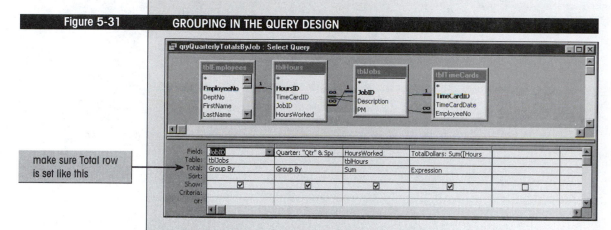

make sure Total row is set like this

7. Run the query to check the results. The query results include 23 records and four columns.

8. Save the query as **qryQuarterlyTotalsByJob** and the close the query.

Now you will create the subreport and add it to the main report. To do this, you drag the query object from the Database window to the desired section of the report. After you've inserted the subreport, you can make formatting changes to it in Design view.

To create the subreport:

1. Open the **rptHoursByJob** report in Design view, size the JobID Footer section to approximately **2½"** tall, and then size and position the report window so that you can see the Database window (see Figure 5-32).

Figure 5-32   **POSITIONING WINDOWS TO DRAG AND DROP THE QUERY OBJECT**

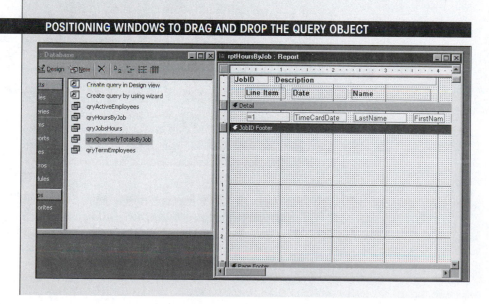

2. Click **Queries** on the Objects bar of the Database window, and then click and drag the **qryQuarterlyTotalsByJob** query to the JobID Footer section of the report. The SubReport Wizard opens, as shown in Figure 5-33.

| Figure 5-33 | SUBREPORT WIZARD DIALOG BOX |

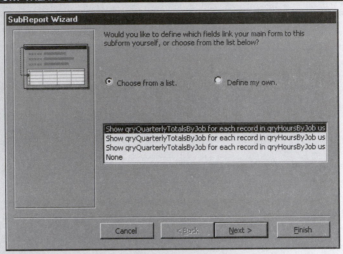

3. Click the **Define my own** option button so that you can identify the field(s) on which the main report and the subreport are linked.

4. Click the **Form/report fields** list arrow, click **JobID**, click the **Subform/subreport fields** list arrow, click **JobID** as shown in Figure 5-34.

| Figure 5-34 | LINKING THE MAIN REPORT AND SUBREPORT |

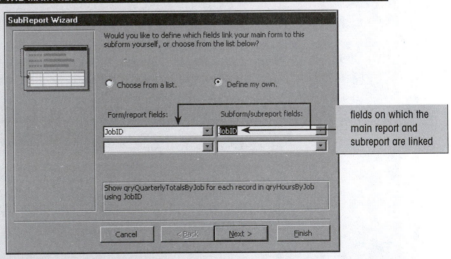

fields on which the main report and subreport are linked

5. Click the **Next** button, type **srptQuarterlyTotalsByJob** as the report name, and then click the **Finish** button.

6. Delete the label **srptQuarterlyTotalsByJob** above the subreport object in the JobID Footer section, save your changes, and close the **rptHoursByJob** report.

Next you will format the subreport and add expressions to the Report Footer section that sum the hours worked and total dollars.

To complete the subreport:

1. From the Database window, open the **srptQuarterlyTotalsByJob** report in Design view.

2. Delete the JobID label in the Report Header section, size the JobID text box to approximately ¼" wide, as shown in Figure 5-35, click the **Properties** button on the toolbar, change the **Visible** property for JobID to **No**.

| Figure 5-35 | RESIZING CONTROLS IN THE SUBREPORT |

resize the JobID text box to approximately ¼"

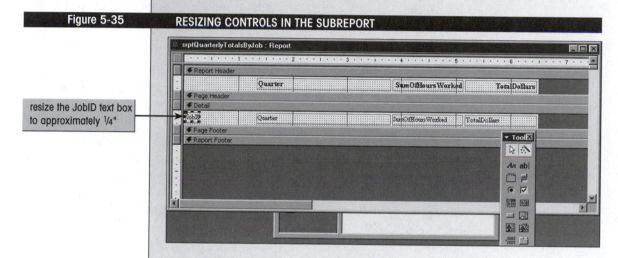

The main report and subreport are linked by the JobID field, so this control must remain on the report; however, it does not need to be visible on the subreport when it's viewed or printed. The JobID field already is located in the JobID Header section of the main report.

3. Delete the **Quarter** label in the Report Header section because the abbreviation Qtr is included in the expression in the Detail section. Change the SumOfHoursWorked label in the Report Header section to **Hours**, and change the TotalDollars label in the Report Header section to **Dollars**.

4. Select the labels. Choose **Arial** from the Font list, **10** from the Font size list, and then click the **Bold** button on the toolbar.

   TROUBLE? If your labels are already bold and/or italic, ignore the instruction to change them. Since this subreport was created using the SubReport Wizard, the font style and color applied to it will be the same as the color and font style you chose for the last report you created using the Report Wizard.

5. Size and reposition the labels in the Report Header section, and the labels and text boxes in the Detail section as shown in Figure 5-36. The Quarter text box will overlap the JobID text box, which is OK because the JobID field is not visible.

| Figure 5-36 | REPOSITIONING AND SIZING CONTROLS IN THE SUBREPORT |

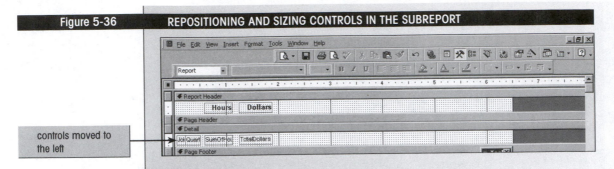

controls moved to
the left

6. Size the Report Footer section of the subreport to approximately ¼" high, and add two text boxes to it, one beneath the SumOfHoursWorked control, and the other beneath the TotalDollars control.

7. If necessary, delete the labels that are drawn with the text boxes.

8. Click the text box control you inserted beneath the SumOfHoursWorked control, click the **Properties** button on the toolbar, change the Name property to **txtTotalHoursWorked**, change the Name property of the text box control to its right to **txtTotalDollars**, and then close the properties dialog box.

9. Click in the **txtTotalHoursWorked** text box control, type **=Sum(SumOfHoursWorked)**, click in the **txtTotalDollars** text box control, type **=Sum(TotalDollars)**, change the Format property of **txtTotalHoursWorked** to **Fixed** and the Format property of **textTotalDollars** to **Currency**, and then change the alignment of both text boxes by clicking the **Align Right** button on the toolbar.

10. Resize the controls and align them with those in the Detail section of the report, as shown in Figure 5-37.

11. Select all the labels and text boxes on the report, change the font to **Arial**, the font size to **8**, the font color to **black** if necessary, and then size the report to be approximately **2"** wide, as shown in Figure in 5-37.

| Figure 5-37 | RESIZING THE SUBREPORT |

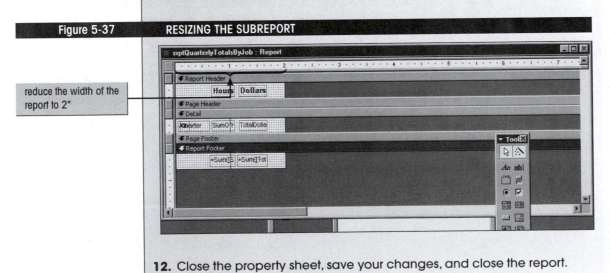

reduce the width of the
report to 2"

12. Close the property sheet, save your changes, and close the report.

Next you'll size the subreport on the main report.

To size the subreport on the main report:

1. Open the **rptHoursByJob** report in Design view, and then maximize the Report window.

2. Size the subreport control on the main report to approximately **2½"** wide by **2"** tall.

3. Size the main report to **6½"** wide, and then position the subreport in the JobID Footer section, as shown in Figure 5-38.

| Figure 5-38 | RESIZING THE MAIN REPORT AND SUBREPORT |

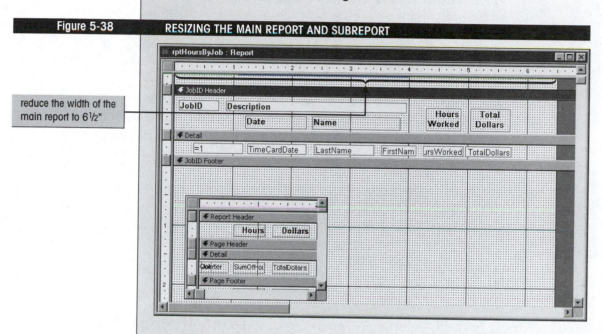

reduce the width of the main report to 6½"

4. Insert a label above the subreport control, type **Quarterly Hours and Dollars**, and then save the report.

5. Preview the report, and move to the second page to see the subreport, as shown in Figure 5-39.

| Figure 5-39 | PREVIEWING THE SUBREPORT IN PRINT PREVIEW |

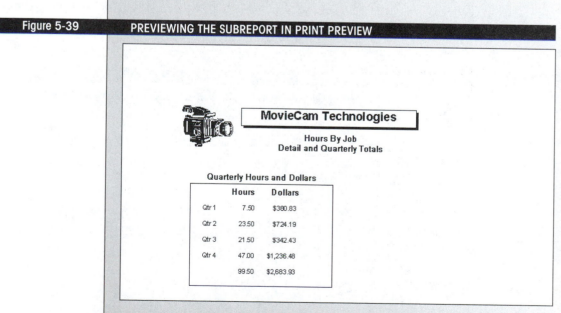

6. Click the **Close** button on the Print Preview toolbar to switch to Design view.

Next you will add a line chart to the report. The chart will graphically illustrate the summary data in the subreport.

Charting

You use the Chart Wizard to add graphs and charts to forms and reports. You must have Microsoft Graph 2000 installed to use the Chart Wizard. You can create two types of charts with the Chart Wizard: a global or unlinked chart that shows the data for each row in the record source; or a record-bound or linked chart that shows the data related to a specific record on the form or report in which it is embedded. Based on the data you specify, the Chart Wizard determines whether to use a global or record-bound chart. You can, however, change the results of a global chart so that it is linked to a specific record.

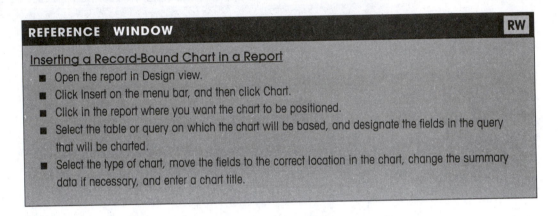

REFERENCE   WINDOW   RW

Inserting a Record-Bound Chart in a Report
- Open the report in Design view.
- Click Insert on the menu bar, and then click Chart.
- Click in the report where you want the chart to be positioned.
- Select the table or query on which the chart will be based, and designate the fields in the query that will be charted.
- Select the type of chart, move the fields to the correct location in the chart, change the summary data if necessary, and enter a chart title.

You and Carolyn will create a record-bound chart that shows summary data about each job. The chart will be based on the qryQuarterlyTotalsByJob query.

To insert a record-bound chart in a report:

1. Click **Insert** on the menu bar, click **Chart**, and then click and drag a rectangle to the right of the subreport in the JobID Footer section. The rectangle should be approximately the same size as the subreport. The Chart Wizard dialog box opens, as shown in Figure 5-40.

Figure 5-40	CHART WIZARD DIALOG BOX

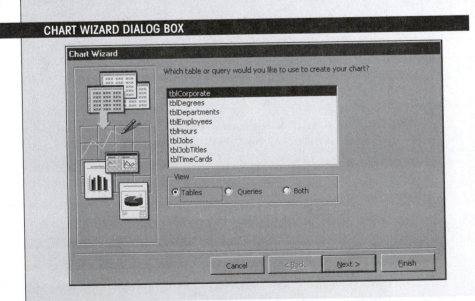

2. Click the **Queries** option button in the View options, click **qryQuarterlyTotalsByJob**, and then click the **Next** button.

3. Add the **Quarter**, **SumOfHoursWorked**, and **TotalDollars** fields to the Fields for Chart list box by clicking each field, and then clicking the [>] button, and then click the **Next** button.

The Quarter, SumofHoursWorked, and TotalDollars fields contain the data you want charted. The chart is linked to the report via the JobID field, but it is not necessary to include the field in the data to be charted. In the next Chart Wizard dialog box, you specify the type of chart you want to create. The line chart will illustrate a comparison of the hours worked and total dollars expended over time. It will be designed so that there is a line for each value with points plotted for each quarter of the year.

4. Click the **Line Chart** button in the third row and third column (see Figure 5-41), and then click the **Next** button.

Figure 5-41	SELECTING THE CHART TYPE

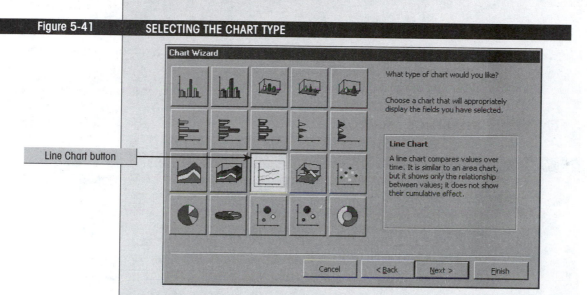

The three fields or field expressions that you selected for this chart appear as buttons at the right of the next dialog box. You drag and drop these buttons to determine where each will be placed in the chart. The x-axis is the horizontal line at the bottom of the chart and currently shows the Quarter. The sum of the SumOfHoursWorked field data is shown on the y-axis (see Figure 5-42). The Chart Wizard automatically generates a SQL statement that totals the data for each field containing numeric values that you are charting—in this case, the SumOfHoursWorked field. You can double-click the button on the y-axis that contains the text SumOfHoursWorked to change the calculation to an Average, Count, or other computation. To add a line to the chart for TotalDollars, you can click and drag the TotalDollars button to a position below the SumOfSumOfHoursWorked button.

Figure 5-42 | **SUMMARIZING AND GROUPING DATA**

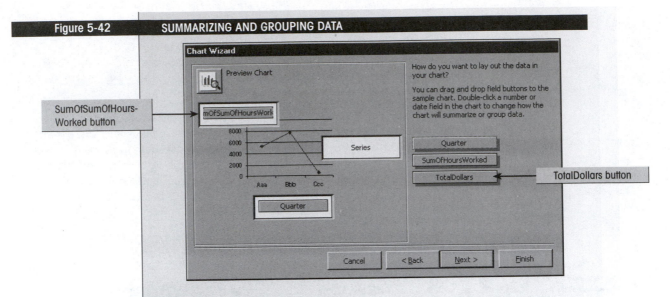

SumOfSumOfHours-
Worked button

TotalDollars button

5. Click and drag the **TotalDollars** button to a position directly beneath the SumOfHoursWorked button, and then click the **Next** button.

6. In the next Chart Wizard dialog box, make sure that **JobID** is displayed in the Report Fields and the Chart Fields list boxes, as shown in Figure 5-43. This specifies JobID as the field on which the chart is linked to the report. Click the **Next** button.

Figure 5-43 | **ESTABLISHING THE FIELD(S) ON WHICH THE CHART AND REPORT ARE LINKED**

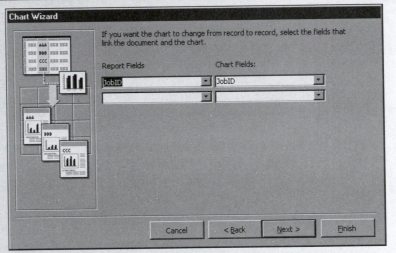

7. Type **Quarterly Job Summary** in the What title would you like for your chart? text box, and make sure the **Yes, display a legend** option button is selected.

8. Click the **Finish** button. Move the subreport and its label to the top of the JobID footer section, and then size the chart as shown in Figure 5-44.

Figure 5-44	LINE CHART INSERTED IN THE REPORT'S DESIGN VIEW

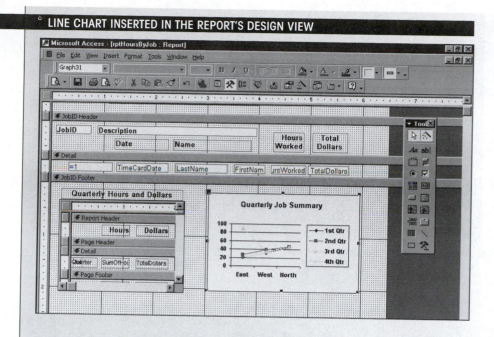

9. Preview the report to test the results, and then return to Design view.

You would like the legend on the chart to identify which line represents dollars and which line represents hours worked. To change the wording, you will modify the query on which the chart is based so that it is a saved query instead of a SQL statement. Then you will change the titles of these dollars and hours worked columns in the query itself.

To create a saved query from the chart SQL statement:

1. Make sure the chart is selected, and then click the **Properties** button 📋 on the toolbar.

2. Click the **All** tab on the property sheet, click the **Row Source** property text box, and then click the **Build** button ⌐⌐⌐. The Query Builder window opens.

3. Right-click the **Table** cell in the SumOfHoursWorked column, and then click **Properties** on the shortcut menu. Type **Hours** in the Caption text box, and leave the property sheet open.

4. Click the **TotalDollars** column, and then type **Dollars** in its Caption text box.

5. Save the query as **qryProductsCharting**.

6. Close the query, and then click the **Yes** button when asked if you want to save the changes and update the property. The name of the saved query is now the setting of the Row Source property on the property sheet.

7. Preview the report and navigate to the second page to see the chart. It should look like that shown in Figure 5-45.

Figure 5-45   MODIFIED LEGEND

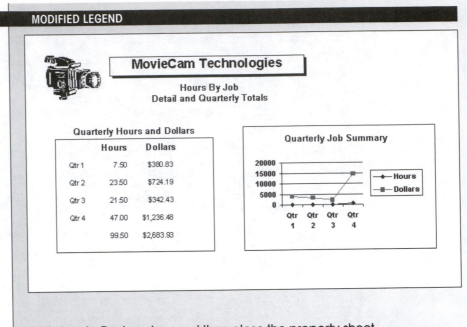

8. Return to Design view, and then close the property sheet.

You want page numbers shown on the report, and you want each product group's page numbers to begin with the number 1. You and Carolyn will add an expression to show page numbers, and then you will write an event procedure to reset the page number to 1 at the beginning of each new product group.

Page Numbering

The Page and Pages properties can be used to print page numbers in forms or reports. The **Page property** specifies the current page number when a page is being printed. The **Pages** property specifies the total number of pages in the report. The Page and Pages properties can be used in an expression, in a macro, or VBA.

An example of an expression in a report that uses these properties is:

```
="Page " & Page & " of " & Pages
```

This expression will display *Page 1 of 15* on the first page of a 15-page report.

When a group of data in a report spans more than one page, you can reset the page numbering so that each group has its own page numbering sequence that starts with page number 1. The report's Page property is **read-write at runtime**, which means that you can reset the Page property at any time by using a macro or code as the report prints.

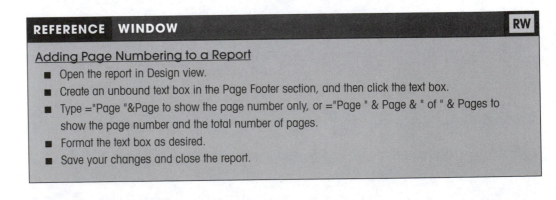

REFERENCE WINDOW   RW

Adding Page Numbering to a Report

- Open the report in Design view.
- Create an unbound text box in the Page Footer section, and then click the text box.
- Type ="Page "&Page to show the page number only, or ="Page " & Page & " of " & Pages to show the page number and the total number of pages.
- Format the text box as desired.
- Save your changes and close the report.

You will use the On Format event property for the JobID Header to reset the Page property to 1. The **Format event** occurs when a header section is formatted, but before it is printed. This event procedure you create for the On Format event property will set the Page property to 1, the header will print, the records in the Detail section and the JobID Footer will print, and the page number will increment until the next JobID Header Format event is recognized.

To add page numbers to the rptHoursByJob report:

1. Add a text box to the Page Footer section.

2. Size the text box so that it is the same width as the report (see Figure 5-46). This allows you to center the page number in the text box, and as a result, center it on the report.

Figure 5-46   **INSERTING PAGE NUMBERS**

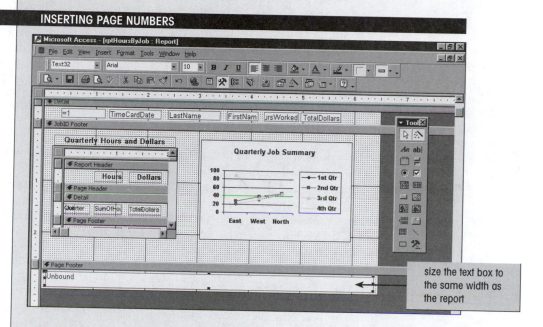

size the text box to the same width as the report

3. Position the insertion point in the text box, type **="Page "&Page**, and then press the **Enter** key.

4. Click the **Center** button on the Formatting toolbar to center the expression in the text box, switch to Print Preview, and scroll down to see the page number. Click the navigation buttons at the bottom of the Print Preview window to move between pages to check the page numbers.

5. Return to Design view, click the **JobID Header** section band, click the **Properties** button on the toolbar, change the Name property to **hdrJobID** if necessary, and then click the **Event** tab on the property sheet.

6. Click the **On Format** text box, click its **Build** button, click **Code Builder** in the Choose Builder dialog box, and then click the **OK** button. The Visual Basic window opens, as shown in Figure 5-47.

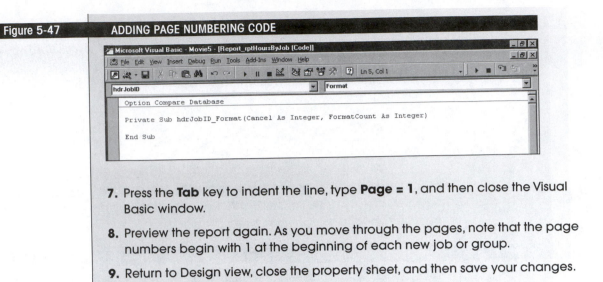

Figure 5-47	ADDING PAGE NUMBERING CODE

```
Option Compare Database

Private Sub hdrJobID_Format(Cancel As Integer, FormatCount As Integer)

End Sub
```

7. Press the **Tab** key to indent the line, type **Page = 1**, and then close the Visual Basic window.

8. Preview the report again. As you move through the pages, note that the page numbers begin with 1 at the beginning of each new job or group.

9. Return to Design view, close the property sheet, and then save your changes.

Next you and Carolyn will add the finishing touches to the report's design.

Adding Blank Rows to a Report

Some reports are easier to read if blank rows are inserted at certain intervals. Access does not provide a method to insert a blank row in the middle of a Detail section. However, you can use VBA code and the properties of controls and sections on a report to insert blank rows.

To add blank rows to a report, you insert a blank unbound text box in the Detail section of the report below the other text boxes, and name it "txtSpacer". Then set the Can Grow and Can Shrink properties of the txtSpacer text box and the Detail section to Yes. Remember that the Can Grow and Can Shrink properties allow controls and sections on a report to grow vertically and shrink vertically when necessary. Wherever you want the blank row to print, txtSpacer needs to contain " ", which is a space between quotation marks. This causes the text box to print, but nothing will be visible inside it. You can write VBA code to insert a blank row after a certain number of records. The VBA code tests which record is being laid out on the page. If you want a blank row after every fifth record, for example, the code tests to see if a record number is evenly divisible by 5. If it is, a blank row is inserted after it. You will use the txtLineItem text box in the rptHoursByJob report to determine which record is going to print.

To add blank rows to the rptHoursByJob report:

1. Drag the Detail section of the report down so that it is approximately ½" high, and insert an unbound text box beneath the LastName text box, as shown in Figure 5-48.

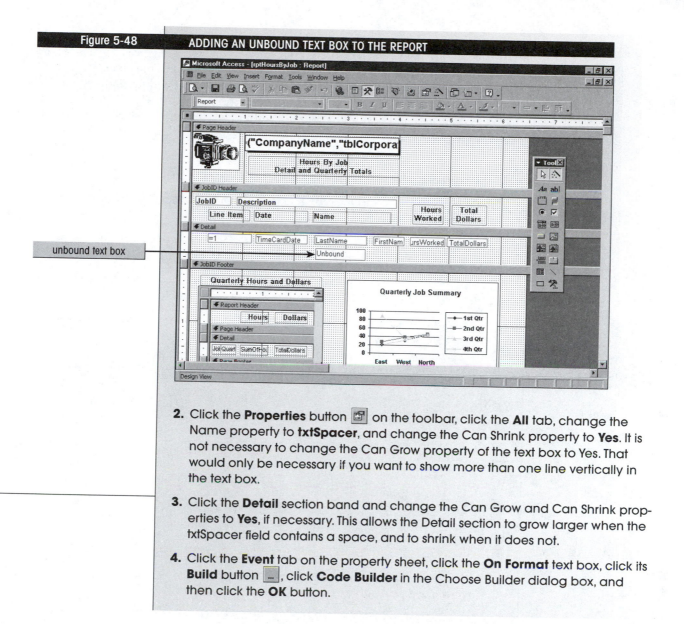

Figure 5-48   **ADDING AN UNBOUND TEXT BOX TO THE REPORT**

unbound text box

2. Click the **Properties** button 🖼 on the toolbar, click the **All** tab, change the Name property to **txtSpacer**, and change the Can Shrink property to **Yes**. It is not necessary to change the Can Grow property of the text box to Yes. That would only be necessary if you want to show more than one line vertically in the text box.

3. Click the **Detail** section band and change the Can Grow and Can Shrink properties to **Yes**, if necessary. This allows the Detail section to grow larger when the txtSpacer field contains a space, and to shrink when it does not.

4. Click the **Event** tab on the property sheet, click the **On Format** text box, click its **Build** button ⌴ , click **Code Builder** in the Choose Builder dialog box, and then click the **OK** button.

Next you will learn how to incorporate a conditional VBA statement to complete the procedure.

Using an If...Then...Else Statement

An **If...Then...Else statement** conditionally executes a group of statements in VBA depending on the results of an expression. This type of conditional statement or control structure will be discussed in greater detail in Tutorial 6. A **control structure** is a series of VBA statements that work together as a unit. A VBA **statement** is a unit that expresses one kind of action, declaration, or definition in complete syntax. A VBA **expression** is a combination of keywords, operators, variables, and constants that yields a string, number, or object. Although you are not yet familiar with some of these terms, they will be introduced as they apply. **Operators** are used to perform arithmetic calculations, perform comparisons, combine strings, and perform logical operations. You have been using the ampersand (&) operator to create expressions in queries and reports that combine fields with other fields and strings of text. (Variables and constants will be introduced in Tutorial 6.) The If...Then...Else statement that you will write includes an expression that uses the Mod operator.

The **Mod operator** is an arithmetic operator used to divide two numbers and return only the remainder. For example, 10 Mod 5 returns 0 because 10 divided by 5 equals 2 with a remainder of 0. And, 10 Mod 3 returns 1 because 10 divided by 3 equals 9 with a remainder of 1.

You will use the Mod operator to determine the result of dividing the contents of the report's txtLineItem field by five. If the remainder (or the result) of the operation is zero, which will occur in multiples of five, you will add a blank space to the txtSpacer control and the blank line will print.

To complete the code for adding a blank line:

1. Press the **Tab** key to indent, type **If (txtLineItem Mod 5) = 0 Then**, and then press the **Enter** key.

2. Press the **Tab** key to indent, type **txtSpacer = " "** (be sure to press the spacebar between the quotation marks), and then press the **Enter** key.

3. Press **Shift+Tab** to outdent, type **Else**, press the **Enter** key, press the **Tab** key to indent, type **txtSpacer = Null**, and then press the **Enter** key.

4. Press **Shift+Tab** to outdent, type **End If** (see Figure 5-49), and then close the Visual Basic window.

Figure 5-49	CODE FOR ADDING A BLANK LINE

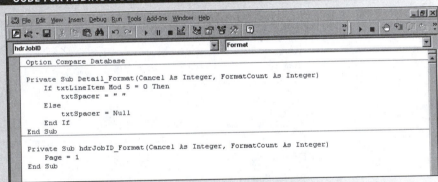

5. Preview the report. A blank line should appear after every fifth record.

6. Return to Design view, close the property sheet, and then save your changes.

7. Close the report, close the **Movie5** database, and then exit Access.

Martin Woodward is pleased with the report. The subreport provides the summary data he needs, and the chart provides a visual representation of that summary data. The detail data is included, and numbered and formatted so that it easy to read.

Session 5.2 QUICK CHECK

1. Which events occur when data is entered, deleted, or changed in a form or control?

2. The _____ event occurs after Access formats a report for printing that has no data, but before the report is printed.

3. What is the first argument of the Msgbox macro action?

4. A(n) _____ procedure returns a value, such as the result of a calculation.

5. Where can VBA functions be used in Access?

6. The Code Builder allows you to create _____ procedures in a class module.

7. The Running Sum property allows you to calculate _____ totals or _____ totals in a report.

8. What does the Page property specify?

9. A(n) _____ in VBA is a unit that expresses one kind of action, declaration, or definition in complete syntax.

REVIEW ASSIGNMENTS

The Hours5 database is similar to the MovieCam Technologies database you worked with in the tutorial. It contains a report template named zsrptTemplate which is identical to the report template in MovieCam. Complete the following:

1. Start Access and open the **Hours5** database located in the Tutorial.05 folder on your local or network drive.

2. Create a table in Design view with the following fields, specifying CompanyID as the primary key, add the new record shown below, and save the table as **"tblCorporate"**.

Field Name	Data Type	Description
CompanyID	Autonumber	1
CompanyName	Text	Technologies Video
Address	Text	1010 West Street
City	Text	Santa Rosa
State	Text	CA
ZipCode	Text	95402
Telephone	Text	(707) 555-5555
FAX	Text	(707) 555-9999

3. Create a new report in Design view. Create an unbound text box in the Report Header section that is approximately 4" wide and ½" tall.

4. Type "=DLookup("CompanyName", "tblCorporate", "CompanyID=1")" inside the text box, and then press the Enter key.

5. Change the font size to 14, the style to bold, and alignment of the text to centered.

6. Save the report as "zsrptMaster" and then close it.

7. Create a new query in Design view, click tblEmployees in the Show Table dialog box, and then click the Add button twice.

8. Close the Show Table dialog box.

9. Click and drag the SupervisorNo field in the tblEmployees field list to the EmployeeNo field in the tblEmployees_1 field list to create a self-join.

10. Right-click the title bar of the tblEmployees_1 field list, click Properties on the shortcut menu, and then type tblSupervisors in the Alias property text box.

11. Close the properties dialog box, drag the EmployeeNo, DeptNo, LastName, HourlyRate, and TimeCard fields from the tblEmployees field list to the design grid.

12. Drag the DeptNo and LastName fields from the tblSupervisors field list to the design grid.

13. Save the query as "qryEmployeesBySupervisor" and then close it.

14. Make sure that Reports is selected on the Objects bar in the Database window, right-click zsrptMaster, click Copy on the shortcut menu, right-click an empty area of the Database window, and click Paste on the shortcut menu.

15. Type "rptEmployeesBySupervisor" in the Report Name text box, and then click the OK button.

16. Open the new report in Design view, and then click the Properties button on the toolbar.

17. Type "qryEmployeesBySupervisor" in the Record Source property text box, and then press the Enter key. Close the properties dialog box, click View on the menu bar, click Sorting and Grouping, click in the first Field/Expression text box, click the list arrow, and then click tblSupervisors.DeptNo. In the Group Properties, change Group Header to Yes and Group Footer to Yes, and then close the Sorting and Grouping dialog box.

18. Drag the tblSupervisor.DeptNo and tblSupervisors.LastName fields to the tblSupervisor.DeptNo Header section. Delete the labels that were created automatically with the text boxes.

19. Drag the EmployeeNo, tblEmployees.DeptNo, tblEmployees.LastName, HourlyRate, and TimeCard fields to the Detail section.

20. Insert appropriate field labels in the tblSupervisors.DeptNo Header section for its corresponding text box in the Detail section. Size and align them with the controls in the Detail section and then apply the bold style to them.

21. Change the style of the tblSupervisorDepts.DeptNo and tblSupervisors.LastName controls in the Header section to bold.

22. Resize the Detail section so that it is approximately ½" tall.

23. Preview the report, return to Design view, and size the text box controls so that the data is visible without being cut off.

Explore   24. Add an unbound text box to the tblSupervisors.DeptNo Footer section that averages the hourly rate paid to employees per supervisor department. Apply the currency format to the text box and include a label to the right of it with the text Average Hourly Rate.

25. Print the report, close it, and save your changes.

CASE PROBLEMS

Case 1. Edwards and Company Jack Edwards has asked you to create a report that contains client names, their phone numbers, and contact names. You've created the report and now need to add some finishing touches to it. Jack wants a total at the bottom of the report of all of the clients on the page, and a count at the bottom of the report of all the clients in the report. (The Edward5 database currently contains only sample records, so the report consists of only one page, but you anticipate that it will eventually be several pages long.)

1. Start Access and open the **Edward5** database located in the Tutorial.05 folder on your local or network drive.

2. Open the rptClientsPhone report in Design view, and, if necessary, display the toolbox.

3. Click the Text Box button on the toolbox, and click in the Page Footer section below the ContactName control.

4. Click the Properties button on the toolbar, and change the Name property to txtCount. Leave the properties dialog box open.

5. Click inside the label to the left of the text box, and type "Total Clients".

6. Click the Page Header section, and then click the Event tab in the properties dialog box.

7. Click in the On Print property, click the Build button, click Code Builder in the Choose Builder dialog box, and then click the OK button.

8. Press the tab key to indent the line, type "txtCount=0", and close the Visual Basic window.

9. Click the Detail section of the report, click the On Print event property text box, click the Build button, click Code Builder, and then click the OK button.

10. Press the Tab key to indent the line, type "txtCount=txtCount + 1", and then close the Visual Basic window.

11. Preview the report.

12. Move the text box and label to the right edge of the report, and then add a new unbound text box to the left side of the Page Footer section.

13. Delete the label that is drawn with the text box, click inside the text box, and type "="Page " & Page & " of " & Pages".

14. Format the label and text boxes in the page footer to be Arial 10 point.

Explore 15. Add an unbound text box to the center of the Page Footer section that displays the current day's date. It should be formatted to display the day and the date.

16. Preview the report to test your changes.

17. Print the report, close it, and save your changes.

18. Close **Edward5** and exit Access.

Case 2. San Diego County Information Systems You have created a new report for your database. The report is named rptEmployeesPhone, and contains a list of all employees sorted alphabetically by last name. You want to add a line item to the report to identify a specific employee, and a blank row after every fourth employee record to make the report easier to read.

1. Start Access, open the **ISD5** database located in the Tutorial.05 folder on your local or network drive, and open the rptEmployeesPhone report in Design view.

2. Make sure that the toolbox is visible, click the Text Box button on the toolbox, and click to the left of the FirstName text box control in the Detail section.

3. Click the Properties button on the toolbar, change the Name property to "txtLineItem", type "=1" in the Control Source property text box, and then change the Running Sum property to Over All.

4. Close the properties dialog box, and size and align the txtLineItem text box so that it is the same height as and aligned with the other controls in the report's Detail section.

5. Add a label in the Page Header section above the txtLineItem control, and type "Line Item". Size and align the label to match the other labels in the Page Header section.

6. Drag the Detail section of the report down so that it is approximately ½" high, insert an unbound text box beneath the LastName text box, click the Properties button on the toolbar, change the name of the text box to txtSpacer, and change the Can Shrink property to Yes.

7. Click the Detail section of the report and change the Can Grow and Can Shrink properties to Yes, click the Event tab in the properties dialog box, click in the On Format property text box, and click the Build button.

8. If necessary, click Code Builder in the Choose Builder dialog box, click the OK button, press the Tab key to indent, type "If (txtLineItem Mod 4) = 0 Then", and then press the Enter key.

9. Press the Tab key to indent, type "txtSpacer = " "" (be sure to press the spacebar between the quotation marks), and then press the Enter key.

10. Press Shift+Tab to outdent, type "Else", press the Enter key, press the Tab key to indent, type "txtSpacer = Null", and then press the Enter key.

11. Press Shift+Tab to outdent, type "End If", close the VB window, and then preview the report.

Explore ▶ 12. Add an image box to the Report Header section that contains the Microsoft Office clip art image Hatecomp. Be sure to adjust the properties of the image box so that the full image displays.

13. Print the report and save your changes.

14. Close the **ISD5** database and exit Access.

Case 3. Christenson Homes The reports for Christenson Homes are not yet completed. Roberta told you that the company is considering incorporating and might change the company name and logo. You created the template for the database, and now need to create a report master that contains the company name and logo. You want these items stored in a table so that you can change them easily if necessary.

1. Start Access and open the **Homes5** database located in the Tutorial.05 folder on your local or network drive.

2. Create a new table in the Design view and define the following fields:

Field Name	Data Type
CompanyID	Autonumber
CompanyName	Text
Logo	OLE Object

3. Set CompanyID as the primary key.

4. Save the table as "tblCorporate".

5. Switch to Datasheet view and then type "Christenson Homes" in the CompanyName field.

Explore   6. Right-click the Logo field, click Insert Object on the shortcut menu, click the Create from File option, click the Browse button, select the **H5Logo** file in the Tutorial.05 folder, and the click OK.

7. Close the table.

8. Create a new report in Design view, and insert a text box in the Report Header section that contains a DLookup function to look up the company name from the tblCorporate table. Delete the label that's automatically created when you add the text box.

9. Format the text box to be Arial, 14 point, bold, and size it to fit the text.

Explore   10. Click the Bound Object Frame button on the toolbox, and click and drag to the left of the text box containing the company name.

Explore   11. Display the properties dialog box, click in the Control Source text box, type =DlookUp ("Logo", "tblCorporate", "CompanyID=1").

12. Change the Size Mode property of the bound object frame to Stretch.

13. Save the report as "zsrptMaster", preview it, and then print it.

14. Close the **Homes5** database and exit Access.

Case 4. Sonoma Farms   The Sonoma Farms database contains a report named rptVisitorsByDistributor. The report contains information about each visitor to the farm, grouped by the distributor name. You want to add a subreport to the Report Footer that shows data that summarizes the number of visitors to the farm, by distributor. You will also add a pie chart that shows the relationship among these numbers.

1. Start Access and open the **Sonoma5** database located in the Tutorial.05 folder on your local or network drive.

2. Open the rptVisitorsByDistribuor report in Design view, and drag the qryVisitorsCount query from the Database window to the Report Footer section of the report.

3. Choose none when asked which fields link the main report to the subreport, and name the subreport "srptVisitorsCount". Delete the label that's automatically created when you insert the subreport.

4. Open the srptVisitorsCount report, and change the CountofVisitorID label to "Total Visitors". Size and align the labels as shown in Figure 5-50, change the font to Arial, and save and close the report.

Figure 5-50   **MODIFYING THE SRPTVISTORSCOUNT REPORT**

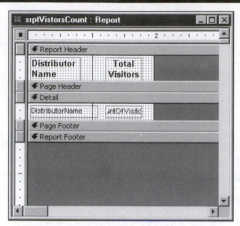

5. Open the rptVisitorsByDistributor report in Design view and size the subreport control as shown in Figure 5-51.

Figure 5-51   **RPTVISTORSBYDISTRIBUTOR**

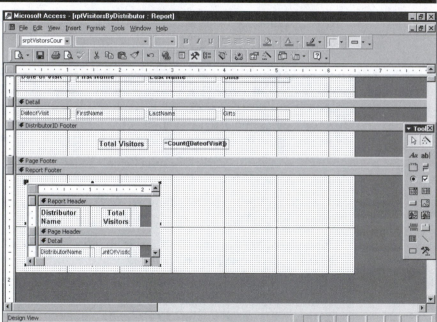

6. Insert a chart in the Report Footer section to the right of the subreport. Base the chart on the qryVisitorsCount query.

7. Choose the pie chart type, and size and align the chart to be approximately the same size as the subreport control.

8. Save the report and print it.

9. Close the **Sonoma5** database and exit Access.

QUICK | CHECK ANSWERS

Session 5.1

1. Domain aggregate functions provide statistical information about a set of records or domain.
2. criteria
3. DAvg returns the arithmetical average of the values in the specified field.
4. An unbound object frame should be used to link to the source file.
5. Page Header
6. The Detail section is the main body of a report.
7. Expressions can be included in Group Footers and the Report Footer.
8. Joining a table to itself is a self-join.
9. The effect of setting the Can Grow property to Yes is that it allows the control to grow vertically in order to display all the data.
10. The advantage to sending a report as a snapshot is that the recipient does not need Access to view the report.

Session 5.2

1. Data events occur when data is entered, deleted, or changed in a form or control.
2. NoData
3. The first argument of the Msgbox macro action is Message.
4. function
5. VBA functions can be used in expressions, property settings, or as criteria in queries and filters.
6. event
7. record-by-record; group-by-group
8. The Page property specifies the current page number when a page is being printed.
9. statement

OBJECTIVES

In this tutorial you will:

- Study properties, events, objects, methods, and collections

- Create an event procedure to validate data entered in a form

- Create an event procedure for the frmDataSwitchboard form

- Learn about If…Then…Else and Select Case conditional statements

- Use the DoCmd object, and learn the syntax of the OpenForm method

- Modify an Access toolbar, and create a custom menu bar and a custom shortcut menu

- Change the Startup properties for the MovieCam database

- Copy VBA code from the Access Help system and use it with an AutoKeys macro

- Split the MovieCam database into a front and back end

CUSTOMIZING THE USER INTERFACE

Redesigning the User Interface in the MovieCam Technologies Database

CASE

MovieCam Technologies

You and Carolyn now have confidence in your ability to write VBA code, so you want to revisit some of the objects you created in the MovieCam database and apply your knowledge to enhance their design. In addition, Amanda asks you and Carolyn to complete the user interface. She wants you to customize menus, toolbars, and the Startup properties to make the database even more user-friendly.

Amanda has also suggested that you split the MovieCam database into a **front end file** containing all the database objects except for the tables, and a **back end file** containing only the tables. You will then move the back end to a shared network drive and distribute copies of the front end to key users for testing the database at its current level of completion. You and Carolyn will continue development of the database in a front end master copy that is unsecured and located on a network drive to which you both have access.

SESSION 6.1

In this session, you will learn more about objects and properties. You will be introduced to VBA methods—specifically, the DoCmd.OpenForm method. You'll study data events and use them to write an event procedure to validate data and to open forms from the frmDataSwitchboard form. You also will learn to work with the If...Then...Else and Select Case conditional statements, as well as work with the DoCmd object.

Objects, Methods, and Properties

You are familiar by now with the term objects. It is used in reference to database tables, queries, forms, controls, fields, relationships, and other components. Objects have certain characteristics called properties. A **property** is a named attribute of an object that defines a certain characteristic, such as size, color, or a behavioral aspect, such as whether the object is visible or whether it is automatically centered.

These objects are referred to as Microsoft Access objects. They are created and maintained by the Access programming environment and are related to the user interface and modules.

In addition to properties, objects have methods. A **method** is a procedure that acts on an object. For example, the Undo method for a control or a form lets you reset the control or the form when its value has been changed. You would use this method in VBA to clear a change to a record that contains an invalid entry. Methods will be introduced as they apply to writing VBA code. Methods are somewhat similar to macro actions.

Collections and Classes

Collections and classes were mentioned briefly in Tutorial 4 when the identifier operators were introduced. A **class** is the definition for an object. It includes the object's name, its properties and methods, and any events associated with it. When you create an **instance** of a class, you create a new object with all of the characteristics defined by that class. The properties and methods associated with one form in the database are the same as the properties and methods of the Form object class. Objects in Access can contain other objects. For example, form objects contain control objects, and table objects contain field objects. In Access, it is common to group related objects together.

Remember from Tutorial 4 that a **collection** is an object that contains a set of related objects (objects of the same class). For example, a Forms collection contains all open forms in the database, and a Reports collection contains all open reports. A collection is not created by the user; it is simply a means of referring to all the open forms or all the open reports. VBA, macros, and queries identify an object by specifying the collection to which it belongs. For example, *Forms!frmDataSwitchboard!grpForms* identifies the option group named grpForms in the frmDataSwtichboard form. The *Forms* collection is followed by the form name, *frmDataSwitchboard*, which is followed by the name of the control, *grpForms*. This is similar to specifying a filename in Windows by typing the name of the drive, the name of the folder, and then the filename itself. For example, *C:\Tutorial.06\Movie6*.

Figure 6-1 summarizes these terms.

Figure 6-1	NEW TERMS AND EXAMPLES	
TERM	**DEFINITION**	**EXAMPLES**
Class	Definition for an object, including the object's name, its properties and methods, and any events associated with it	The Form object class is the definition for forms in the database.
Collection	An object that contains a set of related objects (objects of the same class)	The Forms collection is all the open forms at any given time.
Method	A procedure that acts on an object	The requery method of a form updates the data in a form by requerying the underlying record source. The Undo method for a control lets you reset the control when its value has been changed.
Property	Named attribute of an object that defines a certain characteristic	The Visible property of a control determines whether you can see it displayed in Form view. The Back Color property of a control determines its background color.

Data Event Properties

You applied a number of Print events to reports in Tutorial 5. In this tutorial you will use Data events to trigger code. These events occur when data is entered, deleted, or changed in a form or control. The various data events are described below.

- *After Del Confirm:* This is a form event that occurs after you confirm record deletions and the records are actually deleted, or after the deletions are canceled.
- *After Insert:* This is a form event that occurs after a new record is added to the database.
- *After Update:* This is a form and control event that occurs after a control or record is updated with changed data. This event occurs when the control or record loses the focus, or you click Save Record on the Records menu or toolbar. This event occurs for new and existing records.
- *Before Del Confirm:* This is a form event that occurs after one or more records are deleted, but before Access displays a dialog box asking you to confirm or cancel the deletion. This event occurs after the Delete event.
- *Before Insert:* This is a form event that occurs when you type the first character in a new record, but before the record is added to the database.
- *Before Update:* This is a form and control event that occurs before a control or record is updated with changed data. This event occurs when the control or record loses the focus or when you click Save Records on the Records menu bar or toolbar. This event occurs for new and existing records.
- *Change:* This is a control event that occurs when the context of a text box or the text box portion of a combo box changes. It occurs when you type a character in the control or change the Text property of a control using a macro or VBA.
- *Current:* This is a form event that occurs when the focus moves to a record, therefore making it the current record, or when you requery a form's source of data. This event occurs when a form is first opened and whenever the focus leaves one record and moves to another.
- *Delete:* This is a form event that occurs when a record is deleted, but before the deletion is confirmed and actually performed.

- *Dirty:* This is a form event that occurs when the contents of a form or the text portion of a combo box change. It also occurs when you move from one page to another page in a tab control.
- *Not In List:* This is a control property that occurs when a value entered in a combo box isn't in the combo box list.
- *Updated:* This is a control property that occurs when an OLE object's data has been modified.

Validating Data Using an Event Procedure

In Tutorial 1, you learned how to apply table and field validation rules. By writing code in a form module, you can also validate data as the user enters it. At MovieCam Technologies, time cards are always dated the Saturday following the work week. The product managers want the database to prevent the data entry clerk from entering a date that does not fall on a Saturday. You and Carolyn will write an event procedure to perform this validation.

Before you write the event procedure, you will change a default setting so that the code window opens automatically when you click the Build button for an event property in a form or report. This will bypass the Choose Builder dialog box (see Figure 6-2) that opens when you click the Build button.

Figure 6-2	CHOOSE BUILDER DIALOG BOX

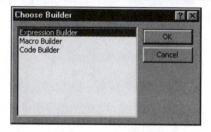

REFERENCE   WINDOW   RW

<u>Bypassing the Choose Builder Dialog Box</u>
- Click Tools on the menu bar, and then click Options.
- Click the Forms/Reports tab in the Options dialog box.
- Click the Always use event procedures check box, and then click the OK button.

You will change the default setting next.

To change default settings so that the Code window opens automatically:

1. Start Access and open the **Movie6** database located in the Tutorial.06 folder on your local or network drive.

2. Click **Tools** on the menu bar, and then click **Options**.

3. Click the **Forms/Reports** tab in the Options dialog box.

4. Click the **Always use event procedures** check box as shown in Figure 6-3.

Figure 6-3 CHANGING DEFAULT SETTINGS IN THE OPTIONS DIALOG BOX

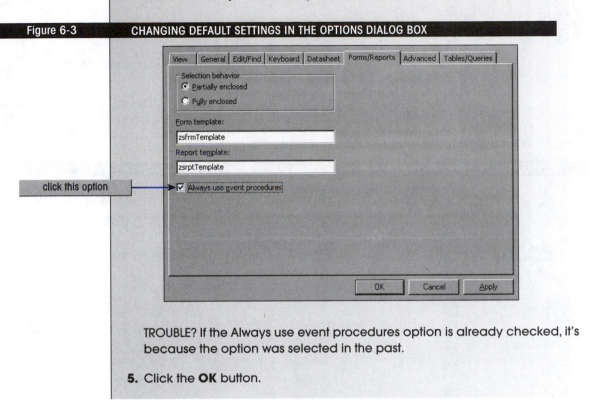

click this option

TROUBLE? If the Always use event procedures option is already checked, it's because the option was selected in the past.

5. Click the **OK** button.

Canceling the Default Behavior Following an Event

After an object recognizes an event, Access carries out the default behavior. For some events, Access runs the event procedure or macro before the default behavior takes place. To cancel the user action for these events, you can include the Cancel Event action in a macro (as you did in Tutorial 5), or the Cancel = True statement in VBA.

One of the events for which Access runs the event procedure before the default behavior takes place is the Before Update event. Others include the Apply Filter, Dbl Click, Delete, and No Data events.

You will use the Before Update event in the frmTimeCards form to test the entry in the TimeCardDate field. If the date entered does not fall on Saturday, the entry is canceled. You'll use the DatePart function to test the day of the week entered in the TimeCardDate field.

The **DatePart function** returns an integer containing the specified part of the given date. For example, you can use it to extract the day of the week, the year, or the day of the month. The syntax of the DatePart function is *DatePart(interval, date [,firstdayofweek[, firstweekofyear]])*.

The *interval* argument is a required string that represents the interval of time you want returned. The *date* argument is the date you are testing. The *firstdayofweek* argument is optional and is used to specify the first day of the week if you don't want Sunday used. The *firstweekofyear* argument is optional and is used to specify the first week of the year, if you do not want the week of January 1 used.

Because Access sets Sunday as day 1 of the week, Saturday is day 7. The procedure you write will test to see if the date entered is any day other than Saturday, and if it is it will cancel the entry and display a message on the screen.

To validate the data entered in the TimeCardDate field in the frmTimeCards form:

1. Open the **frmTimeCards** form in Design view.

2. Select the **TimeCardDate** text box, and then click the **Properties** button 🗔 on the toolbar.

3. If necessary, click the **Event** tab on the property sheet, click the **Before Update** property, and then click the **Build** button ⸱⸱⸱ . Your screen should look like that shown in Figure 6-4.

Figure 6-4	CODE WINDOW IN THE VISUAL BASIC WINDOW

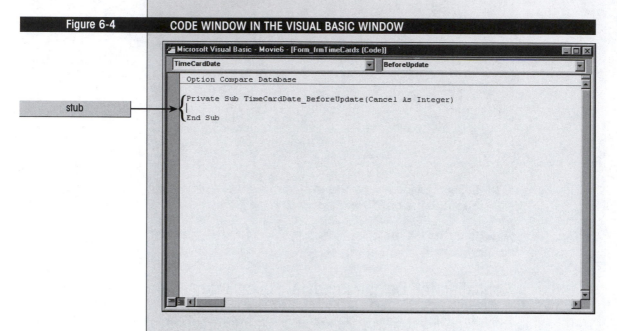

stub

TROUBLE? If other windows such as the Immediate window are displayed in the Visual Basic window, click their Close buttons ☒ to close them.

The insertion point is positioned between the first statement of the event procedure and the last. The first and last statements of the event procedure are called the **stub** (as noted in Figure 6-4). The statements you will use in the code include an If...Then...Else conditional statement to test the entry. This statement will be discussed in greater detail later in this tutorial and is similar to using the Condition column in a macro. You will also include a MsgBox statement to give the user an error message if the date entered does not fall on a Saturday.

4. Press the **Tab** key to indent the line, and type **If DatePart(**. A banner opens below the function and provides syntax information for the DatePart function. See Figure 6-5.

Figure 6-5	TYPING THE SUB PROCEDURE

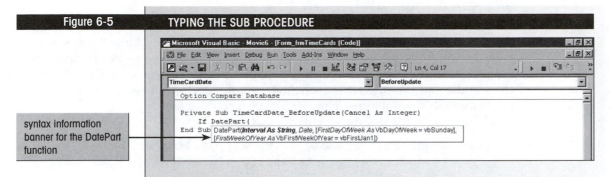

syntax information banner for the DatePart function

TROUBLE? If the banner does not open, click Tools on the menu bar, click Options, click the Editor tab, click the Auto Quick Info check box to select it, and click the OK button. Backspace and retype the open parenthesis in the DatePart function.

5. Type **"w", TimeCardDate) <> 7 Then** and then press the **Enter** key.

6. Press the **Tab** key, type **Cancel = True**, press the **Enter** key to move to the next line, and then type **MsgBox "You must enter a date that corresponds to a Saturday."**

7. Press the **Enter** key, press **Shift+Tab** to outdent the line, and then type **End If**.

8. Click **Debug** on the menu bar, and then click **Compile MovieCam**. The process of translating modules from VBA to a translated form is called **compilation**. (Compilation will be discussed in greater detail in Tutorial 7.) Access will compile all the modules in the MovieCam database and check them for syntax errors.

TROUBLE? If Access identifies any errors in your code, correct the errors and repeat Step 8.

9. Close the Visual Basic window, close the property sheet, and switch to Form view to test the procedure.

10. Add a new record, type **200** in the Time Card No field, type **2/1/02** in the Time Card Date field, and then press the **Enter** key. You will see the error message shown in Figure 6-6.

Figure 6-6	DATA VALIDATION ERROR MESSAGE

11. Click the **OK** button, and then press the **Esc** key twice to cancel the entry.

12. Save your changes and close the form.

Now that you have completed the validation procedure for the frmTimeCards form, you will focus on converting the macros in the MovieCam database forms switchboard. To understand the VBA code needed to open the forms, you will learn about the DoCmd object and its Open Form method. You also will learn about writing conditional statements in VBA, such as If…Then… Else and Select Case statements.

The DoCmd Object

The DoCmd object carries out macro actions in VBA procedures. Most macro actions have corresponding DoCmd methods, and the arguments correspond to the action arguments found in the macro window. For example, the DoCmd.OpenForm method in VBA is equivalent to the OpenForm macro action. You will use the DoCmd object and its methods to create the code to open forms in the frmDataSwitchboard form.

The syntax for the DoCmd.OpenForm object is:

```
DoCmd.OpenForm "formname"[, view][, filtername]
[, wherecondition][, datamode][, windowmode][, openargs]
```

The *formname* argument is the only required argument, and it must be included in quotation marks. The bracketed arguments are optional. If you include an optional argument, you must include a comma for each argument that precedes the optional argument, even though the argument itself is not typed. You do not need to include commas after the optional argument. For example, if you were to include a wherecondition argument, the Docmd.OpenForm statement would be written as follows:

```
DoCmd.OpenForm "formname",,,wherecondition
```

The commas between *formname* and *wherecondition* represent the view and filtername arguments. No commas are required after the wherecondition. The OpenForm method arguments are as follows:

- *Formname:* A string expression that is the valid name of a form in the current database.

- *View:* One of the following intrinsic constants (an **intrinsic constant** is a word that has particular meaning in VBA; for example, in the list that follows, the intrinsic constant acDesign means Design view):
  - acDesign (Design view)
  - acFormDS (Form Datasheet view)
  - acNormal (Form view, which is the default)
  - acPreview (Print Preview)

- *Filtername:* A string expression that is the valid name of a query in the current database.

- *Wherecondition:* A string expression that is a valid SQL where clause without the word *where*.

- *Datamode:* One of the following intrinsic constants:
  - acFormAdd (the form will accept only new records)
  - acFormEdit (the form allows entering, editing, and deleting records)
  - acFormPropertySettings (the form opens based on the form's property settings; this is the default)
  - acFormReadOnly (the form is read-only)

- *Windowmode:* One of the following intrinsic constants:
  - acDialog (the Modal and Pop Up properties are set to Yes)
  - acHidden (form is open but hidden from view)
  - acIcon (form opens minimized as a small title bar at the bottom of the screen)
  - acWindowNormal or acNormal (form opens in the mode set by its properties; this is the default)

■ *OpenArgs:* Use this to set the OpenArgs property of the form. The OpenArgs property lets you specify a particular record you want to move to, and then you use the OpenArgs property in another line of code to move to the specified record.

Control Structures for Decision Processing

VBA provides you with several different control structures for looping. A control structure is a series of VBA statements that work together as a unit. You often need to test for specific conditions in your procedures. VBA provides a number of ways to test for specific values using decision structures, such as If...Then...Else, If...Then...ElseIf, and Select Case.

If...Then...Else

The If...Then...Else construct lets you specify a condition to be evaluated, and then specify the action(s) to take if the condition is true, and the action(s) to take if the condition is false. In the following example, if the value of grpForms is equal to 1, the frmDegrees form is opened; otherwise a screen message prompts the user to select a form. The Else portion of the construct is optional, so if no action is required when the condition is false, it can be omitted.

```
If grpForms = 1 Then
        DoCmd.OpenForm "frmDegrees", acNormal, "", "", , acNormal
Else
        Msgbox "Select a form to open"
End If
```

ElseIf

You use the If...Then...ElseIf structure to test for multiple conditions. To understand the order in which Access evaluates the conditions, review the following example:

```
If grpForms = 1 Then
        DoCmd.OpenForm "frmDegrees"
ElseIf grpForms = 2 Then
        DoCmd.OpenForm "frmDepartments"
ElseIf grpForms = 3 Then
        DoCmd.OpenForm "frmEmployees"
End If
```

Access evaluates the first condition, *grpForms = 1*, and if it is true, the *DoCmd.OpenForm "frmDegrees"* line is executed. Its execution is directed to any code following the End If statement. If *grpForms = 1* evaluates to false, Access proceeds to grpForms = 2, and so on.

Select Case

You might want to use the Select Case statement instead of multiple If...Then...Else statements. Access evaluates the expression that follows the Select Case statement to produce a result, and then compares the result of the expression to each Case statement. The advantage of using the Select Case construct is that is easier to read than multiple If...Then...Else constructs, and the code performs better because only one statement is evaluated. Following is an example:

```
Select Case grpForms
    Case 1
        DoCmd.OpenForm "frmDegrees"
    Case 2
        DoCmd.OpenForm "frmDepartments"
    Case 3
        DoCmd.OpenForm "frmEmployees"
End Select
```

Adding an Event Procedure to the frmDataSwitchboard Form

Access can automatically convert macros to VBA procedures that perform equivalent actions using Visual Basic code. You can convert macros on a form or report, or you can convert global macros that aren't attached to a specific form or report. You and Carolyn want to learn more about writing VBA in lieu of macros, and decided to use the Macro Converter to help you.

Carolyn ran the Macro Converter to convert the mfrmDataSwitchboard macro to VBA code. The results are shown in Figure 6-7.

Figure 6-7   THE MACRO CONVERTED TO VBA CODE

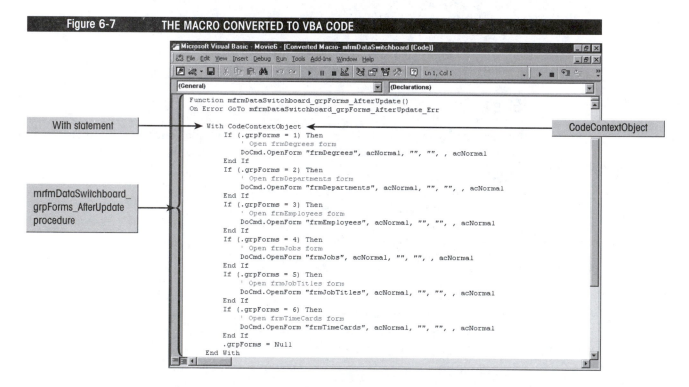

Notice that a series of If...Then...Else statements were created in the conversion. There is no Else statement because there is no action required if the condition evaluated is false. These statements test the value of the grpForms option group, which is set when the user clicks one of the option buttons in the group. The DoCmd.OpenForm method is then used to open the form specified by the option button. All the arguments in the DoCmd.OpenForm statement after the form name are the default choices, and are not required. When Access converts a macro to VBA, it includes the default arguments in the statements even if they are not required.

The With Statement

Also notice the With statement in Figure 6-7. The With statement lets you perform a series of statements on a specified object, such as a form or a control on a form, without restating the name of the object.

Recall from Tutorial 4 that the bang and dot identifier operators are used in VBA code to specifically identify objects and their properties. The bang is used to separate one object from another or from the object class, and the dot is used to separate an object from its property or method. In the following example, the dot (period) is used to separate the lblFirstName object from its BackColor, Caption, and BorderStyle properties.

```
lblFirstName.BackColor = 12632256
lblFirstName.Caption = "First Name"
lblFirstName.BorderStyle = Solid
```

In the above example, the BackColor property is set to gray, the Caption property is set to First Name, and the BorderStyle property is set to Solid.

You can achieve the same effect by using a With statement and identifying the control one time, as shown below:

```
With lblFirstName
     .BackColor = 12632256
     .Caption = "First Name"
     .BorderStyle = Solid
End With
```

Notice the CodeContextObject property referenced in the With statement in Figure 6-7. This property's purpose is to determine the object in which a macro or VBA code is executing. In this instance, the CodeContextObject property represents the frmDataSwitchboard form.

In the converted macro, the CodeContextObject property is used because the mfrmDataSwitchboard_grpForms_AfterUpdate() procedure is a function. Remember that a function in a standard module can be run from properties, expressions, and other procedures. As a function in a standard module, the mfrmDataSwitchboard_grpForms_AfterUpdate() procedure can be run from any form in the database, and the CodeContextObject property will then represent the form that called the function. The grpForms=Null at the end of the procedure sets the option group back to null after the form opens so that the next time the switchboard is used, a new form can be selected.

If the procedure in Figure 6-7 were a form module in the frmDataSwitchboard form, then the With statement and CodeContextObject property would not be necessary, and the procedure would look like this (the indentation and comments identifying the form that will open have been removed to save space):

```
Private Sub grpForms_AfterUpdate()
If grpForms = 1 Then
     DoCmd.OpenForm "frmDegrees", acNormal, "", "", , acNormal
End If
If grpForms = 2 Then
     DoCmd.OpenForm "frmDepartments", acNormal, "", "", ,
acNormal
End If
If grpForms = 3 Then
     DoCmd.OpenForm "frmEmployees", acNormal, "", "", , acNormal
End If
If grpForms = 4 Then
     DoCmd.OpenForm "frmJobs", acNormal, "", "", , acNormal
End If
```

```
If grpForms = 5 Then
     DoCmd.OpenForm "frmJobTitles", acNormal, "", "", , acNormal
End If
If grpForms = 6 Then
     DoCmd.OpenForm "frmTimeCards", acNormal, "", "", , acNormal
End If
grpForms = Null
End Sub
```

A more efficient way to write the same code would be to use the ElseIf form of the If…Then… Else statement, and to leave off the default arguments of the DoCmd.OpenForm as shown below:

```
Private Sub grpForms_AfterUpdate()
     If grpForms = 1 Then
          DoCmd.OpenForm "frmDegrees"
     ElseIf grpForms = 2 Then
          DoCmd.OpenForm "frmDepartments"
     ElseIf grpForms = 3 Then
          DoCmd.OpenForm "frmEmployees"
     ElseIf grpForms = 4 Then
          DoCmd.OpenForm "frmJobs"
     ElseIf grpForms = 5 Then
          DoCmd.OpenForm "frmJobTitles"
     ElseIf grpForms = 6 Then
          DoCmd.OpenForm "frmTimeCards"
     End If
grpForms = Null
End Sub
```

Next you will add the code to the frmDataSwitchboard form and use the Select Case statement discussed above to open a particular form, based on the users choice from the switchboard.

To add code to the frmDataSwitchboard form:

1. Open the **frmDataSwitchboard** form in Design view.

2. Click the frame of the option group once to select it, click the **Properties** button 🖻 on the Form Design toolbar, and then click the **Event** tab on the property sheet. See Figure 6-8.

Figure 6-8	DISPLAYING PROPERTIES FOR THE OPTION GROUP

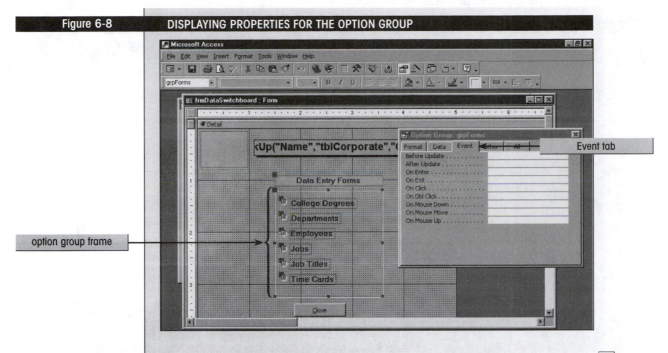

option group frame

Event tab

3. Click the **After Update** property text box, and then click its **Build** button ![Build]. The Code window opens in the Visual Basic window. The new event procedure for the option group's AfterUpdate event property contains the Private Sub and End Sub statements. You can now enter the statements to open a form, based on the option the user selects in the option group.

TROUBLE? If more than one code window opens, close those that you are not currently working with. Make sure that you type in the Form_frmDataSwitchboard (Code) window.

4. Type **Select Case grpForms**, press the **Enter** key, press the **Tab** key to indent, and then type **Case 1**.

5. Press the **Enter** key, press the **Tab** key, and then type **DoCmd.OpenForm "frmDegrees"**.

6. Press the **Enter** key, copy the **Case 1** and **DoCmd.OpenForm** statements and paste them in the blank line you just created before the End Sub statement, change Case 1 to **Case 2**, and then change frmDegrees to **frmDepartments**. If necessary, indent or outdent these statements so that they are aligned as shown in Figure 6-9.

7. Repeat Step 6, and change the Case to **3**, and the form to **frmEmployees**

8. Repeat Step 6, and change the Case to **4**, and the form the **frmJobs**.

9. Complete the code (starting with the Case 5 statement) as shown in Figure 6-9.

| Figure 6-9 | COMPLETED GRPFORMS_AFTERUPDATE PROCEDURE |

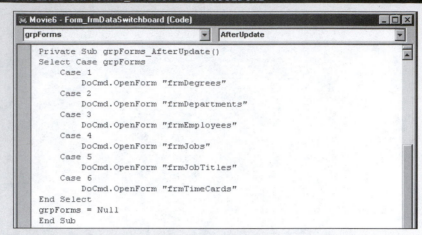

```
Movie6 - Form_frmDataSwitchboard (Code)
grpForms                              AfterUpdate
    Private Sub grpForms_AfterUpdate()
    Select Case grpForms
        Case 1
            DoCmd.OpenForm "frmDegrees"
        Case 2
            DoCmd.OpenForm "frmDepartments"
        Case 3
            DoCmd.OpenForm "frmEmployees"
        Case 4
            DoCmd.OpenForm "frmJobs"
        Case 5
            DoCmd.OpenForm "frmJobTitles"
        Case 6
            DoCmd.OpenForm "frmTimeCards"
    End Select
    grpForms = Null
    End Sub
```

TROUBLE? If you mistype code, position the insertion point in the Code window to the right of the error. Use the Backspace key to delete characters. Reenter any incorrect statements until your screen looks like Figure 6-9.

10. Close the Visual Basic window, close the property sheet, and switch to Form view to test the procedure.

11. Click each of the forms in the option group to be sure that the correct form opens, and then close each form to return to the switchboard.

12. Save the form, and then close it to return to the Database window.

The product managers are pleased with the validation of data entered in the TimeCardDate field in the frmTimeCards form, and you and Carolyn are pleased with your ability to code using VBA. The frmDataSwitchboard form works well, and you are ready to customize toolbars and menus, change Startup properties, and split the database.

Session 6.1 QUICK CHECK

1. A(n) _____ is a named attribute of an object that defines a certain characteristic, such as size or color.

2. A(n) _____ is a procedure that is similar to a statement or function that operates on an object.

3. When does the After Update event occur?

4. What does the DatePart function return?

5. What is the DoCmd object?

6. The _____ argument in Docmd.OpenForm is a string expression that is a valid SQL where clause without the word *where*.

7. The _____ is a good alternative to the ElseIf form of the If…Then…Else statement.

8. What is the purpose of the CodeContextObject property?

9. What is the purpose of using a With statement?

SESSION 6.2

In this session, you will learn how to modify an existing toolbar, create a custom menu bar, and create a custom shortcut menu. You will learn how to modify Startup properties to control user access to objects in the database. You also will learn to work with AutoKeys macros.

Introduction to Menus and Toolbars

Menus and toolbars are common in most Windows-based programs. Commands, such as opening, saving, and closing files, exiting a program, printing, and more, are organized on toolbars and menus so that you can quickly and easily access them.

Access automatically "personalizes" menus and toolbars based on how often you use the commands they contain. When you first start Access, the most basic commands appear on the menus, and are represented by buttons on the toolbars. As you work, Access adjusts the menus and toolbars to display the commands and buttons you use most often. As you already know, clicking the double arrow at the bottom of a menu expands the menu to show all the commands it contains. You can also double-click the menu to expand it. For example, when you double-click Tools on the menu bar, the entire menu is visible. When you click a command on the expanded menu, it is automatically placed on the personalized menu the next time you open it. A command is dropped from your personalized menu if you use Access many times without using that command. You can change settings so that the full set of commands is always on the menus; however, if you are working in the Office 2000 suite, changing this setting in Access affects the other programs in the suite.

REFERENCE WINDOW   **RW**

Displaying the Full Set of Menu Commands
- Click Tools on the menu bar, and then click Customize.
- Click the Options tab in the Customize dialog box.
- Click the Menus show recently used commands first check box to clear the option.
- Click the Close button.

You will now change the menu settings so that all menu commands are available when the menu is opened. You will also explore **menu animation**, the term used to describe how the menu opens. For example, a menu can slide down or it can unfold when you click it.

To display the full set of menu commands and explore menu animation:

1. Click **Tools** on the menu bar, click **Customize**, and then click the **Options** tab in the Customize dialog box.

2. If necessary, click the **Menus show recently used commands first** check box to clear the option, as shown in Figure 6-10.

Figure 6-10   CHANGING MENU OPTIONS

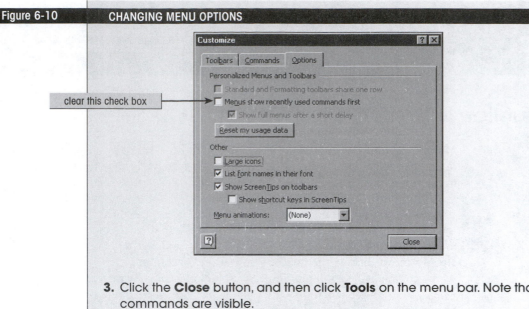

clear this check box

3. Click the **Close** button, and then click **Tools** on the menu bar. Note that all the commands are visible.

4. With the Tools menu still open, click **Customize**. The Options tab should still be selected.

5. Click the **Menu animations** list arrow, click **Slide**, and then click the **Close** button.

6. Click **Tools** on the menu bar to test the change. The animation is a bit distracting, so you will remove it.

7. Click **Tools** on the menu bar, click **Customize,** change the Menu animations back to **(None)**, and then click the **Close** button.

Access 2000 provides you with the flexibility to move and position toolbars. You can position them side by side by clicking the move handle along the left edge of the toolbar and then dragging the toolbar so that it is positioned to the right or left of another toolbar. See Figure 6-11.

Figure 6-11   POSITIONING TOOLBARS SIDE BY SIDE

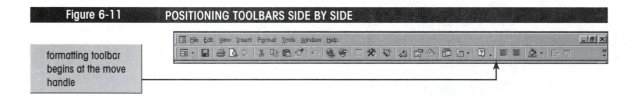

formatting toolbar begins at the move handle

When you position toolbars side by side, however, there might not be enough room for all the buttons. In this case, only the buttons you have used most recently are visible. To resize a toolbar when it is positioned on the same row as another toolbar, click the move handle and then drag the edge of the toolbar. See Figure 6-12.

Figure 6-12   SIZING A TOOLBAR

drag the move handle

To see a list of the buttons that are not visible on a built-in, docked toolbar, click the More Buttons button ⟨»⟩ at the end of the toolbar. When you use a button that is not visible on the toolbar, that button is moved to the toolbar, and a button that has not been used recently is dropped to the More Buttons list, as shown in Figure 6-13.

Figure 6-13   BUTTONS THAT DON'T FIT ON THE TOOLBAR

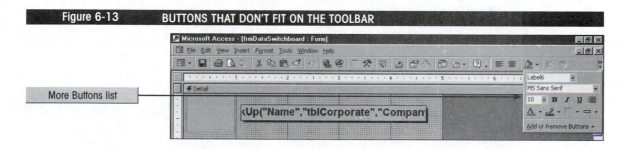

More Buttons list

Because the menus and toolbars are personalized to show the commands that you use most often in Access, you might find at some point that you want to return them to their original state. To do this, open the Customize dialog box from the Tools menu, and click the "Reset my usage data" button, as shown in Figure 6-14.

Figure 6-14   RESETTING THE TOOLBAR

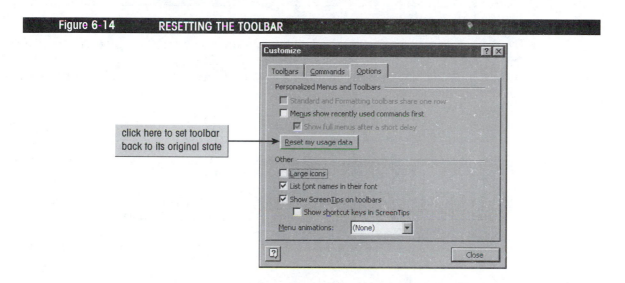

click here to set toolbar back to its original state

You can further customize the built-in menu bar by adding or removing menu items, or by moving a menu to a different location. You also can create your own custom toolbars, menu bars, and shortcut menus.

Creating and Customizing Menus and Toolbars

Creating custom menus and toolbars in a program is an important part of the database development process. In many instances, you will want to restrict access to certain features and objects so that users cannot inadvertently delete data, view sensitive data, modify the design of an object, modify macros or VBA code, and so forth. A simple way to do this is to customize existing menus and toolbars, or create new ones.

You and Carolyn determine that it is in the best interest of MovieCam Technologies to give database users access to only those menu commands and toolbar buttons that they need to enter and edit records. You will restrict access to the default toolbars, and create a custom shortcut menu so that the command to switch to an object's Design view is not available. You also will restrict access to the default toolbars, and will create a custom toolbar that contains only those buttons users need to work in the database. In addition, you will customize shortcut menus so the command to switch to an object's Design view is not available.

Customizing Toolbars

Access stores customized toolbars in a file named System.mdw. This file contains preference and security information, and will be discussed in greater detail in Tutorial 9.

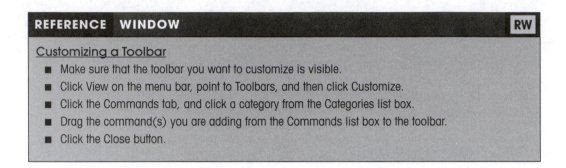

REFERENCE WINDOW   **RW**

Customizing a Toolbar
- Make sure that the toolbar you want to customize is visible.
- Click View on the menu bar, point to Toolbars, and then click Customize.
- Click the Commands tab, and click a category from the Categories list box.
- Drag the command(s) you are adding from the Commands list box to the toolbar.
- Click the Close button.

Before you modify the menus and toolbars for users, you and Carolyn want to customize the menus and toolbars you're using to design and develop the database. Because you spend a lot of time aligning controls on forms, you will add Align Left and Align Top buttons to the Formatting toolbar.

To customize a toolbar:

1. Make sure that **Forms** is selected on the Objects bar in the Database window, and open the **frmJobs** form in Design view.

2. Be sure the Formatting toolbar is visible, as shown in Figure 6-15. If it is not, click **View** on the menu bar, point to **Toolbars**, and then click **Formatting (Form/Report)**.

Figure 6-15	CUSTOMIZING A TOOLBAR

the Formatting toolbar →

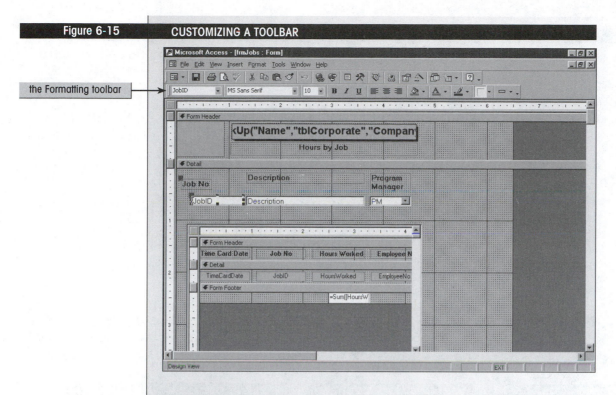

3. Click **View** on the menu bar, point to **Toolbars**, click **Customize**, and then click the **Toolbars** tab. See Figure 6-16. The first tab of the dialog lists the existing toolbars and menu bars in the program. Those that are currently visible are checked.

Figure 6-16	CUSTOMIZE DIALOG BOX

4. Click the **Commands** tab. The Categories list is comparable to the names of existing menus and toolbars; the Commands list box lists the commands that can be added to menus or toolbars.

5. Click **Form/Report Design** in the Categories list box, scroll in the Commands list box to the Align Left command, as shown in Figure 6-17.

| Figure 6-17 | TOOLBAR COMMANDS |

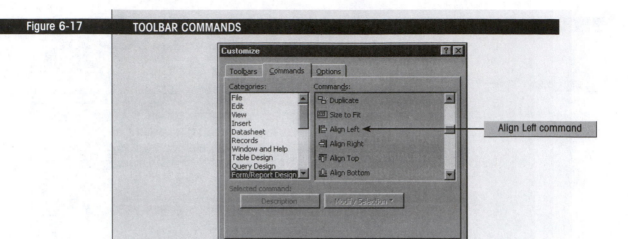

Align Left command

6. Drag the **Align Left** command from the Commands list box to the end of the Formatting toolbar, drag the **Align Top** command from the Commands list box to the right of the Align Left command, and then click the **Close** button. Your toolbar should look like that shown in Figure 6-18.

| Figure 6-18 | FORMATTING (FORM/REPORT) TOOLBAR |

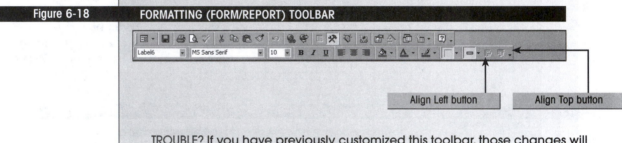

Align Left button   Align Top button

TROUBLE? If you have previously customized this toolbar, those changes will remain in effect until you select the toolbar in the Customize dialog box and click the Reset button.

7. Click the **Job No** label in the main form, hold down the **Shift** key, click the **Description** label in the main form, and then click the **Align Top** button 🔲 on the toolbar.

8. Deselect both controls, click the **Job No** label in the main form, hold down the **Shift** key, click the **JobID** text box in the main form, and then click the **Align Left** button 🔲 on the toolbar. The results are shown in Figure 6-19.

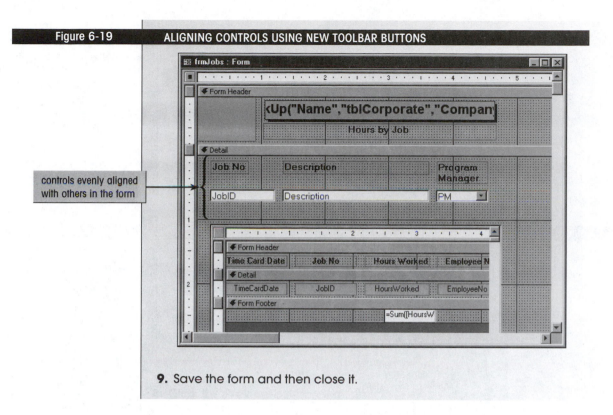

Figure 6-19   ALIGNING CONTROLS USING NEW TOOLBAR BUTTONS

controls evenly aligned
with others in the form

9. Save the form and then close it.

Next you and Carolyn will design a custom menu for the MovieCam database. You then will need to identify the new menu in the Startup properties.

Creating a Custom Menu Bar

When you create a new menu, it's a good idea to follow the standards used by most programs in the Windows environment. That is, for each of the menu items on the menu bar use names that users are familiar with, such as File and Edit. You also should display the menu items in the order that users are accustomed to seeing them.

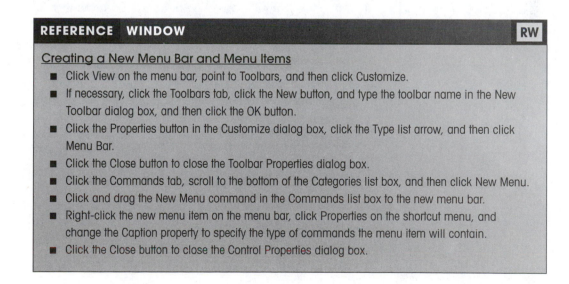

REFERENCE WINDOW   **RW**

Creating a New Menu Bar and Menu Items
- Click View on the menu bar, point to Toolbars, and then click Customize.
- If necessary, click the Toolbars tab, click the New button, and type the toolbar name in the New Toolbar dialog box, and then click the OK button.
- Click the Properties button in the Customize dialog box, click the Type list arrow, and then click Menu Bar.
- Click the Close button to close the Toolbar Properties dialog box.
- Click the Commands tab, scroll to the bottom of the Categories list box, and then click New Menu.
- Click and drag the New Menu command in the Commands list box to the new menu bar.
- Right-click the new menu item on the menu bar, click Properties on the shortcut menu, and change the Caption property to specify the type of commands the menu item will contain.
- Click the Close button to close the Control Properties dialog box.

The new menu that you and Carolyn want to create will contain some of the same menu items that are currently available on the File, Edit, and Records menus. It will not contain any menu items that are on the View, Insert, Window, and Tools menus.

To create a new menu bar:

1. Click **View** on the menu bar, point to **Toolbars**, and then click **Customize** to display the Customize dialog box.

2. Click the **Toolbars** tab, click the **New** button, type **mnuMovieCam** in the New Toolbar dialog box, and then click the **OK** button. The mnuMovieCam toolbar is visible, as shown in Figure 6-20.

Figure 6-20	CREATING A NEW TOOLBAR

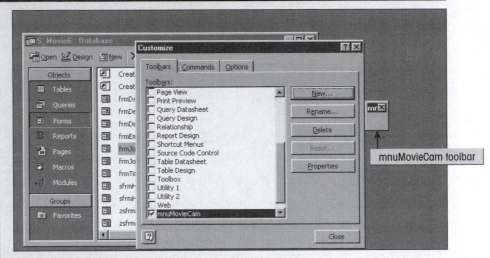

3. Click the **Properties** button in the Customize dialog box to display the Toolbar Properties dialog box.

4. Click the **Type** list arrow, click **Menu Bar**, and then click the **Close** button.

   Now the toolbar will appear as a menu bar rather than as a standard toolbar. Next you will add a New Menu command to the menu bar.

5. Click the **Commands** tab in the Customize dialog box, scroll to the bottom of the Categories list box, and then click **New Menu**.

6. Click and drag the **New Menu** command in the Commands list box to the **mnuMovieCam** menu bar. Next you will name the new menu item on the toolbar.

7. Right-click the **New Menu** item on the mnuMovieCam menu bar, as shown in Figure 6-21.

Figure 6-21   **RENAMING THE NEW MENU ITEM**

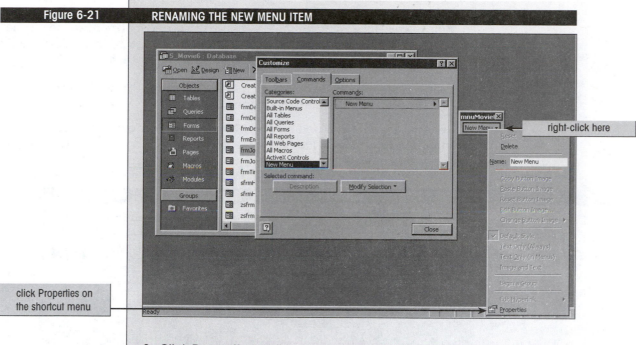

click Properties on
the shortcut menu

right-click here

8. Click **Properties** on the shortcut menu.

9. Change the Caption property to **&File** and then click the **Close** button. The ampersand preceding the F in File enables a keyboard shortcut to open the menu.

The next step in building the custom menu bar is to add commands to the new menu items. To do this you click and drag a command from the Commands list box in the Customize dialog box to the menu item on the menu bar.

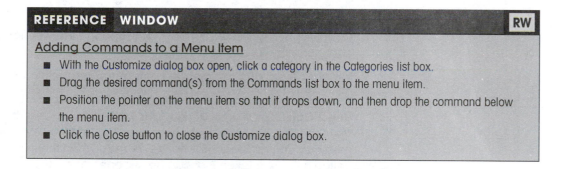

REFERENCE   WINDOW   **RW**

Adding Commands to a Menu Item
- With the Customize dialog box open, click a category in the Categories list box.
- Drag the desired command(s) from the Commands list box to the menu item.
- Position the pointer on the menu item so that it drops down, and then drop the command below the menu item.
- Click the Close button to close the Customize dialog box.

You and Carolyn agree to include the Close, Save Record, Page Setup, Print, Print Preview, and Exit commands on the new File menu.

To add commands to a new menu:

1. Click **File** in the Categories list box.

2. Drag the **Close** command in the Commands list box to the mnuMovieCam menu bar, and drop it below the File menu name.

TROUBLE? Make sure that you position the pointer first on File so that the menu drops down, move it below the File menu name, and then release the mouse button. If you drop the command on the menu bar itself, drag the command to a blank area of the screen to delete it, and then repeat Step 2.

3. Drag the **Save Record** command in the Commands list box to the menu bar, and drop it below the Close command.

4. Repeat this process to add the **Page Setup**, **Print Preview**, **Print**, and **Exit** commands, in that order, to the File menu. The menu should look like that shown in Figure 6-22.

| Figure 6-22 | ADDING COMMANDS TO THE FILE MENU ON THE MNUMOVIECAM MENU BAR |

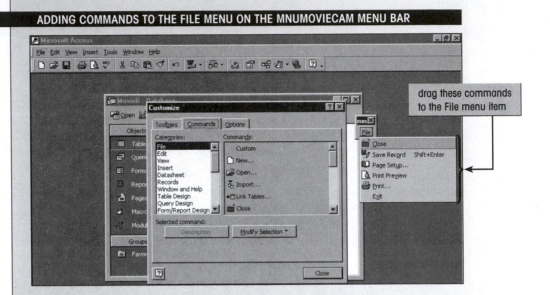

5. Click **New Menu** in the Categories list box, drag the **New Menu** command in the Commands list box to the right of the File menu on the mnuMovieCam menu bar, and then right-click the **New Menu** item.

6. Click **Properties** on the shortcut menu, change the Caption property to **&Edit**, and then click the **Close** button.

7. Repeat Steps 5 and 6 to create a new menu item with a caption of **&Records**.

8. Click **Edit** in the Categories list box of the Customize dialog box, and drag the **Undo**, **Cut**, **Copy**, **Paste**, **Delete**, and **Find** commands, in that order, to the Edit menu on the mnuMovieCam menu bar. The Undo button will appear on the menu as Can't Undo. It will change to Undo when the menu is used and an action has been taken that can be undone.

9. Click **Records** in the Categories list box, and drag the **Sort Ascending**, **Sort Descending**, **Filter By Selection**, **Filter By Form**, **Apply Filter/Sort**, **Remove Filter/Sort**, and **Spelling** commands, in that order, to the Records menu in the mnuMovieCam menu bar, as shown in Figure 6-23.

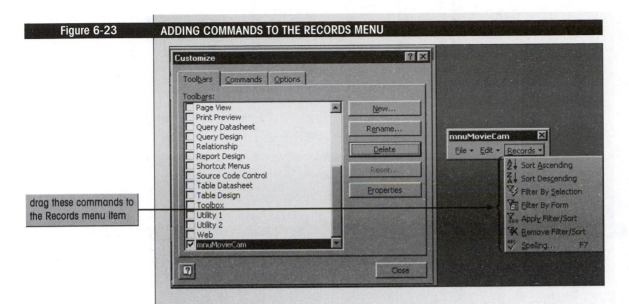

Figure 6-23   ADDING COMMANDS TO THE RECORDS MENU

drag these commands to the Records menu item

10. Click the **Toolbars** tab in the Customize dialog box, scroll down to the bottom of the toolbars list box, click **mnuMovieCam** to turn off the menu, and then click the **Close** button in the Customize dialog box.

Next you and Carolyn will create the shortcut menu that will replace the default shortcut menu in Access.

Creating a Custom Shortcut Menu

A shortcut menu opens when you click the right mouse button. You'll create a custom shortcut menu for your database.

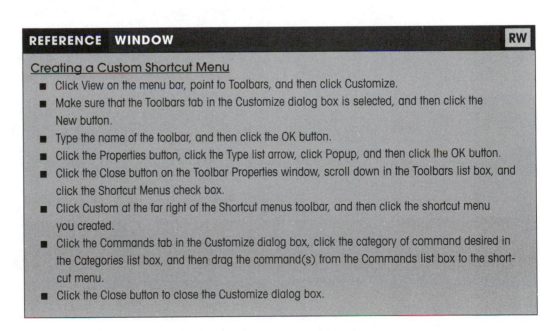

REFERENCE WINDOW   RW

Creating a Custom Shortcut Menu

- Click View on the menu bar, point to Toolbars, and then click Customize.
- Make sure that the Toolbars tab in the Customize dialog box is selected, and then click the New button.
- Type the name of the toolbar, and then click the OK button.
- Click the Properties button, click the Type list arrow, click Popup, and then click the OK button.
- Click the Close button on the Toolbar Properties window, scroll down in the Toolbars list box, and click the Shortcut Menus check box.
- Click Custom at the far right of the Shortcut menus toolbar, and then click the shortcut menu you created.
- Click the Commands tab in the Customize dialog box, click the category of command desired in the Categories list box, and then drag the command(s) from the Commands list box to the shortcut menu.
- Click the Close button to close the Customize dialog box.

The default shortcut menus in Access contain commands to open forms and reports in Design view, to open the Relationships window, and so on. You and Carolyn do not want users to have access to these commands.

To create a custom shortcut menu:

1. Click **View** on the menu bar, point to **Toolbars**, click **Customize**, and then click the **Toolbars** tab in the Customize dialog box

2. Click the **New** button, type **MovieCam**, and then click the **OK** button.

3. Click the **Properties** button, click the **Type** list arrow, and then click **Popup**. The message box shown in Figure 6-24 opens.

Figure 6-24   POPUP MESSAGE BOX

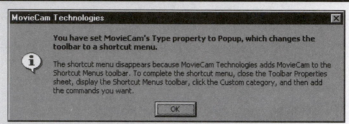

---

4. Click the **OK** button, click the **Close** button in the Toolbar Properties window, scroll down in the Toolbars list box, and click the **Shortcut Menus** check box. The Shortcut Menus toolbar appears.

5. Click **Custom** on the Shortcut Menus toolbar, and then click **MovieCam**. See Figure 6-25.

Figure 6-25   CREATING THE SHORTCUT MENU

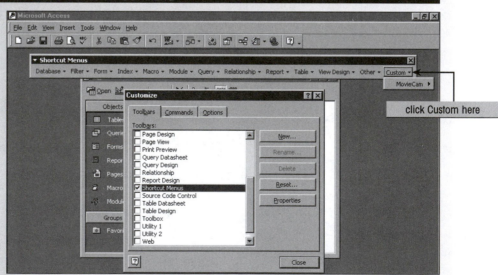

---

6. Click the **Commands** tab in the Customize dialog box, click **Edit** in the Categories list box, and drag the **Undo** command from the Commands list box to the MovieCam shortcut menu.

7. Add the **Copy**, **Paste**, and **Find** commands from the Commands list to the shortcut menu, as shown in Figure 6-26.

| Figure 6-26 | **ADDING COMMANDS TO THE MOVIECAM SHORTCUT MENU** |

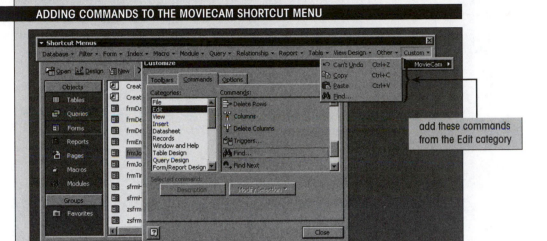

8. Click **Records** in the Categories list box, and then add the **Sort Ascending**, **Sort Descending**, and **Filter by Selection** commands to the shortcut menu.

9. Close the Customize dialog box.

Carolyn points out that the shortcut menu you created is not named properly. For consistency, you should add a tag to the menu name specifying that it is a shortcut menu as you did with the menu bar you created earlier. You decide to delete the shortcut menu and re-create it.

Deleting a toolbar or a menu bar is simple. In the Customize dialog box, you select the toolbar to be deleted, and then click the Delete button. Deleting a shortcut menu is more complicated, you must first convert it to a toolbar, and then delete it.

To delete a shortcut menu:

1. Click **View** on the menu bar, point to **Toolbars**, and then click **Customize**.

2. Make sure that the **Toolbars** tab in the Customize dialog box is selected, and then click the **Properties** button.

3. Click the **Selected Toolbar** list arrow, and then click **MovieCam** from the list, as shown in Figure 6-27.

| Figure 6-27 | CHANGING THE MOVIECAM SHORTCUT MENU TO A TOOLBAR |

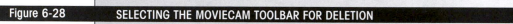

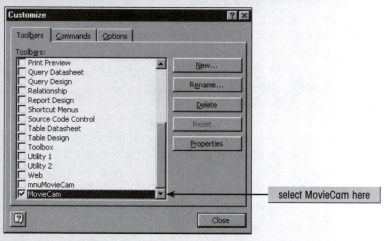

4. Click the **Type** list arrow, and then click **Toolbar** to change MovieCam from a shortcut menu to a toolbar.

5. Click the **Close** button to return to the Customize dialog box, click **MovieCam** in the Toolbars list box to select it, as shown in Figure 6-28.

| Figure 6-28 | SELECTING THE MOVIECAM TOOLBAR FOR DELETION |

6. Click the **Delete** button, and then click the **OK** button to confirm the deletion.

7. Re-create the shortcut menu, naming it **smnuMovieCam**, following Steps 2 through 8 in the previous set of steps.

8. Close the Customize dialog box.

Now that you have completed the custom menus and toolbar, you will change the Startup properties in the MovieCam database so that these menus and toolbar appear by default. You also will set the frmDataSwitchboard form to open automatically when the database opens. Although it is not the Main Switchboard, frmDataSwitchboard will be used as the startup form to test the menus and some of the other startup features.

Startup **Properties**

The Startup properties control user access to areas of the database. These properties are set in the Startup dialog box, which you open by selecting Startup on the Tools menu. The changes you make to the Startup properties apply only to the database in which they are set; changing Startup properties in MovieCam will not affect any other databases. In addition, changing the Startup properties for the database does not override the property settings for a custom toolbar, menu bar, or shortcut menu that's been created for a specific form or report. When you specify a menu bar or shortcut menu in the Startup dialog box, it appears when the database opens.

The Startup properties include:

- *Application Title:* A program name that displays in the database title bar.
- *Application Icon:* A bitmap or icon file of an image that you use as the application icon in the Windows title bar. See Figure 6-29.

Figure 6-29   **APPLICATION ICON**

icon

Windows title bar

- *Menu Bar:* A menu bar that will appear as the default menu bar for the current database.
- *Allow Full Menus:* Allows the use of all Access menu commands. If this option is not selected, a predefined subset of the full built-in menus is shown. This subset of menus doesn't include menus and commands that enable users to change the design of the database objects. Clearing this option also disables the toolbar buttons that correspond to the disabled menu items.
- *Allow Default Shortcut Menus:* Use this property to specify whether or not the program allows the display of built-in shortcut menus. Clearing Allow Full Menus does not disable the shortcut menus, so if you want to keep users from changing the database design, this option also must be deselected.
- *Display Form/Page:* A form or data access page that you want shown when the database opens. Usually a switchboard or splash screen is specified here.
- *Display Database Window:* Deselecting this check box means the Database window will not be visible when you open the database. You can still see it, however, by pressing the F11 key.
- *Display Status Bar:* Deselect this option to hide the status bar.
- *Shortcut Menu Bar:* Use this property to specify a custom shortcut menu that you want to appear in your application. If you want to restrict users from Design view of the database objects, you should also clear Allow Default Shortcut Menus.
- *Allow Built-in Toolbars:* Deselect this option to disable the built-in toolbars.
- *Allow Toolbar/Menu Changes:* Deselect this check box to lock toolbars. This disables the feature that allows you to right-click the toolbar to open the Customize dialog box. It also disables the Toolbars command on the View menu, and the Close button on toolbars.

■ *Use Special Access Keys:* Click the Advanced button in the Startup dialog box so this option is visible. Deselect this option to prevent users from pressing the F11 key to show the Database window, from pressing the Ctrl+F11 keys to toggle to the Database window, from pressing Ctrl+Break to enter the break mode in a Visual Basic module, or from pressing Ctrl+G to display the Immediate window. (Break mode and the Immediate window are discussed in Tutorial 8.)

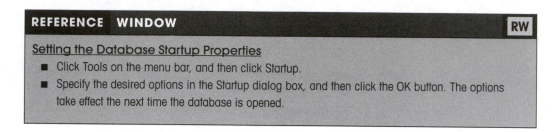

REFERENCE WINDOW **RW**

Setting the Database Startup Properties
■ Click Tools on the menu bar, and then click Startup.
■ Specify the desired options in the Startup dialog box, and then click the OK button. The options take effect the next time the database is opened.

You and Carolyn now will set the Startup properties to display the new menu you created. You will also change some of the other Startup properties.

To change Startup properties:

1. Click **Tools** on the menu bar and then click **Startup**. The Startup dialog box opens, as shown in Figure 6-30.

Figure 6-30 **STARTUP DIALOG BOX**

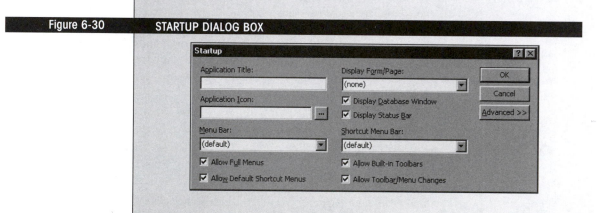

2. In the Application Title text box, type **MovieCam Technologies**, and then click the **Build** button ⬜ at the right of the Application Icon text box. The Icon Browser dialog box opens.

3. Navigate to the **Tutorial.06** folder on your local or network drive, click the **MovieCam** file, and then click the **OK** button. This is an icon of a camera that you will insert as the application icon in the Windows title bar and taskbar.

4. Click the **Menu Bar** list arrow, and then click **mnuMovieCam** to select your custom menu.

5. Click the **Display Form/Page** list arrow, click **frmDataSwitchboard**, clear the **Display Database Window** check box, click the **Shortcut Menu Bar** list arrow, and then click **smnuMovieCam**.

6. Click the **Allow Built-in Toolbars** and the **Allow Toolbar/Menu Changes** check boxes to deselect these options, click the **Advanced** button, and then click the **Use Access Special Keys** check box to deselect it. See Figure 6-31.

Figure 6-31	CHANGING STARTUP PROPERTIES

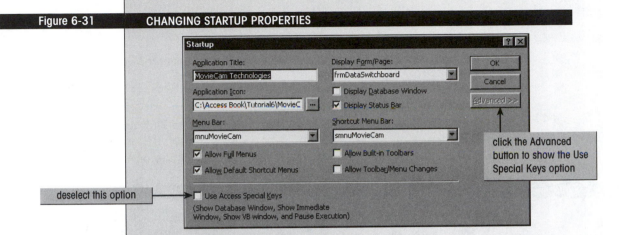

7. Click **OK** to close the Startup dialog box, and then exit the database. You must reopen the database to test your changes.

8. Open the database to see the effect of changing the Startup properties.

9. Right-click anywhere on the switchboard to open the custom shortcut menu.

10. Click **File** on the custom menu bar, and then click **Exit**.

11. Start Access, click the **Movie6** database in the list box, press the **Shift** key and hold it down while you click the **OK** button. The Startup properties are bypassed, and the database opens with the original Startup options in effect.

You and Carolyn do not want users to be able to bypass the Startup properties that you have set, so you will now disable the Startup properties bypass feature.

Disabling the Bypass Key

Access database programmers refer to the Shift key as the bypass key. Disabling the bypass key is a common method for securing a database; however, you must understand that most savvy database users are familiar with this security measure.

You also can disable the bypass key by writing VBA code, which is more difficult for users to undo. The trick here is that the VBA code must also include a method to enable the Shift key, so that you and other authorized users can get into the design and programming areas of the database.

One method to trigger the code that enables or disables the bypass key is to include transparent command buttons on the switchboard. As the developer, you know where they are located and can click them to perform the desired operation. Another method is to trigger the code with a series of keystrokes. An AutoKeys macro provides this functionality and is the method you and Carolyn decide to use.

Using Code Samples in Visual Basic Help

The code to disable or enable the bypass key is somewhat complex. However, Access Help contains many code samples that can be copied and pasted into your database application.

To copy code from Access Help:

1. Click **Help** on the menu bar, and then click **Microsoft Access Help**.

2. If the Office Assistant opens, type **Disable Shift Key**, click the **Search** button, and then click **AllowBypassKey Property**.

3. If the Office Assistant does not open, type **Disable Shift Key** in the **What would you like to do?** text box, and then click the Search button. The first topic, AllowBypassKey Property is visible as shown in Figure 6-32.

Figure 6-32	LOOKING UP CODE IN THE HELP SYSTEM

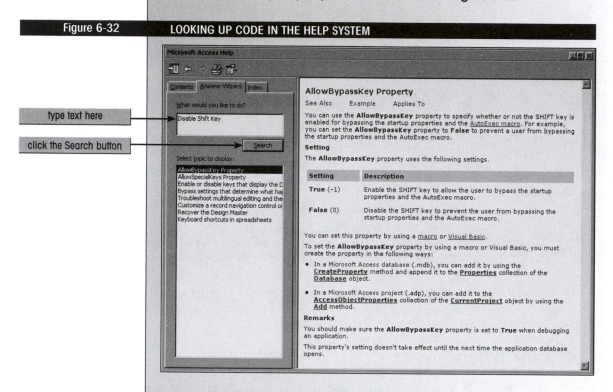

4. Click the **Example** link, make sure that the **AllowBypassKey Property Example** is selected, and then click the **Display** button.

5. Select the entire code sample, as shown in Figure 6-33, from the Sub SetBypassProperty() line to the End Function line, and then press **Ctrl+C** to copy this code to the Clipboard.

| Figure 6-33 | SELECTING THE SETBYPASSPROPERTY CODE |

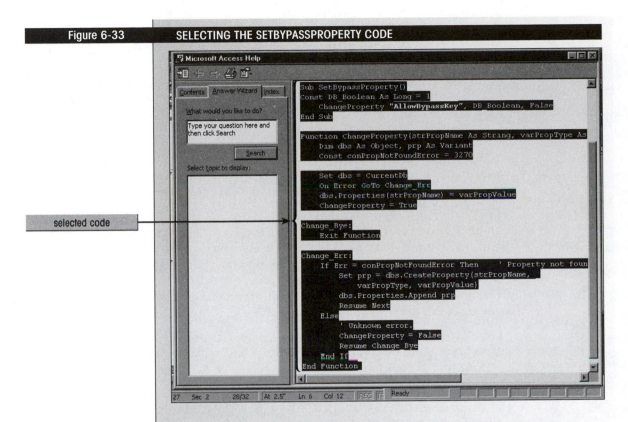

selected code

6. Close the Help window, click **Modules** on the Objects bar of the Database window, and then click the **New** button to create a new standard module.

7. Right-click to display the shortcut menu, and then click **Paste**.

8. Click the **Save** button 🖫 on the toolbar, type **basFunctions** in the Module Name text box, and then click the **OK** button.

As was discussed in Tutorial 5, you can call a function from a macro, an event property, and an expression. The code that you copied into the basFunctions module contains two procedures. One is a sub procedure and the other is a function. The sub procedure calls the function. Again, this code is somewhat complex, which is why you copied it from Help instead of writing it yourself. Because you want to call the SetBypassProperty sub procedure from a macro, you need to change the sub procedure to a function.

9. Double-click the word **Sub** in the first line of the code to select it, type **Function**, and then press the ▼ key. Note that End Sub line of code changes automatically to End Function.

TROUBLE? If both procedures are not visible in the Visual Basic window, click **Tools** on the menu bar, and then click **Options**. If necessary, click the **Editor** tab in the Options dialog box, click the **Default to Full Module View** checkbox, and then click the **OK** button.

To use this function effectively, you need to be able to set the AllowBypassKey Property to false, and also to set it to true. One way to set the AllowBypassKey Property to true or to false using the code you copied from the Help system, would be to include two functions—one sets the AllowBypassKey Property to false, as shown below:

```
Function SetBypassPropertyFalse()
Const DB_Boolean As Long = 1
     ChangeProperty "AllowBypassKey", DB_Boolean, False
End Function
```

The other function sets the AllowBypassKey Property to true, and is shown below:

```
Function SetBypassPropertyTrue()
Const DB_Boolean As Long = 1
     ChangeProperty "AllowBypassKey", DB_Boolean, True
End Function
```

Another way to set the AllowBypassKey Property to true or to false is to include in the function an argument to be supplied when the function is called. If you include an argument in the function that represents true or false, and then supply that true or false argument when the function is called by the macro, it is not necessary to write two separate functions.

The following code sample shows what this function would look like if you included the bValue argument for the reason stated previously:

```
Function SetBypassProperty(bValue As Boolean)
Const DB_Boolean As Long = 1
     ChangeProperty "AllowBypassKey", DB_Boolean, bValue
End Function
```

The argument name is *bValue*. The *b* prefix indicates that it is Boolean, which is the data type for True/False or Yes/No data, and Boolean is the argument data type required in the ChangeProperty function. You and Carolyn determine that passing true or false from the macro is the most efficient way to write the function procedure.

To add a variable to the SetBypassProperty function:

1. Position the insertion point between the parentheses in the first line of the SetBypassProperty function.

2. Type **bValue As**, and press the **spacebar**. Note the banner that opens.

3. Type **B**, and the list shows the items that begin with the letter B.

4. Double-click **Boolean** to complete the statement.

5. Select the word **False** in the ChangeProperty statement, and then type **bValue**. The function should look like that shown in Figure 6-34.

Figure 6-34 **MODIFYING THE SETBYPASSPROPERTY CODE**

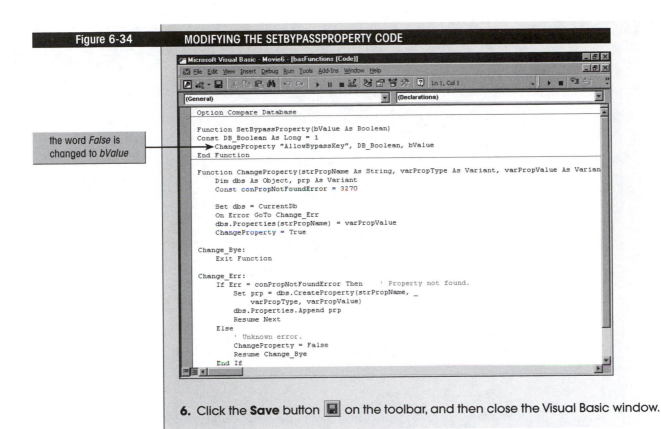

the word *False* is
changed to *bValue*

```
Option Compare Database

Function SetBypassProperty(bValue As Boolean)
Const DB_Boolean As Long = 1
   ChangeProperty "AllowBypassKey", DB_Boolean, bValue
End Function

Function ChangeProperty(strPropName As String, varPropType As Variant, varPropValue As Variant
    Dim dbs As Object, prp As Variant
    Const conPropNotFoundError = 3270

    Set dbs = CurrentDb
    On Error GoTo Change_Err
    dbs.Properties(strPropName) = varPropValue
    ChangeProperty = True

Change_Bye:
    Exit Function

Change_Err:
    If Err = conPropNotFoundError Then     ' Property not found.
        Set prp = dbs.CreateProperty(strPropName, _
            varPropType, varPropValue)
        dbs.Properties.Append prp
        Resume Next
    Else
        ' Unknown error.
        ChangeProperty = False
        Resume Change_Bye
    End If
```

6. Click the **Save** button 🖫 on the toolbar, and then close the Visual Basic window.

Now that you have completed the code, you need to create a way to execute it. You decide that using a series of keystrokes to enable the Shift key, and a different series to disable the key is the best approach. You and Carolyn will be the only ones who know the appropriate key combinations.

AutoKeys Macro Group

You can create a macro group to assign custom commands to key combinations. You use the special name *AutoKeys*, to name the macro group. When you press a key combination, Access searches for an AutoKeys macro, and then runs the macro assigned to that combination. You can use an AutoKeys macro to make key assignments that replace the default key assignments (such as F11, which you can press to display the Database window), or you can create entirely new key combinations.

You also can specify in the macro Conditions column if you want the key to be effective under only certain circumstances. Not all key combinations are available for assignment in the AutoKeys macro. Figure 6-35 lists the key combinations that can be used.

Figure 6-35   **KEY COMBINATIONS FOR AUTOKEYS MACRO**

KEY COMBINATION	AUTOKEYS SYNTAX
Ctrl+Any letter or number key	^A or ^4
Any function key	{F1}
Ctrl+Any function key	^{F1}
Shift+Any function key	+{F1}
Ins	{INSERT}
Ctrl+Ins	^{INSERT}
Shift+Ins	+{INSERT}
Del	{DELETE} or {DEL}
Ctrl+Del	^{DELETE} or ^{DEL}
Shift+Del	+{DELETE} or +{DEL}

To create an AutoKeys macro:

1. Click **Macros** on the Objects bar of the Database window, and then click **New** to create a new macro.

2. If the Macro Name column is not visible, click **View** on the menu bar, and then click **Macro Name**.

3. Click the first row's **Macro Name** text box, type **^{F4}**, and then press the **Tab** key to move to the Action column.

4. Click the **Action** list arrow, click **RunCode**, press the **Tab** key, and then type **Set Bypass property to true**.

5. Press the **F6** key to move to the Function Name text box in the Action Arguments pane, and then click the **Build** button ⬜ so the Expression Builder is visible.

6. Double-click the **Functions** folder in the first column. The Built-In Functions and Movie6 folders appear, as shown in Figure 6-36.

Figure 6-36   **EXPRESSION BUILDER**

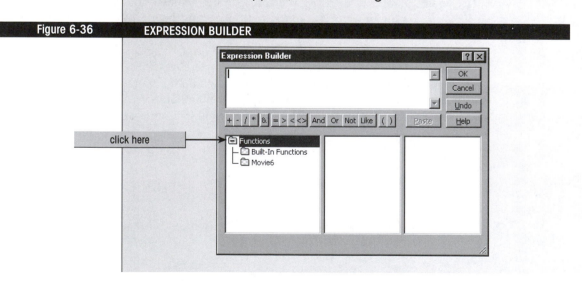

click here

7. Click the **Movie6** Functions folder. A list of standard module names is shown in the center column, and the third column shows the functions within the selected module.

8. Click **basFunctions**, click **SetBypassProperty**, and then click the **Paste** button. Your screen should look like that shown in Figure 6-37.

Figure 6-37   SELECTING THE FUNCTION

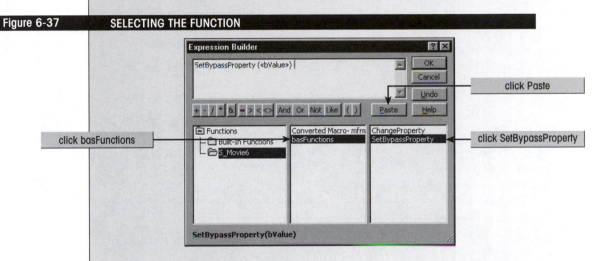

9. Click the **bValue** argument in the Expression window to select it, type **True**, and then click the **OK** button.

10. Click the **Save** button 🖫 on the toolbar, type **AutoKeys** in the Macro Name text box, and then click **OK**.

Next you will complete the macro group by adding the macro to run the SetBypassProperty function with the false argument to disable the bypass key.

To complete the AutoKeys macro:

1. Click in the third row **Macro Name** text box, type **^{F5}**, and then press the **Tab** key to move to the Action column.

2. Click the **Action** list arrow, scroll through the list, click **RunCode**, press the **Tab** key, and then type **Set Bypass property to false**.

3. Press the **F6** key to move to the Function Name Action Argument, and type **SetBypassProperty (False)**, as shown in Figure 6-38.

Figure 6-38   **COMPLETING THE AUTOKEYS MACRO**

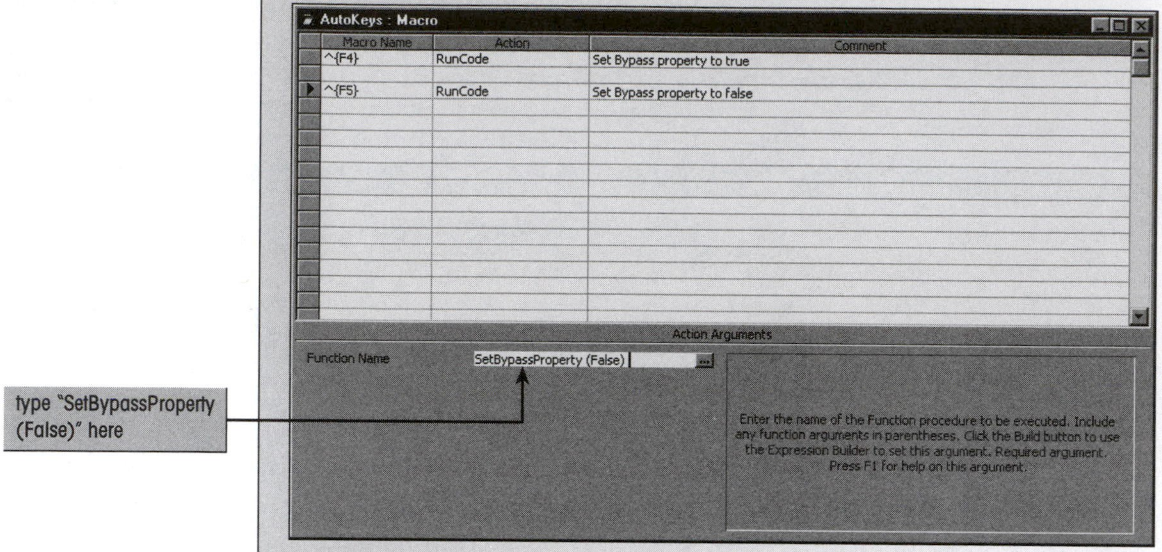

type "SetBypassProperty (False)" here

4. Save your changes and close the macro group.

Next you'll test the code you wrote and the AutoKeys macro. First, be sure that you have a back-up copy of the entire database file. You might need to go to Windows Explorer and make a copy before you continue.

To test the AutoKeys macro and SetBypassProperty function:

1. Press **Ctrl+F5** to disable the Shift key, and then close the Movie6 database.

2. Hold down the **Shift** key as you reopen the Movie6 database. The bypass key doesn't work.

3. Press **Ctrl+F4** to enable the Shift key, and then close the Movie6 database.

4. Open the Movie6 database, again while you hold down the **Shift** key. The bypass key works this time, and the Startup property settings are bypassed.

The final step in the process is to split the MovieCam Technologies database. After this is completed, you and Carolyn can make copies of the front end for users, and continue development in the master front end.

Splitting the Database

Most Access developers agree that Access databases should be split into two files: one containing only Access tables, often called the back end, and another containing all other objects, often called the front end.

Splitting a database like this allows you to link tables from the shared back end to the front end, which is often placed on local drives. Keeping the front end on the user's computer minimizes network traffic and improves performance. The major benefit, however, is that ongoing development of the database objects can be done without interfering with users working in the database. If one file is placed on a shared network drive, the forms and reports cannot be modified when users are working in them. If the database is split, however, changes can be made to a master copy of the front end and then copied to an individual user's machine.

Finally, splitting the database and providing users with a unique copy of the front end allows them to develop their own forms and reports without affecting the database of other users. If a user accesses Design view of a form or report and damages it, only that user's copy is affected.

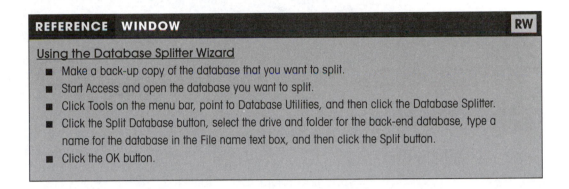

REFERENCE WINDOW   RW

Using the Database Splitter Wizard
■ Make a back-up copy of the database that you want to split.
■ Start Access and open the database you want to split.
■ Click Tools on the menu bar, point to Database Utilities, and then click the Database Splitter.
■ Click the Split Database button, select the drive and folder for the back-end database, type a name for the database in the File name text box, and then click the Split button.
■ Click the OK button.

Now you'll use the Database Splitter Wizard to split the MovieCam database. Before you do, make a back-up copy of the database containing the work that you have done up to this point.

To split the Movie6 database:

1. Close the **Movie6** database, but do not exit Access.

2. Right-click the **Start** button on the taskbar, and then click **Explore** on the shortcut menu to open Windows Explorer.

3. Navigate to the **Tutorial.06** folder containing the Movie6 database, right-click the **Movie6** file, click **Copy**, right-click an empty area of the window, and then click **Paste**. A file named **Copy of Movie6** is created in the Tutorial.06 folder.

4. Open Access and open the **Movie6** database while holding down the **Shift** key to bypass the Startup properties options.

5. Click **Tools** on the menu bar, point to **Database Utilities**, and then click **Database Splitter**. The Database Splitter dialog box opens, as shown in Figure 6-39.

Figure 6-39   DATABASE SPLITTER DIALOG BOX

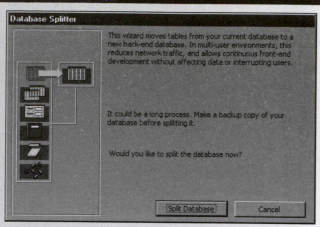

TROUBLE? If a dialog box opens and asks if you want to install the Database Splitter feature, insert your Office 2000 CD in the correct drive, and then click the Yes button. If you do not have the Office 2000 CD, see your instructor or technical support person for assistance.

6. Click the **Split Database** button. The Create Back-end Database dialog box opens. The back-end database will contain the tables from the MovieCam database. You will use the default filename for the back-end database.

7. Click the **Save in** list arrow, navigate to the **Tutorial.06** folder, and then click the **Split** button.

8. Click the **OK** button when the message box opens and tells you that the database has been successfully split.

Now that the database is split, you and Carolyn want to move the back-end database to the shared drive of the network. If you move the back-end database to a new folder or drive, the links to the front-end database will need to be refreshed.

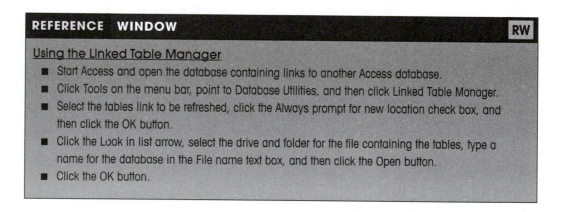

REFERENCE WINDOW   RW

Using the Linked Table Manager
- Start Access and open the database containing links to another Access database.
- Click Tools on the menu bar, point to Database Utilities, and then click Linked Table Manager.
- Select the tables link to be refreshed, click the Always prompt for new location check box, and then click the OK button.
- Click the Look in list arrow, select the drive and folder for the file containing the tables, type a name for the database in the File name text box, and then click the Open button.
- Click the OK button.

The Linked Table Manager is a utility that allows you to refresh links to tables that are contained in a separate database. To see how this feature works, you will move the back-end database to the My Documents folder on your computer. Then you will open the Movie6 front-end database, test the linked tables, and then refresh the links to the back-end database.

To move Movie6_be to the My Documents folder:

1. Close the **Movie6** database and exit Access.

2. Right-click the **Start** button, and then click **Explore** on the shortcut menu.

3. Navigate to the **Tutorial.06** folder, drag the **Movie6_be** database to the **My Documents** folder on the same drive as your Tutorial.06 folder. Do not drag the file to a different drive or you will copy it and this exercise will not work.

   TROUBLE? If you do not have a My Documents folder on the same drive as the Tutorial.06 folder or you don't have copy access to it, check with your instructor or technical support person to see which folder to use. The name of the folder is not important here, only that the file is moved to a new location.

4. Close Windows Explorer, start Access, and then open the **Movie6** database while holding down the **Shift** key.

5. Click the **Tables** button on the Objects bar of the Database window, and then double-click the **tblEmployees** table. An error message is shown.

6. Click the **OK** button in the error dialog box, click **Tools** on the menu bar, point to **Database Utilities**, and then click **Linked Table Manager**. The Linked Table Manager dialog box displays, as shown in Figure 6-40.

Figure 6-40	LINKED TABLE MANAGER DIALOG BOX

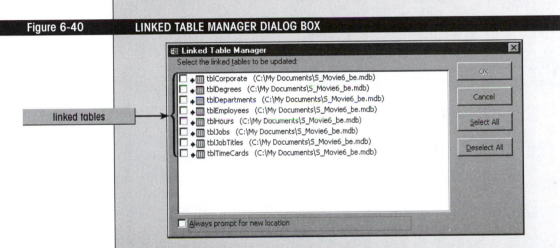

7. Click the **Select All** button to select all the tables in the database, and then click the **Always prompt for new location** check box so that the Linked Table Manager will prompt you for the location of the back-end file.

8. Click the **OK** button, click the **Look in** list arrow and navigate to the **My Documents** folder, click **Movie6_be** to select it, and then click the **Open** button.

9. Click the **OK** button when the message box opens and tells you that all selected linked tables were successfully refreshed, and then click the **Close** button in the Linked Table Manager.

10. Close the Movie6 database, and then exit Access.

11. If you are working in a lab and need to move the Movie6_be database back to the Tutorial.06 folder, repeat Steps 2 through 9, dragging the file from the My Documents folder back to the Tutorial.06 folder and running the Linked Table Manager again.

The database is split into a front and back end, and is ready to be copied for use on individual computers. The menus and switchboards are in place, and the Startup property settings cannot be bypassed by users.

Session 6.2 QUICK CHECK

1. In what way are built-in menus and toolbars personalized?

2. Access stores custom toolbars in a file called _____.

3. To delete a shortcut menu, you must first convert it to a(n) _____.

4. After you change the Startup property settings in Access, how do you test the results?

5. What is an AutoExec macro?

6. Which executes first, Startup property settings or the AutoExec macro?

7. What function does the bypass key perform?

8. What is the purpose of the AutoKeys macro?

9. After splitting the database, the file containing the tables is called the _____.

REVIEW ASSIGNMENTS

The Hours6 database is similar to the MovieCam Technologies database you worked on in the tutorial. You'll modify the switchboard to include VBA code and create a custom menu bar.

1. Start Access and open the **Hours6** database located in the **Tutorial.06** folder on your local or network drive.

2. Make sure that Forms is selected in the Objects bar of the Database window.

3. Open the **frmMainSwitchboard** form in Design view.

4. Click the frame of the option group once to select it, click the Properties button on the toolbar, and then click the Event tab in the properties dialog box.

5. Click in the After Update property text box, and click the Build button. The Visual Basic window opens with the beginning and ending line of the procedure.

6. Type the following code:

```
Select Case grpForms
    Case 1
        DoCmd.OpenForm "frmDepartments"
    Case 2
        DoCmd.OpenForm "frmEmployees"
    Case 3
        DoCmd.OpenForm "frmJobTitles"
End Select
grpForms = Null
```

7. Click File on the menu bar of the Visual Basic window, and then click Print to print the code.

8. Close the Visual Basic window, switch to Form view to test the procedure, and then save your changes and close the form.

9. Click View on the menu bar, point to Toolbars, and then click Customize so the Customize dialog box is visible.

10. Click the New button, type "mnuHours" in the New Toolbar dialog box, click the OK button, and then click the Properties button.

11. Click the Type list arrow, click Menu Bar, click the Close button, and then click the Commands tab.

12. Scroll to the bottom of the Categories list box, click New Menu, click New Menu in the Commands list box, and drag and drop it to the mnuHours menu bar.

13. Right-click New Menu on the mnuHours menu bar, click Properties on the shortcut menu, change the Caption property to &File, and then click the Close button.

14. Scroll to the top of the Categories list box, click File, drag the Close command to the mnuHours menu bar, and drop it below File.

15. Repeat the above process to add the Page Setup, Print Preview, Print, and Exit commands to the menu.

16. Add a new menu item named "Edit" that contains commands for Cut, Copy, and Paste.

17. Add a new menu item named "Records" that contains commands for Sort Ascending and Sort Descending.

Explore 18. Create a new custom toolbar named tlbHours (the *tlb* tag stands for toolbar). Add the Save Record, Page Setup, Print Preview, and Print commands from the File category. Add the Undo, Find, and Find Next commands from the Edit category. Add the Sort Ascending, Sort Descending, Filter by Selection, and Toggle Filter commands from the Records category.

19. Close the **Hours6** database and exit Access.

CASE PROBLEMS

Case 1. Edwards and Company Jack asks you to create a custom shortcut menu to use in the frmClients data entry form. He wants the shortcut menu to contain the following commands: Undo, Copy, Paste, Delete, Find, Sort Ascending, Sort Descending, and Filter by Selection.

1. Start Access and open the **Edward6** database located in the Tutorial.06 folder on your local or network drive.

2. Click View on the menu bar, point to Toolbars, and then click Customize.

3. If necessary, click the **Toolbars** tab, click the New button, type "smnuClients", and then click the OK button.

4. Click the Properties button, click the Type list arrow, click Popup, and then click the OK button.

5. Click the Close button in the Toolbar Properties dialog box, scroll down in the Toolbars list box, and click the Shortcut Menus check box.

6. Click Custom on the Shortcut Menus toolbar, and then click smnuClients.

7. Click the Commands tab in the Customize dialog box, click Edit in the Categories list box, and drag the Undo command from the Commands list box to the shortcut menu.

8. Add the following commands from the Edit category: Copy, Paste, Delete, and Find.

9. Add the following commands from the Records category: Sort Ascending, Sort Descending, and Filter by Selection.

10. Close the Customize dialog box.

11. Open the **frmClients** form in Design view, and then click the Properties button on the toolbar.

12. If necessary, click the All tab in the properties dialog box, click in the Shortcut Menu Bar property text box, click the list arrow, and select smnuClients.

13. Switch to Form view and right-click to test the shortcut menu.

Explore ▶ 14. Switch to Design view. Create a new custom menu named mnuClients that contains File, Edit, and Records menu items. Add Close, Save Record, and Exit to the File menu item. Add Undo, Cut, Copy, Paste, and Find to the Edit menu item. Add Sort Ascending, Sort Descending, and Spelling to the Records menu item. Deselect the mnuClients menu on the Toolbar tab of the Customize dialog box so that it does not display automatically. Open the form's properties dialog box, click the Menu Bar property list arrow and select mnuClients. Close the form and save your changes.

15. Close the **Edward6** database and exit Access.

Case 2. San Diego County Information Systems In the ISD database, classes are stored and entered into the system using the frmClasses form. Because classes are always held on Monday and Wednesday, you decide to add validation code to this form to test the data entered.

1. Start Access and open the **ISD6** database located in the Tutorial.06 folder on your local or network drive.

2. Open the **frmClasses** form in Design view, click the Date text box, and then click the Properties button on the toolbar.

3. If necessary, click the Event tab in the properties dialog box, position the insertion point in the Before Update property text box, and then click the Build button.

4. Type the following code:

```
If DatePart("w", Date) <> 2 Then
        If DatePart("w", Date) <> 4 Then
            Cancel = True
            MsgBox "Classes must be on Monday or Wednesday!"
        End If
    End If
```

5. Click File on the menu bar of the Visual Basic window, click Print to print the code, close the Visual Basic window, and switch to Form view to test the procedure.

6. Navigate to a new record, type "10/15/02" (a Tuesday) in the Date field, and then press the Enter key. The error message is shown. Click the OK button.

7. Type "10/16/02" (a Wednesday) in the Date field, and then press the Enter key.

8. Delete the new record.

9. Save your changes and close the form.

10. Close the **ISD6** database and exit Access.

Case 3. Christenson Homes   Roberta Christenson primarily uses the frmLots form in the Homes6 database. She asks you to set it as the default form for the database. She wants you to modify the database design so she doesn't see the Database window, and also wants you to create a custom menu that includes only the File, Edit, and Records commands.

1. Start Access and open the **Homes6** database located in the Tutorial.06 folder on your local or network drive.

2. Create a custom menu named **mnuHomes** that contains the following menu items: File, Edit, and Records.

3. Add the following commands to the File menu: Close, Print Preview, and Exit.

4. Add the following commands to the Edit menu: Cut, Copy, Paste, and Find.

5. Add the following commands to the Records menu: Sort Ascending, Sort Descending, Filter By Selection, and Filter By Form.

6. On the MnuHomes custom menu, add a command to the File menu just above the Exit command that opens the frmLots form. (Hint: Click All Forms in the Categories list box in the Customize dialog box.)

7. Change the Startup options to meet the following conditions:
   a. The Application Title is Christenson Homes.
   b. The Menu Bar is mnuHomes.
   c. The frmLots form opens automatically.
   d. The Database window does not display.
   e. Displaying default toolbars and changing any toolbar is not allowed.

8. Close the **Homes6** database and exit Access.

Case 4. Sonoma Farms   The frmMainSwitchboard form in the Sonoma Farms database contains an option group named grpForms. You will add the VBA code to automate this form, and then set the Startup properties so that this form opens automatically when the database opens. You also will create code to turn off the bypass feature of the Shift key when the database opens.

1. Start Access and open the **Sonoma6** database located in the Tutorial.06 folder on your local or network drive.

2. Open the **frmMainSwitchboard** form in Design view, select grpForms, display the properties dialog box, and click the After Update event.

3. Using the instruction in this tutorial as a guide, write the code using the Select Case statement to open each form in the option group, and then set the value of the option group back to null.

4. Test the form to be sure it works.

5. Set the Startup property options in the database so that the frmMainSwitchboard form opens automatically. Clear the options to allow full menus, built-in toolbars, and toolbar/menu changes. Disable the function keys so that pressing the F11 key will not display the Database window. (Remember to click the Advanced button in the Startup dialog box so that the Use Access Special Keys option is shown.)

6. Copy and paste the SetBypassProperty code from the Help system that you learned about in the tutorial exercise to a new module. Save the module with the name **basFunctions**. Modify the code so that it is written exactly as it was in the tutorial exercise and then print it by clicking File on the menu bar and then Print.

7. Write an AutoKeys macro that sets the bypass key to true when the F11 key is pressed.

8. Write an AutoKeys macro that sets the bypass key to false when the Ctrl+F11 keys are pressed.

9. Test the changes to the database.

10. Close the **Sonoma6** database and exit Access.

QUICK | CHECK ANSWERS

Session 6.1

1. property
2. method
3. The After Update event occurs after a control or record is updated with changed data.
4. The DatePart function returns an integer that contains the specified part of the given date.
5. DoCmd is a special object that you use to carry out macro actions in Visual Basic procedures.
6. wherecondition
7. Select Case statement
8. The CodeContextObject property's purpose is to determine the object in which a macro or VBA is executing.
9. The With statement allows you to perform a series of statements on a specified object, such as a form or a control on a form, without restating the name of the object.

Session 6.2

1. Access automatically personalizes menus and toolbars based on how often you use the commands.
2. system.mdw
3. toolbar
4. By closing the database and reopening it.
5. An AutoExec macro runs automatically when the database opens.
6. The Startup properties execute before the AutoExec macro.
7. The bypass key bypasses the Startup property setting changes, and the database opens normally.
8. The AutoKeys macro is a macro group used to assign custom commands to key combinations.
9. back end

OBJECTIVES

In this tutorial you will:

- Examine the syntax of the DoCmd.OpenReport method

- Build the switchboard form for reports

- Construct an OpenReport wherecondition in VBA code

- Study variables and constants

- Use variables in your code

- Use the Immediate window

- Set breakpoints in code

- Step through code and check variable contents at different points

USING VISUAL BASIC FOR APPLICATIONS

Creating the Reports Switchboard for the MovieCam Database

CASE

MovieCam Technologies

Amanda asks you to talk with the managers who will be using the MovieCam application. She wants you to determine the variations on reports that they will need. Amanda does not want managers to have access to the Database window, so she wants you to design a switchboard form that will give managers access to the reports they need. She wants you to use VBA procedures to design the switchboard form.

Richard Jenkins in Personnel told you and Carolyn that he wants to be able to print a report that is based on whether an employee is terminated or not, another based on whether an employee is salaried or hourly, and a third according to department. He also wants to be able to generate these reports using filters. Martin Woodward in Production wants to be able to print job reports that are based on job number. He wants to be able to specify the first few digits in a job number, such as "92" or "99", so that he can print a report of the jobs that start with those numbers. He also needs to run reports that are based on time card date and on a range of dates, such as a month or a year.

You and Carolyn will create a switchboard form that looks like the one shown in Figure 7-1. It will contain two option groups: one for Employee Reports and one for Job Reports. You anticipate that you will add more reports to each option group. The switchboard will contain check box, combo box, and text box controls from which users can select the criteria for the report they need to run. One set of controls will apply to Employee Reports, and another set of controls will apply to Job Reports. Because the reports in each category are based on the same tables or queries, the controls for selecting criteria will be nearly the same for each report in a category.

Figure 7-1	SWITCHBOARD FORM FOR REPORTS

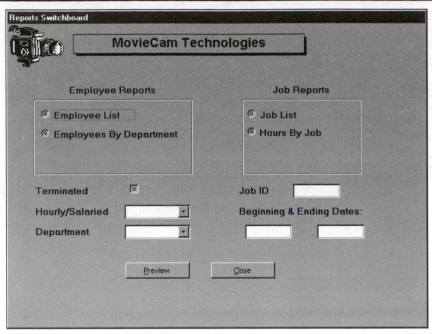

SESSION 7.1

In this session you will learn the syntax of the DoCmd.OpenReport method and use this method to begin coding the frmReportsSwitchboard form. You also will learn to declare variables and constants, study their scope or lifetime, and use a variable in the procedure you write.

Introduction

In earlier tutorials you worked with creating simple Sub procedures using the Code Builder and copied and pasted VBA code from a Help topic. In this tutorial, you will review terms and concepts that were introduced in previous tutorials, and study new terms and concepts that are fundamental to programming in VBA.

All Windows applications are event driven, which means that an event, such as a mouse click on a command button or the change of focus on a form, executes individual blocks of application programming code. VBA 6.0 is a programming language that relies upon the Windows operating system and, as you have seen from writing macros and VBA code in previous tutorials, uses this event-driven model.

Modules

A **module** is an object that contains VBA code. Modules were discussed briefly in Tutorial 1 and you created modules in previous tutorials. Recall that you imported a standard module, basUtilities, into Access from another database, created a new standard module, basFunctions, by copying and pasting sample code from the Help system, and created form and report class modules using the Code Builder. These three types of modules are defined further following:

- *Standard:* You create a standard module the same way you create any other new object in a database. Click Module on the Objects bar of the Database window, and then click New. You use a standard module to store procedures that apply to more than one form or report in the database, or that you want to call from a query expression or a macro. For example, the basUtilities module you imported in Tutorial 3 was a standard module. You imported it so that you could use its ProperCase function in an update query to change first and last names to the proper case. See Figure 7-2.

Figure 7-2	STANDARD MODULE

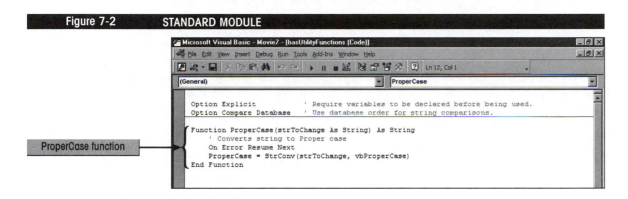

ProperCase function

- *Form class:* You create a form class module when you add VBA code to a form. The code can be triggered by the event properties of the form, its sections or controls, or by other code contained within the module. Code in a form class module cannot be called or triggered by code or events in another form or report. The code is available only to the specific form in which it is contained. The event-handling procedures that you create when you write Sub procedures or functions in a form are the form's new methods; hence, the term class module. You open a form class module by clicking the Code button on the Form Design toolbar, or by selecting the Code command on the View menu. You created form class modules when you wrote the Sub procedures for the frmTimeCards and frmDataSwitchboard forms in previous tutorials.

- *Report class:* You create a report class module when you add code to a report. The code can be triggered by the event properties of the report, sections of the report, or by other code contained within the module. Controls on reports do not have event properties and therefore do not trigger code or macros. Code in a report class module cannot be called or triggered by code or events in another form or report. The code is available only to the specific report in which it is contained. A report module is considered a class module for the same reasons as is a form module. You open a report class module the same way you open a form class module. You created report class modules in Tutorial 5 when you wrote code to add line numbers to a report, and when you calculated a total in a page footer.

Sub Procedures and Functions

Modules are made up of procedures. **Procedures** in any programming language perform actions and tasks. Procedures are ideal for automating repetitive or complex tasks, so in some ways they are comparable to macros. In addition, they are commonly used in building a user interface, as you discovered in earlier tutorials.

Sub procedures and functions are the most commonly used types of procedures. These types of procedures are similar in that they both contain VBA statements, accept arguments, perform operations or calculate values, and can be called from other Sub procedures or functions. They differ in that a function can return a value, can be called from a macro, and can be executed from event properties on forms and reports. In Tutorial 6, you changed a

Sub procedure to a function for disabling and enabling the bypass key. You did that so the procedure could be called from the AutoKeys macro.

Indenting and Spacing Procedures

You've already had a little practice entering code in a readable format. In the procedures you've written so far, you indented some of the code lines, specifically those with decision structures like Select…Case and If…Then…Else. Procedures are easier to read and understand when you indent code. It is also helpful to add blank lines between groups of statements that perform a specific task. Indentations and blank lines do not affect the compilation or performance of your code; they simply make it easier to read.

Procedure Scope

You now know that all procedures are created and stored in modules. Although you could create and store all procedures in one module, your application will be better organized if you group the procedures logically according to their function. In addition, procedures should be stored in different modules so that you can determine their scope.

Scope describes the visibility and accessibility of one procedure from another procedure. For example, a procedure in a form class module is only visible and accessible to the specific form in which it is contained. The **Public** keyword indicates that the procedure can be called from outside the module in which it is contained. The **Private** keyword indicates that the procedure can be called only from within the module in which it is contained. You can declare procedures to be Public or Private by inserting the keyword *Public* or *Private* at the beginning of the first line of the procedure. All procedures are Public by default unless you specify otherwise. So why would you want to declare a procedure to be Private? Take a look at the procedures you copied and pasted from the Visual Basic Help topic in Tutorial 6. Two function procedures exist in the basFunctions standard module, as shown in Figure 7-3.

Figure 7-3	BASFUNCTIONS STANDARD MODULE

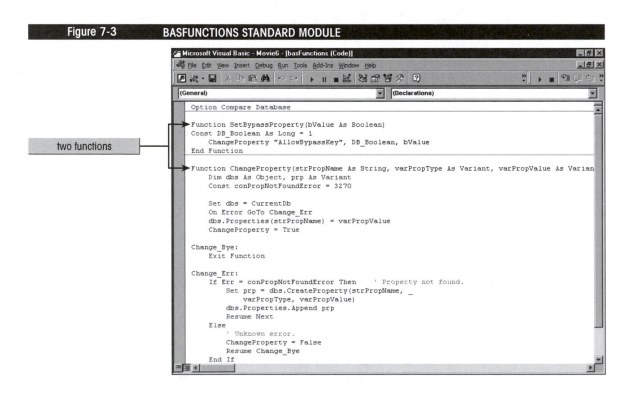

two functions

One function calls the other from within the same module. The first function, SetBypassProperty, needs to be called from a macro, so it should be Public. However, the SetBypassProperty function then calls the ChangeProperty function from within the module, so the ChangeProperty function could be declared Private. Declaring a procedure Private cuts down on the global space needed for the procedure and therefore is a more efficient use of memory. Recall from the discussion of modules that procedures in a form or report class module are only available to the form or report in which they were created. Declaring these procedures Public does not make them available to other forms or reports.

Creating the Reports Switchboard

Carolyn has started work on the reports switchboard. It currently looks like that shown in Figure 7-4. It contains two option groups—grpEmployees and grpJobs—and each option group contains two option buttons. Each option button represents a report.

Figure 7-4	REPORTS SWITCHBOARD

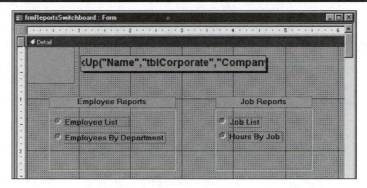

When the reports switchboard is completed, clicking the Employee List button in the Employee Reports group will open the rptEmployeesList report shown in Figure 7-5. This report is identical to the rptActiveEmployees report you worked on in Tutorial 5 except that it no longer filters out the terminated employees. You plan to design the switchboard so that the user can open a report that shows records for active employees or terminated employees. To do that you need to add a check box to the frmReportsSwitchboard form. You will test the value of this check box in the event procedure that you will write later in this tutorial, and use its value to filter the records for the report when it opens. Recall that an event procedure is a procedure that is triggered by an event in a form or report and is stored in the form or report class module.

Figure 7-5	RPTEMPLOYEESLIST REPORT

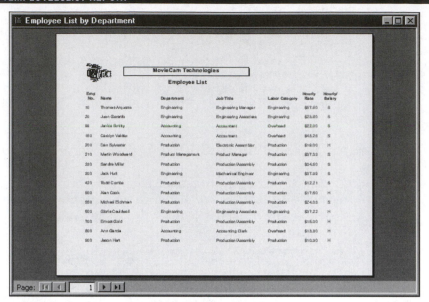

To add a check box to the frmReportsSwitchboard form:

1. Start Access and open the **Movie7** database located in the **Tutorial.07** folder on your local or network drive.

2. Open the **frmReportsSwitchboard** form in Design view and then make sure the toolbox is open.

3. Click the **Check Box** button ☑ on the toolbox, and then click the form below the grpEmployees option group to insert the check box, as shown in Figure 7-6.

Figure 7-6	INSERTING A CHECK BOX CONTROL

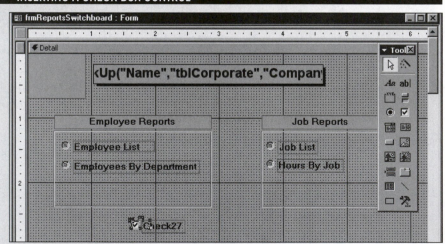

4. Click the **Properties** button on the toolbar, change the Name property of the check box to **chkTerm**, and change the Default Value property to **No**. This sets the check box so that it will not default to No. Later in this tutorial when you write code to test the value of the check box, you will want it to default to No if nothing has been checked on the form.

5. Change the check box label's Caption property to **Terminated**, and move the label to the left of the check box as shown in Figure 7-7. Resize the label so that the entire label text is visible.

Figure 7-7   LABELING AND ALIGNING THE CHECK BOX CONTROL

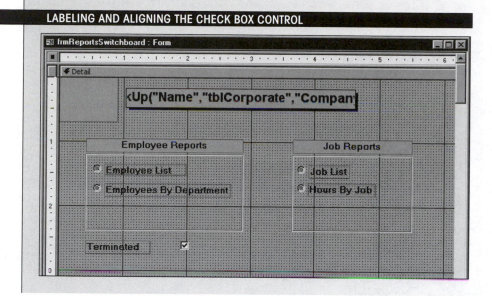

Before you write the event procedure for opening the reports, you will review the syntax of the OpenReport method of the DoCmd object.

OpenReport Method

You will use the OpenReport method of the DoCmd object to open reports from the reports switchboard. The OpenReport method contains a wherecondition argument that will be used to filter the records of the report that is being opened. The syntax of this method is as follows:

```
DoCmd.OpenReport reportname[, view][, filtername]
[, wherecondition]
```

The OpenReport method arguments are as follows:

- *Reportname:* a string expression that is the valid name of a report in the database.
- *View:* one of the following intrinsic constants. (Recall from Tutorial 5 that an intrinsic constant is a word that has particular meaning in VBA.) For example, in the list that follows, the intrinsic constant acDesign means Design view.
  - *acViewDesign:* Design view
  - *acViewNormal:* prints the report immediately and is the default, so if you leave this argument blank the report will print without allowing you to preview it first
  - *acViewPreview:* Print preview
- *Filtername:* a string expression that is the valid name of a query in the current database.
- *Wherecondition:* a string expression that is the valid name of a SQL WHERE clause without the word WHERE. The maximum length of this argument is 32,768 characters. (Remember from Tutorial 3 that the WHERE clause is

used to specify the criteria or condition for which you are querying.) The wherecondition argument must query fields contained in the underlying record source (table or query) of the report you are opening.

Just as with the DoCmd.OpenForm method, you can leave an optional argument blank in the middle of the syntax, but you must include the argument's comma. For example, the following statement will open the rptEmployeeList report in Print Preview and display the data for all employees who are terminated:

```
DoCmd.OpenReport "rptEmployeeList" ,acViewPreview, ,
"Terminated = Yes"
```

REFERENCE WINDOW   **RW**

Adding an Event Procedure
- Open the form or report in Design view, select the control for the event property you want to set, and then open the property dialog box for that control.
- Position the insertion point in the appropriate event property, and then click the Build button.
- Enter the Sub procedure statements in the Code window.
- Compile the procedure, fix any statement errors, and then save the event procedure.

You will use the OpenReport method in the code you write for the reports switchboard next.

To add an event procedure to the frmReportsSwitchboard form:

1. Click the **grpEmployees** option group, click the **Event** tab in the properties dialog box, click in the **After Update** property text box, and then click the **Build** button ☐. The Visual Basic window opens, and the insertion point is positioned between the two lines of the stub.

   TROUBLE? If the Choose Builder dialog box opens, click Code Builder and then click OK.

2. Indent the first line, and then type the following code with additional indenting as indicated:

```
Select Case grpEmployees
   Case 1
      DoCmd.OpenReport "rptEmployeesList",
      acViewPreview, , "Terminated = " & chkTerm
   Case 2
      DoCmd.OpenReport "rptEmployeesByDept", acView
      Preview, , "Terminated = " & chkTerm
End Select
grpEmployees = Null
```

   The code should look like that shown in Figure 7-8.

Figure 7-8	ADDING CODE FOR THE CHECK BOX

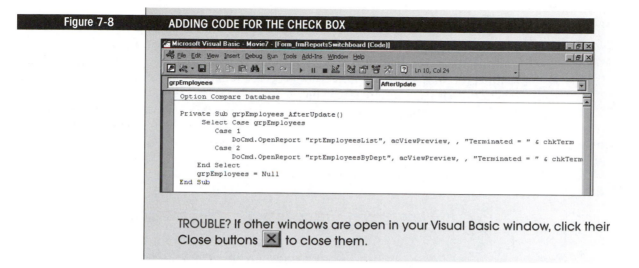

TROUBLE? If other windows are open in your Visual Basic window, click their Close buttons ⊠ to close them.

The WHERE clause argument in each OpenReport method concatenates, or joins, the string "Terminated = " to the value of the chkTerm check box control. If the value of the check box is Yes, the report will show the records for all employees for whom the Terminated field in the tblEmployees table is Yes. If the value of the check box is No, the report will show the records for all employees for whom the Terminated field in the table is No.

Figure 7-9 shows a query that searches the tblEmployees table for records where the Terminated field is equal to Yes.

Figure 7-9	DESIGNING A QUERY TO FIND RECORDS WITH YES IN THE TERMINATED FIELD

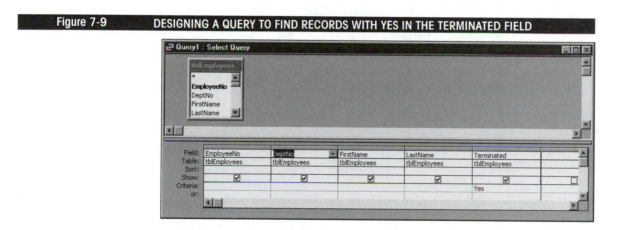

Figure 7-10 shows the SQL view of the same query. Note the syntax of the WHERE clause. If you have trouble constructing the WHERE clause, you can always write a query using the QBE grid and then switch to SQL view to copy and paste the WHERE clause (without the word WHERE) into your code.

Figure 7-10	SQL VIEW OF QUERY TO FIND RECORDS CONTAINING YES IN THE TERMINATED FIELD

SQL WHERE clause →

Compiling Code

Access checks each line of code as you enter it to make sure that it doesn't contain errors. Sometimes errors aren't obvious until each line of code is written and then compared to the entire procedure. Although Access doesn't check the entire procedure as you enter it, it does check the entire procedure when you run it.

When the program is run, Access checks for overall consistency and translates the VBA statements into a language that the computer understands. This process is called **compilation**. If you want to check the code for errors before it is run, you can select the Compile command on the Debug menu.

Next you will compile the code you have just written.

To compile and test the code in the frmReportsSwitchboard form:

1. Click **Debug** on the menu bar, and then click **Compile MovieCam**.

   TROUBLE? If Access identifies any errors in your code, correct the errors and repeat Step 1.

2. Click the **Save** button 🖫 on the toolbar, and close the Visual Basic window.

3. Switch to Form view. Test the code by clicking the **Terminated** check box, and then the **Employee List** button. The report opens with only three records.

4. Close the report, clear the **Terminated** check box, and click the **Employee List** button. The report opens with 12 records.

5. Close the report to return to the switchboard.

Adding Comments

A **comment** is text included in a procedure, and briefly describes what the procedure does. *Commenting* your code is useful to help you remember why you did something a particular way, or what a variable does. In addition, comments provide valuable information to future developers. A comment at the beginning of a procedure should simply explain what the procedure does, rather than how it actually works, because these details might change over time. Additional inline or local comments in your code are used to describe the details of how the code actually works.

To designate a comment in a procedure, you start each comment line with the apostrophe character, as shown in the following example:

```
Sub cmdCustomer_OnClick
        'This Sub procedure opens the frmCustomer form and then maximizes it.
        DoCmd.OpenForm "frmCustomers"
        DoCmd.Maximize
End Sub
```

You and Carolyn realize that you did not include comments in the code you wrote for the frmReportsSwitchboard form. You will now add a descriptive comment to the beginning of the code. You already have some changes in mind for the code itself, so you won't add other comments until the Sub procedure is complete.

To add a comment to the code in the frmReportsSwitchboard form:

1. Switch to Design view and then click the **Code** button 🖾 on the toolbar.

2. Position the insertion point at the end of the first line of the Sub procedure, and then press **Enter** twice.

3. Press **Tab** to indent the line, type **'Open rptEmployeesList or rptEmployeesByDept**, and then press the **Enter** key.

4. Type **'based on criteria entered into the form by the user.** (Type the period.) Press the **Enter** key. Your code should look like that shown in Figure 7-11. Notice that the comments are a different color than the code itself. You can change the color of the comments to suit your preference.

Figure 7-11	ADDING COMMENTS TO YOUR CODE

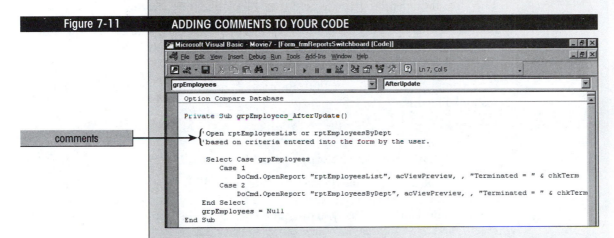

comments

5. Click **Tools** on the menu bar, and then click **Options**.

6. Click the **Editor Format** tab, and then click **Comment Text** in the Code Colors list box.

7. Click the **Foreground** list arrow, and then click **bright blue**.

8. Click the **OK** button to see the results. Your comment text should now be in a shade of blue that is easier to distinguish from black on the screen.

You and Carolyn are satisfied with your progress, but you both think that if you were to add variables to your coding, you could cut down on some of the repetitive statements. You study how to declare variables first.

Variables

VBA lets you store values temporarily in memory. These values are called **variables,** which are named locations in memory that are used to store data of a particular type. For example, suppose you wanted to calculate the sales tax for an order and add it to the cost of the order. To do this without variables for a $150.00 order, you would type the following statements:

```
150 * .075 = 11.25
11.25 + 150.00 = 161.25
```

The disadvantage here is that you have to obtain the result of the first calculation before you can perform the second calculation. However, if you use variables you can simplify the process and make it more generic. Simply changing the value of Sale will compute the value of the TotalSale as shown below:

Sale = 150
SalesTax = Sale *.075
TotalSale = Sale + SalesTax

Another advantage to using variables is that they reduce the amount of coding necessary. For example, suppose you wanted to use a long and complex wherecondition argument like the following in more than one DoCmd.OpenReport statement.

```
"Terminated = " & chkTerm & "AND HourlySalaried = " & "'" &
cboHS & "'"
```

The DoCmd.OpenReport statement would look like the following:

```
DoCmd.OpenReport "rptEmployeesList, acViewPreview, ,
"Terminated = " & chkTerm & "AND HourlySalaried = " & "'" &
cboHS & "'"
```

When you use the variable strSQL in place of the wherecondition argument, the statements look like this:

```
strSQL = "Terminated = " & chkTerm & "AND HourlySalaried = "
& "'" & cboHS & "'"
DoCmd.OpenReport "rptEmployeesList, acViewPreview, , strSQL
```

You can implicitly or explicitly declare a variable. With **implicit declaration** you don't need to declare a variable before using it. You simply use it in a procedure. The problem with implicit declaration is that you might misspell a variable name the second or third time you use it, and as a result create a new variable rather than refer to an existing one.

For example, if implicit declaration were used, the following would result in four variables instead of three:

Sale = 150
SalesTax = Salee *.075
TotalSale = Sale + SalesTax

The misspelled *Salee* (vs. Sale) represents the fourth variable.

Explicit declaration requires that you declare a variable before you use it. To force explicit declaration, you include the *Option Explicit* statement in the Declarations section of the module. See Figure 7-12.

| Figure 7-12 | VBA MODULE |

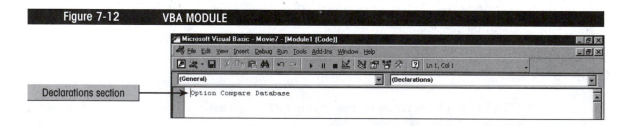

When Option Explicit is set for a module, all variables must be defined before they can be used in a procedure. If Option Explicit had been set in the preceding example, the three variables—Sale, SalesTax, and TotalSale—would have been declared at the beginning of the procedure, and if you attempt to use a variable named Salee, you would receive an error message.

Although variables are typically defined at the beginning of a Sub procedure or function, they can be declared at any point as long as they are declared before they are used.

To be sure that Option Explicit is included every time you create a code module, you can set this option in the Visual Basic window. You will do that next.

To require variable declaration:

1. Click the **Code** button [icon] on the toolbar to display the Visual Basic window.

2. Click **Tools** on the menu bar, and then click **Options**.

3. Make sure the **Editor** tab is selected, and then click the **Require Variable Declaration** option, as indicated in Figure 7-13.

Figure 7-13	REQUIRING VARIABLE DECLARATION

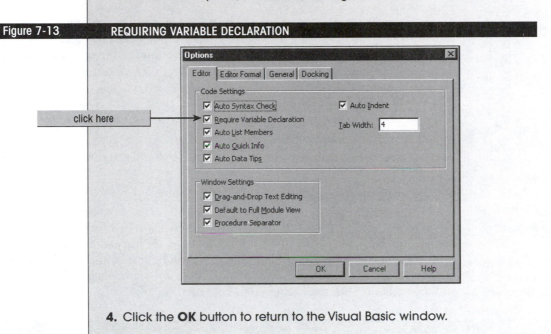

4. Click the **OK** button to return to the Visual Basic window.

Variable Scope

Variable scope is similar to the procedure scope discussed earlier in this tutorial. When you define a variable, you also define the scope of the variable. The time during which a variable retains its value is known as its **lifetime**. Although the value of a variable may change over its lifetime, it still retains some value. When a variable loses scope, it no longer has a value. Scope can be thought of as the variable's lifetime or life span. Once a variable goes out of scope, you cannot refer to its contents. Variable scope is determined by its declaration and its location in a module. You can use four different scopes of variables for declaration: Public, Private, Static, and Dim.

Declaring Variables

You normally use a Dim statement (Dimension statement) to declare variables. For example:

```
Dim strSQL As String
```

This declares the *strSQL* variable as a string data type variable. Data types will be discussed in the next section.

This declaration statement can be placed within a procedure to create a procedure-level variable, or it can be placed at the top of a module in the Declarations section to create a module-level variable. A **procedure-level variable** exists only when the procedure is running. When the procedure is finished executing, the variable is removed from memory. A **module-level variable** can be referenced by another function or Sub procedure within the same module.

The *Static* keyword can be used only in a function or Sub procedure, and can only be referred to by that same function or Sub procedure. The Static keyword differs from the Dim keyword in that the variable retains its value after the procedure has finished running, so that the next time the procedure is run you can refer to the previous value of the variable. Use the Static keyword as follows:

```
Static strSQL As String
```

The *Private* keyword can be used only in the General Declarations section of a module. It has the same effect as using the Dim keyword in the General Declarations section; that is, the variable is available to any function or Sub procedure in the module. For example:

```
Private strSQL As String
```

The *Public* keyword also can be used only in the General Declarations section of the module. The variable can then be referenced from any module anywhere within the database application. For example:

```
Public strSQL As String
```

Variable Data Types

All variables, whether explicitly or implicitly defined, are of a specific data type. When you declare a variable, you declare its scope as you have just learned. In addition, you declare its data type, which defines the kind of values that will be stored in the variable and how much memory space to allocate for the variable. Figure 7-14 summarizes the variable data types and the amount of memory required to hold each variable.

Figure 7-14	DATA TYPES	
DATA TYPE	**MEMORY**	**RANGE**
Byte	1 byte	0 to 255
Boolean	2 bytes	True or False
Integer	2 bytes	-32,768 to 32,767
Long (long integer)	4 bytes	-2,147,483,648 to 2,147,483,647
Single (single-precision floating-point)	4 bytes	-3.402823E38 to -1.401298E-45 for negative values; 1.401298E-45 to 3.402823E38 for positive values
Double (double-precision floating-point)	8 bytes	-1.79769313486231E308 to -4.94065645841247E-324 for negative values; 4.94065645841247E-324 to 1.79769313486232E308 for positive values
Currency (scaled integer)	8 bytes	-922,337,203,685,477.5808 to 922,337,203,685,477.5807
Decimal	14 bytes	+/-79,228,162,514,264,337,593,543,950,335 with no decimal point; +/-7.9228162514264337593543950335 with 28 places to the right of the decimal; smallest non-zero number is +/-0.0000000000000000000000000001
Date	8 bytes	January 1, 100 to December 31, 9999

Figure 7-14	DATA TYPES (CONTINUED)	
DATA TYPE	**MEMORY**	**RANGE**
String (variable-length)	10 bytes + string length	0 to approximately 2 billion
String (fixed-length)	Length of string	1 to approximately 65,400
Variant (with numbers)	16 bytes	Any numeric value up to the range of a Double data type
Variant (with characters)	22 bytes + string length	Same range as for variable-length String data type

Normally when a procedure begins running, all variables (except static variables) are initialized. A number variable is initialized to zero, a variable-length string is initialized to a zero-length string (""), and a fixed-length string is filled with the ASCII character code 0. Variant variables are initialized to Empty. An Empty variable is represented as 0 in a numeric context, or a zero-length string ("") in a string context.

Variant Data Type

If no data type is defined for a variable, the Variant data type is assigned by default and VBA automatically performs any necessary conversions. Although you might be tempted to code your procedures using the Variant data type, there is a drawback. It uses a greater amount of memory and thus, can make your application less efficient.

Variables that are declared implicitly will be variant data types unless the Deftype statement is used. This statement allows you to specify that variables that begin with a particular letter will be a particular data type. For example, *DefStr L-Z* would cause all variables that begin with letters L through Z to default to a String type variable. This statement can be overridden by explicit declaration with a Dim statement. For more information on Deftype statements, open the Help system in the Visual Basic window, click the Answer Wizard tab, and then search for *Deftype*.

Variable Naming Conventions

A naming convention for variables is a good idea because it helps you to easily identify the data type or object type of a variable. (Object variables will be discussed in greater detail in Tutorial 9.) For the steps in this tutorial you will use a three-character prefix to identify the data type of the variable, followed by the base name. Some developers use a single-character prefix. However, for the sake of consistency, you will use three characters. Figure 7-15 defines the variable name prefixes that are used in this tutorial.

Figure 7-15	THREE CHARACTER PREFIXES USED IN VARIABLE NAMES

PREFIX	DATA TYPE
ary	Array
bln	Boolean
cur	Currency
dbl	Double
dtm	Date and Time
lng	Long
int	Number/Counter/Integer
str	String
udt	User-defined
vnt	Variant

Declaring Constants

A **constant** is a meaningful name that takes the place of a number or string. It is like a variable except that you can't change its value after you declare it. You might want to use a constant for a string that occurs frequently in your code or for numbers that are difficult to remember and have no obvious meaning. You have already used some Access predefined constants, such as acViewPreview, in your code. Constants that you create yourself work the same way, except that you name them and you assign the value to them. You declare constants with the Const statement. For example:

```
Const conAppName = "MovieCam Technologies"
```

Constants, like variables, have scope. Declaring a constant in the Declarations section allows you to use it throughout the module. Declaring a constant in a procedure makes it available to only that procedure. The Public and Private keywords are used to declare constants, just as they are used to declare variables.

Because you created the Sub procedure grpEmployees_AfterUpdate() before you selected the option to require variable declaration, the Option Explicit statement is not included in the Form_frmReportsSwitchboard class module. You will correct that next, and then substitute a variable for the wherecondition argument in the OpenReport statement.

To modify the code in the frmReportsSwitchboard form:

1. Position the insertion point at the end of the Option Compare Database statement in the Declarations section, and press the **Enter** key.

2. Type **Option Explicit**, click at the end of the Private Sub grpEmployees_AfterUpdate() line, and then press the **Enter** key.

3. Type **Dim strSQL As String**. Your Sub procedure should look like that shown in Figure 7-16.

Figure 7-16	DECLARING VARIABLES

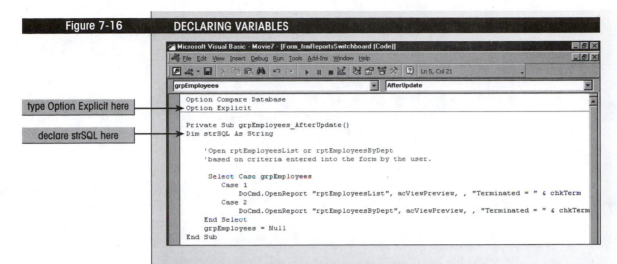

4. Position the insertion point at the end of the comment *based on criteria entered into the form by the user*, press **Enter** twice, and then type **strSQL = "Terminated ="** & **chkTerm**.

5. Delete the string **"Terminated = " & chkTerm** in each of the DoCmd.OpenReport statements, and type **strSQL** in its place. Your code now should look like that shown in Figure 7-17.

Figure 7-17	USING A VARIABLE IN CODE

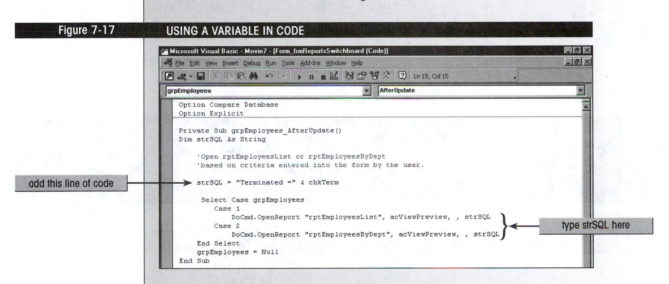

6. Click **Debug** on the menu bar, and then click **Compile MovieCam** to compile the code and check for errors.

7. Click the **Save** button 🖫 on the toolbar to save your changes, and then close the Visual Basic window.

8. Switch to Form view and test the form by running the Employee List report for terminated employees, closing it, and then running it again for active (nonterminated) employees. The list of terminated employees should include three records, and the list of active employees should include 12.

TROUBLE? If a report does not contain the correct number of records, return to Design view, open the code window and check the code carefully against that shown in Figure 7-17. Make any corrections necessary and then repeat Steps 5 through 7.

9. Return to **Design** view.

Now you plan to add more flexibility to the switchboard. In the next session you will modify the code you've written so that users can use more than one condition or criteria to open the reports they need.

Session 7.1 QUICK CHECK

1. VBA 6.0 is a(n) _____ programming language.

2. What is a form class module?

3. What term describes the visibility and accessibility of one procedure from another procedure?

4. What does the term *compiling* mean?

5. In _____ declaration you don't need to declare a variable before using it.

6. The time during which a variable retains it value is known as its _____.

7. How does the Static keyword differ from the Dim keyword when it is used to declare variables?

8. How does a constant differ from a variable?

SESSION 7.2

In this session you'll learn how to write the VBA code to create a multiple condition wherecondition for the DoCmd.OpenReport method. You will use the Immediate window to test code, and learn to use breakpoints to run your procedure up to a particular point. You also will use the Locals window to see the contents of variables and step through code one line at a time so you can watch it execute.

Creating the Wherecondition for Employee Reports

You and Carolyn are going to modify the code for the frmReportsSwitchboard form. Richard Jenkins in the Personnel department told you that he will need to run the employee reports for various conditions. He wants to be able to print reports of all active employees or all terminated employees. At other times, he might need reports on all terminated employees who were salaried, or all active employees who are salaried. And occasionally he needs to see all the salaried, active employees for one department only.

Creating Combo Boxes

Before modifying the code for the frmReportsSwitchboard form, you need to add some controls to the form. First you will add a combo box from which Richard can choose either Hourly or Salaried. You plan to use a combo box because the data is stored in this field as *H* for Hourly or *S* for Salaried, and that is what needs to be typed in on the form. You are concerned that Richard might input the word *Hourly* or the word *Salaried* if you simply use a text box. You will use a combo box with a value list, which stores the value selected in memory for later use, rather than storing it in an underlying table or query.

You also will add a combo box with the DeptName and DeptNo fields so that the appropriate department can be selected from the list, and the user does not type in a department that does not exist.

To create a combo box:

1. Make sure that Access is running, that the **Movie7** database from the **Tutorial.07** folder on the local or network hard drive is open, and that the frmReportsSwitchboard is open in Design view.

2. Make sure that the toolbox is open and that the **Control Wizards** button ![icon] is selected in the toolbox, as shown in Figure 7-18.

Figure 7-18	CREATING THE COMBO BOX

make sure the Control Wizards button is selected

3. Click the **Combo Box** button ![icon] on the toolbox, and then click beneath the Terminated check box to insert a combo box. The Combo Box Wizard opens.

4. Select the **I will type in the values that I want** option, and then click the **Next** button.

5. Type **2** in the Number of columns text box, position the insertion point in the first row of Col1, and then type **H**.

6. Tab to Col2, type **Hourly**, and then press the **Tab** key. This allows you to display the word *Hourly* but store the *H* for use in the wherecondition.

7. Type **S**, press the **Tab** key, type **Salaried** as shown in Figure 7-19, and then click the **Next** button. The next Combo Box Wizard dialog box asks you to specify the column that contains the value you want to store or use later.

Figure 7-19   **SPECIFYING COLUMN VALUES IN THE COMBO BOX WIZARD**

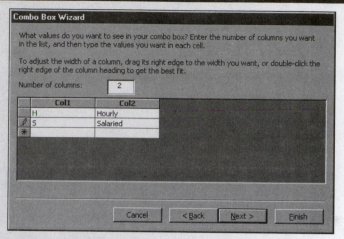

8. Make sure that **Col1** is selected, and then click the **Next** button. This will save H or S to be used later. The last dialog box prompts you to enter a label for the combo box.

9. Type **Hourly/Salaried** and then click the **Finish** button.

10. Click the **Properties** button 🖾 on the toolbar, change the Name property to **cboHS**, change the Column Widths property to **0";1"**, change the List Width property to **1"**, and close the properties dialog box. These changes will hide the first column, which contains H and S, although the first column values will be retained for later use.

11. Size the label to the left of the combo box so that all of the text is visible.

12. Switch to Form view and test the combo box. It has Hourly and Salaried in the list.

Next you'll create the combo box to show the DeptNo and DeptName field values. You will set the combo box properties so that the values are looked up in the tblDepartments table.

To create the cboDept combo box:

1. Switch to Design view, click the **Combo Box** button 🖾 on the toolbar, and then click below the cboHS combo box control to create the combo box.

2. Click the **Next** button in the first dialog box to accept the default option, click **tblDepartments** in the next dialog box, and then click the **Next** button.

3. Add the **DeptNo** and **DeptName** fields to the Selected Fields list box, click the **Next** button, and widen the **DeptName** column by dragging the edge of the column to the right.

4. Click the **Next** button, type **Department**, and then click the **Finish** button.

5. Click the **Properties** button 🖾 on the toolbar, and change the Name property to **cboDept**.

6. Save the form, and close the properties dialog box.

7. Size and align the controls on the form to look like those shown in Figure 7-20.

| Figure 7-20 | ADDING CONTROLS TO THE FRMREPORTSSWITCHBOARD FORM |

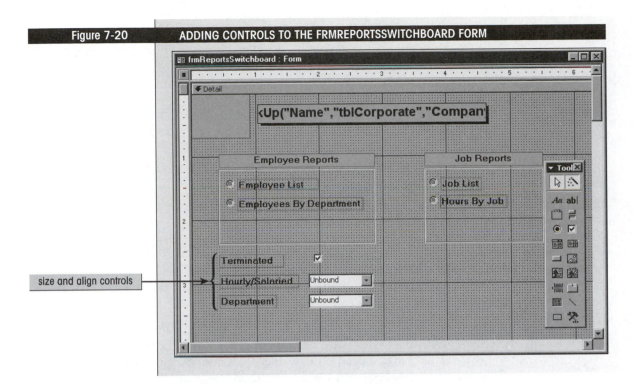

Now that you have completed the controls for the Employee Reports portion of the form, you are ready to plan the code that you will need.

Building the WhereCondition

Recall that the wherecondition argument in the OpenReport method is a SQL WHERE clause without the word WHERE. You and Carolyn have created a query to determine what this argument will look like when it is completed. The OpenReport method will open a report based on the tblEmployees table, and the wherecondition argument will supply the condition for opening the report. Essentially, the wherecondition argument will substitute for a query underlying the report.

The query contains the Terminated, HourlySalaried, and DeptNo fields from the tblEmployees table. The design for this select query, named qryWhere, is shown in Figure 7-21.

| Figure 7-21 | QRYWHERE |

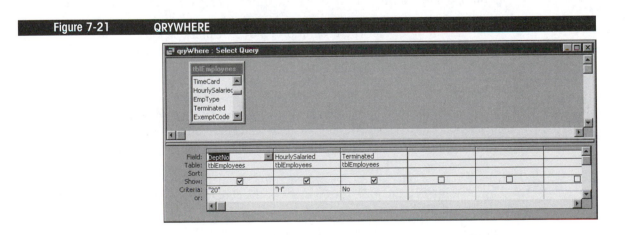

The results of the query after switching to SQL view are as follows:

```
SELECT tblEmployees.DeptNo, tblEmployees.HourlySalaried,
tblEmployees.Terminated
FROM tblEmployees
WHERE (((tblEmployees.DeptNo)="20") AND
((tblEmployees.HourlySalaried)="H") AND
((tblEmployees.Terminated)=No));
```

Take a closer look at the WHERE clause. After you remove the SELECT and FROM clauses and the word WHERE from the WHERE clause, it looks like this:

```
(((tblEmployees.DeptNo)="20") AND
((tblEmployees.HourlySalaried)="H") AND
((tblEmployees.Terminated)=No));
```

Next you remove the parentheses, which are unnecessary syntax in this wherecondition, and the expression looks like the following:

```
tblEmployees.DeptNo="20" AND tblEmployees.HourlySalaried="H"
AND tblEmployees.Terminated=No
```

When Access displays a query in SQL, it includes the complete syntax, just like the Expression Builder does when you create an expression in it. The table names are necessary only if there is more than one table in the query. Because this query has only one table, the field names are all you need in the wherecondition argument of the DoCmd.OpenReport statement. After you remove the references to the table name, you have the following:

```
DeptNo="20" AND HourlySalaried="H" AND Terminated=No
```

Your switchboard form now contains the cboDept combo box, the cboHS combo box, and the chkTerm check box. If you Substitute the names of these controls for the actual data in the previous expression, you get the following:

```
DeptNo="cboDept" AND HourlySalaried="cboHS" AND Terminated=ch
kTerm
```

To construct the above statement so that it can be used as the wherecondition argument in the OpenReport method, you must construct a string expression that joins together strings of text and special characters with the values contained in the cboDept, cboHS, and chkTerm controls in the frmReportsSwitchboard form.

To understand the syntax of this expression, you will examine it in various stages of completion. Each new string added to the end of the expression is in boldface to make it easier for you to identify.

The beginning of the wherecondition follows. It must be enclosed in quotation marks because it is a string that you are going to concatenate to another string, and then to the contents of the cboDept combo box.

```
"DeptNo = "
```

In the following code, a quotation mark has been concatenated to the DeptNo = string because the contents of the cboDept combo box are text and must be surrounded by quotation marks. A single quotation mark is used inside the double quotation marks to make it easier to read.

```
"DeptNo = " & "'"
```

In the following example, the contents of the cboDept combo box are now concatenated to the end of the expression.

```
"DeptNo =  " & "'" & cboDept
```

In the next example, another quotation has been concatenated to the end of the expression. The quotation marks are necessary because DeptNo is a text field. Recall that this is the correct syntax for a text field value in a SQL statement.

```
"DeptNo = " & "'" & cboDept & "'"
```

The following example now concatenates the string *AND HourlySalaried* = to the end of the expression.

```
"DeptNo = " & "'" & cboDept & "'" & " AND HourlySalaried = "
```

The next example shows another quotation mark concatenated to the end of the expression. The contents of the cboHS combo box are text, and therefore must be surrounded by quotation marks. A single quotation mark is used inside the double quotation marks to make it easier to read.

```
"DeptNo = " & "'" & cboDept & "'" & " AND HourlySalaried = "
& "'"
```

The completed expression follows. Note that *chkTerm* is not surrounded by quotation marks in the original SQL statement, and therefore you do not have to concatenate the additional quotation marks to it here.

```
"DeptNo = " & "'" & cboDept & "'" & " AND HourlySalaried = "
& "'" & cboHS & "'" & " AND Terminated = " & chkTerm
```

You are still a bit confused by this. Carolyn has written down each string inside quotation marks and joined it to the next string where an ampersand exists. She substituted a value for cboDept, cboHS, and chkTerm so that you can see the string expression as shown in Figure 7-22.

Figure 7-22	STRING EXPRESSION

DeptNo = '10' AND HourlySalaried = 'H' AND Terminated = Yes

Writing the Code

Now that you and Carolyn have determined what the completed wherecondition should look like, you will write the code so that the user can choose any combination of the three options on the form. To do this, you will first test to see if each of the controls is null. You will use the IsNull function.

The IsNull syntax is IsNull(expression). This function tests the expression to see whether it is null or not. In this case, you want to know if the expression (value of the control) is not null, that is, whether it contains a value, so you will include the *Not* operator before the function. Then you will set a variable called strWhere. At the beginning of the procedure you will declare that variable equal to whatever is already contained in strWhere, and equal to the part of the wherecondition string that applies to the control you are testing.

You will then use a series of If...Then...Else statements to test each of the three controls on the form.

To write the code for building the wherecondition:

1. Click the **Code** button [icon] on the toolbar to display the Visual Basic window, position the insertion point at the end of the Dim strSQL As String line, and then press **Enter**.

2. Type **Dim strWhere As String** to declare another string variable. It will be used to build the wherecondition. The variable strSQL will be used to trim off leading characters after you build the wherecondition.

3. Press **Enter** twice, and type the following comment: **'Build the wherecondition to use in the OpenReport method**.

4. Press **Enter** twice and type the following:

```
If Not IsNull(cboDept) Then
     strWhere = strWhere & " AND  DeptNo= " & "'" & cboDe
pt & "'"
End If
```

5. Select the **strSQL = "Terminated=" & chkTerm** line of code, press the **Delete** key, and then press the **Backspace** key to delete the blank line.

6. Compare your code to that shown in Figure 7-23 to be sure that it is correct.

Figure 7-23   ADDING TO THE WHERECONDITION

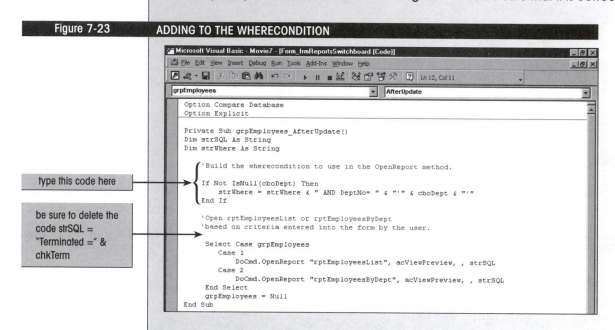

type this code here

be sure to delete the code strSQL = "Terminated =" & chkTerm

You are not certain from which of the three controls (cboDept, cboHS, or chkTerm) the user will choose. To allow for this, you will construct the wherecondition so that it always concatenates whatever is already contained in the strWhere variable to the string " AND " and then to the remaining string expression for that particular control. This way, no matter which of the three controls is chosen, they are joined together with the word AND. Once you have finished building strWhere, you will use a function to trim off the leading string " AND ".

7. Position the insertion point at the end of the End If statement, press the **Enter** key twice, and type the following:

```
If Not IsNull(cboHS) Then
     strWhere = strWhere & " AND  HourlySalaried = " & "'"
 & cboHS & "'"
End If
```

8. Press the **Enter** key twice and type the following:

```
If Not IsNull(chkTerm) Then
     strWhere = strWhere & " AND  Terminated = " & chkTerm
End If
```

9. Click the **Save** button 🖫 on the toolbar. Your code should look like that shown in Figure 7-24.

| Figure 7-24 | COMPLETING THE WHERECONDITION |

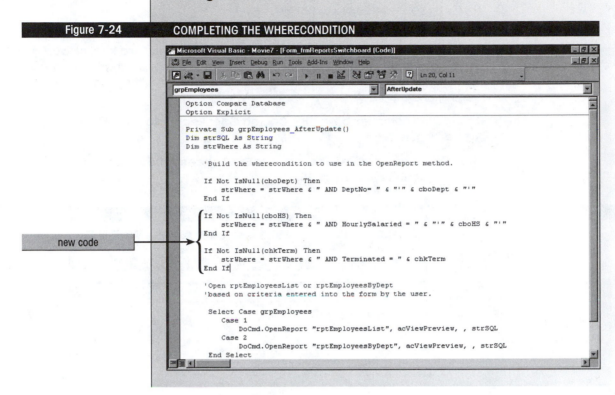

new code

Next you will test the contents of the strWhere variable to determine if it is not null. If it is not null—that is, it contains a string of text—you will trim the leading AND along with the spaces surrounding it. You will use the Mid string function to do this. Some VBA functions have two versions: one that returns a variant data type and another that returns a string data type. When the function name is followed by a dollar sign, it returns a string rather than a variant. Remember that the drawback to variant data types is that they use more memory, which is inefficient. You will use the Mid$ version of this function so that a string is returned.

The Mid function returns a variant or string with a specified number of characters from a string. The syntax of the Mid function is as follows (the bracketed argument is optional):

```
Mid(string, start[, length])
```

The *string* is the variable or string from which you are taking the new string. The *start* is the character position in the string where the part to be taken begins. The *length* is the total number of characters to return. The *length* argument is optional, so if it is left blank the remaining portion of the string is returned, beginning with the character designated by the *start* argument.

To add code to trim leading characters and spaces from the strWhere variable:

1. Press **Enter** twice to add space after the End If statement, and then type the following comment: **'Trim the leading " AND " off strWhere and store the new string in strSQL**.

2. Press **Enter** twice and then type the following code:

```
If Not IsNull(strWhere) Then
    strSQL = Mid$(strWhere, 6)
End If
```

The start argument in the Mid function is 6 because " AND " is a total of five characters, and you want the string to now begin at the sixth character. The strSQL variable will now contain the contents of strWhere without unnecessary leading characters.

3. Change the comment before the Docmd.OpenReport statement to the following (see Figure 7-25):

```
'Open rptEmployeesList or rptEmployeesByDept based on
'the contents of strSQL.
```

Figure 7-25	CHANGING A COMMENT IN THE CODE

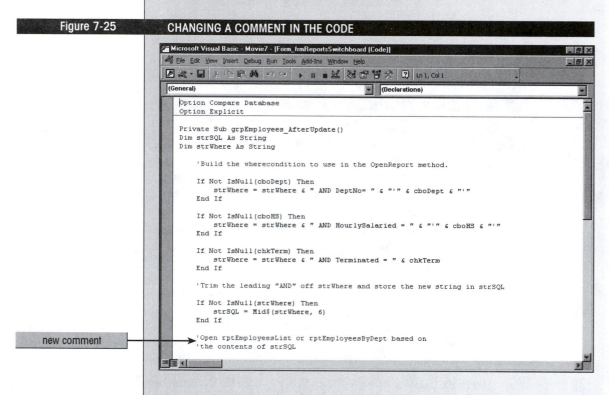

new comment

4. Position the insertion point at the end of the *End Select* statement, and press **Enter** twice.

5. Type the following comment: **'Set the option group, combo boxes, and check box back to null**.

6. Press **Enter**, position the insertion point at the end of the grpEmployees = Null statement, press **Enter**, and then type the following:

```
cboDept = Null
cboHS = Null
chkTerm = Null
```

These statements set the option group, combo boxes, and check boxes back to null after the report opens, so that the user can make a different choice without any residual value left in any of the controls.

7. Press **Enter** to add space between these statements and the End Sub statement, as shown in Figure 7-26.

Figure 7-26   ADDING BLANK LINES TO MAKE THE CODE EASIER TO READ

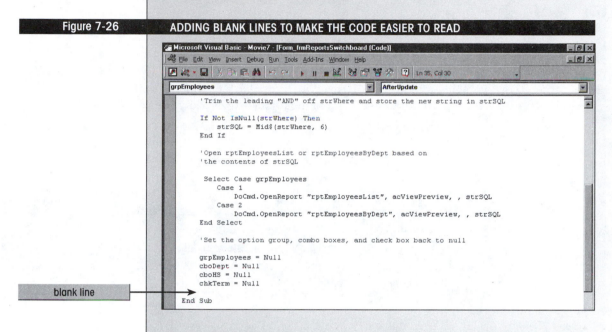

blank line

8. Click **Debug** on the menu bar, and then click **Compile MovieCam**. If any of your variables are misspelled, you should correct them now.

9. Click the **Save** button on the toolbar.

10. Close the Visual Basic window, switch to Form view, and test the reports. Switch back to Design view, and click the **Code** button on the toolbar.

The procedure that you have written is working fine, but you are still a bit confused about the wherecondition. Carolyn suggests using the Immediate window so that you can see the value of each of the variables when you run the procedure. You use the Immediate window to look for errors that are not caught during compilation. (The types of errors you might encounter—including syntax and logic errors—are discussed in more detail in Tutorial 8.) For now you would like to see the contents of the variables during testing.

Using the Immediate Window

The **Immediate window** shows information that results from debugging statements in your code or from commands typed directly into the window. To see the Immediate window in the Visual Basic window, you select Immediate Window on the View menu, or press Ctrl+G on the keyboard. You can use the Immediate window to check results of a line of code, and to check the value of a control, field, property, or variable. You might think of it as a scratch pad on which statements, methods, and Sub procedures can be evaluated immediately.

You can view the results of an expression or a variable in the Immediate window by entering the Print method of the Debug object, followed by the expression. For example:

```
Debug.Print Mid$(strWhere, 6)
```

would display the results of the expression.

The Debug.Print method also can be represented by the question mark character, as shown below:

```
?Mid$(strWhere,6)
```

You also can use the Debug.Print method (or the question mark character) to run a function and display its results in the Immediate window. Recall the basUtilityFunctions module that you imported into the database in Tutorial 3. The module contained a function named ProperCase. To run this function in the Immediate window you would type:

```
?ProperCase("TEST")
```

The function would return *Test*.

REFERENCE WINDOW   **RW**

Testing a Function in the Immediate Window
- In the Code window, press Ctrl+G to open the Immediate window.
- Type a question mark (?), the name of the function, and the function's arguments in parentheses.
- Press the Enter key and the answer is shown.

First you'll test the Immediate window by typing in some simple formulas and running the ProperCase function.

To test the Immediate window:

1. To see the Immediate window, press **Ctrl+G**.

2. Type **Debug.Print 2+3** and then press **Enter**. The result is shown on the next line.

3. Type **?2+3** and then press **Enter**.

   The database contains the basUtilityFunctions module, so you'll now run the ProperCase function.

4. Type **?ProperCase("THIS IS A TEST")** and then press the **Enter** key. The results should look like those shown in Figure 7-27.

Figure 7-27   **USING THE IMMEDIATE WINDOW**

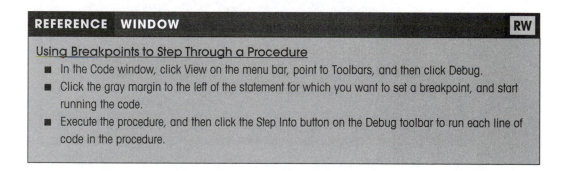

results from simple formulas and the ProperCase function

Now that you've tested the Immediate window, you need a way to stop the code at a particular point so that you can test the value of expressions and variables before the procedure finishes running.

Setting Breakpoints in Code

A **breakpoint** is a selected line of your program at which execution automatically stops. There are various reasons you might want to set a breakpoint to suspend execution at a specific statement in a procedure. You might want to stop running the procedure at a statement where you suspect a problem exists. You might use a breakpoint to suspend execution so that you can use the Immediate window to test the value of variables or expressions at a particular point in the program. When you no longer need them to stop execution, you clear breakpoints. Breakpoints are not saved with your code.

REFERENCE   WINDOW   **RW**

Using Breakpoints to Step Through a Procedure

- In the Code window, click View on the menu bar, point to Toolbars, and then click Debug.
- Click the gray margin to the left of the statement for which you want to set a breakpoint, and start running the code.
- Execute the procedure, and then click the Step Into button on the Debug toolbar to run each line of code in the procedure.

Next you will use breakpoints in conjunction with the Immediate window to see the value of the variables in your code, and to test the Mid$ expression. Carolyn assured you that this will help you better understand the wherecondition code she helped you write.

Testing the code using the Immediate window:

1. Click the gray margin to the left of the Select Case grpEmployees line to set a breakpoint, as shown in Figure 7-28.

Figure 7-28   **SETTING A BREAKPOINT IN CODE**

click the gray margin to the left of the Select Case

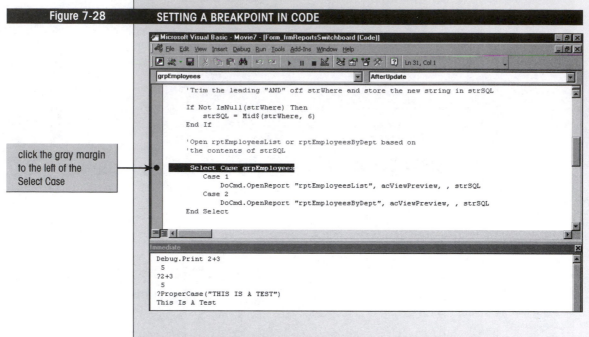

2. Minimize the Visual Basic window, and then switch to Form view to test the frmReportsSwitchboard form.

3. Select **Salaried** from the Hourly/Salaried combo box, and **Engineering** from the Department combo box.

4. Click the **Employee List** option in the Employee Reports option group. The Visual Basic window will show a highlighted line where you created the breakpoint.

5. Type **?Mid$(strWhere, 6)** in the Immediate window to test the Mid function, and then press **Enter**. The results are visible as shown in Figure 7-29.

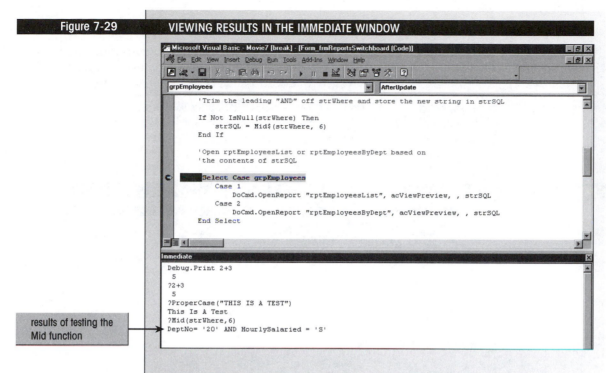

| Figure 7-29 | VIEWING RESULTS IN THE IMMEDIATE WINDOW |

results of testing the Mid function

6. Type **?strSQL** in the Immediate window, and then press **Enter**. The contents of the strSQL variable are shown.

7. Click the **Continue** button ▶ on the Standard toolbar to continue running the code. The Employee List report shows the records that meet the criteria entered on the form.

8. Close the report to return to the switchboard.

You're still a bit confused at how the procedure works, so Carolyn is going to show you how to step through the code one line at a time. This is useful for finding errors that don't show up during compilation, because you can check the value of your variables at various points in the execution of the code.

Reviewing Code Line by Line

Access provides tools that enable you to step through your code line by line. After you have seen the code run through the lines necessary, you can step out of the code. This means that it finishes running. You will use breakpoints and commands on the Debug menu or on the Debug toolbar to step through the procedure. In addition, you will use the Locals window to see the contents of the strWhere and strSQL variables as each line of code executes.

The Locals Window

The Immediate window is useful for running functions, testing expressions, and displaying variables. You should use the Locals window if you need to see only the contents of the variables. In the **Locals window**, Access automatically displays the name, current value, and type of all the variables and objects in the current procedure. The values in the Locals window are updated each time you suspend code execution. If you step through the code, execution is suspended after each statement executes. With the Locals window open, you are able to see the variables change at each step.

To step through code one line at a time:

1. Restore the Visual Basic window by clicking its icon on the taskbar, and then close the Immediate window by clicking its **Close** button in the upper-right corner. It is simpler to step through the code if the Debug toolbar is visible.

2. If necessary, click **View** on the menu bar, point to **Toolbars**, and then click **Debug**. The toolbar, which contains a Step Into button that you can click each time you want to run another line of code, will probably be floating, as shown in Figure 7-30.

Figure 7-30	THE DEBUG TOOLBAR

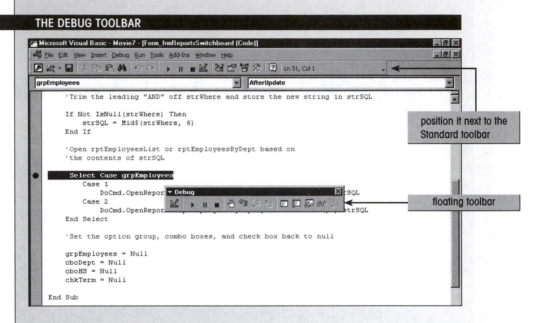

3. If necessary, drag the Debug toolbar by its title bar to the top of the screen, and dock it next to the Standard toolbar. The breakpoint that you set earlier should still exist. You will clear it and set another breakpoint now.

4. If necessary, clear the breakpoint by clicking the dot in the gray margin to the left of the Select Case grpEmployees line Scroll to the top of the code, and set a breakpoint at the Private Sub grpEmployees_AfterUpdate() line, as shown in Figure 7-31. This will stop the code at the beginning of the procedure so that you can step through it one line at a time.

Figure 7-31   SETTING A BREAKPOINT AT THE BEGINNING OF THE PROCEDURE

set the new
breakpoint here

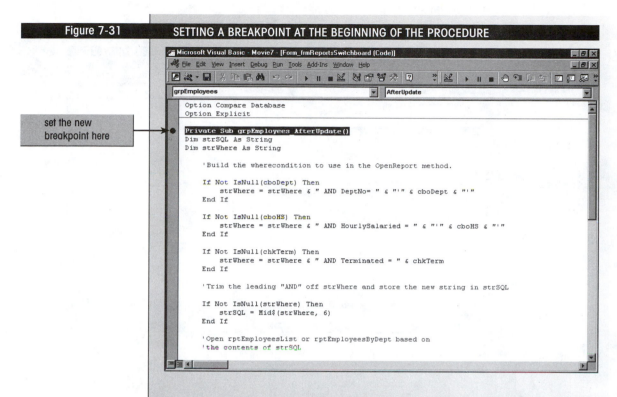

```
Option Compare Database
Option Explicit

Private Sub grpEmployees_AfterUpdate()
Dim strSQL As String
Dim strWhere As String

    'Build the wherecondition to use in the OpenReport method.

    If Not IsNull(cboDept) Then
        strWhere = strWhere & " AND DeptNo= " & "'" & cboDept & "'"
    End If

    If Not IsNull(cboHS) Then
        strWhere = strWhere & " AND HourlySalaried = " & "'" & cboHS & "'"
    End If

    If Not IsNull(chkTerm) Then
        strWhere = strWhere & " AND Terminated = " & chkTerm
    End If

    'Trim the leading "AND" off strWhere and store the new string in strSQL

    If Not IsNull(strWhere) Then
        strSQL = Mid$(strWhere, 6)
    End If

    'Open rptEmployeesList or rptEmployeesByDept based on
    'the contents of strSQL
```

5. Click **View** on the menu bar, and then click **Locals Window**. The Locals window opens at the bottom of the Visual Basic window.

6. Minimize the Visual Basic window, select **Hourly** from the Hourly/Salaried combo box, select **Production** from the Department combo box, and then click the **Employee List** option. The Visual Basic window is visible, and the code stopped running at the beginning of the procedure.

7. Click the **Step Into** button on the Debug toolbar, and the first statement of code is highlighted as shown in Figure 7-32.

Figure 7-32 | STEPPING INTO THE FIRST LINE OF CODE

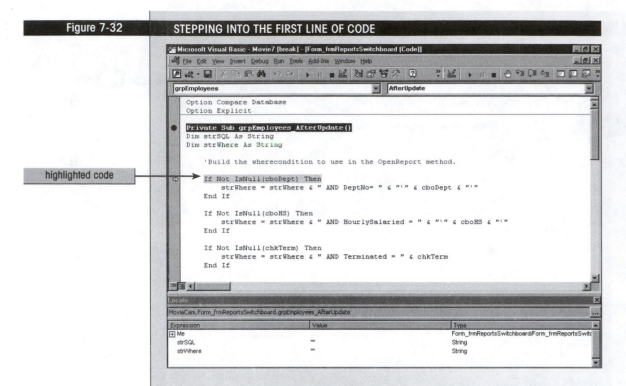

highlighted code

8. Click the **Step Into** button 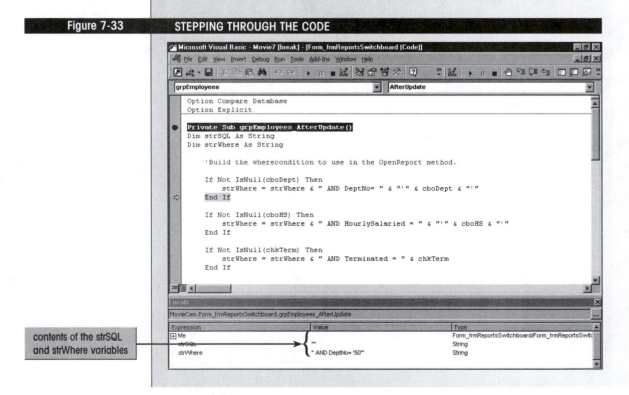 to step through each of the three lines of the first If...Then...Else statement. Note the contents of the strWhere and strSQL variables, as shown in Figure 7-33. The first portion of the wherecondition is complete.

Figure 7-33 | STEPPING THROUGH THE CODE

contents of the strSQL and strWhere variables

You also can see the code execute as you step through it. For example, to begin running the procedure, you chose a value from the Hourly/Salaried combo box and from the Department combo box, but you did not mark the Terminated check box on the frmReportsSwitchboard form. As you step through the If...Then...Else statements, note that Access steps through each line of code when the condition is True, and skips over the line with chkTerm, in which the condition is False.

To continue stepping through the code:

1. Click the **Step Into** button [icon] again to step into the first line of the next If...Then...Else statement, and then click [icon] twice. The contents of the Locals window change to show the new contents of the strWhere variable. The strSQL variable is still a zero-length string.

2. Click [icon] to move to the first line of the next If...Then...Else statement. This If statement should evaluate to False, and Access should skip over the next line.

3. Click [icon] again, and the End If line is highlighted as shown in Figure 7-34.

Figure 7-34	WATCHING THE EXECUTION OF THE PROGRAM

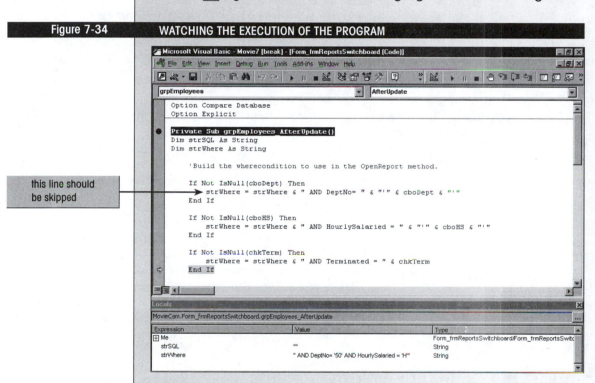

4. Step through the next If...Then...Else statement. The value of the strSQL variable has now changed, as shown in Figure 7-35.

Figure 7-35 | STEPPING THROUGH THE CODE

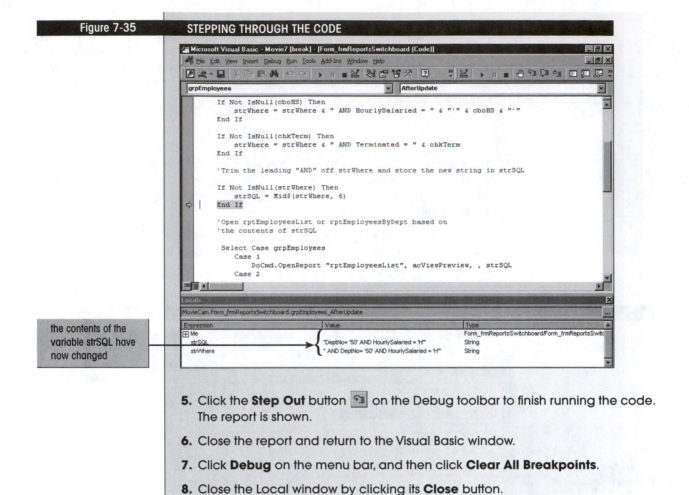

the contents of the variable strSQL have now changed

5. Click the **Step Out** button 🔄 on the Debug toolbar to finish running the code. The report is shown.

6. Close the report and return to the Visual Basic window.

7. Click **Debug** on the menu bar, and then click **Clear All Breakpoints**.

8. Close the Local window by clicking its **Close** button.

You and Carolyn want to make one more change to the design of the Employee Reports section of the frmReportsSwitchboard form. You are concerned that users might click an option button to run a report before first choosing conditions from the three controls. Carolyn suggests adding a command button to preview the report after the report is chosen from the option group and the conditions are selected from the other controls on the form. You agree and next will make the code changes to accomplish this.

Modifying the Code for Employee Reports

If you add a command button to the form that triggers the DoCmd.OpenReport method, you will use that command only once. This is another case where a variable will come in handy. If you declare a variable, such as strReport, for the report name, you can then set the variable equal to the name of the report in the Select Case statement. Then the command button will trigger a DoCmd.OpenReport statement that uses the variable for the report-name argument.

To add a command button to the frmReportsSwitchboard form:

1. Minimize the Visual Basic window, switch to Design view, and make sure the toolbox is open.

2. Make sure that the Control Wizards is *deselected*, click the **Command Button** button ▭, and then click below the cboDept control.

3. Click the **Properties** button 🖼 on the toolbar, change the Name property to **cmdPreview**, and type **&Preview** in the Caption property text box.

4. Click the **Save** button 💾 on the toolbar, and then restore the Visual Basic window.

5. Click the **Object** list arrow as shown in Figure 7-36, and then click **cmdPreview**. The stub is created, and the insertion point is positioned between the two lines of code.

Figure 7-36   **CREATING THE CMDPREVIEW_CLICK STUB**

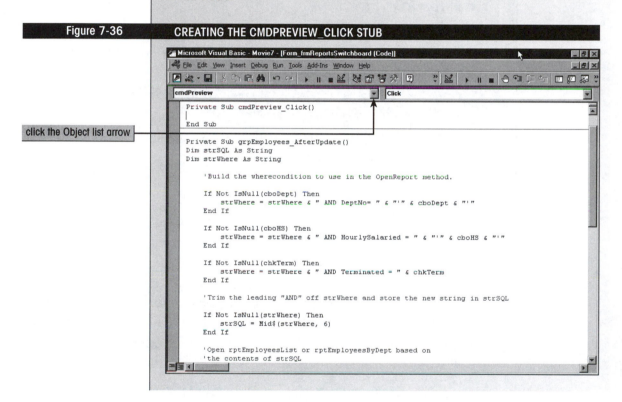

click the Object list arrow

Before you continue, consider the rest of the code. Because the statement to preview the report will be a separate Sub procedure triggered by the cmdPreview button that you just created on the form, the code to populate the wherecondition also needs to be included in this procedure. This is determined by the order of operations that the user will take:

1. The user will click a button in the grpEmployees option group to choose a report. The name of that report will be stored in a new variable named strReport.

2. The user will select Terminated, Hourly or Salaried, and/or the Department. These values need to remain in the controls until the report is previewed.

3. The user will click the Preview button.

As you can determine from these steps, the code to build the wherecondition must be run after the user selects Terminated, Hourly or Salaried, and/or the Department from the controls on the form. If this portion of the code remains in the AfterUpdate procedure, the wherecondition will be built before these choices are made, because the AfterUpdate event fires as soon as an option is selected in the option group.

You will include the code for populating the strWhere and strSQL variables and the Docmd.OpenReport statement in the new Sub cmdPreview_Click() procedure. You also will need to declare these variables at the beginning of this new procedure.

Recall from the discussion of variables that a variable must be declared in the Declarations section if you want it to be available to the entire module. This, as you learned, is because the lifetime of a variable declared in a procedure ends when the procedure stops running. The new strReport variable needs to be declared in the Declarations section of the module because it will be referred to in both procedures.

To complete the coding for the Employee Reports section of the switchboard form:

1. Position the insertion point at the end of the Option Explicit statement in the Declarations section, and then press the **Enter** key.

2. Type **Private strReport As String**.

3. Change Case 1 in the Select Case statement in the Private Sub grpEmployees_AfterUpdate() procedure to:

```
strReport = "rptEmployeesList"
```

4. Change Case 2 in the Select Case statement to:

```
strReport = "rptEmployeesByDept"
```

5. Cut the following statements from the Private Sub grpEmployees_AfterUpdate() procedure, and paste them under the Private Sub cmdPreview_Click() statement:

```
Dim strSQL As String
Dim strWhere As String
```

6. Cut the following comments and statements from the Private Sub grpEmployees_AfterUpdate() procedure, and paste them below the two Dim statements in the Private Sub cmdPreview_Click() procedure (see Figure 7-37):

```
'Build the wherecondition to use in the OpenReport
method
If Not IsNull(cboDept) Then
    strWhere = strWhere & " AND  DeptNo= " & "'" & c
boDept & "'"
 End If
If Not IsNull(cboHS) Then
    strWhere = strWhere & " AND  HourlySalaried = " &
"'" & cboHS & "'"
End If
If Not IsNull(chkTerm) Then
    strWhere = strWhere & " AND  Terminated = " & chkTerm
End If
```

```
'Trim the leading "AND " off strWhere and store the
new string in strSQL
If Not IsNull(strWhere) Then
        strSQL = Mid$(strWhere, 6)
End If
```

Figure 7-37	MODIFYING THE CODE IN THE FRMREPORTSSWITCHBOARD FORM

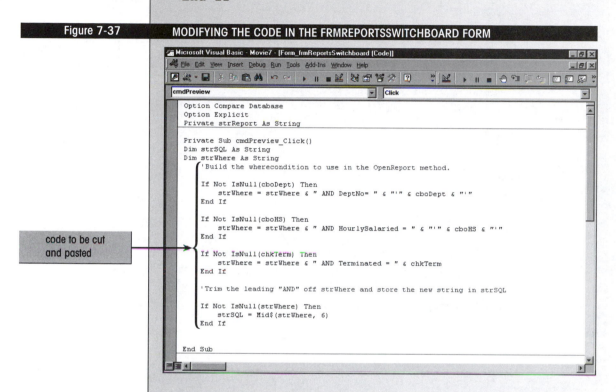

code to be cut
and pasted

7. Press **Enter** twice after the End If statement, and type the following comment and statement:

```
'Open report based on the contents of strSQL.
DoCmd.OpenReport strReport, acViewPreview, , strSQL
```

8. Press the **Enter** key twice, cut the following comment and statements from the Private Sub grpEmployees_AfterUpdate() procedure, and paste them at the end of the Private Sub cmdPreview_Click() procedure between the DoCmd.OpenReport strReport, acViewPreview, , strSQL statement and the End Sub statement as shown in Figure 7-38:

```
'Set the option group, combo boxes, and check box back
to null
grpEmployees = Null
cboDept = Null
cboHS = Null
chkTerm = Null
```

Figure 7-38   CUTTING AND PASTING MORE CODE IN THE FRMREPORTSSWITCHBOARD FORM

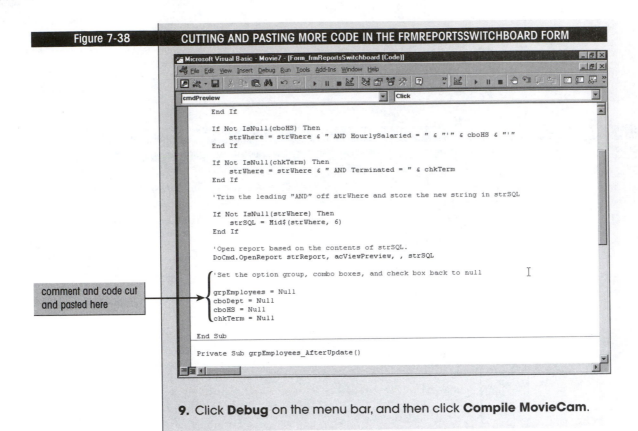

comment and code cut
and pasted here

9. Click **Debug** on the menu bar, and then click **Compile MovieCam**.

Now that you've completed the coding for the grpEmployees option group, you need to test it again. You'll run through various conditions for each of the reports.

To test the frmReportsSwitchboard form:

1. Close the Visual Basic window and then switch to Form view.

2. Click **Employee List**, click the **Terminated** check box, and then click the **Preview** button. The report opens, and shows the records for three employees.

3. Close the report to return to the switchboard, click **Employee List**, select **Salaried** from the Hourly/Salaried combo box, **Engineering** from the Department combo box, and then click the **Preview** button. The report matching these criteria opens.

4. Close the report, click **Employees By Department**, select **Hourly** from the Hourly/Salaried combo box, **Production** from the Department combo box, and then click the **Preview** button. The results match the condition you specified.

5. Close the report, and then click the **Preview** button without selecting a report. Notice that the last report selected is shown with all records. This is fine for now, but in the future you and Carolyn want to include a method that forces the user to choose a report in order to avoid confusion. (You will work on this in Tutorial 8.)

6. Close the open report.

Next you will address Martin Woodward's request that he be able to run job reports according to JobID and by a range of dates. To do this, you will add a text box for the JobID field, another one for a beginning date, and another for an ending date.

To add text boxes to the frmReportsSwitchboard form:

1. Switch to Design view, and make sure that the toolbox is open.

2. Click the **Text Box** button on the toolbox, and then click below the Job Reports option group to create a text box.

3. Click the **Properties** button on the toolbar, change the Name property to **txtJobID**, type **Job ID** in the label control, and move the label to the left of the text box. Size and align the label and text box controls as shown in Figure 7-39.

Figure 7-39   SIZING AND ALIGNING THE JOBID CONTROLS

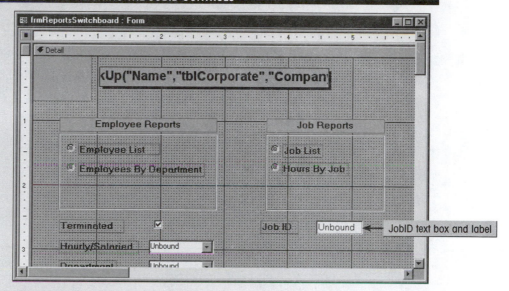

4. Create two more text boxes on the form, delete the label from one of them, and position them as shown in Figure 7-40. Change the Name property of the text box on the left to **txtStartDate**, and change the Name property of the other text box to **txtEndDate**.

Figure 7-40   ADDING THE TEXT BOXES FOR DATES

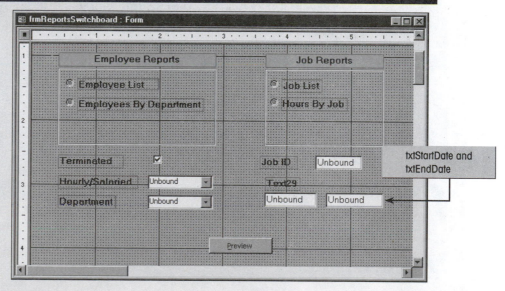

5. Change the Caption property of the label control to **Beginning && Ending Dates:**. You must include two ampersands to display one in the label. Recall that one ampersand is a shortcut key combination and is used to indicate that the character following it is underscored.

6. Size and align the controls as shown in Figure 7-41, and then save the form.

| Figure 7-41 | SIZING AND ALIGNING THE BEGINNING AND ENDING DATES CONTROLS |

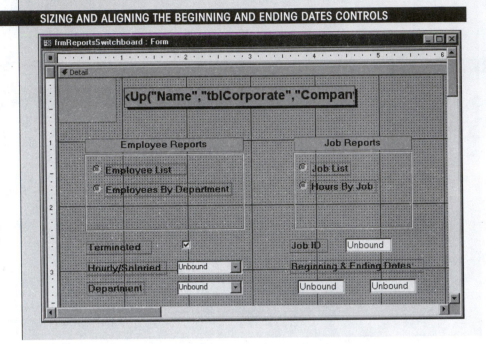

Next you need to add the code necessary to open reports from the Job Reports option group. First you will add a Sub procedure that is triggered by the AfterUpdate event property of the grpJobs option group.

To add a Sub procedure to open the job reports:

1. Click the **grpJobs** option group, display the properties dialog box, click the **Event** tab, click in the **After Update** property text box, and click the **Build** button .

2. Complete the code as shown in Figure 7-42.

Figure 7-42	COMPLETED GRPJOBS_AFTERUPDATE EVENT PROCEDURE

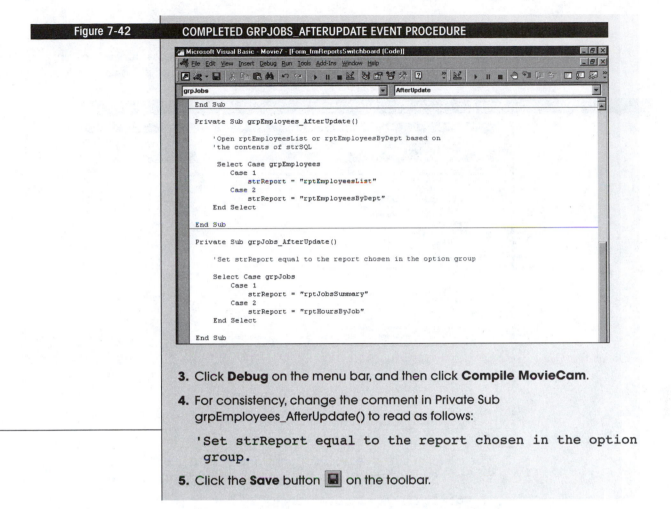

3. Click **Debug** on the menu bar, and then click **Compile MovieCam**.

4. For consistency, change the comment in Private Sub grpEmployees_AfterUpdate() to read as follows:

   ```
   'Set strReport equal to the report chosen in the option
    group.
   ```

5. Click the **Save** button 🖫 on the toolbar.

Adding to the Wherecondition for Job Reports

Now that you have a feel for working with the wherecondition, you will add more conditions to it. Recall that Martin said he wants to run reports for specific job numbers by typing in the first few numbers of the job. For example, if he types "92", he wants all the jobs that begin with those numbers to run. His other request is that he be able to run job reports by a single date or range of dates. The SQL WHERE clause that searches for records where the JobID field starts with "92" and includes any characters following it, looks like this:

```
WHERE JobID Like "92*"
```

You might remember from working with simple queries that the asterisk **wildcard** stands for any group of characters, and that the **Like** operation must be used in conjunction with a wildcard.

The SQL WHERE clause to query for records that include a single date for the TimeCardDate field looks like this:

```
WHERE TimeCardDate =  #11/9/2002#
```

Finally, the SQL WHERE clause to query for records that include a range of dates for the TimeCardDate field looks like this:

```
WHERE TimeCardDate Between #1/1/2002# And #12/31/2002#
```

You will start by adding the code for the JobID field.

To add code to query Job Reports:

1. Position the insertion point at the end of the third End If statement in the Sub cmdPreview_Click procedure as shown in Figure 7-43, and press **Enter** twice.

Figure 7-43   ADDING TO THE WHERECONDITION CODE

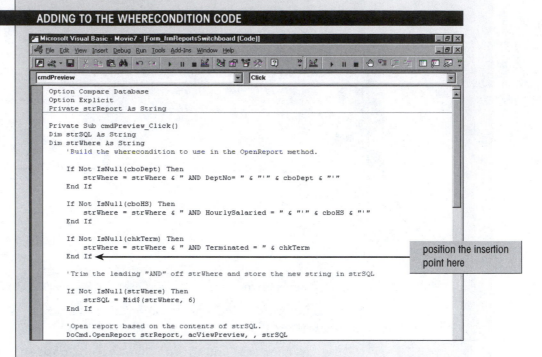

2. Type the following code (you can copy and paste one of the other If...Then...Else statements, and then make the changes that are necessary):

```
If Not IsNull(txtJobID) Then
    strWhere = strWhere & " AND JobID Like " & "'" &
txtJobID & "*'"
End If
```

3. Position the insertion point at the end of the grpEmployees = Null statement, press **Enter**, and type **grpJobs = Null**.

4. Position the insertion point at the end of the chkTerm = Null statement, press **Enter**, and type **txtJobID = Null**.

5. Compile the code and save your changes.

6. Check your code carefully against Figure 7-44 and make any changes necessary.

Figure 7-44   **ADDING TO THE WHERECONDITION CODE**

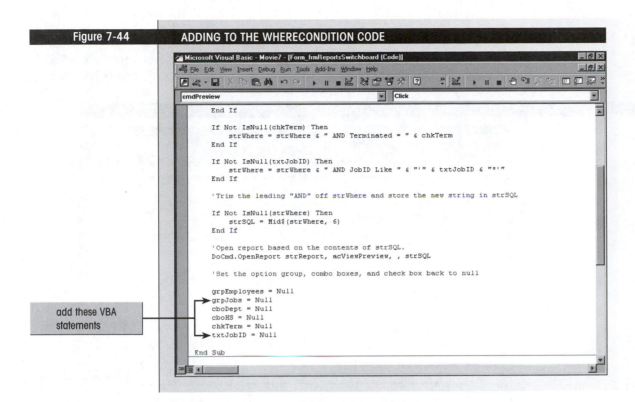

add these VBA
statements

Next you need to plan the remaining statements to query for dates. If the user enters the beginning date in the txtStartDate text box and enters nothing in the txtEndDate text box, you want the report to show records for only one date. The following WHERE clause would accomplish this:

```
WHERE TimeCardDate =  #11/9/2002#
```

If both a start date and an end date are entered, you want to display that range of dates on the report, as this WHERE clause would do:

```
WHERE TimeCardDate Between #1/1/2002# And #12/31/2002#
```

If the start date is left blank and an end date is specified, you want to provide an error message that tells the user to enter both dates for a range, then clear the controls on the form, and exit the sub procedure without previewing a report. To do this, you will use a nested If…Then…ElseIf statement inside an If…Then…Else statement. The first If statement will test to see if the txtStartDate field has an entry (If Not IsNull(txtStartDate)). If it does, the nested If statement will test to see if the txtEndDate field has an entry. If it does not, you add a string to the wherecondition to query for only one date. If the txtEndDate field has an entry, you will add a different string to the wherecondition that queries for the range of dates.

Using the Line Continuation Character

Up to this point, it has not been necessary to extend a statement over more than one line. However, the wherecondition for a range of dates is quite long. In VBA, an underscore serves as a **line continuation character** that you can use when your code is too long to fit on a single line. An ampersand is required to concatenate strings, so if a string extends beyond one line, use an underscore and an ampersand. The following example shows how you will use the underscore in the next series of steps:

```
strWhere = strWhere & " AND TimeCardDate Between " & "#" & _
 & txtStartDate & "#" & " AND " "#" & txtEndDate & "#"
```

To complete the code to query Job Reports:

1. Position the insertion point at the end of the fourth End If statement in the Sub cmdPreview_Click procedure, as shown in Figure 7-45, and press **Enter** twice.

Figure 7-45   COMPLETING THE WHERECONDITION CODE

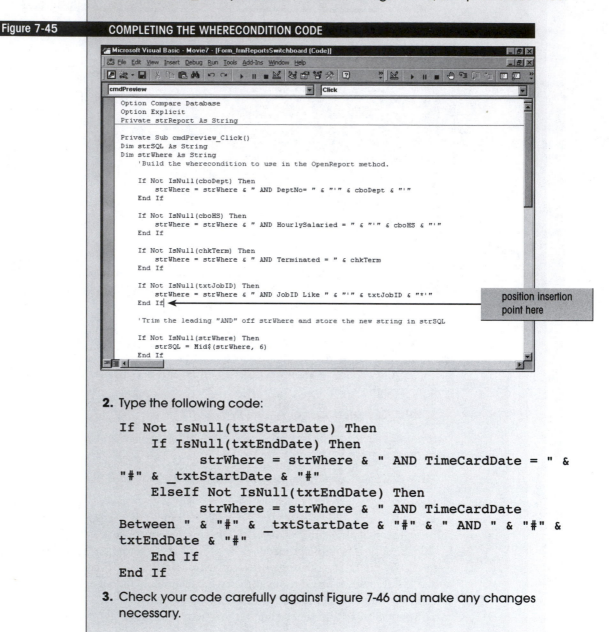

2. Type the following code:

```
If Not IsNull(txtStartDate) Then
    If IsNull(txtEndDate) Then
          strWhere = strWhere & " AND TimeCardDate = " &
"#" & _txtStartDate & "#"
    ElseIf Not IsNull(txtEndDate) Then
          strWhere = strWhere & " AND TimeCardDate
Between " & "#" & _txtStartDate & "#" & " AND " & "#" &
txtEndDate & "#"
    End If
End If
```

3. Check your code carefully against Figure 7-46 and make any changes necessary.

| Figure 7-46 | ADDING THE WHERECONDITON CODE FOR TXTSTARTDATE AND TXTENDDATE |

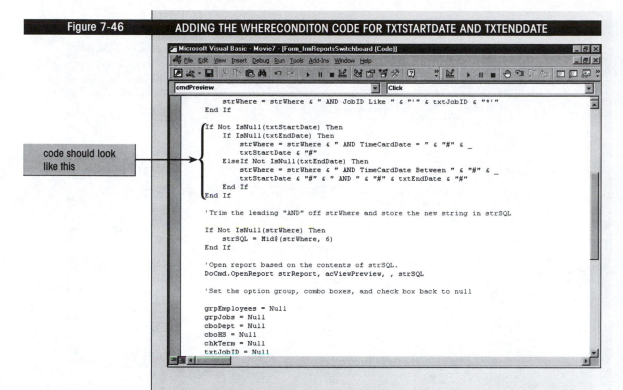

code should look like this

```
            strWhere = strWhere & " AND JobID Like " & "'" & txtJobID & "*'"
        End If

    If Not IsNull(txtStartDate) Then
        If IsNull(txtEndDate) Then
            strWhere = strWhere & " AND TimeCardDate = " & "#" & _
            txtStartDate & "#"
        ElseIf Not IsNull(txtEndDate) Then
            strWhere = strWhere & " AND TimeCardDate Between " & "#" & _
            txtStartDate & "#" & " AND " & "#" & txtEndDate & "#"
        End If
    End If

    'Trim the leading "AND" off strWhere and store the new string in strSQL

    If Not IsNull(strWhere) Then
        strSQL = Mid$(strWhere, 6)
    End If

    'Open report based on the contents of strSQL.
    DoCmd.OpenReport strReport, acViewPreview, , strSQL

    'Set the option group, combo boxes, and check box back to null

    grpEmployees = Null
    grpJobs = Null
    cboDept = Null
    cboHS = Null
    chkTerm = Null
    txtJobID = Null
```

4. If necessary, position the insertion point at the end of the last End If statement you just typed, press **Enter** twice, indent and type the following code (the Clear_Controls code represents the name of a portion of the code that you will add in Step 5):

```
If IsNull(txtStartDate) And Not IsNull(txtEndDate) Then
    MsgBox "You must enter a starting date to run the
report for a range"
    GoTo Clear_Controls
End If
```

5. Position the insertion point at the beginning of the grpEmployees = Null line, and press **Enter**.

6. Position the insertion point on the blank line above the grpEmployees = Null statement, and type **Clear_Controls:** as shown in Figure 7-47. This names this series of statements so that after the message box is shown, you continue at this point in the program.

| Figure 7-47 | ADDING THE CLEAR_CONTROLS: STATEMENT |

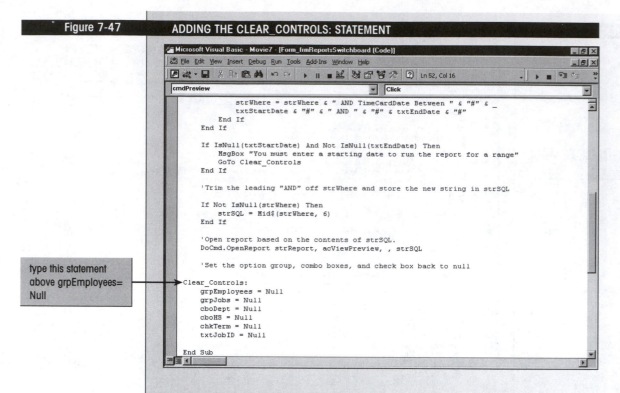

7. Position the insertion point at the end of the txtJobID = Null statement, press **Enter**, and type **txtStartDate = Null**.

8. Press **Enter**, and type **txtEndDate = Null**.

9. Check your code carefully against Figure 7-48 and make any necessary changes.

| Figure 7-48 | SETTING THE TXTSTARTDATE AND TXTENDDATE FIELDS TO NULL |

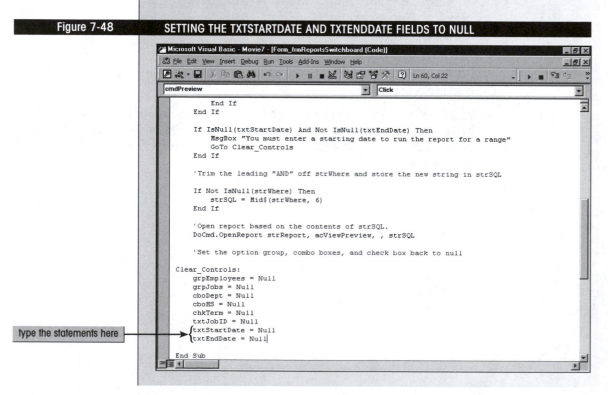

10. Close the Visual Basic window, switch to Form view, and test the form by opening **Hours By Job** for a single date and then for a date range in the year 2002. Open the **Job List** form using **92** and **99** as the Job ID numbers.

Carolyn points out to you that there is one key feature missing from the frmReportsSwitchboard form. You need to provide the users with a way to exit or close the switchboard. They will not have access to the default menu that you and Carolyn are now using when the database is completed, and even then, it would still be more convenient for the user to have a button on the form. You will use the Command Button Wizard to complete this feature.

To add a Close button to the frmReportsSwitchboard form:

1. Switch to Design view, click the **cboDept** combo box on the form, hold down the **Shift** key, select the **Preview** command button, right-click the command button, point to **Align** on the shortcut menu, and then click **Left**.

2. Make sure that the **Control Wizards** button on the toolbox is selected, click the **Command Button** button, and then click to the right of the Preview command button.

3. In the Command Button Wizard dialog box, click **Form Operations** in the Categories list box, click **Close Form** in the Actions list box, and then click the **Next** button.

4. Click the **Text** option button, type **&Close** in the text box, and then click the **Next** button.

5. Type **cmdClose** in the text box to name the button, and then click the **Finish** button.

6. Size and align the button with the Previous command button on the form.

7. Click the **Save** button on the toolbar to save the form, switch to Form view, and then click the **Close** button to test the button and close the form.

TROUBLE? If an error message displays after you click the Close button, switch to Design view, display the properties for the Close button, and be sure that [Event Procedure] is displayed in the On Click text box. If it is not, click the text box list arrow, and select [Event Procedure].

8. Close the **MovieCam7** database and exit Access.

Richard and Martin are pleased with the reports switchboard. They have requested a few additions, such as an option to print directly to the printer without opening the Print Preview window, and access to the Page Setup options so that they can change margins and other page elements. The Page Setup request can be addressed with a menu or a toolbar.

You have compiled notes on features that you want to add or change. Amanda is happy with your work because it is structured in a way that can be easily updated and modified.

Session 7.2 QUICK CHECK

1. The _____ argument in the OpenReport method is a SQL WHERE clause without the word WHERE.

2. You can view the results of an expression or a variable in the Immediate window by entering the _____ method of the Debug object, followed by the expression.

3. What is the shortcut method for viewing the results of an expression in the Immediate window?

4. A(n) _____ is a selected line of your program at which execution automatically stops.

5. What is the Locals window?

6. What does "stepping through" your code refer to?

7. What does a dollar sign following the name of a function mean?

8. In VBA, a(n) _____ serves as a line continuation character that you can use when your code is too long to fit on a single line

REVIEW ASSIGNMENTS

The Hours7 database is similar to the MovieCam Technologies database you worked on in this tutorial. A form named frmReportsSwitchboard has been created in the database. It contains a check box named chkTerm and a combo box named cboDept so that employee reports can be filtered by these criteria. You will write the code to set the strReports variable equal to the report name and then write the code to build the wherecondition and print the report.

1. Start Access and open the **Hours7** database located in the Tutorial.07 folder on your local or network drive.

2. Open the frmReportsSwitchboard form in Design view, click the option group frame to select it, and then click the Properties button on the toolbar.

3. Click the Event tab, click in the After Update event property, and then click the Build button.

> TROUBLE? If the Choose Builder dialog box opens, click **Code Builder**, and then click **OK**.

4. Indent, and add blank lines as appropriate while you type the following comment and code:

```
'Set strReport equal to report chosen in the option group
Select Case grpEmployees
Case 1
strName = "rptEmployeesList"
Case 2
strName = "rptEmployeesByDept"
End Select
```

5. Position the insertion point at the end of the Option Explicit statement, press the Enter key, and type Private strName As String.

6. Select cmdPreview from the Object list to create the sub.

7. Indent, and add blank lines as appropriate while you type the following comments and code:

```
Dim strSQL As String
Dim strCondition As String
'Build the wherecondition to use in the OpenReport method
If Not IsNull(chkTerm) Then
strCondition = strCondition & " AND  Terminated = " & chkTerm
End If
If Not IsNull(cboDept) Then
strCondition = strCondition & " AND  DeptNo= " & "'" &
cboDept & "'"
End If
'Trim the leading "AND " off strCondition and store the new
string in strSQL
If Not IsNull(strCondition) Then
strSQL = Mid$(strCondition, 6)
End If
'Open report based on the contents of strSQL.
DoCmd.OpenReport strName, acViewPreview, , strSQL
'Set the option group, combo boxes, and check box back to
null
grpEmployees = Null
cboDept = Null
chkTerm = Null
```

8. Compile the code, correct any errors, click File on the menu bar in the Visual Basic window, and then click Print.

9. Switch to Form view to test the code. Open both reports using different combinations of conditions.

10. Save the changes and close the form.

11. Close the **Hours7** database and exit Access.

CASE PROBLEMS

Case 1. Edwards and Company Jack Edwards asks you to create a method to make it simple for him to find specific clients in the Clients form. He wants to search based on Company Name and/or Contact Name, and does not want to input the entire name to conduct the search.

To do this, you have created a form named frmCriteria that is similar to the frmReportsSwitchboard form you worked with in this tutorial. It contains a text box named txtCompany and a text box named txtContact. It also contains a Search button that can be used to search for a particular record in the form. The DoCmd.OpenForm method contains a wherecondition argument that works the same way as the wherecondition argument in the Docmd.OpenReport statement. You will write the code needed to populate the wherecondition and open the frmClients form.

1. Start Access and open the **Edward7** database located in the Tutorial.07 folder on your local or network drive.

2. Open the frmCriteria form in Design view, click the Search button, and click the Properties button on the toolbar.

3. Click the Event tab, click in the On Click event property text box, and then click the Build button.

   > TROUBLE? If the Choose Builder dialog box opens, click **Code Builder** and then click **OK**.

4. Indent, and add blank lines as necessary while you type the following Sub procedure:

```
Dim strSQL As String
Dim strWhere As String
'Build the wherecondition to use in the OpenForm method
If Not IsNull(txtCompany) Then
strWhere = strWhere & " AND CompanyName Like " & "'" &
txtCompany & "*'"
End If
If Not IsNull(txtContact) Then
strWhere = strWhere & " AND ContactName Like " & "'" &
txtContact & "*'"
End If
'Trim the leading "AND " off strWhere and store the new
string in strSQL
If Not IsNull(strWhere) Then
strSQL = Mid$(strWhere, 6)
End If
'Open form based on the contents of strSQL.
DoCmd.OpenForm "frmClients", , , strSQL
'Set the text boxes to null
txtCompany = Null
txtContact = Null
End Sub
```

5. Compile the code, correct any errors, click File on the menu bar in the Visual Basic window, and then click Print.

6. Save the code, close the Visual Basic window, and switch to Form view.

7. Test the form by typing West in the Company Name text box, and clicking Search. The frmCriteria form is a modal form, which means it remains on top of other forms. You can move it by dragging it by the title bar.

8. Click in the Contact Name text box, type T, and then click the Search button.

9. Save your changes and close the forms.

10. Close the **Edward7** database and exit Access.

Case 2. San Diego County Information Systems   You have started to create a report switch-board in the ISD database, but are having trouble getting it to work properly. Each time you try to display the Student Phone List report for a particular department, you see all departments. You will troubleshoot the problem.

1. Start Access and open the **ISD7** database located in the Tutorial.07 folder on your local or network drive.

2. Open the frmReportsSwitchboard form in Design view, and click the Code button on the toolbar.

3. Click in the gray margin to the left of the Private Sub cmdPreview_Click() procedure to set a breakpoint.

4. Minimize the Visual Basic window, and switch to Form view.

5. Click the Student Phone List option button, select Information Systems from the Department combo box, and then click the Preview button.

6. Redisplay the Visual Basic window, and display the Debug toolbar if necessary.

7. Click the Step Into button twice, and note that the If…Then… Statement is not executed. Looking more closely, you realize that this is because the NOT operator is missing.

8. Click the Step Out button in the toolbar to complete running the code.

9. Click Debug on the menu bar, and then click Clear All Breakpoints.

10. Change the statement If IsNull(cboDept) Then to If Not IsNull(cboDept) Then.

11. Compile the code, correct any errors, click File on the menu bar of the Visual Basic window, click Print, and then close the Visual Basic window.

12. Switch to Form view, save your changes, close the form, and reopen it to reset the controls.

13. Test the form by clicking the option for the Student Phone List, selecting Sheriff from the Department combo box, and then clicking the Preview button.

14. Close the report, and then close the form.

15. Close the **ISD7** database and exit Access.

Case 3. Christenson Homes   Roberta Christenson asks you to create a method to make it sim-ple for her to find specific lots in the frmLots form. She wants to search based on any part of the address, and/or on any plan. Recall that the data for each lot in a subdivision is stored with a street address and a plan number to identify it.

To grant Roberta's request, you have created a criteria form named frmCriteria that con-tains a text box named txtAddress, and a text box named txtPlan. The form also contains a Search button. The DoCmd.OpenForm method contains a wherecondition argument that works the same way as the wherecondition argument in DoCmd.OpenReport. You will write the code needed to populate the wherecondition and open the frmLots form.

1. Start Access and open the **Homes7** database located in the Tutorial.07 folder on your local or network drive.

2. Open the frmCriteria form in Design view, click the Search button, and click the Properties button on the toolbar.

3. Click the Event tab, click in the On Click event property text box, and then click the Build button.

4. Indent, and add blank lines as necessary while you type the following comment and statements:

```
Dim strSQL As String
Dim strWhere As String
'Build the wherecondition to use in the OpenForm method
If Not IsNull(txtAddress) Then
 strWhere = strWhere & " AND Address Like " & "'*" &
txtAddress & "*'"
End If
```

5. Write another If…Then…Else statement to concatenate the strWhere text for txtPlan.

6. To complete the code, type the following comments and statements:

```
'Trim the leading "AND " off strWhere and store the new
string in strSQL
If Not IsNull(strWhere) Then
strSQL = Mid$(strWhere, 6)
End If
'Open form based on the contents of strSQL.
DoCmd.OpenForm "frmLots", , , strSQL
'Set the text boxes to null
txtAddress = Null
txtPlan = Null
```

7. Compile the code, correct any errors, click File on the menu bar of the Visual Basic window, click Print, and close the Visual Basic window.

8. Switch to Form view and test the form.

9. Close the **Homes7** database and exit Access.

Case 4. *Sonoma Farms*   The Sonoma Farms database contains a report named rptVisitorsByDistributor. You have been asked to create a switchboard that can be used to open the report. The switchboard should be based on two types of criteria: the distributor name and the contact name.

1. Start Access and open the **Sonoma7** database located in the Tutorial.07 folder on your local or network drive.

2. Create a switchboard form named frmReportsSwitchboard that contains an option group named grpReports. Add the label Reports to the option group.

3. Use the Option Group Wizard to create the option group. It should contain one option button that should be labeled Visitor By Distributor.

4. Add text boxes named txtDistributor and txtContact below the option group.

5. Add a command button named cmdPreview that triggers the code to open the report.

6. Complete the code for opening the rptVisitorsByDistributor report from the switchboard. Base the code on the contents of the txtDistributor and txtContact text boxes. The code for the Sub procedures is shown below. Be sure to add spacing and indenting as well as comments to complete the code.

```
Private strReport As String
Private Sub cmdPreview_Click()
Dim strSQL As String
Dim strWhere As String
If Not IsNull(txtDistributor) Then
strWhere = strWhere & " AND DistributorName Like " & "'" &
txtDistributor & "*'"
End If
If Not IsNull(txtContact) Then
strWhere = strWhere & " AND ContactName Like " & "'" &
txtContact & "*'"
End If
If Not IsNull(strWhere) Then
strSQL = Mid$(strWhere, 6)
End If
DoCmd.OpenReport strReport, acViewPreview, , strSQL
'Set the option group, combo boxes, and check box back to null
Clear_Controls:
grpReports = Null
txtDistributor = Null
txtContact = Null
End Sub
Private Sub grpReports_AfterUpdate()
Select Case grpReports
Case 1
strReport = "rptVisitorsByDistributor"
End Select
End Sub
```

7. Compile the code, correct any errors, click File on the menu bar of the Visual Basic window, click Print, and then close the Visual Basic window.

8. Switch to Form view and test the code by typing ABC Distribution in the Distributor Name text box.

9. Save the form.

10. Close the **Sonoma7** database and exit Access

QUICK CHECK ANSWERS

Session 7.1

1. event-driven
2. A form class module is created when you add code to a form.
3. Scope describes the visibility and accessibility of one procedure from another procedure.
4. Compiling is the process of checking for overall consistency and translating the VBA statements into a language that the computer can understand.
5. implicit
6. lifetime
7. The Static keyword differs from the Dim keyword in that the variable that is declared with it retains its value after the Sub procedure or function has finished running.
8. You cannot change the value of a constant after you declare it.

Session 7.2

1. wherecondition

2. Print

3. Typing the question mark instead of Debug.Print prior to the expression is the shortest method for viewing the results of an expression in the Immediate windows.

4. breakpoint

5. The Locals window is a window where Access automatically displays the name, current value, and type of all the variables and objects in the current procedure.

6. Stepping through code means that execution is suspended after each statement executes.

7. The dollar sign means that the function returns a string data type.

8. underscore

OBJECTIVES

In this tutorial you will:

- Review VBA decision structures

- Learn VBA looping structures

- Test a switchboard form for errors

- Learn about the *Me* keyword and use it in code

- Study error types, including syntax, run-time, and logic errors

- Study collections and the bang vs. dot notation

- Write code to handle a VBA error

- Write code to handle Access errors

- Create a combo box for selecting a record on a form

- Learn about ActiveX controls

- Create a form using the Calendar control

TRAPPING ERRORS AND AUTOMATING ACTIVEX CONTROLS WITH VBA

Trapping Errors and Refining Forms in the MovieCam Database

CASE

MovieCam Technologies

Amanda is pleased with the frmReportsSwitchbord form you created, but she is concerned that users might encounter error messages. She asks you to test the switchboard form for potential problems, and design the VBA code necessary to handle them. Amanda also wants you to test the other forms in the database for possible errors, and write error-trapping code for them.

In a recent meeting, Martin Woodward requested that you add some features to the frmTimeCards data entry form. Specifically, he wants to be able to easily search for the record of a particular time card. In addition, Carolyn wants to add a form feature that allows users to enter dates more easily.

SESSION 8.1

In this session you will study decision structures and looping structures. You will test the frmReportsSwitchboard form for errors and add code to it so users cannot choose criteria that do not exist for a specific report. You will learn the difference between the Visible property and the Enabled property. You will review Collections, and compare bang vs. dot notation used to specify objects in Access. You also will write code that uses a looping structure and the Controls collection on a form.

Control Structures for Decision Processing and Looping

VBA provides you with several different control structures for looping and decision processing. A **control structure** is a series of VBA statements that work together as a unit. You use decision structures to test for specific conditions in your procedures. You studied the three most common decision structures in Tutorial 6 —If...Then...Else, If...Then...ElseIf, and Select Case. In this tutorial you will learn about commonly used structures for looping.

Frequently, you will need to execute certain lines of a program multiple times. Rather than writing the line of code multiple times, you can write the code to be executed inside a loop. The most commonly used loop structures are Do...Loop, For...Next, and For Each...Next.

Do...Loop

You use the **Do...Loop** structure to repeat statements in your procedure until a specified condition is true. When Access encounters a Do statement in your procedure, it tests the specified condition. If the condition is true, Access performs the statements contained within the loop. If the condition is false, Access continues the program's execution at the first statement after the Loop keyword.

The Do...Loop construct has several variations. For example:

```
Dim intCounter As Integer
intCounter = 1
Do While intCounter < 5
     MsgBox intCounter
     intCounter = intCounter + 1
Loop
```

The first line of the code declares a variable as an integer, and the next line sets the variable equal to 1. The looping construct performs the loop as long as the variable intCounter is less than 5, and contains a statement that increments the variable each time the loop statements are executed.

The above example does not ensure that the code executes at least once. If the intCounter variable is 5 or greater, the code will not execute at all. To be sure that the code executes unconditionally at least once, the code should look like the following:

```
Dim intCounter As Integer
intCounter = 5
Do
     Msgbox intCounter
     intCounter = intCounter + 1
Loop while intCounter < 5
```

The difference between the two examples is that in the first example, the Do While...Loop evaluates before the code is executed. In the second example, the Do...Loop While is evaluated at the end of the loop so that execution at least once is guaranteed. This code would execute at least once even though the variable is set to 5.

For...Next Loop

Unlike the Do...Loop, the **For...Next loop** executes statements of code a specified number of times. When you use the Do...Loop construct you do not know how many times it will be executed. You use the For...Next loop construct when you have an exact number of iterations you want to perform. Unlike with the Do...Loop, you'll specify the number of times through the loop at the Do...Loop's beginning. The loop shown below will execute 5 times, once for each value specified in the *For intCounter = 1 to 5* statement.

```
Dim intCounter As Integer
For intCounter = 1 To 5
      MsgBox intCounter
Next intCounter
```

The start and stop values, which are 1 and 5 in the example above, also can be variables. A For...Next construct can also be given a step value. A **step value** lets you increment the loop by a given amount. For example:

```
Dim intCounter As Integer
For intCounter = 1 To 5 Step 2
      MsgBox intCounter
Next intCounter
```

The preceding loop repeats three times: once when intCounter equals 1; once when intCounter equals 3; and once when intCounter equals 5.

For Each...Next Loop

The **For...Each...Next** construct executes a group of statements on each member of an array or collection. (Recall from Tutorial 6 that a collection is an object that contains a set of related objects.) For example, the Controls collection contains all of the controls found on an open form. An **array** is a series of variables of the same data type, arranged contiguously in memory. Arrays can be useful for storing a series of values.

The For...Each...Next construct works similarly to the For...Next construct. It iterates through a collection or array, and moves through each object until it reaches the end of the collection. For example, if you want to set the Enabled or Visible property to False for all of the controls on a form, you can use For Each...Next structure to loop though each control in the collection and make the change to its property. The following example sets the Fore Color property (the text color) of all of the controls on the form to red:

```
Dim ctl As Control
      For Each ctl In Controls
      ctl.Fore Color = 255
Next ctl
```

The first statement declares ctl as a control object variable. The next statement specifies that for each control in the Controls collection the next statement(s) should execute. The ctl.Fore Color part of the statement sets the Fore Color property of each control to 255, which is red.

Testing and Refining the Reports Switchboard

Carolyn has tested the frmReportsSwitchboard form. She is concerned that when users choose combo box and text box options, that they'll choose options that do not apply to the report they are trying to run. She suggested disabling the controls that don't apply to specific reports in the class module, and then enabling those controls after the report is run.

Carolyn has also found that an error occurs if the user does not choose a report from one of the two option groups. She wants you to review these problems, so you'll test the switchboard next.

To test the frmReportsSwitchboard form:

1. Start Access and open the **Movie8** database located in the **Tutorial.08** folder on your local or network drive.

2. Make sure that **Forms** is selected on the Objects bar in the Database window, and double-click the **frmReportsSwitchboard** form.

3. Click the **Employee List** option button, type **92** in the Job ID text box, and then click the **Preview** button.

4. An Enter Parameter Value dialog opens, as shown in Figure 8-1, because Access cannot find the JobID field in the rptEmployeesList report.

Figure 8-1	ENTER PARAMETER VALUE DIALOG BOX

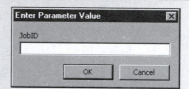

5. Click the **OK** button. The report opens, but no records are visible, as shown in Figure 8-2.

Figure 8-2	RPTEMPLOYEESLIST REPORT

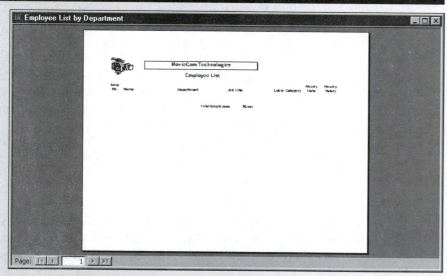

6. Close the report, and then close the switchboard by clicking **File** on the menu bar and then click **Close**. (Closing and reopening the frmReportsSwitchboard form resets it.)

7. Open the **frmReportsSwitchboard** form in **Form** view, and click the **Preview** button. You should see an error message like that shown in Figure 8-3.

Figure 8-3	RUN-TIME ERROR MESSAGE

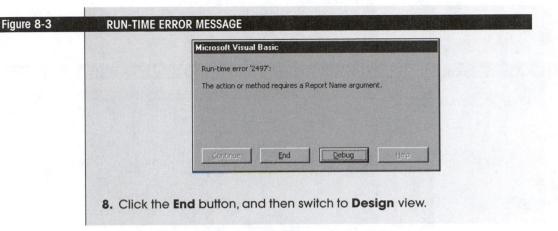

8. Click the **End** button, and then switch to **Design** view.

You can use a couple of ways to rectify an error that's caused when a user specifies criteria that do not apply to a given report. One way is to set the Visible property for the controls that do not apply to the selected report to False, thus making the controls "invisible." Another way is to leave the controls visible, but disable them by changing the Enabled property to False.

You also can use the Visible property to show or hide a form, report, data access page, or a section or control in a form or report. This property can be set in macros or in VBA code; you can also change it in the properties dialog box for some objects.

The Enabled property specifies whether a control can have the focus in form view. Focus, as you have learned, means that a control can receive user input through the mouse or keyboard. In the Windows environment, only one item at a time can have the focus. When the Enabled property is set to False, the control on the form is dimmed.

Figure 8-4 shows the frmReportsSwitchboard form with the Visible property set to False for all the controls related to the Job Reports option group.

Figure 8-4	SWITCHBOARD FORM WITH CONTROLS' VISIBLE PROPERTY SET TO FALSE

Figure 8-5 shows the Enabled property set to False for the controls related to the Employee Reports option group.

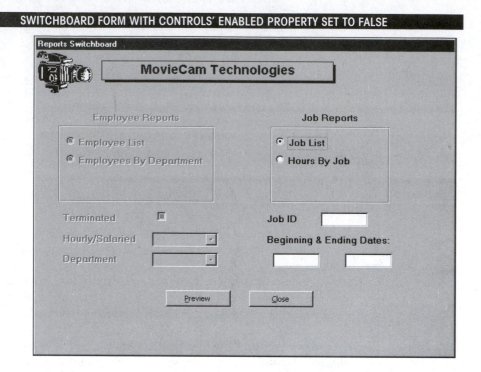

| Figure 8-5 | SWITCHBOARD FORM WITH CONTROLS' ENABLED PROPERTY SET TO FALSE |

After reviewing the two options, you and Carolyn decide that you don't want to confuse or alarm users by having controls disappear completely from the form. Therefore, you will set the Enabled property to False for all controls that don't apply to particular reports in each option group.

Next you will write the code to set the Enabled property to False. The code will execute so that the Enabled property for the controls for the Employee Reports option group is set to False *after* the user selects a Job Report from the grpJobs option group.

To use code to set the Enabled property to False:

1. Click the **Code** button on the Form Design toolbar.

2. Click **grpJobs** from the Object list, and then click **AfterUpdate** from the Procedure list.

3. Position the insertion point at the end of the End Select statement, as shown in Figure 8-6.

Figure 8-6	VISUAL BASIC WINDOW

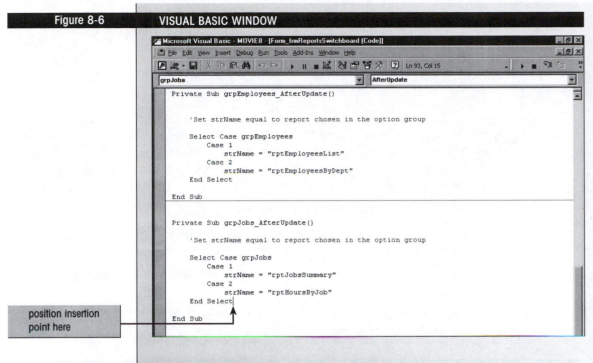

position insertion
point here

4. Press **Enter** twice, and then type the following comment and statements, indenting and spacing as shown in Figure 8-7.

```
'Disable controls for Employee Reports after a Job
'Report is selected
grpEmployees.Enabled = False
cboDepartment.Enabled = False
cboHourlySalaried.Enabled = False
chkTerminated.Enabled = False
```

Figure 8-7	MODIFYING THE GRPJOBS_AFTERUPDATE PROCEDURE

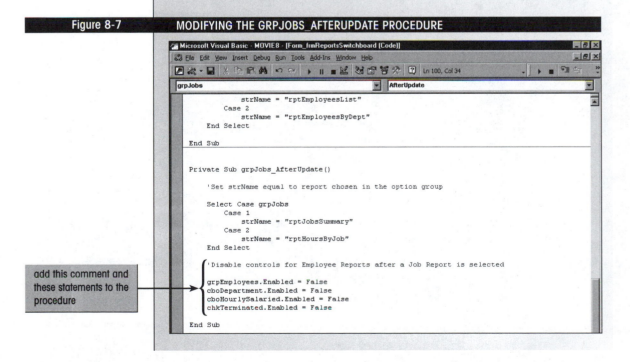

add this comment and
these statements to the
procedure

5. Close the Visual Basic window, switch to **Form** view, and click the **Job List** option. Your switchboard should look like that shown in Figure 8-5.

6. Switch to **Design** view and click [icon] on the toolbar.

Job List, the first report in the Job Reports option group, does not contain a TimeCardDate field. If the user attempts to type in dates and then run this report, the Enter Parameter Value dialog box will open. To prevent this, you will disable the txtStartDate and txtEndDate text boxes for this report, and also disable the Job text boxes when an option from the Employee Reports group is selected.

To disable the date text boxes:

1. Position the insertion point at the end of the strName = "rptJobsSummary" line in the grpJobs_AfterUpdate() Sub procedure, and then press **Enter**.

2. Type the following code. Your code should look like that shown in Figure 8-8 when you are finished.

```
txtStartDate.Enabled = False
txtEndDate.Enabled = False
```

Figure 8-8	ADDING CODE TO DISABLE DATE TEXT BOXES

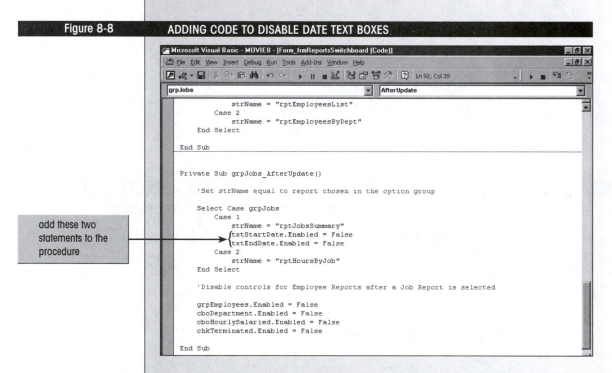

add these two statements to the procedure

3. Click **grpEmployees** in the Object list. The **AfterUpdate** property should already be selected in the Procedure list.

4. Position the insertion point at the end of the End Select statement in the grpEmployees_AfterUpdate() Sub procedure.

5. Press **Enter** twice, and then type the following comment and code statements, indenting and spacing as shown in Figure 8-9.

```
'Disable controls for Job Reports after Employee Report
'is selected
grpJobs.Enabled = False
txtJobID.Enabled = False
txtStartDate.Enabled = False
txtEndDate.Enabled = False
```

Figure 8-9   ADDING CODE TO THE GRPEMPLOYEES_AFTERUPDATE PROCEDURE

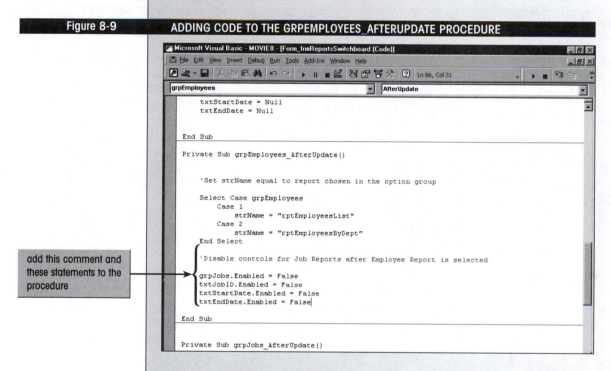

add this comment and these statements to the procedure

6. Click the **Save** button 🖫 on the toolbar, and then close the Visual Basic window.

7. Switch to **Form** view and test the form by clicking the **Job List** option. The Employee Reports options and the Beginning and Ending Date text boxes are dimmed. Close the form.

   TROUBLE? If you receive the error message "You can't disable a control while it has the focus", be sure that the code to disable the grpJobs, txtJobID, txtStartDate, and txtEndDate controls is in the grpEmployees_AfterUpdate() Sub procedure and *not* in the grpJobs_AfterUpdate() Sub procedure.

8. Open the **frmReportsSwitchboard** form, and click the **Employee List** option. All the Job Reports controls are now dimmed.

9. Switch to **Design** view.

The controls that you have disabled now need to be enabled before the frmReportsSwitchboard form is used again. To do this you will add code that sets the Enabled property for the controls back to True *after* the selected report is previewed.

Rather than typing a line of code for each control, you will use a loop construct to loop through each control—except for the label controls—in the Controls collection. Label controls do not have an Enabled property, and the code will not execute if a label control is included in the procedure.

Collections

You know that a collection is a group of objects of the same type or class. The Forms collection contains open forms, and the Reports collection contains open reports. Even though forms and reports are similar, they are not the same and you must refer to them in separate collections. Many different collections are available when you are programming in Access (see Figure 8-10), and collections can contain other collections.

Figure 8-10	ACCESS OBJECTS AND COLLECTIONS

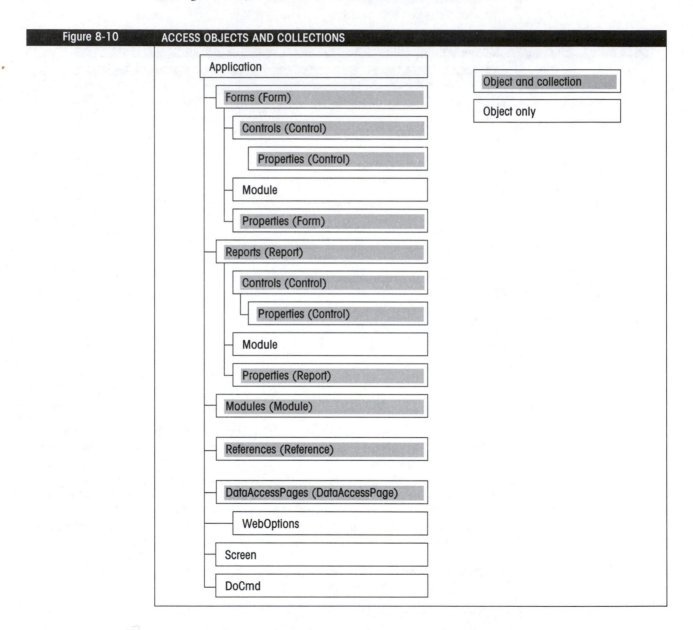

For example, each form object has a Controls collection that contains all of the controls on the form. The name of a collection is often the starting point in the path for a particular object. For example, *Forms!frmReportsSwitchboard* specifies the frmReportsSwitchboard form that is a part of the Forms collection. There is more than one correct notation that can specify the path to an object or property. Understanding each type of notation will make it easier to understand the syntax that you see in sample code in the VBA Help system, and the code that you use in this tutorial.

Dot vs. Bang Notation

Dot notation uses the dot (.) operator to indicate that what follows is an item defined by Access. For example, the properties of an object are items defined by Access. In the step exercise where you referred to the Enabled property by typing *grpEmployees.Enabled*, you used dot notation to refer to properties.

Dot notation also is used to indicate the sequence of steps that you take to specify a particular object. Consider, for example, the steps required to change the Enabled property of the grpEmployees control on the frmReportsSwitchboard form to False. First you open the frmReportsSwitchboard form in Design view, then you click the grpEmployees option group, display the properties dialog box for that control, find the Enabled property, and, finally, change the property to False. Dot notation enables you to simply provide a path to a particular property. Using dot notation, the preceding example looks like the following:

```
Forms("frmReportsSwitchboard").Controls("grpEmployees").Enabled
```

As you can see, dot notation can result in long paths. The collection is specified, then the specific item in the collection, then the next collection, and then the specific item in it, and so on. Default collections and properties reduce the size of dot notation. For example, Controls is the default collection of a form, so the word *Controls* does not need to appear in the path. Therefore, the following statement has the same meaning as the previous one:

```
Forms("frmReportsSwitchboard")("grpEmployees").Enabled
```

You can use **bang notation**, which uses the bang operator (!), in place of dot notation when the collection referenced by an object is the default collection. Therefore, the following statement is the same as the previous two examples:

```
Forms![frmReportsSwitchboard]![grpEmployees].Enabled
```

Note that the brackets do not need to be typed as long as there are no spaces in the object names. You can see why developers are encouraged to use bang notation over dot notation. It is much shorter. In addition, you can use keywords and special objects to make the path shorter still.

Me Keyword

In a VBA class module, the **Me** keyword can be used to refer to the associated form or report that the class module is in. *Me* always refers to the object that is running the code. For example, using the Me keyword in the frmReportsSwitchboard form refers to this form even if other forms are currently open or have the focus. Using the Me keyword, you could shorten the example used in the preceding section to the following:

```
Me!grpEmployees.Enabled
```

CodeContextObject Property

The **CodeContextObject** property determines the object in which a macro or VBA code is executing. When you converted a macro to VBA code in Tutorial 5, the CodeContextObject property was used in the resulting procedure. The CodeContextObject is mentioned again here because it has the same functionality as the Me keyword, except that it can be used in a class module *or* a standard module. Functions using the CodeContextObject can be called from an event property in either a form or report. In this instance, the name of the form or report calling the procedure containing CodeContextObject will be substituted for CodeContextObject. The Me keyword can only be used in a class module in which it substitutes for the name of the form or report that contains the class module. The CodeContextObject property can be used in standard modules, but the Me keyword cannot.

The Screen Object

The **Screen object** is the particular form, report, or control that currently has the focus. The Screen.ActiveForm and Screen.ActiveReport objects refer to the form or report that currently has the focus. The Screen.ActiveControl object refers to the control that currently has the focus. The Screen objects can be used only when a form or report is active, or an error will result.

For example, the following statement refers to the switchboard form in the database that has the focus, and changes the form's Caption property to Current Switchboard:

```
Screen.ActiveForm.Caption = Current Switchboard
```

Controls Collection

You can refer to a control on a form either by implicitly or explicitly referring to the **Controls collection**. It is faster to refer to a control implicitly, as demonstrated in the following examples (these two examples also use the dot and bang notation discussed earlier):

```
Me!grpEmployees
Me("grpEmployees")
```

You also can refer to a control by its position in the collection index. The **collection index** is a range of numbers that begin with a zero, and in turn represent each object in the collection. Most indexes are zero-based, meaning they begin counting with a zero. Recall that the Column property of combo boxes discussed in earlier tutorials was zero-based. The following example refers to the control by its position in the collection index:

```
Me(0)
```

To refer to the same control explicitly, use any of the three following examples:

```
Me.Controls!grpEmployees
Me.Controls("grpEmployees")
Me.Controls(0)
```

The Me keyword can only be used to refer to code in a form or report class module. If you refer to a form or report from a standard module, or a different form's or report's module, you must use the full reference to the form or report.

You and Carolyn will use the Controls collection of the frmReportsSwitchboard form and set the Enabled property for all the controls (except for the label controls) in the collection to True. You will use the For...Each...Next loop construct to do this. To test the form controls to determine if they are *not* labels, you will use the If...Then... Else decision construct and include the *Type Of* expression. You also will need to declare an object variable in your code to represent the controls in the Controls collection. Object variables are discussed next.

Object Variables

You use **object variables** when you want to declare variables in your procedures to use in place of object names. For example, to refer to the frmReportsSwitchboard form, you could declare a variable as follows:

```
Dim frmMyForm As Form_frmReportsSwitchboard
```

You must precede the name of the form or report with *Form_* or *Report_* when you define the object variable, because forms and reports share the same name space. For example, the name *Customers* could be used for both a form and report in a database that does not follow the naming conventions used in this tutorial.

Another way to declare an object variable and to assign a particular object to it is to declare the variable, and then use the Set statement to initialize it as illustrated in the following example:

```
Dim frmMyForm As Form
Set frmMyForm = frmReportsSwitchboard
```

You can then use the frmMyForm object variable to manipulate the frmReportsSwitchboard form properties and/or methods.

Object variables do, however, use memory and associated resources. Setting an object variable equal to *Nothing* discontinues the association and frees these resources. In addition, setting an object variable to Nothing when you finish using it prevents you from accidentally changing the object by changing the variable. To set the object variable referred to in the preceding example to Nothing, simply include the following:

```
Set frmMyForm = Nothing
```

Now you are ready to write the code to set the Enabled property to True for the controls on the form.

To set the Enabled property to True for controls on the form:

1. Click the **Code** button [image] on the toolbar.

2. Position the insertion point at the end of the Dim strSQL As String in the cmdPreview_Click() Sub procedure, and then press the **Enter** key.

3. Type **Dim ctl As Control** to declare the variable ctl an object variable. See Figure 8-11.

| Figure 8-11 | DECLARING THE OBJECT VARIABLE |

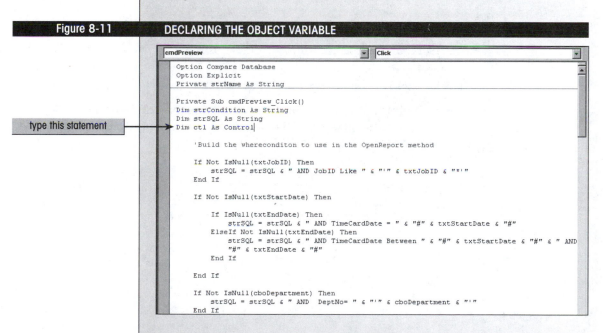

type this statement

4. Position the insertion point at the end of the txtEndDate = Null line, and then press the **Enter** key twice.

5. Type the following comment and statements, indenting and spacing as shown in Figure 8-12.

```
'Enable all of the controls except labels
For Each ctl In Me.Controls
If Not TypeOf ctl Is Label Then
ctl.Enabled = True
End If
Next ctl
```

Figure 8-12   ADDING THE CODE TO ENABLE ALL THE CONTROLS

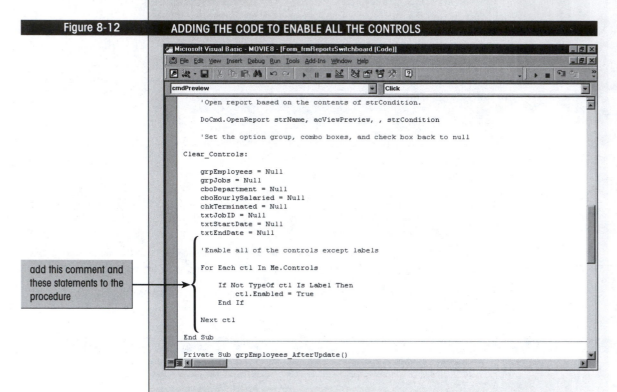

add this comment and
these statements to the
procedure

6. Click the **Save** button 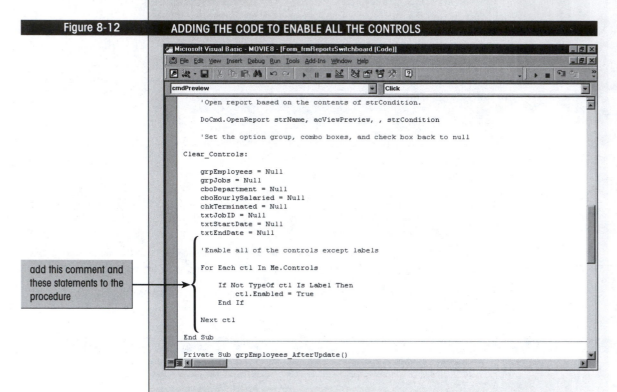 on the toolbar, and then close the Visual Basic window.

7. Switch to **Form** view, and test the form by clicking the **Job List** option. The Employee Reports options and the Beginning and Ending Date text boxes are now dimmed, as shown in Figure 8-13.

| Figure 8-13 | SETTING THE ENABLED PROPERTY |

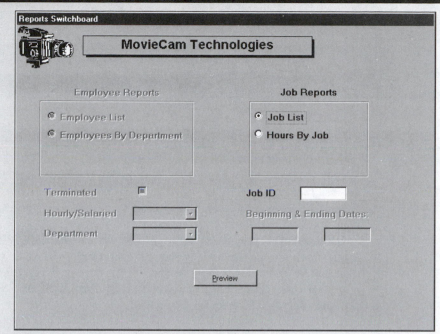

8. Click the **Preview** button, and then close the report. The controls are now enabled.

9. Switch to **Design** view.

You and Carolyn have completed the necessary coding to prevent one type of user error. Next you need to address the problem that occurs when the user does not select a report from one of the option groups. You will review error types and error handling in the following session.

Session 8.1 QUICK CHECK

1. What is a control structure in VBA?

2. The _____ is used to repeat statements in your procedure until a specified condition is true.

3. The _____ will execute statements a specified number of times.

4. How does the Visible property differ from the Enabled property?

5. Which type of control does not have an Enabled property?

6. The _____ operator indicates that what follows is an item defined by Access.

7. Which notation—dot or bang—results in a shorter path to an object or property?

8. What is the Me keyword used for?

9. What advantage does CodeContextObject have over the Me keyword?

10. What is the Screen object?

SESSION 8.2

In this session you will learn about the different types of errors that can occur in Access and VBA. You will write error-trapping code for a VBA run-time error, and learn how to identify an Access run-time error and write code to handle it. You also will learn about the Event and NotInList properties and how they can be used to trap Access errors. You will create a combo box and write code to synchronize records on a form to the record chosen in the combo box. You will learn about ActiveX controls and create a form that incorporates the Calendar control.

Syntax Errors

Syntax errors occur when you violate the VBA syntax rules. For example, a syntax error occurs if you misspell a keyword such as *Msgbox*, forget the End Select statement in a Select…Case decision structure, or omit necessary punctuation, such as a required comma in a DoCmd.OpenReport statement.

Syntax errors are detected either as you write code in the VBE (Visual Basic Editor), or immediately before the code is run. All syntax errors must be corrected before the procedure can be executed. To be sure that VBA is checking for syntax errors, click Tools on the menu bar in the Visual Basic window, click Options, click the Editor tab, and make sure that the Auto Syntax Check option is selected.

Run-Time Errors

Run-time errors occur while the application is running. A run-time error also occurs if the user attempts an operation that the system cannot perform. For example, you might write code that opens a particular report, and then later you change the name of that report. If you do not change the report's name in your coding procedures, a run-time error will occur when the user tries to run the code.

When Access encounters a run-time error during program execution, it selects the line of code that caused the error and prompts you with a dialog box. For example, you would receive the error message shown in Figure 8-14 if you renamed the rptEmployeesList report to rptEmployees and then attempted to open the report from the frmReportsSwitchboard form.

Figure 8-14	RUN-TIME ERROR

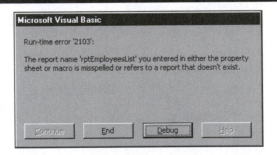

Clicking the Debug button in the error dialog box will open the Visual Basic Editor so that you can attempt to fix the error. Clicking the End button will immediately terminate the program, and clicking the Help button will open related Help topics.

Run-time errors are generally more difficult to fix than syntax errors because there can be many sources of these errors and those sources might not always be obvious. For example, an application might run fine under normal circumstances, but when a user enters a particular type of data, an error results. It also might not always be possible to anticipate run-time errors.

Logic Errors

Logic errors occur when your procedures execute without failure, but their results are not what you intended. A logic error can occur when code has been assigned to the wrong event procedure, or when the order of operations in a procedure is incorrect.

Recall Tutorial 7 when you created procedures for the frmReportsSwitchboard form. You moved the statements that set the controls back to null from the grpEmployees_AfterUpdate( ) procedure to the cmdPreview_Click( ) procedure. You moved that code so that the controls on the switchboard were set to null *after* the report opened, rather than after the user chose an option from the option group. If you had not moved those statements, a logic error would have occurred. The controls would have been set back to null, and the report would have opened showing all records instead of the records specified by what you entered in the text boxes. Logic errors can be quite difficult to find, but stepping through code (as discussed in Tutorial 7), is a good way to locate them.

Trapping Run-Time Errors

It's a fact in the programming world that errors will occur. So it's important that you protect your programs and data from the effect of those errors. You can accomplish this by the use of error handling, also known as **error trapping**.

By trapping run-time errors, you will make your application more tolerant of them. If a run-time error is generated by a VBA procedure, you handle the error by adding error-handling code to the procedure itself. If the run-time error is generated by the interface, the run-time error triggers the Error event for the active form or report. You can handle this error by creating a VBA procedure for the Error event. The NotInList event property of combo boxes on forms also can be used to create an error handler for a specific type of interface error.

Without error handling in place, the user can be forced to abruptly exit the application, often without knowing why. However, applications that trap run-time errors can handle common user errors without stopping the application. The better you are at anticipating common errors and protecting against them, the less likely that your application will fail.

VBA Errors

To write an error-handling routine to trap the run-time error that occurs when no report is chosen from the option group, you need to learn about the On Error statement, the Err object and its properties, and the Resume statement.

The On Error Statement

You can enable error handling in a procedure by using the **On Error statement**. When VBA encounters a run-time error, it searches for an On Error statement that indicates there is an error-handling routine included in the procedure. If VBA finds an On Error statement, the error is handled, and execution of the procedure resumes either at the statement that caused the error or at a different statement, depending on how the error handler is enabled.

If VBA cannot find an On Error statement, execution halts and a run-time error message is received.

The On Error GoTo Statement enables an error-handling routine in the procedure and also specifies the routine's location in the procedure. For example, Access would stop execution when an error occurs and go to the statements labeled TestError, if the following statement was used:

```
On Error GoTo TestError
```

Execution would then resume, based on the Resume statement used.

The Resume Statement

The Resume statement resumes execution after an error-handling routine is finished. It can have any of the following forms:

- *Resume:* If the error occurred in the same procedure as the error handler, execution resumes with the statement that caused the error. If the error occurred in a called procedure, execution resumes at the statement that last called out of the procedure to the error-handling routine.

- *Resume Next:* If the error occurs in the same procedure as the error handler, execution resumes with the statement that immediately follows the statement that caused the error. If the error occurred in a called procedure, execution resumes with the statement immediately following the statement that last called out of the procedure that contains the error-handling routine, or execution resumes at the On Error Resume Next statement.

- *Resume line:* Execution resumes at the line specified in the required line argument. The **line argument** is a line label or line number and must be in the same procedure as the error handler. A **line label** is used to identify a single line of code and can be any combination of characters that starts with a letter and ends with a colon (:). Line labels are not case-sensitive and must begin in the first column of the code window. A **line number** is also used to identify a single line of code and can be any combination of digits that is unique within the module where it is used. Line numbers also must begin in the first column of the Code window.

The Err Object

The **Err object** contains information about an error that has just occurred. When a run-time error occurs, the properties of the Err object are filled with information that both uniquely identifies the error and that can be used to handle it. The properties of the Err object are reset to zero or a zero-length string after the Exit Sub or Exit Function statement executes in an error-handling routine. The properties of the Err object are as follows:

- *Err.Number:* The number property is an integer value that specifies the last error that occurred. You can use this property in error-handling code to determine which error has occurred. Each error has a unique number; by default the error's (Err's) number property is set to zero to indicate that no error has occurred.

- *Err.Description:* This property is a string that contains a description of the error. The Description property contains the Access error message. Once an error is trapped, you can replace this message with a custom message that is more user-friendly.

- *Err.Source:* The source property contains the name of the object application that generated the error. For example, if you open Excel from Access and Excel generates the error, Excel sets the Err.Source property to Excel Application.

- *Err.HelpFile:* You can use this property to specify a path and filename to a VBA Help file. The HelpFile property is useful for displaying information about a particular error. That information is more user-friendly and more complete than just the description. By default, the HelpFile property displays more information about a particular error by returning the default Help file that Access uses.

■ *Err.HelpContext:* This property is used to specify the Help topic that is identified by the path in the HelpFile argument. The HelpContext property must be used in conjunction with the HelpFile property before a particular Help topic can be shown. By default, the HelpContext property offers more information on a particular error by returning the default Help file that Access uses.

■ *Err.LastDLLError:* This property contains the system error code for the success or failure of the last call to a dynamic link library. A **dynamic link library (DLL)** is a file containing a collection of Windows functions designed to perform a specific class of operations. Most DLLs have a .dll extension, but some use the .exe extension. Functions within DLLs are called by applications as needed to perform desired operations.

Using objects and statements, you can build the following error handler to respond to the error that occurs if a report is selected that does not exist in the database:

```
Private Sub grpJobs_AfterUpdate()
    'Set strName equal to report chosen in the option group
On Error GoTo TestError
    Select Case grpJobs
      Case 1
            strName = "rptJobsSummary"
      Case 2
            strName = "rptHoursByJob"
    Exit Sub
TestError:
    If Err.Number = 2103 Then
        Msgbox "The report selected does not exist in this database"
        Resume Next
    End If
End Sub
```

Error number 2103 is the error that occurs if you attempt to open a report that does not exist in the database. The *OnError Goto TestError* line tells Access to stop execution and go to the code labeled *TestError* if an error occurs. The If…Then…Else construct tests the error number, and then returns an appropriate message box. The *Resume Next* statement causes execution to resume at the Case 2 statement because the report does not exist.

Next you will add an error handler to the frmReportsSwitchboard form. The error handler is similar to the one in the preceding example. It will test for run-time error 2497, which indicates that the action or method requires a Report Name argument.

To add an error-handling routine to the frmReportsSwitchboard form:

1. Make sure that Access is running, that the **Movie8** database from the **Tutorial.08** folder on your local or network drive is open, and that frmReportsSwitchboard is open in Design view.

2. Click the **Code** button on the toolbar to show the Visual Basic window.

3. Position the insertion point at the end of the Dim ctl As Control statement, as shown in Figure 8-15, and press **Enter** twice.

Figure 8-15 ADDING ERROR-HANDLING CODE TO THE CMDPREVIEW_CLICK PROCEDURE

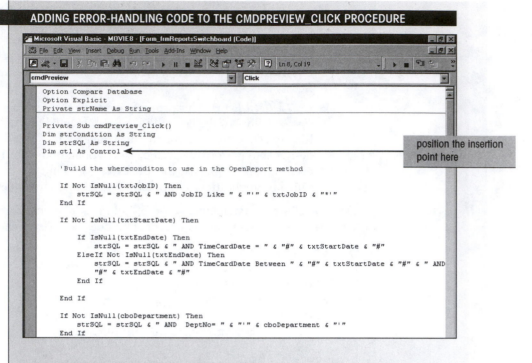

4. Press **Tab** to indent, and then type **On Error GoTo PrintError**.

5. Scroll down, position the insertion point at the end of the Next ctl statement, and then press **Enter** twice.

6. Type the following comment and code, indenting as shown in Figure 8-16:

```
PrintError:
If Err.Number = 2497 Then
'No report was selected from the option groups
MsgBox "You must select a report from one of the option
groups"
Resume Next
End If
```

Figure 8-16	ERROR HANDLER

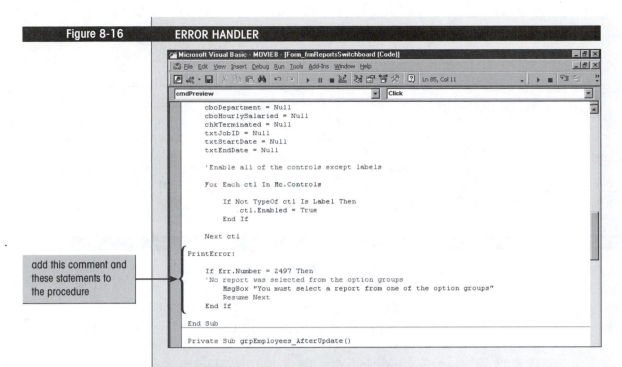

add this comment and
these statements to
the procedure

```
cboDepartment = Null
cboHourlySalaried = Null
chkTerminated = Null
txtJobID = Null
txtStartDate = Null
txtEndDate = Null

'Enable all of the controls except labels

For Each ctl In Mc.Controls

    If Not TypeOf ctl Is Label Then
        ctl.Enabled = True
    End If

Next ctl

PrintError:

    If Err.Number = 2497 Then
    'No report was selected from the option groups
        MsgBox "You must select a report from one of the option groups"
        Resume Next
    End If

End Sub

Private Sub grpEmployees_AfterUpdate()
```

7. Click **Debug** on the menu bar, and then click **Compile MovieCam**. If you have any syntax errors, correct them now.

8. Close the Visual Basic window, click the **Save** button 🖫 on the toolbar, and then close the frmReportsSwitchboard form.

9. Open the frmReportSwitchboard form in **Form** view, and click the **Preview** button *without* selecting a report from either option group. You receive your custom error message, as shown in Figure 8-17.

Figure 8-17	CUSTOM ERROR MESSAGE

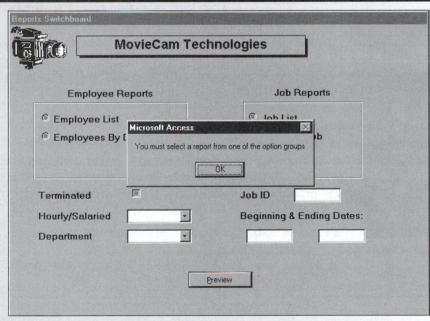

10. Click the **OK** button and then close the form.

Now that you have completed the error handler for the VBA error, you will focus on errors that might occur in the interface.

Access Errors

In the section on error trapping, you learned that Access errors can be handled with the Error event. Remember that Access errors occur in the user interface, as opposed to those that occur in your VBA code.

Carolyn has tested some of the other forms in the database, and has run across a potential problem with the frmTimeCards form. If the user does not enter a time card number, the error message shown in Figure 8-18 is received.

Figure 8-18   ACCESS ERROR MESSAGE

This is an Access error and you will use the Error event to trigger error-handling code to deal with it.

Error and Timing Events

Recall that many types of events exist in Access, including the Print events and Data events discussed in earlier tutorials. Error and Timing events are another category of events, and include the following:

- *Error:* This event occurs when an Access run-time error occurs in a form or report. (This does not include run-time errors in VBA.) To run an event procedure when the Error event occurs, set the OnError property to the name of the Event Procedure.

- *Timer:* This event occurs when a specified time interval passes as specified by the TimeInterval property of the form. To keep data synchronized in a multiuser environment, you use this event to refresh or requery data at specified intervals.

Determining the Error Number

To determine the error number of the Access error shown in Figure 8-18, you and Carolyn will add code to the frmTimeCards form that is triggered by the Error event. The Error event procedure includes several arguments that will help you find out more about the error. The syntax of the Error event procedure is:

```
Private Sub Form_Error(DataErr As Integer, Response As
    Integer) OR
Private Sub Report_Error(DataErr As Integer, Response As
    Integer)
```

The Error event procedure arguments are:

- *DataErr:* DataErr is the error code returned by the Err object when an error occurs.

- *Response:* Response is the setting that determines whether or not to display an error message. It can be one of the following constants:

  - *AcDataErrContinue:* Use this to ignore the error and continue without displaying the default Access error. You can use this setting in conjunction with a custom error message.

  - *AcDataErrDisplay:* This is the default setting and specifies that the default Access error message will be shown.

You will use the DataErr argument to determine the code number of the error. You must add code to be triggered by the Error event procedure that in turn instructs Access to display the error number in the Immediate window.

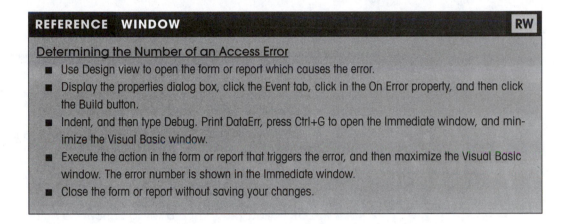

REFERENCE WINDOW   RW

Determining the Number of an Access Error
- Use Design view to open the form or report which causes the error.
- Display the properties dialog box, click the Event tab, click in the On Error property, and then click the Build button.
- Indent, and then type Debug. Print DataErr, press Ctrl+G to open the Immediate window, and minimize the Visual Basic window.
- Execute the action in the form or report that triggers the error, and then maximize the Visual Basic window. The error number is shown in the Immediate window.
- Close the form or report without saving your changes.

After you and Carolyn identify the error number, you can write the code necessary to trap it.

To determine the error number of an Access error:

1. Open the **frmTimeCards** form in **Design** view, and then click the **Properties** button on the toolbar.

2. Click the **Event** tab, click in the **On Error** property text box, and then click the **Build** button .

3. If necessary, click the **Code Builder**, click the **OK** button, press **Tab**, type **Debug.Print DataErr**, and then press **Ctrl+G** to open the Immediate window, as shown in Figure 8-19.

Figure 8-19   **DETERMINING THE ERROR NUMBER**

type this statement

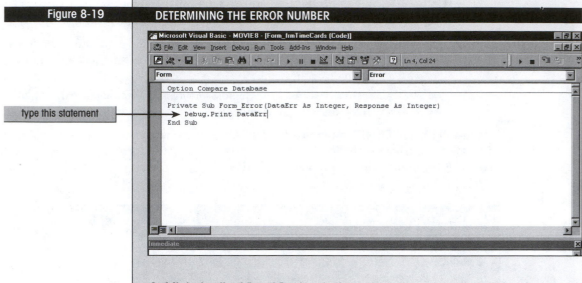

4. Minimize the Visual Basic window, close the properties dialog box, and then switch to **Form** view.

5. Click the **New Record** button on the toolbar, press **Tab** to go to the Time Card Date field, type **11/9/2002**, and then press **Tab**.

6. Type **20** and then press **Tab**. The error message *Index or primary key cannot contain a Null value* is shown.

7. Click the **OK** button, press the **Esc** key to cancel the entry, and then switch to **Design** view.

8. Redisplay the Visual Basic window by clicking its icon on the taskbar. You will see error number 3058 in the Immediate window, as shown in Figure 8-20.

Figure 8-20   **ERROR NUMBER IDENTIFIED IN THE IMMEDIATE WINDOW**

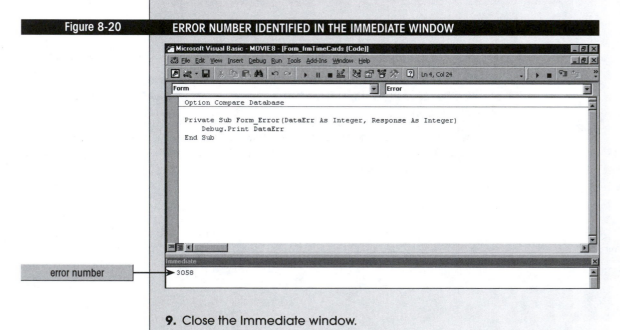

error number

9. Close the Immediate window.

Now you'll delete the statement you used to identify the error and replace it with an error-handling routine. You will use an If…Then…Else construct to test the error number. If the error is 3058, you will display a custom message, position the insertion point in the Time Card No text box, and suppress the default error message. If the error is other than error 3058, you will display the default Access error message.

To write an error handler for error 3058:

1. Delete the **Debug.Print DataErr** statement from the Form_Error(DataErr As Integer, Response As Integer) event procedure.

2. Type the following comment and code, spacing and indenting as shown in Figure 8-21.

```
'Display a custom error message for missing TimeCardNo
If DataErr = 3058 Then
MsgBox "You must type a Time Card No to continue"
Response = acDataErrContinue
DoCmd.GoToControl "TimeCardID"
Else
Response = acDataErrDisplay
End If
```

Figure 8-21	ERROR-HANDLING CODE FOR MISSING TIME CARD NUMBER

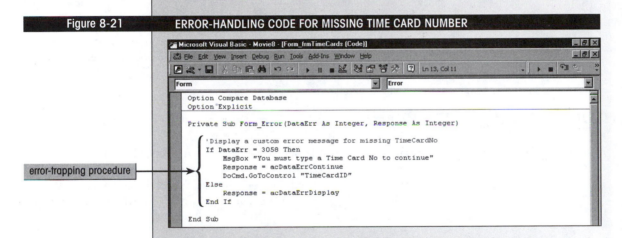

error-trapping procedure

3. Close the Visual Basic window, and then switch to **Form** view.

4. Click the **New Record** button ▶* on the toolbar, press **Tab** to go to the Time Card Date field, type **11/9/2002**, and then press **Tab**.

5. Type **20** and then press **Tab**. You will see the custom error message shown in Figure 8-22.

Figure 8-22   CUSTOM ERROR MESSAGE

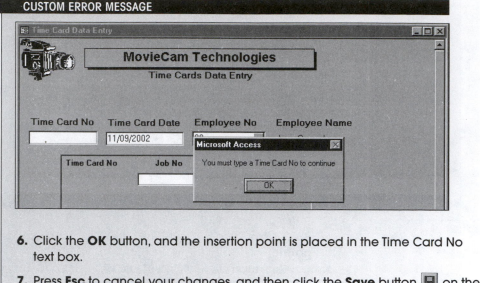

6. Click the **OK** button, and the insertion point is placed in the Time Card No text box.

7. Press **Esc** to cancel your changes, and then click the **Save** button 🖫 on the toolbar.

8. Switch to **Design** view.

You have completed the code for the error that occurs if a user does not enter a time card number. Now you will work on the other changes that Martin Woodward requested for the frmTimeCards form.

Combo Box Programming

Martin asked you to modify the frmTimeCards form so that a record can be "looked up" by the TimeCardNo field. He wants to be able to type a time card number in a text box or select a time card number from a list and then be able to go directly to that record. You and Carolyn decide to include a combo box on the frmTimeCards form to accomplish this.

To create the combo box:

1. Make sure that the toolbox is visible, and that the Control Wizards button is *not* pressed in.

2. Click the **Combo Box** button 🔲 on the toolbox, and then click in the Form Header section above the Time Card Date label to insert the combo box.

3. Click the label to select it, display the properties dialog box, change the Name property to **lblLookup**, the Caption property to **Lookup**, and the Fore Color property to **255** (red), as shown in Figure 8-23.

Figure 8-23	LBLLOOKUP PROPERTIES

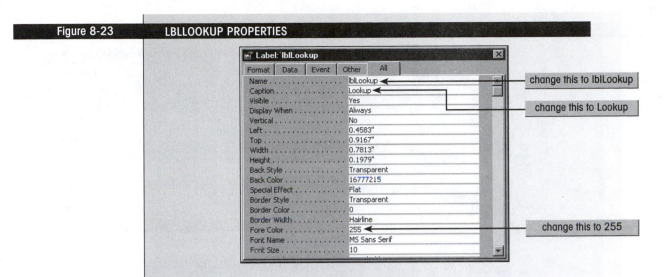

4. Click the **combo box**, change the Name property to **cboLookup**, click in the **Row Source property text box**, and click the **Build** button .

5. Add the **tblEmployees** and **tblTimeCards** tables to the Query Builder window, and close the Show Table dialog box. The Query Builder window should look like that shown in Figure 8-24.

Figure 8-24	QUERY BUILDER WINDOW

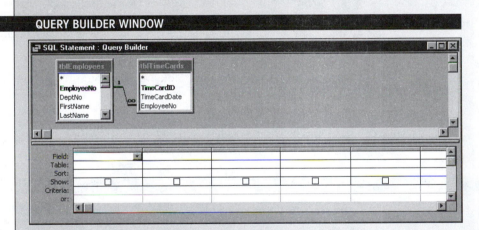

6. Add the **TimeCardID** field from the tbltimeCards table and the **LastName** field In the tblEmployees table to the query grid as shown in Figure 8-25.

Figure 8-25   ADDING FIELDS TO THE QUERY GRID

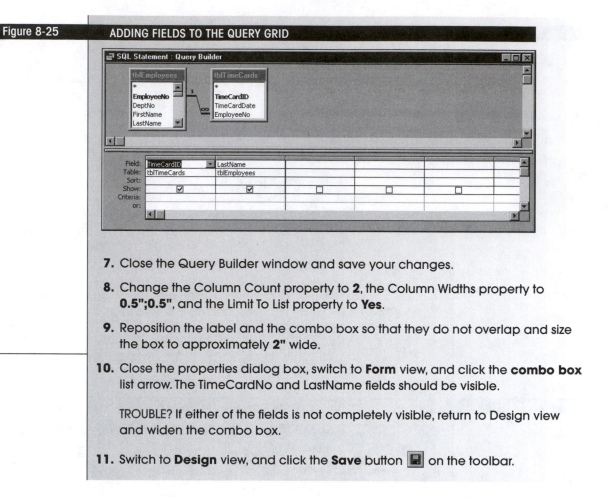

7. Close the Query Builder window and save your changes.

8. Change the Column Count property to **2**, the Column Widths property to **0.5";0.5"**, and the Limit To List property to **Yes**.

9. Reposition the label and the combo box so that they do not overlap and size the box to approximately **2"** wide.

10. Close the properties dialog box, switch to **Form** view, and click the **combo box** list arrow. The TimeCardNo and LastName fields should be visible.

    TROUBLE? If either of the fields is not completely visible, return to Design view and widen the combo box.

11. Switch to **Design** view, and click the **Save** button 🖫 on the toolbar.

Now you will add the Sub procedure to synchronize the record on the form to the one the user chooses from the combo box. The procedure you will write is shown in Figure 8-26.

Figure 8-26   CBOLOOKUP_AFTERUPDATE() PROCEDURE

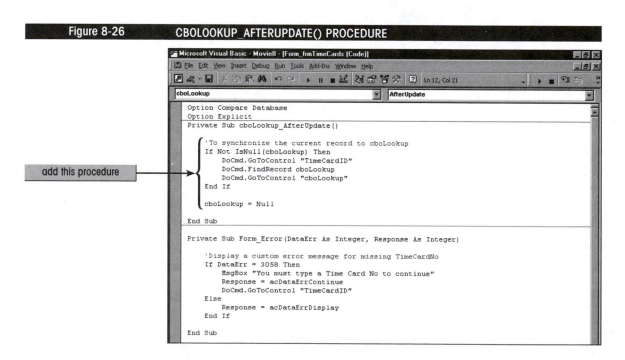

The Sub procedure will test whether there is a value in the combo box. If there is, the sub procedure will move the focus to the TimeCardID control. Next the FindRecord method will look up the contents of the cboLookup combo box in the TimeCardID field, and finally return the focus to the combo box with another DoCmd.GoToControl statement.

The code uses two methods of the DoCmd object: DoCmd.GoToControl and DoCmd.FindRecord. These are discussed next.

DoCmd.GoToControl

You can use the GoToControl method to move the focus to a specified field or control in the current record of the open form or table. You can use this method when you want the field or control to have the focus for comparison purposes or to use the FindRecord method. You also can use this method to navigate in a form according to certain conditions. The syntax of this method is:

```
DoCmd.GoToControl controlname
```

Its single argument is controlname, which is a string expression that is the name of a control or field on the active form or table.

DoCmd.FindRecord

You can use the FindRecord method to find the first instance of data that meet the criteria you specify in the FindRecord arguments. This method also can be used to find records in a form or table. The syntax of this method is:

```
DoCmd.FindRecord findwhat[, match][, matchcase][, search]
[, searchasformatted][, onlycurrentfield][, findfirst]
```

The DoCmd.Find Record arguments are:

- *Findwhat:* This argument is required and is the data for which you are searching. It can be an expression that evaluates to text, a number, or a date.
- *Match:* Use acAnywhere to specify that you are searching for data contained in any part of the field. Use acEntire (the default) to specify that you are searching for data that fills the entire field. Or use acStart to specify that you are searching for data located at the beginning of the field. The Match argument is not required.
- *Matchcase:* Use this argument to specify whether or not the search is case-sensitive. Use True (-1) for a case-sensitive search, and False (0) for a search that's not case-sensitive. This argument is not required and the default is false.
- *Search:* Use this argument to specify the direction of the search. Use acUp to specify that the search starts at the current record and goes back to the beginning of the records. Use acDown to start at the current record and search down to the end of the records. Or use acSearchAll to search all of the records. This argument is not required and the default is acSearchAll.
- *Searchasformatted:* Use True in this argument to search for data as it is formatted, and False to search for data as it is stored in the database. This argument is not required and the default is False.
- *Onlycurrentfield:* Use acAll to specify that the search include all the fields, or use acCurrent to specify that the search is confined to the current field. The current field search is faster and is the default. This argument is not required.
- *Findfirst:* True specifies that the search should start at the first record, and False specifies that the search should start at the record that follows the current record. The default is True and this argument is not required.

Next you will add the code to the form and test to be sure it works properly.

To add a sub procedure to the frmTimeCards form:

1. Click the **cboLookup** combo box to select it, and then click the **Properties** button 🖾 on the toolbar.

2. Click the **Event** tab in the properties dialog box, click in the **After Update** property text box, click the **Build** button ⌐ , if necessary, click the **Code Builder**, and then click the **OK** button. The insertion point is positioned between the stub.

3. Type the following comment and code, indenting and spacing as shown in Figure 8-26:

```
'To synchronize the current record to cboLookup
If Not IsNull(cboLookup) Then
DoCmd.GoToControl "TimeCardID"
DoCmd.FindRecord cboLookup
DoCmd.GoToControl "cboLookup"
End If
cboLookup = Null
```

4. Click **Debug** on the menu bar, and then click **Compile MovieCam**. Close the Visual Basic window, close the properties dialog box, and then switch to **Form** view.

5. Test the combo box by clicking the list arrow, and then clicking **11**. The record for time card number 11 is shown.

6. Type **125** in the text box portion of the Lookup field, and then press the **Enter** key. The record for time card number 125 is shown.

7. Type **500** in the text box portion of the Lookup field, and then press the **Enter** key. Because there is no such time card number, you receive the error message shown in Figure 8-27.

Figure 8-27	ACCESS ERROR MESSAGE

8. Click **OK** to return to the form, and then press the **Esc** key to cancel the entry.

The error message shown in Figure 8-27 is an Access error rather than a VBA run-time error. An Access error occurs when the LimitToList property is set to Yes and a user chooses a value that does not exist. You will use a special event procedure to handle this error.

NotInList Event Procedure

While the Error event helps you respond to many errors, the NotInList event can be used to trigger code to respond to the specific error shown in Figure 8-27. The NotInList event applies *only* to controls on a form and does not trigger the Error event. This is important for you to understand because you used code in the Error event procedure in this form, and that code shows the default Access error message if the error is *not* number 3058.

The NotInList event property has the following syntax:

```
Private Sub controlname_NotInList(NewData As String, Response
As Integer)
```

The arguments are:

- *Controlname:* The name of the control whose NotInList event procedure you want to run.

- *NewData:* A string that Access uses to pass the text the user entered in the text box portion of the combo box to the event procedure.

- *Response:* This setting indicates how the NotInList event was handled. The Response argument can be one of the following constants:

  - *acDataErrDisplay:* This is the default and displays the default message to the user. You can use this constant when you don't want to allow the user to add a new value to the combo box list.

  - *acDataErrContinue:* This constant specifies that the default error message is not shown. You can use this when you want the user to receive a custom message and you want to skip the default error message.

  - *acDataErrAdded:* This constant specifies that the message is not shown to the user. It enables you to add the entry to the combo box list in the NotInList event procedure.

You and Carolyn will use the acDataErrContinue Response argument to provide your own error message and suppress the default message.

To add the NotInList event procedure to the frmTimeCards form:

1. Switch to **Design** view, click the **combo box** if necessary to select it, and then click the **Properties** button ▣ on the toolbar.

2. Click the **Event** tab, click in the **On Not in List property** text box, click the **Build** button ▣, if necessary click **Code Builder**, and then click the **OK** button.

3. Type the following comment and code, indenting and spacing as shown in Figure 8-28.

```
'Display a custom error message and suppress the
default message
MsgBox "The time card number you entered does not exist.
Press Esc and enter the correct number."
Response = acDataErrContinue
```

| Figure 8-28 | CBOLOOKUP_NOTINLIST PROCEDURE |

```
Microsoft Visual Basic - Movie8 - [Form_frmTimeCards [Code]]
File  Edit  View  Insert  Debug  Run  Tools  Add-Ins  Window  Help
(General)                                    (Declarations)

          DoCmd.GoToControl "TimeCardID"
          DoCmd.FindRecord cboLookup
          DoCmd.GoToControl "cboLookup"
     End If

     cboLookup = Null

End Sub

Private Sub cboLookup_NotInList(NewData As String, Response As Integer)

     'Display a custom error message and suppress the default message
     MsgBox "The time card number you entered does not exist. Press Esc and enter the correct
     Response = acDataErrContinue

End Sub

Private Sub Form_Error(DataErr As Integer, Response As Integer)

     'Display a custom error message for missing TimeCardNo
     If DataErr = 3058 Then
          MsgBox "You must type a Time Card No to continue"
          Response = acDataErrContinue
          DoCmd.GoToControl "TimeCardID"
     Else
          Response = acDataErrDisplay
     End If

End Sub
```

type this procedure →

4. Click **Debug** on the menu bar, click **Compile MovieCam**, close the Visual Basic window, close the properties dialog box, and then switch to **Form** view.

5. Type **500** in the Lookup text box, and then press the **Enter** key. You will see the custom error message shown in Figure 8-29.

| Figure 8-29 | CUSTOM ERROR MESSAGE |

Microsoft Access
The time card number you entered does not exist. Press Esc and enter the correct number.
OK

6. Click **OK**, press **Esc**, and then close the form and save your changes.

The last change that you make to the frmTimeCards form will be to set the Time Card Date text box so that when a user double-clicks it, a calendar menu will appear, and the user can click the date. You will use an ActiveX control for this purpose.

ActiveX Controls

In addition to the standard built-in controls in the toolbox, Access supports ActiveX controls. In previous versions of Access these were referred to as OLE controls or custom controls. An **ActiveX control** is similar to a built-in control in that it is an object that you place on a form or report to display data or perform an action. However, unlike a built-in control, the code that supports the ActiveX control is stored in a separate file or files that must be installed for you to be able to use it.

You can install the Calendar ActiveX control when you install Access. There are more than 100 other ActiveX controls available in Microsoft Office 2000, and even more controls are available from third-party vendors.

Other programs, such as Word, Excel, and VBA, support ActiveX technologies. Because each program might support a different set of ActiveX controls, controls that work in some programs might not work in others. If you use a control that hasn't been certified for use in Access, you can receive unpredictable results. If you insert an ActiveX control on an Access form and get the "No Object in this Control" error message, you might have selected a control that is not supported. If you distribute an Access application that uses ActiveX controls, you must make sure that the controls are installed on each computer that runs your application.

To find third-party ActiveX controls, search the Internet using the keywords *ActiveX controls*. Two examples of third-party sites that provide controls and documentation regarding their use are: *http://www.coolstf.com/activex.html* and *http://www.taxupdate.com/software/*. The documentation provided with third-party controls should indicate whether or not they are compatible with Access.

ActiveX controls have methods and properties associated with them, just as built-in controls do. You can use these methods and properties to manipulate the control's behavior and appearance. To set the properties for an ActiveX control, display the Access properties dialog box, click in the Custom property text box, and then click the Build button. Custom properties of an ActiveX control also can be manipulated by using VBA the same way you use it to manipulate properties for built-in controls.

Registering an ActiveX Control

The Calendar control is automatically registered with the system when you install the control file. Many ActiveX controls are registered automatically, but some are not. To add a control to a form in Design view, it must be registered.

To determine whether an ActiveX control is registered, open a form in Design view, click Insert on the menu bar, and then click ActiveX Control. If the control you want to use is included in the list, you can add it to a form. If it's not listed, you must register it first. To register an ActiveX control, click Tools on the menu bar, and then click ActiveX Controls. Click the Register button. In the Add ActiveX Control dialog box, navigate to the ActiveX control file, and then click Open.

Using the Calendar ActiveX Control

You and Carolyn want to use the Access Calendar ActiveX control to build a menu form that can be accessed from any other forms in your application. The calendar form will appear when the user double-clicks a date text box on a form. It will then store the date that the user double-clicks on the calendar control in the text box on the form.

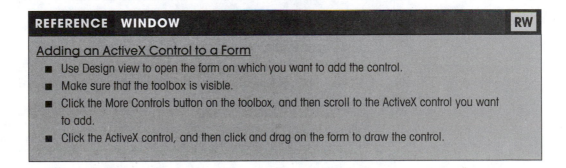

REFERENCE WINDOW | RW

Adding an ActiveX Control to a Form
- Use Design view to open the form on which you want to add the control.
- Make sure that the toolbox is visible.
- Click the More Controls button on the toolbox, and then scroll to the ActiveX control you want to add.
- Click the ActiveX control, and then click and drag on the form to draw the control.

Your first step will be to create the calendar form.

To create the frmCalendar form:

1. Create a new unbound form in **Design** view.

2. If necessary, click **View** on the menu bar, and then click **Form Header/Footer** to eliminate them from the form.

3. Size the form so that it is **2"** wide by **1½"** high, as shown in Figure 8-30.

Figure 8-30   SIZING THE FRMCALENDAR FORM

4. Click the **Properties** button 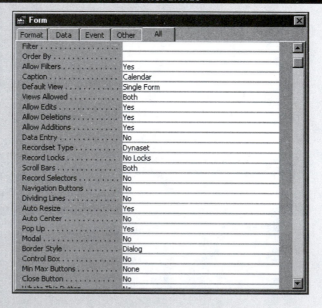 on the toolbar, and type **Calendar** in the Caption property text box. Change the Navigation Buttons property to **No**, the Pop Up property to **Yes**, the Border Style property to **Dialog**, the Control Box property to **No**, the Min Max Buttons property to **None**, and the Close Button property to **No**. See Figure 8-31. You are setting the Pop Up property to Yes so the form will remain on top of any other open forms.

Figure 8-31   CHANGING THE FRMCALENDAR FORM PROPERTIES

5. Make sure the toolbox is visible, and then click the **More Controls** button.

6. Click **Calendar Control 9.0**, and then click and drag to draw a calendar that fits on the form.

7. Right-click the **calendar control**, point to **Calendar Object**, and then click **Properties**. The Calendar Properties dialog box opens, as shown in Figure 8-32.

Figure 8-32 | **CALENDAR PROPERTIES DIALOG BOX**

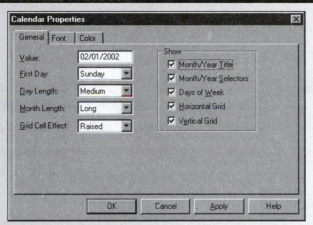

8. Clear the **Month/Year Title** check box so there is more room on the calendar, and then click the **OK** button. The form should look like that shown in Figure 8-33.

Figure 8-33 | **CALENDAR FORM**

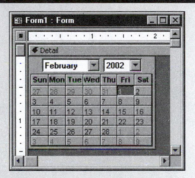

9. If necessary, click the **Properties** button on the toolbar to display the property sheet for the control, and change the Name property to **actlCalendar**. The *actl* prefix is for ActiveX control.

10. Save the form as **frmCalendar**.

   Next you will add a Sub procedure to the DblClick event of the calendar control on the frmCalendar form. The procedure will store the value of the calendar in a dtmDate variable, and then close the frmCalendar form. It will then set the active control on the form that opened the frmCalendar form so the control is equal to the value of the dtmDate variable.

To add the Sub procedure to the frmCalendar form:

1. Click the **Code** button on the toolbar to show the Visual Basic window.

2. Click **actlCalendar** in the Object list, and click **DblClick** in the Procedure list.

3. Type the following comment and code, spacing and indenting as shown in Figure 8-34.

```
Dim dtmDate As Date
'To set the date control to date selected on the calendar
dtmDate = Me.ActiveControl.Value
DoCmd.Close acForm, Me.Name
Screen.ActiveControl.Value = dtmDate
```

Figure 8-34   **ACTLCALENDAR_DBLCLICK() SUB PROCEDURE**

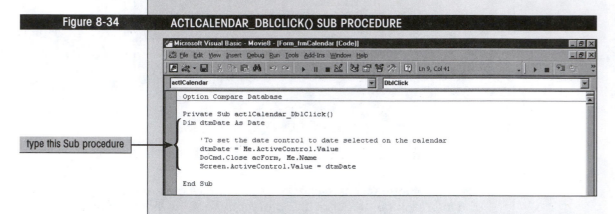

type this Sub procedure

4. Click **Debug** on the menu bar, and then click **Compile MovieCam**.

5. Save the form and close the Visual Basic window.

6. Close the form.

Now that the frmCalendar form is created, you can open it from any other form in the database by adding a sub procedure to that form. You will do this next in the frmTimeCards form. You want the user to be able to double-click the Time Card Date field and have the frmCalendar form open.

To add code to open the frmCalendar form in the frmTimeCards form:

1. Open **frmTimeCards** in **Design** view, and click the **TimeCardDate** text box control.

2. If necessary, click the **Properties** button on the toolbar to display the property sheet for the control, and then click the **Event** tab.

3. Click in the **On Dbl Click** property text box, click the **Build** button , if necessary click **Code Builder**, and then click the **OK** button.

4. Press **Enter** to insert a blank line, and then press the **Tab** key to indent.

5. Type **DoCmd.OpenForm "frmCalendar"** and then press the **Enter** key to add a blank line, as shown in Figure 8-35.

Figure 8-35   TIMECARDDATE_DBLCLICK SUB PROCEDURE

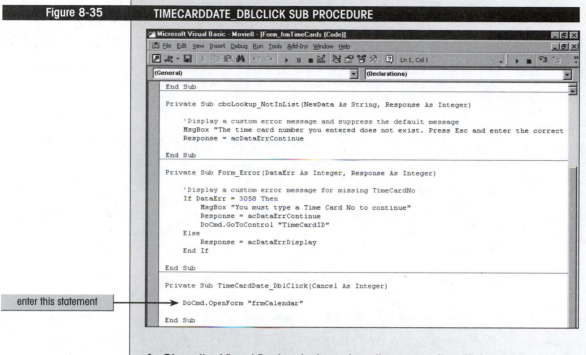

enter this statement

6. Close the Visual Basic window, close the properties dialog box, and then switch to **Form** view.

7. Click the **New Record** button on the toolbar, and double-click the **Time Card Date** text box. The frmCalendar form opens.

8. Double-click any date on the calendar to populate the text box.

9. Press the **Esc** key to cancel the entry.

10. Click the **Save** button on the toolbar to save your changes.

Next you will test the functionality of this new date feature.

To test the frmCalendar form:

1. Double-click the **Time Card Date** text box to open the frmCalendar form.

2. If necessary, drag the **frmCalendar form** so you can see the Employee No field, and then click in the **Employee No** text box.

3. Double-click a date on the frmCalendar form. The date is entered into the Employee No text box.

4. Press the **Esc** key to cancel the entry.

5. Close the frmTimeCards form to return to the Database window.

Your test found that the focus can be changed from the frmCalendar form back to the frmTimeCards form before the date is entered in the correct text box. This allows the user to click other parts of the form, and then double-click the date on the calendar. A number of different errors could result from this problem. The user could enter a date into the Time Card No text box or into the Employee No text box. He or she could click on a label and then double-click the date, which would result in run-time error 2448—"You can't assign a value to this object."

Rather than attempt to write code to prevent this situation, you will change the Modal property of the frmCalendar form. This will prevent the user from clicking on any other object and changing the focus until the frmCalendar form is closed.

To change the Modal property for the frmCalendar form:

1. Open the frmCalendar form in **Design** view.

2. Click the **Properties** button [icon] on the toolbar.

3. Click the **Other** tab in the properties dialog box, and change the Modal property to **Yes**.

4. Close the properties dialog box, and then save your changes and close the form.

5. Open the **frmTimeCards** form in **Form** view, and click the **New Record** button [icon] on the toolbar.

6. Double-click the **Time Card Date** text box to open the frmCalendar form.

7. Try to click on another part of the frmTimeCards form. The focus does not change.

8. Double-click a date on the calendar, and then press the **Esc** key to cancel the change.

9. Close the frmTimeCards form.

10. Close the Movie8 database and exit Access.

You and Carolyn are pleased with the way the new frmCalendar form works. You plan to add code to open the calendar in other data entry forms in the database as well. Martin is satisfied with the functionality you have added to the frmTimeCards form. The combo box provides him with an easy method for finding data, and he likes the visual effect of the calendar feature.

Session 8.2 QUICK | CHECK

1. Misspelling a key word is an example of a(n) _____ error.

2. What is a run-time error?

3. When VBA encounters a run-time error generated by a procedure, it searches for a(n) _____ statement.

4. What does the Resume statement do?

5. A run-time error that is generated by the interface triggers the _____ event.

6. What is the purpose of the NotInList event?

7. A(n) _____ control is similar to a built-in control, in that it is an object that you place on a form to display data or perform an action.

8. Which ActiveX control included in Microsoft Office is an Access control?

REVIEW ASSIGNMENTS

The Hours8 database is similar to the MovieCam Technologies database you worked on in this tutorial. A form named frmReportsSwitchboard has been created to open reports in the database. You will add some code to this switchboard to deal with errors.

1. Start Access and open the **Hours8** database located in the **Tutorial.08** folder on your local or network drive.

2. Open the frmReportsSwitchboard form in Form view, and then click the Preview button *without* selecting a report. Run-time error message 2497 is shown.

3. Click the End button to close the error dialog box.

4. Switch to Design view, and then click the Code button on the toolbar.

5. Position the insertion point at the end of the Dim strCondition As String statement, and press the Enter key twice.

> TROUBLE? If all procedures are not visible in the Visual Basic window, click **Tools** on the menu bar, and then click **Options**. If necessary, click the **Editor** tab in the options dialog box, click the **Default to Full Module View** check box, and then click the **OK** button.

6. Type "On Error GoTo ReportError", and then press the Enter key.

7. Click at the end of the chkTerminated = Null statement, and press the Enter key twice.

8. Type the following comment and code:

```
ReportError:
If Err.Number = 2497 Then
'No report was selected from the option groups
MsgBox "You must select a report from one of the option groups."
Resume Next
End If
```

9. Compile the code, click File on the menu bar, and then click Print to print the code.

10. Close the Visual Basic window and switch to Form view.

11. Click the Preview button. The new error message is shown.

12. Save your changes and close the form.

13. Close the **Hours8** database and exit Access.

CASE PROBLEMS

Case 1. Edwards and Company   The frmClient data entry form contains a combo box for ConsultantID. The user can enter the ConsultantID number or select an item from the list. Because this combo box is based on the data in the tblConsultants table, an error results if the wrong number is entered. You will determine the error number and write code to deal with it.

1. Start Access and open the **Edward8** database located in the **Tutorial.08** folder on your local or network drive.

2. Open the frmClients form in Form view, and click the New Record button on the toolbar.

3. Click in the Consultant text box, type "800", and press Enter.

4. Click OK when the Microsoft Access error message box is shown, and then press the Esc key to cancel the entry.

5. Switch to Design view, open the properties dialog box, click the Event tab, click in the On Error property text box, and then click the Build button.

6. Press Tab, type "Debug.Print DataErr", and then press Ctrl+G to open the Immediate window.

7. Minimize the Visual Basic window, close the properties dialog box, and then switch to Form view.

8. Click the New Record button on the toolbar, tab to the Consultant field, type 800, and then press Tab.

9. Click the OK button to close the error dialog box, press the Esc key to cancel the entry, and then switch to Design view.

10. Redisplay the Visual Basic window. The error number 3201 is shown in the Immediate window.

11. Delete the Debug.Print DataErr statement and add the following code:

```
'Display a custom error message for incorrect Consultant ID
If DataErr = 3201 Then
MsgBox "You must type a Consultant ID that is in the list.
Press Esc to cancel the entry."
Response = acDataErrContinue
Else
Response = acDataErrDisplay
End If
```

12. Compile the code, click File on the menu bar, and then click Print to print the code.

13. Close the Visual Basic window and switch to Form view.

14. Click the New Record button, type "800" in the Consultant text box, and press Enter. Your error message is shown.

15. Save your changes and close the form.

16. Close the **Edward8** database and exit Access.

Case 2. San Diego County Information Systems   The frmClasses form is used to enter all the classes into the tblClasses table in the ISD8 database. It also contains a field for the class date. You have decided to create an ActiveX calendar control on the form so you can enter a date by double-clicking the date on the calendar control.

1. Start Access and open the **ISD8** database located in the **Tutorial.08** folder on your local or network drive.

2. Open the frmClasses form in Design view, display the toolbox if necessary, and click the More Controls button.

3. Click Calendar Control 9.0, and then click and drag to draw a calendar to the right of the other controls on the form.

4. Right-click the calendar, point to Calendar Object, and then click Properties.

5. Clear the Month/Year Title check box, and then click the OK button.

6. Size the calendar control so that you can read the dates.

7. Click the Properties button on the toolbar to display the properties dialog box for the control, and change the Name property to actlCalendar.

8. Click the Code button on the toolbar, and add the following Sub procedure:

```
Private Sub actlCalendar_DblClick()
Dim dtmDate As Date
'To set the date control to date selected on the calendar
dtmDate = Me.ActiveControl.Value
Date.Value = dtmDate
End Sub
```

9. Click Debug on the menu bar, click Compile ISD Training, click File on the menu bar, and then click Print to print the code.

10. Close the Visual Basic window and switch to Form view.

11. Test the calendar by double-clicking a date.

12. Save your changes and close the form.

13. Close the **ISD8** database and exit Access.

Case 3. Christenson Homes   The frmLots form in the Homes8 database contains a combo box for entering the subdivision. As you test this form, you note that if the user types an item that is not in the list, the following error message is received: *The text you entered isn't an item in the list.* You will replace this error message with your own to make the form more user-friendly.

1. Start Access and open the **Homes8** database located in the **Tutorial.08** folder on your local or network drive.

2. Open the frmLots form in Form view, and click the New Record button on the toolbar.

3. Press the Tab key, and type the word "test" in the Subdivision text box.

4. Press the Enter key; you will see the error message. Click OK.

5. Press the Esc key to cancel the entry, and switch to Design view.

6. Create a Sub procedure that is triggered by the On Not In List event of the SubdivisionID combo box. The code will be similar to the following code used in this tutorial:

```
'Display a custom error message and suppress the default mes-
sage
MsgBox "The subdivision you entered does not exist. Press Esc
and enter the correct subdivision."
Response = acDataErrContinue
```

7. Compile the code, test it, and then print it.

8. Save the changes and close the form.

9. Close the **Homes8** database and exit Access.

Case 4. Sonoma Farms   The Sonoma Farms database contains a form named frmVisitors. You would like to add a form to this database that contains the Access ActiveX calendar control that you can access to enter a date in the Date of Visit text box in the frmVisitors form.

1. Start Access and open the **Sonoma8** database located in the **Tutorial.08** folder on your local or network drive.

2. Create an unbound form in Design view, and add the Calendar Control 9.0 ActiveX control to the form.

3. Click the Properties button on the toolbar, and type "Calendar" for the caption. Change the Navigation Buttons property to No, the Pop Up property to Yes, the

Modal property to Yes, the Border Style property to Dialog, the Control Box property to No, the **Min Max Buttons** property to None, and the Close Button property to No.

4. Right-click the calendar, point to Calendar Object, click Properties, clear the Month/Year Title check box, and then click the OK button.

5. Change the Name property of the control to actlCalendar.

6. Using the code in this tutorial as a sample, write the VBA code so that clicking a date on the calendar control enters that date into the Date of Visit text box on the frmVisitors form.

7. Save the form as "frmCalendar" and close it.

8. Using the code from the frmTimeCards form in this tutorial as a guide, add the code to the frmVisitors form to open the frmCalendar form when the Date of Visit text box is double-clicked.

9. Switch to Form view and test the two forms.

10. Return to the Visual Basic window and print the code.

11. Save your changes and close the frmVisitors form.

12. Close the **Sonoma8** database and exit Access.

QUICK | CHECK ANSWERS

Session 8.1

1. A control structure is a series of VBA statements that work together as a unit.
2. Do…Loop
3. For…Next loop
4. The Visible property can be used to show or hide a control, while the Enabled property specifies whether a control can have the focus in Form view.
5. Label controls do not have an Enabled property.
6. dot
7. Bang notation results in shorter pathnames to an object or property.
8. The Me keyword is used to refer to the associated form or report that the class module is in.
9. CodeContextObject can be used in a standard module, but the Me keyword cannot.
10. The Screen object refers to the particular form, report, or control that currently has the focus.

Session 8.2

1. syntax
2. A run-time error is an error that occurs while the application is running.
3. On Error
4. The Resume statement resumes execution after an error-handling routine is finished.
5. Error
6. The purpose of the NotInList event is to trigger code to respond to the specific error in which the item selected is not in the list.
7. ActiveX
8. The Calendar control is an Access control.

OBJECTIVES

In this tutorial you will:

- Compare the ActiveX Data Object (ADO) and Data Access Object (DAO) models

- Study the DAO model collections and objects

- Test DAO object code in the Immediate window

- Use the DAO Recordset object in VBA code

- Identify the different levels of security in Access

- Learn to work with the Workgroup Administrator, and create and join workgroup information files

- Establish user-level security in the MovieCam database

- Create users and assign permissions

- Learn to set and clear user passwords

- Create a shortcut on the desktop to a secured database

WORKING
WITH OBJECT MODELS AND SECURING THE DATABASE

Working with DAO and Implementing User-Level Security in the MovieCam Technologies Database

CASE

MovieCam Technologies

In Tutorial 8, you added a combo box to the frmTimeCards form. The combo box you added can be used to look up a particular time card number and then show it on the form. Martin Woodward requested that you change the search feature so it shows employee last names, time card numbers, and the date. He wants the data to show records sorted by last name and then by time card number. He likes the pop-up frmCalendar form you created and wants the time card search to operate similarly. You plan to create a pop-up form that contains a list box that looks up time card records in the frmTimeCards form. You and Carolyn have researched coding with Recordset objects in DAO, and you have determined that using Recordset objects is a more efficient way to program the pop-up form feature.

Amanda has reevaluated the method that you and Carolyn developed for controlling user access to the database. More users than you anticipated will be using the database, so you need to determine the various levels of rights that users will have to the data and objects. Amanda wants you and Carolyn to implement user-level security on the database, so you also need to create user groups for data entry personnel, for managers that need read-only access, and for administrators, such as you and Carolyn.

**SESSION
9 .1**

In this session, you will study the Data Access Object (DAO) and ActiveX Data Object (ADO) models and compare the two of them. You will learn to manipulate DAO objects in the Immediate window and study the DAO Recordset object, in particular. You will create a form for looking up data. The form you create will contain a list box. You also will learn some of the methods and properties of the Recordset object, and, in turn, use these methods and properties to write the VBA code for looking up data on a form.

Introduction to Object Models

The VBA code that you have written in earlier tutorials fits into a logical framework called the Access object model. The **Access object model** (which was diagrammed in Tutorial 8), contains all the items such as the forms collection, forms, and controls collection that you use in an application. You use the object model to interact programmatically with the Access user interface.

Up to this point, changes you have made to the application's data have been handled by Access behind the scenes. For example, if a user changed the data in a form, Access changed the data in the underlying table.

To write VBA code that works directly with the data in your application, you must work with a different object model. To create tables and queries and manipulate records programmatically, you must work with either the DAO library or the ADO library provided with Access.

DAO vs. ADO

The **DAO** interface has been used to programmatically manipulate data, create tables and queries, and manage security in Access databases since Access 2.0 was released. (Version 1.0 contained DAO 1.0, but it was very restrictive.) DAO is a reliable interface for working with native Access data (data stored in an Access database).

Company databases have data that was created in programs other than Access, however. For example, many companies use SQL Server, Sybase, or Oracle, which are large client-server databases. In these instances, Access is often used as the front-end, or client, to the data stored in these databases, and is attached to the data in back-end tables or providers. In this configuration, the attached tables appear just like Access tables and can be accessed programmatically using DAO in the same way that native Access tables are accessed. The problem with using DAO to manipulate the data in these tables is that it is not particularly efficient. DAO has to communicate with Open Database Connectivity (ODBC), which is the technology, or glue, that is used to attach tables from client-server databases. While ODBC can be used to connect to relational databases, it cannot be used to connect to data that is not relational, such as the Microsoft Exchange mail system.

To address this issue and some of the ODBC efficiency problems, Microsoft has developed the OLEDB technology that provides access to both relational and nonrelational data. This new technology has a single programmatic interface—called **ADO**—and this is what client applications use, regardless of the type of data provider. What this means is that you use the same syntax whether you are connecting to tables in SQL Server, tables in Access, or data that is in Microsoft Exchange.

Microsoft has made it clear that ADO is the interface they will use in the future, and that DAO will ultimately be abandoned. There will be no further development of DAO; Microsoft has stated that the presence of DAO in Access 2000 is only to ease the transition to ADO.

It is the opinion of many developers that while ADO is a simpler data model in some ways, DAO is a better programmatic interface. This is a logical assumption if you consider the problems inherent in any new software. While ADO has been touted as the wave of the future, it is new and lacks much of the functionality of DAO, particularly in dealing with recordsets. A **recordset** is simply a set of records, and manipulating recordsets is one of the major uses of ADO and DAO technology. In this tutorial, you will use DAO to manipulate recordsets.

The ADO object model is shown in Figure 9-1.

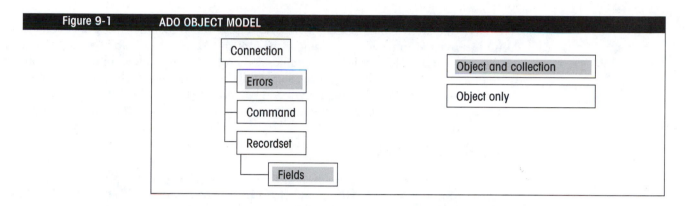

Figure 9-1   ADO OBJECT MODEL

The DAO object model is shown in Figure 9-2.

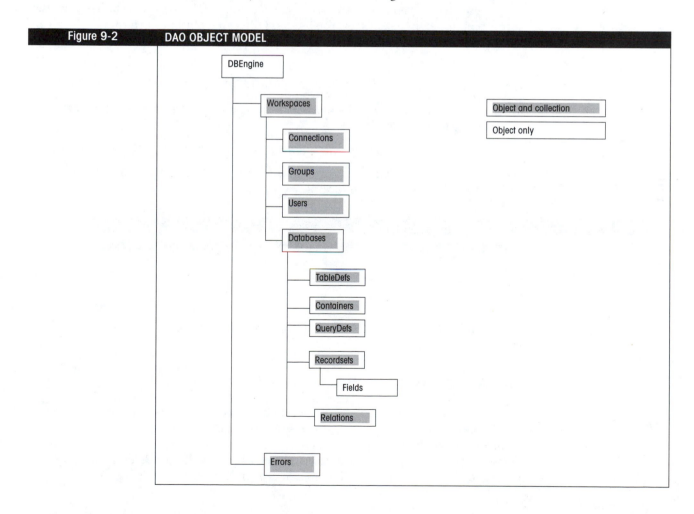

Figure 9-2   DAO OBJECT MODEL

ADO

The ADO hierarchy is simpler than the DAO hierarchy, and starts with the Connection object that represents a connection to any database engine. The Connection object contains an Errors object, Command object, and Recordset object. Both the ADO and DAO object models have a Recordset object for working with data in tables and queries, but the rest of each hierarchy is different.

DAO

The DAO hierarchy contains a number of objects, grouped together into collections. The DAO hierarchy is arranged in the same manner as the Access object model with collections of objects, each of which has its own methods and properties. Recall that in the Access object model there is a Forms collection that contains all the open forms, each form has a controls collection, and so on. Look at Figure 9-2 and you can see that DAO also has collections. It contains an Errors collection, Workspaces collection, Databases collection, and so forth.

The DBEngine Object

In the Access object hierarchy, the Application object representing the Access application is the topmost object; in ADO the Connection object is the topmost object; and in DAO the DBEngine object is at the top. The **DBEngine object** represents the DAO interface into the JET engine and ODBCDirect technology. The JET engine is the database engine that Access uses for all its native database management. ODBCDirect technology is used to access remote ODBC databases. You use the DBEngine object to determine which version of DAO you are using, and to access the collection contained in it.

To use the DBEngine object to determine the DAO version:

1. Start Access and open the **Movie9** database located in the **Tutorial.09** folder on the local or network drive.

2. Press **Ctrl+G** to open the Immediate window in the Visual Basic window.

3. Type **?DBEngine.Version** and then press the **Enter** key. Version 3.6 should be visible in the Immediate window, as shown in Figure 9-3.

Figure 9-3   TESTING THE DBENGINE

```
Immediate
?DBEngine.Version
3.6
```

The DBEngine object default collection is the Workspaces collection, which is discussed next.

The Workspace Object

The Workspaces collection contains all active Workspace objects of the database engine. A **Workspace object** represents a single session or instance of a user interacting with the database engine. For example, to find out the name of the user currently logged on to the database, you could use the Workspace object. (As you will learn later in this tutorial, you are logged in by default as the Admin user, even in an unsecured database.)

To determine the current user of the database:

1. Type **?DBEngine.Workspaces(0).UserName** in the Immediate window, and then press the **Enter** key. The user name admin is returned, as shown in Figure 9-4.

| Figure 9-4 | TESTING THE WORKSPACES COLLECTION |

```
Immediate                                                              ×
?DBEngine.Version
3.6
?DBEngine.Workspaces(0).UserName
admin
```

The Workspace object contains a Users collection and a Groups collection that, in turn, contain details of all users and groups defined in the current system database. The Workspace object also contains a Databases collection, which is discussed next.

The Database Object

Because you normally have only one database open at a time, there will be only one Database object in the Databases collection for the current workspace. Next you will test the Database object in the Immediate window.

To determine the current database:

1. Type **?DBEngine.Workspaces(0).Databases(0).Name** in the Immediate window, as shown in Figure 9-5.

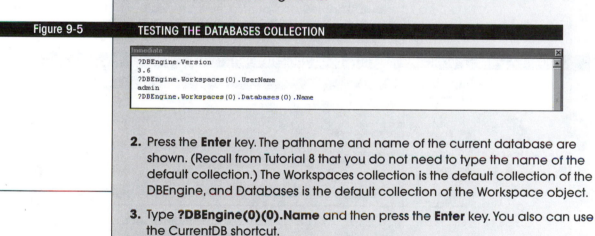

| Figure 9-5 | TESTING THE DATABASES COLLECTION |

```
Immediate                                                              ×
?DBEngine.Version
3.6
?DBEngine.Workspaces(0).UserName
admin
?DBEngine.Workspaces(0).Databases(0).Name
```

2. Press the **Enter** key. The pathname and name of the current database are shown. (Recall from Tutorial 8 that you do not need to type the name of the default collection.) The Workspaces collection is the default collection of the DBEngine, and Databases is the default collection of the Workspace object.

3. Type **?DBEngine(0)(0).Name** and then press the **Enter** key. You also can use the CurrentDB shortcut.

4. Type **?CurrentDB.Name()** in the Immediate window, and then press the **Enter** key. The Immediate window should look similar to that shown in Figure 9-6.

Figure 9-6   DETERMINING THE CURRENT DATABASE

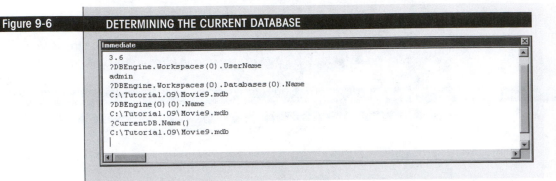

The **Database object** contains five collections: Containers, QueryDefs, Recordsets, Relations, and TableDefs. The Containers collection holds one container object for each collection of documents. The documents contain information about objects in the database and their owners and permissions.

The QueryDefs collection contains one QueryDef object for every saved query that exists within the database. The Relations collection contains one Relation object for every relationship defined between tables in the database. The TableDefs collection contains one TableDef object for every table (including system tables, but excluding linked tables) in the database. Next you'll use the TableDefs collection to find the number of tables in the database, and the QueryDefs collection to find the number of queries in the database.

To determine the number of tables and queries in the database:

1. Type **?CurrentDB.TableDefs.Count** in the Immediate window, and then press the **Enter** key. The result should be 13, as shown in Figure 9-7.

Figure 9-7   USING THE TABLEDEFS COLLECTION TO COUNT TABLES

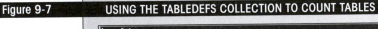

2. Close the Visual Basic window, click **Tables** on the Objects bar of the Database window, and count the tables. You should count eight tables.

3. Click **Tools** on the menu bar, and then click **Options**.

4. Click the **View** tab if necessary, make sure **System objects** check box is marked, and then click the **OK** button. You should now see five additional system tables listed in the Database window. **System tables**, such as the MSysObjects table, are database objects that are defined by the user or by the system. You can create a system object by using *USys* as the first four characters in the object name.

5. Press **Ctrl+G** to open the Immediate window, type **?CurrentDB.QueryDefs.Count**, and then press the **Enter** key. The result is 15, as shown in Figure 9-8.

Figure 9-8 | **USING THE QUERYDEFS COLLECTION TO COUNT QUERIES**

```
Immediate                                                    ×
C:\Tutorial.09\Movie9.mdb
?DBEngine(0)(0).Name
C:\Tutorial.09\Movie9.mdb
?CurrentDB.Name()
C:\Tutorial.09\Movie9.mdb
?CurrentDB.TableDefs.Count
 13
?CurrentDB.QueryDefs.Count
 15
```

6. Close the Visual Basic window. If you look at the queries listed in the Database window, you'll see that there are only five. The reason for this is that each time you create a combo box, a list box, a form, or a report that uses a SQL statement as its source, a saved query is created, but is not shown in the Database window.

7. Click **Tools** on the menu bar, click **Options**, click the **View** tab, clear the **System objects** check box, and then click the **OK** button.

The Recordset Collection

One of the collections used most often in the Database object is the Recordsets collection. The **Recordsets collection** contains one Recordset object for every recordset that is currently open in the database. The Recordset object represents the records in an underlying table or query, and can be considered simply a set of records. Following are the types of Recordset objects you can use:

- *Table:* This is the default type of Recordset object and represents a table that you can use to add, change, or delete records from a single table in an Access database. The table can be local or attached.

- *Dynaset:* This type of Recordset object can be the results of a query that contains records that can be updated. This object can be used to add, change, or delete records from the underlying table or tables. It also can contain fields from one or more Access database tables that are either local or attached. A dynaset can be edited and those results will be reflected in the underlying tables. While a dynaset is open, Access updates the records in the dynaset to reflect changes that other people are making in the underlying tables.

- *Snapshot:* This type of Recordset object cannot be updated and does not reflect changes other users make to the underlying tables. Snapshot is a static representation of the data from one or more Access database tables that are local or attached. One advantage of snapshots is that they are generally faster to create than dynasets.

- *Forward-only:* This type of Recordset object is identical to a snapshot, except that you can only scroll forward through the records; you can read the records one after another, but you cannot go back to previous records. This object also is read-only and does not reflect user changes.

- *Dynamic:* This type of Recordset object is used for accessing data in remote OBDC databases, as opposed to Access databases. Dynamic is a query result from one or more tables in which you can add, change or delete records. Records that others add, change, or delete also appear in the recordset.

You will test the Recordset object in the Immediate window next.

To test the Recordset object:

1. Press **Ctrl+G** to open the Immediate window.

2. Type **?Currentdb.OpenRecordset("tblTimeCards").RecordCount** and then press the **Enter** key. This opens the recordset underlying the tblTimeCards table and returns a count of the records. The number of records returned is 25, as shown in Figure 9-9.

Figure 9-9	USING THE RECORDSET COLLECTION TO COUNT RECORDS IN A TABLE

```
Immediate                                                           ☒
C:\Tutorial.09\Movie9.mdb
?CurrentDB.Name()
C:\Tutorial.09\Movie9.mdb
?CurrentDB.TableDefs.Count
 13
?CurrentDB.QueryDefs.Count
 15
?CurrentDB.OpenRecordset("tblTimeCards").RecordCount
 25
```

3. Close the Visual Basic window, and open the **tblTimeCards** table from the Database window. There are 25 records.

4. Close the table.

You and Carolyn decide to use a pop-up form containing a list box to look up time cards from the frmTimeCards form, rather than using the combo box you created in Tutorial 8. You think this will make the feature more user-friendly, because a list box shows more columns and rows. The program managers typically search for a time card based on the employee last name, time card number, and date. A list box will more easily show this data. Also, the menu form format keeps the form from being visible while it is not used. You will use DAO Recordset code to program the list box on the menu form. Before you can do that, however, you need to complete the frmFindTimeCards form that Carolyn began.

Carolyn set the form properties so that they are similar to the frmCalendar form you created in Tutorial 8. The Pop Up and Modal properties are both set to Yes, the Border Style property is Dialog, and the Navigation Buttons, Control Box, Min Max Buttons, and the Close Button properties are set to No. Carolyn removed the form header and footer sections from the form, and sized the form so that it is approximately 4" wide by 2" tall, as shown in Figure 9-10.

Figure 9-10   FRMFINDTIMECARDS

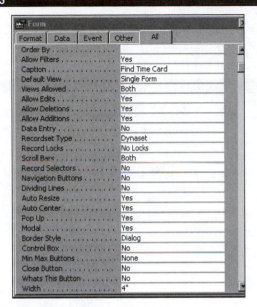

Next you will add the list box to the form, and then change some of its properties.

To add the list box to the frmFindTimeCards form:

1. Open the **frmFindTimeCards** form in **Design** view, make sure that the toolbox is visible, and that the **Control Wizards** button is selected.

2. Click the **List Box** button on the toolbox, and then click in the upper-left corner of the form to create the list box. The first dialog box of the List Box Wizard appears, as shown in Figure 9-11.

Figure 9-11   LIST BOX WIZARD

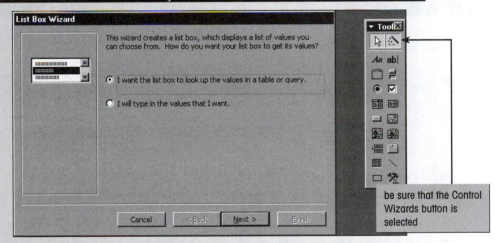

be sure that the Control Wizards button is selected

3. Accept the default selection, and then click the **Next** button.

4. Click **tblTimeCards** from the list of tables in the next dialog box, and then click the **Next** button.

5. Add **TimeCardID** and **TimeCardDate** in the list of Available Fields to the Selected Fields list box, as shown in Figure 9-12, and then click the **Next** button. You will add the LastName field from the tblEmployees table after you have completed the List Box Wizard.

Figure 9-12   SELECTING FIELDS FOR THE LIST BOX

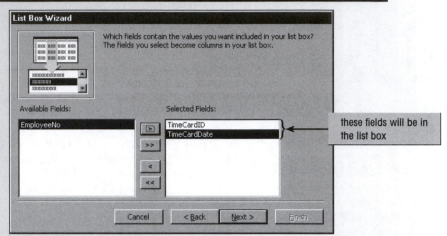

these fields will be in the list box

6. Clear the **Hide key column (recommended)** check box because you want the TimeCardID field to be visible in the list box, and then click the **Next** button.

7. Make sure that **TimeCardID** is selected in the dialog box that asks which value you want to use later to perform an action, and then click the **Next** button. Later on, you will use the TimeCardID field in your code to look up the record on the frmTimeCards form.

8. Type **Select Time Card** as the label for the list box, as shown in Figure 9-13, and then click the **Finish** button.

Figure 9-13   ENTERING THE LABEL FOR THE LIST BOX

Next you need to change the Row Source of the list box so that it also shows the last name of the employee. You will change the list box properties so that the field saved for later use is the second column. Then you will create two command buttons. One will be used to search for the time card after it is chosen from the list box. You will name the button cmdFind. You will change the Enabled property for the cmdFind button to No, so that it is not enabled by default. Later, you will add a Sub procedure to the form class module to set the Enabled property of the button to Yes after a user has chosen a time card from the list box. The other command button you create will be used to close the form.

To change the list box properties:

1. Click the **Properties** button 📓 on the toolbar, click in the Row Source property text box, click the **Build** button ⋯ , click **Query** on the menu bar, and then click **Show Table**.

2. Click **tblEmployees** in the Show Table dialog box, click the **Add** button, and then click the **Close** button.

3. Drag the **LastName** field to the first column of the query grid, click the **Sort** list arrow, click **Ascending**, click the **Sort** list arrow for the TimeCardID field, and then click **Ascending**, as shown in Figure 9-14.

Figure 9-14	MODIFYING THE LIST BOX SQL STATEMENT

drag LastName to the first column of the grid

click Ascending

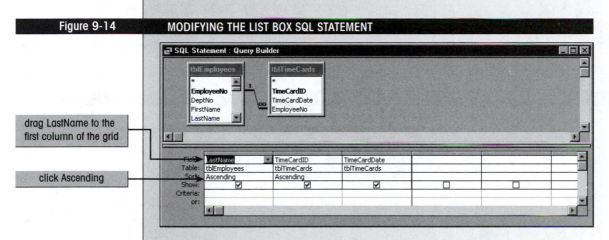

4. Close the Query Builder window and save the changes.

5. Change the Name property to **lstFind** (be sure to type the letter "l" and *not* the number 1 as the first character), the Column Count property to **3**, the Column Widths property to **1";0.5";0.5"**, and the Bound Column property to **2**. These changes allow you to show the LastName field in the first column, and use the TimeCardID field in the second column to look up the record on the frmTimeCards form.

6. Size the lstFind control and its label as shown in Figure 9-15, and then deselect the **Control Wizards** button ⟋ to turn it off.

Figure 9-15	SIZING THE LIST BOX

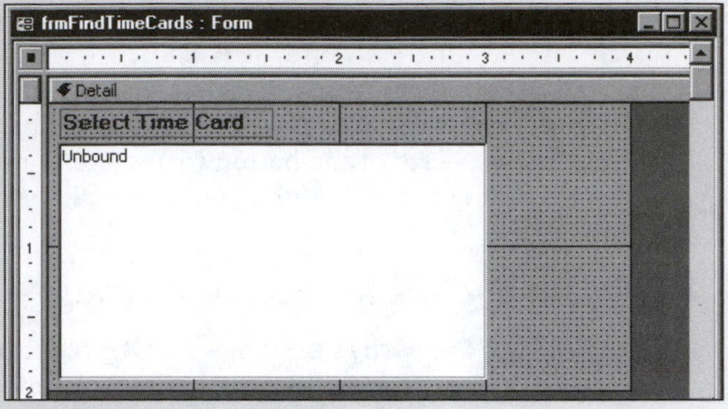

7. Click the **Command Button** button ▭ on the toolbox, click to the right of the list box to create a command button, click **Edit** on the menu bar, and then click **Duplicate**. A second command button is created below the first.

8. Change the Name property of the first command button to **cmdFind**, the Caption to **&Find Record**, and the Enabled property to **No**. Then change the Name property of the second command button to **cmdCancel** and the Caption to **&Cancel**.

9. Size and align the buttons as shown in Figure 9-16, and then save the changes to the form.

Figure 9-16	ADDING THE COMMAND BUTTONS

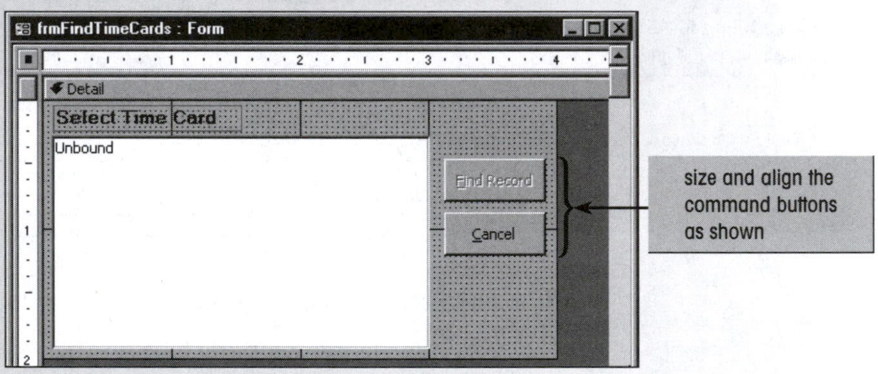

size and align the command buttons as shown

You are ready to begin writing the code for the list box, but first you must make sure that the DAO library is available because the code will use the DAO Recordset object, rather than the ADO Recordset object. You will do that next.

Changing the Object Library Reference

An **object library** is a collection of prebuilt objects and functions that you can use in VBA code. By default, the ADO library is selected in Access 2000.

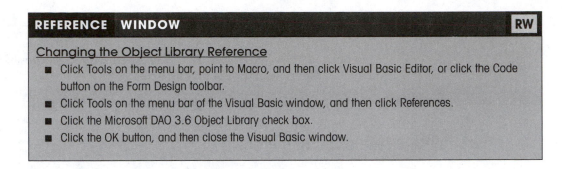

REFERENCE   WINDOW   **RW**

Changing the Object Library Reference

- Click Tools on the menu bar, point to Macro, and then click Visual Basic Editor, or click the Code button on the Form Design toolbar.
- Click Tools on the menu bar of the Visual Basic window, and then click References.
- Click the Microsoft DAO 3.6 Object Library check box.
- Click the OK button, and then close the Visual Basic window.

Next you will add the DAO library so that you can use its objects in your code.

To add the DAO library:

1. Click the **Code** button 📷 on the Form Design toolbar to open the Visual Basic window.

   TROUBLE? If the Choose Builder dialog box opens and asks you to select a builder, close the Visual Basic window, click Tools on the menu bar, click Options, click the Forms/Reports tab, click the Always use event procedures check box, and then click the OK button. Click the Code button 📷 to return to the Visual Basic window.

2. Click **Tools** on the menu bar of the Visual Basic window, and then click **References**.

3. Click the **Microsoft DAO 3.6 Object Library** check box, as shown in Figure 9-17.

Figure 9-17   SELECTING THE DAO OBJECT LIBRARY

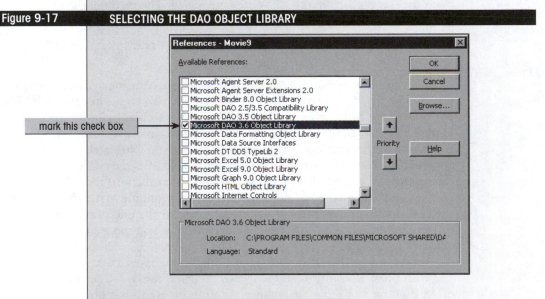

4. Click the **OK** button, and then close the Visual Basic window.

Writing Code Using the Recordset Object

The completed VBA Sub procedure that will find the record chosen in the list box on the frmTimeCards form is shown in Figure 9-18.

To understand this code, you need to understand the RecordsetClone property, the FindFirst method of DAO Recordset objects, and the Bookmark property of forms and recordsets.

RecordsetClone Property

Every form has a **RecordsetClone property** that you can use to get a copy of the form's underlying recordset. By creating a copy of the table or query on which the form is based, you can navigate or operate on the form's records independently of the form itself. After you have navigated to or modified the record in the copy, you set the actual recordset of the form equal to the copy. One advantage of using a form's RecordsetClone property is that you then can use the DAO Find methods—that cannot be used with forms—to navigate through records. You will learn about these methods in the next section.

The Sub procedure will include the following line of code:

```
Dim rst As DAO.Recordset
```

The preceding statement declares an object variable as a DAO Recordset object. The following line of code sets the object variable to the RecordsetClone property of the frmTimeCards form:

```
Set rst = Forms!frmTimeCards.RecordsetClone
```

FindFirst, FindLast, FindNext, and FindPrevious Methods

These methods locate the first, last, next, or previous record in a dynaset or snapshot Recordset object according to the criteria specified. The methods then make that record the current record. The syntax for these methods is:

```
recordset.{FindFirst | FindLast | FindNext | FindPrevious}
criteria
```

The *recordset* is an object variable that represents an existing dynaset or snapshot recordset object. The *criteria* is a string used to locate the record and is like the WHERE clause in a SQL statement without the word WHERE. (This is similar to the wherecondition argument in the DoCmd.OpenReport object that you worked with in Tutorial 7.)

If a record that matches the criteria isn't located, the NoMatch property is set to True. If the recordset contains more than one record that satisfies the criteria, the FindFirst method locates the first record, the FindNext method locates the next record, and so on.

The FindFirst method begins searching at the beginning of the recordset and searches to the end. The FindLast method begins searching at the end of the recordset and searches to the beginning. The FindNext method begins searching at the current record and searches to the end of the recordset. The FindPrevious method begins searching at the current record and searches to the beginning of the recordset.

When a new Recordset object is opened, its first record is the current record. If you use one of the Find methods to make another record in the Recordset object current, you must synchronize the current record in the Recordset object with the form's current record. You do this by assigning the value of the Recordset's bookmark property to the form's bookmark property.

The statement in the procedure you will write looks like the following:

```
rst.FindFirst "TimeCardID = " & "'" & lstFind & "'"
```

This statement uses the FindFirst method of the Recordset object to find the first record. It searches from the beginning of the recordset to the end.

Bookmark Property

When a bound form is open in Form view, each record is assigned a unique bookmark. The **Bookmark property** contains a string expression created by Access. You can get or set the form's Bookmark property separately from the DAO Bookmark property of the underlying table or query.

Bookmarks are not saved with the records they represent, and are valid only while the form is open.

In the procedure you will write, you will enter the following statement to set the Bookmark property of the form equal to the Bookmark property of the Recordset object, thus synchronizing the records:

```
Forms!frmTimeCards.Bookmark = rst.Bookmark
```

To write the code for the cmdFind button:

1. Right-click the **Find Record** button on the form, and then click **Build Event** on the shortcut menu.

2. If necessary, select **Code Builder** in the Choose Builder dialog box, and type the following comment and statements, indenting as shown in Figure 9-18.

```
Dim rst As DAO.Recordset
'Find the record and then close the dialog box
Set rst = Forms!frmTimeCards.RecordsetClone
rst.FindFirst "TimeCardID = " & "'" & lstFind & "'"
Forms!frmTimeCards.Bookmark = rst.Bookmark
DoCmd.Close acForm, "frmFindTimeCards"
```

Figure 9-18	WRITING THE CMDFIND CODE

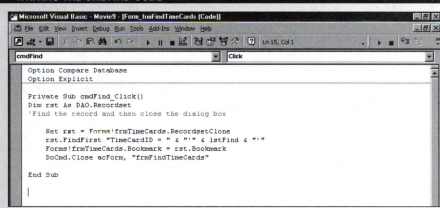

TROUBLE? The control name is lstFind, with the letter "l" as the first character, not the number 1. If you typed the number one (1), change it to the letter "l" and complete the procedure.

3. Click the **Object** list arrow, click **lstFind**, click the **Procedure** list arrow, and then click **AfterUpdate**.

4. Type **cmdFind.Enabled = True**.

5. Click the **Object** list arrow, click **cmdCancel**, and then type **DoCmd.Close**.

6. Click **Debug** on the menu bar, and then click **Compile Movie9**.

7. Click the **Save** button on the toolbar, and then close the Visual Basic window.

8. Minimize the form, open the **frmTimeCards** form from the Database window, restore the **frmFindTimeCards** form, and switch to **Form** view. Both forms are now open in Form view, as shown in Figure 9-19.

Figure 9-19   TESTING THE FRMFINDTIMECARDS FORM

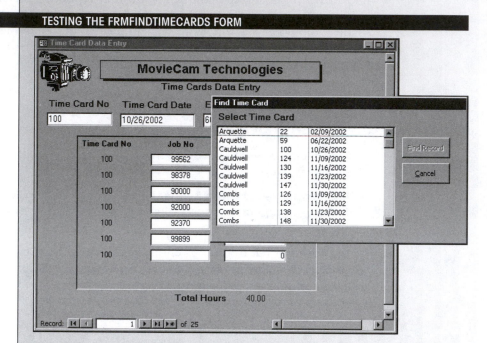

9. Click time card number **139** from the list box, and then click the **Find Record** button. The button is enabled when a selection is made from the list box, the record is shown in the frmTimeCard form, and the frmFindTimeCards form closes.

Next you will add code to the frmTimeCards form. The code will open the frmFindTimeCards form when the Time Card No text box is double-clicked.

To open the frmFindTimeCards form from the frmTimeCards form:

1. Switch to **Design** view.

2. Click the **TimeCardID** text box, click the **Properties** button on the toolbar, click the **Event** tab, click in the **On Dbl Click** property text box, click the **Build** button [...], and if necessary, click **Code Builder** in the Choose Builder dialog box.

3. Type **DoCmd.OpenForm "frmFindTimeCards"** as shown in Figure 9-20.

Figure 9-20	ADDING THE CODE TO THE FRMTIMECARDS FORM

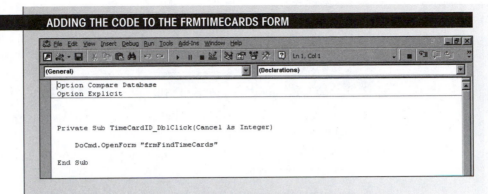

4. Close the Visual Basic window, close the Properties dialog box, and then switch to **Form** view.

5. To test the code, double-click the **Time Card No** text box, and then click the **Cancel** button on the frmFindTimeCards form to make sure that it works.

6. Save the **frmTimeCards** form, and then close it.

The last thing you will do is add code to the frmFindTimeCards form, so that if a user double-clicks a time card in the list box, the time card will be found as if the user had clicked the Find button.

To complete the frmFindTimeCards form:

1. Open the **frmFindTimeCards** form in **Design** view.

2. Show the properties for the lstFind list box, click the **Event** tab, click in the **On Dbl Click** property text box, click the **Build** button ⬜ , and if necessary click **Code Builder**.

3. Type the following comment and code, indenting as shown:

```
'Find the record that is double-clicked
    If Not IsNull(lstFind) Then
            cmdFind_Click
    End If
```

4. Save your changes, close the Visual Basic window, and close the form.

5. Open the **frmTimeCards** form in **Form** view, double-click the **Time Card No** text box to open the frmFindTimeCards form, and then double-click time card **126**. The record is shown in the frmTimeCards form, and the frmFindTimeCards form is closed.

6. Close the **frmTimeCards** form.

7. Close the **Movie9** database and exit Access.

The new frmFindTimeCards form meets all of Martin's requirements and is more efficient than the combo box that you created in Tutorial 8. You and Carolyn are pleased with the results, and now will turn your attention to assigning security levels to the database.

Session 9.1 QUICK CHECK

1. To write VBA code that works directly with the data in your application, you must work with ADO or _____.

2. When is it a good idea to use DAO rather than ADO?

3. The _____ is the database engine that Access uses for all of its native database management.

4. What is the object at the top of the DAO hierarchy? What object is at the top of the ADO hierarchy?

5. What are the types of Recordset objects?

6. How can a user create a system object?

7. Every form has a(n) _____ property that you can use to get a copy of the form's underlying recordset.

8. The _____ method of the Recordset object begins searching at the beginning of the recordset and continues to the end.

9. What is an object library?

SESSION 9.2

In this session, you will learn the different security options in Access and will implement user-level security on the MovieCam database. You will learn about the Workgroup Administrator and create a new workgroup information file. You will use the Security Wizard to create groups and users and to set permissions for them in the database. You also will set and clear passwords for users, and create a desktop shortcut to open the MovieCam database.

Overview of Security

You can apply a number of different security options to an Access database. In Tutorial 6, you changed the Startup properties and disabled the Bypass key to restrict users from opening database objects in Design view. This method is fine for a small application without lots of users, but it is not foolproof. In addition, it does not allow for various permissions for different users or groups of users.

The simplest method for protecting an Access database is to set a password on it. Once a password is set, a dialog box request that password whenever a user attempts to open the database. Users can open the database only if they enter the correct password in the dialog box. After the database is open, the user has access to all objects in it.

The most flexible and extensive method for securing a database is called user-level security. With **user-level security**, a database administrator can grant specific permissions to individual users and/or groups of users for any database object, except data access pages and modules.

User-level security prevents users from changing tables, queries, forms, reports, and macros, and also protects sensitive data in the database.

Workgroup Information File

An Access **workgroup** is a group of users in a multiuser environment who share data. If user-level security is defined, the members of a workgroup are recorded in an Access **workgroup information file** that is read at startup. This file contains the users' names, passwords, and the group to which they belong.

When you install Access, the Setup program automatically creates an Access workgroup information file that is identified by the name and organization information you provide during the installation process. Technically, security is established by default for each Access database you create. The only user in the database is Admin. Admin, by default, has full rights to all objects in the database and has no password. Therefore, each time you open an unsecured database, you open it as Admin with full rights, and no password is required. Each time you create a new database in Access, you create it as Admin, so, by default, Admin is the owner of each database. Owners and administrators have full rights to the database objects.

You will want to create a new workgroup information file for two critical reasons. The first is that Admin is the default owner and administrator of all databases in Access according to the default workgroup information file. If you do not create a new workgroup information file, users will not be able to use *any* Access database on the system without knowing the Admin password you created in the default workgroup information file. You must create a new workgroup information file that contains the name and password of a new user who is both owner and administrator.

The second reason is that the default workgroup information file simply contains the name and organization that was provided when the Access software was installed. This information is easy to obtain, and anyone who has it can re-create the default workgroup information file, identify themselves as an administrator account, and gain full rights to the database. To guard against this, you should create a new file that is protected by a workgroup ID.

A **workgroup ID** is a case-sensitive string that contains letters and/or numbers and is 4 to 20 characters long. Think of the workgroup ID as a password for the workgroup information file. Only someone who knows the workgroup ID can re-create the workgroup information file.

The workgroup information file can be created in one of two ways. You can create it by running the Wrkgadm.exe program that is installed with Access. You run this program by clicking the MS Access Workgroup Administrator shortcut in the Office folder, or by double-clicking the Wrkgadm.exe file, which, depending on the software installed, may be in the Languages folder or the Office\1033 folder. You can also create a new workgroup information file while running Access. The User-Level Security Wizard contains a dialog box that asks whether you want to use the existing workgroup information file or create a new one.

Creating a Workgroup Information File

Carolyn has read up on user-level security and suggests creating the workgroup information file as a separate step from running the User-Level Security Wizard. She has a good reason for this. When the wizard is run, the user currently logged into the database becomes the new owner of the database and all of the objects in it. Remember that the owner has full rights. If you create the workgroup information files as a part of running the User-Level Security Wizard, the new owner of the database becomes unknown user. Carolyn thinks it's best to create the new workgroup information file, create a new administrative user named MovieAdmin, log in as MovieAdmin, and then run the wizard. This will make MovieAdmin the new administrator and the new owner of the database.

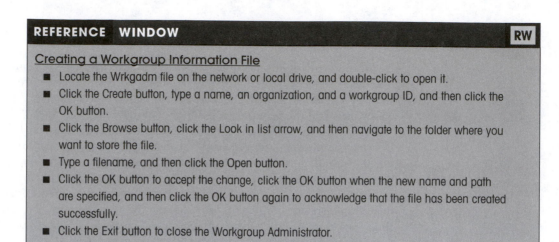

REFERENCE WINDOW   RW

Creating a Workgroup Information File
- Locate the Wrkgadm file on the network or local drive, and double-click to open it.
- Click the Create button, type a name, an organization, and a workgroup ID, and then click the OK button.
- Click the Browse button, click the Look in list arrow, and then navigate to the folder where you want to store the file.
- Type a filename, and then click the Open button.
- Click the OK button to accept the change, click the OK button when the new name and path are specified, and then click the OK button again to acknowledge that the file has been created successfully.
- Click the Exit button to close the Workgroup Administrator.

You will create the new workgroup information file next.

To create a new workgroup information file:

1. Right-click the **Start** button, and then click **Find** on the shortcut menu if you are using Windows 98, or **Search** if you are using Windows 2000.

2. Type **Wrkgadm** in the Named text box, click the **Look in** list arrow, and select the local hard drive or the network drive containing the application files. (Check with your instructor if you are unsure which to select.)

3. Click the **Find Now** or **Search Now** button, and the Wrkgadm file is shown in the list box.

4. Double-click the **Wrkgadm** file to open the Workgroup Administrator dialog box, as shown in Figure 9-21.

| Figure 9-21 | WORKGROUP ADMINSTRATOR |

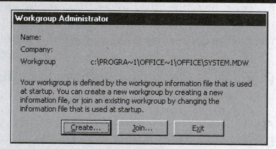

5. The Workgroup Administrator dialog box should show the default workgroup information file, SYSTEM.MDW, preceded by its path on the local or network drive, the name associated with it, and the company associated with it. Write down this information now. You will need to know the location of SYSTEM.MDW later in order to make it the active file (rejoin it). If an error is made, you may also need to recreate the default workgroup information file later and all of this information will be required to recreate it. As an added precaution, you may want to copy the SYSTEM.MDW file to a floppy disk so that you can simply copy it back to the local or network drive later. See your instructor or technical support person if you need assistance to do this.

6. Click the **Create** button, type *your name* in the Name text box, and then type **MovieCam Technologies** in the Organization text box.

7. Type **Movie1234** in the Workgroup ID text box, and then click the **OK** button.

8. Click the **Browse** button, click the **Look in** list arrow, and navigate to the **Tutorial.09** folder.

9. Change the filename to **moviesecure** as shown in Figure 9-22, and then click the **Open** button.

Figure 9-22	NAMING THE WORKGROUP INFORMATION FILE

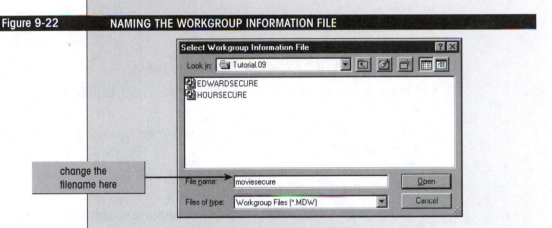

change the filename here

10. Click the **OK** button to accept the change, click the **OK** button when the new name and path are specified, and then click the **OK** button again to acknowledge that the file has been created successfully. Make sure that the new workgroup information file specified is MOVIESECURE.MDW.

11. Click the **Exit** button to close the Workgroup Administrator.

Rebuilding a Workgroup Information File

If a workgroup information file is damaged or deleted, you can re-create it as long as you have the exact, case-sensitive information that you used when you initially created the file. This information includes the name, company name, and workgroup ID.

Make sure that once you have created the new workgroup information file, you have users rejoin or modify their shortcuts if you've stored the file in a new location or if you have changed the name.

Security Accounts

The workgroup information file you create or use by default contains the following predefined user and group accounts:

- *Admin:* This is the default user account. This account is exactly the same for every copy of Access and for other applications such as VBA and Excel.
- *Admins:* This is the adminstrator's account group. Users in this group have full rights to all objects in the database. The group must have at least one user at all times. The Admin user is in the Admins group.

■ *Users:* This group account contains all user accounts. Access automatically adds user accounts to the Users group when a member of the Admins group creates them. This account is the same for any workgroup information file, but it contains only user accounts created by members of the Admins group of that workgroup and the Admin user. A user account can be removed from the Users group only if an Admins group member deletes that user.

Creating a New User

Before you and Carolyn make any changes to the users and groups, you decide to make a copy of the database. You will do that next.

To make a copy of the Movie9 database:

1. Right-click the Windows **Start** button, and then click **Explore** on the shortcut menu.

2. Navigate to the **Tutorial.09** folder containing the **Movie9** database, and then right-click the file.

3. Click **Copy** on the shortcut menu, right-click an empty area of the window, and then click **Paste** on the shortcut menu.

4. Right-click the **Copy of Movie9** file, click **Rename** on the shortcut menu, type **MovieSecure.mdb**, and then press the **Enter** key.

5. Close Windows Explorer, open **Access**, and then open the **MovieSecure** database.

You and Carolyn want to determine the user and group accounts and the database owner. You will then make the changes necessary to establish a new owner and administrator.

To create a new owner and administrator:

1. Click **Tools** on the menu bar, point to **Security**, and then click **User and Group Accounts**. The User and Group Accounts dialog box opens, as shown in Figure 9-23. The Admin user is shown in the Name box, and the Admins and Users groups are shown in the Available Groups list box. The Member Of list box shows that Admin is currently a member of both the Users and Admins group.

Figure 9-23   **USER AND GROUP ACCOUNTS DIALOG BOX**

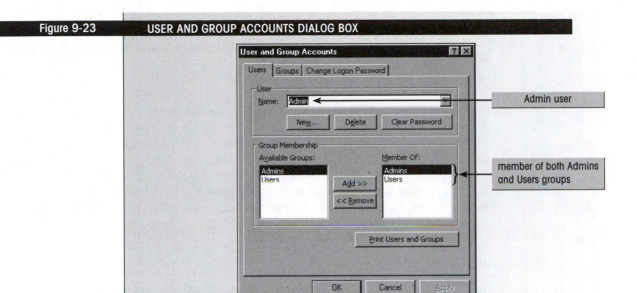

2. Click the **New** button to create a new user, and then type **MovieAdmin** in the Name text box.

3. Press the **Tab** key, type **Movie1234** in the Personal ID text box, and then click the **OK** button. The Personal ID is not the same as a password. It is a case-sensitive, alphanumeric string of 4 to 20 characters that Access combines with a user account name to identify a user or group in a workgroup.

4. With **Admins** selected in the Available Groups list box, click the **Add>>** button to make MovieAdmin a member of the Admins group, as shown in Figure 9-24. Recall that there must always be at least one member of the Admins group. You are adding the new user to this group. Next you will take the Admin user out of the Admins group.

Figure 9-24   **MAKING MOVIEADMIN A MEMBER OF THE ADMINS GROUP**

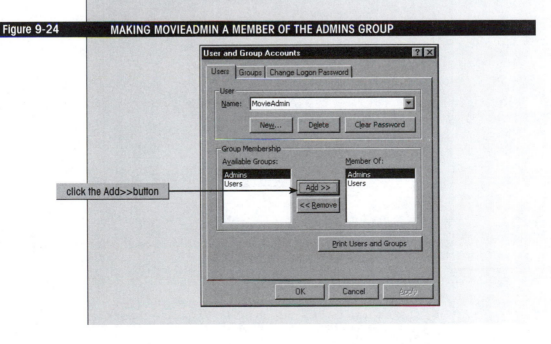

5. Click the **Name** list arrow, and then click **Admin**.

6. Make sure that **Admins** in the Member Of list box is selected, and then click the **<<Remove** button.

If you decide later to give database rights to the Users group, you need to guard against the possibility that someone might create a new workgroup information file with the Admin user in it. You also want to guard against a user joining the default workgroup information file, SYSTEM.MDW, in which Admin exists but does not require a password. Setting a password now requires a user to use it to log into MovieSecure as Admin. In addition, you must set an Admin password for Access to prompt you for a logon name. Because you will want to log on as MovieAdmin before you run the User-Level Security Wizard, you want that prompt to display.

Setting a Password

Next you'll change the logon password for the Admin user. Currently the Admin user is only a member of the Users group.

To add a password for the Admin user:

1. Click the **Change Logon Password** tab in the User and Group Accounts dialog box, as shown in Figure 9-25.

Figure 9-25   **CHANGING THE ADMIN PASSWORD**

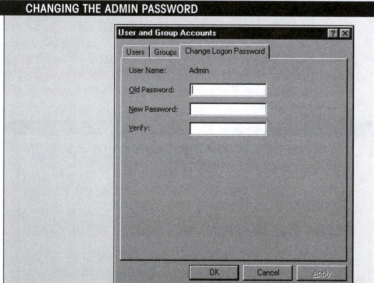

2. Press the **Tab** key to move to the New Password text box.

3. Type **moviecam**, press the **Tab** key, and then type **moviecam** again to confirm.

4. Click the **OK** button. Now you will test the password.

5. Exit Access.

6. Start **Access**, and then open the **MovieSecure** database.

7. In the Logon dialog box, click in the Name text box, type **Admin**, and then press the **Tab** key.

8. Type the password, **moviecam**, and then press the **Enter** key.

9. Close the **MovieSecure** database, and exit Access.

The next step in the process is to log on as the new administrator of the MovieAdmin database, and assign a password to this account. You also will run the User-Level Security Wizard to secure the database.

User-Level Security Wizard

The User-Level Security Wizard performs the following tasks:

- Gives you the option to create a new workgroup information file.
- Secures the objects you select in the database that is open when you run the wizard.
- Lets you add new groups with predefined levels of security to the database.
- Lets you add new users and passwords to the database.
- Assigns ownership of the database and the objects in it to the user who is currently logged in.
- When you are finished, print a User-Level Security Wizard report that contains passwords and user names you create.
- Makes a back-up copy of the database using the same name and the .bak extension.

Running the User-Level Security Wizard

You will now log back on to the database as MovieAdmin. Although you defined a Personal ID (PID) for this user when you created the MovieAdmin user, a PID is not the same thing as a password. A password is used to access the application; the PID is used as a part of the encryption process. After you create a password for the MovieAdmin user, you will run the User-Level Security Wizard.

To create a password for the MovieAdmin user and run the User-Level Security Wizard:

1. Start **Access** and then open the **MovieSecure** database.

2. In the Logon dialog box, type **MovieAdmin** in the Name text box, and then click the **OK** button to open the database.

3. Click **Tools** on the menu bar, point to **Security**, and then click **User and Group Accounts**.

4. Click the **Change Logon Password** tab in the User and Group Accounts dialog box. Note that the current user is now MovieAdmin, as shown in Figure 9-26.

Figure 9-26   **MOVIEADMIN IS THE CURRENT USER**

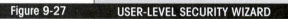

User and Group Accounts	? X

Users | Groups | Change Logon Password

User Name: MovieAdmin ←————————————————   **user name**

Old Password: [   ]

New Password: [   ]

Verify: [   ]

OK   Cancel   Apply

5. Press the **Tab** key, type **moviecam** in the New Password text box, press the **Tab** key, type **moviecam** in the Verify text box, and then click the **OK** button. Note that you are using simple passwords and repeating them. In a personal or business situation, you should create passwords that are at least six characters in length, and use a combination of letters and numbers that makes your passwords difficult to determine.

6. Click **Tools** on the menu bar, point to **Security**, and then click **User-Level Security Wizard**. The first dialog box, which is shown in Figure 9-27, gives you the option of creating a new workgroup information file or modifying the existing one.

Figure 9-27   **USER-LEVEL SECURITY WIZARD**

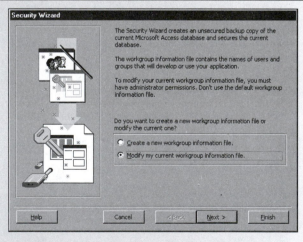

Security Wizard

The Security Wizard creates an unsecured backup copy of the current Microsoft Access database and secures the current database.

The workgroup information file contains the names of users and groups that will develop or use your application.

To modify your current workgroup information file, you must have administrator permissions. Don't use the default workgroup information file.

Do you want to create a new workgroup information file or modify the current one?

○ Create a new workgroup information file.

● Modify my current workgroup information file.

Help   Cancel   < Back   Next >   Finish

7. Make sure that the **Modify my current workgroup information file** option is selected, and then click the **Next** button. The next dialog box contains a list of objects in the database. All are selected by default to be secured. If you want an object to be unsecured, you would deselect it now.

8. Click the **Next** button.

The next dialog box in the User-Level Security Wizard lets you choose from a list of pre-defined groups with varying levels of security. Clicking an item in the list displays an explanation of the Group Permissions for that group. This dialog box creates the group so that you, as database administrator, are then able to add users to the group as you create them. You and Carolyn decided to add the Full Data Users group for the data entry employees, and the Read-Only Users group for some of the managers. You will add these groups next, and also complete the User-Level Security Wizard.

To complete the User-Level Security Wizard:

1. Click the **Full Data Users** and **Read-Only Users** check boxes, as shown in Figure 9-28, and then click the **Next** button. The next dialog box lets you grant permissions to the Users group. You will not give the Users group any permissions because you have two groups selected.

Figure 9-28	ADDING PREDIFINED GROUPS

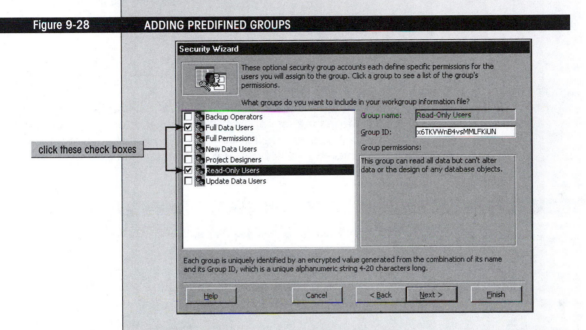

2. Make sure the **No, the Users group should not have any permissions** option is selected, and then click the **Next** button. The next wizard dialog box, which is shown in Figure 9-29, lets you add new users and passwords for these users. A PID is automatically provided. You will add Martin and Carolyn as new users, but you will not add passwords. The users can set their own password the first time they log on to the database.

Figure 9-29 ADDING USERS

users can be added here

a PID is automatically provided

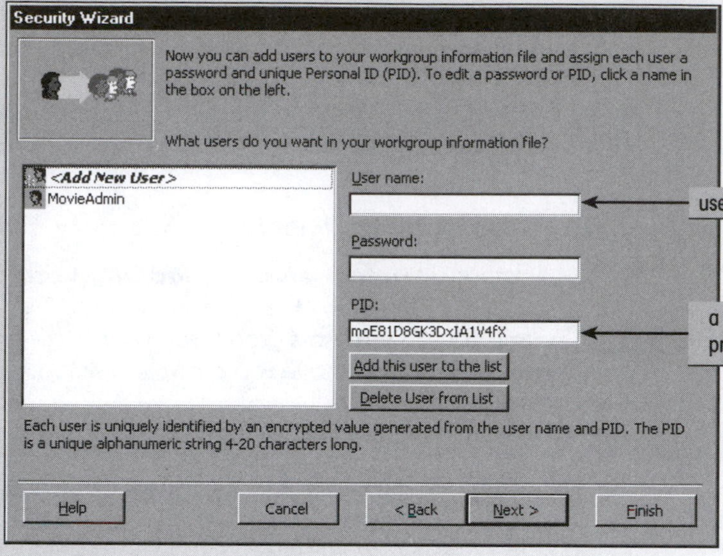

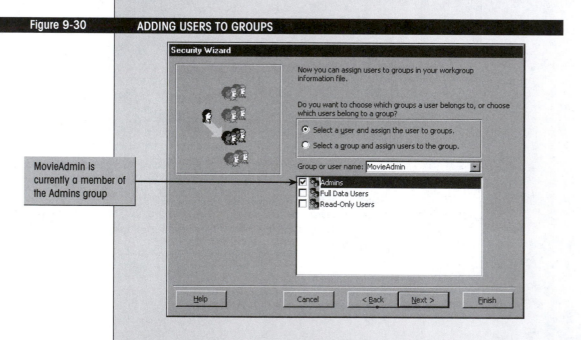

3. Type **mwoodward** in the User name text box , click the **Add this user to the list** button, type **cwhite** in the User name text box, click the **Add this user to the list** button, and then click the **Next** button. The next dialog box, which is shown in Figure 9-30, lets you add database users to specific groups. As you see, MovieAdmin is currently in the Admins group.

Figure 9-30 ADDING USERS TO GROUPS

MovieAdmin is currently a member of the Admins group

4. Click the **Group or user name** list arrow, click **mwoodward**, check the **Read-Only Users** option, click the **Group or user name** list arrow, click **cwhite**, check the **Full Data Users** option, and then click the **Next** button. The final wizard dialog box, which is shown in Figure 9-31, asks you to choose a name and location for the back-up file the wizard will create.

Figure 9-31 **SAVING THE BACK-UP FILE**

5. Click the **Finish** button to accept the default name and location. The One Step Security Wizard Report is shown in Print Preview. This report contains the information you need to re-create the workgroup information file, and the users of the database. You will export it to Word so that you can print it later.

6. Click the **OfficeLinks** button list arrow on the toolbar, and click **Publish It with MS Word** to export the report to a Word document.

7. Close the Word document, which is assigned the name *swz_rptSecure*, and then close the report. A dialog box appears and asks if you want to save the report as a Snapshot file.

8. Click the **No** button to return to the Database window.

9. Close the **MovieSecure** database and exit Access. You are exiting because you are currently logged on as MovieAdmin. To log on as another user, you must exit Access and then open it again.

Next you and Carolyn will test the security of the database.

Testing User-Level Security

To test the MovieSecure workgroup information file that is currently in use, you will log on as *cwhite* and test this user's access to various objects in the database. Recall that this user is a member of the Full Data Users group.

To test the security of theMovieSecure database:

1. Start **Access**, open the **MovieSecure** database, type **cwhite** in the Name text box, and then click the **OK** button. Recall that you have not assigned a password to this user.

2. Click **Forms** on the Objects bar in the Database window, click **frmReportsSwitchboard**, and then click **Open**. The form opens fine. Now you'll test to be sure that reports can be previewed.

3. Click the **Employee List** option, and then click the **Preview** button. The Employee List report opens in Print Preview.

4. Click the **Close** button to close the report, and then click the **Design** button in the Database window to open the **frmReportsSwitchboard** form in Design view. You receive the error message shown in Figure 9-32.

Figure 9-32	TESTING USER-LEVEL SECURITY ON THE FRMREPORTS SWITCHBOARD FORM

5. Click the **OK** button, and then close the **frmReportsSwitchboard** form.

6. Click **Tables** on the Objects bar in the Database window, click **tblEmployees**, and then click the **Design** button. You receive the error message shown in Figure 9-33.

Figure 9-33	TESTING USER-LEVEL SECURITY ON THE TBLEMPLOYEES TABLE

7. Click the **No** button to close the dialog box. You will conduct one more test to determine whether users can make changes to their own permissions.

8. Click **Tools** on the menu bar, point to **Security**, and then click **User and Group Permissions**.

9. Make sure that **cwhite** is selected in the User/Group Name list box, that **Table** is selected in the object list box, that **tblEmployees** is selected in the Object Name list box, and then click the **Read Design**, **Modify Design**, and **Administer** check boxes.

10. Click the **OK** button. You receive the error message shown in Figure 9-34.

Figure 9-34	TESTING USER-LEVEL SECRUITY ON DATABASE PERMISSIONS

11. Click the **OK** button in the error message, and then click the **Cancel** button in the User and Group Permissions dialog box.

Carolyn is curious how this new workgroup information file, MovieSecure, will affect users' access to other databases on which the User-Level Security Wizard has not been run. For example, what would happen if you were to close the secure database, MovieSecure, and then open the Movie9 database, which is an unsecured copy? You will test this next.

To test an unsecured database:

1. Close the **MovieSecure** database, but do not exit Access. This way the current user, *cwhite,* is still logged on.

2. Open the **Movie9** database from the **Tutorial.09** folder on your local or network drive. This is the original file you copied at the beginning of this tutorial.

3. Click **Forms** on the Objects bar of the Database window, click **frmReportsSwitchboard**, and click **Design** to open this form in Design view. It opens as it normally would without security implemented.

4. Close the **frmReportsSwitchboard** form, click **Tables** on the Objects bar of the Database window, and open the **tblEmployees** table in **Design** view. Again note that it opens as it normally would. To investigate why these objects open with no error messages, you'll take a look at the security settings.

5. Close the **tblEmployees** table, click **Tools** on the menu bar, point to **Security**, and then click **User and Group Accounts**. Note that the same users and groups that were defined for the MovieSecure database exist in this database as well, as shown in Figure 9-35. This is because you are still using the new MovieSecure workgroup information file. Recall that the users and groups, passwords, and PIDs are all stored in this file.

Figure 9-35	MOVIESECURE WORKGROUP INFORMATION FILE ON ORIGINAL DATABASE

6. Click the **Name** list arrow, and then click **cwhite**. Note that cwhite is a member of two groups: the Full Data Users group and the Users group. Recall that all new users created by the database administrator are automatically added to the Users group. In MovieSecure, the Users group has no permissions to any of the database objects. Next you'll see what rights the Users group has in this database.

7. Click **OK** to close the User and Group Accounts dialog box, click **Tools** on the menu bar, point to **Security**, and then click **User and Group Permissions**.

8. Click the **Groups** option button, click **Users** in the User/Group Name list box, click the **Object Type** list arrow, click **Table**, and then click **tblEmployees** in the Object Name list box. See Figure 9-36. Note the permissions that all Users group members have in an unsecured database. They have permissions to read, write, and change all of the objects. However, in the MovieSecure database, members of the Users group have no permissions.

| Figure 9-36 | PERMISSIONS FOR USERS GROUP MEMBERS IN AN UNSECURED DATABASE |

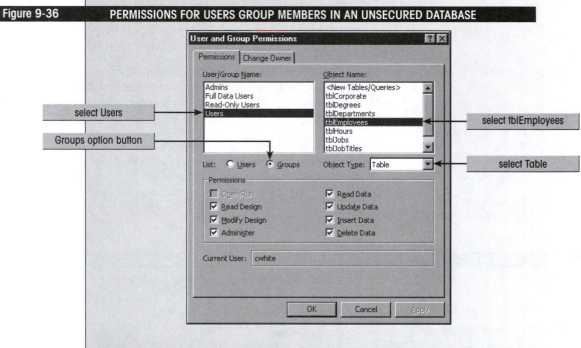

9. Click **OK** to close the User and Group Permissions dialog box.

10. Close the database and exit Access.

Joining the Default Workgroup

Next, you and Carolyn will rejoin the default workgroup information file, SYSTEM.MDW so that it can be used with other Access databases. You will then create a shortcut to the secured MovieSecure database which uses the Workgroup information file created for it.

To join the default workgroup information file:

1. Right-click the **Start** button, and then click **Find** on the shortcut menu if you are using Windows 98, or **Search** if you are using Windows 2000.

2. Type **Wrkgadm** in the Named text box, click the **Look in** list arrow, and select the local hard drive or the network drive containing the application files. (Check with your instructor if you are unsure which to select.)

3. Click the **Find Now** or **Search Now** button, and the Wrkgadm file is visible in the list box.

4. Double-click the **Wrkgadm** file to open the Workgroup Administrator.

5. Click the **Join** button in the Workgroup Administrator dialog box.

6. Click the **Browse** button, and navigate to the SYSTEM.MDW location that you wrote down near the beginning of this session.

7. Click **SYSTEM.MDW**, click **Open**, and then click the **OK** button. You receive the message dialog box shown in Figure 9-37.

| Figure 9-37 | JOINING THE DEFAULT WORKGROUP INFORMATION FILE |

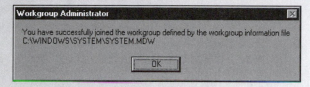

8. Click the **OK** button, and then click the **Exit** button in the Workgroup Administrator dialog box.

Next you'll open an unsecured database to see the effect of using the default SYSTEM.MDW workgroup information file.

To open an unsecured database while the default workgroup information file is in use:

1. Start **Access** and then open the **Movie9** database.

2. Click **Tools** on the menu bar, point to **Security**, and then click **User and Group Accounts**. The default user and groups are visible, as shown in Figure 9-38. The only user is Admin and the only groups are Admins and Users. These are the default user and groups specified earlier in this tutorial.

Figure 9-38   **DEFAULT USERS AND GROUPS**

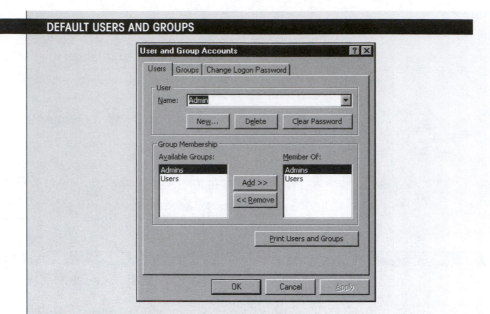

3. Click **OK** to close the User and Group Accounts dialog box, close the database, and exit Access.

Creating a Shortcut to an Access Database and its Workgroup Information File

You and Carolyn want to leave the default workgroup information file in use and use the moviesecure.mdw file specifically when you work in the MovieSecure database. To do this, you can create a shortcut on the desktop that opens Access and the MovieSecure database using the workgroup information file specified by the shortcut.

An example of the Target property of a shortcut that opens a database with a specific workgroup information file is:

"C:\Program Files\Microsoft Office\Office\Msaccess.exe"
"C:\Tutorial.09\MovieSecure.mdb" /wrkgrp "C:\Tutorial.09\MovieSecure.mdw"

The *"C:\Program Files\Microsoft Office\Office\Msaccess.exe"* portion of the property specifies the program to open—*Msaccess.exe* is located in the *Office* folder, which is in the *Microsoft Office* folder, which is in the *Program Files* folder on the *C* drive.

The *"C:\Tutorial.09\MovieSecure.mdb"* segment specifies the name of the Access database to open—*MovieSecure.mdb* located in the *Tutorial.09* folder on drive *C*.

The */wrkgrp "C:\Tutorial.09\MovieSecure.mdw"* segment specifies that the workgroup information file of the Access database is *MovieSecure.mdw*, located in the *Tutorial.09* folder on drive *C*.

To create the shortcut, you'll use the Find/Search feature in Windows to locate the Msaccess.exe program file. Then you'll add the remaining string necessary to complete the Target property of the shortcut.

To create a shortcut to the MovieSecure database:

1. Right-click the **Start** button, and then click **Find** on the shortcut menu if you are using Windows 98, or **Search** if you are using Windows 2000.

2. Type **Msaccess** in the Named text box, click the **Look in** list arrow, and select the local hard drive or the network drive containing the application files. (Check with your instructor if you are unsure which to select.)

3. Click the **Find Now** or **Search Now** button, and the Msaccess file is shown in the list box.

4. Right-click the name of the file, and then click **Create Shortcut** on the shortcut menu. You will receive the message dialog box shown in Figure 9-39. It asks if you want to place the shortcut on the desktop.

Figure 9-39	CREATING THE MOVIESECURE SHORTCUT

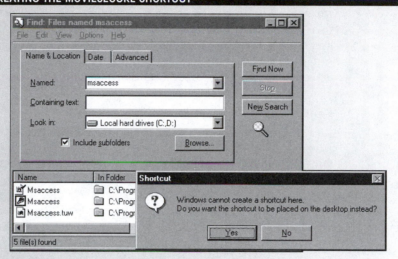

5. Click **Yes**, and then close the Find dialog box or Search Results window.

6. Right-click the **Shortcut to Msaccess** icon on the desktop, and then click **Properties** on the shortcut menu.

7. Click at the end of the target text and type **"C:\Tutorial.09\MovieSecure.mdb" /wrkgrp "C:\Tutorial.09\MovieSecure.mdw"**. This is the path to the MovieSecure file and the MovieSecure workgroup information file, assuming that they are located on the local hard drive in a folder named Tutorial.09. If these files are in another location, you will have to specify it in the path you type. Click **OK** to close the properties dialog box.

8. Right-click the **Shortcut to Msaccess** icon, click **Rename** on the shortcut menu, type **MovieSecure**, and then press the **Enter** key.

9. Test the shortcut by double-clicking it. Access launches, the MovieSecure database opens, and you are prompted to log on.

10. Type **MovieAdmin** in the Name text box, press the **Tab** key, type **moviecam** in the password text box, and then click the **OK** button.

You and Carolyn plan to put a shortcut on the desktops of all employees who use the database. Then they will not have to join the appropriate workgroup information file because that will happen automatically via the shortcut.

Assigning Permissions

You can assign two types of permissions in user-level security: explicit and implicit. **Explicit permissions** are granted directly to a user account and no other account is affected. **Implicit permissions** are granted to a group account. When you add a user to a group, the group's permissions are granted to that user; removing a user from a group takes away those permissions.

A user's security level is based on both the implicit and explicit permissions of that user, and that level is always the least restrictive of the two. This means that you can add a user to a group that has a particular level of permissions, yet still give that user less restrictive permissions than those of group to which he or she belongs. The simplest way to administer a workgroup of users is to create new groups and assign permissions to the group. You can then add users to the group that has restrictions that are closest to what you want for that user, and, if necessary, add additional permissions to the individual user.

Only a member of the Admins group, or a user who has Administer permission for an object, or the owner of an object, can change permissions.

Owners

The user who creates a table, query, form, report, or macro is the **owner** of that object. The same group previously identified as having the ability to change permissions can also change ownership of the database or the objects in it. The simplest way to change ownership of all the objects in the database is to create a new database and import all of the objects, or run the User-Level Security Wizard. The user who is logged on will then have ownership.

Group accounts cannot own databases, but can own database objects. In this case, all the members of the group own the object.

Changing Permissions

You and Carolyn decide that the Read-Only Users group should have read-only rights to all data except that in the tblEmployees table. Because this table contains salary information, you want only a small group of users to have access to it.

REFERENCE WINDOW
<u>Changing Permissions</u>
■ Click Tools on the menu bar, point to Security, and then click User and Group Permissions.
■ Select the Users or Groups option button to select whether you are changing permissions for a user or a group, and then select the user or group from the User/Group Name list box.
■ In the Object Name list box, select the object for which you want to change permissions.
■ Click the appropriate permissions, and then click OK to close the User and Group Permissions dialog box.

Your first step will be to remove the group's rights to this data. Then you will test the change and assign an individual user the rights to that data.

To change permissions for a group:

1. Click **Tools** on the menu bar, point to **Security**, and then click **User and Group Permissions**.

2. Click the **Groups** option button, and then click **Read-Only Users** in the User/Group Name list box.

3. Click **tblEmployees** in the Object Name list box, and clear the **Read Design** check box if necessary, as shown in Figure 9-40.

Figure 9-40   CLEARING THE PERMISSIONS FOR READ-ONLY USERS

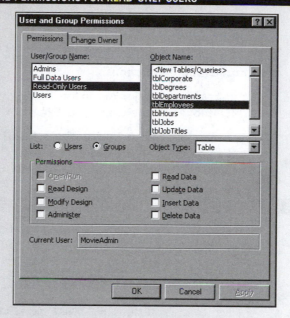

4. Click **OK** to close the User and Group Permissions dialog box.

5. Close the **MovieSecure** database and exit Access.

6. Start **Access** and open the **MovieSecure** database by double-clicking the shortcut on the desktop.

7. Type **mwoodward** in the Name text box, and then click the **OK** button. This user is a member of the Read-Only Users group.

8. Click **Tables** on the Objects bar in the Database window, click **tblEmployees**, and then click **Open**. This user does not have permission to modify this object.

9. Click the **OK** button to close the message box and return to the Database window.

10. Close the **MovieSecure** database and exit Access.

You now know that the change to the Read-Only Users group took effect, so you will add another user to the group—rjenkins. Richard Jenkins is a manager in Human Resources and needs access to the employee data. You will modify his permissions to include the tblEmployees table. You also want to enable his rights to modify data in the tblEmployees table.

To add a new user and change permissions:

1. Double-click the **shortcut** to MovieSecure on the desktop, type **MovieAdmin** in the Name text box, type **moviecam** in the Password text box, and then click the **OK** button. You need to log on as an administrator or owner to add users and change permissions.

2. Click **Tools** on the menu bar, point to **Security**, and then click **User and Group Accounts**.

3. Click the **New** button, type **rjenkins** in the Name text box, and then type **rjmovie2468** in the Personal ID text box.

4. Click **OK**, click **Read-Only Users** in the Available Groups list box, and then click the **Add** button.

5. Click **OK**, click **Tools** on the menu bar, point to **Security**, and then click **User and Group Permissions**.

6. If necessary, click **rjenkins** in the User/Group Name list box, and then click **tblEmployees** in the Object Name list box.

7. Click the **Read Data**, **Update Data**, **Insert Data**, and **Delete Data** check boxes, as shown in Figure 9-41. The Read Design check box is checked automatically when you click the Read Data option.

Figure 9-41   **CHANGING PERMISSIONS FOR RJENKINS**

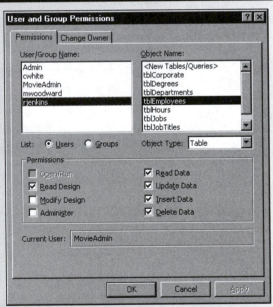

8. Click the **OK** button to accept the changes.

9. Close the **MovieSecure** database and exit Access.

Now that you have made the necessary changes to the user account, you need to log on as rjenkins to test them. You will do that next. In addition, you need to determine the method for a user to set up a password when he or she first logs on.

Setting Passwords

Passwords for the user security accounts are created so that no other user can log on using that name. You and Carolyn plan to have users establish their own passwords the first time they log on to the new system. As you have seen, by default Access assigns a blank password to any new user in the workgroup. For a new user to establish a password, they must start Access, log on with that user name, and then open User and Group Accounts from the Security menu. The password can be entered on the Change Logon Password tab.

REFERENCE WINDOW   **RW**

Clearing a Password

- Click Tools on the menu bar, point to Security, and then click User and Group Accounts.
- Click the Name list arrow, scroll down, and then click the name of the user for whom you want to clear the password.
- Click the Clear Password button, and then click OK to close the User and Group Accounts dialog box.

A password can be 1 to 20 characters in length, can include any combination of numbers and special characters, and is case-sensitive. Neither you nor your users can recover a password if they forget it. If a user forgets a password, an administrative user must log on and then clear the password for that user.

Next you will test the changes to the rjenkins permissions, set a password as rjenkins, and then log back on as the administrative user to clear the password.

To set and clear a password:

1. Double-click the **shortcut** to MovieSecure on the desktop, type **rjenkins** in the Name text box, and then click the **OK** button.

2. Click **Tools** on the menu bar, point to **Security**, click **User and Group Accounts**, and then click the **Change Logon Password** tab.

3. Type **test** in the New Password text box, press the **Tab** key, and then type **test** in the Verify text box.

4. Click the **OK** button to accept the change, open the **tblEmployees** table in Datasheet view, tab to the **Hourly Rate** field for Thomas Arquette, and then type **60.00**. Note that the change is accepted.

5. Press the **Esc** key to cancel the change, close the **tblEmployees** table, close the **MovieSecure** database, and exit Access.

6. Double-click the **shortcut** to MovieSecure on the desktop, type **MovieAdmin** in the Name text box, type **moviecam** in the Password text box, and then click the **OK** button.

7. Click **Tools** on the menu bar, point to **Security**, and then click **User and Group Accounts**.

8. Click the **Name** list arrow, scroll down, and then click **rjenkins** from the list, as shown in Figure 9-42.

| Figure 9-42 | CLEARING THE PASSWORD FOR RJENKINS |

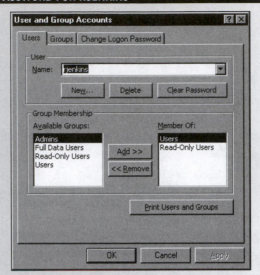

9. Click the **Clear Password** button, and then click **OK** to close the User and Group Accounts dialog box.

10. Close the **Movie9** database and exit Access.

Removing **User-Level Security**

There are times when you might need to remove user-level security from a secured database. This is a two-step process. First, log on to the database as a workgroup administrator, and give the Users group permissions on all tables, queries, forms, reports, and macros. Then return ownership of the database and objects to the default Admin user. To do this, exit, log on as Admin, create a blank database, and then import all of the objects from the original database into the blank database. You also should clear any password that you set for the Admin user if the users will not be using the default workgroup information file. Recall that in the default workgroup information file, Admin has no password.

Now that you and Carolyn have set up the groups for the new database, you can add users as necessary. Users will be able to create their own passwords for the system and, as administrators, you and Carolyn can make modifications and changes as necessary to the database objects. You plan to use the menus and switchboards that you developed in earlier tutorials as the user interface to the system, but you will not need to use code to disable the Bypass key now that user-level security is in place.

Session 9.2 QUICK | CHECK

1. What is a workgroup?

2. In an unsecured database, the default user is _____.

3. The default workgroup information file is named _____.

4. What is the simplest method for setting up database security?

5. The workgroup information file you create or use by default contains what prede-fined user and group accounts?

6. What is the difference between a PID and a password?

7. The user who creates a table, query, form, report, or macro is the _____ of that object.

8. Who can change permissions for a user or group?

9. If a user forgets a password, is it possible to recover it?

REVIEW ASSIGNMENTS

The Hours9 database is similar to the MovieCam Technologies database you worked on in this tutorial. You want to implement user-level security on the database. You will create the users and run the User-Level Security Wizard to accomplish this task.

1. Right-click the Start button, and then click Find or Search on the shortcut menu.

2. Type Wrkgadm in the Named text box, click the Look in list arrow, and select the local hard drive or the network drive containing the application files. (Check with your instructor if you are unsure which to select.)

3. Click the Find Now or Search Now button, and the Wrkgadm file is shown in the list box.

4. Double-click the Wrkgadm file to open the Workgroup Administrator dialog box. Make sure that you write down the location of the default workgroup information file, SYSTEM.MDW, so that you can rejoin it later.

5. Join the workgroup named HOURSECURE located in the Tutorial.09 folder on your local or network drive.

6. Start Access, and open the **Hours9** database located in the Tutorial.09 folder on your network or local drive.

7. Click Tools on the menu bar, point to Security, and then click User and Group Accounts.

8. Click the New button to create a new user, and then type "HoursAdmin" in the Name text box.

9. Press the Tab button, type "Hours1234" in the Personal ID text box, and then click the OK button.

10. With Admins selected in the Available Groups list box, click the Add>> button to make HoursAdmin a member of the Admins group.

11. Click the Name list arrow, and then click Admin.

12. Make sure that Admins is selected, in the Member Of list box and then click the <<Remove button.

13. Click the Change Logon Password tab, press the Tab key to move to the New Password text box, type "hours", press the Tab key, type "hours" again to confirm, and then click the OK button.

14. Exit Access, then restart it, open the **Hours9** database, type "HoursAdmin" in the Name text box, and then press the Enter key.

15. Click Tools on the menu bar, point to Security, click User-Level Security Wizard, make sure that the Modify my current workgroup information file option is selected, and then click the Next button. All the objects should be checked in the next dialog box. Click the Next button, click the Full Data Users check box, click the Next button, make sure the No, the Users group should not have any permissions option is checked, and then click the Next button.

16. Type "tjames" in the User Name text box , click the Add this user to the list option, click the Next button, click the Group or user name list arrow, click tjames, check the Full Data Users option, and then click the Next button.

17. Click the Finish button to accept the default name and location. The One Step Security Wizard Report is shown in Print Preview.

18. Click the Print button and then close the report.

19. Close the **Hours9** database and exit Access.

20. Repeat Steps 1-4 to open the Workgroup Administrator, and then join the default workgroup information file SYSTEM.MDW.

CASE PROBLEMS

Case 1. Edwards and Company   User-level security has been established on the Edwards and Company database. The administrative user and owner of the database is EdwardAdmin. No password has been established. You need to create two new users and add them to the Read-Only Users group.

1. Right-click the Start button, and then click Find or Search on the shortcut menu.

2. Type "Wrkgadm" in the Named text box, click the Look in list arrow, and select the local hard drive or network drive containing the application files. (Check with your instructor if you are unsure which to select.)

3. Click the Find Now or Search Now button. The Wrkgadm file is visible in the list box.

4. Double-click the Wrkgadm file to open the Workgroup Administrator dialog box. Note the location of the default workgroup information file, SYSTEM.MDW, so that you can rejoin it later.

5. Join the EDWARDSECURE workgroup information file located in the Tutorial.09 folder on your local or network drive.

6. Start Access, and open the **Edward9** database located in the Tutorial.09 folder on the network or local drive.

7. Type "EdwardAdmin" in the Name text box, and then click the OK button.

8. Click Tools on the menu bar, point to Security, and then click User and Group Accounts.

9. Click the New button to create a new user and then type "jedwards" in the Name text box.

10. Press the Tab button, type "Edwards1234" in the Personal ID text box, and then click the OK button.

11. Select Read-Only Users in the Available Groups list box, and click the Add>> button to make jedwards a member of the group.

12. Click the New button to create a new user, and then type "medwards" in the Name text box.

13. Press the Tab button, type "Edwards5678" in the Personal ID text box, and then click the OK button.

14. Select Read-Only Users in the Available Groups list box, and click the Add>> button to make medwards a member of the group.

15. Click OK to close the User and Group Accounts dialog box, close the **Edward9** database, and then exit Access.

16. Restart Access, open the **Edward9** database, type "jedwards" in the Name text box, and then press the Enter key.

17. Click Tools on the menu bar, point to Security, and then click User and Group Accounts.

18. Click the Change Logon Password tab, type "edwards" in the New Password text box, type "edwards" in the Verify text box, and then click the OK button.

19. Close the **Edward9** database and exit Access.

20. Repeat Steps 1-4 to open the Workgroup Administrator, and then join the default workgroup information file SYSTEM.MDW.

Case 2. San Diego County Information Systems You are going to implement user-level security on the training database and need to create a workgroup information file to store the new users and passwords. You will create this file next.

1. Right-click the Start button, and then click Find or Search on the shortcut menu.

2. Type "Wrkgadm" in the Named text box, click the Look in list arrow, and select the local hard drive or network drive containing the application files. (Check with your instructor if you are unsure which to select.)

3. Click the Find Now or Search Now button. The Wrkgadm file is shown in the list box.

4. Double-click Wrkgadm to open the Workgroup Administrator. Note the location of the default workgroup information file, SYSTEM.MDW, so that you can rejoin it later.

5. Click the Create button, type "*your name*" in the Name text box, and then type "San Diego County ISD" in the Organization text box.

6. Type "ISD1234" in the Workgroup ID text box, click the OK button, click the Browse button, click the Look in list arrow, and navigate to the Tutorial.09 folder.

7. Change the filename to "ISDSECURE" and then click the Open button.

8. Click the OK button to accept the change, click the OK button when the new name and path are specified, and then click the OK button again to acknowledge that the file has been created successfully.

9. Click the Exit button to close the Workgroup Administrator, start Access, and open the **ISD9** database located in the Tutorial.09 folder on the network or local drive.

10. Click Tools on the menu bar, point to Security, and then click User and Group Accounts.

11. Click the New button to create a new user, and then type "ISDAdmin" in the Name text box.

12. Press the Tab button, type "ISD1234" in the Personal ID text box, and then click the OK button.

13. With Admins selected in the Available Groups list box, click the Add>> button to make ISDAdmin a member of the Admins group, click the Name list arrow, and then click Admin.

14. Make sure that Admins in the Member Of list box is selected, and then click the <<Remove button.

15. Click Tools on the menu bar, point to Analzye, and then click Documentor.

16. Make sure that the Tables tab is selected, click the Select All button, click the Options button, click the Permissions by User and Group check box, click the Nothing option for Include for Fields, click the Include for Indexes option and make sure that the Properties and Relationships boxes are not checked.

17. Click the OK button, and then click the OK button again to preview the report.

18. Print the report, close the **ISD9** database, and exit Access.

19. Repeat Steps 1-4 to open the Workgroup Administrator, and then join the default workgroup information file SYSTEM.MDW.

Case 3. Christenson Homes   The frmLots form in the Homes9 database is used for entering data into the tblLots table and the tblCustomers table. Roberta wants to be able to look up a record by the subdivision and then by the address. On the frmLotSearch form you will create a list box to display the subdivision and lot address. You will open the list box by double-clicking the Address text box on the frmLots form.

1. Start Access, and open the **Homes9** database located in the Tutorial.09 folder on the network or local drive. A blank form named frmFindLots has been created in the database.

2. Open the frmFindLots form, and create a list box on the form that looks up the Subdivision name and the Lot address from the tblSubdivision and tblLot tables, respectively.

3. Create a button to find the record on the frmLots form. Type the following code to look up the data:

```
Private Sub cmdFind_Click()
Dim rst As DAO.Recordset
'Find the record and then close the dialog box
Set rst = Forms!frmLots.RecordsetClone
rst.FindFirst "Address = " & lstFind
Forms!frmLots.Bookmark = rst.Bookmark
DoCmd.Close acForm, "frmFindLots"
End Sub
```

4. Create a button to cancel (close) the frmFindLots form. You can use the Command Button Wizard for this.

5. Add the following code to the frmLots form that will open the frmFindLots form when the Address text box is double-clicked.

```
Private Sub Address_DblClick(Cancel As Integer)
    DoCmd.OpenForm "frmFindLots"
End Sub
```

6. Close the **Homes9** database and exit Access.

Case 4. Sonoma Farms   You plan to implement user-level security on the Sonoma Farms database. You need to create a workgroup information file named SONOMASECURE. You will run the User-Level Security Wizard to do this. In addition to the Admin group and Users group, you plan to create a Read-Only Users group. You will create a new Admin user name—SonomaAdmin—but will not assign a password. You also will create one new user name—jdowney—and add him to the Read-Only Users group.

1. Run the Workgroup Administrator to create a new workgroup information file named "SONOMASECURE", and save it in the Tutorial.09 folder. Type "*your name*", "Sonoma Farms", and "Sonoma1234" as the ID. Be sure to note the location of the default workgroup information file, SYSTEM.MDW, so that you can rejoin it later.

2. Open Access, and then open the **Sonoma9** database from the Tutorial.09 folder on the local or network drive.

3. Create a new administrator named "SonomaAdmin" with a PID of "Sonoma1234", add this user to the Admins group, and remove Admin from the Admins group.

4. Create a password, "Sonoma", for Admin, close the **Sonoma9** database, and exit Access.

5. Open Access, open the **Sonoma9** database from the Tutorial.09 folder on the network or local drive, and log on as SonomaAdmin.

6. Run the User-Level Security Wizard, create a Read-Only Users group, make sure that the Users group has no permissions, and create one new user named "jdowney" with no password.

7. Add jdowney to the Read-Only Users group.

8. Print the User-Level Security report.

9. Close the **Sonoma9** database and exit Access.

10. Repeat Step 1 to join the default workgroup information file, SYSTEM.MDW.

QUICK | CHECK ANSWERS

Session 9.1

1. To write VBA code that works directly with the data in your application, you must work with ADO or DAO.

2. Use DAO to write code that makes changes to the structure of tables and queries in a JET (.mdb) database or to manipulate recordsets behind forms.

3. The JET engine is the database engine that Access uses for all of its native database management.

4. The object at the top of the DAO hierarchy is the DBEngine object. The Connection object is at the top of the ADO hierarchy.

5. The types of Recordset objects are table, dynaset, snapshot, forward-only, and dynamic.

6. A user can create a system object by using *USys* as the first four characters in the object name.

7. Every form has a RecordsetClone property that you can use to get a copy of the form's underlying recordset.

8. The Findfirst method of the Recordset object begins searching at the beginning of the recordset and continues to the end.

9. An object library is a collection of prebuilt objects and functions that you can use in VBA code.

Session 9.2

1. An Access workgroup is a group of users in a multiuser environment who share data.
2. In an unsecured database, the default user is Admin.
3. The default workgroup information file is named SYSTEM.MDW.
4. The simplest method for protecting an Access database is to set a password on it.
5. The workgroup information file you create or use by default contains Users and Admins Group accounts and an Admin user.
6. A password is used to access the application; the PID is used as a part of the encryption process.
7. The user who creates a table, query, form, report, or macro is the owner of that object.
8. The owner of the database or any member of the Admins group can change permissions for a user or group.
9. No. However, their account can be reset so that they can create a new password.

OBJECTIVES

In this tutorial you will:

- Learn how hyperlinks are used in Access

- Create hyperlinks on a form to other database objects

- Create hyperlinks that address e-mail

- Add hyperlinks to a menu bar

- Learn about data access pages and how to use them

- Use grouping levels to create a data access page

- Format controls on a data access page

- Apply a theme to a data access page

- Export a query to an HTML document

CONNECTING TO THE WORLD WIDE WEB

Working with Hyperlinks and Data Access Pages in the MovieCam Technologies Database

CASE

MovieCam Technologies

You and Carolyn recently met with Amanda to review your progress on the MovieCam technologies database. Amanda wants you to create the database main switchboard form that users will use to navigate to other switchboards.

Many users have Internet access, and all of them have access to the company intranet. Amanda wants you to use the Web features of Access to provide a method for navigating to the Web from within the database. To accomplish this, you and Carolyn decide to add some Web options to the custom menu bar that you already created.

One of the original objectives for the database was to integrate it with the company intranet. This integration would be beneficial to MovieCam employees in several ways. Amanda wants employees who don't have access to the MovieCam database to be able to view their time card records online. She also wants all employees to have the ability to go online and modify certain portions of their employee record, including current mailing address, phone number, and emergency contact information.

Finally, you and Carolyn want to experiment with exporting data to the Web. At times, managers need to see query results so they can complete quarterly or annual reports. It occurs to you that exporting a query to an HTML document might be a simple way to handle infrequent requests for specific data.

SESSION 10.1

In this session you will study hyperlinks and how they are used in Access. You will insert hyperlinks on a form to objects in the database. You also will insert a hyperlink to an e-mail address. You will complete the MovieCam menu bar by adding Web-related commands to it, and include a hyperlink to the Microsoft Home Page.

Introduction

Access contains a number of features designed to let you take advantage of the resources on the World Wide Web (WWW). You can embed hyperlinks on forms, assign hyperlinks to a toolbar or menu command, create data access pages (a new object in Access 2000), and so forth. A **hyperlink** is text or an image that you click to navigate to other parts of a file, to other documents on your computer or network, or to Internet addresses. A **data access page** is an object in the database that lets you display, edit, and manipulate other objects, such as tables, forms, and reports, so that they can be published to the Web using the Internet Explorer Web browser. (Data access pages do not work with all Web browsers.)

You and Carolyn still need to complete the main switchboard form for the MovieCam Technologies database. You want to be able to use the main switchboard to open the frmDataSwitchboard form and the frmReportsSwitchboard form. You also plan to add a button for exiting the database to the main switchboard.

Carolyn has suggested that you try a lightweight form for the main switchboard form. A **lightweight form** contains hyperlinks to the objects in the database that you want to open, rather than having controls that trigger VBA code. The form is called lightweight because it opens faster than a form containing VBA code.

Using Hyperlinks on a Form

You can create a hyperlink on a form to a Web site, another file, an e-mail address, or an object in the database. You create it by inserting a command button, label, or image control, and then setting the control's properties to tell the hyperlink where to jump. The address—the pathname to the file or URL—associated with the control is saved with the form and doesn't change, even if you move from one record to another. You also can store hyperlinks in a field in a table and then create a text box on a form that is bound to that field. In this instance, the hyperlink changes with each record as the user navigates through them. If the hyperlink address points to a Web site, the user's Web browser automatically opens when the hyperlink is clicked.

You use the Hyperlink Address and the Hyperlink SubAddress properties to design the hyperlink control. Use the **Hyperlink Address property** to specify the path to a document on the local or network drive or a Web site address. Use the **Hyperlink SubAddress property** to specify a particular location in a document, such as a bookmark in a Word document, or a particular object like a form or report in an Access database. Hyperlinks can be used to navigate to:

- *Word or Excel files:* A hyperlink can open any file created in a Microsoft Office application. Specify the path and filename of the document, such as *C:\MyDocuments\Report*, in the Hyperlink Address property text box.

- *HTML documents:* A hyperlink can navigate to an HTML file on the Web or on a network or local computer. The file is visible in a Web browser regardless of whether it's on a local drive, an intranet, or the Internet.

- *Internet addresses:* A hyperlink can navigate to other areas of the Internet besides the WWW. You can set a hyperlink address to transfer a file from an FTP server or to send electronic mail. To send e-mail, you specify the address in the Hyperlink Address property text box as follows: *mailto:krisoxford@msn.com*.

■ *Access database objects*: hyperlink can open any object, such as a form or a report, in the same database or in a different database. If the object is in the same Access database as the hyperlink, you leave the Hyperlink Address property blank and specify the name of the form or report (preceded by the word *Form* or *Report*) in the Hyperlink SubAddress property text box.

Creating a Lightweight Switchboard

You will create a main switchboard form that looks like the one shown in Figure 10-1. It will contain a button to open the frmDataSwitchboard form and a button to open the frmReportsSwitchboard form. The form also will contain a button to exit the application, and a hyperlink to e-mail Carolyn in case a user needs help with the database or has questions.

Figure 10-1	MOVIECAM MAIN SWITCHBOARD FORM

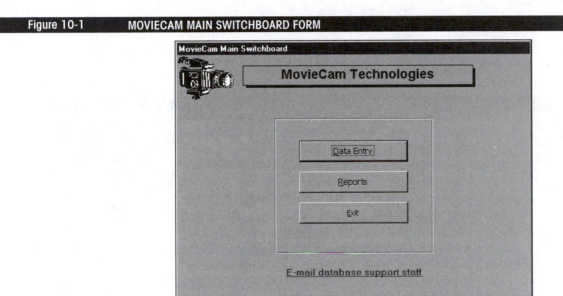

The Data Entry and Reports command buttons will be designed as hyperlinks to the specified switchboard form in the database. Hyperlinks can be formatted to look like standard command buttons and can include a keyboard shortcut just like command buttons that execute VBA code or macros.

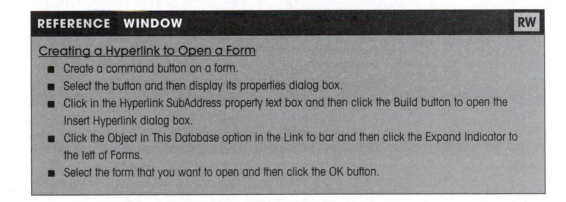

REFERENCE   WINDOW   **RW**

Creating a Hyperlink to Open a Form

■ Create a command button on a form.
■ Select the button and then display its properties dialog box.
■ Click in the Hyperlink SubAddress property text box and then click the Build button to open the Insert Hyperlink dialog box.
■ Click the Object in This Database option in the Link to bar and then click the Expand Indicator to the left of Forms.
■ Select the form that you want to open and then click the OK button.

You'll create the Exit button with the Command Button Wizard, and then write a VBA Sub procedure to exit the database. The label at the bottom of the switchboard will be a hyperlink to Carolyn's e-mail address. Clicking it will open Microsoft Outlook Express and address the e-mail if it is installed on your computer.

To create the frmMainSwitchboard form:

1. Start **Access**, and open the **Movie10** database located in the **Tutorial.10** folder on your local or network drive.

2. Click **Forms** on the Objects bar in the Database window, right-click **zsfrmMasterSwitchboard**, and then click **Copy** on the shortcut menu.

3. Right-click an empty area of the Database window, click **Paste** on the shortcut menu, type **frmMainSwitchboard** in the Paste As dialog box, and then click the **OK** button.

4. Open the new form in **Design** view, and maximize the form window. It should look like that shown in Figure 10-2.

Figure 10-2	MAIN SWITCHBOARD FORM IN DESIGN VIEW

5. Drag the bottom of the Detail section of the form down to the **4-inch** mark, show the toolbox if necessary, make sure the Controls Wizards button is *not* pressed in, click the **Command Button** button on the toolbox, and drag to draw a command button, as shown in Figure 10-3.

| Figure 10-3 | RESIZING THE MAIN SWITCHBOARD FORM |

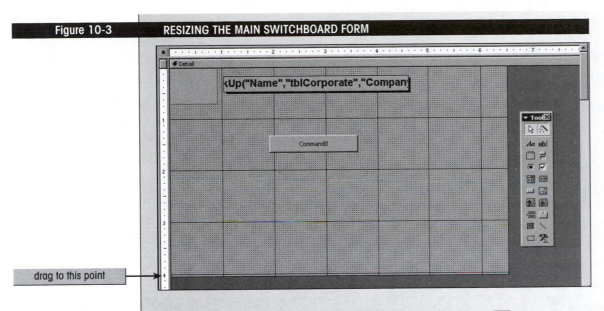

drag to this point

6. Click the button to select it, click the **Properties** button 🖭 on the toolbar, click the **All** tab if necessary, change the Name property to **cmdForms**, the Caption property to **&Data Entry**, click in the Hyperlink SubAddress property text box, and click the **Build** button ⟦…⟧. The Insert Hyperlink dialog box opens, as shown in Figure 10-4.

| Figure 10-4 | INSERT HYPERLINK DIALOG BOX |

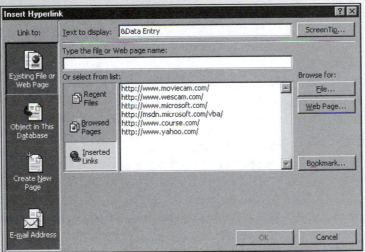

TROUBLE? Your list of recently used hyperlinks may be different than those displayed in Figure 10-4 depending on the sites that you have visited recently.

7. Click the **Object in This Database** option in the Link to bar, and then click the **Expand Indicator** ⟦+⟧ to the left of Forms. All the forms in the current database are shown.

8. Click **frmDataSwitchboard**, and then click the **OK** button. The Hyperlink SubAddress property text box now contains *Form frmDataSwitchboard*.

9. In the properties dialog box, scroll to and change the Fore Color property to **0** (this changes the text on the button to black), the Font Size property to **10**, and the Font Underline property to **No**. These changes make the hyperlink on the button look like a standard command button.

Next you will add the command button to open the frmReportsSwitchboard form. You will simply duplicate the button you just created, and make the necessary changes to the new button's properties.

To add the command button for the frmReportsSwitchboard form:

1. Make sure that the **Data Entry** button control is still selected, click **Edit** on the menu bar, and then click **Duplicate**. A duplicate button is created below the Data Entry button, as shown in Figure 10-5.

Figure 10-5   DUPLICATING THE COMMAND BUTTON

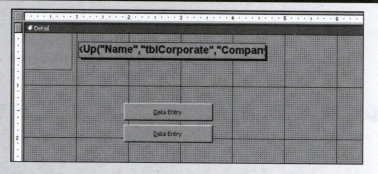

TROUBLE? You might see two menu bars: the mnuMovieCam toolbar you created earlier, and the default menu bar. Click View on the menu bar, point to Toolbars, and then click Customize. Scroll to mnuMovieCam, and click the check box to clear it.

2. Change the Name property of the new button to **cmdReports**, the Caption property to **&Reports**, the Hyperlink SubAddress to **Form frmReportsSwitchboard**, and then close the properties dialog box.

3. Switch to **Form** view and click each button to test it, and then use each button's keyboard shortcut key. These are **Alt+D** for the Data Entry button, and **Alt+R** for the Reports button.

4. Switch to **Design** view, click the **Control Wizards** button on the toolbox, click the **Command Button** button, and click and drag to draw a third button below the first two. The Command Button Wizard opens.

5. Click **Application** in the Categories list box, make sure that **Quit Application** is selected in the Actions list box, click the **Next** button, type **&Exit** in the Text box, click the **Next** button, type **cmdExit** in the text box that requests a name, and then click the **Finish** button.

6. Select all three buttons, right-click the buttons, point to **Size** on the shortcut menu, click **To Widest**, right-click the buttons again, point to **Size**, click **To Tallest**, right-click the buttons, point to **Align**, and then click **Left**. (You could also use the Align Left button [🅑] you added to the toolbar in Tutorial 6 if you are working on the same computer you used for Tutorial 6.)

7. Click **Format** on the menu bar, point to **Vertical Spacing**, click **Make Equal**, click the **Rectangle** button [▫] on the toolbox, and click and drag around the buttons, as shown in Figure 10-6.

Figure 10-6   **CREATING A RECTANGLE AROUND THE BUTTONS**

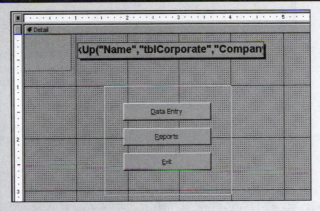

8. Click the **Save** button [💾] on the toolbar to save your changes, switch to **Form** view, and then click the **Exit** button to test it. The Access program closes. If a message box displays asking if you want to exit Access and empty the clipboard, click **Yes** to continue.

The switchboard needs a few finishing touches. You want to add a hyperlink label for sending e-mail to Carolyn, and you want to change the Caption property of the form so that it reads MovieCam Main Switchboard. You'll also add a few ScreenTips to the buttons.

To complete the frmMainSwitchboard form:

1. Start **Access**, open the **Movie10** database located in the **Tutorial.10** folder on your local or network drive, open the **frmMainSwitchboard** form in **Design** view, and then click the **Properties** button [📑] on the toolbar.

2. Type **MovieCam Main Switchboard** as the Caption property, click the **Data Entry** button, type **Open the data entry forms switchboard** in the ControlTip Text property, click the **Reports** button, type **Open the reports switchboard** in the ControlTip Text property, click the **Exit** button, type **Exit Access** in the ControlTip Text property, and then close the properties dialog box.

3. Change the form width to **5½"** and then click the **Save** button [💾] on the toolbar. Your form should look like that shown in Figure 10-7.

Figure 10-7	SIZING THE FORM

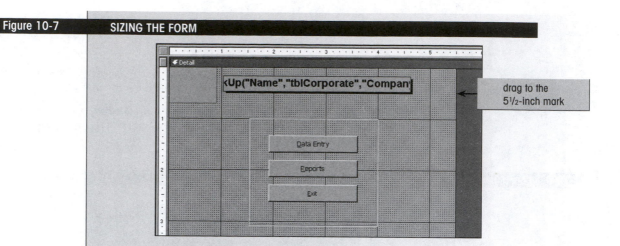

4. Click the **Insert Hyperlink** button [icon] on the Form Design toolbar. The Insert Hyperlink dialog box opens.

5. Click **E-mail Address** in the Link to bar, type **E-mail database support staff** in the Text to display text box, position the insertion point in the E-mail address text box, and then type **cwhite@moviecam.com**. Notice that the mailto: portion is added automatically to the beginning of the entry, as shown in Figure 10-8.

Figure 10-8	CREATING THE E-MAIL HYPERLINK

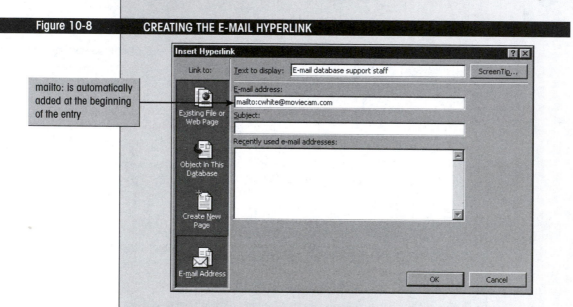

6. Click the **OK** button, and drag the label containing the hyperlink to approximately ¼" below the rectangle around the command buttons.

7. Click the **rectangle** to select it, hold down the **Shift** key, and click the new label containing the hyperlink so that both are selected.

8. Right-click the selected controls, point to **Size**, click **To Widest**, right-click the selected controls, point to **Align**, and then click **Left** (or **Right**, depending on how the label is positioned). Your form should look like that shown in Figure 10-9.

Figure 10-9	SIZING THE LABEL CONTROL

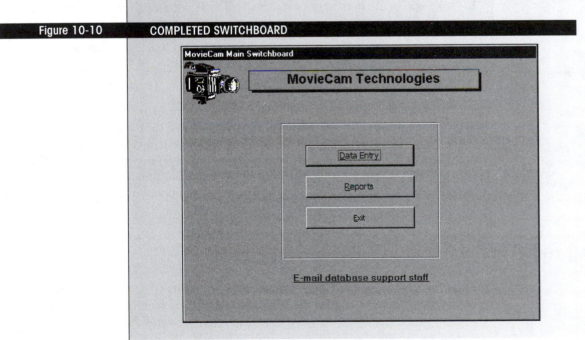

9. Click the **Detail** section of the form to deselect the two controls, click the **label containing the hyperlink** to select it, click the **Center** button on the toolbar to center the label text inside the box, and then click the **Save** button on the toolbar to save your changes.

Next you will test the hyperlink and the property changes that you made to the switchboard.

To test the frmMainSwitchboard form:

1. Switch to **Form** view. Your form should look like that shown in Figure 10-10.

Figure 10-10	COMPLETED SWITCHBOARD

2. Click the hyperlink **E-mail database support staff**. Microsoft Outlook Express opens (if it is installed) and you will see a new e-mail message addressed to cwhite@moviecam.com, as shown in Figure 10-11.

TROUBLE? If Outlook Express is not installed you may need to skip this step. If another e-mail program is the default e-mail system, a dialog box may display asking if you want to make Outlook Express your default mail client. If this happens, click No and continue without performing this step or Step 3.

Figure 10-11	ADDRESSED E-MAIL

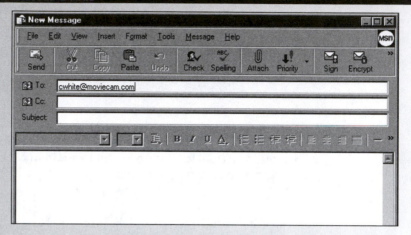

3. Close the New Message window to return to the switchboard.

4. Position the pointer over the Data Entry button. The ControlTip text is shown.

5. Test each of the two other command buttons to be sure that the ControlTip property settings work properly.

6. To close the form, click **File** on the menu bar, and then click **Close** to return to the Database window.

You and Carolyn are pleased with the frmMainSwitchboard form. It effectively controls the parts of the database to which users have access. When the database is ready for use, you plan to set the Startup properties to open the frmMainSwitchboard form when the database is opened. You also will set other options to hide the Database window, disable the shortcut menus, and set the mnuMovieCam menu bar as the default menu bar. Rather than disable the Bypass key, you will use the Startup settings in conjunction with the secured database and workgroup information file you created in Tutorial 9 to truly secure the system.

Using Hyperlinks on a Menu Bar

Carolyn has added some additional menu items to the mnuMovieCam menu bar that you created in Tutorial 6. She added the menu items Web and Help, as shown in Figure 10-12.

Figure 10-12	MNUMOVIECAM MENU BAR

The choices on the Help menu include two commands for working with the Access Help system. You want to add Web menu commands to search the Web and to go to the Microsoft Home Page so that users can browse for online training, classes, and other product information.

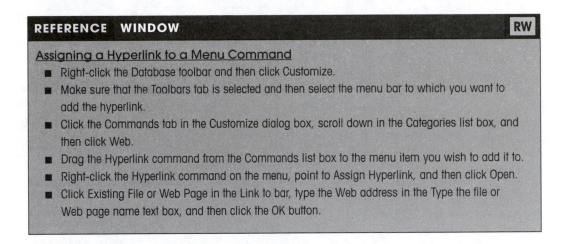

REFERENCE   WINDOW   RW

Assigning a Hyperlink to a Menu Command
- Right-click the Database toolbar and then click Customize.
- Make sure that the Toolbars tab is selected and then select the menu bar to which you want to add the hyperlink.
- Click the Commands tab in the Customize dialog box, scroll down in the Categories list box, and then click Web.
- Drag the Hyperlink command from the Commands list box to the menu item you wish to add it to.
- Right-click the Hyperlink command on the menu, point to Assign Hyperlink, and then click Open.
- Click Existing File or Web Page in the Link to bar, type the Web address in the Type the file or Web page name text box, and then click the OK button.

To assign a hyperlink to a toolbar button or menu command, you must add a button or a menu command, and then add the hyperlink to replace the command that is currently assigned to it. You will do this next.

To complete the mnuMovieCam menu bar:

1. Right-click the **Database** toolbar, and then click **Customize** on the shortcut menu, as shown in Figure 10-13. The Customize dialog box opens.

| Figure 10-13 | DATABASE TOOLBAR SHORTCUT MENU |

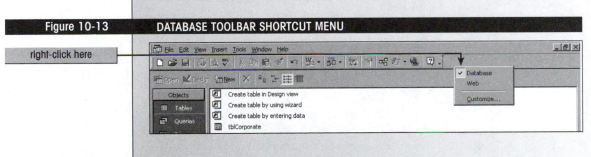

right-click here

2. Make sure that the **Toolbars** tab is selected, scroll down to the bottom of the list, and click the **mnuMovieCam** check box. The toolbar is shown.

3. Click the **Commands** tab in the Customize dialog box, scroll down in the Categories list box, and click **Web**.

4. Drag the **Search the Web** command from the Commands list box to the Web menu item, as shown in Figure 10-14.

Figure 10-14 ADDING THE SEARCH THE WEB COMMAND

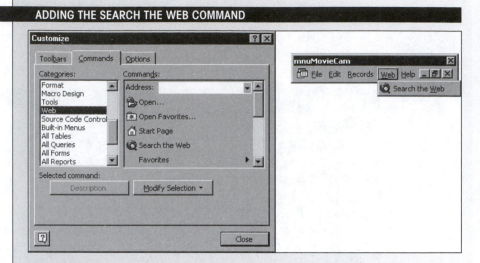

5. Scroll down in the Commands list box, click the **Hyperlink** command, and drag it below the Search the Web command on the Web menu.

6. Right-click the **Hyperlink** command, point to **Assign Hyperlink**, and then click **Open**. The Assign Hyperlink: Open dialog box opens, as shown in Figure 10-15.

Figure 10-15 ASSIGN HYPERLINK: OPEN DIALOG BOX

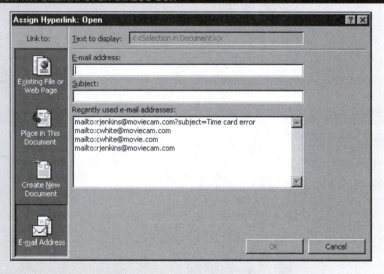

7. Click **Existing File or Web Page** in the Link to bar, type **www.microsoft.com** in the Type the file or Web page name text box, and then click the **OK** button.

8. Right-click the **Hyperlink** command, click the **Name** command, type **&Microsoft**, click outside the menu, and then close the Customize dialog box. You must be connected to the Web for the next step to work.

9. Click **Web** on the mnuMovieCam menu bar, and then click **Microsoft**. Internet Explorer launches and the home page for Microsoft is shown.

10. Close Internet Explorer to return to Access. Right-click the **Database** toolbar, click **Customize** on the shortcut menu, make sure that **Toolbars** is selected. Scroll down to the bottom of the list, click the **MnuMovieCam** check box to deselect it, and then close the Customize dialog box.

The Web commands that you added to the menu bar work well. Amanda is satisfied that the custom menu bar provides the options that users will need from within the database. The main switchboard works well and loads quickly because it has very little VBA code. Now that these items are completed, you and Carolyn are ready to work on the data access pages. In the next session, you will create two data access pages that will be placed on the company intranet.

Session 10.1 QUICK CHECK

1. What is a hyperlink?

2. What is a data access page?

3. The _____ property is used to specify the path to a document on the local or network drive or a Web site address.

4. The _____ property is used to specify a particular location in a document, such as a bookmark, or a particular Access database object such as a form or report.

5. What is the advantage of a lightweight switchboard?

6. A lightweight switchboard contains little or no _____.

7. How can you assign a hyperlink to a menu bar or toolbar?

SESSION 10.2

In this session you will create read-only and updateable data access pages. You will apply a theme to the pages, learn to format controls on a page, and work with grouping levels. You will create a hyperlink to e-mail an employee of MovieCam and create a hyperlink on one page that opens another page. You will open the data access pages in Internet Explorer, navigate between them, learn to edit data in a page, and you will export a query to an HTML document.

Data Access Pages

Not all MovieCam employees will have access to or be using the MovieCam database; however, they still need access to some of the database information. You can make this information available via the company's intranet by placing it in data access pages that can then be viewed in the Internet Explorer Web browser.

At Amanda's direction, you and Carolyn will create two data access pages: one read-only page that displays employee, time card, and hours data, and one updateable page that displays employee name, address, telephone number, and emergency contact information. Both pages will be uploaded to the MovieCam intranet.

Data access pages are Web pages that are separate from your Access database file and allow users with Web access to view and edit data in your tables. You create data access pages in much the same way that you create forms and reports.

Creating a Read-Only Data Access Page

The first data access page you create is based on the qryHoursByEmployee query, which Carolyn has already designed. Figure 10-16 shows the query in Design view.

Figure 10-16   QRYHOURSBYEMPLOYEE QUERY IN DESIGN VIEW

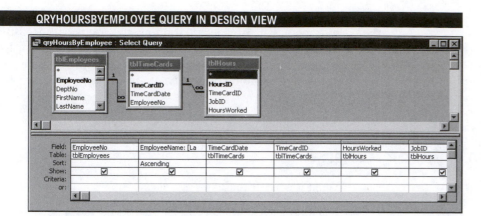

The query contains the EmployeeNo field and the EmployeeName field, and is an expression that concatenates the FirstName and LastName fields from the tblEmployees table, the TimeCardDate and TimeCardID fields from the tblTimeCards table, and the HoursWorked and JobID fields from the tblHours table. Running the query produces the results shown in Figure 10-17.

Figure 10-17   QRYHOURSBYEMPLOYEE RESULTS IN DATASHEET VIEW

Employee No	EmployeeName	Time Card Date	Time Card No	Hours Worked	Job No
10	Arquette, Thomas	06/22/2002	59	11	99899
10	Arquette, Thomas	06/22/2002	59	10	90000
10	Arquette, Thomas	06/22/2002	59	9	92370
10	Arquette, Thomas	02/09/2002	22	8	99899
10	Arquette, Thomas	06/22/2002	59	3	98378
10	Arquette, Thomas	02/09/2002	22	4	92000
10	Arquette, Thomas	02/09/2002	22	5	92370
10	Arquette, Thomas	02/09/2002	22	4	90000
10	Arquette, Thomas	02/09/2002	22	12	98378
10	Arquette, Thomas	02/09/2002	22	7	99562
10	Arquette, Thomas	06/22/2002	59	7	99562
600	Cauldwell, Gloria	11/09/2002	124	10	90000
600	Cauldwell, Gloria	11/16/2002	130	13	92370
600	Cauldwell, Gloria	11/16/2002	130	10	98378
600	Cauldwell, Gloria	11/16/2002	130	7	99562
600	Cauldwell, Gloria	11/09/2002	124	7	99899
600	Cauldwell, Gloria	11/09/2002	124	6	92370
600	Cauldwell, Gloria	10/26/2002	100	8	99899
600	Cauldwell, Gloria	10/26/2002	100	4	92370
600	Cauldwell, Gloria	10/26/2002	100	10	92000
600	Cauldwell, Gloria	10/26/2002	100	8	90000

Record: |◄| ◄ | 1 | ► | ►| | ►* | of 115

The data access page you create from the query will contain grouping levels similar to grouping levels you specify in reports. Grouping levels will be discussed in detail later. For now, you should know that pages that contain them cannot be updated; they are read-only. If an employee finds an error in the hours listed for a particular time card, that employee can click a hyperlink that you will insert on the page and e-mail the timekeeper about the error.

You will use the Page Wizard to create this page.

To create a data access page:

1. Click **Pages** on the Objects bar of the Database window, and then double-click **Create data access page by using wizard**. The Page Wizard opens, as shown in Figure 10-18.

Figure 10-18   **PAGE WIZARD OPENING DIALOG BOX**

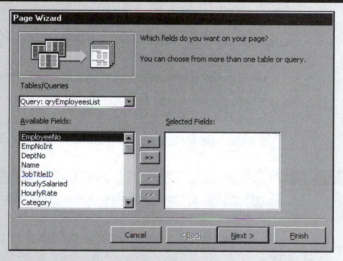

2. Click the **Tables/Queries** list arrow, click **qryHoursByEmployee**, click the **>>** button to move all the fields in the Available Fields list box to the Selected Fields list box, and then click the **Next** button. The next Page Wizard dialog box, shown in Figure 10-19, asks if you want to add any grouping levels, and assumes that you want to use the JobID field to group the items in this page.

Figure 10-19   SECOND PAGE WIZARD DIALOG BOX

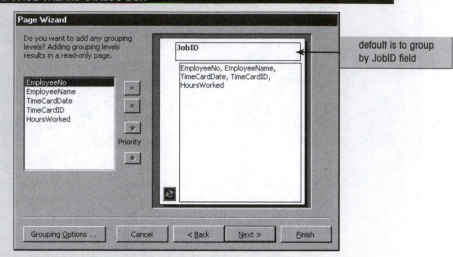

default is to group
by JobID field

However, you want to group by the EmployeeName field so that all the time cards and hours for a particular employee will be visible on one page. Grouping in data access pages automatically creates an expand control in the page. (This control will be discussed in more detail later in this tutorial.)

3. Click the **<** button to move JobID back to the list of fields, click **EmployeeName**, click the **>** button, and then click the **Next** button. The next screen of the Page Wizard asks for the sort order. You are not sure in what order you want to sort the detail records, so you will leave this blank.

4. Click the **Next** button. The next dialog box prompts you for a name for your page.

5. Type **dapTimeCards** and then click the **Finish** button. The data access page and the field list are visible in Design view, as shown in Figure 10-20.

Figure 10-20   COMPLETED DATA ACCESS PAGE

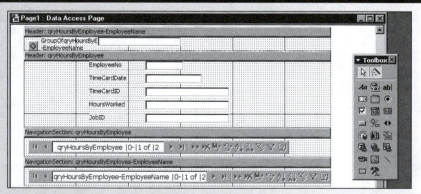

6. Switch to **Page** view by clicking the **View** button 🖽 on the toolbar. You see that the data access page needs a lot of work.

7. Click the **View** button 🔲 ▾ to switch back to **Design** view.

8. Click **File** on the menu bar, click **Save As**, type **dapTimeCards**, click the **OK** button, navigate to the **Tutorial.10** folder on your local or network drive, and then click the **Save** button. Recall that the data access page is saved outside the database, so you must tell Access where you want it saved.

Although a data access page looks like an Access form, it is quite different. The controls on the page work differently, the tools for designing pages are not as advanced as those for forms and reports, and you cannot use any of the wizards or expressions that you have used on forms and reports.

Formatting the Data Access Page

Next you will make some changes to the default formatting that the Page Wizard applied to the data access page. You will add a title, change the text inside the labels on the page, and move one of the controls on the data access page to a different section.

To format the data access page:

1. Click the text placeholder at the top of the page that says "Click here and type title text," and type **Time Cards Page**.

2. Click the **GroupOfqryHoursByEmployee-EmployeeName** label in the qryHoursByEmployee-EmployeeName header section, click the **Properties** button on the toolbar, click the **All** tab if necessary, and then change the InnerText property to **Employee Name**.

3. Click the **EmployeeNo** label in the qryHoursByEmployee section, and change the InnerText property to **Employee No**.

4. Repeat Step 3 to change the remaining labels as follows: TimeCardDate to **Time Card Date**, TimeCardID to **Time Card No**, HoursWorked to **Hours Worked**, and JobID to **Job No**.

5. Right-click the **Employee No** text box as shown in Figure 10-21, click **Cut** on the shortcut menu, right-click the **qryHoursByEmployee–EmployeeName** header, and then click **Paste**.

Figure 10-21	CUTTING AND PASTING THE EMPLOYEE NO TEXT BOX

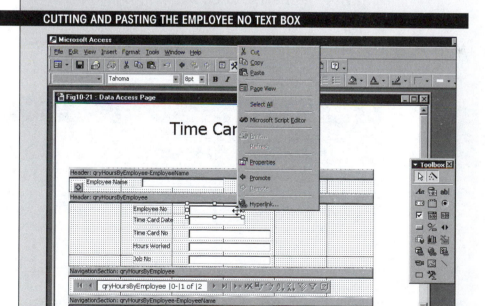

Note that in a data access page when you click the text box (and *not* the label) and then cut, copy, or move it, the label is included in the action. When you click the label and cut, copy, or move it, only the label is affected by your action. This is different from the way you cut, copy, and move labels and text boxes on forms and reports.

6. Make sure the **Employee No** text box is selected, and move it to the right of the Employee Name control. It should look like Figure 10-22.

Figure 10-22   **MOVING THE EMPLOYEE NO TEXT BOX AND LABEL**

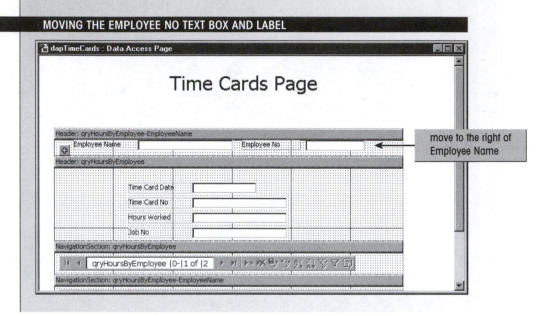

Applying Themes to Data Access Pages

A **theme** is a set of design elements and color schemes for background, font, horizontal lines, bullets, hyperlinks, and controls. Using a theme helps you quickly create professional, attractive data access pages.

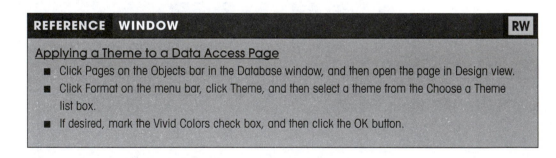

REFERENCE WINDOW   **RW**

Applying a Theme to a Data Access Page
- Click Pages on the Objects bar in the Database window, and then open the page in Design view.
- Click Format on the menu bar, click Theme, and then select a theme from the Choose a Theme list box.
- If desired, mark the Vivid Colors check box, and then click the OK button.

A theme can be applied and then changed at any point in the page development. Themes are installed with Access; additional themes can be downloaded from the Web. In addition to Access themes, you can apply a Microsoft FrontPage theme to data access pages. A number of Web sites offer free themes for FrontPage.

When applying a theme, you can select options to brighten colors, animate graphics, and apply a background to the data access page. Next you will apply a theme to the data access page.

Applying a theme to the data access page:

1. Click **Format** on the menu bar, and then click **Theme**. You will see the Theme dialog box shown in Figure 10-23.

Figure 10-23   THEME DIALOG BOX

TROUBLE? Your Choose a Theme list box may have different themes displayed depending on those installed on the computer you are working on. If Expedition is not included in the list, choose another theme and advise your instructor that it was not available.

2. Click **Expedition** from the Choose a Theme list box, click the **Vivid Colors** check box, and then click the **OK** button.

3. Click the **View** button on the toolbar to switch to Page view. Next you will make some changes to the text boxes, fonts, and labels.

4. Switch to **Design** view, click the **Employee Name** label, click the **Font Size** list arrow on the toolbar, click **10**, and then click the **Bold** button on the toolbar.

5. Repeat Step 4 with the **Employee No** label.

6. Click the **Employee Name** text box, click the **Properties** button on the toolbar if necessary, click the **Format** tab, type **none** for the BorderStyle property, and then change the Font Size to **10**.

7. Repeat Step 6 with the **Employee No** text box.

8. Click the **Time Card Date** text box, change the BorderStyle property to **none**, and then do the same to the **Time Card No**, **Hours Worked**, and **Job No** text boxes in the detail section.

9. Click the **View** button on the toolbar to switch to **Page** view, and then click the **expand** indicator to the left of Employee Name. Your page should now look like that shown in Figure 10-24.

Figure 10-24 **TIME CARDS PAGE**

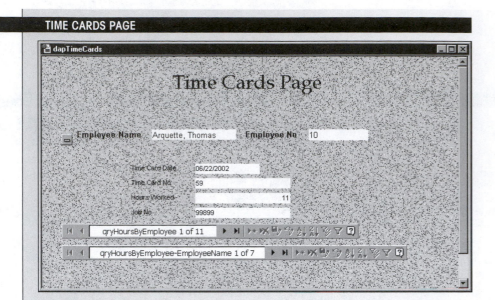

TROUBLE? If your labels wrap to two lines, widen the label in Design view so that it fits on one line, as shown in Figure 10-24.

Grouping in Data Access Pages

Grouping data in data access pages is much like grouping data in a report. When you specify groups in the page, Access automatically adds an expand control so that users can expand or collapse the records in a group. The page contains a Sorting and Grouping dialog box that allows you to add or delete groups, and define exactly how you want the groups to appear.

Pages have some advantages over printed reports. Pages are interactive so the user can move through the records online and view the data they desire. Plus, pages always contain the most current data because they are connected to the database, whereas a printed report is only as current as the database was at the time the report was printed. Finally, pages can be distributed electronically by using e-mail.

The expand indicator and the record navigation toolbar are added automatically to a data access page for each group specified. They can be removed or modified. Groups can be easily added to, or deleted from, a data access page by selecting a text box, and then choosing Promote or Demote from the shortcut menu.

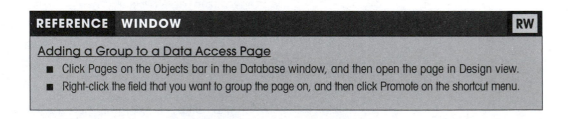

REFERENCE WINDOW RW

Adding a Group to a Data Access Page
- Click Pages on the Objects bar in the Database window, and then open the page in Design view.
- Right-click the field that you want to group the page on, and then click Promote on the shortcut menu.

You and Carolyn are satisfied with the page so far, but you want to group the data in the page so that each time card number and time card date are visible, and so the user can expand a particular time card to view its detail. This way, when there are many time cards in the system, it will be easier to find the specific time card and expand it to see the hours and jobs. Next you will add a new group to the data access page.

To add a group to the data access page:

1. Return to **Design** view, right-click the **Time Card Date** text box, and then click **Promote** on the shortcut menu. A new group is added to the page.

2. Right-click the **Time Card No** text box, click **Cut** on the shortcut menu, right-click inside the new group header, and then click **Paste**.

3. Move the **Time Card No** label and text box to the right of Time Card Date, as shown in Figure 10-25.

Figure 10-25	MOVING THE TIME CARD DATE AND TIME CARD NO TEXT BOXES AND LABELS

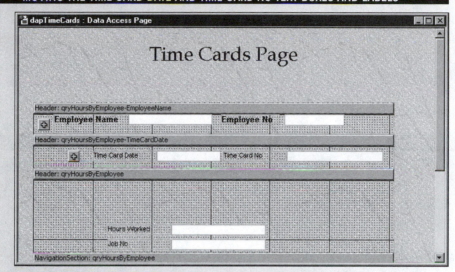

4. Size the **Hours Worked** text box and the **Job No** text box so that each is approximately **1"** wide.

5. Move the **Hours Worked** label and text box and the **Job No** label and text box to the top of the Header: qryHoursByEmployee section, and position them next to each other as shown in Figure 10-26.

Figure 10-26	MOVING THE HOURS WORKED AND JOB NO TEXT BOXES AND LABELS

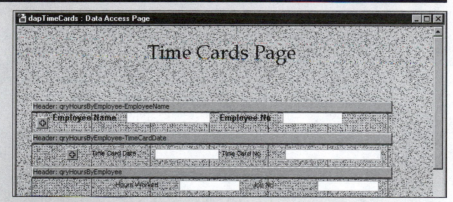

6. Click the **Header: qryHoursByEmployee** section, position your pointer over the handle on the bottom center of the section so that it looks like ↕, and then click and drag the section up to the bottom of the controls.

7. Return to **Page** view, and click the **Expand Indicator** ⊞ to the left of Employee Name to show the time cards for that employee.

8. Click ⊞ to the left of the first Time Card Date to show the hours for that particular time card.

9. Return to **Design** view.

Changing Sorting and Grouping Properties

Now you want to modify the way the data in the groups is shown on the page. First you will eliminate the NavigationSection: qryHoursByEmployee section below the Header: qryHoursByEmployee section. Each time card will have only 5 to 10 entries, so the user does not need a toolbar to navigate through these records. You also will eliminate the NavigationSection: qryHoursByEmployee-TimeCardDate section because at this time the number of time cards per employee is not excessive. You can always add this later if it becomes necessary. See Figure 10-27.

Figure 10-27	NAVIGATION TOOLBARS

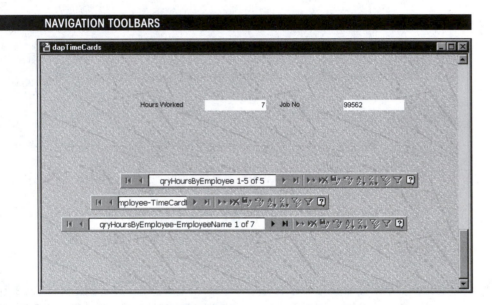

You also will modify the remaining record navigation toolbar in the NavigationSection: qryHoursByEmployee-EmployeeName section to eliminate unused buttons.

Finally, you will change some of the sorting and grouping properties to determine the number of records shown on each page and to determine which sections you want expanded by default. This will eliminate the need to click the expand indicator. You also will add a caption section to eliminate the repetitive labels in the two innermost sections, qryHoursByEmployee and qryHoursByEmployee-TimeCardDate.

To change the sorting and grouping properties:

1. Click **View** on the menu bar, and then click **Sorting and Grouping**. The Sorting and Grouping dialog box opens, as shown in Figure 10-28.

Figure 10-28 | **SORTING AND GROUPING DIALOG BOX**

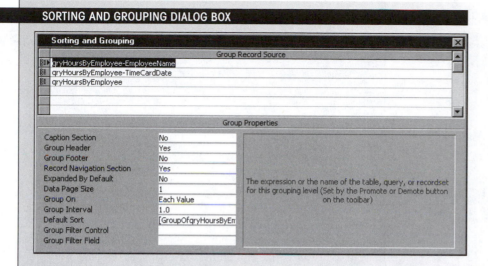

2. Click **qryHoursByEmployee**, change the Caption Section property to **Yes**, the Record Navigation Section property to **No**, and the Data Page Size property to **All**.

3. Close the Sorting and Grouping dialog box. Your data access page should look like that shown in Figure 10-29. It now contains a new section, Caption: qryHoursByEmployee, that you can use for the labels so they don't repeat for each section entry. The Navigation Section is gone.

Figure 10-29 | **DATA ACCESS PAGE WITH CAPTION SECTION ADDED**

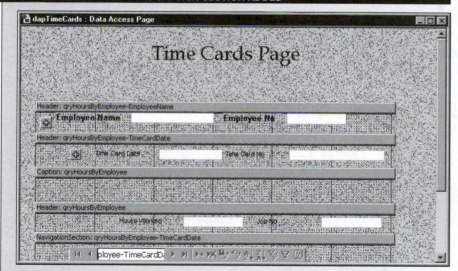

4. Right-click the **Hours Worked** label, click **Cut**, right-click the **Caption qryHoursByEmployee** section, click **Paste**, and then move the label so that it is positioned directly above the Hours Worked text box.

5. Repeat Step 4 for the **Job No** label. You might need to make the label smaller to position it above the Job No text box.

6. Move the pasted labels to the top of the Caption: qryHoursByEmployee section, and then drag the section up beneath them, as shown in Figure 10-30.

Figure 10-30   MOVING THE LABELS IN THE CAPTION SECTION

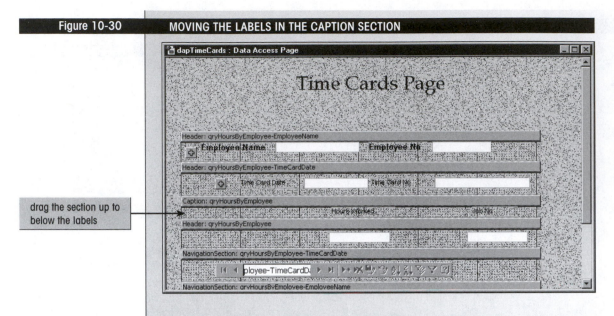

drag the section up to below the labels

7. Click **View** on the menu bar, click **Sorting and Grouping**, and then click **qryHoursByEmployee-TimeCardDate**.

8. Change the Caption Section property to **Yes**, the Record Navigation Section property to **No**, the Data Page Size property to **10**, and then close the Sorting and Grouping dialog box.

9. Cut and paste the **Time Card Date** and **Time Card No** labels into the Caption: qryHoursByEmployee-TimeCardDate section.

10. Switch to **Page** view and test the page. Click the **expand indicators** to see the various levels.

Changing Navigation Toolbar Properties

Now that you have completed the changes to the Sorting and Grouping properties, you and Carolyn want to modify the remaining record navigation toolbar. It currently contains a label that identifies the qryHoursByEmployee-EmployeeName, and is followed by a string that shows the record number and the total number of records. You want this to read "Employee Name" instead, but you won't change the record number display. You also will eliminate the buttons, including the Delete and Sort Ascending buttons, on the record navigation toolbar that do not work in this type of page.

To change the properties of the navigation toolbar:

1. Switch to **Design** view, click the **navigation toolbar**, and then display its properties dialog box, if necessary.

2. Click the **All** tab, click in the **RecordsetLabel property** text box, and then press **Shift+F2** to open the Zoom window.

3. Delete the **qryHoursByEmployee-** string at the beginning of the entry, click between Employee and Name, and press the **spacebar**. The Zoom window should now look like that shown in Figure 10-31.

Figure 10-31	CHANGING THE RECORDSETLABEL PROPERTY

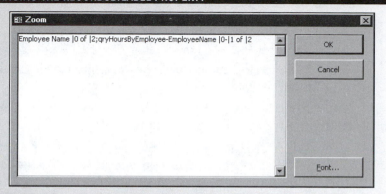

4. Click the **OK** button, change the ShowDelButton property to **False**, the ShowFilterBySelectionButton property to **False**, the ShowNewButton property to **False**, and the ShowSaveButton property to **False**. Change the ShowSortAscendingButton property to **False**, the ShowSortDescendingButton property to **False**, the ShowToggleFilterButton property to **False**, and the ShowUndoButton property to **False**.

5. Size the record navigation toolbar to approximately **3"** wide, and center it as shown in Figure 10-32.

Figure 10-32	SIZING THE RECORD NAVIGATION TOOLBAR

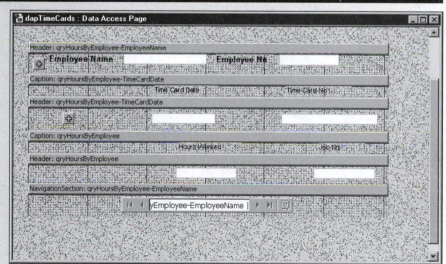

6. Switch to **Page** view. You and Carolyn want the Employee Name group to expand automatically when a new record is viewed.

7. Switch to **Design** view, click **View** on the menu bar, and then click **Sorting and Grouping**.

8. Change the Expanded By Default property for qryHoursByEmployee-EmployeeName to **Yes**. Then the expand indicator will not have to be clicked each time the user navigates to a new employee record. Close the Sorting and Grouping dialog box.

9. Switch to **Page** view to test your changes.

To complete the dapTimeCards page, you will create a hyperlink to e-mail the timekeeper in case an employee discovers an error in the data.

To add a hyperlink to a data access page:

1. Switch to **Design** view, make sure that the toolbox is visible, and then click the **Hyperlink** button 📇.

2. Click approximately 1 inch below the record navigation toolbar. The Insert Hyperlink dialog box opens.

3. Click **E-mail Address** in the Link to bar, type **E-mail Timekeeper** in the Text to display text box, and then type **rjenkins@moviecam.com** in the E-mail address text box.

4. Type **Time card error** in the Subject text box as shown in Figure 10-33, and then click the **OK** button.

Figure 10-33	CREATING THE E-MAIL HYPERLINK

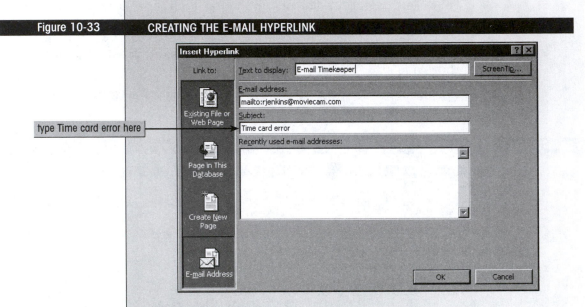

type Time card error here

5. Position the pointer on the handle on the right side of the hyperlink text box. Click and drag to make the box the same width as the body of the data access page, as shown in Figure 10-34.

Figure 10-34   **MAKE THE HYPERLINK THE SAME WIDTH AS THE BODY OF THE PAGE**

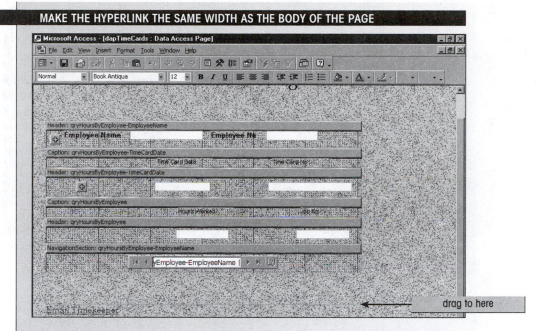

6. Click the **Center** button 🔳 on the toolbar to center the text inside the box.

7. If necessary, drag the handle on the bottom of the hyperlink text box down so that the text displays completely.

8. Switch to **Page** view and click the hyperlink to test it. Outlook Express opens, and an e-mail is addressed automatically.

9. Save your changes, close Outlook Express, and close the page.

Creating an Updateable Data Access Page

One of the original objectives for the database was to create a data access page to allow employees to update their personal information on the company intranet. Amanda sent a memo to all employees to let them know that if they do not want their home address, telephone number, and emergency contact information available on the company intranet, they should send a written request. No one made the request, so you can create a data access page based on the tblEmployees table.

If you want to be able to edit the records in a data access page, you must base the page on a single table, make sure there are no grouping levels, and make sure that only one record at a time is visible. The page that you planned will allow employees to change their address and emergency contact information.

You want to provide users with quick access to their individual record, so you will include a combo box to filter the records by last name. You will apply the same theme to this page as you used on the time cards page, and you also will provide a link on this page to the dapTimeCards page.

You will use the AutoPage: Columnar Wizard to create this page.

To create an updateable data access page:

1. Make sure **Pages** is selected on the Objects bar in the Database window, and double-click **Create data access page by using wizard**.

2. Click the **Tables/Queries** list arrow, click **Tables: tblEmployees**, and then move the following fields from the Available Fields list box to the Selected Fields list box: **EmployeeNo**, **FirstName**, **LastName**, **Address1**, **Address2**, **City**, **State**, **Phone**, **ZipCode**, **EmergencyContact**, and **EmergencyPhone**.

3. Click the **Next** button, and then click **Next** again. You do not want to add any grouping levels.

4. Select **LastName** as the field to sort by, click the **Next** button, type **dapMovieEmployees**, and then click **Finish**.

5. Click the placeholder **Click here and type title text**, and then type **Employees Contact Information Page**. Click **Format** on the menu bar, click **Theme**, click **Expedition**, click the **Vivid Colors** check box, and then click the **OK** button.

6. Click **View** on the menu bar, click **Sorting and Grouping**, change the Caption Section property to **Yes**, and then close the Sorting and Grouping dialog box.

7. Make sure the toolbox is visible and that the **Control Wizards** button is selected, click the **Dropdown List** button, and then click in the center of the Caption: tblEmployees section to create a drop-down list. (The drop-down list looks just like a combo box on a form.)

8. In the Combo Box Wizard dialog box, click **Next** to accept the default selection to look up the values in a table or query, click the **Tables** option button, click **tblEmployees** in the list box, and then click the **Next** button.

9. Double-click **LastName** from the Available Fields list box, click **Next**, click **Next** again because the column does not need to be wider, type **Last Name** for the label, and then click the **Finish** button. Your page should look like that shown in Figure 10-35.

Figure 10-35   ADDING THE COMBO BOX TO THE DAPEMPLOYEES PAGE

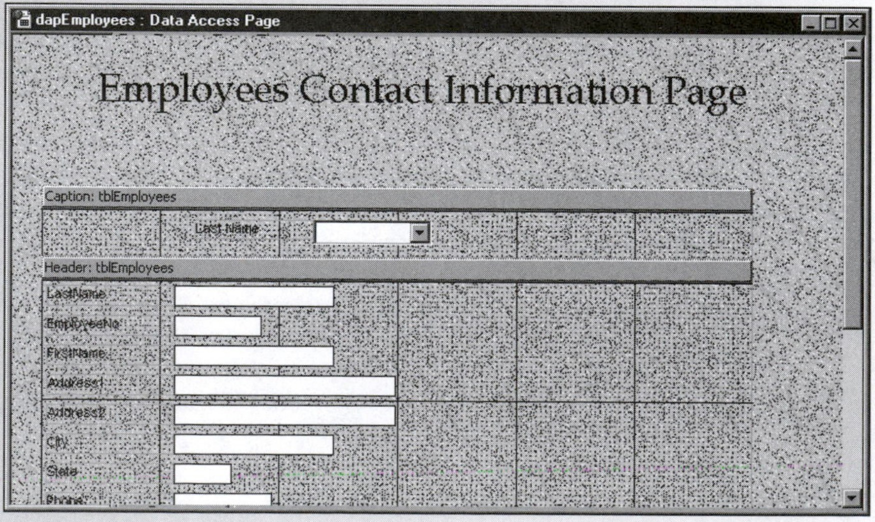

dapEmployees : Data Access Page

Employees Contact Information Page

Caption: tblEmployees

Last Name

Header: tblEmployees

LastName
EmployeeNo
FirstName
Address1
Address2
City
State
Phone

Now you need to set the page to filter the records. If this were a form or report, you would write VBA code to synchronize the combo box record to the record on the page, but data access pages do not require any programming to do this. And, because data access pages are designed to run in Internet Explorer, which does not use the same language or event model as Access, you would have to use a scripting language like VBScript or JavaScript rather than VBA.

To set the data access page to filter the records:

1. Make sure that the drop-down list text box is selected and that its properties dialog box is open.

2. Click the **All** tab, and change the ID property to **cboLastName**.

3. Click **View** on the menu bar, and then click **Sorting and Grouping**.

4. Type **cboLastName** in the Group Filter Control property text box, and then type **LastName** in the Group Filter Field property text box. The Group Filter Control property is used to specify the combo box or list box that filters the page. The Group Filter property is the name of the field on which this control is filtered.

5. Close the Sorting and Grouping dialog box and the properties dialog box, and switch to **Page** view. Test the combo box by clicking the list arrow and choosing a last name from the list. The record in the page will synchronize to chosen name.

6. Return to **Design** view and click the **Save** button 🖫 on the toolbar, type **dapMovieEmployees**, navigate to the **Tutorial.10** folder on your local or network drive, and then click the **Save** button.

Because the new data access page is linked directly to the tblEmployees table, you and Carolyn want to be sure that records cannot be deleted from the table. Although the Cascade Delete Related Records option is not in effect between the tblEmployees and tblTimeCards tables, an employee who does not have a record in the tblTimeCards table could be inadvertently deleted. You also don't want the user to navigate to a new record and try to add data. You will make these changes to the record navigation toolbar next.

To complete the dapMovieEmployees page:

1. Click the **Last Name** label in the Caption: tblEmployees section, show the properties dialog box, change the InnerText property to **Last Name Search**, close the properties dialog box, and then click the **Bold** button 🄱 on the toolbar. The text wraps in the label.

2. Drag the left edge of the label to make it large enough so the text fits on one line, and if necessary, click **View** on the menu bar, point to **Toolbars**, and then click **Alignment and Sizing**. The alignment and sizing feature in a data access page is different from that on forms and reports. You need to click the control that is the size you want the other controls to be, click the button to size a particular direction, and then click the control to be sized.

3. Click the **cboLastName** combo box, click the **Size Height** button 🄸 on the Alignment and Sizing toolbar, and then click the label containing **Last Name Search**.

4. With the cboLastName combo box still selected, click the **Align Top** button 🖫 on the Alignment and Sizing toolbar, and then click the label containing **Last Name Search**. If you want to size or align multiple controls, you can click the control that is the size you want the rest to be, double-click the button on the toolbar, and then click each control to be sized.

5. Move the combo box and label to the left edge of the page as shown in Figure 10-36, click the **record navigation toolbar**, and then click the **Properties** button 🖼 on the toolbar.

Figure 10-36   **MOVING THE COMBO BOX AND LABEL**

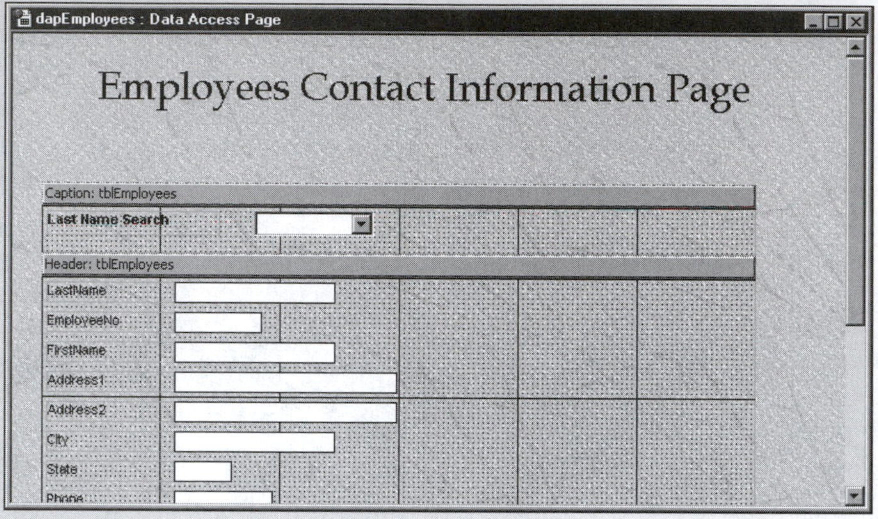

---

6. Delete **tbl** from the beginning of the RecordsetLabel property, and change the ShowDelButton property and the ShowNewButton property to **False**.

7. If the page is maximized, click the **Restore** button 🖻 so that you can see the title bar of the data access page. Click the **title bar** to select the page, and then change the Title property (the second property listed) to **Employee Contact Information**.

8. Close the properties dialog box, select the title **Employees Contact Information Page**, and then click the **Align Left** button 🔳 on the toolbar.

9. Switch to **Page** view to test the page, click the **Last Name Search** list arrow, and then click **Garcia**. Your data access page should look like that shown in Figure 10-37.

| **Figure 10-37** | **THE DAPEMPLOYEES PAGE IN PAGE VIEW** |

10. Save your changes and close the page.

Testing the Data Access Pages

Now that you have completed the dapEmployees page, it is time to test it. You will open it in Access and then open it in Internet Explorer. The editing features work a bit differently in data access pages than in forms. When you make a change to a record, you need to use the Save Record button on the toolbar to save it. Pressing the Enter key does not move you from text box to text box, so you need to use the mouse to navigate.

You will open the updateable page in Access first.

To edit data in a data access page:

1. Make sure **Pages** is selected on the Objects bar in the Database window, and then double-click **dapMovieEmployees**.

2. Click the **Last Name Search** list arrow, click **Eichman** from the list, select **722 Blair Place** in the Address1 text box, and then press **Delete**.

3. Type **1555 Starr Road** and then press the **Enter** key. The entry disappears.

4. Click in the text box and the address reappears.

5. Click the **Save Record** button [icon] on the record navigation toolbar to save your change.

6. Click the **City** text box, backspace over Santa Rosa, and type **Windsor**. Do *not* press Enter.

7. Click the **ZipCode** text box, change the entry to **95492**, and then click [icon] on the record navigation toolbar.

8. Close the dapEmployees page.

To complete the next set of steps, you do not need to be connected to the Internet, but you do need a copy of Internet Explorer. You will launch Internet Explorer, and open both data access pages to see how they look.

To test data access pages in Internet Explorer:

1. Launch Internet Explorer. (Check with your instructor or technical support person if you are not sure how to do this, or to find out if Internet Explorer is installed.)

2. Click **File** on the menu bar and then click **Open**. You will see the Open dialog box, as shown in Figure 10-38.

Figure 10-38	OPENING A DATA ACCESS PAGE FROM INTERNET EXPLORER

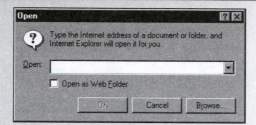

3. Click the **Browse** button and the Microsoft Internet Explorer dialog box opens.

4. Navigate to the **Tutorial.10** folder containing the data access pages, click **dapTimeCards**, and then click the **Open** button.

5. Click the **OK** button in the Open dialog box.

6. Repeat Steps 2-5 to open the **dapMovieEmployees** page.

7. Click the **Last Name Search** list arrow, click **Gerardo**, type **Joyce Gerardo** in the Emergency Contact text box, click in the Emergency Phone text box, type **707 555-4999**, and then click the **Save Record** button 🖫 on the record navigation toolbar.

8. Click the **Back** button ⇐ on the toolbar to navigate to the dapTimeCards page.

9. Click the **Next record** button ▶ on the record navigation toolbar until you reach the record for Todd Combs, and then click the expand indicator for the **5/25/2002** time card. The page should look like that shown in Figure 10-39.

Figure 10-39	TIME CARDS PAGE IN INTERNET EXPLORER

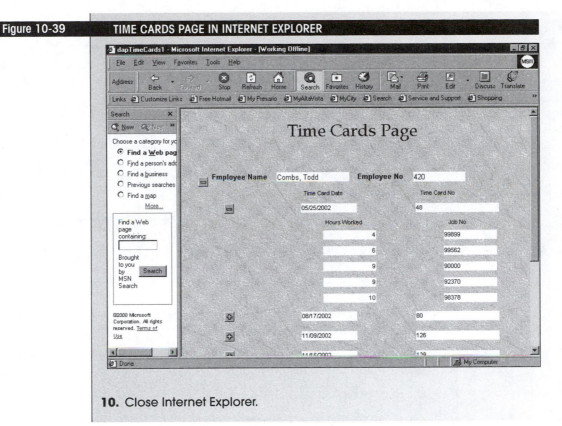

10. Close Internet Explorer.

Adding a Hyperlink to Another Page

You want to provide a link in the dapEmployees page to open the dapTimeCards page. You will do that next.

> ### To add a hyperlink to a data access page:
>
> **1.** Make sure **Pages** is selected on the Objects bar in the Database window, and then open the **dapMovieEmployees** page in **Design** view.
>
> **2.** If necessary, display the toolbox and maximize the window, click the **Insert Hyperlink** button 🖳 on the toolbox, and then click about an inch below the record navigation toolbar on the page.
>
> **3.** Click **Page in This Database** in the Link to bar, and then click **dapTimeCards** from the Select a page in this database list box.
>
> **4.** Type **Time Cards Page** in the Text to display text box, click the **OK** button, and then widen the hyperlink text box so that it the same width as the body of the page, as shown in Figure 10-40.

Figure 10-40   **POSITIONING THE HYPERLINK LABEL**

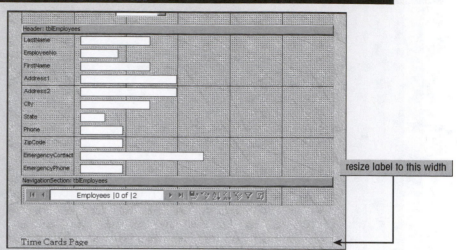

5. Click the **Center** button ☰ on the toolbar, size the hyperlink text box so that all the text is visible, and then save your changes.

6. Switch to **Page** view, and then click the hyperlink. Internet Explorer launches and the dapTimeCards page opens.

7. Close Internet Explorer.

8. Close the **dapMovieEmployees** page to return to the Database window.

The data access pages work well. You plan to have users test them more before you put the pages on the company intranet server. Because data access pages are stored in files that aren't in your database, Access needs to know where to find these database files on your hard disk anytime you open a page. If you have moved the files to a different location, Access will prompt you to locate the files by navigating to the New folder when you try to open the data access page.

Exporting to the Web

You can export tables, queries, forms, or reports to a Web-ready format by using the Export command on the File menu. To save a table, you can use the HTML Documents format, which is readable with any browser.

REFERENCE WINDOW   **RW**

Exporting an Access Query to an HTML Document
- Click Queries on the Objects bar in the Database window, and then open the query you want to export.
- Click File on the menu bar, and then click Export.
- Click the Save in list arrow and navigate to the drive and folder in which you wish to save the document.
- Click the Save as type list arrow, click HTML Documents, and then click the Save All button.
- Close the query.

The qryJobsTotalDollars query groups all of the jobs and shows totals to date of hours and dollars for each job. The product managers need this information from time to time, but do not need the printed output. One option is to provide the managers with read-only rights to the query. Another option is to export the file to an HTML document on a shared drive of the network where the managers can open the file from their browser. You will export the query now.

To export a query to an HTML document:

1. Click **Queries** in the Objects bar in the Database window, and then double-click the **qryJobsTotalDollars** query to open it.

2. Click **File** on the menu bar, and then click **Export**.

3. Click the **Save in** list arrow, and navigate to the **Tutorial.10** folder on your hard drive or network drive.

4. Click the **Save as type** list arrow, click **HTML Documents**, and then click the **Save All** button.

5. Close the query to return to the Database window.

6. Launch Internet Explorer, click **File** on the menu bar, and then click **Open**.

7. Click the **Browse** button, and the Microsoft Internet Explorer dialog box opens.

8. Navigate to the **Tutorial.10** folder, click **qryJobsTotalDollars**, and then click the **Open** button.

9. Click the **OK** button in the Open dialog box. The query appears in Internet Explorer.

10. Close Internet Explorer, close the **Movie10** database, and exit Access.

You and Carolyn are satisfied with this solution for providing data to managers. You plan to train managers on how to open exported queries from Internet Explorer. When the managers have a one-time request for summary data, they can e-mail you or Carolyn. You can then write the query, run it, and export the results to an HTML document. With this approach, you won't need to generate a report or change the switchboard or rights in the database to give the managers access to the data.

Importing from the Web

Access includes other Web-related features. To incorporate data from the Internet or an intranet into your database, you can import or link to HTML files. If you import, you create a static table in Access. If you link to an HTML table, the most current data is shown in your database. Importing and linking to HTML tables is similar to importing text and spreadsheet data, which was discussed in Tutorial 3. Use the Get External Data command on the File menu, and then select HTML Documents from the Files of type list box to import and link to HTML tables.

Session 10.2 QUICK CHECK

1. How is data viewed or edited in a data access page?

2. Data access pages that contain _____ cannot be updated.

3. A(n) _____ is a set of design elements and color schemes for background, font, horizontal lines, bullets, hyperlinks, and controls.

4. The _____ for designing data access pages are not as advanced as those for designing forms and reports.

5. Programming Web pages requires that you use a scripting language like _____ or _____.

6. What are the requirements for an updateable data access page?

7. How is editing data different on a data access page than it is in a form?

8. Which Access objects can you export to an HTML document file?

9. It is possible to import or _____ to HTML tables on the Web.

REVIEW ASSIGNMENTS

The Hours10 database is similar to the MovieCam Technologies database you worked with in this tutorial. You want to create a data access page so that employees can update their address, telephone, and contact information via the company intranet.

1. Start Access, and open the **Hours10** database located in the Tutorial.10 folder on your local or network drive.

2. Select Pages on the Objects bar in the Database window, double-click Create data access page by using wizard, click the Tables/Queries list arrow, click Tables: tblEmployees, and then move the following fields from the Available Fields list box to the Selected Fields list box: FirstName, LastName, Address1, City, State, Phone, ZipCode, EmergencyContact, and EmergencyPhone.

3. Click the Next button, click Next again to skip the step for adding grouping levels, select LastName as the field to sort by, click the Next button, type "dapEmployees", and then click Finish.

4. Click the placeholder Click here and type title text, type "Employees Page", click Format on the menu bar, click Theme, click Industrial, click the OK button, click View on the menu bar, click Sorting and Grouping, change the Caption Section property to Yes, and then close the Sorting and Grouping dialog box.

5. Make sure the toolbox is visible and that the Control Wizards button is selected. Click the Dropdown List button, and click in the center of the Caption: tblEmployees section to create a drop-down list.

6. Click Next to accept the default selection to look up the values in a table or query, click the Tables option button, click tblEmployees in the list box, and then click the Next button.

7. Double-click LastName from the Available Fields list box, click Next, click Next again because the column does not need to be widened, type "Last Name Lookup" for the label, and then click the Finish button.

8. If necessary, select the drop-down list text box, click the Properties button on the toolbar, change the ID property to "cboLastName", click View on the menu bar, and then click Sorting and Grouping.

9. Type "cboLastName" in the Group Filter Control property, type "LastName" in the Group Filter Field property, and then close the Sorting and Grouping dialog.

10. Move the combo box and label to the left edge of the page, and click the record navigation toolbar.

11. Delete tbl from the beginning of the RecordsetLabel property, and change the ShowDelButton property and the ShowNewButton property to False.

12. Click the Save button 🖫 on the toolbar, type **dapEmployees**, navigate to the Tutorial.10 folder on your local or network drive, and then click Save.

13. Switch to Page view and test the page.

14. Close the **Hours10** database and exit Access.

CASE PROBLEMS

Case 1. Edwards and Company Jack Edwards wants you to create a company intranet Web page that consultants can browse for their particular clients. He wants the client name, address, telephone, and contact information displayed so that he does not have to provide each consultant with access to this information in the database itself. The Edwards and Company database contains a query named qryClientByConsultant that contains the fields that you will need to complete the page. The data access page will be grouped by the consultant name and will contain all the fields in the query.

1. Start Access, and open the **Edward10** database located in the Tutorial.10 folder on your local or network drive.

2. Click Pages on the Objects bar in the Database window, and then double-click Create data access page by using wizard.

3. Click the Tables/Queries list arrow, click qryClientByConsultant, click the >> button to move all of the fields in the Available Fields list box to the Selected Fields list box, and then click the Next button.

4. Click ConsultantName, click the > button, click the Next button, click the Sort list arrow, and then click CompanyName.

5. Click the Next button, type "dapClients", and then click the Finish button.

6. Click File on the menu bar, click Save As, type "dapClients", navigate to the Tutorial.10 folder, and then click the OK button.

7. Click the text placeholder at the top of the page that says Click here and type title text, and then type "Clients Page".

8. Click the label in the header that reads GroupOfqryClientByConsultant-ConsultantName, click the Properties button on the toolbar, click the All tab if necessary, and then change the InnerText property to "Consultant Name".

9. Click the CompanyName label in the qryClientByConsultant section, and change the InnerText property to "Company Name".

10. Repeat Step 10 to change the remaining labels as follows: Address1 to "Address", ZipCode to "Zip Code", and ContactName to "Contact Name".

11. Click Format on the menu bar, and then click Theme.

12. Click Capsules from the Choose a Theme list box, click the Vivid Colors check box, and then click the OK button.

13. Click the navigation toolbar in the qryClientByConsultant section.

14. Click in the RecordsetLabel property text box, and then press Shift+F2 to open the Zoom window. Delete the qryClientByConsultant- string, and then type "Client Name".

15. Click the OK button, and change the ShowDelButton, ShowFilterBySelectionButton, ShowNewButton, ShowSaveButton, ShowSortAscendingButton, ShowSortDescendingButton, ShowToggleFilterButton, and the ShowUndoButton properties to "False".

16. Size the record navigation toolbar to approximately 3" wide, and center it.

17. Repeat Steps 14–16 for the navigation toolbar in the qryClientByConsultant-ConsultantName section. Change Client Name to Consultant Name.

18. Save your changes, switch to Page view, and test the page.

19. Close the **Edward10** database and exit Access.

Case 2. San Diego County Information Systems   You use the built-in menu bar in the ISD database rather than a custom menu bar, and want to modify it to include some Web options. You want to add two menu choices: one to navigate to the Microsoft Home Page, and another to navigate to the County home page.

1. Start Access, and open the **ISD10** database located in the Tutorial.10 folder on your local or network drive.

2. Right-click the Database toolbar, and then click Customize on the shortcut menu.

3. Click the Commands tab in the Customize dialog box, scroll down in the Categories list box, and then click Web.

4. Drag Hyperlink from the Commands list box to the bottom of the Window menu item, and then drag another Hyperlink to the Window menu below the menu item you just added.

5. Right-click the first Hyperlink command, point to Assign Hyperlink, and then click Open.

6. Click Existing File or Web Page in the Link to bar, type "www.microsoft.com" in the Type the file or Web page name text box, and then click the OK button.

7. Right-click the Hyperlink command, change the Name to "&Microsoft", and then press Enter.

8. Right-click the second Hyperlink command, point to Assign Hyperlink, and then click Open.

9. Click Existing File or Web Page in the Link to bar, type "www.sandiego-county.org" in the Type the file or Web page name text box, and then click the OK button.

10. Right-click the Hyperlink command, change the Name to "&SDCounty", press the Enter key, and then close the Customize dialog box

11. Click the Microsoft menu choice. Your default browser opens the Microsoft Home Page.

12. Close the **ISD10** database and exit Access.

Case 3. Christenson Homes   Roberta asked you to develop a read-only Web page for customers to view the various subdivisions under construction. The Homes10 database contains the query you wrote for this purpose. The query—named qryLotsBySubdivision—has subdivision and lot information.

1. Start Access, and open the **Homes10** database located in the Tutorial.10 folder on your hard drive or network drive.

2. Create a data access page using the wizard that contains all the fields in the qryLotsBySubdivision query.

3. Group the data in the page by Sudivision name, and save the page as "dapLots" when prompted by the Wizard.

4. Type "Lots Web Page" as the title for the page.

5. Modify the labels so that they contain the names of the fields. Use spaces between words in the field names.

6. Format the label and text box in the grouping header so they are 10-point size and bold.

7. Size the Subdivision Name label so that the text fits on one line.

8. Apply the Expedition theme to the data access page.

9. Delete the Record Navigation Section from the qryLotsBySubdivision section.

10. Add a Caption Section to the qryLotsBySubdivision section, and move the labels in this section.

11. Move the text boxes in the qryLotsBySubdivision section so that they are lined up in a row, rather than a column, and then align their labels over them.

12. Click the navigation toolbar in the qryLotsBySubdivision-SubdivisionName section.

13. Click in the RecordsetLabel property text box, and then press Shift+F2 to open the Zoom window. Delete the qryLotsBySubdivision string, and then insert a space between Subdivision and Name.

14. Remove all of the buttons except the ones used to navigate between records (ShowFirst, ShowNext, ShowLast, and ShowPrevious).

15. Click View on the menu bar, and then click Sorting and Grouping. Change the Expanded By Default property of the qryLotsBySubdivison-SubdivisionName section to Yes.

16. Save the data access page as "dapLots", close the Sorting and Grouping dialog box, and close the properties dialog box.

17. Switch to Page view and test the page.

18. Close the **Homes10** database and exit Access.

Case 4. Sonoma Farms The Sonoma Farms database contains the frmCustomers, frmDistributors, and frmVisitors forms. You have decided to use a lightweight switchboard in this database to open each of these forms. You will include hyperlinks on command buttons for each form and also include a button designed with VBA code to exit the database.

1. Start Access, and open the **Sonoma10** database located in the Tutorial.10 folder on your local or network drive.

2. Create a new unbound form in the database and save it as "frmMainSwitchboard".

3. Change the properties of the form to eliminate record selectors, navigation buttons, the Close, Minimize, and Maximize/Restore buttons, and dividing lines.

4. Create a label at the top of the form, and type "Sonoma Farms Main Switchboard" as the Caption property.

5. Add three command buttons to the form. Create hyperlinks on the buttons to open each of the three data entry forms in the database: Customers, Distributors, and Visitors.

6. Include a shortcut key for each button, and format the buttons so that they look like standard command buttons rather than hyperlinks.

7. Use the wizard to add a command button to exit the database.

8. Add a label hyperlink at the bottom of the form. Use your e-mail address as the hyperlink, so the user can click it if there are problems or questions.

9. Test the form to be sure that it works properly.

10. Save the form.

11. Close the **Sonoma10** database and exit Access.

QUICK | CHECK ANSWERS

Session 10.1

1. A hyperlink is text or an image that you click to navigate to other parts of a file, to other documents on your computer or network, or to Internet addresses.

2. A data access page is an object in the database that lets you display, edit, and manipulate other objects, such as tables, forms, and reports, so those objects can be published to the Web using the Internet Explorer Web browser.

3. The Hyperlink address property is used to specify the path to a document on the local or network drive or to a Web site address.

4. The Hyperlink subaddress property is used to specify a particular location in a document, such as a bookmark, or a particular Access database object such as a form or report.

5. A lightweight switchboard opens faster than a regular switchboard.

6. A lightweight switchboard contains little or no VBA code.

7. To assign a hyperlink to a toolbar button or menu command, you must add a button or a menu command, and then add the hyperlink to replace that command.

Session 10.2

1. Data access pages are Web pages that are separate from your Access database file, and allow those who have Web access to use Internet Explorer to view and edit data in your tables.

2. Data access pages that contain grouping levels cannot be updated.

3. A theme is a set of design elements and color schemes for background, font, horizontal lines, bullets, hyperlinks, and controls.

4. The tools for designing data access pages are not as advanced as those used for designing forms and reports.

5. Programming Web pages requires that you use a scripting language like VBScript or JavaScript.

6. An updateable page must be based on a single table, there must be no grouping levels, and only one record is visible at a time.

7. When you make a change to a record, you need to use the Save Record button on the toolbar to save it. Pressing the Enter key does not move you from text box to text box, so you need to navigate using the mouse.

8. You can export tables, queries, forms, or reports to a Web-ready format.

9. It is possible to import or link to HTML tables on the Web.

A

Access object model

A model that contains all the items you use in an application (such as the forms collection, forms, and controls collection), and is used to interact programmatically with the Access user interface

actions

The individual commands in a macro

ActiveX control

Similar to a built-in control, it is an object you place on a form or report to display data or perform an action; unlike a built-in control, the code that supports ActiveX control is stored in a separate file or files that must be installed for use

ADO

A single programming interface used by client applications, regardless of the type of data provider

***After Del Confirm* event**

A form event that occurs after you confirm record deletions and the records are actually deleted, or occurs after the deletions are canceled

***After Insert* event**

A form event that occurs after a new record is added to the database

***After Update* event**

A form and control event that occurs for new and existing records after a control or record is updated with changed data

allow zero length

A field property, when set to Yes, that allows a zero length string to be entered; applies to Text, Memo, and Hyperlink fields

array

A series of variables of the same data type, arranged contiguously in memory

B

back end

A file that contains tables

bang notation

Uses the bang (!) operator, in place of dot notation when the collection referenced by an object is the default collection

bang operator

An exclamation point (!) used to separate one object from another or from the object collection

***Before Del Confirm* event**

A form event that occurs after one or more records are deleted, but before Access displays a dialog box asking you to confirm or cancel the deletion

***Before Insert* event**

A form event that occurs when you type the first character in a new record, but before the record is added to the database

***Before Update* event**

A form and control event that occurs for new and existing records before a control or record is updated with changed data

bound forms

Forms that are tied to a table or a query, and are used for editing, entering, and reviewing data in that underlying table or query

breakpoint

A selected line of a program where execution automatically stops

C

caption

Field property that displays text other than the field name in Datasheet view

Cascade Delete

Deleting a record in the primary table automatically deletes any related records in a related table

Cascade Update

A change in the primary key of the primary table will automatically be updated in a related table

***Change* event**

A control event that occurs when the context of a text box or the text box portion of a combo box changes

class

The definition for an object, including the object's name, its properties and methods, and any events associated with it

CodeContextObject property

Determines the object in which a macro or VBA code is executing

collection

An object that contains a set of related objects (objects of the same class)

collection index

A range of numbers that begin with a zero, and in turn represent each object in the collection

combo box

A drop-down list of items from which you can select; limits entries in a field

comment

Text included in a procedure; briefly describes what the procedure does

compilation

Process in which Access checks for overall consistency when a program is run and translates the VBA statements into a language that the computer understands

composite key

A primary key that consists of two or more fields

concatenates

Joins—used in the context of joining two tables

constant

A meaningful name that takes the place of a number or string

Controls collection

Group of controls of the same type

control structure

A series of VBA statements that work together as a unit

Current **event**

A form event that occurs when the focus moves to a record, therefore making it the current record; also occurs when you requery a form's source of data

D

DAO

An interface that has been used in programs to manipulate data, create tables and queries, and manage security in Access databases since the release of Access 2.0

data access page

An object in the database that lets you display, edit, and manipulate objects such as tables, forms, and reports so that they can be published to the Web using the Internet Explorer Web browser

data dictionary

A list and definition of the individual fields included in each table in a database

data events

Events that occur when data is entered, deleted, or changed in a form or control; they also occur when the focus moves from one record to another

Database Documenter

Allows you to create a data dictionary quickly and easily by generating a document that clearly identifies the database objects and their related properties

database management system

An application used to manage, store, retrieve, and order large amounts of information

Database window

The command center for working with objects

Database window toolbar

Contains buttons for opening, creating, and deleting objects, and for changing views

data-definition query

A query that uses the data-definition language component of SQL to create objects such as tables and indexes

DatePart function

A function that returns an integer containing the specified part of the given date

DAvg()

A domain aggregate function that returns the mathematical average of the values in the specified field

DBEngine object

Represents the DAO interface into the JET engine and ODBCDirect technology

DCount()

A domain aggregate function that returns the number of records with nonnull values in a specified field

decimal places

Field property that applies to Number and Currency fields and determines the number of decimal places shown to the right of the decimal point

default value

Value, when entered in the Default Value text box, that Access automatically enters into each new record

Delete **event**

A form event that occurs when a record is deleted, but before the deletion is confirmed and actually performed

delimiter

The characters in a text file that identify the end of one field and the beginning of another field

Detail

Section that represents the main body of the report or form

DFirst()

A domain aggregate function that returns the value in the specified field from the first physical record

Dirty **event**

A form event that occurs when the contents of a form or the text portion of a combo box change, or when you move from one page to another page in a tab control

DLast()

A domain aggregate function that returns the value in a specified field from the last physical record

DLookup()

A domain aggregate function that returns the value in a specified field

DMax()

A domain aggregate function that returns the maximum value in a specified field

DMin()

A domain aggregate function that returns the minimum value in a specified field

Do...Loop

A structure used to repeat statements in a procedure until a specified condition is true

domain

A set of records

dot notation

Uses the dot (.) operator to indicate that what follows is an item defined by Access

DSum()

A domain aggregate function that returns the sum of the values in a specified field

dynamic link library (DLL)

File containing a collection of Windows functions designed to perform a specific class of operations

E

Err object

Contains information about an error that has just occurred

error and timing events

Events that are used for error-handling and synchronizing data on forms or reports

error trapping

A way of protecting programs and data from the effect of errors

event procedure

A group of statements that execute when an event occurs and is part of a larger category of procedures called Sub procedures

event property

Associated with each event, it specifies how an object responds when the event occurs

event-driven programming

The use of event properties to run macros or execute VBA code

events

Actions that are recognized by an object and for which a response can be defined

explicit declaration

Process in which it is necessary to declare a variable before using it

explicit permissions

Permissions in user-level security that are granted directly to a user account and affect no other account

expression

A combination of symbols and values that produces a result

F

field size

The number of characters a field can contain

field validation rules

Allow you to validate a field compared to a constant

filter events

Events that occur when a filter is applied or created on a form

focus

The ability to receive mouse or user input through mouse or keyboard actions

focus events

Events that occur when a form or control loses or gains the focus

For Each...Next Loop

A structure that executes a group of statements on each member of an array or collection

For...Next Loop

A structure used to execute statements of code a specified number of times

foreign key

The join field in the secondary table in relationships

form class module

Saved as part of a form, and which contains one or many procedures that apply specifically to that form

form master

A form that contains the controls that are common to all forms in the database

form template

A form on which to base other forms created in the database

format

Predefined standards for entering Number, Date/Time, and other types of fields. Does not affect the way data must be entered, only how it will appear after it is entered

format event

Event that occurs when Access determines what data goes in a report section, but happens before the section is formatted for previewing or for printing

front end

A file that contains the queries, forms, reports, macros, and modules

function

A built-in procedure that returns a value and usually requires you to specify one or more pieces of information, called arguments

G

Group Footer

The section that appears at the end of a group of records; it might contain information that can be used to show calculations, such as a total or an average of the records in the group

Group Header

The section that appears at the beginning of a new group of records; it might contain information such as a group name or a picture that applies to the group

Groups bar

Organizes database objects according to subject

H

hyperlink

Text or an image that you click to navigate to other parts of a file, to other documents on your computer or network, or to Internet addresses

I

identifier operators

Operators that are used in expressions, macros, and VBA code to identify objects and their properties

Immediate window

A window that shows information that results from debugging statements in the code or from commands typed directly into the window

implicit declaration

Process in which it is not necessary to declare a variable before using it

implicit permissions

Permissions in user-level security that are granted to a group account

importing

A way to bring data into Access, usually into a new table; a good alternate if the data will be used only in Access and not in its original format

index

A separate hidden table that consists of pointers to records or groups of records, and is designed to make sorting and searching more efficient

indexed

Field property that can speed up the process of searching and sorting on a particular field, but also can slow updates

input mask

Composed of a string of characters that act as placeholders for the characters that will be entered into the field; controls how data is actually entered into a field, not how it appears after it is entered

instance

A new object with all the characteristics defined by the class on which it is created

junction table

Contains common fields from two tables; is on the many side of a one-to-many relationship with those two tables

keyboard events

Events that occur when you type on a keyboard, and when keystrokes that use the Sendkeys macro action or the Sendkeys statement in VBA are sent to a form or a control on a form

lifetime

The time during which a variable retains its value

lightweight form

A form that contains hyperlinks to the objects in the database that you want to open, rather than having to use controls designed with VBA code

line continuation character

A character that is used when the code is too long to fit on a single line

linking

A way to use outside data in Access; it leaves data in its current format and location outside Access, and is a good alternate method if the data is going to be used both in its original format and in Access

literal

A character in the input mask that you don't have to type, such as dashes in a Social Security number

Locals window

Displays the name, current value, and type of all the variables and objects in the current procedure

logic errors

These occur when your procedures execute without failure, but the results are not what you intended; can occur when code has been assigned to the wrong event procedure or when the order of operations in a procedure is incorrect

macro

A command or series of commands, used with forms and reports, that automate database operations

Me keyword

In a VBA class module, it can be used to refer to the associated form or report that contains the class module; always refers to the object that is running the code

menu animation

A term used to describe how the menu opens

method

A procedure that acts on an object

mod operator

An arithmetic operator used to divide two numbers and return only the remainder

module

An object in an Access database that is used to store VBA functions and procedures; a small compact program written in VBA

mouse events

Events that occur in a form or in a control on a form as a result of a mouse action, such as pressing down or clicking the mouse button

new value

Field property that can be applied only to fields of AutoNumber data type

NoData event

Event that occurs after Access formats a report for printing when the report has no data, but before the report is printed

Not In List event

A control property that occurs when a value entered in a combo box isn't in the combo box list

object library

A collection of prebuilt objects and functions that you can use in VBA code

object variables

Used when you want to declare variables in your procedures to use in place of object names

Objects bar

Contains buttons for viewing each database object

object shortcuts

Provide a quick method for creating an object

On Error statement

A statement that enables error handling in a procedure

one-to-many relationship

Exists when a related table has many records that relate to a single record in the primary table

one-to-one relationship

Exists when one entry in each table corresponds to only one entry in the other table

operators

Used to perform arithmetic calculations, perform comparisons, combine strings, and perform logical operations

orphan record

A record in the related table that does not contain a record in the primary table

owner

In a group, the user who creates a table, query, form, report, or macro

page event

Event that occurs after Access formats a page for printing, but before the page is printed

Page Footer

The section that appears at the bottom of every page of a report and may contain information such as date, time, and page numbers

Page Header

The section that prints at the top of every page in a report and may include column headers or the report title

page property

Property that specifies the current page number when a page is being printed

pass-through query

A query that passes an uninterrupted SQL statement to an external database server

precision

Field property that can be applied only to fields of Number data type where the Field Size property has been changed to Decimal; defines the total number of digits used to represent a numeric value

primary key

The field (or fields) that uniquely identifies a record in a table

primary table

Table that contains data about a person or object when there is only one record that can be associated with that person or object

print events

Events that are found on reports and report sections, and occur when a report is being printed or is being formatted for printing

print print event

Event that occurs after Access has formatted the data in a report section, but before the section is printed

Private keyword

A keyword that indicates that the procedure can be called only from within the module where it is contained

procedures

In any programming language, a group of statements that perform actions and tasks

property

A named attribute of an object that defines a certain characteristic

Public keyword

A keyword that indicates that the procedure can be called from outside the module where it is contained

 R

records

A set of field values

recordset

A set of records; the results (or the records found) of a query; manipulating recordsets is one of the major uses of ADO and DAO technology

redundancy

Duplication of data

referential integrity

Requires that a foreign key value in a related table matches the value of the primary key for some row in the primary table, and prevents the occurrence of orphaned records

related table

In a relationship, it is the table(s) that is not the primary table

relational database management system (RDBMS)

An application that links tables through a common field, and thereby combines data in new objects and minimizes data duplication; also can store a large amount of information

Report Footer

The section that appears once at the end of a report and may be used to show the results of expressions such as totals or averages

Report Header

The section at the beginning of a report that may contain information such as company logo, report title, and company name and address

reports

Used primarily for printing records in an organized, attractive

format; might be based on the contents of a table, the results of a saved query, or a SQL statement

required

Field property, when set to Yes, that requires text or a value be entered into the field

Resume statement

A statement that resumes execution after an error-handling routine is finished

retreat print event

Event that occurs when Access must back up past one or more report sections on a page in order to perform multiple formatting passes

run-time errors

These occur while the application is running, or when the user attempts an operation that the system cannot perform

 S

scale

Field property that can be applied only to fields of Number data type where the Field Size property has been change to Decimal; also determines the number of decimal places to the right of the decimal point

scope

The visibility and accessibility of one procedure from another procedure

Screen object

The particular form, report, or control that currently has the focus

ScreenTip

A message that appears when the pointer is positioned on a control, form, or button on a toolbar

self-join

The process of joining a table to itself in a query

splash screen

A type of unbound form that opens automatically when a database is opened; it is designed to give the user something to do while the application is loading

step value

Value that lets you increment a For…Next loop by a given amount

Structured Query Language (SQL)

The most common complete database query language that offers the capability to create components of a database as well as to manipulate them

Sub procedure

A series of VBA statements that performs actions but does not return a value

subdatasheet

A datasheet that allows you to view or edit related data in another table

subreport

A report that is inserted in another report

switchboard

An unbound form that is used to navigate to other forms and reports in the database

syntax errors

These occur when you violate the rules of VBA syntax

tab-delimited

Text files in which the fields are separated by a tab; each record begins on a new line

table validation rules

Allow you to test the validity of one field compared to another

theme

A set of design elements and color schemes for background, font, horizontal lines, bullets, hyper-links, and controls

transactional table

Table in which the data entry process is ongoing

trap errors

When a developer anticipates an error that could occur, the default response of Access can be trapped and replaced with custom messages and actions

unbound forms

Forms that are not tied to a table or query; used to create an interface that provide users with controlled access to the application

unicode compression

Each character is represented by two bytes instead of by a single byte; represents data in Text, Memo, or Hyperlink fields

union query

A query that creates the union of two or more tables

***Updated* event**

A control property that occurs when an OLE object's data has been modified

user interface

The mechanism by which the user communicates and interacts with the application

user-level security

The most flexible and extensive method for securing a database

validation rule

An optional expression (formula) that can be created at the table or field level

validation text

Appears in the warning message box that opens if the validation rule is violated

variable scope

The lifespan of a variable that is determined by its declaration and its location in a module

variables

Named locations in memory that are used to store data of a particular type

VBA expression

A combination of keywords, operators, variables, and constants that yields a string, number, or object

VBA statement

A unit that expresses one kind of action, declaration, or definition in complete syntax

W

window events

Events that occur when you open, resize, or close a form or report

workgroup

A group of users in a multiuser environment who share data

workgroup ID

Case-sensitive string that contains letters or numbers and is 4 to 20 characters long

workgroup information file

A file that, if user-level security is defined, records the members of a workgroup; it contains the user's names, passwords, and the group to which they belong, and is read at startup

Workspace object

Represents a single session or instance of a user interacting with the database engine

Special Characters

! (exclamation point), AC 130, AC 329

* (asterisk), AC 305

_ (underscore), AC 307–311

. (period), AC 130, AC 329

A

Access errors, AC 340–344

  determining error number, AC 340–343

  Error events, AC 340

  Timing events, AC 340

Access object models. *See* object models

action queries, AC 17

ActiveX controls, AC 350–356

  Calendar, AC 351–356

  registering, AC 351

Admin account, AC 381

Admins account, AC 381

ADO interface, AC 362–364

After Del Confirm event, AC 219

After Insert event, AC 219

After Update event, AC 219

Allow Zero Length property, AC 14

appending data to tables, AC 95–96

archived records, deleting, AC 100–101

archiving data, AC 97–102

asterisk (*), wildcard, AC 305

B

back end files, AC 76, AC 217

bang notation, AC 329

bang operator (!), AC 130, AC 329

Before Del Confirm event, AC 219

Before Insert event, AC 219

Before Update event, AC 219

blank rows, adding to reports, AC 206–207, AC 208

bound forms, AC 118

breakpoints, setting in code, AC 291–293

buttons. *See* command buttons

Bypass key, disabling, AC 247–251

C

Calendar ActiveX control, AC 351–356

Can Grow property, reports, AC 175–181

Can Shrink property, reports, AC 175–181

Caption property, AC 14

Cascade Delete option, AC 45–48

Cascade Update option, AC 45–48

Change event, AC 219

charts, reports, AC 200–204

check boxes, adding to switchboards, AC 268–269

classes, AC 218–219

clauses, SQL, AC 105–109

clearing passwords, AC 399–400

Clnt function, AC 16–17

CodeContextObject property, AC 329

collection(s), AC 130, AC 218, AC 219, AC 328–330

  CodeContextObject property, AC 329

  Controls, AC 330

  dot versus bang notation, AC 329

  Me keyword, AC 329, AC 330

  Screen object, AC 330

collection index, AC 330

combo boxes, AC 51–57, AC 344–350

  creating, AC 51–53, AC 280–283, AC 344–347

  creating SQL statements, AC 54–55

  DoCmd.FindRecord method, AC 347–348

  DoCmd.GoToControl method, AC 347

  Lookup Wizard, AC 51–53

  NotInList event procedure, AC 348–350

command(s)

  adding to menus, AC 239–241

  menus, AC 231–232

command buttons
   adding to data entry forms,
      AC 151–152
   adding to switchboards, AC 299
   assigning macros, AC 153
   creating using Command Button Wizard, AC 153–156
**Command Button Wizard,
   AC 153–156**
   VBA code, AC 157–158
comments, VBA, AC 272–273
compiling VBA code, AC 272
**composite keys, AC 38,
   AC 40–41**
concatenation, fields, AC 15
**Condition column, Macro
   window, AC 143**
constants, AC 278–280
controls, forms
   changing properties,
      AC 132–133
   moving, AC 141–142
Controls collection, AC 330
**control structures, AC 207,
   AC 320–321**
   decision processing,
      AC 225–226
   Do...Loop, AC 320
   For Each...Next, AC 321
   For...Next, AC 321
copy and paste method, table structure, AC 97–98
creating queries, AC 79–88
   append queries, AC 98–99
   Expression Builder, AC 80–83
   self-joins, AC 170–175
   text-manipulation functions,
      AC 80, AC 83–84
   update queries, AC 90–91
crosstab queries, AC 17
Current event, AC 219
customizing
   menu bars, AC 237–241
   toolbars, AC 234–237
Cycle property, forms, changing, AC 20–21

D

**DAO interface, AC 362–363,
   AC 364**
**data access pages, AC 29,
   AC 408, AC 419–440**
   changing navigation toolbar properties, AC 430–433
   changing sorting and grouping properties, AC 428–430
   filtering records, AC 435

   formatting, AC 423–424
   grouping data, AC 426–428
   hyperlinks to other pages,
      AC 439–440
   read-only, creating, AC 419–423
   testing, AC 437–439
   themes, AC 424–426
   updatable, creating, AC 433–437
database(s)
   current, determining,
      AC 365–366
   determining current user, AC 365
   determining number of tables and queries, AC 366–367
   documenting, AC 61–66
   opening, AC 5
   splitting, AC 254–258
   tables. *See* entering records in tables; relationships; tables
database design, AC 34–36
Database Documenter, AC 61, AC 62–66
   exporting reports to Word,
      AC 64–65
   printing reports, AC 65–66
database management systems (DBMSs), AC 4–5
Database object, AC 365–367
**database object(s). *See also* form(s); module(s); report(s);
   tables**
   naming conventions, AC 5–7
Database window, AC 7–8
   hiding objects, AC 101–102
Database window toolbar, AC 7
data-definition queries, AC 103
data dictionaries, AC 61
data entry, tables. *See* entering records in tables
data entry forms
   adding command buttons,
      AC 151–152
   creating, AC 127–135
   identifier operators, AC 130–133
   subforms, AC 133–135
   switchboards, AC 138
Data event(s), AC 182
data event properties, AC 219–220
Datasheet view, creating tables, AC 36–37
data type(s)
   fields, changing, AC 78
   variables, AC 276–277
data type conversion functions, AC 80
**date(s), entering in tables,
   AC 58–61**
date and time functions, AC 79
DAvg function, AC 167
DBEngine object, AC 364
DBMSs (database management systems), AC 4–5
DCount function, AC 167

Decimal Places property, AC 13

decision processing, control structures, AC 225–226

declaring variables, AC 275–276

default behavior, following events, canceling, AC 221–223

default options, macros, changing, AC 148

default properties, toolbox controls, changing, AC 123–124

Default Value property, AC 14

Delete event, AC 219

deleting records
archived records, AC 100–101
referential integrity, AC 44

deleting shortcut menus,
AC 243–244

delimiters, AC 76

Design view, changing queries of reports, AC 178–180

Dest Connect Str property, queries, AC 94

Destination DB property, queries, AC 94

Destination Table property, queries, AC 94

Detail section, reports, AC 169
numbering lines, AC 192–193

DFirst function, AC 167

Dirty event, AC 220

disabling
Bypass key, AC 247–251
text boxes, AC 326–327

DISTINCT keyword, SQL,
AC 104

DISTINCTROW keyword, SQL, AC 104

DLast function, AC 167

DLLs (dynamic link libraries),
AC 337

DLookup function, AC 167–169

DMax function, AC 167

DMin function, AC 167

DoCmd.FindRecord method,
AC 347–348

DoCmd.GoToControl method,
AC 347

DoCMD object, AC 224–225

documenting databases,
AC 61–66

Do...Loop control structure,
AC 320

domain aggregate functions,
AC 167–169

dot notation, AC 329

dot operator (.), AC 130, AC 329

DSum function, AC 167

dynamic link libraries (DLLs),
AC 337

E

editing, data in data access pages, AC 437

entering records in tables,
AC 49–61
combo boxes, AC 51–57
dates, AC 58–61
subdatasheets, AC 57–58

Err object, AC 336–339

error(s)
Access. See Access errors
logic, AC 335
run-time, AC 334, AC 335
syntax, AC 334
VBA. See VBA errors

Error events, AC 182, AC 340

error handlers, writing,
AC 343–344

error trapping, run-time errors, AC 335

event(s), AC 143
canceling default behavior following, AC 221–223

event-driven programming,
AC 143

event procedures, AC 157
adding to switchboards,
AC 226–230, AC 270–271
validating data. See validating data using event procedures

event properties, AC 143,
AC 182–191
assigning VBA functions to,
AC 188
converting macros to VBA code, AC 186–189
NoData event, AC 183–186
Print events, AC 183

Excel
analyzing query results, AC 110
importing spreadsheets, AC 91–96
sorting and subtotaling data,
AC 110–111

exclamation point (!), bang operator, AC 130, AC 329

explicit permissions, AC 396

exporting
Database Documenter reports to Word, AC 64–65
to Web, AC 440–441

Expression Builder, creating queries, AC 80–83

F

field(s)
changing data types, AC 78
concatenation, AC 15

foreign keys, AC 39

primary keys, AC 38, AC 39, AC 40–41

properties, AC 9–14

field expressions, queries, AC 16–17

Field Size property, AC 13

field validation rules, AC 9–10, AC 12–13

Filter events, AC 183

filtering records, data access pages, AC 435

FindFirst method, Recordset object, AC 374–375

FindLast method, Recordset object, AC 374

FindNext method, Recordset object, AC 374

FindPrevious method, Recordset object, AC 374

focus, AC 183

Focus events, AC 183

Force New Page property, reports, AC 26–27

For Each...Next control structure, AC 321

foreign keys, AC 39

form(s), AC 8–25, AC 117–158

adding expressions, AC 131–132

adding list boxes, AC 369–370

adding pictures, AC 125–126

adding rectangles, AC 22–23

adding sub procedures, AC 353–354

adding text expressions, AC 23–24

bound, AC 118

changing names, AC 24–25

code to open, AC 354–355

Cycle property, AC 20–21

data entry. *See* data entry forms

design, AC 119–126

form masters, AC 124–126

hyperlinks, AC 409–416

lightweight, AC 408, AC 409–416

macros. *See* macro(s)

moving controls, AC 141–142

ScreenTip messages, AC 120

switchboard. *See* switchboards

templates, AC 121–123

toolbox control default properties, AC 123–124

unbound, AC 118

Format events, AC 183

Format property, AC 13

formatting

data access pages, AC 423–424

reports, AC 176–178

form class modules, AC 189–191, AC 265

form masters, creating, AC 124–126

form templates, creating, AC 121–123

For...Next control structure, AC 321

FROM clause, SQL, AC 105

front end files, AC 76, AC 217

functions, AC 186–188, AC 265–266

assigning to event properties, AC 188

data type conversion, AC 80

date and time, AC 79

text-manipulation, AC 80, AC 83–84

G

group(s), macros, AC 251–254

Group Footer section, reports, AC 170

Group Header section, reports, AC 170

grouping data in data access pages, AC 426–428

grouping properties in data access pages, changing, AC 428–430

Groups bar, AC 7

H

hiding objects in Database window, AC 101–102

hyperlink(s), AC 408–419

forms, AC 409–416

menu bars, AC 416–419

to other data access pages, AC 439–440

uses, AC 408–409

Hyperlink Address property, AC 408

Hyperlink SubAddress property, AC 408

I

identifier operators, AC 130–133

If...Then...ElseIf statement, decision processing, AC 225

If...Then...Else statements, AC 207–208

decision processing, AC 225

Immediate window, AC 289–293

testing, AC 290–291

implicit permissions, AC 396

importing
data, Import Text Wizard,
AC 76–78
modules, AC 88–89
spreadsheets, AC 91–96
from Web, AC 441

**Import Spreadsheet Wizard,
AC 91–96**

Import Text Wizard, AC 76–78

indenting procedures, AC 266

index(es)
collection, AC 330
tables, AC 39–40

Indexed property, AC 14

input mask(s), entering dates in tables, AC 60–61

Input Mask property, AC 13

instances, AC 218

Internet Explorer, testing data access pages, AC 438–439

JOIN clause, SQL, AC 107–109
junction tables, AC 43

Keyboard events, AC 183
keys, tables. *See* **tables**
keywords. *See also specific keywords*
SQL, AC 104

L

lifetime, variables, AC 275

**lightweight forms, AC 408,
AC 409–416**

Like operation, AC 305

line arguments, AC 336

**line continuation character (_),
AC 307–311**

line labels, AC 336

line numbers, AC 336

linking data, AC 76

list boxes
adding to forms, AC 369–370
changing properties,
AC 371–372

lists, numbered, AC 191–193

literals, AC 60

Locals window, stepping through code, AC 293–298

logic errors, AC 335

Lookup Wizard, creating combo boxes, AC 51–53

M

macro(s), AC 29, AC 142–158
assigning to command buttons, AC 153
changing default options, AC 148
comparing to VBA, AC 157–158
converting to VBA code,
AC 186–189
creating, AC 143–153,
AC 252–254
events, AC 143
groups, AC 251–254
Macro window, AC 142–143
naming, AC 143

**Macro Name column, Macro
window, AC 143**

Macro window, AC 142–143

**many-to-many relationships,
AC 43**

**margins, reports, changing,
AC 28**

masters
creating data entry forms,
AC 127–129
switchboards, AC 136–137

Me keyword, AC 329, AC 330

menu(s), AC 231–232
adding commands, AC 239–241
shortcut, creating, AC 241–243

menu bars
customizing, AC 237–241
hyperlinks, AC 416–419

methods, AC 218, AC 219

Mod operator, AC 208

module(s), AC 29, AC 264–267
functions. *See* functions
importing, AC 88–89
sub procedures. *See* sub
procedures
types, AC 264–265

module-level variables, AC 276

Mouse events, AC 183

moving
    controls on forms, AC 141–142
    toolbars, AC 232

N

names
    database objects, AC 5–7
    forms, changing, AC 24–25
    macros and macro groups,
        AC 143
    variables, AC 277–278

navigation toolbar properties, data access pages,
    AC 430–433

New Value property, AC 13

NoData events, AC 183–186

Not In List event, AC 220

NotInList event procedure,
    AC 348–350

numbered lists, AC 191–193
    Running Sum property,
        AC 191–193

numbering pages in reports,
    AC 204–206

O

object(s). *See also* database object(s); form(s);
    report(s); tables
    hiding in Database window,
        AC 101–102
    owners, AC 396

object collections, AC 130

object libraries, changing reference, AC 372–373

object models, AC 362–373
    changing object library reference, AC 372–373
    DAO versus ADO interface,
        AC 362–364
    Database object, AC 365–367
    DBEngine object, AC 364
    Recordset object. *See* Recordset object
    Workspace object, AC 364–365

Objects bar, AC 7

Object shortcuts, AC 7

object variables, AC 330–333

On Error statement, AC 335

one-to-many relationships,
    AC 42–43

one-to-one relationships, AC 42

opening
    databases, AC 5
    forms, AC 354–355

OpenReport method,
    AC 269–271

operators, AC 207–208

options, adding options groups to switchboards, AC 139–140

ORDER BY clause, SQL,
    AC 106–107

orphan records, AC 43

Output All Fields property, queries, AC 94

owners of objects, AC 396

P

page(s), data access. *See* data access pages

Page events, AC 183

Page Footer section, reports,
    AC 169

Page Header section, reports,
    AC 169

page numbering, reports,
    AC 204–206

Page property, reports, AC 204

Pages property, reports, AC 204

parameter queries, AC 17

pass-through queries, AC 103

passwords
    clearing, AC 399–400
    setting, AC 384–385, AC 399–400

period (.), dot operator, AC 130

permissions, AC 396–400
    changing, AC 396–398
    explicit, AC 396
    implicit, AC 396
    owners, AC 396
    setting passwords, AC 399–400

pictures, adding to forms,
    AC 125–126

Precision property, AC 13

previewing reports, AC 25

primary keys, AC 38, AC 39,
    AC 40–41
    referential integrity, AC 45

primary tables, AC 42

Print events, AC 183

printing Database Documenter reports, AC 65–66

Private keyword, AC 266

procedure(s), AC 265–267
  comments, AC 272–273
  indenting, AC 266
  scope, AC 266–267
  spacing, AC 266
procedure-level variables,
  AC 276
programming, event-driven,
  AC 143
properties, AC 218, AC 219
Public keyword, AC 266

Q

queries, AC 15–17
  action, AC 17
  analyzing results in Excel, AC 110
  changing from Design view,
    AC 178–180
  creating. *See* creating queries
  crosstab, AC 17
  determining number, AC 366–367
  field expressions, AC 16–17
  parameter, AC 17
  properties, AC 94–96
  saved, creating SQL statements,
    AC 203–204
  select, AC 15–17
  SQL-specific. *See* SQL-specific queries
  subreports, AC 194–195

R

RDBMSs (relational database management systems),
  AC 4
read-only data access pages,
  creating, AC 419–423
record(s), AC 8
  archived, deleting, AC 100–101
  deleting, referential integrity, AC 44
  entering in tables. *See* entering records in tables
  filtering, data access pages,
    AC 435
  grouping in reports, AC 170
  orphan, AC 43
record-bound charts, inserting in reports, AC 200–204
Record Locks property, queries, AC 94
RecordsetClone property, Recordset object, AC 374

Recordset object, AC 367–372
  Bookmark property, AC 375–377
  FindFirst, FindLast, FindNext, and FindPrevious methods,
    AC 374–375
  RecordsetClone property, AC 374
  writing code using, AC 374–377
recordsets, AC 15, AC 363
rectangles, adding to forms,
  AC 22–23
redundancy, database design,
  AC 34
referential integrity, AC 43–48
  Cascade Update and Cascade Delete options, AC 45–48
  deleting records, AC 44
  primary keys, AC 45
registering, ActiveX controls,
  AC 351
related tables, AC 42
relational database management systems (RDBMSs), AC 4
relationships, AC 41–48
  creating, AC 46–48
  many-to-many, AC 43
  one-to-many, AC 42–43
  one-to-one, AC 42
  referential integrity, AC 43–48
removing user-level security,
  AC 400
report(s), AC 25–28
  adding blank rows, AC 206–207, AC 208
  Can Grow and Can Shrink properties, AC 175–181
  changing queries from Design view, AC 178–180
  changing sort order, AC 25–26
  crating expressions, AC 28
  Database Documenter, exporting to Word, AC 64–65
  Force New Page property,
    AC 26–27
  formatting, AC 176–178
  form class modules, AC 189–191
  grouping records, AC 170
  inserting charts, AC 200–204
  margins, changing, AC 28
  numbered lists, AC 191–193
  page numbering, AC 204–206
  previewing, AC 25
  sections, AC 169–170
  sizing, AC 27–28
  subreports. *See* subreports
report class modules, AC 265
Report Footer section, AC 170
Report Header section, AC 169
report masters, AC 166–169
  domain aggregate functions,
    AC 167–169

Report Snapshot feature, AC 180–181

Required property, AC 14

resetting toolbars, AC 232

Resume statement, AC 336

Retreat events, AC 183

rows, blank, adding to reports, AC 206–207

Running Sum property, AC 191–193

run-time errors, AC 334

    trapping, AC 335

S

Scale property, AC 13

Screen object, AC 330

ScreenTips, AC 120

sections, reports, AC 169–170

security, AC 378–400

    permissions. *See* permissions

    security accounts. *See* security accounts

    shortcuts to databases and workgroup information files, AC 394–395

    user-level, removing, AC 400

    User-Level Security Wizard. *See* User-Level Security Wizard

    workgroup information files. *See* workgroup information files

security accounts

    creating new users, AC 382–384

    setting passwords, AC 384–385

    types, AC 382–383

Select Case statement, decision processing, AC 225–226

select queries, AC 15–17

SELECT statement, SQL, AC 104

self-joins, creating queries, AC 170–175

SetBypassProperty function, adding variables, AC 250–251

Shift key, disabling as Bypass key, AC 247–251

shortcut(s)

    databases, AC 394–395

    workgroup information files, AC 394–395

shortcut menus

    creating, AC 241–243

    deleting, AC 243–244

sizing

    reports, AC 27–28

    subreports, AC 199

    toolbars, AC 232

snapshot format, reports, AC 180–181

sorting data in Excel, AC 110–111

sorting properties in data access pages, changing, AC 428–430

sort order, changing in reports, AC 25–26

Source Connect Str property, queries, AC 94

Source Database property, queries, AC 94

spacing procedures, AC 266

splash screens, AC 118–119

splitting databases, AC 254–258

spreadsheets, importing, AC 91–96

SQL (Structured Query Language), AC 103

    queries. *See* SQL-specific queries

SQL-specific queries, AC 17, AC 103–111

    data-definition queries, AC 103

    keywords, AC 104

    pass-through queries, AC 103

    SQL statements and clauses, AC 104, AC 105–111

    union queries, AC 103–104

SQL statements, combo boxes, AC 54–55

standard modules, AC 264–265

Startup properties, AC 245–247

statements

    SQL, AC 104, AC 109–110

    VBA, AC 207

stepping through code, AC 293–298

    Locals window, AC 293–298

Structured Query Language (SQL), AC 103

    queries. *See* SQL-specific queries

subdatasheets, AC 57–58

subforms, AC 133–135

    inserting in forms, AC 133–134

    referring to subforms in expressions, AC 134–135

sub procedures, AC 157, AC 186, AC 265–266

    adding to forms, AC 353–354

subreports, AC 194–200

    creating, AC 195–198

    creating queries, AC 194–195

    sizing on main report, AC 199

subtotaling, Excel, AC 110–111

switchboards, AC 118, AC 136–142

    adding command buttons, AC 299

    adding event procedures, AC 226–230

    adding option groups, AC 139–140

    adding text boxes, AC 303

changing form properties,
AC 137–138
creating, AC 267–273
creating masters, AC 136–137
data entry forms, AC 138
moving controls on forms,
AC 141–143
refining, AC 323–327
testing, AC 302, AC 321–323
syntax errors, AC 334

tab-delimited files, AC 76
importing to databases, AC 76–78
tables, AC 8–14, AC 36–61
appending data, AC 95–96
creating in datasheet view, AC 36–37
determining number, AC 366–367
entering records. *See* entering records in tables
foreign keys, AC 39
indexes, AC 39–40
junction, AC 43
modifying design, AC 37
primary, AC 42
primary keys, AC 38, AC 39,
AC 40–41
properties, AC 9–13
related, AC 42
relationships. *See* relationships
transactional, AC 40
table structure, copy and paste method, AC 97–98
**table validation rules, AC 9–10,
AC 11**
**templates, forms, creating,
AC 121–123**
testing
Immediate window, AC 290–291
switchboards, AC 302,
AC 321–323
user-level security, AC 389–392
text, validation, AC 9
text boxes
adding to switchboards, AC 303
disabling, AC 326–327
text expressions, adding to forms, AC 23–24
text-manipulation functions, creating queries, AC 80, AC 83–84
**themes, data access pages,
AC 424–426**
Timing events, AC 182, AC 340

toolbars, AC 231, AC 232–233
customizing, AC 234–237
positioning, AC 232
resetting, AC 232
sizing, AC 232
toolbox controls, changing default properties, AC 123–124
transactional tables, AC 40
**trapping run-time errors,
AC 335**

unbound forms, AC 118
underscore (_), line continuation character, AC 307–311
Unicode Compression property, AC 14
union queries, AC 103–104
**UNION statement, SQL,
AC 109–110**
Unique Records property, queries, AC 94
Unique Values property, queries, AC 94
**updatable data access pages,
creating, AC 433–437**
Updated event, AC 220
user(s), new, creating, AC 382–384
user interfaces, AC 119–120
**user-level security, removing,
AC 400**
**User-Level Security Wizard,
AC 385–394**
joining default workgroup,
AC 392–394
running, AC 385–389
testing security, AC 389–392
Users account, AC 382

**validating data using event
procedures, AC 220–225**
canceling default behavior following events, AC 221–223
DoCMD object, AC 224–225
**validation rules, AC 9–10,
AC 11–13**
validation text, AC 9
variables, VBA, AC 273–278

data types, AC 276–277

declaring, AC 275–276

lifetime, AC 275

naming conventions, AC 277–278

object variables, AC 330–333

scope, AC 275

Variant data type, AC 277

VBA, AC 263–311

adding comments, AC 272–273

adding to conditions, AC 305–311

building conditions, AC 283–289

Command Button Wizard,
  AC 157–158

compiling code, AC 272

converting macros to,
  AC 186–189

crating combo boxes, AC 280–283

creating switchboards,
  AC 267–273

declaring constants, AC 278–280

functions. *See* functions

Immediate window, AC 289–293

methods. *See* methods

modifying code for reports,
  AC 298–305

modules. *See* module(s)

setting breakpoints, AC 291–293

statements, AC 207

stepping through code,
  AC 293–298

sub procedures. *See* sub
  procedures

variables. *See* variables, VBA

VBA errors, AC 335–339

Err object, AC 336–339

On Error statement, AC 335

Resume statement, AC 336

W

WHERE clause, SQL,
  AC 105–106

wildcards, AC 305

Window events, AC 183

With statement, adding event
  procedures to switchboard forms, AC 227–230

Word, exporting Database Documenter reports to,
  AC 64–65

workgroup(s), AC 379

default, joining, AC 392–393

workgroup IDs, AC 379

workgroup information files,
  AC 379–381

creating, AC 379–381

rebuilding, AC 381

shortcuts, AC 394–395

Workspace object, AC 364–365

World Wide Web

exporting to, AC 440–441

importing from, AC 441

Z

zero-based values, AC 130

TASK	PAGE #	RECOMMENDED METHOD
Access objects, display hidden	AC 102	Click Tools on the menu bar, click Options, click the View tab, click the Hidden objects check box
Access objects, hide	AC 101	Right-click the object in the Database window, click Properties, click the Hidden check box
Access objects, import	AC 89	See Reference Window: Importing Access Objects
ActiveX control, register	AC 351	Click Tools on the menu bar, click ActiveX Controls, click the Register button, navigate to the folder containing the ActiveX control, click on it, click Open
ActiveX control, use	AC 351	See Reference Window: Adding an ActiveX Control to a Form
Ampersand, display on a control	AC 150	Type &&
Append query, create	AC 87	See Reference Window: Creating an Append Query
Breakpoint, use	AC 291	See Reference Window: Using Breakpoints to Step Through a Procedure
Chart, create	AC 200	See Reference Window: Inserting a Record-Bound Chart in a Report
Choose Builder dialog box, bypassing	AC 220	See Reference Window: Bypassing the Choose Builder Dialog Box
Code Builder, use	AC 189	See Reference Window: Using the Code Builder
Combo Box Wizard, use	AC 281	Click the Control Wizards button ⬚ on the toolbox, click the Combo Box button ⬚ on the toolbox, click on the form to create the control
Combo box, create	AC 51	See Reference Window: Adding a Combo Box to a Table Using the Lookup Wizard
Command Button Wizard, use	AC 154	See Reference Window: Using the Control Wizard to Add a Command Button to a Form
Command button, create	AC 151	Click the Command Button ⬚ on the toolbox, click on the form or report to create the control
Command button, duplicate	AC 151	Select a command button, click Edit on the menu bar, click Duplicate
Comment text, change color	AC 273	From the VBA window, click Tools on the menu bar, click Options, click the Editor Format tab, click Comment Text
Composite Primary key, create	AC 40	See Reference Window: Specifying a Composite Primary Key
Controls, align	AC 132	Select two or more controls, right-click the selected controls, click Align
Copy, field contents	AC 49	Press Ctrl+' (Ctrl+apostrophe)
Data Access Page Wizard, use	AC 421	Click Pages on the Objects bar of the Database window, double-click Create data access page by using wizard
Database Documenter, use	AC 62	See Reference Window: Using the Database Documenter
Database Splitter Wizard, use	AC 255	See Reference Window: Using the Database Splitter Wizard

TASK	PAGE #	RECOMMENDED METHOD
Database window, display	AC 245	Press the F11 key
Date, insert automatically	AC 50	Press Ctrl+; (Ctrl+semicolon)
Dates, displaying a four-digit year	AC 59	*See* Reference Window: Forcing a Four-Digit Year
Default control properties, change	AC 123	Click the control to be changed on the toolbox, display the Properties window
Delete query, create	AC 100	*See* Reference Window: Creating a Delete Query
Design View, switch to	AC 11	Click the Design View button
Errors, determine the number	AC 341	*See* Reference Window: Determining the Number of an Access Error
Event procedure, create	AC 270	*See* Reference Window: Adding an Event Procedure
Expression Builder, opening	AC 81	Click the Build button
Expression Builder, use	AC 81	*See* Reference Window: Using the Expression Builder
Expression, create in form or report	AC 131	*See* Reference Window: Creating an Expression in a Form
Field Expression, create	AC 16	Click in the Field text box, type the expression name, type a colon, type the expression
Field Validation Rule, create	AC 12	*See* Reference Window: Creating a Field Validation Rule
Fields, dragging all to the query design grid	AC 98	Double-click the title bar of the table field list, drag the selected fields to the first column of the design grid
Form, Creating from a master	AC 127	*See* Reference Window: Creating a form from a Master
Form Name, change	AC 24	Right-click the form in the Database window, click Rename
Form Properties, change	AC 20	*See* Reference Window: Changing Form Properties
Form section, size	AC 125	Position the pointer at the bottom edge of the section until it changes to the ⊥ shape, click and drag
Form template, create	AC 121	*See* Reference Window: Creating a Form Template
Form, select	AC 142,144	Click the Form Selector box in the upper-left corner of the form in Design view
Group, create	AC 8	Right-click in the Groups bar, click New Group
Immediate window, open	AC 290	Press Ctrl+G
Immediate window, use	AC 290	*See* Reference Window: Testing a Function in the Immediate Window
Import Spreadsheet Wizard, use	AC 92	*See* Reference Window: Using the Import Spreadsheet Wizard
Import Text Wizard, use	AC 76	*See* Reference Window: Using the Import Text Wizard
Index, create	AC 40	Click the field to be indexed, click the list arrow of the Indexed property
Keyboard shortcut, create on a control	AC 150	Type a Caption for the control that includes a single ampersand before a character

TASK	PAGE #	RECOMMENDED METHOD
Label, create on a form or report	AC 128	Click the Label button 𝐴𝑎 on the toolbox, click on the form or report to create the control
Linked Table Manager, use	AC 256	*See* Reference Window: Using the Linked Table Manager
Locals window, open	AC 295	From the VBA window, click View on the menu bar, click Locals Window
Macro action argument pane, move to	AC 145	Press the F6 key
Macro builder, use	AC 149	Display the Properties window, position the insertion point in an Event property, click the Build button ..., click Macro Builder
Macro, converting to VBA	AC 186	*See* Reference Window: Converting a Macro to VBA
Macro, displaying Name and Condition columns	AC 147	*See* Reference Window: Changing Default Macro Settings
Menu, create	AC 237	*See* Reference Window: Creating a New Menu Bar and Menu Items
Menu, customize	AC 239	*See* Reference Window: Adding Commands to a Menu Item
Menu, display full	AC 231	*See* Reference Window: Displaying the Full Set of Menu Commands
Object library, add	AC 373	*See* Reference Window: Changing the Object Library Reference
Option Group Wizard, use	AC 139	*See* Reference Window: Using the Option Group Wizard
Page numbers, add to a report	AC 204	*See* Reference Window: Adding Page Numbering to a Report
Password, clear	AC 399	*See* Reference Window: Clearing a Password
Password, set	AC 385	Click Tools on the menu bar, point to Security, click User and Group Accounts, click Change Logon Password tab
Permissions, change	AC 396	*See* Reference Window: Changing Permissions
Picture, add to a form	AC 125	*See* Reference Window: Adding a Picture to a Form
Properties window, open	AC 126	Click the Properties button
Query, exporting to Excel	AC 110	Click OfficeLinks list arrow, click Analyze It with MS Excel
Query, opening from the report window	AC 178	*See* Reference Window: Modifying the Query from the Report Window
Query, run	AC 16	Click the Run button !
Relationship, create between tables	AC 46	*See* Reference Window: Creating a Relationship Between Tables
Relationships, print report	AC 66	Click File in the menu bar of the Relationships window, click Print Relationships
Report page break, add	AC 26	*See* Reference Window: Applying the Force New Page Property
Report sort order, change	AC 25	Click View, click Sorting and Grouping
Report, number items in	AC 192	*See* Reference Window: Using the Running Sum Property to Number Items in a Report

TASK REFERENCE

TASK	PAGE #	RECOMMENDED METHOD
Report, preview	AC 25	Click the Print Preview button 🔍
Report, sizing	AC 27	Position the pointer on the right border of the report so that it looks like ↔, click and drag to the right or left.
Retangles, add	AC 22	*See* Reference Window: Adding a Retangle to a Form
Self-join, create	AC 171	*See* Reference Window: Creating a Self-Join Query
Shortcut menu, create	AC 241	*See* Reference Window: Creating a Custom Shortcut Menu
Snapshot, create	AC 180	*See* Reference Window: Sending a Report in Snapshot
SQL query, create	AC 105	*See* Reference Window: Creating a Query Using SQL
Startup properties, bypass	AC 247	Open Access, press the Shift key, open the database with Shift key held down
Startup properties, change	AC 246	*See* Reference Window: Setting the Database Startup Properties
Subdatasheet, display related records	AC 58	Click the Expand Indicator ⊞
Subdatasheet, hide related records	AC 58	Click the Collapse Indicator ⊟
Subreport Wizard, use	AC 195	Drag the query or table on which the subreport will be based to the main report from the Database window
Table Validation Rule, create	AC 10	*See* Reference Window: Creating a Table Validation Rule
Table, copying	AC 97	*See* Reference Window: Copying and Pasting a Table Structure
Table, create in Datasheet view	AC 36	Click Tables in the Object bar, double-click Create table by entering data in the Database window
Text box, create on a form or report	AC 23	Click the Text Box button ⧉ on the toolbox, click on the form or report to create the control
Theme, applying to data access page	AC 424	*See* Reference Window: Applying a Theme to a Data Access Page
Toolbar, customize	AC 234	*See* Reference Window: Customizing a Toolbar
Toolbar, display more buttons	AC 233	Click the More Buttons button ⧉
Toolbar, resize	AC 232	Click the move handle and drag the edge of the toolbar
Unique values, finding	AC 95	*See* Reference Window: Querying for Unique Values
Update query, create	AC 90	*See* Reference Window: Creating an Update Query
Variable declaration, require	AC 275	From the VBA window click Tools on the menu bar, click Options, click the Editor tab, click Require Variable Declaration to select it
Visual Basic window, open	AC 249	Click the Code button 🖳
Zoom window, open	AC 83	Right-click the text box, click Zoom

File Finder

Location in Tutorial	Name and Location of Data File	Student Creates New File
Tutorial 1		
Session 1.1	Movie1.mdb	
Session 1.2	(Continued from Session 1.1)	
Review Assignments	Hours1.mdb	
Case Problem 1	Edward1.mdb	
Case Problem 2	ISD1.mdb	
Case Problem 3	Homes1.mdb	
Case Problem 4	Sonoma1.mdb	
Tutorial 2		
Session 2.1	Movie2.mdb	
Session 2.2	(Continued from Session 2.1)	doc_rptObjects
Review Assignments	Hours2.mdb	
Case Problem 1	Edward2.mdb	
Case Problem 2	ISD2.mdb	
Case Problem 3	Homes2.mdb	
Case Problem 4	Sonoma2.mdb	
Tutorial 3		
Session 3.1	Movie3.mdb Movie3.txt	
Session 3.2	(Continued from Session 3.1) Movie3.xls	
Session 3.3	(Continued from Session 3.2)	
Review Assignments	Hours3.mdb	
Case Problem 1	Edward3.mdb Edward3.txt	
Case Problem 2	ISD3.mdb ISD3.xls	
Case Problem 3	Homes3.mdb	
Case Problem 4	Sonoma3.mdb Sonoma3.xls	
Tutorial 4		
Session 4.1	Movie4.mdb Logo	
Session 4.2	(Continued from Session 4.1)	
Review Assignments	Hours4.mdb	
Case Problem 1	Edward4.mdb	
Case Problem 2	ISD4.mdb	
Case Problem 3	Homes4.mdb H4Logo	
Case Problem 4	Sonoma4.mdb	
Tutorial 5		
Session 5.1	Movie5.mdb Logo	
Session 5.2	(Continued from Session 5.1)	
Review Assignments	Hours5.mdb	
Case Problem 1	Edward5.mdb	
Case Problem 2	ISD5.mdb	
Case Problem 3	Homes5.mdb H5Logo	
Case Problem 4	Sonoma5.mdb	

File Finder

Location in Tutorial	Name and Location of Data File	Student Creates New File
Tutorial 6		
Session 6.1	Movie6.mdb	
Session 6.2	(Continued from Session 6.1)	
Review Assignments	Hours6.mdb	
Case Problem 1	Edward6.mdb	
Case Problem 2	ISD6.mdb	
Case Problem 3	Homes6.mdb	
Case Problem 4	Sonoma6.mdb	
Tutorial 7		
Session 7.1	Movie7.mdb	
Session 7.2	(Continued from Session 7.1)	
Review Assignments	Hours7.mdb	
Case Problem 1	Edward7.mdb	
Case Problem 2	ISD7.mdb	
Case Problem 3	Homes7.mdb	
Case Problem 4	Sonoma7.mdb	
Tutorial 8		
Session 8.1	Movie8.mdb	
Session 8.2	(Continued from Session 8.1)	
Review Assignments	Hours8.mdb	
Case Problem 1	Edward8.mdb	
Case Problem 2	ISD8.mdb	
Case Problem 3	Homes8.mdb	
Case Problem 4	Sonoma8.mdb	
Tutorial 9		
Session 9.1	Movie9.mdb	
Session 9.2	(Continued from Session 9.1)	MOVIESECURE.mdw Movie9.bak
Review Assignments	Hours9.mdb HOURSECURE.mdw	Hours9.bak
Case Problem 1	Edward9.mdb Edward9.bak EDWARDSECURE.mdw	
Case Problem 2	ISD9.mdb	
Case Problem 3	Homes9.mdb	
Case Problem 4		SONOMASECURE.mdw Sonoma9.bak
	Sonoma9.mdb	
Tutorial 10		
Session 10.1	Movie10.mdb	
Session 10.2	(Continued from Session 10.1)	dapMovieEmployees dapTimeCards dapEmployees
Review Assignments	Hours10.mdb	
Case Problem 1	Edward10.mdb	dapClients
Case Problem 2	ISD10.mdb	
Case Problem 3	Homes10.mdb	dapLots
Case Problem 4	Sonoma10.mdb	